Engineering Constitutional Change

This volume provides a holistic presentation of the reality of constitutional change in 18 countries (the 15 old EU member states, Canada, Switzerland and the USA). The essays offer analysis on formal and informal constitutional amendment, bringing forth the overall picture of the parallel paths constitutional change follows, in correlation with what the constitution means and how constitutional law works. To capture the patterns of constitutional change, multifaceted parameters are explored, such as the interrelations between form of government, party system, and constitutional amendment; the interplay between constitutional change and the system of constitutionality review; the role of the people, civil society, and experts in constitutional change; and the influence of international and European law and jurisprudence on constitutional reform and evolution. In the extensive final, comparative chapter, key features of each country's amendment procedures are epitomized and the mechanisms of constitutional change are explained on the basis of introducing five distinct models of constitutional change. The concept of constitutional rigidity is re-approached and broken down into a set of factual and institutional rigidities. The classification of countries within models, in accordance with the way in which operative amending mechanisms connect, leads to a succinct portrayal of different modes of constitutional change engineering.

This book will prove to be an invaluable tool for approaching constitutional revision either for theoretical or for practical purposes and will be of particular interest to students and scholars of constitutional, comparative and public law.

Xenophon Contiades is Professor of Public Law, Dean of the School for Social and Political Sciences of the University of Peloponnese, and Director of the Centre for European Constitutional Law-Themistocles and Dimitris Tsatsos Foundation, Athens, Greece.

Routledge Research in Constitutional Law

Available titles in this series include:

Weak Constitutionalism
Democratic legitimacy and the question of constituent power
Joel I. Colon-Rios

Engineering Constitutional Change
A comparative perspective on Europe, Canada and the USA
Xenophon Contiades, Centre for European Constitutional Law

Engineering Constitutional Change

A Comparative Perspective on Europe, Canada and the USA

Edited by

Xenophon Contiades

Routledge
Taylor & Francis Group
LONDON AND NEW YORK

First published 2013
by Routledge
2 Park Square, Milton Park, Abingdon, Oxon OX14 4RN

Simultaneously published in the USA and Canada
by Routledge
711 Third Avenue, New York, NY 10017

Routledge is an imprint of the Taylor & Francis Group, an informa business

British Library Cataloguing in Publication Data
A catalogue record for this book is available from the British Library

Library of Congress Cataloging in Publication Data
A catalog record for this book has been requested

ISBN 978-0-415-52976-1 (hbk)
ISBN 978-0-203-09499-0 (ebk)

Typeset in Baskerville
by RefineCatch Limited, Bungay, Suffolk

MIX
Paper from responsible sources
FSC
www.fsc.org
FSC® C004839

Contents

Notes on Contributors

Abraham Barrero Ortega, Professor of Constitutional Law, University of Seville

Christian Behrendt, Professor of Public and Constitutional Law, University of Liege

Robert Blackburn, Professor of Constitutional Law, King's College London

Xenophon Contiades, Professor of Public Law and Dean, University of Peloponnese, Director, Centre for European Constitutional Law

Thomas Fleiner, Professor Emeritus of Public Law, University of Fribourg, former Director, Institute of Federalism

Alkmene Fotiadou, Dr. iur, Research Associate, Centre for European Constitutional Law

Jörg Gerkrath, Professor of European Law, University of Luxembourg

Tania Groppi, Professor of Public Law, University of Sienna

Allan C. Hutchinson, Distinguished Research Professor of Law, Osgoode Hall Law School, York University

Liliane Icher, Lecturer, University of Toulouse I Capitole

Markus Kotzur, Professor of Public and European Law, University of Leipzig

Helle Krunke, Professor of Constitutional Law, University of Copenhagen

Fiona de Londras, Professor of Law, Durham University

Jónatas E. M. Machado, Associate Professor of Constitutional Law, University of Coimbra

Lars-Göran Malmberg, Professor of Public Law, University of Gothenburg

Wanda Mastor, Professor of Public Law, University of Toulouse I Capitole

David Gwynn Morgan, Professor Emeritus of Law, University College Cork

Tuomas Ojanen, Professor of Constitutional Law, University of Helsinki

Irene Sobrino Guijarro, Assistant Professor of Constitutional Law, University of Seville

Manfred Stelzer, Professor of Public Law, University of Vienna

Ioannis Tassopoulos, Associate Professor of Public Law, National and Kapodistrian University of Athens

John R. Vile, Professor of Political Science and Dean, University Honors College, Middle Tennessee State University

Wim J.M. Voermans, Professor of Constitutional and Administrative Law, Director, Institute of Public Law, University of Leiden

Acknowledgments

This book is dedicated to the memory of Professor Dimitris Th. Tsatsos, who focused an important part of his academic work on Comparative Constitutional Law in his capacity as Professor of Constitutional Law both in Germany and Greece, and later drawing from his experience as a Member of the European Parliament. Dimitris Tsatsos was my friend and my mentor, and he is greatly missed. The most valuable thing he did for me, besides endowing me with his friendship, was giving me the opportunity to work with him for more than 20 years.

Of great value has been the support of the Centre for European Constitutional Law – Themistokles and Dimitris Tsatsos Foundation, under the auspices of which a workshop was held in September 2011 and in which all contributors to this volume participated, within the context of the annual summer seminars organised by the Centre. The book benefited greatly from these discussions.

My wife, Alkmene Fotiadou, besides being the co-author of the final comparative chapter, was present throughout all the stages of putting together this volume and organising the workshop. I would like to thank her, not only for her participation in this project, but mostly for striking the difficult balance between writing together and being family.

1 Constitutional change engineering

Xenophon Contiades

The meaning of a question is the method of answering it.

Ludwig Wittgenstein, *Philosophical Remarks*

On narratives of constitutional change

A new narrative has gradually been evolving, a narrative shared by constitutional literature, which focuses on the concept of constitutional change. As opposed to the less attractive technical terms "revision" and "amendment," change corresponds to images of transformation through the perpetual interaction of formal and informal mechanisms, and suggests fluidity encompassing the correlation between political antagonism, judicial identity and the constitution. Amending procedures dictate how constitutional change is supposed to take place, and the success or failure in the accomplishment of their intended difficulty level affects the relationship between explicit and implicit changes. Still, the reality of change is determined through the impact of other factors as well, such as the structure of the political system, the effect of civil or common law tradition, the system of judicial review, and constitutional ethos.

It seems that constitutional theory is making a return to basics. Notions of sovereignty, constitutional reform and evolution, entrenchment and constitutional design are revisited. The question posed is why the issue of constitutional revision and constitutional change is becoming increasingly intriguing. The answer is multifaceted. Amending formulas are no longer perceived as clauses in hibernation remaining in sleep mode, coming out only when the amending process is initiated, but on the contrary are omnipresent, exerting continuous influence on constitutional and political theory and practice. This phenomenon is enhanced as it is apparent that states still remain the main locus of sovereignty, since supranational institutions have not absorbed state functions, and EU constitution-making did not proceed as smoothly as envisaged in the recent past.

Still, the heart of the issue lies elsewhere. Recent preoccupation with constitutional change stems from, and also marks a new era of, constitutionalism, where the existence of constitutions is regarded as a self-evident reality. In this new context the constitution, not imperiled by enemies, is demystified (and can afford to be demystified), while amending procedures can be treated as modes of adaption to changing circumstances rather than imaginary simulations of the constitutive moment. They can therefore be subjected to scrutiny with regard to their efficiency in performing the task they were designed to perform, in light of their ratio and the results they produce. Constitutional reform is neither taboo nor an extraordinary process, but part of normal constitutional life, reflecting that constitutions are no longer perceived as mystical, sacred documents but as indispensable tools used regularly and interminably. This undisputed normativity and indispensability of the constitution goes hand in hand with the necessity of adaptability to changing circumstances that include state transformation, new threats against rights, and supranational co-operation.

The need for adjustability to new requirements as a trigger for constitutional change does not automatically render the process routine. Strong conflicts regarding the allocation of powers may underlie constitutional change. Not regarded as sacrilegious anymore, formal change may signal serious reforms in the operation of the state, providing the means for resolving conflicts between political elites, the people, and the judiciary, as well as between federal states and subnational entities. In the comparative approach of engineering constitutional change, journeys of sovereignty unravel, revealing winners and losers in the incessant conflict that takes place between constitutional actors, and betraying conscious or unconscious choices between constitutionalism and democracy.

Comparative assessment of constitutional change: alternative methods

Comparative constitutional law and political science have taken very important steps in the field of constitutional change theory. Comparisons are often conducted on the basis of quantitative analysis using information such as the age and length of the constitutions under assessment, and the number of constitutional revisions that have been performed, then compiling indexes of rigidity. Several approaches are continuing the effort to explain constitutional amendment through the analysis of empirical data, an effort originated in the 1990s in the USA, while different theories and methodologies are applied to draw conclusions from such data. Criticism targeted against these methodologies stresses the danger of ignoring other, non-measurable aspects that determine the route of constitutional change. Disregarding or bypassing comparability and commonality is another potential pitfall, related to the difficulty of maintaining coherency in multi-level approaches that aim to place country-specific amendment processes in their wider constitutional, socio–political, and historical context.

This volume attempts an holistic presentation of the reality of constitutional change in 18 countries, which, despite their important differentiations, also share profound commonalities (after all, the 15 old member states of the EU along with the USA, Canada and Switzerland are the core of what is traditionally referred to as the West). Constitutions emerged in Europe and North America in the eighteenth and nineteenth century, in correlation with a specific type of state; constitutions and states becoming inescapably interrelated as historical phenomena marking the passage from feudalism to the nation state. This common background facilitates evading any misconceptions that may occur when juxtaposing constitutions that resemble each other in form or content but are applied in totally different cultural, socio–political, and legal contexts.

The 18 contributions in this volume offer analysis regarding how constitutional amendment takes place in different legal orders, by addressing the multifaceted issues set out by an outline designed to bring forth the overall picture of the parallel paths that constitutional change follows in each country, in correlation to what the constitution means and how constitutional law works. It is not mere coincidence that some contributions begin with a discussion on what the constitution is, finding it necessary before approaching constitutional change to talk about the constitution *per se*; in others, the weight is placed on history in order to explain constitutional evolution, while several others focus on the particularities of the political system or on the tension between the legislator and the judiciary. In that sense, this volume is not a compilation of national contributions, but hosts through a common spectrum different theories and comprehensions.

Characteristic of the varying conceptions of constitutional change, even in countries that share common understandings of constitutionalism, are several terminological issues that emerged by addressing the outline. The terms "revision" and "amendment" have different connotations in each legal order: "revision" indicates extensive constitutional makeover, whereas "amendment" indicates lesser interventions; or, "revision" meaning formal change and "amendment" either formal or informal change, while common lawyers feel much more at home with the notion of "change." These differences were particularly apparent where scholars had to decide how to translate the term used in their own language to indicate amendment/revision. For the purposes of this volume, authors were left free to choose the terms that best corresponded to their legal culture, priority therefore being given to allowing differentiations to surface instead of pursuing uniformity.

Here follows the outline which endeavored to capture the reality of constitutional change in the examined legal orders:

- History and evolution of the amending procedure
- The amending formula: analysis and interpretation of constitutional provisions regarding constitutional revision
- The role of the people, civil society and experts in constitutional change
- Judicial review of constitutional amendments
- Informal methods of constitutional change
- Correlations between constitutional change and the system of constitutional review
- Interrelations between form of government, party system, and constitutional amendment
- The influence of international and European law and jurisprudence on constitutional reform and evolution
- Criticisms on the amendment procedure and constitutional entrenchment
- Contemporary debate on constitutional reforms

The outcome of responding to the above outline suggests that underlying any narrative of constitutional change is the relationship between constitutions and time as forged through the succession of episodic and incremental changes, while multiple constitutional actors fight over taking the lead. In case the link between the way in which change actually happens and the amending processes is missing, the analysis of constitutional change disregards the fragmentation of power and the underlying tensions over the final outcome, and so fails to capture the essence of the constitution (i.e. the allocation and delimitation of powers). Constitutional amendment seen under the prism of the intended and unintended consequences of amending formulas reveals how mechanisms of constitutional change work, exploring the perpetual confrontations taking place between constitutional lawmaker and judge, between formal and informal change, and between constitutionalism and democracy.

Modelizing constitutional change

The common outline was put together in order to guide the comparative analysis through a series of questions that attempt to grasp the essence of the way in which constitutional change is engineered. Questions are important for revealing commonalities and divergences, yet can sometimes be self-defeating by imposing discipline of thought whereas riskier approaches can lead to revealing answers. The choice of questions is crucial for the directions that thought and observation follow. The main questions employed to facilitate the comparative exploration are:

- Does the amending procedure reveal or express a specific understanding of what the constitution is?
- Is the way in which the constitution organizes political power, allocates authority and regulates fundamental rights interrelated with the amending formula?
- Do stringent and complex amending procedures cause devaluation of the constitution or lead to its mystification, and to what extent is this determined by the features of informal change?
- Do demanding amending processes nurture the living constitution or are they detrimental to it?
- Is it possible that unamendable provisions are furnished with the charm of the forbidden, becoming unspeakably desirable, symbolizing reversal?
- Is it possible for amending formulas to be irrational, and what are the criteria for assessing amending formulas?
- Does the formula achieve the goal it is designed to serve (i.e. stability, consent, consistency, continuity, adaptability, etc.)?
- Can constitutional change be considered a process of cultural development?
- How does legal culture and constitutional ethos affect the equilibrium between formal and informal change?

- Do differences between civil law and common law traditions affect modes of constitutional change?
- How does volatility of the political system relate to constitutional change?
- Is there a tendency towards less complex amending processes?
- Can the enhancement of the role of the people counterbalance the role of political elites and judges in constitutional change?
- Is the role of experts in constitutional amendment related to the dominant constitutional ethos, and how does their involvement impact the "level of rigidity"?
- Are experts necessarily allies to political elites or can they be allies of the people?
- How does the relationship between lawmaker and judge influence the route of constitutional change?
- Who has the final word in the dialogue between constitutional legislator and courts, and what are the limits of the judicial review of amendments?
- How does the formation of a common European legal culture influence constitutional change?
- How did participation in the EU and seceding sovereignty affect formal and informal change?
- What triggers the debate on future amendments?

Despite the differences in constitutional culture, political history, form of government, judicial review systems and amending formulas, the existence of important convergences came forth through comparative analysis. Constitutional theory in the countries approached seems to share similar agonies, although these agonies are faced in completely different ways. Within each legal order, there are various mechanisms of formal and informal change, operated by multiple actors. Studying mechanisms of constitutional change inevitably touches upon the whole spectrum of constitutional law and allocation of powers.

Multifarious responses to the issues raised by the above questions can be explained on the basis of models of constitutional change. The range of diversity corresponds to the existence of very distinct models. The modelization of constitutional change is based on the correlation of mechanisms and the role of actors within different political systems and constitutional orders. This addition to the comparative constitutional law toolkit provides an alternative way to approach amendment, but also to understand diverse constitutional cultures through the way in which change is effected. Once models are built, the plot thickens as it becomes possible to discern what determines the profile of constitutional change in each polity, and the traditional notion of rigidity is re-examined to reveal the existence of differing multiple rigidities. Based on holistic approaches of constitutional narratives, modelizing constitutional change demands the comparative analysis of multiple parameters and factors. The process of change is where constitutions precariously cross paths with reality, and it is through the conceptual lens of constitutional change models that the different modes and effects of this encounter are revealed.

2 Constitutional change in Austria

Manfred Stelzer[1]

History and evolution of the constitutional amendment procedure

This section aims to demonstrate how the current amendment rules of the Austrian Constitution ensued from the specific historical situation in which the Constitution was framed. Major amendments of the Constitution will be discussed, emphasizing that their rising number after World War II was largely due to the governmental structure of the system, which frequently mandated the two-thirds majority required for such amendments.

History of the amendment regulation

The contemporary Austrian system of government is still based on the Constitution of 1920.[2] It was re-enacted after World War II and has been amended more than a hundred times, yet its core elements are still in force today. This Constitution, which designates Austria as a federal state and a parliamentary republic (features of a presidential system were added only by a 1929 amendment) emerged after the collapse of the Austro-Hungarian Empire. Its amendment procedures reflect the common attitude to the newly formed republic, as its democratic government was largely seen as a government in transition. When the multi-ethnic monarchy collapsed, it immediately became clear that the non-German-speaking population would disengage. Those people were already in the process of forming independent national states. The subsequent changes in territorial configuration reduced the center of power for the former Austro-Hungarian Empire to a small republic. Because it was deprived of vast agricultural and industrial resources as well as its traditional markets, few believed that the new republic was economically viable. Furthermore, influential groups within the main political parties (the Christian Socialists, the Social Democrats and the German Nationalists[3]) were convinced that democracy was only a transitional phase to ultimately be replaced by an authoritarian regime, whether by the re-establishment of the monarchy, a fascist regime or a socialist regime, based on Marxism–Leninism. The groups embraced different totalitarian movements,[4] making it difficult—sometimes impossible—for them to agree on substantive issues of the Constitution. The failure to enact a new bill of fundamental rights is probably the most prominent example of the effects of their contentious attitude.

After initial attempts to join Germany were quashed by the Treaty of Saint Germain,[5] a Constituent National Assembly (*Konstituierende Nationalversammlung*) was entrusted by law with the drafting of a new Federal Constitution.[6] Although this law envisaged that the new Constitution should provide for amendments to be ratified by means of a referendum only, it was later decided otherwise. As the framers believed in its mere provisional function, amendments to the new Constitution were to be passed by a two-thirds majority of the National Council. Furthermore, it was not deemed necessary to incorporate amendments into the original document. Only a "total revision" of the Constitution was to be submitted to a compulsory referendum (Art. 44 para 2, later para 3 of the Federal Constitution). The Federal Constitution (*Bundesverfassungsgesetz, B-VG*)[7] was passed by Parliament on 1 October 1920 and entered into force on 10 November of the same year. However, the extensive and highly neurotic conflicts between the political parties led to a civil war, and the parliamentary system was replaced in 1934 by the Catholic authoritarian *Ständestaat* (corporate state). This Constitution was not introduced by following the total revision procedures of the 1920 Constitution, but by a governmental decree.[8]

In 1938, Austria was occupied by German troops after almost no resistance and subsequently annexed to the German Reich (*Anschluss*). The 1934 Constitution was not formally abolished, but was set aside by German law. After World War II, the 1920 Constitution (in its amended 1929 version) was re-enacted.

Despite the tension and conflicts between the two dominant political parties—the Socialist Party[9] and the Conservative People's Party[10]—they nevertheless vowed to co-operate. They often joined together to form a grand coalition and, in this way, easily commanded the two-thirds majority needed for a constitutional amendment during most of the "Second Republic." Occasionally, their then sole opponent, the Freedom Party (FPÖ), was reduced to 5 per cent of parliamentary seats.[11]

It was part of the nature of this post-war co-operation for each of the dominant parties to identify issues of great importance to them and entrench amendments, by means of this favorable procedure. As long as a compromise was reached, the Constitution could be altered and amended almost at will. The main function of the Constitution was, therefore, to assist the two parties in finding such a compromise. Austrian public-law scholars and the Constitutional Court largely supported this system, as both interpreted the Constitution in a retrospective way, focusing on the legal background against which a constitutional provision was designed and the circumstances under which it was enacted.[12] This practice was, of course, not purely incidental: careers at universities and on the bench of the Constitutional Court were often influenced by party affiliation. However, this method required additional amendments, as problem-solving was deferred to Parliament rather than attempted by finding a more imaginative or inventive interpretation. The only threshold was a "total revision" of the Constitution, which was identified by scholars and the Constitutional Court to result from an amendment of the principles of the Constitution. The principles could only be altered by submitting the bill to a referendum.

Notwithstanding the discussions revolving around various cases of constitutional amendments, only Austria's accession to the European Union (EU) qualified as an amendment of constitutional principles and was consequently submitted to a referendum. All other constitutional amendments were enacted by Parliament. There were hundreds of constitutional alterations, including constitutional laws and constitutional provisions, making it impossible even for experts and constitutional scholars to list them all. Already in the 1960s, constitutional scholars had coined the phrase "shattered constitution" or "constitution in tatters."[13] It is impossible to discuss all these amendments within this chapter—an overview of the most important laws will have to suffice.[14]

A 1984 amendment of the Constitution (BGBl. 490/1984) slightly altered the amendment procedure by strengthening the position of the states and the Federal Council respectively. According to the 1920 version of the Constitution, the Federal Council could not block such a bill, only veto it. The National Council could overrule the veto. The only exception was a constitutional law that altered the position of the Federal Council, which required the consent of the Federal Council and, within the Federal Council, not only the majority of its members but also the majority of the delegates of at least four states. This 1984 amendment assigned power to the Federal Council to effectively block any bill that limited the power of the states (BGBl. 490/1984). Such a bill could only be passed with a two-thirds majority in the Federal Council; but, as the members of the Federal Council cast their votes along party lines rather than state interests, this power has never been used.

A 2008 amendment of the Constitution (BGBl. I 2/2008) abolished the option to alter the Constitution by means of state treaties. Until then, it was possible (and common) to alter the Constitution by adopting an international treaty or some selected provisions at the rank of a constitutional law. Since the 2008 amendment, this is no longer the case. International treaties may only be adopted at the rank of ordinary laws. Should an alteration of the Constitution be necessary or desirable to fulfill the duties imposed by the treaty, a specific constitutional provision is required.

Overview on major constitutional amendments

Constitutional amendments before World War II

Although constitutional amendments did not occur frequently during the 1920s, two major amendments were very important for the development of the Constitution. The 1925 amendment (BGBl. 268/1925) mainly provided for the allocation of powers between the Federation and the states (*Kompetenzverteilung*), already overdue since the enactment of the Constitution in 1920. The 1929 amendment (BGBl. 392/1929) partly changed the character of the Constitution. Meant as a reaction to the emerging civil war, it tried to (re)establish law and order. It provided for the general election of the Federal President, furnishing this institution with further responsibilities, such as the appointment and the dismissal of the Federal Chancellor and (on her or his proposal) the appointment and/or dismissal of all other Cabinet members. Since 1929, the Federal President has been furnished with the power to dissolve Parliament and to govern on the basis of so-called "emergency decrees" (*Notverordnungen*) in times when the National Assembly cannot be convened in due course.

The 1934 Constitution abolished democracy, replacing it with the co-operation of corporations in the lawmaking process. Laws had to be discussed first by Corporate Councils, which delegated members into a "Parliament" where laws already agreed upon by the Councils could be passed (or rejected) without further discussion. It is remarkable that similar procedures were part of the efficient Constitution after World War II. The renowned system of social partnership, largely seen as a guarantee of social peace and economic progress in post-war Austria, worked on a similar basis: laws agreed upon by the social partners. Therefore, decisions based on a so-called "social partner's compromise" were rarely challenged in Parliament. These organizations were highly influential, as their representatives (sometimes even their presidents) held seats in Parliament. Being members of the respective political parties, they had to run as candidates for general elections according to party statutes.

Constitutional amendments after World War II

As already mentioned, the 1920 Constitution (in its 1929 version) was re-enacted after World War II. Other than in Germany, no discussion about designing a new constitution emerged, basically due to the political aim of preventing Austria from being separated into two parts (as Germany had been) and to avoid Soviet influence in such discussions. One of the first additional constitutional laws enacted was a law prohibiting the recurrence of National Socialism (StGBl. 13/1945). A breach of that law would constitute severe punishment. It may be argued that the Constitution was thereby enriched by a moral (anti-fascist) concept.

Following the 1955 State Treaty of Vienna, which officially ended the control of the Allied Forces and restored Austria's sovereignty, the eternal neutrality of Austria was declared by law (*Neutralitätsgesetz*, BGBl. 211/1955). It significantly shaped the post-war politics and the international role of this country. Neutrality was probably the only substantial political concept providing an identity that both major parties could subscribe to. Of course, the accession to the EU jeopardized the principle of neutrality,[15] which (formally) is still in force.

In 1958, Austria became a member of the European Convention on Human Rights (ECHR). Rather than agreeing on a new domestic fundamental bill of rights, the Convention was adopted at the level of a constitutional law and made directly applicable (albeit this intended effect had to be achieved by a 1964 constitutional revision with retrospective effect). Although initially reluctant, the Constitutional Court followed the ever-evolving jurisprudence of the European Court of Human Rights (ECtHR), which effectively changed the reading of the Austrian Constitution and triggered further significant amendments.

A 1975 amendment of the Constitution extended the power of the Constitutional and Administrative Court, filling some loopholes regarding the concept of legal protection (BGBl. 302/1975). More interesting, however, is the 1975 Act on Political Parties (BGBl. 404/1975), which contains a constitutional provision on the formation of political parties that, in practice, excludes only the formation of National Socialist movements. This Act mainly provides for the public funding of political parties in a way that has helped to significantly change Austria's political landscape. As it favors smaller parties, the Act can be held partially responsible for the rise of the Freedom Party.[16] Following the Swedish example, an Ombudsman Board was introduced by a 1977 amendment (BGBl. 121/1977).

In 1988, Parliament reacted to the ever-evolving jurisprudence of the ECtHR concerning Art. 6 ECHR. As this article was modeled on the Anglo-Saxon system rather than the Central European Administrative State, it jeopardized the far-reaching competences of Austrian administrative bodies in the areas of civil rights and criminal charges. Although the Constitution allowed the establishment of independent administrative bodies in specific cases, a solution on a more general level seemed to be desirable. Thus, Independent Administrative Tribunals were introduced by a 1988 amendment (BGBl. 685/1988) and established at state level. Originally furnished with the responsibility to decide on matters of administrative criminal charges and the exercise of direct administrative power, their competences were extended by a 2001 amendment (BGBl. 137/2001) to cover fields of civil rights and obligations according to the jurisprudence of the ECtHR.

The 1995 accession to the EU has significantly changed the design of Austria's Constitution. Because it represented a "total revision" of the Constitution in the eyes of many legal scholars, the government, and the Constitutional Court, it was first considered necessary to submit it to a referendum. But the bill submitted to the referendum only provided for Austria's accession to the EU.[17] It is therefore unclear to what extent the principles of Austria's Constitution have effectively been altered. It might be questionable whether future amendments of the European Treaty were to trigger a further amendment to constitutional principles (and therefore a total revision) or not. Some scholars, for instance, argued that the "Constitution Treaty" would have represented a further "total revision" of Austria's Constitution, whilst the Lisbon Treaty did not.[18] Second, the EU Treaty shifted powers from the states to the Federation, from Parliament to the Federal Cabinet, and effectively curtailed the power of the Constitutional Court.

Third, to counterbalance some shifts in power, the accession to the EU triggered formal amendments to the Constitution (BGBl. 1013/1994). They provided for the participation of the states and the Federal Parliament in EU lawmaking procedures, by confirming the obligation of the Federal Cabinet to inform both the states and the Federal Parliament about EU lawmaking projects (a similar provision had already been in force accompanying the accession process[19]). Furthermore, the power to issue statements with binding effect on the voting of the Federal Minister representing Austria in the Council was vested in them. Fourth, EU law taking precedence over Austrian constitutional law (with the possible exception of its principles) allows for further and unforeseeable changes of Austria's Constitution.

Shortly after the accession to the EU, it was questioned whether the Austrian Constitution, already described as "shattered" in the 1960s, still stood the test of time. Structural deficits were arguably detected. On the model of the European Constitutional Convention, a Constitutional Convention was established that worked on a complete overhaul of the Austrian Constitution (2003–2005).[20] It produced a comprehensive draft version including a redistribution of power between the Federation and the states, as well as a new bill of rights including social rights. Although all parties participated in this convention, and an all-party compromise seemed to be within reach, the idea to replace the current Constitution with a new one was quickly dropped. However, the Constitution has been partially altered since. A 2007 amendment (BGBl. I 27/2007) further changed the electoral system, introducing the possibility of postal voting. A 2008 amendment established the Asylum Court, thus curtailing the power of the Administrative Court (BGBl. I 2/2008) and abolished the possibility of adopting international treaties at the level of constitutional law. This only half-heartedly addressed the problem that constitutional provisions are spread over the whole legal system, although an overwhelming number of constitutional provisions and/or laws were re-ranked as ordinary laws or held to have expired. Another amendment reformed the law on the Federal Budget (BGBl. 1/2008).

A comprehensive redistribution of powers between the Federation and the states, albeit elaborated in a Cabinet bill,[21] has not yet been established. A 2010 Cabinet bill on the establishment of Administrative Courts in the states, replacing the Independent Administrative Tribunals and over 100 independent administrative bodies, is still under consideration.[22] Thus, it might be said that Austria's Constitution was, and probably always will be, a Constitution in the making.

Informal methods of constitutional change

The brief overview on the formal amendments of the Austrian Constitution has already revealed that, allegedly apart from its core principles, Austria has a very flexible constitution, which has easily been amended throughout the decades. It might be surprising to learn, therefore, that many informal amendments have also been made, most notably in fields in which the two dominant parties failed to find a compromise.

Informal amendments occur when the Constitution is changed without altering or amending the text in accordance with the formal procedure entrenched in the Constitution. It might therefore be regarded as an informal amendment when laws that are not passed according to these procedures change the Constitution. This situation might be the case when European or international law effectively changes the Constitution. These cases are covered below. Moreover, ordinary laws passed by Parliament might also change the Constitution. This process is possible because not all constitutional laws are entrenched: there are ordinary laws that are regarded as constitutional laws in a substantive, albeit informal, sense. One prominent example is the law on the election of the National Council. As this law was, for instance, significantly altered in the early 1970s (BGBl. 194/1971), it facilitated changes in the party system.[23] Apart from these cases, academic literature emphasizes that informal methods of changing the Constitution can be seen in judicial interpretation and/or shifts in political practice and convention.[24] Both cases can be observed in Austria, although most Austrian scholars would uphold a strong distinction between "interpretation" and "amendment." The argument would be that the cases discussed below cannot be seen as changes but rather as the breakthrough of the Constitution's original meaning.

Changes in state practice

Alterations in state practice provide one example of how informal amendments of the Constitution are instigated. Two cases will be discussed here: the first case concerns the power of the Federal President. Article 47 para 1 of the Federal Constitution grants the President the power to authenticate the constitutional enactment of any federal law. The wording of this constitutional provision has led to a discussion on the extent of the President's power of review and thus influence on the legislative process.[25] Two facts enjoy general consensus among public lawyers. First, the Federal President has the right, and in fact the duty, to formally review lawmaking procedures. To be precise, the President is to ensure that procedural rules have been observed; for example, that a vote was held according to the Standing Orders of the National Council. Second, the Federal President does not have the right to veto a bill on political grounds, unlike the American President, for example.

Constitutional theory is divided on whether the Federal President may or may not refuse his or her signature to laws passed by Parliament on substantive grounds.[26] However, the President's refusal would effectively terminate the lawmaking procedure as the Constitution provides neither the National Council with the power to overturn the President's decisions, nor a court the jurisdiction over this issue. In the event that the Federal President refuses to sign a law, the National Council would have two options: to alter the offending provision or to initiate rather complicated proceedings to remove the Federal President from office. These proceedings are so complicated that they are quite unlikely to occur, especially with regard to the failure to sign one law.

Austrian Federal Presidents initially were reluctant to claim the power to review a law on substantive constitutional grounds. One former Federal President, Rudolf Kirchschläger, even explicitly denied the existence of such a power, arguing that, in light of the legal circumstances described above, he would otherwise block a law that had been supported by a majority in Parliament and hinder its enactment. For the sake of democracy, he would rather leave it to the Constitutional Court to pronounce on its constitutionality and to rescind it if necessary.[27] However, given the different interpretations and intentions of his successors, this view was not always shared. Some Federal Presidents wished to play a more active part in domestic policies and occasionally delayed the process of signing a bill or even threatened not to sign it at all. A more recent case occurred in January 2008, when President Heinz Fischer withheld his signature from a bill[28] already passed by Parliament, on the grounds that it constituted a violation of Art. 7 ECHR. The

National Council deferred to the Federal President's view and redrafted the bill, omitting the offending provision. Once passed, the Federal President provided his signature. This example may indicate that the state organs accepted the Federal President's power to refuse to sign a law on substantial constitutional grounds. In any case, a precedent has been created and it may already be argued that state practice has changed the Constitution informally.

The second case discussed under this section concerns the role of state constitutions. One decisive feature of Austria's federal system is not only the fact that most of the power is vested in the Federation, but also that the Federal Constitution provides for substantive guidelines for state constitutions, although states are theoretically seen as sovereign entities.

State constitutions may only be amended or enacted insofar as the Federal Constitution is not thereby affected (Art. 99 para 1 of the Federal Constitution). It was initially assumed that states merely had to implement those parts of the Federal Constitution that were tailored to the state constitution, leaving little or no leeway. For a long time, states therefore merely copied the rather comprehensive federal law on principles, thus the need to respect regional differences was not overwhelming. This interpretation muted the notion of a state as a sovereign entity and consequently also contradicted the nature of a federal state. The late 1970s saw a change in this attitude,[29] which was strengthened by the increasing self-confidence of the states. Today, a "relative constitutional autonomy of the states" has been established, strengthening the above-mentioned practice that states, although strictly speaking bound by the Federal Constitution, legislate freely in areas where the Federal Constitution is silent on matters of the state constitution. Indeed, some state constitutions even provide for civil rights or a welfare-state principle.[30]

It is noteworthy that in both cases discussed above, the change in state practice was initiated and underpinned by scholarly analysis and academic discussion.

Judicial interpretation

Law court decisions have also informally amended the Austrian Constitution, especially in the field of fundamental rights. Here, the two dominant political parties could not agree on a compromise for enacting a new bill, despite having set up a Fundamental Rights Reform Committee (*Grundrechtsreformkommission*) in the 1960s, and despite the recommendations of the Constitutional Convention. Only recently has the Supreme Court declared itself the guardian of fundamental rights in criminal law cases and, by doing so, effectively altered the significance of human rights in criminal law suits.[31]

According to Austria's centralized system of constitutional review, it is mainly the responsibility of the Constitutional Court to review laws. Already furnished with this power in 1919, the Court has made extensive use of this mandate, not only with regard to reviewing but also rescinding laws. For decades it has adhered to more formal, retrospective methods of reading and interpreting the Constitution, thereby supporting the requirement for political parties to compromise. In the 1980s, however, the Court introduced different methods of reading the

Constitution, foremost with regard to the fundamental rights provision. Based on the example of the European Court of Human Rights (ECtHR) and the German Federal Constitutional Court and, again, initiated and underpinned by legal writing, the Constitutional Court started to apply the principle of proportionality when scrutinizing alleged infringements of freedom rights.[32] This had two effects: freedom rights were at once working thresholds that Parliament could not cross by enacting ordinary laws; constitutional amendments were necessary. Further, sometimes even more importantly, ordinary laws had to be interpreted in the light of the proportionality principle, thus reducing the leeway of the administration.

It is noteworthy that as long as the Constitutional Court maintained traditional methods of reading the Constitution, its competence to review laws was generally accepted. However, politicians and academics alike started criticizing the result of the Court's considerations in the 1980s, when the Court started promoting freedom of rights and introduced the principle of proportionality.[33] The power of the Court was especially questioned with regard to the democratic principle enshrined in the Constitution.[34] Its methodological turnaround not only challenged the traditional approach of reading the Constitution, but also the political system. As a result, as long as the People's Party and the Social Democrats enjoyed a two-thirds majority in Parliament, it became a habit to enact constitutional provisions for the sole purpose of preventing the Court from scrutinizing the law. This move was not only a reaction to a specific court ruling, promoting freedom rights or the principle of equality, but also a means of prohibiting the Court from scrutinizing a legal provision.[35] However, in hindsight, the Court's introduction of the proportionality principle prepared Austria's legal system for the accession to the EU. To a certain extent, of course, it has broken the tradition that constitutional changes should stem from party compromises rather than from a more imaginative and inventive interpretation.

Formal constitutional amendment process

The procedures to formally amend the Constitution do not substantially differ from enacting ordinary laws; merely a majority of two-thirds in Parliament with half of its members present is required. Against the background of the Austrian political system, the Constitution has proved to be rather flexible. The principles of the Constitution, which may only be altered by means of a "total revision" triggering a mandatory referendum, might be seen as a rather rigid core element.

The authority to amend Austrian Constitutional Law is derived from Art. 44 of the Federal Constitution. Under Art. 44 para 1, constitutional laws or constitutional provisions contained in ordinary laws can be passed by the National Council, by a two-thirds majority of the votes cast and with a quorum of at least half the members present.[36] The wording of Art. 44 of the Federal Constitution provides for a specific observation. When addressing the amendment procedure, this Article speaks of "constitutional laws or constitutional provisions contained in ordinary law," thus providing the possibility of enacting formal constitutional legislation outside the Constitution in individual constitutional Acts (*Bundesverfassungsgesetze*) or in constitutional provisions (*Verfassungsbestimmungen*) in ordinary laws. The Federal Constitution, for example, does not contain a bill of rights; however, provisions for civil liberties are included in various bills and (additionally) in various legislative Acts.

Drafting methods and ordinary amending procedure

In line with the legal and political situation already outlined, amendments of the Constitution almost became part of the Parliament's daily routine. The amendment procedures do not substantially differ from the general procedures to enact a law, which need the co-operation of Parliament and the executive branch of government, as laws have to be signed by the Federal President and published by the Federal Chancellor. Initially, there must be a legislative proposal considered and passed by the National Council and subsequently, in most cases (and always when an amendment to the Constitution is envisaged), by the Federal Council.

The impetus to pass a new law often derives from sources outside Parliament. The Federal Cabinet proposes a vast majority of bills and adopted texts. The preparation of the legislative texts—and this procedure also applies to constitutional amendments—are mostly the task of the administration. There are several informal procedural steps that can be taken. A draft might be circulated to relevant ministries to obtain expert opinions. Ministerial proposals may in turn be provided to interested parties and expert groups, whereby expert reviews are formulated. The ministry may—but is not obliged to—amend its draft based on the expert review before submitting it to the Federal Cabinet. A special department within the Federal Chancellery, the so-called *Verfassungsdienst* (which might translate as "Constitutional Service Department") will be involved in drafting constitutional provisions and/or laws and will scrutinize other bills against the Constitution, possibly suggesting constitutional provisions. According to the Austrian tradition of grand coalition governments, the verdict that a law or a specific legal provision might violate the Constitution would not necessarily result in abandoning it but in proposing a constitutional amendment already at this stage of the lawmaking procedure.

Once a legislative initiative has been successfully launched and approved by the Federal Cabinet (*Ministerrat*), it is subject to an assessment procedure[37] in which a number of institutions may comment on the draft. Subsequently, the National Council considers the bill in the course of the two main procedures. The draft bill is (after a general assessment) first discussed in committees. Committees often consult members of the civil service and external experts. During these preliminary deliberations, a committee may also make amendments to the original draft if these committees do not wish to be bound by a compromise of the social partners or a strong commitment to the government. Consultations in the committees normally take place *in camera*. During what is called the "second reading," draft bills are further considered in the plenary meetings of the National Assembly, after the bill has been dealt with in the committee. This discussion is open to the public. The legislation procedure in the National Council ends with voting on the bill, which in the case of a constitutional law or constitutional provision needs a majority of two-thirds with at least half of the members present.[38]

As a rule, the Federal Council will deliberate on possible amendments to the Constitution that have already been adopted by the National Council. In most cases the Federal Council has the right to veto. Under Art. 44 para 2, an amendment to the Constitution restricting the competence of the states (*Länder*) has, since 1984, required the approval of the Federal Council by a two-thirds majority in the presence of at least half the members. Such approval has never been refused. An amendment to the provisions regarding the status and the composition of the Federal Council (Arts. 34 and 35 of the Federal Constitution) requires approval by the Federal Council, and additionally the majority of the representatives of at least four states. Attempts to change the status and/or composition of the Federal Council have been discussed extensively,[39] yet have never been formally made.

When the Federal Council has not been given the right to approve, only the right to veto, it may delay the legislative process but cannot prevent the enactment of a law. Here, the Federal Council may raise a "reasoned objection" within eight weeks, but only to the effect that the National Council may overrule it. For reasons that cannot be discussed here, but which have led to intensive considerations to alter the status, composition, and responsibilities of the Federal Council (and even its abolishment), it has never really represented state interests. Instead, votes have been cast along party lines. Since constitutional amendments needed the support of the dominant parties, both of which always enjoyed a comfortable majority in the Federal Council, constitutional amendments never failed to satisfy Federal Council procedures or were thereby delayed.

When considering the ease with which amendments can be made and subsequently designated as constitutional law, it could be held that the Austrian Federal Constitutional Law is highly flexible in nature. Of course, the post-war political system plays a significant role in this observation. Major changes in the political system may lead to a more rigid Constitution.

"Total revision" of the Constitution

A more inflexible procedure has to be observed under Art. 44 para 3 of the Federal Constitution. Here, the Austrian Constitution provides for a specific procedure if a "total revision" (*Gesamtänderung*) of the Constitution is envisaged. In this case, a referendum is also needed. The same applies to partial amendments (*Teiländerung*), although only if one-third of the members of the National Council or the Federal Council deems a referendum necessary. By way of interpretation, Austrian scholars as well as the Constitutional Court believe that the Constitution undergoes a total revision whenever principles of the Constitution are altered or seriously affected.[40] Austrian scholars are still divided on questions of how many such principles exist and what their exact meaning might be. The Constitutional Court has accepted three principles:[41] the democratic principle, the federal principle, and the principle of *Rechtsstaat*. Precisely what falls under these principles must still be assessed. However, some decisions of the Constitutional Court allow at least some basic understanding on their substance, which will be briefly outlined below.[42]

The democratic principle primarily protects certain constitutional institutions and their powers. At the core of this principle rests the Austrian Parliament and its legislative powers. Alterations to the position of the Austrian Parliament, especially with regard to the legislative powers of the National Council, may constitute a modification of the democratic principle. Austria's accession to the EU transferred a large set of legislative powers from the Parliament to the EU's political bodies, and was therefore seen as a total revision of the Constitution.[43]

The core element of the federal state principle lies in the division of powers between the Federation and the states.[44] Transferring a large set of powers from the states to the Federation might therefore violate this principle, while selective transfers have always constituted only partial revisions. As such partial revisions frequently happened as a consequence of the retrospective interpretation of the Constitution, the gradual transfer of powers has been termed a "creeping total revision" (*schleichende Gesamtänderung*)[45] by Austrian constitutional lawyers, albeit with no effect so far on the Constitutional Court.[46]

According to the reading of the Constitutional Court, a *Rechtsstaat* must guarantee legal certainty (*Rechtssicherheit*) and, above all, legal protection (*Rechtsschutz*). The Austrian Constitution, for example through the establishment of the Administrative Court and the Constitutional Court, provides for the latter. From the Constitutional Court's point of view, the principle of legal protection was endangered when regulations were enacted as constitutional law and the Constitutional Court was subsequently prevented from scrutinizing them. This was primarily the case in the late 1980s, when the Parliament overruled decisions of the Constitutional Court by enacting constitutional provisions. With these decisions, the Court had rescinded laws that disproportionally inhibited the establishments of businesses. The Constitutional Court noted that such measures could potentially undermine its powers if taken (too) frequently, and thus interfere with the principle of *Rechtsstaat*.[47] But again, the Court did not take any action with regard to single and selective constitutional entrenchments. Ultimately, however, it rescinded a law on the basis of these arguments, which allegedly undermined its power to scrutinize laws in the field of the public procurement law of the states.[48]

However, there is still only one practical example in which a constitutional amendment was seen as a total revision by the government and resulted in a referendum: Austria's accession to the EU. It might therefore be said that the principles of the Austrian Constitution form a rather rigid core element. Austrian scholars even express the view that European law may not override this core element.[49] This interpretation might be supported by the Lisbon Treaty, which stipulates that the EU would respect its member states' "national identities inherent in their fundamental structures, political and constitutional."[50] This clause may be read as a guarantee that member states can uphold core elements of their constitutions that may not be overridden by EU law.

Effective substantive limits?

According to a general reading of the Austrian Constitution, which reflects its initial understanding as a Constitution governing a transitional period, it is held that all its principles can be changed, and even abolished, by means of a referendum. This fact was especially considered true for the democratic principle: in contrast to the German "eternity clauses," Austrian democracy might lawfully be abolished by a referendum. For the past two decades, some Austrian scholars have questioned this view.[51] As no attempts were made to completely abolish one or other principle, the question of whether there may be substantial limits to the principles remains an ongoing academic debate.

The role of the people

The Austrian Constitution provides for direct involvement of the people in the amending procedures. The electorate may initiate an amending procedure and may be asked to vote on the bill. However, these are not frequent events. Apart from that, governmental and non-governmental institutions are consulted during an assessment procedure following a Cabinet initiative, thereby allowing for their informal participation in the amendment process.

Austria's democracy is focused on Parliament. Direct participation of the electorate in the lawmaking procedure is only foreseen additionally. Three instruments cover this issue: the popular initiative (*Volksbegehren*), the referendum (*Volksabstimmung*), and the public consultation (*Volksbefragung*).

Popular initiatives

The popular initiative is a formal request by the citizens to introduce a matter for legislative action in Parliament. It has been questioned whether the people are entitled to initiate an amendment to the Federal Constitution. The phrasing of the Constitution (Art. 41 para 2) is ambiguous, as it states that a popular initiative may only relate to subject matters to be regulated by a federal law, thus leaving it open to interpretation whether only ordinary laws fall under this provision or it extends to constitutional laws as well. In the case of the latter, the separation of powers between the Federation and the states may be overridden and a subject matter might be concerned that falls under the responsibility of the states. Nevertheless, it is current state practice to allow a popular initiative, even pertaining to a constitutional provision, which is occasionally the case. One illustrative example is a fairly recent law on animal protection that needed a constitutional alteration to furnish the Federation with the power to enact it. This law was initiated in 1996 by several non-governmental organizations (NGOs) committed to animal protection. It was hugely supported by Austria's largest-selling daily newspaper and was eventually enacted by the Federal Parliament in 2004 (BGBl. 118/2004).

Currently, the support of one per million of the electorate is required to start the proceedings. Until a 1998 amendment to the law on popular initiatives (BGBl. I 160/1998), it was possible to replace the initial support of citizens by the vote of a few members of the National Council and state parliaments respectively. Therefore, this instrument was designed as a means for opposition parties rather than the electorate. Although this option has been abandoned by the said amendment, it still might be observed that opposition parties rather than civil society have primarily organized the most popular initiatives filed so far.

Despite the possibility of the electorate instigating and partaking in a popular initiative, the initiative is not a binding instrument; Parliament is under no obligation to render any legislative decision. This fact has led to an ongoing discussion to introduce the obligation to submit the subject matter to a referendum, should Parliament refuse to legislate.

Assessment procedure

As already outlined, in all cases concerning a Cabinet bill, an assessment or consultation procedure will be observed (*Begutachtungsverfahren*).[52] This procedure is not entrenched; no specific rules apply as to who has to be consulted and what time limits might be set. Basically informal in character, it reflects the system of social partnership, but the consultation extends beyond the social partners. During this assessment procedure, state, non-state actors, and institutions may comment on the draft. The aim is to enable those with a particular interest in the draft bill to issue opinions. Participants may range from social partners, namely the Austrian Federal Economic Chamber (*Österreichische Bundes-Wirtschaftskammer*), the Chamber of Agriculture (*Landwirtschaftskammer*), the Chamber of Labour (*Arbeiterkammer*) and the Austrian Trade Union Federation (*Österreichischer Gewerkschaftsbund*), various other chambers, NGOs, and state parliaments to single persons (such as experts) or groups of people. Anyone aiming to influence a particular legislation in Austria would, therefore, try to get an invitation to issue an opinion. The submitted opinions are not made available to the public.

Although issued opinions are not binding, it is of note that the co-ordinated views and compromises of the participants are given particular consideration. Co-ordinated views and compromises by the social partners used to be upheld in Parliament.[53] Again, it might be noted that the assessment procedure does not address the civil society as such, but various chambers and other organizations, many of which are affiliated with the party system.

Referenda

Unlike the popular initiative, a referendum is a binding instrument. It is used as an electorate device allowing eligible citizens to have a direct vote on bills that have already been passed by Parliament. The procedure follows the model for conducting general elections. Depending on the circumstances, a referendum may either be rendered compulsory by federal law (in the case of a total revision) or be otherwise initiated by Parliament.[54]

Although Austrian scholars have argued numerous times that constitutional provisions have violated constitutional principles and therefore would have required a referendum for the reasons outlined previously, only two referenda have been carried out during the Second Republic. The first referendum was held in 1978, following a large public debate on the operation of an already completed nuclear power plant in the village of Zwentendorf. This issue has been the only non-mandatory referendum held on a law that initially was an ordinary law. The results of the votes were duly implemented by Parliament. A new law prohibiting the "peaceful exploitation of nuclear power" (*Atomsperrgesetz*, BGBl. 676/1978) was passed, and only in 1999 (BGBl. I 149/1999) was it transferred into the rank of constitutional law. To this day, there are no nuclear power plants operating in Austria.

The second was held in 1994, in the course of Austria's accession to the EU. This was the only situation in which the government was willing to accept the idea of a total revision and to submit a constitutional law to a referendum, which subsequently was successfully concluded.[55]

Public consultation

Apart from the above, for the purpose of exploring public opinion, the Constitution has foreseen another direct democratic instrument, the consultation of the people (*Volksbefragung*). According to Art. 49b of the Federal Constitution, the National Council may decide to consult the people on a matter of fundamental and national importance that lies within the power of the federal legislator. The result would not be binding on Parliament. No such consultation has been held so far.

Influence of international and European law

Both international and European law may have the power to directly amend the Constitution. Until 2008, the government had the option to adopt international treaties at the rank of constitutional law. In any case, international and European law may trigger a constitutional amendment when necessary or desired to fulfill Austria's obligation imposed by a treaty or a European law. Such an amendment might also be informed by ECtHR jurisprudence. This section focuses on the impact of international and European law and jurisprudence on the Austrian Constitution. There are basically two ways in which the Austrian Constitution is affected both by international and European law. First, it is possible that international and European law may directly amend the Austrian Constitution. Second, the obligations imposed on Austria by international or European law may render a constitutional amendment necessary, or at least desirable. Sometimes, this need or desire may follow a ruling of an international court, most likely the ECtHR. As a consequence, both the Federal constitutional law and numerous federal statutes supplementing it have been amended in light of international duties and obligations. Austria's entry into the EU joined its legal system with EU law in the form of a dual constitution.

International law

With regard to international law, a distinction has to be made between customary international law and international treaties. The Austrian Constitution is open to customary international law, as it provides for the transformation of the "general principles of international law" into the Austrian legal system according to Art. 9 para 1 of the Federal Constitution. Some scholars believe that these general principles might directly alter the Constitution as they might take the rank of a constitutional law according to the subject matter to which they are related.[56] Should regulating the subject matter in question require its imposition in a constitutional law, these principles would be ranked at the level of constitutional law, thus directly amending the Constitution. Other scholars hold the view that general principles of international law could only be positioned below the rank of constitutional law, but above ordinary law, thus placing them on a specific position within the step pyramid.[57] As a consequence, general principles of international law would not have the power to silently amend the Constitution. The Constitutional Court has never settled this dispute; there is still an ongoing debate that would also concern the ranking of decisions of international bodies directly affecting Austria.

As already outlined, the Austrian Constitution could have been amended by adopting international treaties or selected provisions of these treaties at the rank of a constitutional law, until a 2008 amendment abolished this option (BGBl. I 2/2008). Such an adoption procedure only required a two-thirds majority in Parliament with at least half of its members present, and the explicit indication that the affected provisions were altering the Constitution. The adoption of the ECHR at the rank of a constitutional law might be the most prominent example, but there were literally hundreds. The 2008 amendment, which changed this practice, also re-ranked international treaties and specific provisions in these treaties as ordinary laws: it lists more than 170 such provisions.[58] In case a constitutional amendment is needed to fulfill an obligation imposed by an international treaty, a specific constitutional law covering this issue would have to be enacted in the future.

Amendments to the Austrian Constitution were also informed by ECtHR jurisprudence. Foremost, the introduction of Independent Administrative Tribunals on a state level can be seen as a reaction to the Court's reading of Art.6 ECtHR. Further, the ECHR and the rulings of the ECtHR have influenced the understanding of fundamental and human rights by the Austrian Constitutional Court, which has adhered to the jurisprudence of the ECtHR. Most certainly, this jurisprudence has, at least partially, underpinned the introduction of the proportionality principle.

European law

Austria became part of the European Union in 1995. As already discussed, this move was probably the most serious amendment of the Constitution, simultaneously amending its core principles. European law may directly amend Austria's Constitution, as the general view is that European law takes precedence over Austrian law, "ordinary" constitutional law included. Only the principles of the Constitution form a core element that cannot be overridden by European law.

Although European law may be supreme over Austrian constitutional law, Parliament has nevertheless incorporated principles of European law into the

Austrian Constitution or amended the Austrian Constitution following amendments to the EU Treaty. For instance, a 2008 amendment (BGBl. I 1/2008), which redrafted the law on the federal budget, incorporated requirements according to the Maastricht Treaty into the Austrian Constitution. A 2010 amendment (BGBl. I 57/2010) altered Art. 23b–23h of the Federal Constitution to ensure that both the National and the Federal Council could raise a claim that the subsidiary principle was violated by an EU bill according to the procedures entrenched in the Lisbon Treaty. Further, the transformation of a directive might still require a constitutional amendment or, at the very least, such an amendment might be felt desirable. The shift in power between the states and the Federation to transform European directions on environmental impact assessment and/or public procurement may serve as examples.[59]

The 2008 amendment on the ratification of international treaties (BGBl. I 2/2008), which abolished the option to adopt international treaties at the rank of a constitutional law, emphasized the specific position of the EU treaties in the Austrian legal system. Until the 2008 amendment, EU treaties were adopted at the rank of a constitutional law and were indicated as "amending the Constitution." According to the 2008 amendment, however, future treaties will no longer be indicated as amending the Constitution, nor will they be adopted at the rank of a constitutional law. Nevertheless, adoption will require a two-thirds majority in the National Council, with at least half of its members present. Additionally, the Federal Council needs to give its consent under the same voting rules; and adoption might be subject to a referendum, which would be mandatory in case of a further amendment to constitutional principles. The power to override Austrian constitutional law is only derived from the European Court of Justice jurisprudence, which Austria accepted by joining the EU in 1995.

The influence of Austria's political system on constitutional revision

Although political parties are hardly mentioned in the written Constitution, they play a decisive part under the efficient Constitution. Thus, it can be argued that the much criticized deficiency of the Austrian Constitution basically mirrors the political system, which has been formed by two "camps" following substantially different ideologies. This section touches on difficult and delicate questions concerning the differences between the "written" and the "efficient" Constitution. According to the "written" Constitution, the actors to engineer a constitutional amendment are the Federal Cabinet, the National and Federal Councils, the Federal President, and the people. Political parties are not listed among those actors, and they were hardly mentioned in the Constitution at all until 1975. Only by the 1975 Political Parties Act (BGBl. 404/1975) was the formation of political parties entrenched. According to this constitutional provision, the participation in the political decision-making process falls within their responsibilities.

In reality, however, the main political parties had already existed before the Republic was founded in 1918 and were re-established after World War II, before

Austria was declared independent from the German Reich. In fact, the declaration of independence was signed by the leaders of the (then) Socialist Party, the People's Party, and the (Soviet-influenced) Communist Party. Austria's party system, which emerged from the Austro–Hungarian Monarchy, completely overrides the power-dividing structures the written Constitution provides for.[60]

Political parties may in general be an essential element in representative democracies, as they act as intermediaries between the state and society. Austrian political parties have always exceeded this role. Together with their affiliated associations, they not only dominated the political sphere, but almost all parts of socialization as well.[61] Thus, the conservative People's Party and the Social Democratic Party formed the center of political camps. Under the "efficient" Constitution, the framing of the Constitution and amendments to it were basically the result of a struggle between those two camps, which adhere, at least in part, to completely different ideologies and values. Herein lies the reason why enacting a more modern bill of rights and restructuring the allocation of powers between the Federation and the states were, and still seem to be, impossible targets to achieve.

Nevertheless, in light of the experience of the 1933 Civil War and the Nazi period, under which representatives of both parties found themselves incarcerated in concentration camps, they vowed to co-operate after the war. This vow did not, of course, mean that all tensions, conflicts, and mutual distrust were abandoned, although much of it could be concealed in times of economic prosperity. The belief in co-operation and the need to compromise, combined with the still lingering mutual distrust,[62] had a serious impact on the Constitution.

As mentioned previously, not only bills bearing an essential "constitutional" character but also other provisions were enacted as constitutional law in Austria. Any matter of special interest for one of the dominant parties could be entrenched, thus safeguarding it against a possible (absolute) majority from the other party, at least as long as one still commanded slightly more than one-third of the seats and therefore had the power to block any amendment to the Constitution. The system was based on reciprocity and worked even in periods when a single party controlled the government.[63] It might therefore be said that, despite the fact that the written Constitution allocates the power to amend to various actors, such as the Federal Cabinet, Parliament and the people, in reality constitutional amendments were engineered by party agreements.

It might be said, therefore, that the state of the Constitution mirrors the political system. The mere "technical" understanding of the Constitution, as incorporating laws that have to be passed according to specific requirements, reflects the highly controversial ideologies and values that the two camps (the Social Democrats and the Conservatives) represent. This conflict has heretofore prevented any structural reform of the Constitution. Over the decades, some controversies might have mellowed, but they have not completely vanished. The recent rise of the Freedom Party, more or less representing the "third camp" (the pre-war German Nationalists), combined with the loss of the two-thirds majority by the two major parties, might significantly and sustainably change the efficient Constitution. Such a change would probably also affect the written Constitution. It can already be seen that since the

2008 elections, in which the two dominant parties lost their two-thirds majority, amending the Constitution has become a more complex affair. Opposition parties have to be invited to vote in favor of an amendment, and they will only do so if their bargaining positions are also met.

The role of experts in the constitutional revisions

Internal and external experts may be consulted at almost every step of the amending procedure. In most cases, however, the ministerial bureaucracy would draft constitutional amendments. On occasions, expert groups were established to draft more comprehensive amendments. Only a small part of this work has actually led to alterations of the Constitution. Experts might participate at many stages of the lawmaking procedures in general, and in the constitutional amendment procedures in particular. As most amendments stem from Cabinet bills, the civil service drafts them. The civil service (most notably in the various Ministries) provides the government with expertise, not only on the subject matter, but also on all technical aspects of drafting a bill. With regard to constitutional amendments, the Constitutional Service Department of the Federal Chancellery would be involved. The influence of the civil service may even go beyond that: as Parliament is not equipped with a comprehensive legal service, (senior) members of the civil service will often attend committee meetings and be asked to help redrafting a Cabinet bill if Parliament so desires. Most notably, the assessment procedure, which regularly follows the submission of a Cabinet bill, is largely held as participatory by experts. The Chamber of Labour and the Federal Chamber of Commerce are regarded as "brains trusts" of the Social Democratic Party and the People's Party respectively.

External experts, such as university professors, may be involved at any stage of the drafting procedure. Their opinions might be requested by the Cabinet Minister, by organizations during the assessment procedure, by political parties or, eventually, by Parliament. As their opinions would not necessarily be published, it is difficult to assess the extent of their influence. In most cases, however, experts would be chosen or recommended by political parties or their affiliates. Those experts are, therefore, often members of the political parties or affiliated with them. Thus, it is even more difficult to assess which part of an opinion is biased by party commitments. In some cases, external experts have been given a more prominent role in preparing constitutional amendments. The fact that in these cases the drafts produced were hardly ever enacted might reveal something about the rather fragile relationship between the political system and external expertise.

By 1964, a group of experts was already established by the Federal Chancellor to draft a modern bill of rights, replacing the 1867 Fundamental Law on the Rights of Citizens.[64] This group (the "Fundamental Rights Reform Commission"—*Grundrechte-Reformkommission*) continued its work until 1974 and was followed by an Editorial Committee, which produced a comprehensive draft version of a fundamental rights bill in 1983. In 1985, a committee was established that consisted of representatives of the political parties holding seats in the National Council; its task was to re-phrase the draft version in order to find a political compromise. The only outcome was an amendment to the 1862 guarantee of personal freedom (which had introduced the *habeas corpus* rule) in light of Art. 5 ECHR, a provision that had already been part of Austria's Constitution. This new law on personal freedom was enacted in 1988 (BGBl. 684/1988). Nothing else followed, the idea to enact a modern bill of rights was dropped, and the committee ended its work without being formally dissolved in 1993, almost 30 years after the establishment of the Reform Commission.

Following Austria's accession to the EU, not only was the idea to pass a more modern bill of rights resurrected, but also a complete overhaul of the Austrian Constitution seemed to be desirable. An Austrian Constitutional Convention was established, based on the model of the European Constitutional Convention. Consisting of various experts—such as law professors, judges, representatives of the social partners, and others—it worked on a draft version of a new Constitution from 2003 to 2005.[65] Its chair, a former chairman of the Public Audit Office, presented the draft version. Hence, the idea to replace Austria's current Constitution with a completely new document (obviously constituting a "total revision" and therefore triggering a referendum) was again dropped. Following the 2006 elections, another committee of experts was established at the Federal Chancellery and entrusted with drafting comprehensive amendments. Since then, several partial revisions of the Constitution have been enacted, avoiding more controversial questions.

Assessing the work of all these experts is difficult. Some of them have boosted their careers, others have probably only wasted their time. Judging by the results, it can be said that they obviously could have been achieved using fewer academic and non-academic resources, albeit that some of this work informed amendments that were ultimately enacted. One expert group, at least, was highly successful. During the mid-1990s, under the chair of the chairman of the Public Audit Office, an expert group designed the so-called "income pyramid," providing for the income of public functionaries such as the Federal President, the Chancellor, the Cabinet Ministers, Members of Parliament, and many others.[66] This income pyramid was adopted by Parliament, parts of it also at the rank of a constitutional law. It establishes a very generous system, second only to Italy within the Organization for Economic Co-operation and Development (OECD) countries: an obviously pleasing result.

Judicial review of constitutional amendments

The Constitutional Court may review a constitutional amendment on two grounds. First, it may scrutinize it against procedural rules; second, it may review it in light of the constitutional principles. The Court has never rescinded a constitutional provision on the grounds that it did not meet procedural requirements, but it has once rescinded a provision that was held to violate the principle of *Rechtsstaat*.

In Austria, the Constitutional Court was already furnished with the power to review laws in 1919. According to the (Austrian) model of centralized judicial review, it is the only court that can rescind a law. All other courts (as well as administrative bodies) do not have the power to rescind or disregard a law that might violate the Constitution. This reading is, of course, different from laws contravening European law: in such cases, all courts and administrative bodies are obliged to set aside genuine Austrian law and even the Austrian Constitution.

Where constitutional amendments are concerned, the Constitutional Court has the power to review them on two grounds. First, it may examine whether the relevant procedural rules have been observed. The Standing Orders of the National Council, for instance, provide for a specific way in which the voting on a bill has to be conducted. It has already been the case, albeit not with regard to a constitutional amendment, that this procedure was not obeyed and the Court subsequently rescinded the law under scrutiny.[67] It is therefore possible that the Constitutional Court may rescind a constitutional amendment in case a similar failure occurs. Second, the Constitutional Court may even review a constitutional amendment on substantive grounds, whenever a violation of a constitutional principle is alleged. An amendment to constitutional principles would mean a "total revision" of the Constitution. A law providing for such a total revision would additionally need a referendum in order to be enacted legally. According to the concept of the "step pyramid" (or "hierarchy of norms", *Stufenbau*), which the Austrian legal system is believed to be built upon, these principles take a higher rank than (ordinary) constitutional laws. Constitutional laws, therefore, may only be passed within the framework provided by these principles. Exceeding this framework would (also) involve a legal question that might be settled by the Constitutional Court.

The Constitutional Court was rather reluctant to use its power to rescind constitutional provisions on substantive grounds. In fact, it has only used it once. Following rescissions of several state law provisions, which all violated the Constitution in similar ways, the Federal Parliament adopted a constitutional provision stating that the public procurement laws of the states, which were in force on a certain day, should be deemed constitutional. Although Parliament only intended to address these certain specific constitutional requirements, which were previously upheld by the Court, the Constitutional Court understood the provision as an abrogation of its power to review statutes in the entire field of state public procurement law. It declared this process to be incompatible with the principle of *Rechtsstaat* and rescinded the provision,[68] noting that a referendum would have been required to introduce it. It is quite obvious that a referendum would never have been held on this kind of constitutional law—not only for financial reasons, but even more importantly for political ones: who would explain to the people why it might be necessary to undermine the principle of *Rechtsstaat*? By means of this decision, the Constitutional Court set an effective limit for amending the Constitution.

A total revision of the Constitution (i.e. an amendment of one or more constitutional principles, like the constitutional law on Austria's accession to the EU) can only be reviewed on procedural grounds. However, this might involve some delicate questions, as a referendum would have to be held according to a specific law,[69] establishing several procedural requirements that may fail to be met. In the only case of such a mandatory referendum so far, no such failure has occurred,[70] albeit that the question as to which way the government was obliged to inform the people was an issue. In this case, however, the government engaged a high-profile advertising agency that designed a campaign similar to those aiming at selling consumer goods, thus ridiculing the political dimension of a referendum.

Criticism and reform

Austrian scholars highlight functional as well as structural deficiencies of the Constitution. Because of the relative ease with which it has been amended, they emphasize that it failed to provide a consistent framework for government policy. Further, they reveal structural deficiencies that partly stem from the 1920 adoption of monarchical institutions. Remedies have long been suggested and discussed; in the light of the current sovereign debt crisis, nothing has ensued so far. Discourse on a substantial reform of the Austrian Constitution, which in some instances dates back to 1848, is still ongoing.

Functional deficiency

Perhaps the most highly criticized component of Austrian constitutional law is the relative ease with which it has been amended throughout post-war Austria, together with the circumstance that the amendments need not be included in the main document of the Constitution.[71] The "shattered Constitution," which split over the entire legal system, was also regarded as a failed Constitution: it failed to provide an efficient framework for government policies.

As established, amendments can exist as external Acts and provisions within Acts that are merely granted the rank of constitutional law. In addressing this deficiency, proposals were made to include a provision effecting the incorporation of such amendments into the constitutional text. Scholars argue that the lack of such a specific mechanism within the constitutional document provides ample leeway for political maneuvers. By virtue of an "incorporation clause" (similar to Art. 79 para 1 Bonner Basic Law), the Act in question would be more transparent. Moreover, systematic aspects would have to be considered.[72] A provision, for instance, with the sole purpose of preventing the Constitutional Court from reviewing a tax law because it is not reconcilable with the principle of equality, can be "hidden" in the law on taxation. With an incorporation clause in place, specific exceptions to the principle of equality would have to be stipulated, making it harder for the government to argue in favor of such a provision, as it would otherwise transpire that the law was intended to violate this principle.

Although it was discussed in the Constitutional Convention, such an incorporation clause has not been enacted so far—and probably never will be. Nevertheless, to tackle the barely manageable inventory of constitutional law, the bill on clearing up the vast body of constitutional laws was adopted by Parliament (*Bundesverfassungsrechtsbereinigungsgesetz*).[73] However, the structural problems were not addressed.

Structural deficiencies: allocation of powers

Functional deficiencies apart, Austrian scholars—and most recently also institutions such as the Public Audit Office—have addressed structural deficiencies,[74] some of which are also a direct result of the fact that the Constitution was built on the heritage of the monarchy. The administrative system, the judiciary, the committees etc. were basically established under the monarchy and, as such, have long raised questions about efficiency and effectiveness. Similar problems stem from the post-war policy of the two dominant parties that aimed to guarantee their spheres of influence on all levels and in all fields of administration.

Federation and the states

Analysis of the federal constitutional system draws attention to the inflexibility and the static design of the allocation of powers between the Federation and the states. Article 15 of the Federal Constitution provides that all competences not allocated to the Federation remain within the autonomous sphere of competence of the states. This general provision seems to safeguard the power of the states. In practice, this allocation of powers and state constitutional autonomy is far more limited than it appears. The areas of competence assigned to the Federation are considerably higher, thus only few areas remain under the jurisdiction of the states. Moreover, although the states are represented in the Federal Council of the Parliament, the representation of their interests is considered to be disproportionate and inefficient.[75] This situation is mainly due to the aforementioned fact that the Federal Council is overshadowed by the party system, with votes being cast along party lines rather than for state interests. Also, one of the competences of the Federation is its right to supervise the lawmaking of the states, which creates the impression that states are somewhat subordinate. As a result, the allocation of powers has long been criticized as too centralistic.

A further criticism with regard to this aspect of allocation of powers is that it is unsuited to the implementation of EU law.[76] Under the current allocation of powers, both the Federation and the states are obliged to implement EU directives in accordance with their respective sphere of authority. However, some matters regulated under EU directives may encompass legal aspects that are covered with varying areas of competency by both Federation and the states. As a result, the implementation process may be significantly complicated, creating overlaps and/or loopholes—or it has to ultimately result in a constitutional amendment re-allocating the powers between the Federation and the states.

All these issues have long been discussed, and several proposals have been submitted; they were also addressed in the Constitutional Convention. With regard to the allocation of power between the Federation and the states, a Cabinet bill was previously submitted.[77] Although the Grand Coalition Government had agreed upon it, it was withdrawn.

Administrative Courts

In Austria, there has been an ongoing debate with regard to the effectiveness and functioning of the Administrative Court. The establishment of administrative state courts to take over some of the Administrative Court's tasks was generally desired, especially with regard to Art. 6 ECHR. It was argued that such an establishment would strengthen federalism, as states would be enabled to exercise judicial functions. In the late 1980s, Independent Administrative Tribunals were established in the states. They are granted the authority to rule on administrative offences, although not with regard to cases in the first instance. These Administrative Tribunals do not have the status of a court. Moreover, numerous administrative authorities were set up in order to meet the standards constituting a tribunal under Art. 6 of the ECHR.[78] An even greater impact on the Austrian legal system is posed by a further requirement under Art. 6 ECHR: the entitlement of an individual to a hearing by an independent and impartial tribunal in the determination of his rights and obligations and of any criminal charge against him.

A 2010 Cabinet bill[79] proposed the introduction of further (lower) Administrative Courts and the dissolution of more than a hundred independent administrative authorities. The bill provides for the introduction of State Administrative Courts and two Federal Administrative Courts. The states would be responsible for organizing their courts. Thus, for the first time, they would be allocated juridical powers in a formal sense. All courts would form the first tier of administrative review, and it is envisaged that they would have the power to decide on the merits of a case. The Administrative Court would form the second tier of administrative review, thus becoming a court of appeal. As the proposed constitutional amendment still restricts the jurisdiction of the Administrative Courts to the review of administrative rulings and the exercising of direct administrative power, a further modernization of the system would be desirable, even if this bill should be passed by Parliament. Thus it is still under consideration.

Fundamental bill of rights

It might not be seen as a fundamental or a structural deficiency of the Austrian Constitution that the two main political parties could not agree on a new, more modern, fundamental bill of rights; albeit that the Fundamental Reform Commission and the Constitutional Court have submitted draft versions. Both the 1867 Basic Law on Fundamental Rights and the ECHR are working instruments and the absence of social rights within the Constitution, though much bemoaned by the Social Democrats, has not prevented Austria from establishing a comprehensive social-welfare system. The inability to pass a new fundamental bill of rights therefore reveals deficiencies within the political system, which is still based on fundamental ideological differences and perceived distrust.

These differences have probably prevented more substantial reforms so far and have also prevented the Austrian Constitution from becoming a more stable, reliable regime. Thus, it was always—and probably will always be—a Constitution in the making; provided, of course, that the political system might not be subject to fundamental and sustainable changes.

Notes

1 My highly committed team at Vienna University—Fabiane Baxewanos, Doris Erker and Nastaran Sharif—has supported me on all technical aspects of drafting this article. Nastaran Sharif has helped to improve the language. I am deeply indebted to all of them.
2 For a more comprehensive analysis of the historical and political background of the framing of the Austrian Constitution, cf. M. Stelzer, *The Constitution of the Republic of Austria. A Contextual Analysis*, Oxford-Portland: Hart Publishing, 2011, pp. 1–18.
3 E. Tálos and E. Horvath, *Facts and Figures*, Vienna: Federal Chancellery, Federal Press Service, 2000, p. 33.
4 For more details see H. Dachs and A. Staudinger, "Parteien und politische Bewegungen", in E. Tálos et al. (eds), *Handbuch des politischen Systems Österreichs. Erste Republik 1918–1933*, Wien: Manz, 1995, pp. 143–76.
5 See also B. Jelavich, *Modern Austria: Empire and Republic, 1815–1986*, Melbourne: Cambridge University Press, 1987, pp. 155–62.
6 *Bundes-Verfassungsgesetz* (BGBl. 114/1918).
7 The English version online. Available HTTP: <http://www.ris.bka.gv.at/Dokumente/Erv/ERV_1930_1/ERV_1930_1.pdf> (accessed 9 December 2011).
8 BGBl. 1/1934.
9 In 1991 they were renamed the Social Democratic Party.
10 They were the successors to the pre-war Christian Socialists.
11 For more details see W.C. Müller, "Das österreichische Parteiensystem: Periodisierung und Perspektiven", in A. Pelinka, F. Plasser and W. Meixner (eds), *Die Zukunft der österreichischen Demokratie. Trends, Prognosen und Szenarien*, Schriftenreihe des Zentrums für Angewandte Politikforschung, 2000, vol. 22, Wien: ZAP, pp. 281–309.
12 Cf. Stelzer, op. cit., p. 194ff.
13 H. Klecatsky, "Hat Österreich eine Bundesverfassung?", *Juristische Blätter*, 1965, p. 544ff.
14 For a more comprehensive and detailed overview on constitutional amendments cf. L.K. Adamovich, B.-C. Funk, G. Holzinger, and S.L. Frank, *Österreichisches Staatsrecht*, band 1: *Grundlagen*, 2nd edn, Wien: Springer, 2011, pp. 106–24.
15 Cf. S. Griller, "Verfassungsfragen der österreichischen EU-Mitgliedschaft (Teil III)", *Zeitschrift für Rechtsvergleichung*, 1995, p. 107ff.; R. Walter, H. Mayer and G. Kucsko-Stadlmayer, *Grundriss des österreichischen Bundesverfassungsrechts*, 10th edn, Wien: Manz, 2007, p. 94.
16 Cf. G. Sandner and H. Sickinger (eds), "Aufstieg und Fall der FPÖ - Zwischen europäischem Trend und österreichischem Sonderweg", *Österreichische Zeitschrift für Politikwissenschaft*, 2003, vol. 33, p. 33ff.
17 See Beitritts-BVG (BGBl. 744/1994).
18 T. Öhlinger, *Warum der EU-Reformvertrag aus verfassungsrechtlicher Sicht keiner Volksabstimmung bedarf*, Rechtsgutachten im Auftrag des Herrn Bundespräsidenten, Wien, 2007. Online. Available HTTP: <http://www.hofburg.at/rte/upload/rechtsgutachten_univ_prof_dr_oehlinger.pdf> (accessed 9 December 2011); T. Öhlinger, "EU: Referendum über Verfassung nötig?", *Die Presse, Rechtspanorama*, 5.7.2004. Online. Available HTTP: <http://diepresse.com/home/recht/rechtspanorama/189680/Referendum-ueber-EUVerfassung-Pflicht-Keine-Argumente-in-Sicht?from=suche.intern.portal>.

19 BGBl. 775/1992.

20 Extensive material on the history and the work of the Constitutional Convention is online. Available HTTP: <www.konvent.gv.at> (accessed 9 December 2011). For a critical conclusion see L. Adamovich, "Nach dem Österreich-Konvent. Bereinigung oder grundlegende Änderung der Verfassung?", in Bundesministerium für Inneres (ed.), *Verfassung - Reform - Rechtsschutz, 3. Rechtsschutztag des Bundesministeriums für Inneres*, Wien: NWV, 2006, pp. 27–37.

21 1706 dB XVII. GP; cf. K. Weber, "Möglichkeiten und Grenzen der Reform der bundesstaatlichen Kompetenzverteilung vor dem Hintergrund der Bemühungen um einen Vertrag über die europäische Verfassung", in M. Akyürek et al. (eds), *Staat und Recht in europäischer Perspektive, Festschrift Heinz Schäffer*, Wien: Manz, 2006, pp. 923 and 934ff.

22 Verwaltungsgerichtbarkeits-Novelle 2010, 129/ME (XXIV. GP).

23 H. Neisser, M. Handstanger and R. Schick (eds), *Das Bundeswahlrecht. Gesetzesausgabe mit Erläuterungen und einer Sammlung der Judikatur*, 2nd edn, Wien: Verlag Österreich, 1994, pp. 33–6.

24 R. Dixon, "Constitutional Amendment Rules: A Comparative Perspective", in T. Ginsburg and R. Dixon (eds), *Comparative Constitutional Law*, Cheltenham: Elgar, 2011, p. 96.

25 See D. Jahnel, "Die Mitwirkung des Bundespräsidenten an der Gesetzgebung", *Juristische Blätter*, 1987, p. 633ff.; F. Koja, "Die Stellung des Bundespräsidenten in der Verfassung. Seine politische Funktion", in F. Weissensteiner (ed.), *Die österreichischen Präsidenten. Leben und Werk*, Wien: Österreichischer Bundesverlag, 1982, p. 9; K. Korinek, "Die Beurkundung der Bundesgesetze durch den Bundespräsidenten", in A. Mock (ed.), *Verantwortung in unserer Zeit*, Linz: Österreichische Staatsdruckerei, 1990, p. 121.

26 Koja, op. cit., pp. 9, 13.

27 For President Kirchschläger's view see Korinek, op. cit.

28 RV 283 BlgNR 23.GP.

29 F. Koja, *Das Verfassungsrecht der österreichischen Bundesländer*, 2nd edn, Wien: Springer, 1988; P. Pernthaler, "Die Verfassungsautonomie der österreichischen Bundesländer", *Juristische Blätter*, 1986, p. 477ff.

30 For a comprehensive overview to the various ways Austrian states have used this constitutional power, see: P. Häberle, "Textstufen in österreichischen Landesverfassungen – einVergleich", in P. Häberle (ed.), *Jahrbuch des öffentlichen Rechts der Gegenwart*, Tübingen: Mohr, 2006.

31 See for example the decisions OGH 13 Os135/06m, 19 Os 16/09s, 14 Os 12/11p.

32 See e.g. VfSlg 10932/1986, VfSlg 11276/1987, VfSlg 11652/1988, VfSlg 11749/1988,VfSlg 12227/1989, and M. Stelzer, *Das Wesensgehaltsargument und der Grundsatz der Verhältnismäßigkeit*, Wien: Springer, 1991.

33 M. Holoubek, "Die Interpretation der Grundrechte in der jüngeren Judikatur des VfGH", in R. Machacek, W. Pahr and G. Stadler (eds), *Grund- und Menschenrechte in Österreich*, vol. I *Grundlagen, Entwicklungen und internationale Verbindungen*, Kehl am Rhein-Straßburg-Arlington: N.P. Engel Verlag, 1991, p. 43ff.; L. Adamovich, B.-C. Funk and G. Holzinger, *Österreichisches Staatsrecht*, band 3: *Grundrechte*, Wien-New York: Springer, 2003, pp. 16–18.

34 T. Öhlinger, "Verfassungsgesetzgeber und Verfassungsgerichtsbarkeit", *Österreichische Juristen-Zeitung*, 1989, vol. 44, pp. 451–2.

35 VfSlg 15373/1998.

36 There are some special cases for which the Constitution requires the same quorum as for constitutional laws, although no constitutional law is involved; Standing Orders of the National Council may be an example of that. They are considered to be part of the Constitution in a "substantive" sense. Further, since a 2008 amendment, all amendments to the EU Treaty will be passed on that requirement without being formally seen as "constitutional law."

37 Only Cabinet bills are subject to such an assessment procedure.

38 Walter, Mayer and Kucsko-Stadlmayer, op. cit., pp. 230–42.
39 See e.g. H. Schambeck (ed.), *Bundesstaat und Bundesrat in Österreich*, Wien: Verlag Österreich, 1997, pp. 497–525; H. Schäffer, "Reformperspektiven für den Bundesrat", *Journal für Rechtspolitik*, 2007, vol. 15(1), pp. 11–22.
40 E. Wiederin, "Gesamtänderung, Totalrevision und Verfassungsgebung", in M. Akyürek et al. (eds), op. cit., p. 961ff.; Adamovich, Funk, Holzinger and Frank, op. cit., band 1: *Grundlagen*, p. 130ff.
41 Austrian scholars have listed up to 11 principles, such as a liberal principle, a principle concerning the division of power, the separation of state and church, and many more: see F. Ermacora, *Österreichische Bundesverfassungsgesetze*, Stuttgart: Reclam, 1985.
42 For a more comprehensive analysis cf. Stelzer, op. cit.
43 Walter, Mayer and Kucsko-Stadlmayer, op. cit., pp. 78, 129; T. Öhlinger, "Die Transformation der Verfassung. Die staatliche Verfassung und die Europäische Integration", *Juristische Blätter*, 2002, p. 2ff.
44 VfSlg 11669/1988.
45 For further details on this term see P. Pernthaler, *Der Verfassungskern*, Wien: Manz, 1998, p. 71.
46 H.P. Rill, "Die österreichische Bundesstaatlichkeit und die Gesamtänderungsschwelle des Art 44 Abs 3 B-VG", in M. Akyürek et al. (eds), op. cit., p. 717.
47 VfSlg 11756/1988.
48 VfSlg, 163278.
49 T. Öhlinger, "Soll über den Vertrag von Lissabon in Österreich das Volk abstimmen?", *Ecolex*, 2008, pp. 290–2; Walter, Mayer and Kucsko-Stadlmayer, op. cit., p. 135.
50 Art. 4 para 2 TEU.
51 P. Oberndorfer, "Artikel 1", in K. Korinek and M. Holoubek (eds), *Österreichisches Bundesverfassungsrecht*, Wien, New York: Springer, 2000, p. 1 and p. 9ff.; Pernthaler, op. cit.
52 Walter, Mayer and Kucsko-Stadlmayer, op. cit., p. 227.
53 See H.P. Rill, "Wie können wirtschaftliche und soziale Selbstverwaltung sowie die Sozialpartnerschaft in der Bundesverfassung verankert werden?", *Journal für Rechtspolitik*, 2005, p. 107ff.
54 For further details see Arts. 43 and 44 of the Federal Constitution.
55 See VfSlg 13839/1994.
56 For an overview see Walter, Mayer and Kucsko-Stadlmayer, op. cit., p. 113ff.
57 H.P. Rill, "Der Rang der allgemein anerkannten Regeln des Völkerrechts", *Zeitschrift für öffentliches Recht*, 1960, vol. 10, p. 439ff.
58 BGBl. I 2/2008.
59 BGBl. 99/2002; BGBl. 153/2004.
60 H. Dachs, "Das Parteiensystem", in Tálos et al. (eds), op. cit., pp. 143–59.
61 This included e.g. sports clubs, hiking associations and car driver clubs.
62 See also Adamovich, Funk, Holzinger and Frank, op. cit., band 1: *Grundlagen*, pp. 125–6 where it is argued that the tradition of distrust plays an important part in the history of Austria's Constitution.
63 For instance, the ÖVP in the 1960s and the SPÖ in the 1970s.
64 Cf. Adamovich, Funk and Holzinger, op. cit., band 3: *Grundrechte*, p. 13.
65 Cf. Adamovich, Funk, Holzinger and Frank, op. cit., band 1: *Grundlagen*, p. 126.
66 B. Wieser, "Politikerbezügepyramide und Landesgesetzgebung", *Journal für Rechtspolitik*, 1998, p. 379ff.
67 VfSlg 16151/2001.
68 VfSlg 16327/2001.
69 Referendum Act, BGBl. 79/1973.
70 VfSlg 13839/1994.
71 Cf., e.g., Adamovich, Funk, Holzinger and Frank, op. cit., band 1: *Grundlagen*, p. 127.
72 Ibid., p. 137.

73 E. Wiederin, "Verfassungsbereinigung", in G. Lienbacher, G. Wielinger (eds), *Öffentliches Recht Jahrbuch 2008*, Wien-Graz: Neuer Wissenschaftlicher Verlag, 2008, pp. 45, 49.
74 Cf. e.g. Adamovich, Funk, Holzinger and Frank, op. cit., band 1: *Grundlagen*, pp. 125–8.
75 Cf. Walter, Mayer and Kucsko-Stadlmayer, op. cit., p. 59.
76 Cf. Adamovich, Funk, Holzinger and Frank, op. cit., band 1: *Grundlagen*, p. 127.
77 1706 dB XVII. GP; see Weiss, op. cit., pp. 497–525.
78 BGBl. 684/1988.
79 Verwaltungsgerichtbarkeits-Novelle 2010, 129/ME (XXIV. GP).

3 The process of constitutional amendment in Belgium

Christian Behrendt

History and evolution of the constitutional amendment procedure

In September 1830, the Belgian revolution broke out and, on 4 October that year, the provisional Government proclaimed the independence of the new state.[1] Two days later, on 6 October, a 14-member Commission was entrusted with the preparation of a draft Constitution, which could serve as a basis for the discussions of the future constitution-making Assembly, the National Congress. The elections to the National Congress (i.e. the first national votes in the history of Belgium) took place on 3 November 1830, and the Congress held its opening session on 10 November. Within less than three months, the National Congress adopted the new Constitution. This impressive speed was mainly due to the fact that the Congress closely followed the draft text of the 14-member Commission, only departing from the text when it found serious reasons to do so. Formally promulgated on 7 February 1831, the Constitution came into force two weeks later, on 25 February.[2] In addition to the text of the Constitution itself, the Belgian National Congress of 1830–1831 adopted two decrees with constitutional force (i.e. the decrees of 18 and 24 November 1830), which are, as the Constitution *sensu stricto*, still in force today.

With the Constitution of 7 February 1831, Belgium has one of the world's oldest Constitutions still in operation: to our knowledge, Belgium is in fourth position, after San Marino (Constitution enacted in 1600), the United States of America (Constitution enacted in 1787) and Norway (Constitution enacted in 1814). Over the decades, the original text of the 1831 Constitution had undergone numerous changes, so it was decided in 1994 to renumber the entire text, without altering its substance. This renumbering operation was called "the co-ordination of the Constitution."[3] To a certain extent, this change is analogous with the renumbering of the EC Treaty (which has been renumbered twice since 1957).

The co-ordination procedure is set out in Art. 198 (formerly 132) of the Belgian Constitution, which provides:

> In agreement with the King, the Houses of Parliament may change the numerical order of articles and of sub-articles of the Constitution, in addition to sub-divisions of the latter into titles, chapters and sections, modify the terminology of provisions not submitted for revision in order to harmonize

> them with the terminology of new provisions and to ensure the concordance of the Dutch, French and German texts of the Constitution. In this case, the Houses may debate provided that at least two-thirds of the members composing each House are present; and no change may be made unless it is supported at least by a two-thirds majority.

Every Article of the Constitution already in existence before the renumbering operation in 1994 is thus known under two numbers: under its old one, applicable until 16 February 1994, and under its new one, applicable since 17 February 1994. This remark is important when one wishes to consult literature or case law in Belgian constitutional law: in reading a comment written from the 1950s onwards, for example, Art. 68 of the Constitution (which lays down the treaty-making power of the King), one has to bear in mind that, in terms of the current Constitution, this text is now vested in Art. 167. And the same is true for the constitutional amendment procedure: originally located in Art. 131 (old numbering), the provision—which has since then never been amended—is today lodged in Art. 195. At the same time as the renumbering operation came into effect (i.e. on 17 February 1994), it was quite inappropriately also decided to abolish the title of the Constitution (which was "Constitution of 7 February 1831") and to replace it by a new one, "Co-ordinated Constitution of 17 February 1994." This change of denomination is, however, misleading since the constitutional text of 1831 is, legally speaking, still in force: the renumbering operation of 1994 does not amount to the creation of a new Constitution. Therefore, it is correct to state that the current Belgian Constitution was enacted in 1831-even if the title of the Constitution as it is published in today's statute books seems to suggest that it was created in 1994.

Birth of the amendment procedure: Art. 195 (ex-Art. 131) of the Belgian Constitution

On 4 February 1831, the National Congress agreed upon the final version of Title VII of the new Constitution. This title, which included only one Article (Art. 131), is dedicated to the amendment procedure of the Constitution.[4] The enactment of this provision did not generate a long discussion. Indeed, at that time, the Constitution-makers' attention was mainly focused on the choice of a King and a royal family for the newly created state (because Belgium did not have a pre-existing dynasty that could have been naturally called to the throne). More generally, the Belgian Constitution of 1831 largely borrows from the French and Dutch constitutional texts that existed at that time.[5] The new Art. 131 is no exception to that rule. It is drafted on the model of the Dutch Constitution of 1815,[6] except for one point: the new Belgian Article imposes, prior to any constitutional amendment, the dissolution of Parliament. Quite paradoxically, it is today precisely this feature of the Belgian amendment procedure—the automatic dissolution of both Houses of Parliament—that is the most exposed to criticism.[7]

Article 131 (nowadays Art. 195) is still in force today, and it figures, together with the American procedure of Art. V of the Constitution of 17 September 1787, among the most rigid amendment rules in the contemporary legal world. It provides:

> The [federal][8] legislative power has the right to declare that there are reasons to amend those constitutional provisions it determines. After such declaration, the two Houses of Parliament are automatically dissolved. Two new Houses are elected, in accordance with the provisions of Art. 46. These Houses then decide, in agreement with the King, on the points submitted for revision. In this case, the Houses may discuss provided that at least two-thirds of the members who compose them are present; and no change to the Constitution may be made unless it is supported by at least two-thirds of the votes cast.

As one can see, the amendment procedure of the Belgian Constitution thus contains three distinct phases.

Evolution of the amendment procedure

As already pointed out, the revision procedure, although criticized, has never been modified. On several occasions, proposals have been made to replace the current version of Art. 195 in order to reduce its rigidity and make it more subtle, but they were all abandoned.[9] Today (December 2011), the debate seems to have died out, largely because of the recent institutional difficulties with which the country has struggled: after the last general election of 13 June 2010, the different political parties of the country needed more than 540 days in which to agree upon the installation of a new government (which was finally sworn in on 6 December 2011). These institutional difficulties have shown the need for—and the usefulness of—a highly rigid amendment procedure.

In this context, recent opinion polls show that in the Dutch-speaking part of the country (Flanders), the Flemish independence party N-VA is credited with approximately 35 per cent of the votes,[10] and the Flemish extremist right-wing party Vlaams Belang with 11 per cent of the votes.[11] Put together, these two parties, both in favor of the independence of Flanders as a sovereign country (although traditional enemies on many other political issues), unite 46 per cent of the Flemish voters. It is thus no surprise that, currently, a vast majority of academics and politicians consider the fact that the Belgian Constitution is endowed with a particularly rigid amendment procedure as an advantage.

Selective overview of constitutional amendments

The first amendment of the Belgian Constitution was enacted in 1893[12] (between 1831 and 1893, no amendment had taken place) and concerned the extension of voting rights in national elections. The second phase of amendments intervened in 1920–1921[13] and was also related to the right to vote in national elections. In order to proceed to the third phase of amendments, one has to advance more than 40 years, to 1967. In other words, if one considers the first century of the existence of the Belgian State (1831–1931), the Constitution was in that period only modified twice. The third period of amendment took place between 1967 and 1971. It is also known as "the first State reform" (in total, there have been five State reforms thus far, and the sixth one is currently in process).[14] The fourth period of amendment occurred between 1980 and 1985 (second State reform), and the fifth between 1988 and 1992 (third State reform). The sixth period of amendment (fourth State reform) occurred between 1993 and 1994 (as with the fifth State reform, which took place in 2001, it did not require an amendment of the Constitution). The sixth State reform, which is about to start, will thus lead to a seventh period of amendment of the Constitution.

The process of constitutional amendment

Formal Constitution—substantive Constitution

In analyzing the Constitutions of different legal systems, it is important to distinguish the word "Constitution" in its formal meaning (*constitution formelle* in French, *formele Grondwet* in Dutch) from its substantive meaning (*constitution matérielle* in French, *materiële Grondwet* in Dutch).[15]

In its formal meaning, a Constitution can be defined as a written document, which sets out the basic rules that give the State its main characteristics and which endows its citizens with fundamental rights. Within the Kelsenian pyramid of legal norms, the Constitution in its formal meaning is located at the highest level of domestic norms; no norm of the national legal system in question can claim to have a higher hierarchical status.[16] In its substantive meaning, a Constitution includes the entire body of essential rules that govern the socio-political entity, without taking into consideration their hierarchical importance. Generally, one considers the body of law that attributes power to state organs, regulates their mutual relations, and the relations between them and the citizens, as pertaining to the substantive Constitution. The procedures applicable for the revision of the rules of the substantive Constitution depend on their respective hierarchical value: insofar as they are also part of the Constitution in its formal meaning, their change will be subject to the formal amendment procedure of the Constitution.

In Belgium, outside the formal Constitution, a lot of important provisions regarding the country's institutional structure are laid down in so-called "special laws" (*lois speciales* in French, *bijzondere wetten* in Dutch). In political terms, these statutes are as difficult to change as the Constitution itself in that they also require a two-thirds majority in both Houses of Parliament.[17]

In the Belgian context, it is highly important to notice that the largest part of the successive State reforms—and also nearly all rules regarding the allocation of competencies, and of monies to the federate entities—are written down in these special laws. In other words, and slightly stretching the point, one could say: as far as the organization of Belgium's institutional structure is concerned, the essential provisions are not to be found in the category of formally constitutional norms, but outside the Constitution, in the category of special laws (this is why they are considered to be part of the Constitution in its substantive meaning).

Of these special laws, four are of particular relevance: the Special Law of 8 August 1980 on Institutional Reforms (since amended), the Special Law of 6 January 1989 on the Constitutional Court (since amended), the Special Law of 12 January 1989 on the Institutions of Brussels (since amended), and the Special Law of 16 January 1989 on the Financing of the Federate Entities (since amended).

Despite their great importance, it remains true that these special laws belong to the category of legislative, not constitutional, enactments. It is thus coherent that the Constitutional Court[18] is competent to review them against the Constitution,[19] and if it finds an unconstitutionality, it can annul them.

Informal methods of constitutional change

Judicial interpretation

In Belgium, the Constitution can be interpreted by all judges in the country, if a lawsuit brought before them requires them to do so. For instance, every judge can assess whether an administrative order issued by the executive power abides by the fundamental rights enshrined in the Belgian Constitution. Article 159 of the Constitution will allow the judge to set aside every administrative rule—issued by the central government, a federate entity or a local municipality—if in his or her view the latter is not in accordance with the provisions of the Constitution. To this extent, one can say that every judge in the country (and not only the Supreme Court,[20] the State Council[21] or the Constitutional Court) is an authentic interpreter of the constitutional text; every time the interpreter's perception of the text changes, we are thus *de facto* faced with a case of informal constitutional change.

Implicit revisions

Another informal method of constitutional change is the implicit revision of the Constitution. This expression designates the situation in which a constitutional provision is not formally amended but in which its scope is indirectly modified (reduced or extended) by the formal amendment of another constitutional provision. In other words, the implicit revision of provision A is an incidental consequence of the formal amendment of a provision. Moreover, this situation can occur when provision A is not listed on the Declaration for Revision of the Constitution and can therefore not be formally amended, whereas provision B *is* mentioned in the Declaration. There are numerous examples of implicit revisions in Belgian constitutional history that can be found elsewhere;[22] discussing them here would oblige us to present a long number of isolated legal situations, which would unnecessarily lead away from the main thread of the paper.

Formal constitutional amendment process

Article 195 of the Belgian Constitution sets out the formal conditions for the constitutional amendment process. Let us now turn to this provision and submit it to closer analysis. As already pointed out, the procedure is highly rigid: it counts among the most cumbersome in the contemporary legal world.

The revision procedure: three distinct stages

In Belgium, in order to amend the Constitution, Parliament is required to pass through three separate and successive stages. The rationale for this phased procedure is to make the Members of Parliament aware of the high normative importance of any constitutional amendment; moreover, the constitution-maker of 1831 wanted to make sure that there would be sufficient time for the maturing of the amendment proposal, so that no change to the Constitution would be made without careful reflection.[23] In this respect, the principal stage, which induces the "slowing down" of the procedure, is the second one: the compulsory dissolution of both Houses of Parliament before any amendment to the Constitution. But let us go through the process in detail.

a) *The legislative power approves a Declaration of Revision of the Constitution (Art. 195 para 1 of the Constitution).* The first step of any constitutional amendment consists of passing, in both Houses of Parliament, a Declaration approved by an absolute majority of votes in each House,[24] affirming that "it is requisite to amend the Constitution." This first Declaration is to be completed by a second one, of identical terms, issued by the King. The King's declaration will naturally need a ministerial counter-signature.[25] These two Declarations for Revision (*déclarations de revision / herzieningsverklaringen*) must indicate precisely which articles of the Constitution are intended to be amended (e.g. "Art. 167" or, even more precisely, "the second paragraph of Art. 151"). In other words, it is not possible to pass a declaration declaring that the Constitution as such, without any further precision, ought to be amended.

   If Parliament wishes to amend the Constitution in order to insert a new article, the Declaration for Revision must indicate the approximate content of the new provision and the title of the Constitution into which it should be placed (the declaration will thus say: "The amendment of the Constitution is requisite in order to insert in it a new article forbidding capital punishment, to be placed into Title II of the Constitution"). Only the Articles mentioned in the two Declarations for Revision can be amended; under Belgian constitutional law, one says that these provisions are, thanks to the vote of the Declarations, "opened up for amendment."[26] If, for any reason, the King's Declaration is not identical to the one issued by Parliament, the lowest common denominator prevails: in other words, in such case, only the provisions listed in both Declarations are amendable. The two Declarations are to be published in the Official Journal.[27] The principal, and very important, legal consequence of this requirement is that at the very moment the Declarations are published in the Official Journal, Parliament is automatically dissolved and general elections are called. It is thus evident that no Member of Parliament would vote in favor of a Declaration for Revision if he or she does not have a very good reason to do so: the approval of the declaration entails the termination of all parliamentary mandates, the legislature comes to a sudden end, and no MP is happy to lose their seat (and losing their seat also means losing the rather comfortable salary and the immunities that are part of the parliamentary function).

The dissolution of the Houses of Parliament has a double purpose. The first, as already seen, is the intention to slow down the constitutional revision process and to guarantee sufficient time for reflection. In other words, it prevents constitutional revision being taken lightly. The second purpose is the installation of an element of representative democratic legitimacy. The people, via their vote, are enabled to express their opinion on the necessity of the intended amendment, and (if affirmative on this question) on the substantive orientation they think the amendment should have.[28] However, nowadays, this second preoccupation seems to have become a legal fiction.[29] Indeed, in practice, issues of constitutional amendment have nearly no influence on the election campaign (even if, formally speaking, the elections are called because a Declaration for Revision has been voted for). Furthermore, over the decades, the Declarations for Revision have become increasingly long (even though many provisions "opened up for amendment" are not changed and are only included in the Declaration in order to increase the possibilities of political bargaining). One can thus say that the requirement of general elections is less and less pertinent if its rationale, in line with what the constitution-maker of 1830 thought, is to secure the amendment procedure with an element of fresh representative legitimacy.[30]

Since 1831, 15 Declarations of Revision have been passed by successive Parliaments. The dates of publication are 23–24 May 1892, 23 October 1919, 14 March 1954, 30 April 1958, 17 April 1965, 2 March 1968, 15 November 1978, 6 October 1981, 9 November 1987, 18 October 1991, 12 April 1995, 5 May 1999, 10 April 2003, 2 May 2007 and 7 May 2010.

b) *The legislative chambers are dissolved and re-elected (Art. 195 paras 2 and 3, and Art. 46 of the Constitution).* With the publication of the two declarations in the Official Journal and the automatic dissolution of both Houses of Parliament, a period of 40 days begins,[31] in which general elections have to take place (in Belgium, general elections are always held on a Sunday morning[32]). The newly elected Houses are then obliged to convene at the latest two months after the dissolution of the former Houses.[33]

c) *The revision* sensu stricto *(Art. 195 paras 4 and 5 of the Constitution).* Finally, the newly elected Houses of Parliament may, if they wish, revise the Article(s) that have been indicated in the Declaration for Revision (and which are therefore amendable). Generally speaking, only a small minority of the Articles will be effectively changed: the Declaration operates as a permission to amend, not as an obligation. In Belgian constitutional history, there have even been Declarations on which, after the renewal of both Houses of Parliament, not a single Article was in the end amended.[34] The revision *sensu stricto* is subject to a two-thirds majority in both Houses: at least two-thirds of the members of each of the Houses must be present, and a majority of two-thirds of the votes is necessary to adopt any modification.[35]

After being agreed upon by both Houses of Parliament, the text is sent to the Royal Palace in order to receive the King's assent (with ministerial countersignature) and to be promulgated. Finally, the constitutional amendment is published in the Official Journal. It comes into force on the very day of its publication, unless the new constitutional provision expressly indicates another date.[36]

Uniform procedure

Belgium has a single constitutional revision procedure, identical in all circumstances. Some scholars have, however, pleaded in favor of the creation of a second procedure, more flexible and reserved for one particular situation. This more subtle amendment procedure would, according to their proposal, be applicable if the Kingdom wishes to ratify a Treaty that is incompatible with the Constitution.[37] The main idea is to avoid, in this specific case, any conflict of norms by permitting a speedy change of the incompatible domestic constitutional provisions without the obligation to dissolve Parliament.[38] In addition, these authors have suggested a systematic preventive verification of the constitutional compatibility of treaties Belgium intends to ratify.[39] In case of inconsistency between the Treaty and the Constitution, the ratification procedure would be suspended until the Constitution is adapted.

Intangibility of certain elements of the Constitution

If one carries out an overview in comparative constitutional law, one will see that some constitutions do contain unamendable provisions (i.e. provisions that are legally precluded from revision). Among the most striking examples in the contemporary world are Art. 1 of the German Basic Law and Art. 139 of the Italian Constitution. Let us now turn to the situation in Belgium.

Articles 17, 18 and 25 of the Constitution. Arts. 17, 18 and 25 of the Belgian Constitution read as follows: "Article 17—The punishment of Confiscation of assets cannot be introduced. Article 18—Civil death is abolished; it cannot be re-established. Article 25—The press is free; censorship can never be introduced. (. . .)" All three articles are related to forms of state action that were commonly used in the Ancien Régime, and of which the constitution-maker of 1831 wanted to ensure would not form part of the legal system of the new Belgian state. In order to underscore the great importance of these prohibitions, the three provisions are formulated in a way that makes them appear unalterable. However, legal theory has consistently considered that the provisions in question are not intangible, so that they could, in theory, be amended.[40] Let us note, in passing, that the three articles have not been modified since 1831, and that, some decades later, they were literally taken over by the Luxembourg constitution-maker.[41]

Decrees of the National Congress. In addition to the constitutional text *sensu stricto*, the Constitution-maker of 1830–1831 also approved two other texts of constitutional force. The first, a decree issued by the National Congress on 18 November 1830, proclaims the Independence of the Belgian provinces.[42] The second, also a decree but issued one week later, on 24 November, excludes the members of the Dutch royal family "for all times to come from any power" in Belgium. Scholars are divided on the question of whether these two constitutional decrees voted by the National Congress can be subject to amendment. In other words, the question is whether the amendment procedure laid down in Art. 195 of the Constitution can be applied to them. According to some authors, all Belgian constitutional rules (and thus also the two decrees) can be subject to amendment.[43] In other words, this group of scholars considers that there are no intangible rules in Belgian constitutional law. It is worth noticing that an advisory note of the Legislative Section of the State Council, issued in 1993, supports this view.[44] On the other hand, the debates of the National Congress of 1830–1831 show that the constitution-maker had the clear intention to render these two decrees intangible and that he wanted to make sure that the constitutional amendment procedure of Art. 195 (formerly 131) could not be applied to them.[45] Very consistently, all early scholars of Belgian constitutional law (i.e. during the first century of the country's existence, between 1830 and 1930) shared this view;[46] not a single author of that period can be found to affirm the contrary.

Elementary constraints preclude me from further discussion of this issue in the setting of this essay, but I can refer the reader who wants to go further on this issue to some other writings I have published on the subject.[47] In any case, in my eyes, the two decrees in question are intangible—even if it is true that, given the process of European unification and the excellent relations that exist at present between Belgium and the Netherlands, a constitutional decree precluding "for all times to come" any member of the Dutch royal family from any power whatsoever in Belgium seems rather hostile and awkward today. But one must not forget the troubled times in which the text was written,[48] and it seems also methodologically questionable to interpret today a constitutional provision in a sense that is persistently contrary to the intention of the "founding fathers" (as our American friends would say): the founder's intention was to establish an unalterable rule. I should also add that the practical consequences of the decrees of November 1830 are next to non-existent;[49] they are, nowadays, of purely theoretical interest.[50]

Article 197 of the Belgian Constitution: the period of a provisional regency. Art. 197 provides: "During regency, no changes may be brought to the Constitution regarding the constitutional powers of the King and Arts. 85 to 88, 91 to 95, 106 and 197 of the Constitution." During a regency (i.e. when the King's functions are temporarily exercised by a Regent), certain articles of the Constitution may not be modified. The provisions at hand are related to the constitutional powers of the King and to his status, to the succession to the throne and to the regency itself.

Article 196 of the Belgian Constitution: the Constitution cannot be amended in times of war, or when the Houses of Parliament are prevented from meeting freely on the federal territory. According to Art. 196, "[n]o constitutional revision may be undertaken or pursued during times of war or when the Chambers are prevented from meeting freely on federal territory." No revision of the Constitution may be initiated or pursued in time of war or when the Houses of Parliament are prevented from meeting freely on the national territory. This article was inserted in 1965–1968 and is inspired by several foreign examples[51] where, in a period of trouble, a dictatorship was established in a perfectly "legal" manner (by "legal," I mean the respect of all formal requirements for constitutional amendment[52]).

The role of the people

Belgian constitutional law does not allow the organization of referenda, be it at the constitutional or the legislative level.[53] It is true that the idea to introduce referendary mechanisms into the framework of domestic public law was raised a number of times.[54] However, several powerful arguments exist within the Belgian context to oppose this idea, at least at the national level.

First, referenda—turning on binary questions (i.e. with "yes" or "no" answers)—sharpen oppositions and hinder the emergence of compromises. A referendum can bring a legislative reform cause to fall, without proposing a valid alternative: it suffices to vote "no," but the "no" can be motivated by the consideration that the proposed bill goes much too far—or that it does not go far enough. In this sense, a referendum can paralyze a reform proposal that appears to be the only possible compromise in a specific situation. In such a situation, referendary techniques can constitute an obstacle to institutional pacification and lead to precisely the reverse: popular polarization and paralysis.[55] Second, in Belgium, a country with 60 per cent Dutch-speaking and 40 per cent French-speaking citizens, national referenda seem unsuited because they would allow the Dutch-speaking citizens, if they vote in large numbers the same way, to make their opinion systematically prevail. This objection is all the more serious since both linguistic communities *do effectively* diverge on a various number of topics. As two leading scholars put it: "[A] referendum would reveal the rift that exists between the two communities, risking to cause [sic] the final break-up of the country."[56]

In summary, the suggestion to endow the Belgian constitutional amendment procedure (or the ordinary legislative process in Parliament) with nationwide referendary techniques has to be analyzed with care and skepticism. We should bear in mind that Belgium has a fragile cohesion[57] and possesses an important tradition of legal norm creation through politically negotiated compromises.[58]

How does international and European law and jurisprudence affect constitutional revision?

Once the Belgian Parliament has given its consent to an international treaty, it becomes part of the national legal order (Belgium thus has a monistic vision of international law[59]). Moreover, it is also recognized that treaty provisions with direct effect (i.e. the directly applicable rules of conventional international law) prevail over national statutory norms (but there is a controversy on the question of which norm should prevail if rule of conventional international law is inconsistent with the Constitution itself[60]). Thus, if a national provision is contrary to an international rule that has direct effect, the national judge must apply the international rule and may not apply the domestic provision (unless the conflict concerns a treaty and a domestic rule of constitutional rank; in this latter situation, the controversy persists).

International law has also influenced—and favored—several constitutional revisions. In 1998, for example, it was primary EU law that led to a constitutional revision. Article 8b para 1 of the Maastricht Treaty provides that "[e]very citizen of the Union residing in a Member State of which he is not a national shall have the right to vote and to stand as a candidate at municipal elections in the Member State in which he resides, under the same conditions as nationals of that State (. . .)." However, Art. 8 para 2 of the Constitution provided at the time that Belgian nationality was a necessary condition for the exercise of any political right (and according to Belgian law, the supreme political right is the *ius suffragii*, the right to participate as a voter or candidate in an election[61]). These two provisions were patently incompatible. On 11 December 1998 (i.e. before the municipal elections of October 2000), Art. 8 of the Belgian Constitution was finally modified, in order to render possible in Belgium the extension of the *ius suffragii* to non-Belgian EU citizens. As already seen, it is precisely in this context—a new obligation of international law that runs contrary to domestic constitutional law—that some scholars advocate the introduction of a second, less rigid amendment procedure (without the dissolution of Parliament), in order to ease the change of the Constitution and to bring to a rapid end its inconsistency with the Treaty.

Judicial review of constitutional amendments

In Belgium, there is no review on constitutional amendments; they are not subject to any judicial control whatsoever. This implies, moreover, that the Constitutional Court is not competent to review them against the other provisions of the Constitution (which is quite logical, since amendments are of no lower rank than the other provisions of the Constitution). One can, however, regret that, in contrast to all projects of legislative norms, projects for constitutional amendments are not even referred, for advice, to the Legislative Section of the State Council.[62] Indeed, such advice could be beneficial in order to ascertain that the amendment proposals are well formulated; moreover, the State Council would be able, as it does when it comes to projects of statute laws, to draw Parliament's attention to a possible conflict between the proposed text and current obligations of the realm under international and European law.[63]

Criticism of the amendment procedure

The Belgian constitutional revision procedure, like more or less every procedure of that kind in the world, can be appreciated both positively and negatively. In its current formulation, it offers a certain number of advantages.[64] Most prominently, the current procedure involves three important institutions: the Houses of

Parliament, the King (in modern terms, the Federal Government) and the people (through the requirement of general elections). The successive intervention of these state organs is undoubtedly a security against extreme or too emotional proposals of amendment. Moreover, the present process prevents the approval of modifications without sufficient discussion; it imposes a maturing of solutions and leads to a moderate rhythm of the amendment procedure. However, the current constitutional revision process as it is laid down in Art. 195 unfortunately also has some (very significant) inconveniences, which are principally due to its exceptionally rigid nature. Three of them in particular can be pointed out.[65]

First, the fact that the amendment process is divided into three distinct and successive phases entails the risk that important and necessary constitutional modifications are not initiated because the political parties that would normally support them fear a possible defeat in the next parliamentary election (since the procedure, if started, necessarily leads to an election). So, in the beginning of a legislature, a reform proposal (and even a highly advisable one) will most probably not lead to the vote of a Declaration for Revision. Secondly, the dissolution of both Houses impairs the normal action of Parliament and Government: many politicians consider the main virtue of Art. 195 to be in the fact that it allows the Government to determine the date of the next general election.[66] The third inconvenience of the procedure is that the newly elected Houses may have a different majority than the previous Houses. This disadvantage can be twofold: either the new Houses do not possess a two-thirds majority to amend a provision that was included in the Declaration for Revision (in which case, the provision cannot be amended), or the new Houses do possess a two-thirds majority to amend a provision that was not included in the Declaration for Revision (in which case, the provision can again not be amended). From a democratic point of view, both situations are detrimental: in the first case, dissolution of Parliament has been triggered for nothing; in the second, a two-thirds majority of validly elected MPs is precluded from altering the Constitution.

Modification of the constitutional revision procedure?

One can certainly state that the actual constitutional revision procedure has positive and negative aspects.[67] At present, considering the Belgian situation and its linguistic tensions and divides, a modification of Art. 195 of the Constitution (into a less rigid procedure) does not seem desirable. However, some improvements, taking into consideration the evolution of time and the evolutions that Belgium has undergone, can be pointed out. The first suggestion, as already seen, is the introduction of a more flexible procedure that would be used when Belgium intends to give assent to a European Treaty that would be incompatible with the Constitution without a prior revision of the domestic Constitution. This specific procedure could avoid the (rather unnecessary) dissolution of the Houses of Parliament, which in its turn would allow a more speedy ratification of the treaty.

The second suggestion concerns the "special law" problematic. As already seen, it is incoherent that special laws, although subordinated to the Constitution, require a special linguistic majority that the Constitution does not contain. In other words, it is—at least under this aspect—more difficult to revise a special law than to modify the Constitution. In my eyes, it would thus be advisable to bring this situation to an end (for which there are, however, historical reasons) and to extend the linguistic requirements applicable to special laws to the procedure of constitutional amendments.

Written in 1831and resisting numerous attempts to amend it, Art. 195 and its highly rigid character amount almost to an historic curiosity: far from perfect, their many inconveniences are too obvious. But the evolution of the country in recent years (and especially in the last domestic crisis, which lasted 20 months, from 26 April 2010 to 6 December 2011) has brought back to the surface the main virtue of the procedure: it contributes to maintaining some sort of stability in a country grounded on an increasingly fragile cohesion. Could it be that historical curiosities sometimes deploy safeguards in the face of contentious modernity?

Notes

1 *Official Bulletin of the Belgian Provisional Government*, no. 4.

2 X. Mabille, *Histoire politique de la Belgique, Facteurs et acteurs de changement*, Bruxelles: CRISP, 4th edn, 2000, p. 108.

3 *La coordination de la Constitution* in French and *De coördinatie van de Grondwet* in Dutch.

4 During the co-ordination operation of 1994, Title VII was renumbered and became Title VIII.

5 Only a dozen articles are genuinely new. They mainly concerned the appointment of senators, the relationships between Church and state, and the people's right to assemble (Mabille, op. cit., p. 116).

6 To be precise, on Art. 229 to Art. 232 of the Constitution of the Kingdom of the United Netherlands of 24 August 1815, *Official Journal of the Netherlands*, no. xxix (the territory of Kingdom of the United Netherlands is nowadays divided into three states: the Netherlands, Belgium and Luxembourg).

7 C. Behrendt, "Les propositions émises dans le passé en vue de modifier l'article 195 de la Constitution belge", in F. Delpérée (ed.), *La procédure de révision de la Constitution*, Brussels: Bruylant, 2003, p. 115.

8 The adjective "federal" was added during the co-ordination operation in 1994, as a matter of clarification. It is the sole alteration of the provision since 1831.

9 For a more complete overview of these abandoned proposals in the history of Belgian constitutional law, see Behrendt, op. cit., pp. 113–35.

10 Poll realized by the *Ipsos* demographic institute, published in the newspaper *Le Soir* of 3 December 2011.

11 Ibid.

12 Amendment of 7 September 1893 (*Belgian Official Journal*, 9 September).

13 Amendments of 15 November 1920 (*Belgian Official Journal*, 3 December); 7 February 1921 (*Belgian Official Journal*, 10 February); 24 August 1921 (*Belgian Official Journal*, 31 August) and 15 October 1921 (*Belgian Official Journal*, 24–25 October).

14 See the *Institutional Agreement on the Sixth State Reform* of 11 October 2011.

15 M. Uyttendaele, *Trente leçons de droit constitutionnel*, Brussels: Bruylant, 2011, pp. 65–6; C. Behrendt and F. Bouhon, *Introduction à la théorie générale de l'état – Manuel*, 2nd edn, Brussels: Larcier, 2011, pp. 199–201.

16 Behrendt and Bouhon, op. cit., pp. 190–1.

17 Special laws are a mechanism designed to protect the French-speaking minority of the country (roughly 60 per cent of the Belgian population is Dutch-speaking and

40 per cent is French speaking; there is also a tiny German-speaking minority, counting for less than 0.8 per cent of the national population).

18 In French, *Cour constitutionnelle*; in Dutch, *Grondwettelijk Hof*. The Court changed its name in 2007; before that date, it was called "Court of Arbitration" (*Cour d'Arbitrage* in French, *Arbitragehof* in Dutch).

19 See under Constitutional Court, decisions 8/90 of 7 February 1990 and 17/94 of 3 March 1994.

20 In French, *Cour de Cassation*; in Dutch, *Hof van Cassatie*.

21 The State Council is the Supreme Administrative Court of the country (in French, *Conseil d'État*; in Dutch, *Raad van State*).

22 A. Alen and F. Meersschaut, "De 'impliciete' herziening van de grondwet", *Présence du droit public et des droit de l'homme – Mélanges offerts à Jacques Velu*, Brussels: Bruylant, 1992, vol. 1, p. 259ff.

23 X. Delgrange and H. Dumont, "Le rythme des révisions constitutionnelles et l'hypothèse de l'accélération du temps juridique", *Administration publique trimestrielle*, 1999, p. 212.

24 At that stage of the procedure, a two-thirds majority is thus not required.

25 Art. 106 of the Constitution.

26 "*Ouvertes à revision*" in French and "*voor herziening vatbaar*" in Dutch.

27 The journal is called *Moniteur Belge* in French and *Belgisch Staatsblad* in Dutch. Online. Available HTTP: <www.moniteur.be> or <www.staatsblad.be>. Since 1 January 2003, the paper version of the Journal has stopped; it is henceforth only available online (except for three paper copies that are still printed for archiving purposes of the Federal administration).

28 J.-C. Scholsem, "Brèves réflexions sur une éventuelle révision de l'article 195 de la Constitution", *Revue belge de droit constitutionnel*, 1999, p. 101.

29 Uyttendaele, op. cit., p. 74.

30 Delgrange and Dumont, op. cit., p. 217.

31 Art. 46, last paragraph of the Constitution.

32 Although Art. 106 of the Electoral Code of 12 April 1894 does not require this; in theory, the elections could take place on another day. But since 1894, this has never been the case; the vote has always taken place on a Sunday.

33 Art. 46, last paragraph of the Constitution.

34 See the Declarations for Revision of 1953 and 1958.

35 Abstentions are taken into account to calculate the quorum of presence, but not to determine the majority of votes.

36 Concurring: A. Alen and K. Muylle, *Compendium van het Belgisch Staatsrecht, Syllabusuitgave*, Mechelen: Kluwer, 2008, 2nd edn, vol. 1, p. 122. See also Constitutional Court, decision 5/2004 of 14 January 2004.

37 F. Delpérée, "La déclaration de révision de la Constitution: le 195, certainement pas, un 195 *bis*, pourquoi pas?", *Journal des Procès*, no. 450, 10 Janvier 2003, pp. 16–17.

38 F. Delpérée, "Le contrôle de constitutionnalité des traités internationaux", *Revue belge de droit constitutionnel*, 1999, pp. 97–8.

39 H. Simonart, "La procédure de révision: Présentation du problème", in Delpérée (ed.), op. cit., 2003, p. 23.

40 Concurring: A. Alen, *Handboek van het Belgisch Staatsrecht*, Deurne: Kluwer, 1995, pp. 70–1; F. Delpérée, *Le droit constitutionnel de la Belgique*, Bruxelles and Paris: Bruylant and LGDJ, 2000, pp. 77–8; M. Uyttendaele, *Précis de droit constitutionnel belge*, 3rd edn, Brussels: Bruylant, 2005, p. 123.

41 See Arts. 17, 18 and 24 of the Luxembourgish Constitution of 17 October 1868.

42 To be precise, it is actually a re-proclamation, because independence had already been proclaimed some weeks earlier, on 4 October.

43 M. Verstraete, "Observations au sujet du caractère révocable ou irrévocable du décret du 24 février 1831 proclamant l'indépendance du peuple belge", *Revue de l'Administration*,

1954, p. 129; A. Mast, *Overzicht van het Belgisch Grondwettelijk recht*, Ghent: Story-Scientia, 1983, 7th edn, p. 480; Alen, op. cit., pp. 70–1, and Delpérée, *Le droit constitutionnel de la Belgique*, op. cit., p. 77.

44 State Council, Legislative Section, avis du 15 Juillet 1993, published in *Documents parlementaires*, Chambre des représentants, 48e législature, session ordinaire 1992–1993, no. 1036/2.

45 B. Beyts, speech before the National Congress on 24 February 1831 (É. Huyttens, *Discussions du Congrès national de Belgique*, Brussels, Société typographique belge, 1844, vol. 2, p. 590).

46 O. Orban, *Le droit constitutionnel de la Belgique*, Liège and Paris: Dessain, Giard and Brière, 1908, vol. 2, p. 731; P. Errera, *Traité de droit public belge*, Paris: Giard and Brière, 1918, p. 4; G. Dor and A. Braas, "La Constitution", *Les Novelles*, vol. II, Brussels: Larcier, 1935, p. 138.

47 Behrendt and Bouhon, op. cit., p. 122 and pp. 181–4.

48 In 1830, Belgium became independent in a revolution fought (and won) against the Dutch army, and in 1831, nine months after the Independence, Belgium was already faced with its first war, launched by the Netherlands.

49 For all the period from 1831 to 2011, I am not aware of a single case in which they have been applied, and I know of no author who would have claimed to have found one.

50 To give the most eloquent illustration of this: some years ago, when I joined the scientific committee of a Belgian statute book series, I realized that, in these books, the decrees were not even published (I thus suggested adding them, which was done). But the statute books, which are edited annually, had been published for more than half a century without the two decrees — and nobody even noticed.

51 For example, the Czechoslovak coup d'état of 1948.

52 It is, however, obvious that the instauration of a dictatorship, even if one supposes that all domestic formal requirements were met, would violate numerous substantive provisions of International Human Rights Law — unless, of course, one also supposes that the country in question were to renounce all its international conventional obligations in this field.

53 Uyttendaele, *Trente leçons de droit constitutionnel*, op. cit., p. 110.

54 Already a century ago, in 1908, my predecessor in the Chair of Constitutional Law in Liège, Oscar Orban, discussed such proposals (*Le droit constitutionnel de la Belgique*, op. cit., pp. 727–8). See also the proposal of F. Perin, *Parliamentary documents*, House of Representatives, ordinary session 1967–1968, no. 563/1 (document of 23 February 1968).

55 M. Uyttendaele, "Le referendum constitutionnel en Belgique ou une réponse inadaptée à une question pertinente", *Administration publique trimestrielle*, 1994, pp. 112–13.

56 Delgrange and Dumont, op. cit., p. 232.

57 See above, footnote 10 and related information in the main text.

58 Scholsem, op. cit., p. 104.

59 Behrendt and Bouhon, op. cit., pp. 477–93.

60 The majority of writers (myself included) believe that in the case of an inconsistency between a norm of a Treaty with direct effect ratified by Belgium on the one hand, and a norm of the Belgian Constitution on the other, the latter should prevail: otherwise, the Constitution could be bypassed — and thus *de facto* revised — by simply agreeing to international treaties (and this although such an agreement does not require a two-thirds majority in Parliament). The complete list of authors favorable to the position of pre-eminence of the Constitution in the case of a conflict with a norm of international law can be found in Behrendt and Bouhon, op. cit., p. 492, footnote 1744. This position of constitutional pre-eminence is not based on any form of obsolete legal nationalism or exaggerated patriotism but on the simple consideration that, in a country abiding by the principles of democracy and the rule of law, it would not be acceptable to bypass, via a simple-majority law agreeing to a treaty, the constitutional rule that any

amendment made to the Constitution must be approved by a two-thirds majority in both Houses of Parliament (Art. 195 of the Constitution). At footnote 1745 of my book, I indicate the writers supporting the opposite view.

61 Orban, op. cit., p. 565.

62 The Belgian Council of State is composed of two Sections: the Section of Legislation (which has a purely advisory function) and the Section of Administrative Litigation (which constitutes the Supreme Administrative Court of Belgium).

63 H. Dumont, X. Delgrange and S. Van Drooghenbroeck, "La procédure de révision de la Constitution: Suggestions", in Delpérée (ed.), op. cit., p. 157.

64 On this subject, see also F. Delpérée and S. Depré, *Le système constitutionnel de la Belgique*, Brussels: Larcier, 1998, p. 263.

65 Delpérée and Depré, op. cit., pp. 263–4.

66 Scholsem, op. cit., p. 101.

67 On this issue see also: C. Behrendt, "La possible modification de la procédure de révision de la Constitution belge", *Revue française de droit constitutionnel*, 2003, vol. 54, pp. 279–308.

4 Constitutional change and constitutional amendment

A Canadian conundrum

Allan C. Hutchinson

When you are through changing, you are through.

Bruce Barton

American Chief Justice John Marshall's admonition that "we must never forget, that it is a constitution we are expounding" is the stuff of jurisprudential apple-pie.[1] Its beauty and banality are indispensable elements of its enduring appeal. As a key to interpretive practice and doctrinal change, it is itself open to varied interpretations. Whereas some jurists draw upon its rhetorical force to justify a program of continuing efforts for "expounding" the Constitution in a way that keeps it current and in tune with a prevailing ethos, others enlist it as part of a campaign to put the constitution beyond generational tampering and to make change a matter for formal amendment of the written document, not for judicial alteration through incremental elaboration. Notwithstanding this division of opinion, there is almost universal recognition that constitutions deserve especial solicitude and should hold special sway in society's understanding of law and politics. The overarching challenge is to offer some account of constitutional meaning and authority that both recognizes the need for stability and the desire for change—how is it possible to establish a practical set of institutional arrangements that treats constitutions as an authoritative and enduring body of super-norms and, at the same time, allows for a certain responsiveness to the changing values and ideas of society?

In this essay, I want to explore this dynamic tension between stability and change that both energizes and enervates the theory and practice of constitutional law in Canada. In so doing, I will develop a critical account that insists upon an inevitable and inseparable relation between law and politics.[2] For me, a constitution is an organic process through which people determine the kind of society and citizens that they are and want to become. In seeking to negotiate and establish the institutional and substantive terms of their collective existence, the process involved, the product achieved, and their dialectical relation are all within constitutionalism's conceptual and practical provenance. While the formal documents and conventions of nationhood represent a privileged resolution of constitutional debate, the continuing and inescapable struggle to interpret and re-interpret that compromise gives fresh meaning and effect to it. Thus, constitutionalism embraces the practical and the utopian, the institutional and the ideological, the real and the imagined, the past and the future. Accordingly, in tracing and appreciating constitutional change, it will be important to examine a variety of strategies, both formal and informal, by which these imperatives have been accommodated. Attention to the written record is only a part of the constitutional story.

While I maintain that these general observations can claim a general validity, they have particular relevance and resonance in the Canadian context. The first section of the essay sets out a theoretical framework for understanding the challenge of understanding constitutional change and the relation of any amendment process to changes made. In the second section, I look at the first phase of Canadian constitutional history and trace the dynamics by which constitutional change was effected and defended. The third section grapples with the more modern phase of Canadian constitutional development and explores efforts made to bring about legal change in a context in which political change proved to be almost impossible. Throughout the paper, I will contend that constitutional law is an organic work-in-progress whose dependable lifeblood is the continuity of change; any distinction between its formal and informal revision or between its fixed and fluid dimensions is mistaken. There is a constitutional tradition of political transformation in which there is development and growth, but not always in gradual ways or predictable directions.

Setting the table

A high-stakes game

Constitutions are considered the foundation on which law and politics are built. Whether made up of formal documents or formalized customs, they are supposed to contain the terms and conditions on which political power is to be obtained, allocated, exercised, and controlled in a legal manner: they are meant to be the institutional and constant matrix within which the ebb and flow of political action occurs. Indeed, great stock is set by the extent to which states subscribe to such constitutional promise and strive to achieve such constitutional practice. Those countries that subscribe to constitutional government will be vindicated as being both politically legitimate and legally sound. And this is no bad thing—good governance ought to be as much about the "what" that is decided as the "how" it is decided. However, the idea and practice of government based on a stable and constant constitution proves more illusory than real: the belief that constitutions can ground anything is a dangerous conceit.

In Canada, constitutional law operates in much the same way as the common law generally, but with two principal differences. First, the stakes are usually high in constitutional interpretation: lives are changed; elected representatives are constrained in what they can and cannot do; citizens' rights against government are vindicated or vanquished; and the like. It is a contested drama in which power and principle, right and wrong, and process and substance vie with each other for popular priority and general acceptance. While courts tend to be front-and-center in the Canadian production, other actors—bureaucrats, police officers, politicians, teachers, the media, etc.—play a major practical set of roles. Second, when dealing with constitutional matters, courts (and others) have to respect in some way the formal and written documents that form the basis for both their own power and the circumstances in which such power can be exercised. However, while these differences ought not to be trivialized, they are insufficient to alter the basic nature of the adjudicative task. The difference is more a matter of emphasis and degree than difference and kind. Constitutional adjudication, therefore, is simply a particular kind of common law adjudication. The basic components of the common law mind-set are adapted to the specialized demands of the constitutional context.

In Canada, therefore, constitutional law is a baffling mish-mash of texts, customs, conventions, ideals, and cases. As such, it is more instructive and more convincing to view constitutional law as an historical and political tour-de-force of the episodic and unpredictable occasions on which judges, jurists, and other members of the political elite contribute to the efforts of Canadians to come to terms with who they are and who they want to be. There is no resolution or finality to that process, and there is certainly no gradual, getting-better-all-the-time progress. Despite the self-understanding of its judicial and juristic practitioners, constitutional interpretation is a volatile tradition of transformative politics. Indeed, David Strauss captures this phenomenon well when he states that "the forces that bring about constitutional change work their will almost irrespective of whether and how the text of the Constitution is changed," and the "constitutional order would look little different if a formal amendment process did not exist." He ascribes the appreciation that the heart of a constitution is in its almost unhindered judicial interpretation to the finding that "constitutional law is best seen as the result of a complex, evolutionary process, rather than of discrete, self-consciously political acts by a sovereign People."[3] I both agree and disagree with this assessment. I agree in that it is not so much that the political arena in itself does not matter, but rather that the same ideological forces play themselves out through the courts. However, I disagree in that, if Strauss means that the constitutional law's "complex, evolutionary process" is gradual and contained, the common law does not change in an incremental and principled way. Common law adjudication is itself a political process, albeit one that is different in dynamics and performance than the legislative branches of government. It is a work-in-progress affected by and responsive to its social, historical, and political environment.

Perhaps surprisingly (or not), while the stakes of constitutional law are very high, the stakes of constitutional theory are even higher. Those who are able to persuade others, particularly judges, what they should be doing when they engage and fulfill their constitutional responsibilities exert a massive influence; they set the informing terms within which disputes are recognized, reflected upon, and resolved. Moreover, constitutional theorists perform this role from the relatively obscure and unaccountable wings of the political and legal stage. This is both an enormous opportunity and a huge responsibility. The theory that is considered to underpin and guide the judicial process will be very influential and occasionally decisive in matters of constitutional application. Of course, the claims of theory will themselves not be politically innocent; theoretical claims of abstract universality and ideological neutrality are suspect.[4]

Constitutions and democracy

The relationship between democracy and constitutions is a long and fractious one. Those who lean towards the constitutionalist side have tended to perceive democracy as a threat to political order and the preservation of important values, whereas those who take a more democratist stance tend to treat constitutions as elite hindrances to popular rule, as much as anything else. However, the prevailing view today is decidedly more constitutionalist than democratist. Theorists, politicians, and judges value the democratic worth of popular participation, but maintain that it must be channeled and disciplined within a larger constitutional structure: complicated amendment procedures, judicial review of legislation that is deemed inconsistent with the constitution, and limited opportunities for direct popular involvement in political decision-making. Indeed, far from negating democracy, constitutionalism is promoted as creating an orderly framework within which democracy can be protected and thrive. So contained, democracy will allow citizens to involve themselves more appropriately in political governance and make reasonable political decisions. As stated by the judges of the Supreme Court of Canada, "viewed correctly, constitutionalism and the rule of law are not in conflict with democracy; rather, they are essential to it."[5]

Democracy is about self-government. Its basic idea is that citizens come together as political equals and decide for themselves the laws that will regulate their conduct and the institutions under which they live. As such, democrats are especially preoccupied with sources.[6] No matter how substantively just a legal principle or rule seems to be, a democrat will always be interested in questions about its origin and, therefore, its legitimacy. A vital dimension in the assessment of any legal norm as being just is the fact that it originated in an exercise of self-legislation by the governed, not simply imposed or made on their behalf: democracy is about rule *by* the people, not simply *for* the people.[7] However, the democratic pedigree of a law is not the only concern of a democrat: democratic lineage is a necessary, if not always sufficient, condition for an initiative's justness. Both the matter and manner of laws are important. Indeed, it is the procedural mode of their creation that bolsters and underwrites the substantive merit of those laws; matter and manner are intimately related and re-enforcing. Although this attention to sources has considerable salience in the legislative arena, its implications are even more pressing in regard to constitutional or fundamental laws, which, by their nature, are often beyond the reach of day-to-day politics.

The amenability of constitutional arrangements and fundamental laws to periodic reconsideration and revision seems an indispensable part of any democratic compact. Even if it requires some trade-offs and compromises to be put into practice in large societies, strong democracy is a regime of popular self-government, which not only allows for, but relies upon, the regular participation by citizens in the formulation and enactment of the laws that govern their lives.

At its most general, it is the rule *of* everyone *by* everyone.[8] For the democrat, a political system that has entrenched the "right" abstract principles in what is thought to be a finished constitution, and that has attempted to freeze in place a particular juridical arrangement, sits uncomfortably with any genuine commitment to democracy. Democracy resists political closure; it fosters, not forecloses, political and popular engagement: a self-governing people must be able to confront and reformulate its commitments on a regular, democratic basis.[9] In that respect, democracy supposes not only ample opportunities for popular participation, but a regime consistent with the ideal of democratic openness: there can be no set of laws whose authority is taken for granted and which are not subject to revision.

Making changes

The well-known North American debate between James Madison and Thomas Jefferson provides the classical example of the tension between democracy and constitutionalism. Madison reacted against Jefferson's insistence in periodic constituent assemblies designed to allow the people to exercise its "right to choose for itself the form of government it believes most promotive of its own happiness."[10] For Madison, Jefferson's proposal recommended to the citizenry that their current system of government was somehow defective, depriving the government of "that veneration which time bestows on every thing, and without which perhaps the wisest and freest governments would not possess the requisite stability."[11] Instead of periodic assemblies that, by opening the constitution to the "decisions of the whole society" interested "too strongly the public passions,"[12] Madison favored a complicated amendment procedure. He favored a process that involved a series of extraordinary majorities at the federal and state levels, which made even minor constitutional changes difficult to propose and unlikely to succeed. Justice Marshall provided judicial support to this approach when he declared that, while the people "have an original right to establish for their future government such principles as, in their opinion, shall most conduce to their own happiness," the exercise of this "original right is a very great exertion; nor can it nor ought it to be frequently repeated." He went on to add that, "since the authority from which they proceed can seldom act," these principles are "designed to be permanent."[13]

The problem, of course, is that no constitution can establish a permanent "just and democratic regime": the very idea of a finished constitution that seeks to prevent instances of popular constitutional change is incompatible with democracy. Instead of treating important constitutional transformations as occasions for establishing more just constitutional forms and superior mechanisms for democratic engagement, most modern constitutions attempt to regulate their own transformation through very limited and highly technical mechanisms. They make change difficult and unlikely, even if supported by great majorities of the population. These amendment rules are driven by an aspiration to consolidate the permanency of the constitutional regime, not by an urgent impetus to maintain and preserve the revolutionary spirit that brought the constitutional regime into existence.

For example, Art. V is the amendment rule of the US Constitution. While it was created by a "democratic revolution," it makes future democratic changes in the constitution extremely difficult to effect. Indeed, it is one of the most demanding constitutional amendment processes in the world.[14] Under Art. V, two-thirds of both Houses of Congress may propose amendments or two-thirds of the state legislatures may apply for a Convention for proposing amendments. These proposals must then be ratified by three-fourths of state legislatures or by three-fourths of special state conventions. With such formidable hurdles, it is not surprising that the US Constitution has been amended only 27 times in over two centuries. Moreover, it is equally telling that the ratification of the Twenty-seventh Amendment took 200 years to be completed; it was ratified in 1992, after being originally presented by James Madison in 1789.[15] All told, Art. V seems to be less an amendment rule and more a non-amendment rule.

Again, from a strong democratic viewpoint, Art. V not only makes constitutional change difficult and unlikely, it also makes it non-participatory; amendment of the constitution is left exclusively in the hands of government officials, albeit elected representatives. This is true even when the initiative to propose constitutional changes is not only placed in Congress, but states are also provided with the initiative of applying for a (until now unprecedented) Convention that would arguably have an unlimited power to propose amendments or even an entirely new fundamental law.[16] Such a Convention, at least in theory, could be seen as an attempt to reproduce the process through which the Constitution was established in the first place. Even leaving aside the difficulties involved in calling a Convention (created in part by the super-majority rules in the initiative and ratification processes, and by the possibility that Congress might refuse to call it or to send its proposals for ratification),[17] there are certain ambiguities in the text of Art. V that make its democratic credentials questionable. For example, would the members of the Convention be democratically elected? If they are elected, would they be elected by the people at large or according to the principle of state equality (e.g. one delegate for each state regardless of the size of the state's population)? Would the Convention have the power to adopt its own internal rules? Does the Convention or Congress have the power to create an alternative ratification procedure (such as a binding national referendum)? Could Congress transform itself into a Convention?[18]

The formal and informal

Of course, the upshot of having a next-to-impossible-to-use amendment process is not that no changes in constitutional arrangements happen. On the contrary, it is that change occurs by other, even less democratic, means than those provided by the written Constitution itself. It is difficult to discover any society whose constitution, even if its form stays the same, remains fixed in substance over any extended period of time. This is especially the case in common law jurisdictions, like the United States, the United Kingdom, and Canada. While jurists and politicians may pay lip-service to a nation's founding and enduring documents, they know that this is only the beginning of the search for constitutional meaning. Amendment is simply one kind of change that is more formal in style, less technical in substance and often, although not always, more significant. Changes, even of a large and significant nature, occur even though the formal process of constitutional change itself remains unused and unchanged. While there is no simple or fixed causal relationship, the informal amendment process is inextricably linked to the formal amendment process in that "an informal amendment process exists because formal amendment is so difficult."[19]

In Canada, like the United States, changes in constitutional law have happened at a steady and continuous pace. While taking place under the guise of interpretation, there have been some monumental changes in the regime of constitutional structures and rights. Constitutional history shows that there is no change so big that it could not be achieved informally (and in spite of the written Constitution) if the political forces are sufficiently aligned to demand or facilitate it. It is only when there is insufficient support for change (particularly from the elites) that the formal amendment process will appear as a brute obstacle to change.[20] Otherwise, change will proceed with little concern for the distinction between legal interpretation and constitutional amendment, and between the formal and informal practices of change. The Canadian experience offers a revealing glimpse into how the formal and informal dimensions combine to effect change.

Most importantly, by exploring how such changes have occurred, it becomes possible to glimpse the fundamental and operative assumptions about political power and democratic legitimacy at any point in history. In particular, the actual institutional levers and location of such constitutional changes disclose where a society situates the actual seat of sovereignty and where it locates the real locus of legitimacy, regardless of what formal constitutional provisions might suggest or recommend. As regards Canada, this site is most definitely not the people themselves. It is the courts, especially the Supreme Court, which have become the preferred site for effecting important changes in the constitutional order. By design and default, they have claimed the ultimate authority to act on behalf of Canadian citizens as a self-governing collective: judges have become the filters and proxies for the citizenry.

However, in a society that claims to be devoted to the ideas and practice of democratic legitimacy, it is far from clear why the courts are the suitable or appropriate institution to speak and act on the people's behalf. To put it more pointedly, if the courts are assumed to have democratic legitimacy, then democratic legitimacy is a very thin device and counts for little in the general political scheme of things. The courts are neither operated nor constituted in line with popular will or representative viewpoints. Indeed, the democratic legitimacy of the courts is somewhat perversely grounded in their willingness to act as a check on popular and direct expressions of constituent power. This seems to put democracy firmly under the control of the Constitution. At best, democracy is reduced to merely one value in a much broader range of constitutional commitments.

In order to put some practical flesh on this skeletal outline of the theoretical issues involved, I will survey and analyze the history of the Canadian Constitution, with particular emphasis on the process of change. It can be usefully and realistically divided into two distinct phases for present purposes. At Canada's founding, the original enabling document was that of a British statute, the British North America Act, in 1867. It was the written part of a much larger constitutional tradition that drew upon the unwritten sources of the common law and customary conventions; change was constant and largely informal. The second stage of constitutional development occurred in 1982 when Canada patriated its Constitution (i.e. established it as a home-based instrument with its own amendment procedures) and incorporated a Charter of Rights and Freedoms. There remained a broader framework of common law principles and customary convention within which its written components functioned: change has continued in much the same way since.[21]

Of trees and nature

A colonial beginning

If the United States came into constitutional being through a decisive act of colonial revolution, then Canada achieved its status as a nation through a more reserved act of colonial forbearance. While this difference in origins has many explanations and consequences, it highlights a vital distinction between the challenge of constitutional interpretation and change in the United States and Canada. Whereas the US Constitution was intended as a break with the past and a popular manifestation of constituent power, the Canadian Constitution was the continuation of an established political tradition and had no greater significance than any other exercise of power by a legislative authority. Moreover, also reflecting its British roots, the formal documents of the Canadian Constitution are not intended to be complete or definitive. The Constitution comprises both formal and informal sources. Indeed, the critical tension between established constitutional documents and developing legal doctrine is at the heart of Canadian constitutional law.

Even before the Canadian Confederation in 1867, a colonial system of responsible government existed and was modeled on the British parliamentary system. This system entailed certain arrangements that established the election and operation of the legislature and a division of power between the executive and legislative branches of colonial government; both branches remained subject to the imperial control of the British Parliament and Crown via various mechanisms. Moreover, it must be emphasized that the British Parliament retained the power to pass imperial statutes in regard to Canada without any requirement for Canadian support or consent; this was the essence of colonial governance. Any Canadian law that was repugnant to an imperial statute was invalid. Also, a Governor-General, appointed by the British Crown, held veto power over all colonial legislative enactments.

In the late 1860s, several colonies in British North America expressed the hope of creating a federation. A document was drafted whose purpose was essentially to enable the continuation of old arrangements and encode a division of power between provincial legislatures and a federal Parliament. The delegates convened in London and requested enactment of the document as an imperial statute. This became the fabled British North America Act. It was prescribed to be "a Constitution similar in principle to that of the United Kingdom." In the British tradition, it was not intended to be a comprehensive constitutional document that codified all the provisions of responsible government. For instance, the composition of the actual executive authority and its relationship to the legislative authority were treated as being regulated by unwritten and traditional conventions; this still remains the case today. Most importantly for our purposes, there was no amending process. As a British statute, it could only be changed at the behest of the British Parliament; Canadian approval was not formally required, even if politically expected. This situation prevailed until 1982.

Political negotiations

Between 1867 and the patriation of the Constitution in 1982, the text of the British North America Act changed little. However, substantial and significant changes occurred regarding matters of judicial interpretation and political convention. Politically, various shifts and alterations were made over the decades. A good example is the virtual elimination of British imperial power. On a reading of the text of the 1867 Constitution, the office of the Governor-General is supposed to occupy an important and powerful place in Canada's constitutional regime. The British North America Act confers on the Governor-General broad discretionary powers, including a discretionary power to withhold royal assent to legislation temporarily (reservation) or completely with royal direction (disallowance). The Governor-General can also veto the legislative appointment of governments, dissolve Parliament, appoint Senators, and perform many more important functions Additionally, the Governor-General or Lieutenant-Governor, not the Prime Minister or Cabinet, possesses the executive discretion to appoint senior judges.

While the Governor-General's appointment is formally made by the Queen on the advice of her ministers, it has been accepted since the Imperial Conference of 1930 that this appointment will be made only on the advice of the Canadian federal government. Similarly, the powers of reservation and disallowance had fallen into disuse by 1930—reservation had occurred 21 times between 1867 and 1878, but had never occurred after 1878, and disallowance had occurred only once (in 1873).[22] It was expressly acknowledged at the Imperial Conference that these powers would not be exercised. With respect to all of the Governor-General's other powers, like the power to prorogue Parliament, convention has developed that all such powers are only to be exercised at the request and with the consent of the Prime Minister. Also, in 1930, it was decided by convention (and, in 1931, codified in the Statute of Westminster) that no new imperial statutes would be made unless explicitly requested; the doctrine of repugnancy, which gave superior legal status to imperial statutes in case of conflict with local laws, was also abandoned.

Given that the British North America Act was simply an imperial statute itself, the implication of such changes was that they would effectively implement the removal of constitutional status of the British North America Act and give Canadian legislatures the power to amend the Constitution at will. Foreseeing this problem, and because no domestic amending formula could be agreed upon, the Canadian and British governments came to a political arrangement that the British North America Act would continue to retain its traditional legal status as the supreme law in Canada. The practice developed that the British North America Act would only be changed at the request and consent of Canada. The form and institution of such a request was not codified, but was understood to involve a joint address of the Canadian House of Commons and the Canadian Senate.

Judicial interpretations

As its name suggests, the British North America Act was simply another statutory enactment of the British government. As such, it was to be interpreted in much the same way as any other piece of legislation. True to form, the Canadian courts went about their business of interpreting the constitutional separation-of-powers provisions of the British North America Act in a methodologically modest way. The received rules of statutory interpretation were relied upon: the words were to be given their ordinary meaning, and reference to legislative intent was considered unnecessary or unacceptable. Although there were some occasional attempts to look to "original intent," the Judicial Committee of the Privy Council (a part of the British House of Lords that was the final court of appeal for most Canadian cases until 1949) had no truck with such deviations from accepted tradition. In *Lambe* in 1887, the Privy Council made it clear that constitutional questions "have been left for the decision of the ordinary courts of law, which must treat the provisions of the (British North America) Act in question by the same methods of construction and exposition which they apply to other statutes."[23]

In fulfilling this mandate, Canadian jurisprudence took a distinctive approach. In one of the most celebrated Canadian cases, the courts had to decide in the late 1920s whether a woman could be a "qualified person" to sit in the Senate. While a contemporary reading would include women, the accepted meaning of "person" at the time of confederation did not; no woman would have been allowed to hold public office in 1867. While the Supreme Court of Canada stayed with the earlier meaning, the Privy Council held that it was not the original meaning that held interpretive sway. Lord Sankey laid out an alternative approach that became and remains the hallmark of constitutional adjudication:

> The British North America Act planted in Canada a living tree capable of growth and expansion within its natural limits (. . .) Their Lordships do not conceive it to be the duty of this Board—it is certainly not their desire—to cut down the provisions of the Act by a narrow and technical construction, but rather to give it a large and liberal interpretation so that the Dominion to a great extent, but within certain fixed limits, may be mistress in her own house.[24]

This embrace of a "living tree" approach to constitutional interpretation gave the lie to any claim that the Constitution stood available and ready for interpretation in its objective "thereness." Indeed, such a static idea of a Constitution is as misleading as it is mistaken. At least as evidenced by the Canadian context, a Constitution is confirmed to be a distinctly organic process in which societies shape and re-shape their institutional arrangements and commitments on the fly. While there is an obvious acknowledgment that change occurs, it is still insisted that such change is to be gradual and progressive. Canadian constitutional law's natural development is treated as a matter of slow growth, not abrupt transformation. However, this process of "growth and development" is much more open-ended and unstructured than the courts and commentators would have us believe. While the law changes to meet new and different political conditions, it does so in a way that confounds any retrospective claims that such historical evolution is gradual and incremental. Canada's Constitution is a place where the nation works through its competing anxieties and shifting aspirations, often in the most abrupt way and with the most unexpected results.

For instance, while almost none of the wording of the Constitution Act 1867 has changed in more than 125 years, the meaning and effect of its provisions on the division of provincial and federal powers have gone through a process of continual redefinition. The bulk of constitutional law comprises the many judicial cases that have sought to interpret and apply constitutional arguments to changing social and political circumstances. Indeed, it is difficult to pin down the difference in the substantive effects of the formal acts of amending the Constitution and the informal acts of interpreting it. In an important sense, the Constitution is changed every time it is judicially reinterpreted; amendment is simply a more formal kind of change. More to the point, these judicially engineered changes are significant in number and effect. But, in a constitution that is as much unwritten and evanescent as it is written and fixed, this should come as no surprise.

Like Canada itself, the terrain is too vast and too variable to do more than sample some of the more striking examples of how the Constitution has changed over the years and how its growth has not been as measured and principled as its common law defenders insist. Some examples of the ways in which constitutional doctrine and, therefore, the Constitution has shifted and changed over the years include:

- *Things that are in the written parts of the Constitution can move in and out of the Constitution over time*—Under ss. 55, 56, and 57 of the Constitution Act 1867, the British government retained the right to "reserve and disallow" Canadian statutes. However, this power has not been exercised since 1878 in the case of reservation, and since 1873 in the case of disallowance. Moreover, under s. 90 of the Constitution Act 1867, the federal government has the powers of reservation and disallowance over provincial laws, although this has not been exercised since 1943. It is the received wisdom that any attempt to utilize these powers would not only be politically objectionable, but would also be legally inoperative. Indeed, in 1981 the Supreme Court of Canada stated that "reservation and disallowance of provincial legislation, although in law still open, have, to all intents and purposes, fallen into disuse."[25] Nevertheless, efforts to amend the Constitution have sought to include provisions that would explicitly delete such powers from the Constitution. This is an instance where the writing has remained, but the meaning has been lost.

Another example of this is the overall division of legislative powers between the federal government and the provinces. Whereas s. 91 of the Constitution Act stipulates the federal powers, s. 92 lays out the provincial powers. While each section states that the powers are granted "exclusively" to each branch of government, the traditional practice is to allow each level of government to legislate on the same issue if the subject matter validly falls under both heads of authority. For instance, traffic laws can fall within both the provinces' "property and civil rights" power and the federal government's "criminal law" power. However, if a valid federal and provincial law conflict, the federal law has paramountcy. The courts have interpreted "conflict" in a very narrow manner and decided that statutes only conflict where "compliance with one law involves breach of the other."[26]

- *Things that are written in the Constitution can take on different and occasionally contradictory meanings over time*—The history of the interpretation of the "peace, order and good government power" ("POGG") granted to the federal government is an object lesson in how words remain but meanings change. Apart from the continuing debate over whether the so-called POGG power is a residuary power or whether it includes the whole of the federal power, the extent and scope of this power has taken on different guises as circumstances demand. For instance, it has been used to transfer powers to the federal government over matters of "national concern" and where there is an "emergency," even if such matters would otherwise fall under provincial jurisdiction.[27] These doctrines seem to have been fashioned from whole cloth.

  Another illustration of this phenomenon is the historical tension between the federal government's "trade and commerce" power under s. 91(2) of the Constitution Act and the provinces' "civil rights and property" power under s. 92(13). While the courts have mapped out different spheres of authority in terms of inter- and intra-provincial trade, there is still much vagueness and confusion surrounding the details of the doctrine.[28]
- *Things that are written in the Constitution can be circumvented by things that are not written in the Constitution*—The problem of delegation exemplifies this well. The key issue is whether the federal and provincial governments can agree to swap powers—in other words, can the federal government give the provinces power to levy indirect taxes, a strictly federal power, in return for the provinces giving the federal government power to establish a pension scheme, a strictly provincial power? The Supreme Court of Canada has said that, as there is no express authority in the constitution, it was not allowed because it would amount to *de facto* constitutional amendment. However, the courts did allow the federal government and provinces to delegate powers to administrative bodies established under the authority of the other.[29] In effect, what could not

be done by legislative delegation could be achieved by administrative delegation; what could not be done directly was done indirectly. The upshot of allowing delegation is that the federal and provincial governments can agree to circumvent the constitution's written division of powers.

Another example of how the written Constitution can be easily end-run is the exercise of the federal spending power—are there restraints on how the federal government can distribute its considerable tax revenues? For instance, while the administration of hospitals comes within provincial competence, the federal government has exercised great influence over healthcare policy by the conditional deployment of federal funds. The debate is whether the federal government can spend only within its designated fields of federal competence or whether it can also fund projects that fall within provincial competence. The prevailing view is that the federal government can indeed fund in provincial areas as it is a choice for any province whether or not to accept such funding under the conditions it is granted. The Supreme Court of Canada has given tacit approval to such practices.[30]

The combined effect of these political negotiations and judicial decisions is that the Canadian Constitution has undergone a constant series of alterations and modifications. Not only were these reforms both large and small, they also occurred entirely outside the democratic theater of politics. It seems almost beside the point to cavil about whether such regular changes are more appropriately classified as "amendments" or "interpretations." Through a variety of modes, the Constitution has remained both constant in form and flexible in meaning. While this is a considerable achievement, there linger questions about the legitimacy of such changes from a democratic viewpoint. The "living tree" that is Canada's Constitution has certainly grown, but the question of whether it has done so within its "natural limits" or whether it has simply responded to the fads and fancies of its judicial gardeners (suitably influenced by more general currents of constitutional propriety) is one for political debate and evaluation.

Of charters and constraints

Coming home

By the 1970s, many Canadians began to complain that it was more than timely for Canada to have its own home-grown Constitution and to cut most formal constitutional ties with the United Kingdom. Apart from formalizing many informal practices, there was a push to include within any new constitutional compact an entrenched commitment to the protection of rights. Led by Pierre Trudeau's federal Liberal Party, a successful campaign was waged to substantially change Canada's constitutional framework. Despite efforts to portray it more as "romantic" nation-building, the whole process of constitutional change was highly politicized. After an extended period of bartering and horse-trading, the end result was a brokered compromise between federal and provincial politicians.

Initially, the federal government's desire to repatriate the Constitution and introduce a Charter of Rights and Freedoms was not matched by some of their provincial counterparts. In particular, there was little agreement on an amending formula. To break the political log-jam, the federal government threatened to act unilaterally. In response, the provinces took the issue to the courts. Eventually, the federal government launched a reference to the Supreme Court on whether constitutional changes brought about without provincial consent could effect changes to the powers of the provinces, and whether there was a legal or conventional obligation to obtain provincial consent before requesting an amendment. This was an occasion of high constitutional and political drama.

The Supreme Court of Canada assumed the role of political arbitrator in the midst of a constitutional crisis. In classic common law tradition, the Court pressed ahead in the absence of any apparent legal rules. The judges acknowledged the legal power of a unilateral federal request to make changes that would affect provincial powers, but found that there existed a non-legally binding convention whereby a "substantial degree of provincial consent" was needed before such a request could be made to the British Parliament. In a moment of realpolitik, the country accepted the force of this non-enforceable convention as a way out of the political and constitutional impasse. Negotiations between the federal government and the provinces were re-opened. Notwithstanding the continued unwillingness of Quebec to engage or participate in such exchanges, an agreement was reached between the federal government and all the other provinces; this was considered to meet the threshold for a "substantial degree of provincial consent."[31] Accordingly, on 15 April 1982, a home-grown Canadian Constitution was introduced. Its main features were the abdication of British parliamentary authority, an entrenched bill of rights, constitutional recognition of aboriginal land rights, and a new amendment formula.

The amending formula

The amending formula under the Constitution Act 1982 is a complex set of rules that attempts to achieve a delicate balance in terms of both facilitating and frustrating change. On the one hand, it allows for relatively easy change when the substantive change is modest and political interests are aligned. On the other hand, it increases the threshold for change considerably when there is a significant modification in the offing and little political consensus. There are four basic procedures under Part V of the Constitution Act 1982:

1. *General formula*—Section 38 is the default formula and is to be used when the proposed amendment does not fall into another section of Part V. This requires support from the federal Parliament and "the legislative assemblies of at least two-thirds of the provinces that have (. . .) at least fifty per cent of the population of all the provinces." However, there are several provisions that can apply to the use of the general formula:
   (a) provinces may make an official dissent by legislative resolution (during a mandated window of time before proclamation) and, as a result, be exempt from the future operation of the applicable amendment;

(b) compensation can be made to provinces which, as a result of exercising the exemption, are maintaining jurisdiction over powers that the rest of the provinces have transferred to the federal government;
(c) under s. 42 amendments "in relation" to a list of specified "matters" (e.g. the principle of proportionality, the powers of the Senate and the method of selecting Senators, the Supreme Court of Canada, and the establishment of new provinces) are to be made under the formula dictated in s. 38, but are not subject to the dissent and exclusion rules, and therefore once in effect shall apply to the whole federation. These are matters that, due to their nature, do not lend themselves to partial application and must apply universally.

2. *Unanimity formula*—Under s. 41, amendments in relation to a list of specified "matters" may only be made after supporting resolutions have been passed by federal Parliament and every provincial legislature. These matters include the status of the monarchy, mandated minimum representation for each province in the House of Commons, and the composition of the Supreme Court.
3. *Some but not all provinces*—An amendment "in relation to any provision that applies to one or more, but not all, provinces" can be made with the agreement of the federal Parliament and "the legislative assembly of each province to which the amendment applies." This s. 43 procedure has been used to bring about some educational reforms in several provinces.
4. *Parliament or provincial legislature alone*—Parliament may amend "the Constitution of Canada in relation to the executive government of Canada or the Senate and House of Commons." This gives the federal Parliament limited power to modify its own arrangements as long as those changes do not impact provincial powers or status and are not properly dealt with under (1) and (2). Also, the legislature of each province may "exclusively make laws amending the constitution of the province." This procedure was used by the federal government to grant the Territory of Nunavut representation in the Canadian Senate; this was done under protest by some political parties, which thought that the general formula in (1) should have been used.

Part V is, of course, rife with ambiguity. This likely only strengthens further the power of the Supreme Court to balance the relevant interests at play within a particular context. However, the Canadian constitutional regime has managed to negotiate this uncertainty because of a political culture that largely maintains a genuine commitment to maintaining the strength of the federation: all three branches of government have shown great restraint and deference when necessary to avoid constitutional crises and to maintain the legitimacy of state institutions. Nevertheless, the constitutional terrain is not as flat or uneventful as might appear to be the case: there is considerable political activity and antagonism just below the legal surface.

Since 1982, there have been several efforts to amend the Constitution, all greeted with varying degrees of success. After the (failed) 1995 Quebec referendum, a special legislative arrangement was established between the federal government and the provinces, whereby a veto was given with respect to future amendments made under the 7/50 formula that are not subject to the dissent and exemption clauses. The statute only applies to amendments proposed by federal ministers and, therefore, not those proposed by a province. However, as the Regional Veto Statute is a piece of federal legislation, it can be repealed by the federal Parliament at any time. It has not been called into action or challenged in the last 15 years or so.

However, there have been several extended and divisive efforts to amend the constitution, which have had a less successful (depending on one's political alignment and views) outcome. In 1987, the Conservative government put forward the Meech Lake Accord. This was a package of constitutional amendments intended to deal with long-standing concerns of Western provinces and demands from the Province of Quebec. After protracted negotiations, the Accord failed in 1990 to be ratified by all 10 provincial governments, as required. This was followed by another effort to fashion a more acceptable and comprehensive package of constitutional amendments; this became known as the Charlottetown Accord. Again, this was defeated in a national referendum in 1992.

Judicial exertions

Up to its patriation in 1982, the formal constitution under the British North America Act was a minimalist document that simply laid the basic framework for confederation: civil liberties were not covered. This did not preclude the courts from using the common law to bridle arbitrary government acts and locate an "implied bill of rights" within the interstices of that Act. These efforts were sporadic and half-hearted, but they spoke to the vibrant possibilities of the common law.[32] However, with the advent of the new Charter of Rights and Freedoms in 1982, the judicial focus shifted from the unearthing of some basic rights to the interpretation of entrenched and explicit rights.

From the get-go, the federal government made it plain that the task of working out the Charter's meaning should be left to the courts: "government intended to avoid the problem of frozen rights by entrenching a broadly worded Charter that would require the judiciary to play a decisive role in defining the content of rights as a way to allow for the continual evolution of their meaning."[33] And, after some initial hesitation, the courts soon warmed to their task. In short order, the Supreme Court made it plain that it did not consider constitutional patriation to have consolidated or codified Canada's constitution completely. Unlike in the United States and other jurisdictions, there is still no one founding document that claims to occupy the whole constitutional field. For instance, although s. 52 of the Constitution Act 1982 contains a definition of "the Constitution of Canada," it is not exhaustive and is merely exemplary. Indeed, in *New Brunswick Broadcasting*,[34] the Supreme Court of Canada expressly confirmed that the Constitution comprised a variety of written and unwritten sources that were far from finite or fixed in definition and number.

So, notwithstanding the important patriation process of 1982, the Constitution continues to be dealt with in line with the familiar methodology of the common law. Constitutional law is a process as much as a product; it is a site for development as much as a completed structure. That said, the challenge over how the courts should go about their interpretive responsibilities under the Charter has, of course, led to considerable debate among judges and jurists. But, following the earlier Canadian constitutional tradition, the courts have shown little interest in an originalist approach and have taken a much more organicist stance in line with the "living tree" imperative.[35] Indeed, the Supreme Court of Canada has been quite vocal about the failings and futility of an originalist approach to constitutional adjudication even when the documentary evidence is both more extensive and more readily available; "the simple fact remains that the Charter is not the product of a few individual public servants, however distinguished, but a multiplicity of individuals who played major roles in the negotiating, drafting and adoption of the Charter."[36] Consequently, most Canadian lawyers and court commentators tend to concur that it is no more of a stretch for judges to be entrusted with the considerable discretion to update the Constitution over time than it is to expect them to ascertain the original meaning of a constitutional document over two centuries later.

The courts have gone about this interpretive responsibility with a certain enthusiasm, albeit occasionally guarded and subdued. Of course, there has not been unanimity or even a general consensus over the correct general approach or the particular interpretation of specific clauses. But the courts have continued to be creative and expansive in the overall attitude to their Charter duties. Indeed, not surprisingly, they have followed much the same path as under the pre-1982 regime. A few examples of the ways in which constitutional doctrine and, therefore, the constitution has shifted and changed over the past 20 years include:

- *Things that are not in written parts of the Constitution can become part of the constitution over time*—A good example of the power of judicial interpretation is *Sparrow*, in which the courts had to interpret the meaning and effect of s. 35 of the Constitution Act 1982, which reads that "existing aboriginal rights . . . are hereby recognised and affirmed."[37] This section is outside the Charter of Rights and Freedoms and so is not governed by the limiting force of s. 1 of the Charter, which states that all the rights and freedoms in the Charter are "subject only to such reasonable limits prescribed by law as can be demonstrably justified in a free and democratic society." Nevertheless, the Supreme Court held that, although the text of s. 35 has no mention of reasonable limits, the federal government has the continuing general power to impose reasonable restrictions on the exercise of any aboriginal rights protected under s. 35. If this is a valid interpretation, it is difficult to imagine in what substantive, as opposed to formal, ways an amendment of the constitution would differ from it.
- *Things that are written in the Constitution can be limited and controlled by things that are not written in the Constitution*—The Canadian Constitution is rife with examples of conventional and customary rules (i.e. restricted powers of the Governor-General in terms of the exercise of royal assent). While such conventions are seen to be the product of accretion over a period of observant practice, there are instances in which conventions seem to have sprung full-grown into

constitutional life. Also, there are said to be unwritten constitutional principles that hold sway over the written Constitution. For example, in the Provincial Judges Reference,[38] it was held that laws contradicting or offending the unwritten principle of judicial independence can be invalidated as unconstitutional.

- *Things that are written in the Constitution can change dramatically in meaning over time*— A good example of this under the Charter is the interpretation of the guarantee of freedom of association in s. 2. In 2007, the Supreme Court of Canada gave its decision in the Health Services and Support case. In a blunt assessment, the Court announced that its earlier ruling denying the constitutional existence of a right to bargain collectively was wrong and to be overturned; "the grounds advanced in the earlier decisions for the exclusion of collective bargaining rights from the Charter's protection of freedom of association do not withstand principled scrutiny and should be rejected . . . The protection enshrined (in the Charter) may properly be seen as the culmination of a historical movement towards the recognition of a procedural right to collective bargaining."[39] This is no small move in the world of constitutional law, politics, and change.

A question of balance

The best way to understand and appreciate the Canadian constitutional context in general, and the dynamics of constitutional change in particular, is to offer an extended analysis of one prominent and high-profile situation. Perhaps more than most, Canada is a country that has a continuing debate about its constitutional arrangements. This debate covers not only the legal structure of such arrangements, but also the process by which such a structure can connect to the political debate for its alteration. Although this leads to more than its fair share of national angst, Canada has at least been obliged to attend to the legitimacy and substance of the basic building blocks in its constitutional tool-kit. Of course, at the heart of this contemporary debate is the persistent problem of French-speaking Quebec's continued relationship with the rest of Canada. This involved the fraught and continuing political debate over whether and, if so, how Quebec might realize its desire for independence and secede from Canada. There can be no greater or more far-reaching constitutional matters for Canada than this.

The written Constitution was silent on such matters. When combined with the fact that Quebec played no part in the patriation of the Constitution in 1982, this in itself is revealing. As seems to have become customary, the issue found its way to the Supreme Court for authoritative guidance on what the Constitution might recommend and require in such circumstances. This brings to the fore a whole host of difficult and enduring concepts and practices—democracy, sovereignty, self-determination, federalism and, of course, the rule of law. Few constitutional challenges call so acutely into question the whole issue of what Constitutions are, where they are to be found, and how they are to be given meaning. The decision of the Supreme Court is an object lesson in the dilemmas that confront any theoretical efforts to give meaningful and legitimate practical content to constitutional law in a modern democracy. Moreover, it underlines the very fluid notion of constitutional change and the relationship between "amendment" and "interpretation."

The main question to be answered was "under the Constitution of Canada, can the National Assembly, legislature or government of Quebec effect the secession of Quebec from Canada unilaterally?" The Supreme Court decided that it could not. Any political decision to secede is constrained by, and must be implemented in accordance with, existing constitutional commitments. However, in a subtle analysis of the relationship between democracy and the rule of law, it also held that, if there was a clear democratic vote in favor of secession, the rest of Canada would be obliged to negotiate with Quebec over the terms of its withdrawal from the Canadian federation. Balancing constitutional rights and obligations with legal structures and political initiatives, the Supreme Court sought to clarify the delicate interplay between law and politics in a democracy and its own role in that dynamic confrontation.

For instance, it decided that, whereas the legal order of the Constitution prevented unilateral acts and required collective action, what constitutes "a clear democratic vote" and "legitimate negotiations" was a political matter that fell outside the legal mandate of the courts. As a unanimous Supreme Court concluded, "the task of the Court has been to clarify the legal framework within which political decisions are to be taken 'under the Constitution' and not to usurp the prerogatives of the political forces that operate within that framework." In order to do that, the Court made it plain that "the Constitution is more than a written text. It embraces the entire global system of rules and principles which govern the exercise of constitutional authority. A superficial reading of selected provisions of the written constitutional enactment, without more, may be misleading." Recognizing, therefore, that the written constitutional rules must be interpreted in light of the underlying unwritten principles that have been developed over time, the Supreme Court insisted that the enacted text is to be understood against the foundational principles of democracy, federalism, the Rule of Law, and respect for minority rights. Constitutional texts are primary, but they do not exhaust the Constitution and there is "an historical lineage" whose underlying principles "inform and sustain the constitutional text."[40]

In adopting such an approach, the Supreme Court recognizes that constitutional law is fluid and evanescent, not fixed and unmoving. Indeed, it sought to turn that fact to its institutional advantage. The decision was long and persuasively written because the judges needed to convince the relevant actors to accept its proposed modification/addition to the constitutional regime. The Court sought to protect the Constitution by making necessary compromises to allow all sides to continue to participate in debate and discussion within the confines and in recognition of the legitimacy of the Constitution. In order to reassure all sides that political debate could continue under the umbrella of the Constitution, the Court presented the Constitution as a flexible and unfolding process that could respond effectively to the country's changing needs.

Of course, all this raises sensitive questions about the role and legitimacy of the Supreme Court itself in a constitutional democracy. This is especially pressing when the Court is balancing the demands and dynamics of a written and unwritten Constitution. This debate is outside the scope of this essay, but it does impact upon the whole question of the courts' pivotal position in matters of constitutional change. Whatever approach the courts take, it tends to be premised on the notion that the courts are the appropriate venue for such debates and decisions about the need for and direction of constitutional change. This is an extremely dubious operating assumption in societies that are supposed to be committed to democracy as a founding principle and civic imperative; it has only served to reinforce the second-class status, at best, of popular participation and civic engagement. [41]

Conclusion

There are many general insights that can be gained about constitutional change more generally from the Canadian experience. But, for present purposes, the most important and telling insight is that constitutional change is as much about contested politics as it is about technical engineering. There is no consistent or detached logic that drives or explains the course of Canada's constitutional odyssey or any other nation's constitutional journey through history. Moreover, that way that politics impacts and shapes constitutional terrain will vary from jurisdiction to jurisdiction and from time to time. Like nature itself, the Constitution's "living tree" grows and expands in response to the contingent forces of the political climate. Indeed, a close analysis of Canada's constitutional history strongly recommends that there are no "natural limits" to change in the sense of there being some pattern or structure to those parameters that is reducible to a fixed or enduring formula.[42] As with much else in law and politics, constitutional change comports to the jurisprudential insight that "anything might go"—and often will.

Notes

1 *McCulloch v Maryland*, 17 U.S. (4 Wheat.) 316, 407 (1819).
2 In this essay, I build on and extend my earlier work. See A.C. Hutchinson, *Waiting for Coraf: A Critique of Law and Rights*, University of Toronto, 1995 and *Evolution and Common Law*, Cambridge University Press, 2005.
3 D. Strauss, "The Irrelevance of Constitutional Amendments", *Harvard Law Review*, 2001, vol. 114, pp. 1458–9, 1505 and 1457.
4 See A.C. Hutchinson, *The Province of Jurisprudence Democratized*, Oxford University Press, 2009.
5 *Reference re Secession of Quebec*, 1998, 2 S.C.R, p. 245.
6 See J. Waldron, "Can There Be a Democratic Jurisprudence?", *Emory Law Journal*, 2009, vol. 58, p. 675.
7 See, for example, F. Michelman, "Constitutional Authorship", in L. Alexander (ed.), *Constitutionalism: Philosophical Foundations*, Cambridge University Press, 1998, p. 76 and *Brennan and Democracy*, Princeton University Press, 1999.
8 M. Hardt and A. Negri, *Multitude: War and Democracy in the Age of Empire*, Penguin Press, 2004, p. 240.
9 See S. Holmes, *Passions and Constraints: On the Theory of Liberal Democracy*, The University of Chicago Press, 1995.

10 Letter from Thomas Jefferson to Samuel Kercheval (12 July 1816) in M.D. Peterson (ed.), *The Portable Thomas Jefferson*, Penguin Classics, 1975, p. 560.

11 The Federalist, no. 49, 1961 p. 256 (James Madison) (Clinton Rossiter, ed.).

12 Ibid.

13 *Marbury v Madison*, 5 U.S. 137, 176 (1803).

14 See D.S. Lutz, "Toward a Theory of Constitutional Amendment", in S. Levinson (ed.), *Responding to Imperfection: Theory and Practice of Constitutional Amendment*, Princeton University Press, 1995, p. 260 and Z. Elkins, T. Ginsburg and J. Melton, *The Endurance of National Constitutions*, Cambridge University Press, 2009.

15 R. Bernstein, "The Sleeper Wakes: The History and Legacy of the Twenty-Seventh Amendment", *Fordham Law Review*, 1992, vol. 61, p. 497.

16 For a discussion, W.E. Dellinger, "The Recurring Question of the 'Limited' Constitutional Convention", *Yale Law Journal*, 1979, vol. 88, p. 1623.

17 In fact, according to some interpretations, the number of applications required to call an Art. V Convention was surpassed in 1993, but Congress did not call the Convention; M. Stokes Paulsen, "How to Count to Thirty-Four: The Constitutional Case for a Constitutional Convention", *Harvard Journal of Law and Public Policy*, 2011, vol. 34, pp. 837, 856. By 2010, the number of states asking for a Convention had decreased from 45 to 33 (34 being the requisite number of states).

18 Some of these questions are considered in M.B. Rappaport, "Reforming Article V: The Problems Created by the National Convention Amendment Method and How to Fix Them", *Virginia Law Review*, 2010, vol. 96, p. 1523.

19 H. Gerken, "The Hydraulics of Constitutional Reform: A Skeptical Response to Our Undemocratic Constitution", *Drake Law Review*, 2007, vol. 55, p. 925.

20 Strauss, op. cit., p. 1464. The work of Reva Siegel and Robert Post focuses on the ways social movements and other socio-political forces shape constitutional culture. See R.C. Post and R.B. Siegel, "Legislative Constitutionalism and Section Five Power: Policentric Interpretation of the Family and Medical Leave Act", *Yale Law Journal*, 2003, vol. 112, p. 1943 and "Protecting the Constitution from the People: Juricentric Restrictions on Section Five Power", *Indiana Law Journal*, 2003, vol. 78, p. 1.

21 The classic text is P. Hogg, *The Constitutional Law of Canada*, 5th edn, Carswell, 2007. The most expansive statement of the Canadian constitutional tradition can be found in *Reference re Secession of Quebec*, op. cit.

22 Hogg, op. cit., pp. 2–3.

23 *Bank of Toronto v Lambe*, 12 App. Cas. 575, 579 (1887) (P.C.). For good discussions of this approach, see L. Tremblay, "*Marbury v Madison and Canadian Constitutionalism*: Rhetoric and Practice", *Revue Juridique Themis*, 2003, vol. 37, p. 374 and I. Binnie, "Interpreting the Constitution: The Living Tree vs. Original Meaning", *Policy Options*, 2007, vol. 28, p. 104.

24 *Edwards v Canada* (Attorney General), (1930) A.C. 124 at 136 (P.C.).

25 *Re Resolution To Amend The Constitution*, (1981) 1 SCR 753 at 802. See also *The Queen v Beauregard*, (1986) 2 SCR 56.

26 *Smith v The Queen*, (1960) SCR 776 at 800. This is the case even if the statutes duplicate each other, see *Multiple Access v McCutcheon*, (1982) 2 SCR 161.

27 See *R v Crown Zellerbach*, (1988) 1 SCR 401; *Anti-Inflation Reference*, (1976) 2 SCR 373 and *R v Hauser*, (1979) 1 SCR 984.

28 See *General Motors v City National Leasing*, (1989) 1 SCR 641.

29 See *Nova Scotia Inter-Delegation Case*, (1951) SCR 31 and *PEI Potato Marketing Board v Willis*, (1952) 2 SCR 392. See also *Brant Dairy v Milk Commission*, (1973) SCR 131 and *R v Furtney*, (1991) 3 SCR 89.

30 *Re Canada Assistance Plan*, (1991) 2 SCR 525.

31 See also *Quebec Veto Reference*, (1982) 2 SCR 793.

32 See *Entick v Carrington*, (1765), 95 E.R. 807 and *Roncarelli v Duplessis*, (1959) SCR 121. On the implied Bill of Rights, see *Alberta Press*, (1938) SCR 100, *Switzman v Elbling*,

(1957) SCR 285, and *Co-operative Committee on Japanese-Canadians v A-G for Canada*, (1947) AC 87.

33 J. Chretien, "Parliamentary Presentation", in J.B. Kelly, *Governing with the Charter: Legislative and Judicial Activism and Framers' Intent*, University of British Columbia Press, 2005, p. 91. See also Hutchinson, *Waiting for Coraf*, op. cit., pp. 15–24.

34 *New Brunswick Broadcasting Co. v Nova Scotia* (Speaker of the House of Assembly), (1991) 1 SCR 319.

35 See e.g. *Law Society of Upper Canada v Skapinker*, (1984) 1 S.C.R. 357, para 11 (Can.) (Estey, J.) ("Narrow and technical interpretation, if not modulated by a sense of the unknowns of the future, can stunt the growth of the law and hence the community it serves") and *Hunter v Southam*, (1984) 2 S.C.R. 145, 155 (Can.) (Dickson, C.J.) ("It must . . . be capable of growth and development over time to meet new social, political and historical realities often unimagined by its framers"). See also A. Kavanagh, "The Idea of A Living Constitution", *Canadian Journal of Law and Jurisprudence*, 2003, vol. 16, p. 55 and W.J. Waluchow, *A Common Law Theory of Judicial Review: The Living Tree*, Cambridge University Press, 2007. That being said, there was some resistance to this way of proceeding. See e.g. F.L. Morton and R. Knopff, "Permanence and Change in a Written Constitution: The 'Living Tree' Doctrine and the Charter of Rights", *Supreme Court Law Review*, 1990, vol. 1(2d), p. 533; G. Huscroft, "The Trouble With Living Tree Interpretation", *University of Queensland Law Journal*, 2006, vol. 25, p. 3 and B.W. Miller, "Beguiled by Metaphors: The 'Living Tree' and Originalist Constitutional Interpretation in Canada", *The Canadian Journal of Law and Jurisprudence*, 2009, vol. 22, p. 331.

36 Reference re *Motor Vehicle Act (British Columbia)* S 94(2), (1985) 2 S.C.R. 486, 508 (Can.) (J. Lamer).

37 *R v Sparrow*, (1990) 1 SCR 1075.

38 *Provincial Judges Reference*, (1997) 3 SCR 3. See also the discussion of the Patriation Reference, *infra*.

39 Reference re *Public Service Employee Relations Act (Alta.), PSAC v Canada, RWDSU v Saskatchewan*; Reference re *Public Service Employee Relations Act (Alta.)*, (1987) 1 S.C.R. 313, *PSAC v Canada*, (1987) 1 S.C.R. 424 and *RWDSU v Saskatchewan*, (1987) 1 S.C.R. 460.

40 See *Quebec Reference*, op. cit., p. 257.

41 For an effort to move beyond the judicial/parliamentary supremacy dichotomy towards an emphasis on popular participation in ordinary law-making and constitutional decision-making, see A.C. Hutchinson, "A 'Hardcore' Case Against Judicial Review", *Harvard Law Review*, 2008, vol. 121, forum 57.

42 *Edwards v Canada*, op. cit.

5 Formal and informal methods of constitutional change in Denmark

Helle Krunke

Setting the scene: the Danish legal and political context

By way of a short introduction to the Danish political and legal system, Denmark is a constitutional monarchy with negative parliamentarianism. Before 1973, Denmark had a few, large political parties in Parliament. This changed with the elections of 1973 when many small, new parties managed to get elected to Parliament. Since then, Denmark has had minority governments, sometimes based on (regular) political support from another party.[1]

Denmark has no Constitutional Court. The ordinary courts can, however, carry out constitutional review if the plaintiff has a specific individual legal interest in the case. The courts do not perform abstract judicial review as Danish courts are, in accordance with the Scandinavian tradition, quite reluctant to pronounce. Separation of powers is interpreted in such a way that legislative power is superior to the executive and the judicial powers. The courts are independent, but usually not very dynamic, and careful that their decisions relate only to legal and not political questions and prioritizations. The reason for this is that courts have no democratic legitimacy, in contrast to the Parliament. As we shall see later, this context has great significance for the way in which constitutional change is carried out in Denmark.

Like the rest of the Nordic legal systems, the Danish legal system is closer to the civil law system than the common law system. The Nordic legal systems do, however, form a special branch of the civil law system but without the civil codes like those of Germany and France.[2] It should also be mentioned that, in Denmark, preparatory work plays an important role in the interpretation of legislation, including the Constitution. This feature is consistent with the previously described interpretation of the separation of powers and the reluctance of courts to pronounce, while it is usually presumed that the older the preparatory work is, the less weight is normally given to it in interpretation.[3] The present Danish Constitution entered into force in 1953. However, many Articles date back to 1849, 1866 or 1915, which means that they were set out in a very different political context to that of 1953 or indeed today. This also raises the question of whether the Constitution must be interpreted fragmentarily, according to the origin and context of the specific articles, or as a coherent framework.[4] Furthermore, it touches upon the question of whether the Constitution should be interpreted on the basis of a black-letter law approach, or on the basis of a contextual interpretation approach. We shall return to this topic, since it is very important in the context of constitutional change. There seem to be different schools of Danish constitutional law. The Copenhagen school represents a contextual approach.[5]

All of the above provides an overall context and framework—the legal and political landscape—for constitutional change in Denmark. We shall draw upon these observations as we go along.

History and evolution of the constitutional amendment procedure

Absolute monarchy was introduced in Denmark in 1660 and finds its "democratic" legitimacy in a conveyance of power from the people to the monarch. The Constitution of the absolute monarchy was called *Kongeloven* (the King's Law) or *Lex Regia* and dates back to 1665.[6] It was a *lex fundamentalis* inspired by Jean Bodin, unifying all power (legislative, executive and judiciary) with a sovereign: the monarch.[7] *Lex Regia* was not published until 1709, as it was initially treated as a state secret (*arcana imperii*).[8] There was no amendment procedure in *Lex Regia*, as it was stated that it was forever unchangeable.[9] Nevertheless, in practice, exceptions were made to it.[10]

Due to the inspiration of the French Revolution, the absolute monarchy was abolished and Denmark was turned into a constitutional monarchy with a new Constitution in 1849. This development took place as a "peaceful revolution," in which the King chose to cede power to the people. Since 1849, the Constitution has been amended in 1866, 1915, 1920, and 1953; in other words, it has only been revised four times over a period of 162 years.

The first constitutional provisions regarding revision of the Constitution conformed to the following pattern: first, the Parliament (the Upper and the Lower House) adopted a bill concerning a revision of the Constitution. Whereas the 1849 procedure required Parliament to adopt the bill twice (Art. 100), the 1866 procedure only required Parliament to adopt the bill once (Art. 95). In both the 1849 and 1866 procedures, only a simple majority was required to vote in favor of the bill. However, the 1849 Constitution contained an exception to this procedure. If a vote concerned the order of succession to the throne, a three-quarters majority of Parliament was required in favor, according to Art. 4. Only the King could introduce such a bill. Article 4 was abolished in the 1866 Constitution.[11] It is interesting that, in the 1849 procedure, Parliament could only adopt the bill at an ordinary gathering, whereas according to the 1866 procedure, Parliament could adopt the bill at both ordinary and extraordinary gatherings. According to Art. 24 of the 1849 Constitution and Art. 19 of the 1866 Constitution, Parliament only sat once a year for an ordinary gathering, which could not last longer than two months without the King's approval. Only the King could call for an extraordinary gathering of Parliament, and he decided its length according to Art. 25 (1849

Constitution) and Art. 20 (1866 Constitution). In this way, the 1866 Constitution made it possible for Parliament to speed up the amendment procedure, compared with the 1849 Constitution.[12] The balance between, on the one hand making change to the Constitution possible and, on the other hand, not allowing change too easily, has always been a difficult issue. Already, in the preparatory work to the 1849 Constitution, this balance is mentioned. It is emphasized that an appropriate balance seems to have been reached in the proposed Constitution. Even though the process might seem complicated at first glance, a change to the Constitution can be carried out within 15 months if the King and the people really are convinced that a change would be beneficial—and according to the preparatory work, such a desire to change the Constitution must wait 15 months.[13] The balancing of political stability and legal resistance on the one hand, and the realistic possibility of changing the Constitution as society changes on the other, is central when designing a constitutional article on the revision/amendment of the Constitution. We shall return to this balance later in this section. At this point, it should be noted that, back in 1849, it was in the King's interest to make it difficult to change the Constitution again. The revolutionary trend stemming from the thoughts of the Age of Enlightenment had a strong influence on many European countries and had forced the King to cede power to the people, although he still played a central role in the 1849 Constitution.

Second, the bill had to be approved by the King in the 1849 procedure. This authority was changed to the Government in the 1866 Constitution, and this wording has been maintained in the subsequent revisions of the Constitution. Third, both Houses were dissolved and elections to both Houses were held. In this way, the voters were indirectly given the opportunity to approve or disapprove of the proposed constitutional change, since they could vote for candidates with views that matched their own.[14] Fourth, the new Parliament had to approve the bill, and the bill then had to receive the royal assent. This wording has remained the same in all Constitutions since 1849, but today royal assent is interpreted as governmental assent, even though formally both the minister and the monarch (on the responsibility of the minister) sign.

With the 1915 Constitution, a referendum on the content of the revision was added to the revision procedure and voters had a direct influence on whether the proposed constitutional change was desirable. In this referendum a majority, and at least 45 per cent of all those who were entitled to vote, had to vote in favor of the bill. The introduction of a referendum on the content of the revision, in 1915, must be viewed as a strengthening of the democratic legitimacy behind the Constitution.[15] It should be noted that an election remained part of the amendment procedure. Involvement of the electorate twice in the amendment procedure was unique at the time and was primarily to be found in some American states.[16] In 1953, the percentage was lowered to 40 per cent in order to make it easier to change the Constitution. The system of two chambers changed to a one-chamber system in 1953, and the wording of the amendment procedure was changed accordingly.

Consequently, the provision for revision in the Constitution from 1953, which has remained unchanged in the present Constitution, has the following content:

> Article 88: If Parliament passes a Bill for a new constitutional provision and the Government wishes to proceed with the matter, a general election is called. If the Bill is passed without amendment by the new Folketing after the election, it must be submitted to the parliamentary electors within six months of its finally being passed for approval or rejection by a direct vote. More detailed rules for this vote are established by an act. If a majority of those voting, and at least 40 per cent of all those entitled to vote, have voted for Parliament's decision, and it is affirmed by the King, it becomes part of the constitutional act.

In conclusion, two developmental tendencies in the amendment procedure from 1849 to 1953 can be seen: 1) the monarch's influence on the amendment of the Constitution has been limited, and 2) the amendment procedure has been made more "democratic," in the sense that Parliament can initiate an amendment process faster, the Government has taken over the monarch's competence, and the people are included in the process not just through an election but also through a referendum on the bill.

Most important aspects of the revisions of the Constitution

In 1866, the Constitution was amended for the first time. This was necessary because Denmark had lost 20 per cent of its territory in a war with Germany in 1864. After that, the next amendment of the Constitution took place in 1915. Between the 1866 Constitution and the 1915 Constitution, an important event had taken place. In 1901, the King had accepted that it was Parliament, and not the King as before, who decided which Government Denmark should have. However, the parliamentary principle was not mentioned in the 1915 Constitution. It was not until 1953 that this principle became written constitutional law.[17] The 1915 Constitution is associated with its popular democratic implications.[18] Until 1915, only about 14 per cent of the Danish population had the right to vote.[19] Women, poor people, and servants were given the right to vote with the 1915 Constitution. The right to vote and the right to be elected were extended to include younger people from the age of 25. An exception to this was elections to the Upper House. Equal rights to vote for the Upper House were introduced in 1915, but one had to be 35 years old to vote or to run for election. The electorate was more than doubled with the new 1915 Constitution.[20] Elections based on proportionality replaced elections based on majority in local constituencies. Furthermore, it was the 1915 Constitution that introduced the referendum as part of the revision process.[21] In addition, the protection of human rights was strengthened.[22]

The 1920 revision of the Constitution was aimed at reuniting *Nordslesvig* (an area in southern Jutland) with Denmark. Originally, the Government also had ambitions to advance the democratic line from 1915.[23] Among other things, it wanted to lower the voting age even further, and make the rules and procedures that applied to the Lower House apply equally to the Upper House; for instance, the possibility of dissolving the chamber. However, most of these proposals were rejected by the Upper House because the two main political parties, *Venstre* and *Konservative*, were against them. After an election in 1920, which gave the two aforementioned political parties a majority in the Lower House, further democratization of the Constitution was not possible. Proposals from the minority to turn Denmark into a republic (i.e. going from a two-chamber to a one-chamber system and lowering the election age to 21) were voted down.[24] Thus, the constitutional amendment ended up being primarily leveled at the reunion of Denmark and *Nordslesvig*. The most important of the other amendments was the reduction of the King's prerogative in foreign affairs. From then on, the monarch was much more constrained by Parliament's consent when exercising his foreign affairs prerogative. The 1920 Constitution was the first to be placed before the electorate, according to the new amendment procedure introduced in the 1915 Constitution. The result was that 47.54 per cent of the voters voted in favor of the proposal.

An attempt to revise the Constitution in 1939 failed, because only 44.46 per cent of those entitled to vote voted in favor of the proposal. According to the contemporary Constitution, a majority and at least 45 per cent of those entitled to vote should have voted in favor of the proposal. The main goal of the 1939 revision was to abolish the Upper House and introduce a one-chamber system in Denmark.[25]

In 1953, another attempt was made to revise the Constitution, this time successfully. Of those entitled to vote, 45.76 per cent voted in favor of the proposal in the referendum. The most important amendment was the abolition of the Upper House. Another important change was the fact that the parliamentary principle became written constitutional law—previously, its legal basis had been a constitutional convention. As we shall see below, it was made easier to cede sovereignty to international organizations in 1953; it was also made easier to hold referendums; and an ombudsman was introduced. Furthermore, the constitutional protection of human rights was strengthened with the 1953 revision. The experience from the failed attempt to amend the Constitution in 1939 resulted in changes to the amendment procedure in the 1953 revision. As mentioned, the original requirement of 45 per cent was changed to 40 per cent in order to make it easier to carry out constitutional change. The question of voting age was transferred to a legislative act; thus, from then on the voting age could be determined by referenda, without having to amend the Constitution.[26]

Finally, according to Art. 2 of the Danish Constitution, royal authority shall be inherited by men and women in accordance with the provisions of the Act of Succession to the Throne, 27 March 1953. In 2009, the Act of Succession to the Throne was amended so that the first-born child becomes heir to the throne, regardless of gender. As Art. 2 of the Constitution specifically refers to the Act of Succession to the Throne from 1953, it has been interpreted in such a way that the amendment procedure in Art. 88 of the Constitution must be applied if the 1953 Act is to be amended.[27] Thus, in 2009 the Art. 88 procedure was applied when amending the Succession Act: 58.5 per cent of the electorate participated in the referendum, and 45.5 per cent of the electorate voted in favor of the amendment.

Informal methods of constitutional change

The Constitution also changes as a result of more informal processes. With reluctant courts, the political actors' role as interpreters of the Constitution becomes significant. There is a gray zone between interpreting the Constitution and changing it. Thus, constitutional interpretation and especially the limits of constitutional interpretation are pivotal for the concept of constitutional change. This circumstance is also one of the reasons for the intense debate between legal scholars on whether constitutional interpretation should follow a contextual line or a line of black-letter law. The answer to this question sets limits for the political actors' interpretation of the Constitution, and in some legal systems also the courts' interpretation, and it highlights the distinction between interpreting existing rules and making new rules.

The political actors' behavior has significance both for interpreting and changing the Constitution. Political practice might result in a constitutional convention, and in Denmark a constitutional convention is legally binding and can enact a new constitutional rule at the same level of the Constitution. The reason a political practice can become a legally binding rule in the form of a constitutional convention in Denmark might very well be explained in the tradition of reluctant courts and a Constitution that is very difficult to change formally. Taking these two parameters into account, constitutional conventions become a way of establishing constitutional rules that are legally binding. In other words, the convention is a way of creating new constitutional law that fits a modern context. Since political practice results in legally binding rules, the conditions for a practice becoming a constitutional convention have been the subject of extensive debate among Danish legal scholars. As was the case with the limits of constitutional interpretation, this question touches upon the delimitation of constitutional law in a legal system—and in both cases, the line will always be blurred. A constitutional convention can have legal status at the same level of the Constitution if it changes or interprets the Constitution, or it can have legal status at the same level as normal legislation if it creates a new constitutional rule that does not alter the Constitution or interpret it.[28]

Thus, the Danish Constitution can be amended by a constitutional convention, but what are the criteria for a practice that turns into a legally binding rule in the form of a constitutional convention? As just mentioned, the criteria for a constitutional convention to evolve have been much debated in constitutional theory. The traditional criteria, having both objective and subjective aspects, are as follows: there must be a common practice that the actors have followed, continuous and long-standing, under the impression that the precedent is necessary or allowed.[29] Later emphasis was put on the actors in the precedent believing that they were bound by the rule.[30] In parts of the more recent theory, the subjective aspects have been criticized, since it is extremely difficult to determine whether the actors feel legally bound by the practice.[31] Empirical studies carried out in order to determine whether the actors feel legally bound by the rule are often uncertain and not scientifically verifiable.[32] In parts of the theory, the subjective criterion has been replaced by criteria focusing on the appropriateness of the practice.[33] This criterion is also to be found in Norwegian theory on constitutional conventions.[34] The interesting question is whether it is the actor's feeling of appropriateness[35] or the interpreter's assessment of appropriateness in the light of general constitutional principles that the criterion builds upon.[36] If one follows the first possibility, the same problems of determining the actor's feelings as in the general problem with the subjective criteria will occur.

Very few constitutional conventions have been accepted as such in legal theory. Three examples will be mentioned: a) The courts have the competence to review the constitutionality of legislation; b) The select committee on financial matters has the competence to accept an expense that is not included in this year's Finance Act; c) In most paragraphs in the Danish Constitution, "the King" is now interpreted as "the Government." These constitutional conventions all have legal status at the same level as the Constitution. There has been much discussion on whether there is a constitutional convention according to which the mandates issued by the European Policy Committee are legally binding on the Government. Legal theory does not agree on this point.[37]

We have discussed constitutional interpretation (by the courts or by politicians) and constitutional conventions as part of the informal processes that can adjust constitutional law to a modern context. A related and much more controversial question is how a state of emergency affects the constitutional order. Can (parts of) the Constitution be set aside in a state of emergency and, if so, under which conditions? Must this be seen as a non-compliance of the Constitution or an exception? We shall not go into details with this discussion, which could be brought to a more philosophical level by including the thoughts of Carl Schmitt and Hermann Heller.

The Danish Constitution has an article that reads:

> In an emergency the King[38] may, when the Folketing[39] cannot assemble, issue provisional laws, provided that they shall not be at variance with the Constitutional Act, and that they shall always, immediately on the assembling of the Folketing, be submitted to it for approval or rejection.

As it appears, this very narrow legal basis for acting in emergencies does not provide the Government with the competence to issue provisional laws that are at variance with the Constitution. This Article has not been used since 1885–1893, when it was used as a political tool in a dispute between the Government and Parliament. In addition to this written regulation, it is normally assumed that there is an unwritten principle on emergency action, which, under extreme circumstances, allows the Government to deviate from the Constitution.[40] There must be a serious danger for the state and its institutions;[41] the deviation must be strictly necessary; the legal values of democracy and human rights that underlie the Constitution must be respected as far as possible;[42] and finally, proportionality must be respected.[43] This very narrow opportunity for deviating from the Constitution must be seen specifically as a "deviation from" and not as a "change to" the Constitution. On the other hand, the effect is obviously the same as long as the emergency lasts.

Formal constitutional amendment process

There are several phases of a constitutional amendment: Parliament passes a bill for a constitutional revision. The Government wishes to proceed with the matter. A general election is called. The bill must be passed without any changes by the new Parliament after the election. The bill must then be submitted for approval or rejection by a direct vote within six months of its finally being passed. A majority of those voting, and at least 40 per cent of all those entitled to vote, must vote in favor of Parliament's decision. Finally, it is affirmed by the Government.

The procedure described above, which has its legal basis in Art. 88 of the Danish Constitution, must be followed if a legislator wants to legislate in accordance with the Constitution or if a legislator wants a certain rule to have legal status at a constitutional level. This procedure is the same regardless of whether the purpose of the constitutional change is to amend the existing Constitution or to carry out a general revision of the Constitution. Thus, the concepts of "amendment" and "revision" do not carry the same weight, as is the case in other European Constitutions.

We shall now go through the procedure and discuss how it is interpreted. A bill on constitutional revision must be introduced in Parliament. As Art. 88 is silent on who has the competence to introduce the bill, one must fall back on the normal rules for introducing bills in Parliament. According to Art. 2,1 the Government can introduce bills, and according to Art. 41 para 1, Members of Parliament can also introduce bills. The bill must state in its title that it is a bill on constitutional revision (Standing Orders of Parliament, Art. 16 para 1). If a majority of Parliament votes in favor of the bill, the amendment procedure continues.

Next, the Government decides whether it wants to proceed with the constitutional revision. It should be noted that the Government is not allowed to use its normal governmental prerogative to affirm bills (Art. 22) at this point, and this move turns the bill into normal legislation instead of a constitutional revision.[44] If the Government decides to stop the revision process at this point and Parliament does not agree with this decision, it must use the parliamentarian principle (Art. 15) to force the Government to call an election. As we shall return to later in this section, it makes a difference whether this political pressure results in the Government calling an election according to Art. 88 or it uses its normal governmental prerogative to call elections (Art. 32 para 2). In the first case, the constitutional revision procedure will continue, whereas in the latter case, the revision procedure comes to an end and a new revision procedure must start after the election, if a majority in the new Parliament supports the idea.[45]

If the Government decides to carry on with the constitutional revision, an election is called, according to Art. 88. There is no time limit for this action in Art. 88. Thus, the Government cannot be criticized for failing to take immediate action. On the other hand, the Government must state that it supports the constitutional revision when calling the election, so it is clear to everyone that it is an Art. 88 election.[46]

After the election, Parliament must once more pass the bill. A particular problem connected with this is who should take the initiative to introduce the bill for the new Parliament. Parts of the literature support the view that the new Government is not obliged to introduce the bill,[47] while other parts of the literature support the view that the new Government *is* obliged to do so.[48] However, the literature agrees that if the Government does not introduce the revision bill, any Member of Parliament can do so.[49] Once again, it demands a majority of Parliament to vote in favor of the bill. The bill cannot be amended at this point as that would be contrary to the whole idea of the amendment procedure, which by its many steps ensures that the amendment is well thought through. If Parliament has new initiatives for the constitutional revision, it must start a new revision procedure. There is no time limit in Art. 88 for the new Parliament passing the bill, but naturally it must be before their mandate as parliamentarians runs out, which is after four years or whenever a new election has taken place, according to Art. 32.

The next step is a referendum on the constitutional revision bill, for which there is a time limit. The referendum must take place within six months of the bill finally being passed by Parliament. Voters are asked to vote in favor of the bill or to reject it. The starting point is that they cannot vote separately on different parts of the bill: it is a "yes" or "no" referendum. However, if from the beginning of the process Parliament and the Government have divided the revision of the Constitution into different issues, treated in different bills, and followed the amendment procedure in Art. 88 for all the bills, it is possible to let the electorate vote on all the bills separately, and thus give them the chance to have a more detailed opinion on the revision.[50] Alternative proposals cannot be put in front of the voters as in an Art. 88 referendum. This dilemma can, however, be solved by using a normal referendum (Art. 42).[51] As for the outcome of the referendum, a majority of at least 40 per cent of the electorate must vote in favor of the bill. If the referendum is positive, the bill on the amendment process moves to the last stage—royal assent. If this is given, the bill becomes an integral part of the Constitution.

In Danish constitutional law, no material limitations to revision exist.[52] The Article in the Danish Constitution that comes closest to an "eternity" clause is Art. 77, on freedom of speech, which declares that "censorship and other preventive measures shall never again be introduced." However, there seems to be no solid basis for interpreting this as an eternity clause.[53]

Alf Ross introduced the following approach to the question of eternity clauses based on the *grundnorm* theory. According to Ross, Art. 88 cannot apply to Art. 88 itself. Amendments of Art. 88 are only valid because they are accepted as such and not because the Art. 88 procedure has been applied. The norm that determines the competence to adopt the Constitution is the presupposed *grundnorm* based on convention. This *grundnorm* was not created through a procedure, so it cannot be changed by a procedure.[54] In other words, Art. 88 is a *grundnorm* that is valid according to a constitutional convention. Article 88 is a linguistic expression of this presupposed *grundnorm*.[55] Alf Ross's theory in this field has not been supported by other parts of Danish legal theory.[56]

The role of the people

A constitutional revision cannot be carried out without the inclusion of the electorate. The electorate plays a double role in the amendment procedure: first, by voting in an election in which it is obvious that the amendment of the Constitution will be one of the major political questions. Second, by voting in a referendum on the proposed amendment. The electorate can vote in favor of the bill or reject it. As mentioned, the requirement is that a majority of those voting, and at least 40 per cent of those entitled to vote, must vote in favor of the revision of the Constitution. Since it is difficult to fulfill this requirement, one might venture that the people have quite a significant role in the Danish constitutional amendment procedure.

The Constitution has very seldom been amended. However, as mentioned earlier, the amendment procedure was used recently (2009). According to Danish constitutional law before 2009, the first-born prince would become King, even if he had an older sister. This procedure was amended in 2009 to introduce gender equality in accession to the throne. There was much public debate before the referendum. For instance, some groups preferred a general revision of the Constitution (which has not been revised since 1953) so recommended that the voters vote "no" to the revision on the succession rule. Other matters of public discussion were gender equality and to what extent a "yes" campaign could be financially supported by the Government. The result of the referendum was a "yes" vote and thus the succession rule was changed.

Denmark elected a new Government in the fall of 2011. It consists of two left-wing parties, *Socialdemokratiet* and *Socialistisk Folkeparti*, and *Det Radikale Venstre*, which is a center party. The Government also has *Enhedslisten* (another left-wing party) as a supporting party. The new Government intends to start a political and public discussion on a general revision of the Constitution.[57] Among other themes, the role of the monarch and human rights have been mentioned as possible areas of amendment. The Government has declared that they will start the discussion by setting up a commission to come up with suggestions for reform. This declaration has already resulted in some debate—both political and public—on whether reform of the Constitution is necessary, or even appropriate, and which areas should be included in such reform.

In conclusion, constitutional amendment is surrounded by public debate in Denmark. The reasons for this might be the following: first, Denmark has a long tradition of democracy. It is a value that is imbued in all layers of Danish society from politics to local associational life and school boards. It is a value taught in schools. Thus, participatory democracy is a general value in the Danish society; therefore, people take part in political discussions on constitutional reform. Having said this, the elite is always more active in public debates than the rest of society. Second, since the electorate plays such an important role in constitutional reform, it is not possible for politicians to change the Constitution without the inclusion of the voters. Therefore, it is necessary for politicians to involve the people in the process and get them sufficiently engaged in the reform so that a majority of those voting, and at least 40 per cent of those entitled to vote, will vote in favor of the revision of the Constitution. This percentage cannot be reached without a public debate and a large amount of public engagement. Third, although the Constitution is old and might not entirely reflect the modern political context, it does have quite an extensive symbolic value, both for the people and for the politicians (it plays a significant role in political rhetoric).

How do international and European law and jurisprudence affect constitutional revision?

When the Constitution was revised in 1953, a new paragraph about supranational organizations (Art. 20) was included in the new Constitution:

> *Section 20, Subsection 1.* Powers that are granted to the authorities of the Kingdom under this Constitution may, by means of an Act and to a specific extent, be transferred to international authorities created by mutual agreement with other States to promote international legal order and cooperation.
>
> *Subsection 2.* A majority of five-sixths of the Members of Parliament is required to pass Bills in this respect. If such a majority is not obtained, but the majority required to pass normal Bills is obtained, and the Government maintains the Bill, it is submitted to the parliamentary electors for approval or rejection in accordance with the rules established for referendums in Section 42.

This provision makes it possible for Denmark to cede sovereignty without using the procedure for amending the Constitution (given that the conditions in Art. 20 are fulfilled, otherwise the Art. 88 procedure must be followed). Before 1953, it was necessary to follow the procedure for amending the Constitution (which was even more demanding as a majority of those voting, and at least 45 per cent of all those entitled to vote, had to vote in favor of Parliament's decision). Thus, in 1953 international cooperation was made easier. This was a natural reaction to the closer international and European cooperation after the Second World War. European Union cooperation is not mentioned in the Danish Constitution as the present Constitution dates back to 1953, and Denmark entered the European Community in 1973.

The Danish constitutional human rights protection is quite arbitrary as seen from a modern point of view, and this fact has meant that the European Convention on Human Rights and practice from the European Court of Human Rights plays an increasingly important role in Danish human rights protection. The democratic legitimacy of the latter has been the subject of both political and public debate. This discussion must be seen in the context of the Danish separation of powers system, in which Parliament is stronger compared to the courts. A dynamic interpretation style, such as that used by both the European Court of Human

Rights and the European Court of Justice, is very different from the Danish tradition. The traditional Danish understanding of "democracy" is defined by a strong Parliament, whereas the courts do not play a strong role in this definition. This understanding of democracy lies close to formal democracy theory, far from a more substantive democracy theory. As mentioned, a modernization of the Danish human rights charter is on the present agenda for constitutional revision. Also, the relationship between Danish law and international law might be the subject of discussion in a reform. The Danish Constitution is interpreted as dualistic, and it does not give priority to international law. In conclusion, the Danish Constitution does not reflect the reality of the importance of EU and international cooperation.

Form of government, political conflict, and constitutional revision

As stated in the preface, Denmark is a constitutional monarchy with negative parliamentarianism. Since 1973, Denmark has had minority governments, sometimes based on (regular) support from a supporting party. Political parties are not mentioned in the Danish Constitution.[58] How does this picture affect constitutional revision?

An amendment procedure starts with a bill on constitutional amendment being introduced in Parliament. This follows the normal procedure for introducing bills, which means that both the Government (Art. 21) and members of Parliament (Art. 41 para 1) can introduce a bill on constitutional amendment. This procedure means that the Government does not have a privileged right to introduce bills on constitutional amendment. The bill must go through three readings in Parliament (Art. 41 para 2) and a majority in Parliament must vote in favor of the bill for the amendment procedure to continue. As Denmark normally has minority governments, the bill cannot be passed without support from political parties outside the Government. This process also means that a majority outside the Government could put forward a bill on constitutional revision and pass the bill through Parliament. Technically, the Government could stop the amendment process at the next level by choosing not to proceed with the matter. However, in reality, since Denmark has negative parliamentarianism (Art. 15), such a Government would not last long and would be forced to call an election. In the election, the voters would show whether they support a constitutional revision. It should be noted that if the Government called the election according to Art. 88, the revision procedure would continue, whereas if the Government used its normal prerogative to call an election (Art. 32 para 2), it would stop the revision procedure.

For the past 10 years, until the fall of 2011, Denmark has had a right-wing minority Government consisting of two political parties, *Venstre* and *Konservative*, with a third party, *Dansk Folkeparti*, as a regular supporting party. Together, this political constellation could have started a constitutional revision if it had decided so, but it was not in favor of doing so. However, the Government did take the initiative on the revision of the Act of Succession to the Throne, mentioned earlier. As noted, some groups of the public viewed this action as a way of blocking a more general constitutional revision. Introduction of gender equality in the right to the throne has always been considered a safe card to gather the required majority, and at least 40 per cent of those entitled to do so, to vote in favor of a constitutional revision. In 2003, the opposition party, *Socialistisk Folkepart,* introduced a bill on constitutional amendment, but they could not provide a majority in favor of constitutional changes. This party is now part of the new left-wing Government, formed in 2011.

The new Danish Government stated in its platform that Denmark needs a new discussion on the Constitution. Thus, it intends to set up a constitutional commission.[59] With the support of *Enhedslisten,* a supporting left-wing party, the Government would be able to start a constitutional revision process. In Parliament, the main issues dividing the left-wing in support of changes and the right-wing against changes are: a) the status of European human rights in the Constitution, and b) the position of the monarch in the Constitution.

Even though the present Government seems willing to reform the Constitution, one might argue that certain elements in the present Constitution from 1953—which contains much older articles, some of which date back to 1849—have a "preserving" effect on a Government. The Constitution still contains a number of royal prerogatives now interpreted as governmental prerogatives. One might argue that many of these prerogatives reflect a different political system, in which the King had a special position. In a constitutional revision, this might not fit a modern democratic society, even though it is now the Government and not the monarch who exercises these prerogatives. Since the EU didn't exist in 1953, EU cooperation is not mentioned in the Constitution. This cooperation, and Parliament's control of Danish EU policy, could also be the subject of a constitutional revision. Thus, the Government might not have an interest in a general constitutional revision.

One last question relating to Denmark being a constitutional monarchy may be posed. What role does the monarch play in constitutional revision? The monarch might not have an interest in a general revision of the Constitution, but still has certain competences, the most important being appointing new governments and signing bills. Even though these competences are in reality formal, the monarch is still present on the political scene. In a new Constitution built on a modern view of democracy, the monarch's role might be very limited. Actually, this topic is on the agenda of some political parties who form the present left-wing majority. One might ask whether the monarch could block such a development. According to Art. 88, the last element of the revision procedure is that the bill must receive royal assent. As is the case in Art. 22 of the Constitution on royal assent, this point must be interpreted as a governmental competence.[60] Formally, the monarch signs all bills in Denmark together with a minister, and on the responsibility of the minister (Art. 14). The monarch has not refused to sign since 1865, and the monarch's role must be viewed as a rather formal procedure.[61]

The role of experts in constitutional revision

The role that lawyers should play in constitutional revision is controversial. On the one hand, political initiative (and public debate) should drive a revision process. Such a process has the most democratic legitimacy. Then, lawyers can help with technical details. On the other hand, one cannot be blind to the fact that constitutional experts have more than a technical knowledge from which the revision can benefit. For instance, they know which articles in the present Constitution have given rise to interpretative problems; in addition, they know how foreign constitutions are designed and how they function; and finally, they have knowledge of EU law and international law, and the relationship between them, etc. Constitutional law experts will often be aware of which new initiatives might be beneficial in a constitutional revision, and thus be able to give advice not just on technical details but also on new constitutional initiatives. It should also be pointed out that the line between technical advice and advice on the content can be blurred. Both politicians and experts on constitutional law can contribute to a revision process, but politicians have a popular mandate, whereas experts do not.

In the last two proposals for revising the Danish Constitution, only politicians were members of the constitutional commissions that were set up. However, constitutional law experts played a more important role in the 1953 revision than in the proposed 1939 revision. In the revision of the Danish Constitution in 1953, the constitutional commission consisted mainly of politicians, but four prominent experts on constitutional law were also assigned. In the report of the 1946 constitutional commission, nine out of 15 appendices are expert opinions from legal scholars. The constitutional commission set up in relation to the 1939 proposal for a new Constitution (which did not get through the referendum and therefore never took effect) consisted of politicians only, and the proposal was characterized by its political rather than its legal identity.[62]

One might ask what role experts played in the original 1849 Constitution. Two politicians, Monrad and Lehmann, played an important role in designing the Constitution. D.G. Monrad, a theologian, wrote the first draft and, as he had no expertise in constitutional law, searched for inspiration in foreign constitutions. After the Government had discussed the draft, Orla Lehmann, a lawyer, worked on the wording of the specific Articles.[63] The proposal was then discussed in the Constitutional Assembly, the members of which were chosen by the electorate. Thus, the process had a strong political identity.

Judicial review of constitutional amendments

As mentioned, Denmark has no constitutional court. Instead, the ordinary courts can carry out constitutional review. However, as a clear starting point, this procedure requires that the plaintiff has a specific individual legal interest in the case. Danish courts do not perform abstract constitutional reviews. In other words, if a citizen can prove that he or she has a specific individual legal interest in constitutional review, the courts can carry out a review. What legal question could a case on constitutional revision concern? As mentioned, there are no material limitations to the revision of the Constitution. Thus, it is not possible to imagine a case in Danish courts on whether the content of a constitutional revision is in accordance with an eternity clause. Since a constitutional revision must follow Art. 88, a case on whether the Art. 88 procedure should have been followed is much more realistic and, indeed, such a case actually exists.[64] Another possibility is a case of whether the Art. 88 procedure has been followed correctly in a specific constitutional revision.

What if a person does not have a specific individual legal interest? The Danish Supreme Court has decided in two cases that even though the plaintiffs did not have a specific individual legal interest that differed from any other Danish citizen, he or she had sufficient legal interest in having the case reviewed. The legal question in *Maastricht*[65] was whether the Art. 88 procedure should have been followed instead of the Art. 20 procedure, when Denmark entered the Maastricht Treaty. The question of legal interest was treated separately. The Supreme Court ruled that:

> . . . the Maastricht Treaty entails a transfer of legal competence within a number of general and significant areas of life and thus it is in itself of extensive importance for the Danish population in general . . . (author's translation)

This case is, of course, very interesting since it concerns a legal question in the field of constitutional revision; namely, whether an Art. 88 procedure should have been followed.

The legal question in *Lisbon*[66] from January 2011 was whether the Art. 20 procedure should have been used instead of Art. 19 (the normal treaty procedure in which Parliament must give its consent), when Denmark entered the Lisbon Treaty. Once again, the question on legal interest was treated separately. The Supreme Court noted that the parties disagreed on the significance of the changes in the rules on competence and voting in the European cooperation that the Lisbon Treaty entails, in relation to Art. 20 of the Danish Constitution. Since this disagreement concerned legislative competence within a number of general and significant areas of life and, thus, circumstances that are of extensive importance for the Danish population in general, and since the dispute had a general and extensive effect, the plaintiffs had sufficient legal interest in having the case reviewed.

Thus, there are two cases in which the Supreme Court has granted the plaintiffs a constitutional review, even though they did not have a specific individual legal interest. One of them even concerned whether an Art. 88 procedure should have been followed. It should be noted, however, that the Supreme Court in two other cases (on whether an Art. 88 procedure should have been followed when Denmark entered a new EC/EU treaty) ruled that the plaintiffs had no specific individual legal interest in the case.[67]

Finally, if a minister was responsible for an Art. 88 procedure not being followed correctly, the Parliament could decide to bring him or her before the Court of Impeachment. The Court of Impeachment most likely falls under the definition of a court.[68]

Criticisms on the amendment procedure and constitutional entrenchment

As mentioned earlier, when designing a constitutional amendment procedure, the challenge is to strike the right balance between stability and room for change. In other words, the procedure must, on the one hand, guarantee legal resistance and, on the other hand, be realistic to change through a well-thought-out process so that it reflects modern society. As is apparent, the Danish Constitution is very difficult to revise. It is extremely difficult to engage such a large proportion of the electorate to take part in a referendum and to vote in favor of a new Constitution. This difficulty is an important reason why Denmark seldom revises its Constitution, even though society changes over time. Another reason has been a lack of political support behind such a project. This shortcoming can result in an outmoded Constitution both in terms of content and language.

This situation causes a number of problems. First, the Constitution will be misleading for a reader without background knowledge about the Danish constitutional system. It might appear slightly undemocratic if ordinary Danes are not able to understand their own Constitution by reading the text. Second, it is obvious that foreigners with no knowledge of Danish constitutional law will be misled when reading the Constitution as the wording does not give a clear or realistic impression of which institutions and actors are important in the modern political system. For instance, the monarch is mentioned throughout the Constitution, even though in reality the Government has taken over the monarch's competence, and the weekly meeting for the ministers, which is a very important forum, is not even mentioned in the Constitution. Third, one might ask whether the content, for instance the human rights protection in the Constitution, lives up to modern standards.

Democratic legitimacy behind a Constitution is important, because the Constitution is the people's document containing rules on and limits of governance. One could venture that democratic legitimacy is an argument for a high percentage of votes (Art. 88). On the other hand, one could ask whether the democratic legitimacy is actually waning as the Constitution ages.[69] Furthermore, one must be aware that, when a Constitution becomes older in both content and language and no longer reflects the modern society, constitutional interpretation and constitutional practice (which might turn into constitutional conventions) will play a larger role; this fact creates a less transparent system and gives more power to political agents and lawyers. Also, it will be left for the international courts to define, for instance, the scope of the protection of human rights, if the Constitution does not provide for detailed protection in this field.

Contemporary debate on the need for a future constitutional revision

The last time the Danish Constitution was subject to a general revision was in 1953. Once in a while, the need for a new constitutional revision is debated. In

1999, when the Danish Constitution reached 150 years old, the Danish Parliament invited a number of legal scholars to discuss the need for revision in different areas. In 2003, when the present Danish Constitution from 1953 turned "50," one of the largest political parties agitated for a general revision of the Constitution. None of these initiatives resulted in a revision of the Constitution. However, as mentioned, the new Danish Government, which was appointed in the fall of 2011, has put forth a new discussion of the Constitution and the establishment of a constitutional commission as part of its government platform. This move seems to be the closest Denmark has come to a revision in recent times. However, the future will show whether it ends with a revision. It is a long process with many obstacles, but the Government, together with its supporting party, does have a majority so the first steps of the process might be possible. Then the people should agree to any constitutional changes.

In more recent debates, it is often emphasized that the protection of human rights in the Danish Constitution has been outdated and overtaken by the protection given by the European Convention on Human Rights. Some political groups would prefer this protection to have its legal basis at the constitutional level. Human rights will be an important issue in the debate that the present Government intends to initiate on constitutional reform.

Two general aspects that are often debated are whether Denmark should have a Constitutional Court and whether church and state should be separated. It has also been mentioned that the Constitution does not reflect the fact that political bodies play an important role in political life and decision-making. Bodies that no longer play any significant role are mentioned in the Constitution (Art. 17 and Art. 18) while, for instance, the weekly meeting of ministers led by the Prime Minister—a forum which plays a much more important role—is not mentioned at all in the Constitution. Neither are the political parties mentioned in the Constitution. The word "King" appears in many paragraphs, and thus one with no background knowledge reading the Danish Constitution would get the impression that the monarch plays a highly important role in the Danish political system. However, most of these paragraphs are today interpreted as government competences. The role of the monarch is an issue that will probably be given much attention in the coming revision discussions, as some of the parties in the left-wing majority are republicans. In addition, it has been suggested that the European Policy Committee and the mandate procedure related to this committee, which has become increasingly significant the closer EU cooperation gets, should be mentioned in the Constitution. Finally, it has been advanced that some of the former royal prerogatives that are now governmental prerogatives have lost their significance.

As follows from the above, it is extremely difficult to reform the Constitution because so many voters must vote in favor of a reform. Thus, the reform must be so "popular" that many people make the effort to vote. Gender equality as regards succession to the throne has always been mentioned as a question that could have been used to engage the voters in a general revision of the Constitution. However, this opportunity was bypassed in 2009 as the referendum dealt with the question of succession only. As mentioned, this topic caused much discussion in 2009. Thus, it is interesting to speculate whether it will be possible to engage the electorate sufficiently in a constitutional debate to carry through a revision of the Constitution.

Notes

1 E. Damgaard, "Parlamentarismens danske tilstande", in E. Damgaard (ed.), *Parlamentarisk forandring i Norden (Parliamentarian change in the Nordic countries)*, Universitetsforlaget, 1990, pp. 23–4.
2 K. Zweigert and H. Kötz, *Comparative Law*, Oxford: Clarendon Press, 1998, p. 277.
3 H. Zahle, *Dansk Forfatningsret*, vol. 1 (*Danish Constitutional Law*), C. Ejlers Forlag, 2001, pp. 72–3.
4 Ibid., p. 63.
5 See for instance Zahle, op. cit., vols 1–3 (especially pp. 73–4 in vol. 1).
6 *Lex Regia*, 14 November 1665, must according to C.G. Holck be categorized as a Constitution; see C.G. Holck, *Den danske statsforfatningsret*, vol. 1 (*Danish Constitutional Law*), published after the author's death by C. Goos and J. Nellemann, Forlaget af den Gyldendalske boghandel, 1869, p. 98. Holck argues that, since *Lex Regia* stated that it was forever unchangeable, it was above ordinary legislation. Holck defines a constitution as a legal document that is protected against amendment in the sense that it cannot be changed in the same way as ordinary legislation; see p. 93. It might be added that *Lex Regia* regulated how the state was organized.
7 D. Tamm, *Retshistorie*, vol. 1: *Dansk retshistorie* (*Legal history: Danish legal history*), Jurist- og Økonomforbundets Forlag, 1990, pp. 116–17.
8 Ibid., pp. 117–18.
9 P. Andersen, *Dansk Statsforfatningsret*, vol. I (*Danish Constitutional Law*), 2nd edn, Gyldendals Boghandel Nordisk Forlag, 1949, p. 16.
10 Holck, op. cit, p. 98.
11 Ibid., p. 100.
12 The process was made easier without increasing the risk of the process not being well considered and well thought out. See Holck, op. cit., p. 100.
13 See the preparatory work to the 1849 Constitution, vol. 1, p. 19.
14 Holck, op. cit., pp. 99–100.
15 This amendment was not the only one that strengthened the democratic legitimacy of the Constitution in the 1915.
16 K. Berlin, *Den danske statsforfatningsret*, anden del, 1. halvbind (*Danish Constitutional Law*, part 2, vol. 1), Nyt Nordisk Forlag. Arnold Busck, MCMXXXIII, p. 54.
17 It is usually presumed that the parliamentary principle had turned into a constitutional convention before it became written law in 1953. See H. Koch, "Retssædvane eller statsskik – kampen om parlamentarismen siden 1901", *Juristen*, 1990, pp. 64–79.
18 H. Koch and K. Hvidt, *Danmarks Riges Grundlove 1849, 1866, 1915, 1953* (*The Constitutions of Denmark 1849, 1866, 1915, 1953*), Christian Ejlers Forlag, 2000, p. 16; Andersen, op. cit., p. 62.
19 Koch and Hvidt, op. cit., p. 16.
20 Ibid.
21 Andersen, op. cit., p. 66.
22 Koch and Hvidt, op. cit., p. 16.
23 Andersen, op. cit., p. 67.
24 Ibid., pp. 67–8.
25 Ibid., pp. 68–72.
26 See Koch and Hvidt, op. cit., p. 18.
27 This interpretation is to be found all the way back to Holck, op. cit., pp. 101–2.
28 A. Ross, *Dansk statsforfatningsret*, vol. 1 (*Danish Constitutional Law*), 3rd edn, O. Espersen, Nyt Nordisk Forlag. Arnold Busck, 1983, pp. 47–8.

29 P. Andersen, *Dansk Statsforfatningsret*, vol. 1 (*Danish Constitutional Law*), Nordisk Forlag, 1944, p. 140; M. Sørensen, *Statsforfatningsret* (*Constitutional Law*), Juristforbundets Forlag, 1973, p. 34.

30 Ross, op. cit., pp. 43–7. According to Ross, the question of whether the actors feel legally bound by a practice must be answered by empirical investigations. Henrik Zahle criticizes Ross, but his own definition of a constitutional convention also includes indirectly a subjective criterion, since the relevant actors must find practice appropriate; Zahle, op. cit., vol. 3, pp. 53–4.

31 See for instance Zahle, op. cit., vol. 3, pp. 53–4.

32 H. Krunke, *Den Udenrigspolitiske Kompetence. Udenrigspolitik og magtfordeling ved overgangen til det 21. århundrede* (*The Foreign Affairs Competence. Foreign affairs and separation of powers at the entry into the 21st century*), Jurist- og Økonomforbundets Forlag, 2003, pp. 86–91.

33 Zahle, op. cit., vol. 3, pp. 53–4; Krunke, op. cit., pp. 92–7. This is actually a criterion that was put forward by Scheel in 1865, by Henry Ussing in 1944, and by Ernst Andersen in 1947, and has been revitalized by Zahle; A.W. Scheel, *Privatrettens almindelige Deel* (*Private Law, general part*) 1865, p. 166; H. Ussing, *Aftaler* (*Agreements*), G.E.C. Gads Forlag, 1944, p. 439 and E. Andersen, *Forfatning og sædvane* (*Constitution and conventions*) G.E.C. Gads Forlag, 1947, pp. 124–7.

34 P. Stavang, *Storting og Regjering* (*Parliament and Government*), 1999, p. 32; P. Helset and B. Stordrange, *Norsk statsforfatningsret* (*Norwegian Constitutional Law*), 1998, p. 81.

35 Zahle takes this standpoint. Zahle, op. cit., vol. 3, pp. 53–4.

36 This standpoint is to be found in Krunke, op. cit., pp. 92–7, and in the Norwegian literature mentioned.

37 Zahle and Krunke find the mandates legally binding (though with a different argumentation), while Albæk Jensen does not find them legally binding. See Zahle, op. cit., vol 2, p. 295; Krunke, op. cit., pp. 200–19; H. Krunke, "Developments in National Parliaments Involvement in Ordinary Foreign Policy and European Policy", *European Public Law*, 2007, vol. 13, pp. 335–48; J. Albæk Jensen, *Parlamentarismens statsretlige betydning* (*The Constitutional Meaning of Parliamentarism*), Jurist- og Økonomforbundets Forlag, 1997, pp. 119–36.

38 The King is now interpreted as the Government.

39 The Danish Parliament is called the Folketing.

40 Zahle, op. cit., vol. 3, p. 286.

41 Sørensen, op. cit., p. 39.

42 Zahle, op. cit., vol. 3, p. 286.

43 H. Koch, *Demokrati – slå til!* (*Democracy – fight back!*), 1994, Gyldendal, p. 414.

44 Zahle, op. cit., vol. 3, p. 40.

45 Ibid.

46 Ibid.

47 Ibid.

48 P. Andersen, *Dansk Statsforfatningsret* (*Danish Constitutional Law*), Gyldendal, 1954, p. 447.

49 Zahle, op. cit., vol. 3, p. 40; Andersen, op. cit. (1954), p. 447.

50 Andersen, op. cit. (1954), p. 449.

51 Zahle, op. cit., vol. 3, p. 41.

52 In the older literature see for instance Holck, op. cit., p. 101, and in more recent literature see Zahle, op. cit., vol. 3, p. 43.

53 The preparatory work does not support such an interpretation. See Andersen, op. cit. (1954), p. 439 and Holck, op. cit., p. 101.

54 A. Ross, *Dansk Statsforfatningsret*, vol. 1 (*Danish Constitutional Law*), Nyt Nordisk Forlag, Arnold Busck, 1966, p. 162.

55 H. Zahle (ed.), *Grundloven. Danmarks Riges Grundlov med kommentarer* (*The Constitution. The Constitution of Denmark with explanatory notes*), Jurist- og Økonomforbundets Forlag, 2006, p. 615.

56 See for instance Sørensen, op. cit., pp. 30–3.

57 See the government platform, 2011, p. 61.
58 On the role of political parties in Danish constitutional law, see J. Albæk Jensen, *De politiske partier i retlig belysning* (*The political parties seen from a legal perspective*), Jurist- og Økonomforbundets Forlag, 2009.
59 See the government platform, op. cit., p. 61.
60 Zahle (ed.), op. cit., p. 614.
61 Ibid., p. 228.
62 For a critical approach to this process, see Andersen, op. cit. (1949), pp. 69–71.
63 Tamm, op. cit., p. 218.
64 See U 1996.1300 H.
65 Ibid.
66 U 2001.984. The case is cited in H. Krunke, "Lissabon-sagen", *Juristen*, 2011, no. 8, pp. 245–51.
67 See U 1973.694 H and U 2001.2065 H. The latter is, of course, the most interesting case because it was delivered after the *Maastricht* case.
68 Zahle, op. cit., vol. 2, p. 84.
69 These two arguments, pro and con, also fit the discussion on whether the Constitution should be interpreted according to the intention of the "founding fathers," or should be a living instrument and interpreted in a modern context.

6 Constitutional amendment in Finland

Tuomas Ojanen

Introduction

The purpose of this chapter is to analyze constitutional amendment processes, as well as constitutional change and dynamism in general, in Finland. While the focus will be on the current state of evolution of the national constitutional amendment procedure, this chapter also seeks to situate the topic within its wider historic–political context as constitutional amendment principles, procedures, and practices are inevitably shaped by the specificities of the Finnish constitutional history and political culture.

The paper is divided into five sections. The initial part provides an historical context, with the emphasis on those idiosyncrasies of Finnish constitutional law that continue to shape constitutional amendment in Finland. There will then follow a discussion of the milestones of constitutional amendments, including the most recent constitutional reform, which enters into force on 1 March 2012. Next, the formal and informal methods of constitutional change, as well as the various modes for reviewing constitutional amendments, will be discussed. The final section includes some summarizing and generalizing observations on the impact of European law and international human rights treaties on constitutional amendments.

Historical background

Usually, the independence of a country predates the emergence of its own legal system, including the Constitution. However, Finland already had her own constitutional–legal system well before her independence in 1917.[1] The roots of the Finnish legal system, including its constitutional foundations, can be traced as far back as the era of Swedish rule. Legal evolution in this period came to provide an historical basis that continued to affect the evolution of Finnish constitutional law and doctrine for a long time after the end of Swedish rule in 1809.

For a century, between 1809 and 1917, Finland was an autonomous Grand Duchy in the Russian Empire, with its own domestic legal system inherited from the period of Swedish rule. What deserves emphasis is that all constitutional enactments under Swedish rule also remained in force during the Grand Duchy era. Since Finland also had its own legislature and central administration, including its own judicial system, Finland was essentially in charge of its domestic affairs, including legal matters. Moreover, significant reforms of the constitutional–political system took place when Finland was still an autonomous Grand Duchy. In 1906–1907, Finland not only adopted a modern, unicameral Parliament elected by universal suffrage but was also the first European country to recognize women's suffrage. In conclusion, Finland did not have to start constructing its constitutional and political system from scratch when it became independent in 1917.

The Grand Duchy era also had other significant influences on the ramifications of the Finnish constitutional system and legal culture. For present purposes, two legacies are particularly worthy of elaboration. The first is the strong tradition of highly formal, rule-focused legalism, characterized by close adherence to the letter of the Constitution. The roots of this tradition originate in the so-called "Russification" between 1899 and 1917. These years were marked by strong Russian efforts to abolish Finland's autonomy. However, one major form of resistance by the Finnish legal and political elite to campaigns of Russification was the claim that all new legislation binding upon Finnish citizens and authorities should be adopted in accordance with the procedures prescribed by the constitutional enactments originating in the Swedish era. This legal positivist resistance turned out to be successful, and ever since those years, the Constitution, as a fundamental legal and political instrument of the country, has been held in high esteem in Finland.[2] In addition, a difference can be detected between the Nordic countries, in that while Scandinavian realism has traditionally been the mainstream philosophy in the other Nordic countries, Finland has maintained a more traditional Kantian–Kelsenian normativist perspective of legal positivism since the late nineteenth and early twentieth century. However, these characteristics of Finnish constitutionalism and legal culture have increasingly been challenged by tendencies towards rights-based constitutionalism and the Europeanization of Finnish law since the late 1980s, as human rights and EU law have impelled the courts to deviate from their traditional, markedly formal and rule-focused legal reasoning toward more principle-based reasoning.[3]

The second constitutional legacy from the Grand Duchy era was the *institution of exceptive enactments*.[4] While the Finns urged the Russians to abide by Finland's constitutional enactments originating in the period of Swedish rule, in the name of the legal positivist spirit, there were simultaneously pressing economic and social reasons to enact modern legislation, which was inevitably at odds with those antiquated constitutional enactments. The solution turned out to be the institution of exceptive enactments. This institution made it possible to adopt legislation that, in substance, was in conflict with the Constitution without amending the text thereof, subject to the proviso that such legislation was approved in accordance with the procedure for constitutional enactments. Although exceptive enactments were adopted in accordance with the procedure for constitutional enactments, they only enjoyed the status of ordinary parliamentary legislation. Consequently, they can be quashed in accordance with the procedure for ordinary enactments and, therefore, by a majority of the votes cast.

Finally, it is important to note that Finland has always been fairly homogeneous and state-centered in its self-understanding about community values. Aside from the

Civil War of 1918, there has been a lack of significant ethnic, cultural, political, or religious controversies that would have split the society into factions or involved severe conflicts of interest that are felt to constitute difficult moral or political issues. Moreover, "consensual pathos" has characterized Finnish political and constitutional culture, particularly in recent decades. These characteristics have contributed not only to the development of Finland as a democratic state based on a rule of law and strong respect for the Constitution, but also to recent constitutional reforms in Finland. It is indicative that all constitutional reforms since the early 1990s have been supported by a very strong consensus across the political leftist–rightist spectrum. However, the most recent constitutional reform entering into force on 1 March 2012 was an exception, as the reform package entailing, *inter alia*, further reductions to the powers of the President was opposed by a relatively broad minority, with 40 MPs voting against it and 40 of the 200 MPs being absent for the vote.

In recent years, however, such issues as immigration and European integration have leapt to the center-stage of politics in Finland in a manner that has increasingly caused friction between political parties and different classes of society. Parliamentary elections in spring 2011 marked a breakthrough for right-wing populism, as the right-wing populist and fiercely Eurosceptic party, the True Finns (*Perussuomalaiset*), gained 19.1 per cent of the votes (34 new seats from 2007) with the outcome that the party is running neck and neck with the traditional big three parties—the National Coalition Party (*Kansallinen Kokoomus*, 20.4 per cent of votes, six new seats from 2007), the Social Democratic Party (*Sosialidemokraattinen Puolue*, 19.1 per cent of votes, three new seats from 2007), and the Center Party (*Keskusta*, 15.8 per cent of votes, 16 new seats from 2007).[5] The National Coalition Party also ended up as the largest party of the country for the first time in history. The support for the True Finns seems to have grown as polls commissioned after parliamentary elections suggest they are on the brink of becoming the largest party in the country.[6] The most significant single reason for the increasing support for right-wing populism seems to be connected to the debate over Finnish actions regarding financially strapped Eurozone countries and European integration in general. The other reasons explaining the trend include increased social inequality, the pension index, the teaching of Swedish[7] in schools, and immigration policy.

Milestones of constitutional reforms

The Constitution Act of 1919

Finland gained independence in 1917. The constitutional framework of the newly independent state was laid down by the adoption of the Constitution Act of 1919 and three other enactments confirming the status of the Constitution between 1917 and 1922.[8]

The Constitution Act of 1919 was drafted and adopted in revolutionary conditions as the class divide, based on socio-economic status, had eventually escalated into Civil War in 1918. After the Civil War, the upper and lower classes remained separated in terms of work, economics, and culture; the working class established its own parallel associations and institutions to counterbalance those of the upper classes. In addition, the constitutional–political setting was characterized by a tension between two opposing ideas of the system of government. On the one hand, there were those favoring a strong presidency for the purpose of providing a counterbalance to the increasing representation of the lower classes in Parliament. On the other hand, there were those who favored the parliamentary focus of authority, with a strong constitutional position for Parliament and government formation based on the result of parliamentary elections and the confidence of Parliament. Simply put, it can be said that the right-wing parties representing mainly the upper classes and the "ruling groups" in general favored a strong presidency, whereas the left-wing parties representing working and other "lower" social classes supported the parliamentary focus of authority.

The outcome turned out to be the "mixed" Constitution Act of 1919 with dimensions of both strong presidential powers and those tending towards a parliamentary form of government. As a consequence, the cycles of constitutional and political life after 1919 were characterized by a search for the appropriate balance between the presidential and the parliamentary focus of authority. Depending on the President and the prevailing political constellation, the constitutional pendulum swung back and forth between parliamentarism and strong leadership of the President of the Republic.

Aside from the tension between parliamentarism and presidential powers, the Constitution Act of 1919 was also characterized by the dualities of flexibility and rigidity; authoritarianism and pluralism; and centralization and decentralization. Due to these combinations and their diversity, the Constitution Act of 1919 was eventually capable of living up to various political and societal needs for eight decades until the new Constitution of Finland came into force in 2000.

Finally, it should be noted that a proposal to authorize the Supreme Court to conduct judicial review over laws passed by Parliament was explicitly rejected when the 1919 Constitution Act was adopted. Although the Constitution Act remained silent on the issue of judicial review of the constitutionality of parliamentary legislation, the rigid interpretive doctrine prohibiting judicial review of laws passed by Parliament was soon adopted. This doctrine was formally based on *e contrario* reasoning about the content of s. 92 ss. 2 of the Finnish Constitution Act, which provided that courts and authorities have a duty not to apply government decrees that conflict with the Constitution or any Act of Parliament. As a result, the structural framework of the Finnish model of constitutional review of legislation assumed the nature of *ex ante* legislative review. In this model, the key role was played by Parliament's Constitutional Law Committee, whose duty was to determine the relationship between a bill and the Constitution whenever doubts about the bill's constitutionality emerged. In addition, certain other actors, such as the Chancellor of Justice, the Speaker of Parliament, and the President of the Republic had certain competences to review the constitutionality of legislative proposals during various stages of the legislative process. However, their role was clearly secondary to that of the Constitutional Law Committee, which had the authoritative word insofar as the constitutionality of legislative proposals was concerned. Hence, for all practical and theoretical purposes, the Committee and its decisions began to assume the same normative significance that constitutional courts usually hold in systems based on judicial review models.

It has been argued that, as with strong presidential powers, this system of legislative review, which was complemented by an equally rigid doctrine prohibiting judicial review over laws passed by Parliament, was actually also a result of the class tensions and socio-political tendencies at the critical stage of the political liberation of Finland in 1918. Moreover, the political and economic elite found out fairly quickly that the parliament-centered review mechanism was capable of insulating the vital property rights issues and vested rights from normal democratic politics.[9] In this sense, as far as the elite were concerned, there was no strategic need for judicial review.

Partial reforms

Traditionally, and even in the early 1990s, Finland fell into the category of presidential democracies where the elected head of state—the President of the Republic—enjoyed strong powers distinct from parliamentary decision-making and the requirement of parliamentary confidence. The most significant bastion of presidential power was in the area of foreign policy, but the Constitution Act of 1919 also acknowledged strong presidential powers in domestic affairs, such as legislation, the formation of the Government, and the appointment of state officials.

The authority of the President reached its zenith during the long-term office of President Urho Kekkonen (1956–1981). His formal constitutional authority was strongly reinforced by his personal leadership. In essence, those years were marked by such an exceptionally strong presidency that the parliamentary powers used at the Parliament–Government axis tended to recede into the background and, occasionally, were more or less dropped from political decision-making. However, the Kekkonen era created a backlash. Since President Mauno Koivisto came to office (1982–1994), the constitutional trend has increasingly moved away from the presidential focus of authority towards parliamentarism. This trend of increasing the parliamentary focus of authority of the Finnish constitutional–political system built on several piecemeal amendments made to the Constitution Act of 1919 and Parliament Act (the other major enactment enjoying constitutional status) in the 1980s and the 1990s. As a result of these amendments, a gradual but continuous empowering of Parliament and the Government, both in domestic and international affairs, took effect. Conversely, the powers of the President were gradually reduced by cutting back on some powers altogether or by linking the exercise of presidential powers to co-operation with the Government.

The accession of Finland to the European Economic Area (EEA) in 1994 and the European Union (EU) in 1995 increased the pressure to reconsider the domestic distribution of powers between Parliament, the Government, and the President. After all, while the constitutional pendulum had already swung towards parliamentarism and, accordingly, decreased the significance of presidential powers on the threshold of EU membership, the "last bastion" of presidential power still remained relatively intact. The President still directed foreign policy by virtue of s. 33 of the Constitution Act of 1919, which provided that "the relations of Finland with foreign powers shall be determined by the President." In the early 1990s, this presidential power was by no means a mere fiction.

Given the strong powers of the President in the sphere of foreign affairs, one of the most important issues to be decided in Finland prior to embarking on the process of European integration was as follows: should European affairs—first EEA affairs and later EU affairs—be considered a domestic or a foreign policy matter? If European affairs were to be considered a matter of foreign policy, they would have fallen within the competence of the President by virtue of s. 33 of the Constitution Act 1919. However, this outcome would have been a severe blow not only to the parliamentary type of government, but also to the participation of Parliament in EU affairs. The constitutional pendulum would have swung back again towards a strong presidency, thereby watering down constitutional amendments since the early 1980s that had nudged the Finnish constitutional system towards parliamentarism. The solution turned out to be that domestic competence constellations were arranged according to the same ratio as those used in domestic legislative affairs, instead of the competence arrangements typical of foreign policy. This solution was justified in light of the fact that, in terms of their substance, most EU affairs feature as domestic matters.

As a consequence, the distribution of power regarding European affairs was regulated by a constitutional amendment founded on the following two basic principles. First, the main responsibility for the national preparation of EEA affairs, and later EU affairs, was given to the Government, whose members are individually and collectively accountable to Parliament. Second, specific constitutional provisions were enacted to ensure the participation of Parliament in considering such EU affairs as would, according to the Constitution, otherwise fall within the competence of Parliament.[10] However, this type of constitutional design, where both the Government and the President have powers relating to foreign and/or European policy, has been prone to tensions, particularly when considering that domestic foreign policies are increasingly co-ordinated at EU level, and that foreign and EU policies are difficult to separate from one another. As a consequence, there has been a great deal of ongoing discussion and debate over the role of the President in EU affairs related to foreign and security policy issues. Although the jurisdiction of the Government covers all EU matters, including common foreign and security policy issues of the Union,[11] the President has tried to legitimize this role in EU affairs, and particularly Common Foreign and Security Policy (CFSP) matters, through the strong links between European and foreign policies. The major argument by the President has been that, in order to genuinely lead foreign policy, the office-holder must also be actively involved in EU policy.[12]

The reform of the domestic system for the protection of constitutional rights

The Constitution Act of 1919 included a brief catalog of fundamental rights (Chapter II of the Constitution Act 1919) and some scattered provisions on such rights elsewhere in the Constitution. These rights were for Finnish citizens only and were almost exclusively classic civil and political rights. For a long time, moreover, fundamental rights were understood to be binding primarily on the legislature. In addition, given the reserved and distrustful Nordic tradition towards rights and judiciaries, as well as the prohibition of judicial review of parliamentary legislation for its compatibility with the Constitution under s. 92 of the 1919 Constitution Act, constitutional provisions on fundamental rights assumed for many years a relatively limited role in court practice and the Finnish scene of constitutionalism in general.[13] Indeed, even cursory references to constitutional provisions on fundamental rights remained rare and sporadic until the 1990s.[14] Hence, the prohibition of judicial review actually resulted in a state of law where courts hardly invoked the Constitution at all. What is more, this passive stance towards fundamental rights extended to international human rights treaties even though they were formally incorporated into the Finnish legal order at the level of ordinary laws.[15] As a result, fundamental rights norms, whether based on constitutional rights provisions or on international human rights treaties already incorporated into the domestic legal order, did not appear in court decisions until the late 1980s. As a result of this constitutional background, there was no genuine tradition of judicial review based on constitutional or human rights in Finland before the 1990s.[16]

However, these developments in the 1980s and early 1990s brought a marked change in the Finnish fundamental rights and human rights culture. One part of this change was that fundamental rights and human rights treaties binding upon Finland started playing a stronger role in the courts. In particular, Finland's accession to the European Convention on Human Rights (ECHR) in 1989, and the incorporation of its provisions into the domestic legal order in 1990, represent one of the most important turns in Finnish constitutional history. In fact, it was the ECHR, with its extensive case law from the European Court of Human Rights, that ultimately convinced the reluctant Finnish courts to regard human rights as legally binding and enforceable rights, and as law by all domestic standards.[17]

Another trend, closely interlinked with the first one, was the growing significance of European-level judicial review as exercised by the European Court of Human Rights (ECtHR) and the European Court of Justice (ECJ), as well as the significance of national courts enforcing European law. These tendencies towards stronger judicial safeguards for fundamental and human rights, and various models of judicial review of parliamentary legislation, were inevitably linked with the issue of the proper division of powers between the legislature and the judiciary, and with tendencies towards "constitutionalization of Finnish law," "politicization of adjudication," and "adjudication of politics."[18]

In 1989, the Government Commission was established to revise Chapter II of the Constitution Act of 1919 relating to fundamental rights. According to the Commission's mandate, human rights treaties binding on Finland, especially the ECHR—which Finland joined in 1990—featured as the prime source of inspiration and stimuli for the reform. After five years of preparation, a complete and extensive amendment of Chapter II of the 1919 Act relating to fundamental rights entered into force on 1 August 1995. The outcome of the reform was, and still is, a broad catalog of fundamental rights, with a range of economic, social and cultural rights, in addition to the more traditional civil and political rights. Moreover, there are specific provisions on responsibility for the environment and environmental rights, as well as for access to documents and the right to good administration. Almost all of the rights are granted to everyone, an exception being made only with regard to the freedom of movement (s. 9) and certain electoral rights (s. 14).

Although international human rights treaties were a major influence on the 1995 Fundamental Rights Reform, the Constitution formulated these rights in a new way and, above all, accorded to them the status of constitutional rights. In addition, it is well established that Finnish authorities and courts should not only interpret and apply constitutional rights and human rights in harmony; they should also try to offer more extensive protection of fundamental rights than that available for corresponding human rights under human rights treaties. As a consequence, human rights obligations binding upon Finland feature as a minimum standard of protection.[19]

On the verge of EU membership, the concern was that EU membership might somehow dilute the domestic standard of protection of fundamental and human rights, particularly in the fields of social rights, transparency, and access to documents. As a consequence, some provisions of the 1995 Fundamental Rights Reform may actually be understood as a self-defense against those problematic tendencies that EU membership might entail in the long run in the field of fundamental rights. A reference can be made to a strict clause on the right of access to information (s. 12, ss. 2), a relatively far-reaching clause on the right to social security in which the guaranteed rights are granted to everyone (not just EU citizens or workers and their families; s. 19). Some social rights, either by means of the relevant constitutional provision itself or by means of Acts of Parliament, have also been guaranteed as subjective rights directly enforceable through the courts.[20]

Finally, it is important to note that the constitutional rights reform of 1995 did not alter the institutional arrangements and power constellations around constitutional rights and human rights. Above all, the prohibition of judicial review of the constitutionality of ordinary legislation remained intact, although the interpretive mandate corresponding to the principle of human rights-friendly interpretation was emphasized.

The Constitution of Finland 2000

Although the Finnish Constitution had already been the subject of several partial constitutional reforms in the 1980s and 1990s, these reforms failed to remove the pressure for a comprehensive constitutional reform aimed at the uniformization and modernization of the constitutional structures, and revision of the distribution of power within the state, so that the parliamentary focus of authority would be further strengthened in the spheres of internal affairs and foreign policy.

In 1990, Parliament required that the Finnish Government should prepare a constitutional reform for the purpose of better balancing the powers of Parliament, the Government, and the President of the Republic, thereby strengthening Parliament's position. In 1992, Parliament obliged the Government to carry on with the process of constitutional reform "for the parliamentarization of the powers of the President of the Republic." In 1994, the Government was assigned the task of launching a wholesale revision of the entire Constitution: the outcome was to be a single and unified constitutional text.[21] After that, the reform proceeded quite rapidly. Within a 17-month period, a parliamentary Commission produced a report that included a government bill on the new Constitution of Finland in 1998. Parliament almost unanimously adopted the new Constitution of Finland, the count in the final vote being 175 for and two against.

The new Constitution of Finland (Act No 731 of 1999) entered into force on 1 March 2000. This new Constitution was, and still is, a modern and unified document with concise and uniform style. Aside from defining the foundations of the constitutional–political system of Finland (Chapter 1), it includes distinct chapters on fundamental rights (Chapter II), the composition and activities of Parliament (Chapters III and IV), the Government and the President of the Republic (Chapter V), legislation (Chapter VI), state finances (Chapter VII), international relations (Chapter VIII), administration of justice (Chapter IX), supervision of legality (Chapter X), administration and self-government (Chapter XI), national defense (Chapter XII), and final provisions (Chapter XIII).

The Constitution of Finland significantly strengthened the Parliament–Government axis and, conversely, entailed further reductions to presidential powers. However, the President of the Republic still figures as a significant authority in the Finnish political–constitutional system. Aside from enjoying some powers in domestic affairs, the foreign policy of Finland is directed by the President "in co-operation with the Government" (in pursuance of s. 93, ss. 1 of the Constitution). Thus, the Constitution still acknowledges the role of the President as the ultimate authority in foreign policy, but binds him or her operatively to co-operation with the Government. The Constitution allows a degree of latitude for the formulation of concrete procedures and practices in the interplay between the President and the Government in the field of foreign policy. Before the Constitution entered into force, Parliament's Constitutional Law Committee observed that—on foreign policy formulation and decision-making—the President "must make all significant foreign policy decisions and actions together with the Government and on the basis of the Government's preparatory work." In addition, the Committee emphasized that the actual forms of co-operation will depend on the significance of the issues. In broad-ranging matters, discussions between the President and the Government are required, even if in more urgent matters it suffices for the President to consult the Cabinet Committee on Foreign and Security Policy or an individual minister, primarily the Prime Minister and Foreign Minister, or the minister responsible for preparing the issue. In practice, co-leadership is executed through the Cabinet Committee on Foreign and Security Policy and, essentially, weekly dialog between the President and the Prime Minister and/or the Foreign Minister.[22] However, it should be emphasized that the Government is responsible for the national preparation of decisions to be made in the EU, including the

Union's common foreign and security policy (under s. 93, ss. 2 of the Constitution). The competence of the Government in EU affairs seeks to secure the participation of Parliament in the European policy of Finland, and it follows from the Government's competence that the Prime Minister represents Finland in the meetings of the European Council. In recent years, the trend has been for Finnish foreign policy to increasingly be shaped in the context of the EU's Common Foreign and Security Policy (CFSP). Consequently, foreign policy powers are increasingly devolved to the Prime Minister and the Government.

However, the constitutional solutions in the area of foreign policy have given rise to debate over the role of the President, particularly insofar as the CFSP of the EU is concerned. In practice, it is difficult—in fact, almost impossible—to draw a clear and unambiguous distinction between EU policy and foreign policy matters. Strong and multifilament links between EU policy and foreign affairs actually make such categorizations inherently unmanageable, because national foreign and security policies are increasingly influenced by co-ordination processes and policy choices at the level of the European Union.

At the level of the daily politics, the problem of constitutional solutions in the area of foreign policy has been manifest in domestic disagreements regarding the Finnish representation in European Council meetings. Although the Finnish Parliament's Constitutional Law Committee has, since 1994, consistently emphasized that the Prime Minister should represent Finland in the European Council,[23] President Martti Ahtisaari (1994–2000) and President Tarja Halonen (2000–2012) both took the view that, as President, they had the right to act, together with the Prime Minister, in those meetings of the European Council at which EU common foreign and security policy affairs are on the agenda. As a result, these Presidents participated in the majority of European Council meetings during the late 1990s and up to the present. In practice, the participation of the President often entailed the Foreign Minister having to leave the meeting room, despite the fact that the Foreign Minister had usually participated in preparing the agenda items, and that all EU affairs belonged to the competence of the Government under the Constitution. In addition, it should be emphasized that the issue of Finland's representation in European Council meetings is of great significance from the point of view of parliamentary participation and accountability. As noted, Parliament enjoys strong rights insofar as the national preparation of EU matters is concerned (s. 96 of the Constitution). Therefore, since the very beginning of Finland's EU membership, the practice has been that the Prime Minister must inform the competent parliamentary committees about issues at the agenda of the European Council meetings both beforehand and afterwards. However, the entry into force of the Lisbon Treaty brought an end to this practice of "dual representation" of Finland in European Council meetings. It was expressly noted by the Constitutional Law Committee that, in view of the changes made by the Lisbon Treaty to the role and powers of the European Council, it is necessary in future for the Prime Minister alone to represent Finland in European Council meetings.[24] The acting President, Mrs Tarja Halonen, has no longer challenged this view. In a recent amendment of the Constitution, which enters into force on 1 March 2012, this new practice is now codified in the new s. 66, ss. 2 of the Constitution, which expressly provides that the Prime Minister represents Finland in the European Council and in other EU meetings where the political leaders of the Member States are represented (such as informal meetings between the leaders of member states and summits between the EU and third countries).

The Constitutional Reform of 2012

Although it is over 11 years since the new Constitution of Finland entered into force, there has been continuous debate and discussion over the need for further changes. The debate has mainly been concerned with divided views on the role of the President in foreign affairs and, in particular, EU affairs. In addition, the discussion has been about the need to say "a bit more" about the EU in the Constitution. The widespread view has been that the Constitution of 2000 failed to resolve these questions satisfactorily. In 2009, a governmental commission with parliamentary composition started considering the need for a reform of the Constitution of Finland. In May 2010, a government bill proposing several amendments to the Constitution was presented to Parliament.[25] The most significant amendments related to the question of mentioning Finland's EU membership in the Constitution, as well as to the procedure for transferring powers to the EU. The proposal is that EU membership should be explicitly mentioned in s. 1 of the Constitution. In addition, it is proposed that the Constitution should be supplemented by a provision providing that a "significant" transfer of state powers to the EU or international organizations would require a two-thirds majority of the given votes in Parliament. Any transfer of powers that were not significant would, *e contrario*, be decided by simple majority.

Moreover, some modifications are proposed as regards the distribution of power between the President and the Government, including the Prime Minister, within the context of European affairs in particular. In general, these modifications entail further reductions to presidential powers. The amendment was accepted in October 2011 by a broad majority of Parliament, with 118 MPs in favor and 40 against, and as many as 40 of the 200 MPs being absent for the vote. The right-wing populist True Finns party and the two members of the Left Faction parliamentary group voted against the constitutional amendment, arguing that the amendment would excessively limit the remaining powers of the President. The new amendment will enter into force on 1 March 2012, simultaneously with the commencement of the next President of the Republic's term of office, following election in January 2012. However, it can already be anticipated that the ongoing debate over the President's role will continue, insofar as foreign policy and EU affairs in particular are concerned. With the approach of the presidential election year of 2012, this debate actually seemed to intensify as disagreements have emerged on the scope of presidential powers during the debates between the presidential candidates. Several presidential candidates seem to be of the view that the recent constitutional amendment has taken too much authority away from the presidency.

Forms of constitutional change

Procedure for constitutional enactment

The procedure for constitutional enactment has remained practically unchanged since the entry into force of the 1919 Constitution Act. Currently, s. 73 of the Constitution of Finland 2000, on the procedure for constitutional enactment, provides as follows:

> A proposal on the enactment, amendment or repeal of the Constitution or on the enactment of a limited derogation of the Constitution shall in the second reading be left in abeyance, by a majority of the votes cast, until the first parliamentary session following parliamentary elections. The proposal shall then, once the Committee has issued its report, be adopted without material alterations in one reading in a plenary session by a decision supported by at least two-thirds of the votes cast. However, the proposal may be declared urgent by a decision that has been supported by at least five-sixths of the votes cast. In this event, the proposal is not left in abeyance and it can be adopted by a decision supported by at least two-thirds of the votes cast.

Thus, the procedure for constitutional enactment requires leaving the bill in abeyance until after elections, provided that the bill is not declared urgent by a decision made by at least five-sixths of the votes cast. In addition, the bill must be adopted by a decision supported by at least two-thirds of the votes cast. It is to be emphasized that there is no need for a referendum in order to approve a constitutional amendment in Finland. However, the amendment procedure can be assessed by the electorate because the bill is left in abeyance until after elections (unless the bill is declared urgent by a decision made by at least five-sixths of the votes cast in Parliament, as mentioned above). Looking back at the history of constitutional amendments, it is normal procedure to leave the bill in abeyance until after elections.

The institution of exceptive enactments

The greatest peculiarity of the Finnish constitutional system is presumably the institution of exceptive enactments.[26] As already noted, the origins of this system can be traced to the Grand Duchy era in the Russian empire. In essence, this institution makes it possible to adopt laws that, in substance, conflict with the Constitution without amending the text thereof, subject to the proviso that such laws are approved in accordance with the procedure for constitutional enactments. Traditionally, constitutional lawyers refer to making a "hole" in the Constitution by an exceptive enactment and filling it with the relevant norms of the exceptive enactment. It should be emphasized that there is no requirement for an emergency when resorting to an exceptive enactment. In addition, for a long time there was a lack of any material or doctrinal limits for the derogation from constitutional provisions by the adoption of exceptive enactments.

According to the well-established constitutional law doctrine, exceptive enactments enjoy the same hierarchical level as ordinary Acts of Parliament. Consequently, an Act of Parliament repealing an exceptive enactment can be adopted through the ordinary procedure of enactment. The procedure for amending exceptive enactments, in turn, depends on the answer to the following question: does the amendment significantly extend the original exception—the "hole"—to the Constitution? If the answer is "yes," the procedure for constitutional enactment becomes necessary; otherwise, the ordinary legislative procedure is sufficient.

Due to the institution of exceptive enactments, no amendment to the Constitution is necessary to enable Finland to enter into an international obligation deemed to be in conflict with the Constitution. However, Acts incorporating international obligations conflicting with the Constitution make a special case among exceptive enactments in the sense that the procedure for their enactment requires no more and no less than a two-thirds majority in Parliament (s. 95, ss. 2). To take an example, the Treaty of Accession of Finland to the European Union of 1994[27] was deemed to be in conflict with the Constitution, the major reason being the incompatibility between Finland's sovereignty and its transfer of powers to the EU.[28] However, no amendment to the Constitution was found appropriate to enable the accession because of the institution of exceptive enactments. Accordingly, the Treaty of Accession was incorporated into Finnish law through an exceptive enactment (Act No 1540 of 1994) approved by a two-thirds majority in Parliament.

The issue of accession was also subjected to a consultative referendum, held on 16 October 1994. However, the referendum was not a constitutional condition for accession. Instead, the issue of accession was put to the people of Finland for the purpose of ensuring the domestic legitimacy of the decision to join the EU. In the referendum, a majority of 56.9 per cent of those who voted answered "yes" to the following question: "Should Finland become a member of the European Union in accordance with the treaty which has been negotiated?" The turnout was 74 per cent.[29] Similarly, the Lisbon Treaty was incorporated into Finnish law through an exceptive enactment (Act No 947 of 2009).

For a long time, the institution of exceptive enactments allowed the practice by which, on the one hand, the Constitutional Law Committee of Parliament—the most authoritative interpreter of the Constitution—was able to uphold a strict interpretation of the Constitution, by requiring the use of the qualified enactment procedure for enacting legislation or implementing enactments of international treaties deemed to be in conflict with the Constitution. Yet, on the other hand, hundreds of exceptive enactments *de facto* derogating from the Constitution were enacted. Since these exceptive enactments usually entailed derogations from constitutional provisions on fundamental rights, the protection of fundamental rights was previously very formal in character. Indeed, if not exclusively then at least predominantly, the protection of fundamental rights was connected with the following question about the proper parliamentary procedure, instead of the material contents or protection of these rights: should normal legislative procedure or the qualified procedure for exceptive enactments be applied? Indeed, some provisions of the Constitution Act of 1919 on fundamental rights, such as the constitutional provision on the protection of property, were eventually subject to so many derogations by exceptive enactments that they actually featured as a kind of an "empty shell" for those numerous derogations that could not be read from the text of the constitutional provision itself.

However, the importance of the institution of exceptive enactments has gradually decreased from the late 1980s onwards. Several reasons have contributed to this constitutional development. First of all, a trend towards the material protection of fundamental rights began in the 1980s. Instead of focusing on the question of the proper parliamentary procedure, the parliamentary Constitutional Law Committee began to be concerned with the material contents and the effective protection of fundamental rights and human rights. In essence, this new approach entailed the Committee making proposals as to how to modify proposed legislation in order to achieve appropriate compliance with fundamental rights and human rights, and with the Constitution in general.[30] Moreover, since the comprehensive reform of the domestic system for the protection of fundamental rights came into force in 1995, the constitutional law doctrine has been that exceptive enactments should only be used to bring domestically into force such international treaties as are deemed to conflict with the Constitution. Conversely, the use of exceptive enactments should be avoided in the context of domestic legislation. As a consequence of this doctrine, the use of exceptive enactments has drastically diminished since the late 1990s. While a total of 888 exceptive enactments were adopted between 1919 and 2000, there have been fewer than 10 exceptive enactments during the last decade.

Last but not least, the Constitution of Finland 2000 introduced two material limits for the derogation from the Constitution by the use of exceptive enactments. On the one hand, s. 73 of the Constitution requires that the enactment of a derogation shall remain "limited." In practice, this precludes the adoption of exceptive enactment that would entail, for instance, an extensive derogation from constitutional provisions on fundamental rights. Furthermore, s. 94 (ss. 3) stipulates that international obligations "shall not endanger the democratic foundations of the Constitution." According to the *travaux préparatoires* of the Constitution, this provision is designed to preclude the ratification of such international treaties, which would endanger such democratic foundations of the Constitution as the status of Parliament as the highest state organ. Up until now, s. 93 (ss. 3) has assumed relevance only twice. The Constitutional Law Committee took the view regarding the Treaty Establishing the Constitution for Europe that this treaty was in accordance with s. 94, ss. 3 and, accordingly, did not endanger democratic foundations of the Constitution.[31] Similarly, the Committee took the view that the Lisbon Treaty remained limited within the meaning of s. 73 of the Constitution.[32]

Informal changes of the Constitution

Amendments to the text of the Constitution through formal procedure for constitutional enactment can be regarded as the primary means by which constitutional reforms come into being. But the process of constitutional change can also be more multifarious and subtle. Once the Constitution is enacted, formal amendment processes are completed, and various doctrinal and interpretive changes are set to commence. The importance of "informal changes" must, therefore, be emphasized as modes of constitutional dynamics and transformations.

The significance of doctrinal changes can be highlighted with reference to those profound transformations that have occurred in Finland within the context of the domestic system for the protection of constitutional rights and human rights, and the institution of judicial review since the late 1980s. Although these transformations have manifested themselves at the level of the text of the Constitution, they have also changed the very foundations of Finnish constitutionalism, including overall constitutional thinking and Finnish legal culture.[33] In essence, these changes have ensured that the traditional characteristics of Finnish constitutionalism—legislative supremacy, democracy as majority rule, presumptions of positivist notions of law, the prohibition of judicial review, and marginal significance of rights in the Finnish scene of constitutionalism—have increasingly been challenged by tendencies towards rights-based constitutionalism and forms of pluralist review since the late 1980s. Finnish constitutionalism has witnessed a clear and significant shift from the legislative sovereignty paradigm to one in which legislative acts are increasingly subordinated to various forms of rights-based judicial review. As a consequence, transformations within the institution of judicial review and the growing role of the judiciary in general have been one of the most significant constitutional developments in Finland in recent years.

One of the most significant outcomes of all these dynamics has been the abandonment of the absolute prohibition of judicial review of the constitutionality of Acts of Parliament. As already noted, there was little, if any, constitutional discussion as to when and how the judicial review of the constitutionality of Acts of Parliament should be exercised before the 1990s. The dominant view was simply that this kind of judicial review was not allowed under the Constitution Act of 1919.[34] However, doubts began to emerge over the viability of the absolute prohibition of this kind of judicial review from the late 1980s onwards. As international human rights treaties were usually formally incorporated into the Finnish legal order at the level of ordinary laws, this not only allowed the direct application of treaty provisions by domestic courts and authorities, but also their precedence in cases where the domestic provision has a hierarchical status lower than an Act of Parliament. In addition, since these treaties assumed the same status as domestic Acts of Parliament, this opened up the possibility for a "weak form" of judicial review and, accordingly, of resolving conflicts between human rights treaties and ordinary domestic legislation through reference to such rules as the *lex posterior* or *lex specialis* rules. In the end, EU membership proved the final straw. By empowering all courts to review all Finnish law—including Acts of Parliament and even the Constitution of Finland—for compatibility with EU law, EU membership provided the decisive incentive to reconsider the prohibition preventing courts from examining the constitutionality of Acts of Parliament. The outcome of this reconsideration was the introduction of concrete *ex post* review by courts under s. 106 of the Constitution of Finland 2000. Section 106, entitled "the primacy of the Constitution," provides:

> If in a matter being tried by a court, the application of an Act would be in evident conflict with the Constitution, the court of law shall give primacy to the provision in the Constitution.

Section 106 of the Constitution acknowledges only a limited role for courts in reviewing the constitutionality of Acts of Parliament. It is not intended to tilt the balance in the review of the constitutionality of Acts of Parliament from the Constitutional Committee toward the judiciary. Instead, the current constitutional premise is that the abstract *ex ante* review carried out by Parliament's Constitutional Law Committee continues to be the primary mechanism for reviewing the constitutionality of legislation. The *travaux préparatoires* of s. 106 are very clear on this point: this section is only intended to amount to a form of weak judicial review, which deliberately seeks to combine the abstract *ex ante* constitutional review of legislation by the Constitutional Law Committee with the concrete *ex post* constitutional review by courts. In this model, the *ex ante* constitutional review by the Constitutional Law Committee is supposed to remain primary, whereas judicial review under s. 106 is basically designed to plug loopholes left in the abstract *ex ante* review of the constitutionality of bills by the Constitutional Law Committee, inasmuch as unprecedented constitutional problems may arise from the courts applying the law in particular cases.[35]

Moreover, s. 106 is designed to apply in extreme cases only, where no other judicial method of giving effect to the Constitution is able to resolve the tension between an Act of Parliament and the Constitution. Indeed, it is explicitly emphasized in the *travaux préparatoires* of s. 106 that the primary method of giving effect to the Constitution remains the "constitution-oriented interpretation approach," in which courts construe Finnish law, including all Acts of Parliament, in accordance with the Constitution. In particular, the criterion of an "evident conflict" is deliberately designated to guarantee the primacy of the constitutional review by the Constitutional Law Committee. The *travaux préparatoires* of s. 106 explicitly state that, as a rule, a court cannot establish the existence of an evident conflict between an Act of Parliament and the Constitution if the Constitutional Law Committee, in its *ex ante* review, has concluded that the relevant Act of Parliament is in harmony with the Constitution. In addition, the requirement of an evident conflict also informs that the courts should not apply s. 106 lightly and frequently, but instead rarely, after a careful judicial analysis and against a backdrop of judicial self-restraint.[36] No wonder, therefore, that there have so far only been four cases involving its actual application by a court.[37]

As already noted, a governmental commission with parliamentary composition recently considered the need for a reform of the Constitution of Finland. Among various questions on the agenda was the issue of whether the criterion of manifest conflict should be removed from s. 106. Although a clear majority of constitutional law scholars appeared to be in favor of eliminating the manifest-conflict criterion from s. 106, the commission ended up concluding that s. 106 should remain intact. In particular, a clear majority of politicians still appeared to entertain doubts about any extension of the scope of judicial review. Indeed, there still seems to be a great deal of disagreement as to when and how the power of judicial review should be exercised, or indeed whether it should be exercised at all.

Supervision of constitutional amendments and the role of experts in constitutional revision

As already noted, Finland's constitutional system has traditionally followed, both formally and in practice, the classic legislative supremacy principles. Thus, Finland does not have a constitutional court, and courts still play a secondary role in reviewing the constitutionality of legislation, although since the 1990s the trend has increasingly been from the classic legislative supremacy towards more pluralist forms of constitutional review.

The primary control mechanism for ensuring the constitutionality of legislation and constitutional amendments, including international obligations and EU affairs, is the (abstract) *ex ante* review carried out by Parliament's Constitutional Law Committee. Consequently, the Committee also plays a key role in supervising constitutional amendments. In practice, the Committee takes a view on the constitutionality of the bills and other matters submitted to it, as well as on their relation to the international human rights treaties binding upon Finland (s. 74 of the Constitution).[38] It should be emphasized that, aside from the constitutional review of legislative proposals and constitutional amendments, the Committee's activities include supervising international treaties and examining proposals for EU measures, such as regulations and directives, for their compatibility with the Constitution.[39] Hence, for all practical and theoretical purposes, the Committee and its decisions assume the same normative role that constitutional courts usually enjoy in systems based on judicial review models. The main difference is that, in the Finnish model, the primary power of review is held by a political organ composed of MPs and acting as an integral part in the political process of legislative action. While in certain models of judicial review the importance of the "political dimension" is reflected in the need to secure a politically balanced composition of a constitutional court, despite all its judges being dressed in judicial gowns, the Finnish model is more open politically, because the Constitutional Law Committee consists solely of members of Parliament, representing both government and opposition parties, and who are often lawyers by education. Yet, in spite of its political constellation, the Committee is supposed to exercise a quasi-judicial function when interpreting the Constitution and reviewing legislative proposals for their conformity with the Constitution and international human rights obligations binding upon Finland. In practice, its work is also characterized by a search for constitutionally well-founded interpretations and consistent use of precedents. The views of the Committee enjoy strong authority, and they are generally treated as binding on Parliament and other authorities.

Before issuing its opinions or reports, the Committee invariably hears academic experts on constitutional law. These experts often provide an important source of interpretive authority and legitimacy for the Committee, particularly in cases in which the experts are unanimous in their views regarding the compatibility of bills and other matters with the Constitution and international human rights obligations binding on Finland. It is not uncommon for the Committee to find a government bill to be unconstitutional or otherwise inappropriate in one or more respects in light of the Constitution. As a consequence, the Committee then requires that appropriate amendments to be made to the bill during its parliamentary consideration.

As already noted, s. 106 of the Constitution acknowledges a limited role for courts in reviewing the constitutionality of Acts of Parliament. Since s. 106 is about reviewing ordinary Acts of Parliament for their compatibility with the Constitution, it does not allow judicial review of constitutional amendments. However, the Supreme Court and the Supreme Administrative Court may feature as consultative bodies in the legislative decision-making process, including those aiming at revising constitutional provisions. According to s. 77 of the Constitution, the President may obtain a statement on the Act from the Supreme Court or the Supreme Administrative Court before its confirmation by the President. Thus, the Supreme Court and the Supreme Administrative Court may act in an advisory capacity if consulted by the President on an Act adopted by Parliament, before its confirmation by the President. As a consequence, these two courts of last instance may also be called to give an opinion about the constitutionality or legality of the legislative proposal, or about the conformity of the proposal with international law or European law *ex ante*. This is also problematic in light of the independence of the judiciary, since these same courts may at a later stage be called to judge on the same legal question *ex post* when applying the Act after its adoption in a concrete case pending before them.

Concluding observations on the sources of constitutional amendments and constitutional change

The previous discussion has already demonstrated that European law and international human rights law have been a significant source of constitutional change and dynamism in Finland. A reference can first be made to the impact of EU membership on the domestic separation of powers between Parliament, the Government, and the President in the field of EU affairs and foreign affairs. As is shown by the most recent constitutional amendment of 2012, EU membership continues to feature as an important source of horizontal relocation of authority between Parliament, the Government, and the President. In addition, this amendment makes EU membership more visible at the level of the text of the Constitution.

International human rights treaties have also featured as a major source of inspiration for the comprehensive reform of the domestic system for protecting fundamental rights in 1995. Furthermore, the impact of European law and international human rights is manifest in the way in which the traditional hard-core doctrine of legislative sovereignty, with the absolute prohibition of judicial review and a legal–positivist statutory law system committed to majoritarian democracy at its apex, became marked by turbulence and by dynamics that were of sufficient magnitude to suggest the emergence of new constitutional structures and patterns. Ultimately, it has been the outcome of the reciprocal influences between various domestic sources of dynamics, EU membership, and international human rights treaties that have entailed a profound shift from the legislative sovereignty paradigm to one in which legislative acts are increasingly subordinated to various forms of rights-based judicial review. At the level of the text of the Constitution, these dynamics have resulted in the adoption of s. 106 of the Constitution, which acknowledges a limited role for the courts in reviewing the constitutionality of Acts of Parliament. However, the constitutional dynamics from the interaction between European law, international human rights law, and certain domestic sources of dynamics transcend s. 106 of the Constitution and also extend to cover the wider and more fundamental changes in the overall constitutional thinking in Finland, as well as the Finnish legal culture in general.

In conclusion, therefore, the most elementary constitutional dynamics have been due to the intricate and multilevel interaction in which EU membership, international human rights treaties, and certain domestic sources of dynamics have contributed and reinforced their respective influences on the very texture of Finnish constitutionalism, including constitutional amendments.

Notes

1 See e.g. A. Jyränki, *Lakien laki*, Lakimiesliiton Kustannus, 1989, pp. 403–72. See also T. Ojanen, "The Europeanization of Finnish Law", in P. Luif (ed.), *Österreich, Finnland, Schweden. Zehn Jahre Mitgliedschaft in der Europäischen Union*, Böhlau Verlag, 2007, pp. 146–50.

2 See also, M. Scheinin, "Constitutionalism and Approaches to Rights in the Nordic Countries", in J. Nergelius (ed.), *Constitutionalism: New Challenges - European Law from a Nordic Perspective*, Martinus Nijhoff, 2008, pp. 135–8.

3 Ojanen in Luif (ed.), op. cit., p. 150.

4 A brief historical review of this institution in English is provided in M. Scheinin, "Constitutional Law and Human Rights", in J. Pöyhönen (ed.), *An Introduction to Finnish Law*, Helsinki: Kauppakaari, 2002, pp. 55–6.

5 According to s. 24 of the Constitution, Parliament is unicameral and consists of 200 representatives, who are elected for a term of four years at a time.

6 See e.g. *Helsingin Sanomat*, "New poll says True Finns are Finland's largest party". Online. Available HTTP: <http://www.hs.fi/english/article/New+poll+says+True+Finns+are+Finland%E2%80%99s+largest+party/1135266268297> (accessed 1 October 2011).

7 Swedish is the national language of Finland alongside Finnish. Section 17 of the Constitution of Finland guarantees the right of everyone to use his or her own language, either Finnish or Swedish, before courts of law and other authorities, and to receive official documents in that language shall be guaranteed by an Act. The same provision also obliges public authorities to provide for the cultural and societal needs of the Finnish-speaking and Swedish-speaking populations of the country on an equal basis.

8 Accordingly, there were four constitutional enactments enjoying constitutional status: the Constitution Act of Finland, the Parliament Act, and two Acts on ministerial liability. All Acts were passed during the first years of independence.

9 See e.g. P. Länsineva, *Perusoikeudet ja varallisuussuhteet*, Suomalainen lakimiesyhdistys, 2002, pp. 43–4.
10 See in more detail, Ojanen in Luif (ed.), op. cit., p. 150.
11 See e.g. the reports by the Constitutional Law Committee of Parliament, PeVM 10/1994 and PeVM 10/1998, p. 26.
12 See e.g. T. Raunio, "Semi-presidentialism and European integration: lessons from Finland for constitutional design", *Journal of European Public Policy – iFirst*, 2011, pp. 1–18.
13 See M. Scheinin, *Ihmisoikeudet Suomen oikeudessa*, Suomalainen Lakimiesyhdistys, 1991, p. 340.
14 Ibid., pp. 358–60.
15 Ibid., pp. 158–69.
16 For a detailed account and a discussion of a paradigm shift in 1988–1991, ibid., pp. 222–8, 246–50, 273–89.
17 See M. Scheinin, "General Introduction", in Scheinin (ed.), *International Human Rights Norms in the Nordic and Baltic Countries*, Martinus Nijhoff, 1996, p. 17ff.
18 For Finnish discussion on constitutionalization of Finnish law and the role of the judiciary, and the proper division of powers between the legislature and the judiciary, see especially J. Lavapuro, *Uusi perustuslakikontrolli*, Helsinki, 2010. See also K. Tuori, *Oikeuden ratio ja voluntas*, WSOYpro., 2007, pp. 249–75; T. Ojanen, "From Constitutional Periphery toward the Center – Transformations of Judicial Review in Finland", *Nordic Journal of Human Rights (Nordisk Tidsskrift for Menneskerettigheter)*, 2009, vol. 27, no. 2, pp. 194–207.
19 See in general, J. Lavapuro, T. Ojanen and M. Scheinin, "Rights-Based Constitutionalism in Finland and the Development of Pluralist Constitutional Review", *International Journal of Constitutional Law*, 2011, vol. 9, pp. 505–31.
20 Finnish courts have treated as "justiciable" several dimensions of social rights. See e.g. the judgments of the Supreme Administrative Court: KHO 2000, p. 36, KHO 2001:35 and KHO 2001, p. 50.
21 See Perustuslakiuudistus. Eri painos. Oikeusministeriön lainvalmisteluosaston julkaisuja 3/2000, p. 5.
22 See PeVM 10/1998 vp, p. 26. See also Raunio, op. cit., pp. 9–10.
23 The Committee already took this view on the verge of Finland's accession to the EU in 1994. See PeVM 10/1994 vp. For subsequent views of the Committee, see e.g. PeVM 10/1998 vp: 26, PeVL 36/2006 vp and PeVL 13/2008.
24 PeVL 2/2010 vp.
25 Government Bill HE 60/2010.
26 A brief historical review of this institution in English is provided from Scheinin in Pöyhönen (ed.), op. cit., pp. 31–57.
27 The instrument concerning the accession of Finland to the European Union is the Treaty between member states of the European Union and the Kingdom of Norway, the Republic of Austria, the Republic of Finland, and the Kingdom of Sweden. O.J. 1994 C 241/14, as adjusted by Council Decision 95/1/EC, Euratom, ECSC, O.J. 1995 L 1/1.
28 See PeVL 14/1994vp.
29 See in more detail Ojanen in Luif (ed.), op. cit., pp. 151–2.
30 See, for instance, Scheinin, op. cit., (1991), p. 362.
31 See PeVL 36/2006 vp.
32 See PeVL 13/2008vp.
33 For an overview, see Ojanen, op. cit., (2009), pp. 194–207. See also Lavapuro, Ojanen and Scheinin, op. cit., pp. 505–31.
34 See Scheinin, op. cit., (1991), p. 358.
35 See government proposal for the new Constitution HE 1/1998, p. 164. See also the Report by the Constitutional Law Committee on government proposal HE 1/1998, PeVM 10/1998, p. 31.

36 For a more detailed discussion of s. 106, see Ojanen, op. cit., (2009), pp. 204–6.

37 See the decision of the Supreme Court KKO 2004:26; the decision of the Supreme Administrative Court 2008:25; the decision of the Insurance Court 6254:2005; and the decision of the Helsinki Administrative Court Helsingin HAO 09.10.2006 T:06/1410/1. However, the last decision was quashed by the decision of the Supreme Administrative Court 2007, p. 77.

38 The supervision by the Constitutional Law Committee is abstract, not concrete, in the sense that the relation between the norm and the circumstances of a particular case is lacking, unlike in the case of concrete (judicial) review, where a court reviews the constitutionality of legislation in the light of all relevant circumstances of a concrete case to be decided.

39 For the participation of Parliament in the national preparation of EU affairs, see N. Jääskinen and T. Kivisaari, "Parliamentary Scrutiny of European Union Affairs in Finland", in M. Wiberg (ed.), *Trying to Make Democracy Work - Nordic Parliaments and the European Union*, Stockholm: Bank of Sweden Tercentary Foundation, 1997, pp. 29–47.

7 Constitutional amendment in France

Wanda Mastor and Liliane Icher

The issue of constitutional amendment has a lot to say about the nature and the functioning of a political regime and about the Constitution itself: "the importance given to the constitutional amendment depends on the notion of Constitution in the history of contemporary constitutionalism."[1] The Constitution, charter of the rule of law, is conceived to survive; there is no doubt that the constituents worked with the idea of eternity in mind. However "paradoxically, it is the possibility of amendment that enables the Constitution's preservation."[2] Indeed, whatever the degree of rigidity of the Constitution, the text has to provide scope for adaptation and evolution, either by superficial alteration or by radical reform.

Methods of constitutional change

Although the Constitution of the Fifth French Republic, promulgated on 4 October 1958, is considered to be rigid given its restrictive amendment clause, it has been modified 24 times. This matter is ruled by Art. 89, the only one in TITLE XVI named "On amendments to the Constitution":

> The President of the Republic, on the recommendation of the Prime Minister, and Members of Parliament alike shall have the right to initiate amendments to the Constitution.
>
> A Government or a Private Member's Bill to amend the Constitution must be considered within the time limits set down in Art. 42 para 3 and be passed by the two Houses in identical terms. The amendment shall take effect after approval by referendum.
>
> However, a Government Bill to amend the Constitution shall not be submitted to referendum where the President of the Republic decides to submit it to Parliament convened in Congress; the Government Bill to amend the Constitution shall then be approved only if it is passed by a three-fifths majority of the votes cast. The Bureau of the Congress shall be that of the National Assembly.
>
> No amendment procedure shall be commenced or continued where the integrity of national territory is placed in jeopardy.

> The republican form of government shall not be the object of any amendment.

According to Professor Guy Carcassonne, this article entitles "a stage manager and four deciding actors"[3] to play a part in the amendment procedure. The stage manager is the Prime Minister, who recommends an amendment to the President of the Republic, puts the question on the agenda of both Assemblies, and supports the project in Parliament, then in front of Congress. The actors are the President, the National Assembly, the Senate, and the people. Article 89 makes several phrases stand out.

Primarily, the initiative belongs to both the President, on the proposal of the Prime Minister, and to the Members of Parliament. In the first case, the suggestion for constitutional amendment takes the form of a government bill; in the second, the form of a parliamentary bill. In fact, all 24 amendments passed since 1958 were originally government bills.

Afterwards, the bills are sent to the Commission of Constitutional Laws, Legislation and the General Administration of the Republic; other commissions can be called upon for an opinion. The shuttle between the National Assembly and the Senate continues until the bill is passed in identical terms by the two Houses, which are of equal importance. Contrary to the ordinary legislative procedure, the Government cannot interrupt the process by asking the Joint Commission or the National Assembly to give a final ruling.

The definitive adoption of the constitutional bill is subordinate to its approval by referendum. However, for the government bills (and only these), the President of the Republic can choose to submit them to a referendum or to Parliament convened in joint session. The Bureau of Congress is that of the National Assembly and meets at Versailles. Since its unique mission is to approve the text adopted by the two Houses, in the name of the sovereign people, it obviously cannot modify the text's content. Hence, the debates are confined to an explanation of the bill by all the political groups of both Assemblies. Then comes the vote, which takes place either by *appel nominal à la tribune*, or—since the modification of the regulation of 28 June 1999—by other methods decided by the Bureau of Congress. To be approved, the government bill has to be passed by a majority of three-fifths of the valid votes. It is interesting to note that, of the 24 amendments passed since 1958, only one has been submitted to a referendum.

Finally, Art. 89 defines the temporal and substantial limits of the amendment. The republican form of government cannot be changed, and no amendment can be initiated or carried out when the integrity of national territory is jeopardized. "It aims at avoiding the possibility of an institutional modification under the pressure of an occupying army like in July 1940."[4] The Constitutional Council deduced from this paragraph the impossibility of amending the Constitution when Art. 16, confederating full power to the President of the Republic, is applied.[5] In addition, the Constitution forbids resorting to the amendment procedure during the vacancy of the Presidency (Art. 7), meaning that the acting President does not have the right of initiative.

France can be proud that only the constituent power, even secondary, is sovereign. The Constitutional Council has mentioned on several occasions that "It is free to abrogate, modify or complete clauses of constitutional value in the form that it considers appropriate (. . .), nothing stands in the way of the introduction in the text of new clauses, which in the provided case, depart from constitutional rules or principles (. . .), this departure can either be express or implicit."[6] Hence, amendment is supposed to be the work of a sovereign power. Nonetheless, this deeply rooted principle has undergone many twists; it seems that the amendment has too often been used as a political weapon, essentially by the executive power.

The amendment: a sovereign work in a dream world

"The constitutional system relies on a theory that is now partly fiction and according to which the Constitution is the achievement of sovereign people, the result of their initial and unconditional power." The French doctrine usually distinguishes the original from the secondary constituent power, the latter being the only one at stake when considering the amendment of the supreme text. However, the sovereign power cannot be absolute.

The delimitation of sovereign power

"Do you want the Assembly elected today to be constituent?" The referendum on 21 October 1945 had the merit of being crystal clear and of bearing significant consequences: a "no" majority would have implied a return to the Third Republic; the "yes" victory led to the formation of the Fourth Republic. Above all, the constituent power is a "political will, that is a concrete political being," according to Carl Schmitt.[7]

"The use of the original constituent power allows a political society to endow itself with a Constitution: this initial power is considered to be sovereign, absolute and discretionary because when it expresses itself, it is, by definition, not linked to any previous or superior rule."[8] In the course of its constitutional history, France has experienced the two expressions of the original constituent power: the constituent referendum and the constituent assembly. The referendum has sometimes been turned into a plebiscite. Napoléon Bonaparte used this trick for the adoption of the Constitution on 13 December 1799, as did Louis-Napoléon Bonaparte on 4 January 1852. Notwithstanding the possibility of misuse, France also held genuine constituent referendums allowing the expression of real choices, such as the ones organized on 21 October 1945 and 28 September 1958, even though the latter simply led to the ratification of a project that the people did not contribute towards elaborating. The 1791 and 1793 Constitutions, and the 1875 constitutional laws, were adopted by a constituent assembly.

Hence, the original constituent power establishes the secondary constituent power, which does not have a concrete autonomous existence: it is defined as "one and indivisible"; it is not one power among others (legislative, executive, and judicial), "it legitimates them all."[9] The secondary constituent power is the expression of a right; the right to modify the supreme text as illustrated by the well-known Art. 28 of the Constitution of 24 June 1793: "The people always have the right to reconsider, to reform and to change their Constitution. A generation cannot subject the future generations to its own laws." Whilst the original constituent power is free, unconstrained by any rules, the secondary constituent power is bounded by limits. On the criteria of these conditions depends the identification of the Constitution either as "flexible" or "rigid." Article 89 of the current Constitution strictly circumscribes the secondary constituent power without blocking it: "the aim is to reconcile the necessity to protect the Constitution against abusive alteration with the concern not to obstruct essential modifications."[10]

Clearly, the people or Congress are the holders of the amendment competence. Since 1958, 24 amendments have occurred. All of the modifications initiated by means of Art. 89 have been passed by Parliament convened in joint session, except for an amendment launched in 2000 to shorten the presidential mandate from seven to five years.[11]

Judicial review of constitutional amendments

Whatever the procedural path followed, the constituent power is sovereign: constitutional laws are definitive and no authority, even the Constitutional Council, can control them. According to the terms of Art. 61 paras 1 and 2, the Council is only competent to control the conformity of ordinary and organic laws with the fundamental norm. Indeed, a constitutional law is the product of sovereignty, and the Council is not granted, in any text, the ability to counter it: "the Council does not hold neither from Art. 61, nor from Art. 89, nor from any other constitutional clause, the power to rule on a constitutional amendment."[12] In this decision, the Constitutional Council clearly puts an end to the interpretations that could have been deduced from the decision rendered on 2 September 1992, the so-called "Maastricht II." The Council then mentioned the sovereign nature of the constituent power, but it is "subject to, first, the limits relative to the period of the initiative as expressed in Arts. 7, 16 and 89 para 4 of the Constitution, and, second, to the respect of Art. 89 para 5 that prohibits an amendment modifying the republican form of the government." If the Constitutional Council cannot control the conformity of the constitutional laws with the supreme text, who can?

The limits of sovereign power

The limits appear in the last two paragraphs of Art. 89: "No amendment procedure shall be commenced or continued where the integrity of national territory is placed in jeopardy. The republican form of government shall not be the object of any amendment." In addition to these restrictions, amendments are forbidden when Art. 16 is applied; that is, when an acting President is in charge "in order not to add uncertainty to the crisis."[13] The last paragraph of Art. 7 of the Constitution states that the initiative right cannot be used: "Neither Articles 49 and 50 nor Article 89 of the Constitution shall be implemented during the vacancy of the

Presidency of the Republic or the period between the declaration of the permanent incapacity of the President of the Republic and the election of his successor." This boundary issue echoes the major doctrinal debate about the existence, or otherwise, of supraconstitutional principles. This matter is particularly important in some countries such as Germany. There, Art. 1 of the Fundamental Law explicitly proclaims: "Human dignity is intangible. All public powers shall respect and protect it."

In France, it is generally agreed that, except for the limits listed in Art. 89, the constituent power is sovereign, as expressed by the Constitutional Council. The supraconstitutionality of the republican form of government seems ridiculous given that, in France, the monarchic movement is marginal; this clause is symbolic. Despite everything, as underlined by Professors Hamon and Troper, "the sovereignty or the limitation of the constituent power issue is not as simple as it seems."[14] They advance at least two difficulties: the first one deals with legitimacy granted to the people by means of referendum that could appear greater to the one given to the Congress; the second one is relative to the uncertainty characterizing fundamental rights, which can always be modified by the constituent power since it is sovereign. The discrepancy between the French Constitutional Council, which refuses to control constitutional laws even when adopted by the Parliament, and some of the national constitutional courts in European countries (such as Italy, Germany, and Austria), which recognize supraconstitutional principles dominating the constituent power, is huge. The cultural and historical context has to be taken into account in this debate: the German constituent keeps in mind its painful past; the French constituent is still influenced by Siéyès' theories claiming that "the national will (. . .) only needs to be real to be legal, it is the very cause of all legality (. . .). However the Nation wishes, it is enough that it wishes and all the forms are right, and its will is always the supreme law." [15]

Given the features of the Fifth Republic, the people and the Congress really are sovereign. The constituent power has "the final word" over the Constitutional Council, as Louis Favoreu pointed out.[16] Moreover, it can contort the absolute authority of the Council's decisions; Georges Vedel explained that "judges do not govern because the sovereign can, at any moment, appear as a constituent majesty and in a bed of justice, break their judgments."[17] The constituent power is an almost absolute ruler since the unique limit it has to comply with is the symbolic ban on modifying the republican form of government. Paradoxically, this prohibition is the only one that has a supraconstitutional force, but its respect cannot be controlled and, subsequently, its eventual infringement cannot be sanctioned. Nonetheless, as Professor Carcassone remarked, "in the absurd case in which the constituent power would want something other than what the Republic and democracy command, what the people agree with or what they consent to, in brief, if the constituent power went mad and denied the rule of law or national sovereignty, the remedy to this folly could not be found in positive law."[18]

No matter who holds the constituent power, how it is used, and within what limits, the real issue is to identify which interests the amendments serve. Quoting the famous expression of Royer-Collard, even if "Constitutions are not tents pitched for the people to sleep in," it is not satisfying to readjust them constantly with more or less important consequences. It is one thing to modernize an aging text; it is another to manipulate the fundamental norm to serve policies of rulers who are not meant to remain in charge in the long run.

The amendment: a political sword in the real world

The relation between political system and constitutional amendment

The frequency of constitutional amendments simultaneously reveals and hides extra juridical considerations. Despite its sovereign nature, the constituent power depends upon the executive power. As explained earlier, the amendment initiative belongs to the President of the Republic and to the Members of Parliament, but, if the truth be told, the executive is in command of the supreme text modification. The figures are striking: all of the constitutional amendments initiated under Art. 89 were governmental bills. The Constitution is not an ordinary norm but the highest in the legal order. As such, it should be modified sparingly and sensibly; in other words, it should not be turned into a frequently used political weapon. The former President of the Constitutional Council, Yves Guéna, took offence at this prospect: "There is probably no Constitution that manages to avoid amendments. They are in a way like the text's breathing. Then, if they quicken, is it difficult not to see the symptom of a disorder or a shift from what was originally wished? On the contrary, the peculiarity of a fundamental norm should be to stand like a beacon facing a storm, facing the wind of change and the spirit of the times (. . .)."[19] However, the French Constitution has been manipulated for better or for worse depending on individual opinions. Some amendments have been useful to the rulers to perpetuate their policy; the 2008 amendment, an important modification adopted by one vote, is a significant example.

The twisted amendment

Several amendments were passed without resorting to Art. 89. First, the constitutional law of 4 June 1960, which enabled the states of the French–African community to reach independence, was ruled by the special procedure of the former Art. 85. This modification has only historical interest.

More significant is the 1962 amendment; it is also the most controversial. Indeed, the context it took place in is referred to as the "plebiscitary Republic."[20] Before the modification, the 1958 Constitution foresaw that the President of the Republic would be elected by a college composed of Members of Parliament, local councilors (rural areas being over-represented), and representatives of overseas territories. This college elected Charles de Gaulle on 21 December 1958 with 78.5 per cent of the votes. The first President of the Fifth Republic clearly announced, in his famous televised speech broadcast on 20 September 1962, that he was planning to reform the presidential election so his successors would not benefit from the same historic legitimacy: "Since the French people officially asked me to take their lead, I feel obliged to consult them upon the issue of my succession, of the mode of electing the head of state (. . .). In order for the President to bear such an office and effectively exercise his role, he needs the explicit trust of the nation."[21] Therefore, the reform looks logical and desirable, but it is the manner of achieving it that was then debated and that is still commented on today. General de Gaulle based its justification upon the democratic argument:

> When my own presidential mandate comes to an end, or if death or illness interrupts it before its term, the President of the Republic will from now on be elected by universal suffrage. Which way, in this matter that affects all French citizens, which way is appropriate for them to express their decision? I believe, by the most democratic way, by referendum. Moreover, it is also the most justified way as the French people detain the national sovereignty and, at the same time, the constituent power as well. Afterwards, he completed his reasoning with a more legal argument by pointing out that the presidential election issue belonged to one of the categories listed in Art. 11, which justified the use of a referendum for any Government Bill, which deals with the organization of the public authorities.

But his critics opposed him with what seems to be an irrefutable argument: whatever the revision, the Constitution can only be amended under Art. 89, the only one in the aptly named title "On amendments to the Constitution." Of course, President de Gaulle did not mention in his speech that, at the time he pronounced it, he was convinced that he no longer had the support of the Senate; he knowingly twisted the spirit and the letter of the supreme text to achieve his goal. On 28 October 1962, the citizens were asked the following question: "Do you approve the government bill submitted to the French people by the President of the Republic relative to the election of the President of the Republic by universal suffrage?" In response, 61.75 per cent answered "yes." The executive power paid a heavy price for this manipulation: a censure motion approved on 4 October led to the collapse of the Pompidou government and, five days later, General de Gaulle dissolved the National Assembly. The 6 November 1962 constitutional law number 62–1292, introducing universal suffrage for the presidential election, was adopted in a stormy context. When the Constitutional Council was asked by the President of the Senate to control the conformity of the referendum law with the Constitution, it declared itself reluctant to rule on a law that was the "direct expression of national sovereignty."[22]

The second attempt to amend the Constitution using Art. 11 was fatal to General de Gaulle. The bill on local organization and on Senate reform submitted by referendum to the French people on 27 April 1969 was rejected by 52.41 per cent. Since the consultation was clearly inscribed in a plebiscitary approach, the President interpreted this result as disapproval and resigned the following day. In the future, another President might try to amend the Constitution using Art. 11 for political reasons, but he or she should remember the lessons of the past: overriding Parliament bears the risk of a rejection by the people. Nevertheless, there remains another way to take advantage of a mandate in order to adopt reforms and employ the Constitution as a political forum.

The swayed amendment

All 24 modifications of the Constitution since 1958 should be put on the same level. Firstly, some of them are "obligatory." The constituent had to reform the French fundamental norm to make it comply with the requirements of international law: the disappearance of the community (4 June 1960); the European construction (25 June 1992, Treaty of Maastricht; 25 January 1999, Treaty of Amsterdam; 1 March 2005, Treaty establishing a Constitution for Europe; 4 February 2008, Treaty of Lisbon); asylum rights (25 November 1993); the International Criminal Court (8 July 1999); and the European arrest warrant (25 March 2003). There is little doubt that the French Constitution will have to undergo further amendments to comply with the extension of international treaties.

Secondly, three changes were specific to overseas territories: 25 June 1992, amendment on organic laws in the overseas territories; 20 July 1998, text on the future of New Caledonia; 23 February 2007, text on the electoral body in New Caledonia.

Thirdly, "technical" amendments constitute a separate and heterogeneous case; some are major (such as the one adopted on 27 July 1993 on the criminal liability of government ministers), others minor (such as the ones adopted on 4 August 1995 on the regime of parliamentary sessions, and on 18 June 1976 on the presidential interim).

It is worth focusing on the "greater" reforms (i.e. those amendments that have significantly changed our institutions). The following catalog is not exhaustive: the election of the President by universal suffrage (6 November 1962); the opening of the Constitutional Council recourse to parliamentary members (29 October 1974); the equality between men and women (8 July 1999); the five-year presidential mandate (2 October 2000); the decentralized organization of the Republic (28 March 2003); and the environment charter (1 March 2005). The amendment adopted on 23 July 2008 deserves special treatment as indicated by its very ambitious title: "comprehensive reform of the institutions." Nine new articles were created and 39 others were modified or completed. When constitutional law experts ponder over an eventual institutional reform, the whole constitutional community is in turmoil. Reports delivered to the President of the Republic, and the flow of information accompanying them, generate a doctrinal dynamism. For instance, the work achieved by the committee directed by Dean Georges Vedel[23] has been taught to many generations of students during the constitutional course in their first year, although some of the recommended reforms have never been voted. The Balladur report has also enjoyed the benefits of this academic advertisement; surely the constitutional law of 28 July 2008 will not eclipse the fact that some of the suggestions were not followed.

The constitutional amendment of 23 July 2008 is, in many respects, significant. Whether defended or criticized, it left no one indifferent because it was not a petty reform but a source of radical change. Observers anticipated the importance of the forthcoming amendment on 18 July 2007, when the President addressed his mission statement to the "comité de réflexion et de proposition sur la modernisation et le rééquilibrage des institutions de la République."

Conclusion

Its "composition is significant of what the political power seems to expect from an expert in constitutional law."[24] Nicolas Sarkozy had the obvious ambition to father a quasi-revolution: "It is admitted that, since (1958), and even more for the past 15 years during which many institutional changes occurred, no overall reflection has been done on the global balance of our democracy."[25] The rebalancing between the two heads of the executive power, the status of the opposition, the modification of the Supreme Council of Magistracy, or the interlocutory question of constitutionality were already considered in the first act of the reform. Most of the innovations adopted by the Congress by one valid vote (538 when 537 were needed) fulfilled the presidential wishes. The priority question of constitutionality that allows the Constitutional Council to be referred to in the case of a concrete recourse, the human rights defender and the limitation of presidential mandates, are carved in presidential stone. The same applies to the referendum on popular initiative—parliamentary initiative, actually—and the possibility for the President to address congress (ability anticipated by President Sarkozy, who gave a speech at Epinal a week before its adoption). Still, Professor Carcassone, who was part of the Balladur committee, regrets that "a bitter aftertaste remains, that of missed opportunities or at least half-grasped ones." He continues: "we could extend this inventory of disappointments and false pretences thanks to the care the government took to minimize some reforms and to deliberately ignore others."[26]

Presidential elections were held in France in April 2012. There is no doubt that when the outgoing President assesses his completed term of office, he will describe this reform as a success. Indeed, the Congress adopted all of the executive power's wishes and ignored some of the recommendations made by the Balladur committee. The most important amendment that the French Constitution experienced was not adopted by referendum but by a one-vote majority. Given its large scale, the question of identifying the constituent power, and more accurately the distinction between the original and secondary constituent power, seems as relevant as it was at the time of Sieyès. Finally, was it not the aim on 23 July 2008 to adopt a new Constitution? Should a modification that creates nine articles and affects 39 others still be called an amendment? In addition to all the questions raised, one thing is certain for the constitutional law experts: no one will benefit from trivialization of the constitutional amendments; everyone will lose from the weakening of our supreme text.

Notes

1 F. Moderne, *Réviser la Constitution, analyse comparative d'un concept indéterminé*, Dalloz, collection thèmes et commentaires, 2001, p. 1.

2 P. Ardant and B. Mathieu, *Institutions politiques et droit constitutionnel*, LGDJ, 2011, p. 89.
3 G. Carcassonne, *La Constitution*, Points, collection Essais, 2009, p. 397.
4 F. Hamon and M. Troper, *Droit constitutionnel*, LGDJ, 2011, p. 490.
5 Constitutional Council, decision no. 92–312 DC of 2 September 1992, *Traité sur l'Union Européenne*, Rec., p. 76.
6 Constitutional Council, op. cit.
7 C. Schmitt, *Théorie de la Constitution*, PUF, collection Léviathan, 1993, p. 212.
8 V. Constantinesco and S. Pierre-Caps, *Droit constitutionnel*, PUF, collection Thémis droit, 2011, p. 206.
9 Schmitt, op. cit., p. 213.
10 Ardant and Mathieu, op. cit., p. 92.
11 Loi constitutionnelle no. 2000–964 of 2 October 2000 (J.O. of 3 October 2000): réduction à cinq ans de la durée du mandat du Président de la République.
12 Constitutional Council, decision no. 2003–469 DC of 26 March 2003, *Loi constitutionnelle relative à l'organisation décentralisée de la République.*
13 Carcassonne, op. cit., p. 78.
14 Hamon and Troper, op. cit., p. 491.
15 E. Sieyes, *Qu'est-ce-que le Tiers-Etat?*, Champs, Flammarion, 1988, pp. 131–2.
16 L. Favoreu, "La légitimité du Conseil constitutionnel", *RIDC*, 1994, no. 2, p. 578.
17 G. Vedel, "Schengen et Maastricht", *Revue française de Droit Administratif*, 1992, no. 2, p. 180.
18 Carcassonne, op. cit., p. 397.
19 *Le Monde*, 25 Janvier 2000.
20 B. Chantebout, *Brève histoire politique et institutionnelle de la Ve République*, Armand Colin, 2004, p. 55.
21 20 September 1962 speech, online. Available HTTP: <http://www.charles-de-gaulle.org/pages/espace-pedagogique/le-point-sur/les-textes-a-connaitre/discours-du-20-septembre-1962.php>.
22 Conseil Constitutionnel, decision no. 62–20 DC of 6 November 1962, Rec. p. 27.
23 G. Vedel (ed.), *Propositions pour une révision de la Constitution*, La Documentation française, collection des Rapports officiels, Paris, 1993, p. 137.
24 X. Magnon, "La composition de la commission Balladur: brèves réflexions sur l'expertise en matière constitutionnelle", *Revue française de droit constitutionnel*, 2008, special issue no. 2, p. 39.
25 Mission statement of the President of the Republic of 18 July 2007, in E. Balladur (ed.), *Une Ve République plus démocratique*, Fayard, La Documentation Française, 2008, p. 207.
26 Carcassonne, op. cit., p. 403.

8 Constitutional amendments and constitutional changes in Germany

Markus Kotzur[1]

Introduction: a cultural concept of a living constitution

What can be described as a constitutional paradox is deeply rooted in constitutional history and reflected in comparative constitutional theory:[2] constitutions are instruments of stabilization as well as transition. Konrad Hesse, one of the "classic" German scholars on constitutional law, found the polarity of "fixedness" and "flexibility" to be an essential constitutional function. It allows openness where social change requires adjustment; it guarantees continuity and consistency where unavoidable change has to be based upon the firm ground of a "basic legal order."[3] In a famous dissenting opinion, US Supreme Court Justice O.W. Holmes went beyond this fixed/flexible dichotomy and emphasized the experimental character of a constitution. According to his approach, a constitution qualifies as a "living instrument": "That, at any rate, is the theory of our Constitution. It is an experiment, as all life is an experiment."[4] Holmes' concept not only refers to Karl Popper's idea of "trial and error" but also to Ernest Renan's famous definition of a nation: "A nation's existence is (. . .) a daily plebiscite, just as an individual's existence is a perpetual affirmation of life."[5] Forming a political community thus relates to a continuing cultural process and so does its constitution.[6] Peter Häberle put it the following way: "A constitution is more than a legal text: a constitution is the expression of a certain level of cultural development, it qualifies as the cultural self-manifestation of the people, it reflects their cultural heritage and is the very basis for their future hopes."[7]

These cultural dynamics are quite the opposite of what the "Fundamental Constitutions of Carolina," going back to a draft by John Locke, solemnly proclaim in their final article: "the sacred and unalterable form and rule of government of Carolina forever."[8] These dynamics are also contrary to another famous quote by the US Supreme Court in *South Carolina v United States*:[9] "The Constitution is a written instrument. As such, its meaning does not alter. That which it meant when it was adopted, it means now." If one does not want to rely on static original intentionalism but wants instead to find the right balance between the rigidity and flexibility of a constitution, one has to look at the constitution's very rationale: being the "supreme law of the land," the constitution legitimates and at the same time limits the exercise of all political powers. It regulates the relationship between political entities as well as the relationship between the State and the citizen. It structures the development of the civil society both for the present and for future generations. To some extent, a constitution has a contractual character (social contract)[10]—a contract, however, that is not completely written once and forever, but something that can be partially rewritten and constantly has to be reread. As John Hatchard says: "Overall a constitution can contribute to the development of a politically active civil society as well as promoting good governance, accountability and the rule of law."[11] To make possible political development in and for a politically active civil society, a constitution regularly enshrines regulations as to a formal amendment procedure on the one hand, and is—to a limited extent—open to informal ways of (historical, socio-political, economical, cultural) change on the other hand. The German Basic Law gives a good example of such "relative elasticity" complementary to "relative stability."[12]

The formal constitutional amendment process

The baseline provisions—Article 79 Basic Law in its constitutional contexts

Article 79 Basic Law: text and context

Article 79 Basic Law renders possible formal amendments of the German Constitution, describes the amending procedure, and limits the power to change the core principles of the Constitution. The norm thus encompasses both instruments of "relative elasticity" and guarantees of "relative stability," and in s 3, even "absolute stability." Before going on with the analysis, a terminological clarification is necessary. One has to carefully distinguish between the original formulation of a constitution, its total revision (e.g. as made possible by Art. 193 Swiss Federal Constitution), its partial revisions (by way of formal constitutional amendments), and its informal change (caused, for example, by changing realities or changing interpretations).[13] The typical amending formula of a constitution is only concerned about the partial formal amendments (or textual changes), which, however, have to be seen in the context of all the other aforementioned types of constitutional formations and reformations. In particular, the amending formula reflects, in parallel to the Preamble,[14] what Bruce Ackermann described as "constitutional moments":[15] all the extraordinary occasions and turning points in history at which a political community "rethinks its constitutional commitments and, in effect, rewrites them outside the formal constitutional amendment process."[16] Consequently, the text of the amendment formula provides for a specific constitutional narrative and resembles all the textual or non-textual contexts shaping the very identity of the Constitution. This is true in particular for Art. 79 Basic Law.

Even though the Basic Law takes on Art. 78 sentence 1 of the 1871 Constitution as well as Art. 76 s 1 sentence 1 of the Weimar Constitution (1919)—both allowing constitutional amendments by the legislature[17]—it makes very clear that after the Weimar Constitution's "silent turnover" by the National Socialist Regime, effective precautionary measures had to be introduced to protect the constitutional core principals and to preclude para-constitutional lawmaking without explicitly changing the text of the Constitution (*Verfassungsdurchbrechungen*).[18] For a human-rights-based democratic restart under the rule of law, a strict line of distinction had to be drawn between the *pouvoir constituant* and the ordinary lawmaking power.[19] Article 79 s 1 sentence 1 Basic Law thus holds: "This Basic Law may be amended only by a law expressly amending or supplementing its text."

Also, the so called "clarifying clause" (Art. 79 s 1 sentence 2 Basic Law), which relates to a certain kind of public international law (peace) treaty, can only be understood by taking into account the specific post-war situation in 1949: "In the case of an international treaty regarding a peace settlement, the preparation of a peace settlement, or the phasing out of an occupation regime, or designed to promote the defense of the Federal Republic, it shall be sufficient, for the purpose of making clear that the provisions of this Basic Law do not preclude the conclusion and entry into force of the treaty, to add language to the Basic Law that merely makes this clarification." The clause, however, only clarifies the validity of the relevant public international law treaties; it cannot change an unconstitutional treaty into one that would be in accordance with the Constitution.[20]

Article 79 s 2 Basic Law requests a qualified majority as a procedural and democratic safeguard of the amendment process; furthermore, it is typical for a federal scheme of government. Any law amending the Constitution "shall be carried by two-thirds of the members of the *Bundestag* and two-thirds of the votes of the *Bundesrat*." The *Herrenchiemsee* Draft Constitution (Art. 106) had been proceeding in a different way and asked for an additional obligatory plebiscite.[21] Whereas this requirement was given up in the final version, the participation of the *Bundesrat* remained strong. It can rely on a longstanding tradition in German constitutional history: see again Art. 78 of the Constitution of 1871 or Art. 76 s 1 sentence 3 of the Weimar Constitution (1919).[22]

Article 79 s 3, although not a unique feature of the German Constitution,[23] is decisive for Germany's constitutional identity: "Amendments to this Basic Law affecting the division of the Federation into *Länder*, their participation on principle in the legislative process, or the principles laid down in Arts. 1 and 20 shall be inadmissible." It is made very clear that even the explicit amendments of the German Constitution may not contravene its spirit, telos, and identity.[24] Thus, the potential alteration of the Constitution has to be structured by effective formal safeguards.

Formal amendments and European integration: the meaning of Art. 23 Basic Law

Today's Art. 23 Basic Law replaces the old version that contained provisions concerning the (temporary) scope of the Constitution and the possible accession of the other parts of Germany.[25] The recent version of Art. 23 Basic Law was introduced into the German Constitution in the run-up to the ratification of the Union Treaty of Maastricht in 1992 as a special provision for the European integration.[26] This is of great symbolical power: the processes of German unification and European integration would not have been possible without each other. Article 23 s 1 standardizes: "With a view to establishing a united Europe, the Federal Republic of Germany shall participate in the development of the European Union that is committed to democratic, social, and federal principles, to the rule of law, and to the principle of subsidiarity, and that guarantees a level of protection of basic rights essentially comparable to that afforded by this Basic Law. To this end, the Federation may transfer sovereign powers by a law with the consent of the *Bundesrat.* The establishment of the European Union (EU), as well as changes in its treaty foundations and comparable regulations that amend or supplement this Basic Law, or make such amendments or supplements possible, shall be subject to ss 2 and 3 of Article 79."

The guidelines for a transfer of national sovereignty to the supranational EU are determined; for this conferral, a formal constitutional amendment procedure is necessary. In that regard, Art. 23 Basic Law qualifies as an exception to the regular procedure of Art. 79 sec. 1. A transfer of sovereignty to the EU requires an "amendment" by ordinary law (*einfaches Gesetz*) in the form of a so-called approving act (*Zustimmungsgesetz*).[27] The very procedure for the transfer of national sovereignty is also the result of the federal and democratic principles laid down in Art. 20 Basic Law. Since the Federal States (*Länder*) must participate in the legislative process to safeguard democracy and federalism, their effective participation in the affairs of the EU needs to be guaranteed. This was also emphasized by the Federal Constitutional Court in its decisions on the Treaties of Maastricht[28] and Lisbon.[29] In *Maastricht*, notwithstanding its rather critical approach, the Court held that the establishment of a political union was compatible with the German Constitution, neither violating the democratic principle nor basic rights standards.[30] The Court also conceded that further, although limited, steps of integration might be constitutional.[31] The EU as such could rely, according to the bench, on a sufficient level of democratic legitimacy.[32] In the controversial *Lisbon* judgment, Karlsruhe once again had to decide on how far European integration might go under the Basic Law. The Court clearly stated that according to Arts. 23 and 79 ss 2 and 3 Basic Law, the European integration process reached its limits. Beyond *Lisbon*, further integration would require constitutional amendments, if not a decision based upon Art. 146 Basic Law.

The historical outset

At the time the Constitution was drafted, Germany lacked full sovereignty and the people in the Soviet-occupied zone—later to become the German Democratic Republic—could not exercise their constitutive power.[33] That had been clearly expressed by the Preamble to the Basic Law in its original version.[34] A provisional Constitution[35] should create provisional political unity for a formerly united but now fragmented Federal State.[36] The very nature of the new Basic Law, however, was anything but transitional: it was an enduring, if not (see Art. 79 sec. 3 Basic Law) everlasting, catharsis—that is to say, an identity-building exercise, turning away from the inhuman, criminal, and "rule of law" National Socialist Regime.[37]

This catharsis includes a new concept of sovereignty. Sovereignty had to be seen no longer as an absolute power, including the unbound decision on war and peace; instead, sovereignty had to be conceived in an instrumental way as serving the human being—as a means to ensure freedom, peace, and security.[38] Consequently, the *pouvoir constituant* of the German people was never unlimited; it was never an "unbound decision *ex nihilo*," as Carl Schmitt and his epigones had implied.[39] Exercising the constituent power qualified as a cultural process in the course of which the people's right to self-determination is realized,[40] whereas the realization itself remains bound by cogent public international law (*ius cogens*), general principles of justice, and first and foremost by the dignity of the human being (see Art. 1 Basic Law).[41]

Germany's "full sovereignty" could only be achieved during the reunification process when the Allied Powers, the former German Democratic Republic, and the Federal Republic of Germany agreed on the so-called "2 plus 4" Treaty (or Treaty on the Final Settlement with Respect to Germany).[42] This "victory" of sovereignty, however, was closely connected with the European integration process. Only a reunited Germany integrated in the then European Community (today, the European Union) could count on a "yes" vote by the Allied Powers and the international community as such.[43] The losses of sovereignty caused by the European integration process made possible a "fully sovereign" Germany, if this paradox is allowed.[44]

Apart from the question of sovereignty, another constitutive moment for the newly drafted Basic Law has to be mentioned. Being very well aware of the classic and fruitful constitutional debates during the Weimar period (e.g. the distinction between "*Verfassung*" and "*Verfassungsgesetz*" by C. Schmitt),[45] the Basic Law should overcome the fundamental weaknesses of the Weimar Constitution. Therefore, not only procedural but also substantial limitations regarding potential constitutional revisions had to be established. The procedural limitations are, in fact, not only in line with many foreign archetypes[46] but also deeply rooted in German constitutional history (especially with respect to a quorum). Substantive limitations, though, were alien to the German Constitution prior to the 1949 Basic Law.[47] The primary motivation for the establishment of substantive limitations is an obvious "lesson learned." The seizure of power (*Machtergreifung*) by the Nazi regime at the end of the Weimar Republic via the enactment of the so-called "Enabling Act" (*Ermächtigungsgesetz*) was in absolute conformity with the formal constitutional requirements of the Weimar Constitution. However, it entitled the government to act beyond the democratic and "rule of law"-based constitutional framework,[48] and betrayed its values in the most outrageous sense.

Finally, a third aspect has to be pointed out. Modern constitutionalism, distinguishing between the *pouvoir constituant* and the *pouvoir constitué*,[49] is closely linked with the doctrine of popular sovereignty (see Art. 20 sec. 1 Basic Law). Given that link, any amendment of the Constitution has to be legitimized by the people. Consequently, most modern constitutions require a (more or less) direct participation of the people in the amending process.[50] In this regard, the German Basic Law is an exception. It is the legislature that can change the Constitution without any direct popular participation.[51] The literature speaks of a unique "monopolization of amendment power by the legislature" being "rare among constitutional democracies," and being based rather on a constitutional than a democratic tradition.[52] Nevertheless, the barriers to amendments are very high, due to the quorum necessary in the *Bundestag* as well as in the *Bundesrat.*[53] Furthermore, changes to the Constitution are no longer subject to the discretion of the constitutional organs[54] but instead have to be in strict accordance with the constitutional requirements.

Boundaries for constitutional revisions

Procedural limitations

a) *Explicit change of the wording of the Constitution* (Art. 79 sec. 1 sentence 1). In contrast to the Weimar Constitution,[55] amendments to the Basic Law require an explicit change of the wording in order to be valid.[56] This is to safeguard that all changes to the Constitution are to be carried out under one umbrella, that of the Constitution ("*Verhinderungformelle Verfassungsdurchbrechungen*").[57] This requirement of incorporation (*Vermeidung von Nebenverfassungen*),[58] moreover, guarantees constitutional transparency and legal certainty. It is disputed whether the provisions of Art. 23 para 1 sentence 3 and Art. 24 para 1 Basic Law constitute exceptions to the principle that constitutional amendments have to be explicit as they provide for the delegation of sovereign rights to other entities.[59]
b) *Quorum* (Art. 79 sec. 2). Any law changing the Constitution requires the support of both the *Bundestag* (Lower House) and the *Bundesrat* (Upper House). By means of involving the *Bundesrat* in the process of constitutional amendments, not only is the participation of the Federal States (*Länder*) guaranteed, but also an additional hurdle is being established for amending the Constitution. The two-fold quorum prevents parties or large coalitions from easily amending the Constitution, even though they represent a vast majority in the *Bundestag*. As the federal level (*Bundestag*) and the State level (*Bundesrat*) are, in terms of the governing political parties, distinct from one another (also due to the overlapping legislative periods), it is highly unlikely that one political party is predominant at both levels. A cross-party consensus is therefore required to successfully amend the Constitution. An empirical fact, however, remains remarkable in this context: whereas the quorum hurdle seems rather high, the huge number of laws changing the German Constitution suggests it is rather a low hurdle.[60]

Substantive limitations

As already stated above, it is a *constitutive part* of Germany's constitutional identity that certain *substantial changes* to the Constitution are inadmissible. This is enshrined in the so-called "Eternity or Perpetuity Clause" of Art. 79 sec. 3, referring to Arts.

1 and 20 Basic Law (and not to the whole bill of rights). Historically, the Norwegian Constitution of 1814 (Art. 112) gives the first example of such a guarantee, which, since then, has caused manifold academic disputes. Nevertheless, a large number of modern constitutions, especially in States that are "in transition" to overcome their authoritarian past, follow the Norwegian and, respectively, the German example.[61] It would, of course, be an illusion to believe that "eternity clauses" could impede revolutionary changes; they can, however, unmask the pseudo-legality of revolutionary upheavals[62] and thus prove the impossibility of legal revolutions.[63] The more a political community needs to assure itself of its well-fortified democracy, the more it might want to rely on the codification of identity-shaping (primarily anti-totalitarian) perpetuity clauses. Countries such as Switzerland, trusting in a constitutional culture, which sustain themselves and self-evidently secure all elements of their identity, do not need written eternity clauses: such constitutional cultures see themselves as "perpetual in and of themselves."[64] France, for example, only guarantees the "Republic" as perpetual (French Constitution of 1958, Art. 89 para 5).[65]

Article 79 s 3 Basic Law can only bind the *pouvoir constitué*, in other words the legislature, but not constitutionally limit the *pouvoir constituant*.[66] The article in itself is, however, in contrast to Art. 79 ss 1 and 2 Basic Law, not subject to any change by the *pouvoir constitué*.[67] Given the strict limits that Art. 79 s 3 Basic Law imposes on the legislature, it has to be construed as well as interpreted in a restrictive way. An extensive interpretation would cause dangerous inflexibility. As shown above, it remains indispensable for a constitution to be able to take into account new developments and to react to changing realities.[68] Consequently, what Art. 79 s 3 Basic Law renders inadmissible is not a change of the wording, especially of Arts. 1 and 20 Basic Law. What must not be changed or, even worse, completely abandoned are merely the principles enshrined in these Articles. At the same time, however, this both limits and extends the scope of application. On the one hand, even Arts. 1 and 20 Basic Law could be changed if only their core principles stay untouched. On the other hand, even beyond the explicitly mentioned Arts. 1 and 20, the change of other articles would be null and void if such a change would affect their core principles. This is true in particular for the guarantee of human dignity being the basis of many human rights (from the prohibition of torture to the right of asylum, from minimum social standards of living to democratic participation), as recently stated in the *Lisbon* decision of the Federal Constitutional Court.[69] Thus, Art. 79 s 3 Basic Law marks a "limit of possible legal regulation" (a "*Schwelle des juristisch Normierbaren*" as an often-cited quote in German constitutional scholarship States).[70] This limit concerns the following contents and thus governs the following fields:

a) *Federalism: division of the federation into states.* Relying on a longstanding tradition of federalism, Art. 79 s 3 Basic Law protects the federal system of government. The norm refers to federalism as such but does not encompass a guarantee of the existence of each Federal State as an entity of its own. The Basic Law itself allows, in Art. 29, a new delimitation of the *Länder* to "ensure that each

Land be of a size and capacity to perform its functions effectively."[71] Theoretically speaking, a federation consisting of two states only could be constitutional. Of course, each federal state has to have a minimum of substantial competences and thus a minimum of material autonomy[72] (such as the free determination of the internal political structure; in particular, the power to enact its own constitution and sufficient participation in the overall tax income to ensure financial independence).[73] Finally, the existing *Länder* may not be deprived of their state quality and become mere territorial partitions.[74]

b) *Participation of the states in the legislative process*. Furthermore, the *Länder* are entitled, in principle, to participate in the formal legislative process at the federal level.[75] The provision does not pose any specific requirement as to how the participation has to be developed. Even indirect participation of the states suffices for this requirement. However, direct involvement of the states is also foreseen by the Constitution (e.g. Arts. 138 and 144 Basic Law). As the participation of the states is only guaranteed in principle, situations are conceivable when their participation is suspended for a limited period of time.[76] The more the decisions are made not by the legislative but by the executive branch, the less effective the *Länder* participation becomes in the federal legislative process. Hence, such tendencies of "executive federalism"[77] (informal lawmaking, intergovernmental or supranational decision-making processes without sufficient parliamentary control) have been harshly criticized.[78] The risk of a "global technocracy" does not only endanger democracy as such, but also democratic decision-making processes in their federal specifications.[79]

c) *Principles laid down in Art. 1 Basic Law*. Whereas the previous substantial limitations restricted the *pouvoir constitué* in its organizational set-up, the restrictions laid down by Art. 1 Basic Law provide for the relationship between the State and the individual.[80] Article 1 provides for three different principles in three paragraphs. Any changes to the Constitution affecting those principles are inadmissible. First and foremost, sec. 1 has to be mentioned: "Human dignity shall be inviolable. To respect and protect it shall be the duty of all state authority." In consequence thereof, and re-emphasizing the promises and commitments given in the Preamble, the "German people therefore acknowledge inviolable and inalienable human rights as the basis of every community, of peace and of justice in the world" (s 2). Finally, s 3 states: "The following basic rights shall bind the legislature, the executive, and the judiciary as directly applicable law."

The universality of human rights becomes most obvious where human dignity is the source of legitimacy.[81] Dignity is granted to any person anywhere, under whatever circumstance. It is granted to the human being just because of being a "human being."[82] By means of establishing that the respect for human dignity shall be the underlying principle of any State authority,[83] the *pouvoir constituant* tried to safeguard that nothing comparable to what happened during World War II in Nazi Germany should ever happen again. In particular, the third paragraph clarifies that in case of doubt, the basic rights entitle people to subjective rights, entitling the individual to claim those rights. It also safeguards that the State is at all times bound by a specific set of basic rights and freedoms. As of today, human dignity provisions have worldwide acceptance.[84] The EU Charter of Human Rights, an integral part of EU primary law, begins with reference to human dignity. The Charter makes clear that human dignity entitles the human being to certain rights.[85]

d) *Principles laid down in Art. 20 Basic Law.* The principles laid down in Art. 20 Basic Law are numerous and find their equivalent in many other provisions in the Constitution. Among these principles are the statehood of Germany, irrespective of any integration efforts (s 1), and the republican form of government. Section 1 clearly states: "Germany is a republic." The federal scheme of government is in addition to the explicit guarantee of federalism also protected via Art. 20 s 1 Basic Law: "Germany is a federal state." Moreover, there is qualification of Germany as a welfare state (s 1). Most fundamentally, however, s 2 enshrines the democratic form of government: "Germany is a democratic state," based upon the sovereignty of the people. A leading principle of democratic decision-making is majority rule.[86] Nevertheless, in a democracy minorities also have to be protected. Article 20 s 3 Basic Law provides for the "rule of law" foundations. This includes a system of effective checks and balances, which furthermore requires that all branches of government (legislature, executive, judiciary) are bound by the constitutional order (s 3).[87] It is interesting to note that the right to resistance (Art. 20 s 4) does not fall within the scope of Art. 79 s 3.[88]

In particular, Art. 79 Basic Law and the process of European integration

Article 79 ss 2 and 3 Basic Law, among others, determine the constitutional amendments for the process of European integration. The famous *Maastricht* and *Lisbon* decisions have already been referred to, but the responsibility for allowing/controlling the supranational integration process (*Integrationsverantwortung*) and protecting the constitutional identity (*Verfassungsidentität*) shall be mentioned once again.[89] Article 79 ss 2 and 3 Basic Law provides the procedural structure for "European" amendments (two-thirds majority in the *Bundestag* as well as the *Bundesrat*). Section 3 formulates the substantive limits that European integration is bound by: the federal structure—including the effective participation of the *Länder*, human dignity as laid down in Art. 1 Basic Law—and the principles enshrined in Art. 20 Basic Law are inviolable.

Revision of the Constitution in its entirety (Art. 146 Basic Law)

From a comparative point of view, Art. 146 Basic Law can be qualified as a unique norm.[90] It might reach even beyond the scope of another prominent example of a constitution opening up to the possibility of its own "total revision" (as opposed to partial formal amendments and informal constitutional changes)—Art. 193

Swiss Federal Constitution: "A total revision of the Federal Constitution may be proposed by the People or by either of the two Councils or be decreed by the Federal Assembly."[91] What Art. 146 Basic Law addresses is a completely new "constitutional formation."[92] The power to instigate this formation is consigned to the people. Accordingly, Art. 146 Basic Law refers to and, at the same time, re-confirms, the pre-constitutional right of a people to give itself a constitution that all legitimate State authority is founded in and all legitimate public power is derived from (the *pouvoir constituant* in the classic terminology of Abbé Sieyès).[93] The citizens do "form the Nation, in the sense of being the moral title holders of sovereignty";[94] it is within their power and right of self-determination to decide upon the very foundations of their political community. Since the East German citizens could not enjoy this right in 1949, Art. 146 Basic Law was originally meant to replace the provisional Basic Law by a then full constitution legitimized by the *pouvoir constituant* of the entire German people.[95] When the occasion came, in the course of the reunification process, that chance—for good political reasons—was ignored. Article 23 Basic Law, in its old version, simply allowed the accession of the five *new Länder* (Brandenburg, Mecklenburg-Western Pomerania, Saxony, Saxony-Anhalt, and Thuringia).[96] Nevertheless, this does not hinder the German people from one day totally revising the old Constitution and giving themselves a (completely) new Constitution. They still possess, as holders of democratic sovereignty, their constitution-making power[97] and could exercise this power via plebiscite.[98]

Examples of formal constitutional amendments that have been made so far

The German Basic Law has undergone many changes since its drafting and its entry into force in 1949.[99] These changes become obvious if a comparison is made between the original text and its up-to-date version. In an analysis on the occasion of the German Constitution's 50th anniversary (1999), Andreas Busch stressed some interesting quantitative aspects: "Comparing today's Grundgesetz with the original text of 1949, it becomes evident at first sight that there were substantial changes in the Constitution. While the Grundgesetz consisted of 146 articles in 1949, it had grown to 171 articles by 1980 . . . Until 1994, another 12 articles had been added to bring the total to 183. Forty articles were added during the course of 50 years, three articles deleted, so that the net growth was 37 constitutional articles. As a consequence, the text length has been substantially altered: from 10,636 words in 1949 it had grown to 17,050 words by early 1994; after the changes initiated by the Joint Constitutional Commission in late 1994 and some further additions, the text length was 19,121 words in the summer of 1998. The text of the Grundgesetz has thus nearly been doubled over that of 1949."[100]

As important as quantitative indicators may be, simply counting the number of formal amendments would neither cover the additional mechanisms of informal change nor shed light on the reasons for formal changes.[101] For a typology of the constitutional amendments, one has to focus on the historical context.

The 1949 Basic Law was hastily created to be a provisional constitutional scheme whilst the German constituent was lacking full sovereignty. Many temporary solutions were incorporated.[102] Thus, the many formal changes that took place afterwards can be perceived as a process of "supplementing and completing a constitution that initially was consciously incomplete," and that "only won its full identity with the peak of the changes in the 1960s and 1970s."[103] In the early years, regulations on a system of financial compensation for losses during wartimes (especially for forced displacement) or on liabilities resulting from the war had to be implemented.[104] Later on, "the development of a state fragment (. . .) to a fully-fledged State" gave rise to the (highly controversial) amendments regarding defense and emergency regulations.[105] More and more powers were concentrated at the federal level (the financial reforms of the late 1960s give only one example) and, for good reasons, Konrad Hesse spoke of an increasingly "unitarian" federal system.[106]

But it is not only national matters (e.g. the German reunification)[107] that influence and promote the change of the Constitution. Due to globalization, the law and especially the Constitution have reacted to external influences. As shown above, Arts. 23 and 24 Basic Law were changed to allow further European integration. A new balance between the national and the supranational level (including institutional adjustments) had to be reached,[108] and even though the wording of Art. 59 s 2 Basic Law remained untouched, the external representation of Germany was strongly influenced "by Europe."[109] Many more examples stemming from different fields of constitutional law could be given, most recently limits on public deficit spending in Arts. 109 and 115 Basic Law. However, it is the overall picture rather than the details that remains decisive: there is indeed a tendency towards a rather overly comprehensive regulation instead of more flexible, abstract, and principle-based standards.[110]

Informal methods of constitutional change

What is meant by "Verfassungswandel"

Following the concept of a "living constitution," the basic and "supreme law of the land" must, notwithstanding its general design for longevity, take into account changing realities and the need to adjust to these realities. The Ukrainian Constitution of 1996 gives one striking example: it has enshrined a hitherto unique Chernobyl Article (Art. 16) after the nuclear disaster in 1986.[111] New Eastern European constitutions invented anti-state-ideology clauses as a clear reaction to their experiences with totalitarian Marxist–Leninist regimes and, in parallel transformation situations, African or Latin American constitutions explicitly recognize political pluralism.[112] However, new realities can also change the meaning of constitutional norms without any alteration of their relevant texts.[113]

This phenomenon is what is meant by "constitutional change" (*Verfassungswandel*).[114] "*Verfassungswandel*" implicitly refers to a changing reference framework of a constitution.[115] It is dependent on many different factors such as judicial activism, political decisions, or social development.[116] Closely related to "constitutional change" is the development of new constitutional customary law ("*Verfassungsgewohnheitsrecht*"). Both forms of constitutional dynamics have one limit in common: changes to a constitution must not lead to an erosion of its substance.[117] And both forms of constitutional dynamics may later require a textual clarification (in Swiss constitutional law, the term "*Nachführung des Verfassungstextes*"—adjusting the text of the constitution to its former unwritten changes—is a very proper description).[118]

External factors causing "Verfassungswandel"

A preliminary remark: the concept of "open statehood" (Offene Staatlichkeit des Grundgesetzes)

External factors such as international and supranational law, the decisions of international courts and tribunals, global lawmaking trends or transnational political debates gain an increasing influence on constitution-building (or constitutional formation), constitutional amendments, and constitutional change.[119] In the twenty-first century, the national State is not closed and autochthonous any more. The German Basic Law reflects this very well. Already in the early years, the German constitutional law literature referred to a "*demokratischen Wendung zu einer internationalistischen Grundeinstellung*" (democratic turn towards an internationally open paradigm).[120] It was Klaus Vogel who had even more accurately foreseen recent "beyond the state" tendencies, when he developed his concept of "*offene Staatlichkeit*" ("open statehood").[121] In the Preamble or in Arts. 23, 25, 26, 59 Basic Law, he found fruitful textual ground for his theory. Even the eternity clause of Art. 79 s 3 Basic Law can be read in the light of the "open-statehood idea": the openness of the Basic Law for the European and international realm is unalterable. The "never again" determination after 1945 is also a "never again" to the closed-nation State.[122]

Today, modern constitutionalism in general has to be aware that the formerly autochthonous Nation State facing the challenges of globalization is integrated in transnational schemes of governance. The most commonly used metaphor for this multilayered structure of overlapping "constitutional regimes" is one of "multi-level constitutionalism."[123] Others speak of constitutional pluralism.[124] Multilevel constitutionalism addresses the "simultaneous presence of various integrated constitutional levels in the same legal space."[125] This presence, however, is not static but delineates an "ongoing process of establishing new structures of government complementary to and building upon—while also changing—existing forms of self-organization of the people or society."[126] Among the most important parameters of this so-called "ongoing process" are the extent of voluntary forfeiture of sovereignty to international organizations and intergovernmental bodies, and the rise and growing influence of non-state actors (such as NGOs, transnational enterprises etc.) respectively, but also the continued viability of the Nation State.

Human relationships (as well as order-building mechanisms necessary for human relationships in freedom, peace, and security) are no longer dependent on only one legal system. Consequently, the normative answer to the internal effects and external dimensions of globalization is given by a model of multiple, intertwined legal systems. Such an overly complex multitude is reflected in terms like *polysystémie normative*[127] or legal pluralism.[128] These theories draw attention to "the possibility that within the same social order, or social or geographical space, more than one body of law, pertaining to more or less the same set of activities, may co-exist." Global legal pluralism, moreover, has to take into account the different and differentiated sets of norms existing on the subnational, the national, the regional, and the international level.

This mixed texture, however, might lead to manifold fragmentations within the legal system.[129] It is the very aim of a constitutional scheme if not to overcome then to integrate the fragmented bodies of the law, human rights law and the rule of law being the most important means of doing so. The governance debate and constitutional theories focusing on private actors, such as Gunther Teubner's "global civil constitutionalism" paradigm,[130] have to be taken into account too.

The global plane

a) *Public international law.* Norms and doctrines of public international law can have a strong impact on national constitutions. This is especially true for the United Nations Charter, other universal UN texts, and universal human rights treaties. Article 26 Basic Law itself translates Art. 2 No. 4 UN Charter into German Constitutional Law.[131] When characterizing the fundamental principles of the constitutional state, Peter Häberle gives some further illustrative examples from a comparative point of view.[132] The specific UN texts on the protection of people with disabilities or children are of worldwide success when reflected in new constitutional provisions (Art. 68 s 3 of the Polish Constitution with regard to those with disabilities, Art. 28 of the South African Constitution, and Art. 72 of the Polish Constitution with regard to the emerging rights of children). National constitutions referring not only to the wording but also to the spirit of international human rights documents have to be particularly emphasized. They "merge" national and international standards in some way. In such a "melting pot," universal principles more easily come into being and create elements of a universal legal order for all humankind.[133] The incorporation and implementation of universal human rights into particular national constitutions helps to make human rights effective. The national legal orders and the international law form an especially co-operative legal order. Human rights are to be made effective in co-operation between national, regional, and international political entities: States, international organizations, and supranational organizations. Of course, the implementation is not a guarantee of immediate effectiveness; it is just a (sometimes very difficult) beginning.

Wherever the framers or "changers" of a constitution take universal standards and worldwide legal networks for granted in the process of globalization—first and foremost because of their own experience—the constitution is open for the world beyond the national State. This openness becomes a key element forming the constitution's very identity.[134]

b) *Comparative constitutional law in a global perspective: universal standards as an incentive for constitutional change.* The same lessons of international "comparative" openness can be learned if one focuses on comparative constitutional law from a global perspective. Innovative constitutional clauses in one State might be the incentive for a constitutional amendment in another State. Doctrines might mutually influence the relevant academic communities. A constitutional court might be inspired by the decisions of other constitutional courts. Today, in particular, human rights form specific constitutional guarantees as well as universal principles. They can give rise to an inter-constitutional global law that again can cause formal as well as informal changes of national constitutions. Furthermore, many classical national policy objectives or basic institutional principles (as, for example, guaranteed by Art. 20 Basic Law) reach far beyond the national State. Public welfare, public services, and public utilities, the protection of the environment, the struggle for security, and so many other duties and obligations cannot be properly fulfilled by the autochthonous national State any more.

Comparison requires cultural sensitivity. A comparative approach not only deals with the comparison of legal texts, but also with the broader cultural, economical, and political "ambience," and so on. Universal principles are the possible outcome of a comparative process, and universality itself is a process rather than an historic idea, a cultural product of real-world interaction—political, scientific, philosophical, and most importantly communicative interaction—rather than Platonic heritage. Or, to put it in slightly simplifying terms, one has to look for certain legal principles common to a vast majority of the legal systems and cultures all over the world.[135] This approach, though, brings up the problem of selection. Since a comparison of everything with everything is impossible, one has to examine which legal cultures to select. Are there some more developed legal systems with a longstanding tradition of human rights, democracy, and a highly developed rule of legal thinking that could play a leading role? Or, on the other hand, are the young and innovative legal systems and constitutions a challenge to re-read, reconstruct or deconstruct even the great classical documents, such as the French Declaration of 1789 or the US Federal Constitution of 1787? One answer is obvious. Given the sovereign equality of all States (Art. 2 No. 1 UN Charter), the formula "civilized nations" in Art. 38 s 1 lit c Statute of the International Court of Justice does not provide for reasonable criteria. A self-centered Eurocentric view has to be overcome.[136]

The European plane

a) *The Council of Europe and its law, in particular the European Convention on Human Rights.* To focus on the European perspective and its law, the European Convention on Human Rights (ECHR) in particular needs to be examined.

The Convention was developed by the Council of Europe and qualifies as the oldest legally binding treaty in the field of regional human rights protection.[137] It establishes at the very least a common minimum standard of human rights protection[138] and aims to safeguard the individual against human rights violations in her or his own State.[139] To do so effectively, the European Court of Human Rights, following the 11th Protocol to the Convention of Human Rights, allows individual complaints.[140] Article 1 of the ECHR clearly determines the scope of application: "The High Contracting Parties shall secure to everyone within their jurisdiction the rights and freedoms defined in Section I of this Convention." When the ECHR entered into force, only States could become parties to the treaty. Protocol No. 14 to the ECHR, which entered into force in June 2010, has now changed this requirement and paved the way for membership of the EU.[141] The legal status the ECHR enjoys differs from Member State to Member State. In Germany, the implementation was achieved by the Approval Law (*Zustimmmungsgesetz*) according to Art. 59 s 2 Basic Law in 1952. Therefore, the Convention does not enjoy constitutional status but applies as a general federal law (*einfaches Bundesgesetz*).[142] Notwithstanding the question of constitutional hierarchy, all domestic laws including the Constitution have to be interpreted in the light of the ECHR (also taking into account the interpretation by the European Court of Human Rights). The consequence of this interpretational standard can be seen in the *Görgülü* case, when the Federal Constitutional Court required German courts to consider, as far as possible, the standards as developed by the European Court of Human Rights.[143]

b) *European Union Law.* The European Charter of Fundamental Rights was developed by a Convention in 1999/2000 and based on the previous legal sources of human rights on the European level, namely the fundamental freedoms as developed by the European Court of Justice (ECJ), the ECHR, and the fundamental rights of the Member States as general principles of law. Primarily, the European Charter of Fundamental Rights qualified as a "solemn proclamation" and thus "soft law" only. When the Treaty of Lisbon entered into force, it became the binding primary law of the European Union (Art. 6 s 1 Treaty on the Functioning of the European Union [TFEU]).[144] As shown above with respect to the ECHR, national constitutional law has to be interpreted in light of the Charter too.[145] Furthermore, the preliminary rulings procedure (Art. 267 TFEU) can serve as a means for constitutional change. When the ECJ decides the question presented with effect *erga omnes*,[146] this might also have some effect on the national constitutions.

c) *Lessons learned: comparative constitutional law in a European perspective.* Given a common European legal culture, determined by historical, socio-political, economic, and cultural aspects,[147] law comparison is a particularly fruitful instrument and might cause constitutional change. One constitutional system can learn from the other and implement domestically what has elsewhere proved to be successful. Preambles of treaties and constitutions give evidence of what the European legal cultures do have in common. The Preamble of the Treaty on European Union (TEU) speaks of the "common cultural, religious and humanistic heritage of Europe." The Preamble of the European Charter on Human Rights addresses the "awareness of the common spiritual–religious and moral heritage in awareness of the undividingly and universal human dignity." Furthermore, it refers to a "common heritage of political traditions, ideals, freedom and the rule of law." The TFEU comprises an Article on culture (167) demanding that "the Union shall contribute to the flowering of the cultures of the Member States while respecting their national and regional diversity and at the same time bringing the common cultural heritage to the fore." Culture, admittedly a rather unspecific and ambiguous term, nevertheless characterizes the reality and identity of Europe. It has to be understood in an open and dynamic way;[148] its dynamics, at the same time, might cause constitutional change and certainly influence legal interpretation.

Internal factors causing "Verfassungswandel"

The internal factors as well as the actors of constitutional change are manifold: judges and judge-made law given the power of judicial review; political actors developing new political strategies; and, last but not least, the citizens bringing their cases to the courts.[149] In particular, judges have a certain margin of appreciation and can actively develop the law.[150] Not infrequently, their decisions also influence the lawmaker. In Germany, this is especially true for the Federal Constitutional Court, due to its high esteem.[151] Among the political actors, political parties, single Members of Parliament, factions, the opposition, lobbyists, or non-governmental organizations have to be mentioned. The citizen is of relevance regarding the aforementioned actors. He or she might start a lawsuit that ends with a "leading case" creating new insights and interpretations, and thus has the potential of constitutional change. He or she furthermore influences the politics participating in periodic elections or by starting a citizens' initiative.

Constitutional amendments and constitutional change in the perspective of European and global constitutionalism

Finally, the concept of multilevel constitutionalism has to be re-addressed. Constitutional change can only be analyzed in the perspective of European, if not global, constitutionalism. It is constitutionalism beyond the Nation State[152] that forces us to rethink mechanisms of constitutional change as reactions to "extra-national" challenges. Ingolf Pernice has examined this with regard to the federal system in Germany and the pre-federal European Union.[153] Parallel structures can be found in the US constitutional system. Binding law on one level influences the law of the others. Binding international law limits the sovereign power of the Nation State and determines the content of internal law. Conversely, constitutional concepts are transferred to the transnational level as the well-known formula of a constitutionalization of the international community implies.[154] These interdependencies form the framework of constitutional changes, which, on the other hand, might reframe the transnational legal order. The complexity might be confusing but "such is reality."

Conclusions

State and society are—as well as all other forms of subnational, national, or transnational political communities—*semper reformanda*; and so are their respective constitutions. The constitution and the constitutional State based upon its very foundations have to be seen as the historical results of revolutions and evolutions.[155] To secure their own future, they require a multiplicity of methods and procedures that allow reforms and make possible change, but also set limits to alteration where identity-shaping, and thus unchangeable, baseline principles such as human dignity, elementary human rights, the rule of law, or a democratic form of government (if not governance) are at stake.[156] Apart from these unmodifiable characteristics, in an open society a constitution will always be a "contested order."[157] Within given limits, possible constitutional changes—the formal as well as the informal ones—thus qualify as the result of order-building contests. In the globalized world of the twenty-first century, such contests always have an international dimension and may also cause a competition between different legal systems and constitutional orders respectively.[158] Consequently, the questions of constitutional amendments and informal constitutional changes require a comparative analysis. They form one chapter in what should become a treatise on global constitutionalism.[159]

The reason for this demanding project is obvious. National constitutions face global interdependencies with other constitutional systems, and are influenced by transnational constitutional schemes. These complex linkages and intertwined structures exist with the very making of a constitution. They continue when constitutional reforms are introduced and where constitutional interpretation takes place. The aforementioned global constitutionalism requires adequate methodological instruments. A culturally sensitive comparison of constitutions, legal enactments, judgments, legal practice, contexts, and, not the least, language become of utmost importance.[160] On the practical side, the previously mentioned competition between different legal systems and legal cultures can be seen as a significant consequence. Given these competitive processes in cultural diversity, one has to be aware that a one-way export of Western ideas (e.g. the Westminster export constitution model bestowed upon the newly independent states without sufficient public debate) would fall short of creating constitutional identities. Constitutional comparison implies the dynamics of mutual learning.[161] "Exported ideas" will not be successful without an indigenous—that is to say, a cultural—adoption.[162] The citizens have to be enabled to recognize a constitutional document as their living constitution and they need to develop what can be called a constitutional ethos.[163] This constitutional ethos also depends on the interpretative process. It is rather doubtful whether rules or principles of interpretation, enshrined in the written constitution, guarantee the necessary interpretative flexibility. The law might sometimes be smarter than the lawmaker, require open means of interpretation, and include all members of an open society as interpreters of a dynamic constitution.[164] Formal constitutional amendments, informal constitutional change, and productive constitutional interpretation go hand-in-hand. They have one aim in common: to secure the constitution for future generations and, at the same time, to secure the future of the constitution.

Notes

1 Many thanks to my scientific research assistant Mrs Giannina-Louisa Wille for her most valuable contributions.

2 P. Häberle, *Europäische Verfassungslehre*, Nomos, 7th edn, 2011, p. 462.

3 K. Hesse, *Grundzüge des Verfassungsrechts der Bundesrepublik Deutschland*, 20th edn, 1995, (reprint 2000), F. Müller, p. 15. Furthermore A. Busch, *The Grundgesetz after 50 Years: Analyzing Changes in the German Constitution*, 1999, Minda de Gunzburg. Center for European Studies, p. 8: "Constitutions therefore are designed for longevity. Thus they are an institutional answer to the demand for stability. Constitutional provisions should not be at the disposition of the government or the parliamentary majority of the day."

4 *Abrams v United States* (250 U.S. 616 [1919]).

5 E. Renan, "What is a Nation? (Qu'est-ce qu'une nation?)", Lecture at Sorbonne, 11 March 1882, in G. Eley and R.G. Suny (eds), *Becoming National: A Reader*, Oxford University Press, 1996, pp. 41–55.

6 The understanding of the "constitution as a public process" has been developed by P. Häberle, *Verfassung als öffentlicher Prozess*, Duncker and Humblot, 1st edn, 1978 and Duncker and Humblot, 3rd edn, 1998. The theory found widespread international reception: see e.g. J. Luther, "La Scienza häberliana delle constituzioni", in P. Comanducci and R. Gustiano *Analisi e diritto*, 2001, p. 105.

7 P. Häberle, *Verfassungslehre als Kulturwissenschaft*, Duncker and Humblot, 2nd edn, 1998, p. 1123.

8 Quoted after H. Dreier, in H. Dreier (ed.), *GG-Kommentar*, Mohr, vol. II, 2nd edn, 2006, Art. 79 s 2 para 1; H. Dreier himself refers to B.P. Poore (ed.), *The Federal and State Constitutions, Colonial Charters, and other Organic Law of the United States*, 2nd edn, Part 2, 1878, p. 1408.

9 *South Carolina v United States* (199 U.S. 437 [1905]).

10 H. Kuriki, "Über den Gedanken des Verfassungsvertrages in der Geschichte der deutschen Verfassungstheorie", in G. Hermes, C. Schönberger and I. Apel, *Öffentliches Recht im offenen Staat. FS R. Wahl*, Dunker and Humblot, 2011, p. 121.

11 J. Hatchard, "Perfecting Imperfections: Developing Procedures for Amending Constitutions in Commonwealth Africa", *The Journal of Modern African Studies*, 1998, vol. 36, p. 381.

12 Hesse, op. cit., p. 16.

13 For a more detailed typology see P. Häberle, "The Constitutional State and its Reform Requirements", *Ratio Juris*, 2000, vol. 13, p. 87. In general, C. Winterhoff, *Verfassung – Verfassunggebung – Verfassungsänderung. Zur Theorie der Verfassung und der Verfassungsrechtserzeugung*, Mohr Siebeck, 2007.

14 Preamble texts—comprising the central narratives of political integration, making reference to the past as well as to the future and often highlighting transformation processes—can be seen as identity-shaping reflections of a political community: P. Häberle, "Präambeln im Text und Kontext von Verfassungen", in *Demokratie in Anfechtung und Bewährung. FS Broermann*, Dunker and Humblot, 1982, p. 245. Furthermore, A.-C. Kulow, *Inhalte und Funktionen der Präambel des EG-Vertrages*, P.C.O. Verlag, 1997; M. Kotzur, *Theorieelemente des internationalen Menschenrechtschutzes*, Duncker and Humblot, 2001, p. 102; L. Orgad, "The Preamble in Constitutional Interpretation", *International Journal of Constitutional Law*, 2010, vol. 8, p. 714.

15 B. Ackermann, *We the People: Foundations*, Harvard University Press, 1991, id., *We the People: Transformations*, Harvard University Press, 1998.
16 P. Horwitz, "Honor's Constitutional Moment: The Oath and Presidential Transitions", *Northwestern University Law Review Colloquy*, 2008, vol. 103, p. 259, also online. Available HTTP: <http://www.law.northwestern.edu/lawreview/ colloquy/2008/47>.
17 Dreier, op. cit., Art. 79 s 1 para 1.
18 H. Ehmke, "Verfassungsänderung und Verfassungsdurchbrechung", *AöR*, 1953–54, vol. 79, p. 396; Hesse, op. cit., p. 291; in detail C. Bushart, *Verfassungsänderung in Bund und Ländern*, F. Vahlen, 1989, p. 32.
19 B.-O. Bryde, "Verfassunggebende Gewalt des Volkes und Verfassungsänderung im deutschen Staatsrecht", in R. Bieber and P. Widmer (eds), *Der europäische Verfassungsraum*, Schulthess, 1995, p. 329, in particular p. 334; H. Dreier, "Grenzen demokratischer Freiheit im Verfassungsstaat", *JZ*, 1994, vol. 49, p. 742.
20 Hesse, op. cit., p. 291; Dreier, op. cit., Vol. II, Art. 79 s 1 para 79, with further reference.
21 K. Bugiel, *Volkswille und repräsentative Entscheidung*, Nomos, 1991, p. 157.
22 Dreier, op. cit., Vol. II, Art. 79 s 2 para 4.
23 There are more constitutions that know or have known a so-called eternity clause (see e.g. the Norwegian Constitution of 1814); M. Herdegen, in T. Maunz and G. Dürig (eds), *GG-Kommentar*, 2011, Vol. 62, Art. 79 s 3 paras 70ff. with further reference.
24 W. Dale, "The Making and Remaking of Commonwealth Constitutions", *The International and Comparative Law Quarterly*, 1993, vol. 42, p. 71: the "basic structure" and the "basic features" of a constitution may not be altered.
25 I. Pernice, in Dreier, op. cit., Vol. II, Art. 23 para 1.
26 R. Streinz, in M. Sachs (ed.), *GG-Kommentar*, 2011, 6th edn, Art. 23 para 9.
27 Dreier, op. cit., Vol. II, Art. 79 s 1 para 16.
28 *BVerfGE* Vol. 89, p. 155ff.
29 *BVerfGE* Vol. 123, p. 267ff.
30 See e.g. P. Hommelhoff and P. Kirchhof (eds), *Der Staatenverbund der Europäischen Union*, Müller, 1994.
31 J. Wieland, "Kaleidoscope – Germany in the European Union – The Maastricht decision of the *Bundesverfassungsgericht*", *European Journal of International Law*, 1994, Vol. 5(1), pp. 259–66.
32 *BVerfGE* Vol. 89, p. 155 para 92.
33 M. Stolleis, "Besatzungsherrschaft und Wiederaufbau deutscher Staatlichkeit", in J. Isensee and P. Kirchhof (eds), *HStR*, Vol. I, Müller, 3rd edn, 2003, para 7; R. Mußgnung, "Zustandekommen des Grundgesetzes und Entstehen der Bundesrepublik Deutschland", in Isensee and Kirchhof (eds), op. cit., para 8.
34 P.M. Huber, in Sachs, op. cit. Preamble paras 4ff. For a detailed documentation see M. Feldkamp, *Der Parlamentarische Rat 1948–1949: Die Entstehung des Grundgesetzes*, Vandenhoeck and Ruprecht, 1998.
35 See e.g. D. Murswiek, *Die verfassungsgebende Gewalt nach dem Grundgesetz für die Bundesrepublik Deutschland*, Duncker and Humblot, 1978, p. 96ff.
36 T. Hertfelder and J. Hess (eds), *Streiten um das Staatsfragment. Theodor Heuss und Thomas Dehler berichten von der Entstehung des Grundgesetzes*, Deutsche Verlags-Anstalt, 1999, introduced the very significant term "*Staatsfragment*" (mere fragment of a formerly united State).
37 Dreier, op. cit., Preamble para 36; Huber, in Sachs, op. cit., Preamble paras 41ff. In general see C. Starck, W. Berg and B. Pieroth, "Der Rechtsstaat und die Aufarbeitung der vor-rechtsstaatlichen Vergangenheit", *VVDStRL*, 1992, Vol. 51, pp. 9, 46, 91. Furthermore M. Bermanseder, *Die europäische Idee im Parlamentarischen Rat*, Duncker and Humblot, 1998.
38 Recently re-emphazised in *BVerfGE*, Vol. 123, p. 346 with reference to C. Starck, *Der demokratische Verfassungsstaat*, Mohr, 1995, p. 356; J.P. Müller, "Wandel des Souveränitätsbegriffs im Lichte der Grundrechte", in Symposion L. Wildhaber, 1997, p. 45.

39 Again *BVerfGE*, Vol. 123, p. 344. Also for the early politics of the Western integration and the European integration under Chancellor K. Adenauer, such thinking about sovereignty was leading the way; cf. W. Weidenfeld, *Konrad Adenauer und Europa. Die geistigen Grundlage der westeuropäischen Integrationspolitik des ersten Bonner Bundeskanzlers*, Europa Union Verlag, 1976; A. Doering-Manteuffel, *Die Bundesrepublik in der Ära Adenauer: Außenpolitik und innere Entwicklung 1949–1963*, Darmstadt, 2nd edn, 1988.
40 Häberle, "The Constitutional State and its Reform Requirements", op. cit., p. 88 (including further reference).
41 K. Stern, *Das Staatsrecht der Bundesrepublik Deutschland*, Beck Juristischer Verlag, Vol. IV/1, 2006, para 97; P. Häberle, "Die Menschenwürde als Grundlage der staatlichen Gemeinschaft", in Isensee and Kirchhof (eds), Vol. II, op. cit., 3rd edn, 2004, para 22; C. Enders, *Die Menschenwürde in der Verfassungsordnung*, Mohr, 1997; P. Mastronardi, "Menschenwürde als materielle 'Grundnorm' des Rechtsstaates?", in D. Thürer, F. Aubert and J.P. Müller (eds), *Verfassungsrecht der Schweiz*, Schulthess, 2001, para 14. In a comparative perspective, P. Ridola, *Diritto comparato e diritto constituzionale europeo*, Giappichelli, 2010, p. 77ff.
42 W. Schäuble, *Der Vertrag. Wie ich über die deutsche Einheit verhandelte*, Deutsche Verlags – Anstalt, 1991; K. Stern, *Der Zwei-plus-Vier-Vertrag*, BayVBl. 1991, p. 523; C. Raap, *Ist das vereinte Deutschland souverän?*, BayVBl. 1992, p. 11.
43 In general K.-P. Sommermann, "Offene Staatlichkeit: Deutschland", in A. v Bogdandy, P. Cruz Villalón and P.M. Huber (eds), *Handbuch Ius Publicum Europaeum*, Vol. II, Müller, 2008, p. 3ff.
44 M. Herdegen, "Extrakonstitutionelle Grundlagen der deutschen Rechtsordnung?", *Staat und Recht*, 1990, vol. 39, p. 697; H. Bauer, "Die Verfassungsentwicklung des wiedervereinigten Deutschland", in Isensee and Kirchhof (eds), vol. I, op. cit., para 14.
45 Ehmke, op. cit., p. 385. For further reference see also Dreier, op. cit., Vol. II, Art. 79 para 3.
46 Cf. P. Häberle in FS Haug, 1986, p. 83ff.
47 See G. Jellinek, *Verfassungsänderung und Verfassungswandlung: eine staatsrechtlich-politische Abhandlung*, O. Häring, 1906.
48 The Government, for example, was entitled to enact laws without being bound to the procedural or to any substantive requirements set forth by the Weimar Constitution, see K.-E. Hein in v. Mangoldt a.o. (eds), *Bonner Grundgesetz*, 2000, Vol. II, 4th edn, Art. 79 s 3 para 29.
49 Hain, op. cit., Art. 79 s 3 para 31. The general distinction was introduced, however, by E.J. Sieyès, *Qu'est-ce que le tiers état?*, 1789, Chapter V *(Dans chaque partie, la constitution n'est pas l'ouvrage du pouvoir constitué, mais du pouvoir constituant)*.
50 B.-O. Bryde, *Verfassungsentwicklung. Stabilität und Dynamik im Verfassungsrecht der Bundesrepublik Deutschland*, Nomos Verlagsgesellschaft, 1982, p. 52.
51 For further details see Busch, op. cit., p. 12.
52 Ibid.
53 See A. Lijphart, *Patterns of Democracy. Government Forms and Performance in Thirty-Six Countries*, Yale University Press, 1999, p. 220.
54 J. Lücke and M. Sachs, in Sachs, op. cit., Art. 79 para 5.
55 Referring to the practice in the Weimar Republic that the constitutional law was, in the end, not reflected by the wording of constitution anymore, Hain in Mangoldt (eds), op. cit., Art. 79 s 1 para 5.
56 U. Hufeld, *Die Verfassungsdurchbrechung – Rechtsproblem der Deutschen Einheit und der europäischen Einigung*, Duncker and Humblot, 1997.
57 P. Häberle in H. Ehmke and P. Häberle (eds), *Beiträge zur Verfassungstheorie und Verfassungspolitik*, Athenäum, 1981, p. 300.
58 Dreier, op. cit., Vol. II, Art. 79 s 1 para 21.
59 See Hain in Mangoldt (eds), op. cit, Art. 79 s 1 paras 13ff.; Dreier, op. cit., Vol. II, Art. 79 s 1 para 26.

60 Dreier, op. cit., Vol. II, Art. 79 s 2 para 17.
61 For further reference see Dreier, op. cit., Vol. II, Art. 79 s 3 paras 9ff.
62 D. Zacharias, "Die sog. Ewigkeitsgarantie des Art. 79 Abs. 3 GG", in M. Thiel (ed.), *Wehrhafte Demokratie*, Mohr, 2003, p. 57.
63 Dreier, op. cit., Vol. II, Art. 79 s 3 para 15.
64 Häberle, "The Constitutional State and its Reform Requirements", op. cit., p. 82; J.P. Müller, "Materielle Schranken der Verfassungsrevision", in F.S. Haug, op. cit., p. 81.
65 Häberle, "The Constitutional State and its Reform Requirements", op. cit., p. 82.
66 Murswiek, op. cit., p. 175.
67 See Dreier, op. cit., Vol. II, Art. 79 s 1 para 27, Art. 79 s 2 para 23, Art. 79 s 3 para 58.
68 Lücke and Sachs, in Sachs, op. cit., Art. 79 para 5.
69 *BverfGE*, Vol. 123, p. 267 para 211.
70 Dreier, op. cit., Vol. II, Art. 79 s 3 para 17.
71 Pernice in Dreier, Vol. II, op. cit., Art. 29 para 20.
72 Dreier, op. cit., Vol. II, Art. 79 s 3 para 22.
73 *BverfGE*, Vol. 34, p. 20 and Vol. 87, p. 196.
74 Lücke and Sachs, in Sachs, op. cit., Art. 79 para 43.
75 Dreier, op. cit., Vol. II, Art. 79 s 3 para 23.
76 Ibid. Differently, S. Blasche, *Die grundsätzliche Mitwirkung der Länder bei der Gesetzgebung*, Nomos, 2006, p. 144ff.
77 Dreier, op. cit., Vol. II, Art. 79 s 3 para 25.
78 M. Herdegen, "Informalisierung und Entparlamentarisierung politischer Entscheidungen als Gefährdungen der Verfassung", *VVDStRL*, 2003, Vol. 62, p. 15ff.
79 E. Forsthoff, *Der Staat der Industriegesellschaft*, Beck, 1971, p. 30ff. Furthermore A.-M. Slaughter, *A New World Order*, Princeton University Press, 2004, p. 219ff.
80 Herdegen in Maunz and Dürig, op. cit., Art. 1 para 1.
81 P. Häberle, "Die Menschenwürde als Grundlage der staatlichen Gemeinschaft", *HStR*, 1995, Vol. I, 2nd edn, para 20, paras 46ff (now 3rd edn, 2004); R. Gröschner, "Die Würde des Menschen", in P. Bavatstro (ed.), *Individualität und Ethik*, 1997, Stuttgart, pp. 15–35.
82 Dreier, op. cit., Vol. I, 2nd edn, 2006, Art. 1 para 55.
83 Cf. Enders, op. cit.
84 For Switzerland see J.P. Müller, *Grundrechte in der Schweiz*, 3rd edn, Stämpfli Verlag, 1999, p. 1ff.
85 Regarding human dignity as a "right to rights" Enders, op. cit.
86 P. Häberle, "Das Mehrheitsprinzip als Strukturelement der freiheitlich-demokratischen Grundordnung", in Häberle (ed.), *Verfassung als öffentlicher Prozess*, op. cit., p. 565ff.
87 Dreier, op. cit., Vol. I, 2nd edn, 2006, Art. 1 para 55.
88 R. Herzog and B. Grzeszick, in Maunz and Dürig, op. cit., Art. 20 para 10.
89 Kirchhof, "Die Identität der Verfassung in ihren unabänderlichen Gehalten", *HStR*, Vol. II, op. cit., para 21.
90 See Dreier, op. cit., Vol. III, 2nd edn, 2008, Art. 146 para 17; in the early years, an important analysis was presented by U. Scheuner, "Art. 146 GG und das Problem der verfassunggebenden Gewalt 1953", in H. Kurz (ed.), *Volkssouveränität und Staatssouveränität, Wissenschaftliche Buchges*, Wissenschaftliche Buchges, 1970, p. 288.
91 See T. Fleiner in this volume. Furthermore R. Schweizer, "Die neue Bundesverfassung: Die revidierte Bundesstaatsverfassung", *AJP*, 1999, p. 666.
92 Häberle, "The Constitutional State and its Reform Requirements", op. cit., p. 87; E.-W. Böckenförde, *Die verfassunggebende Gewalt des Volkes. Ein Grenzbegriff des Verfassungsrechts*, Metzner, 1986; P. Häberle, "Die verfassunggebende Gewalt des Volkes", *AöR*, 1997, vol. 112, p. 54.
93 Dreier, op. cit., vol. III, 2nd edn, 2008, Art. 146 para 21; *BverfGE*, Vol. 5, p. 131.
94 F. Borella, "Nationalité et citoyenneté en droit français", in D. Colas (ed.), *L'Etat de droit. Travaux de la mission de la modernisation de l'Etat*, Presses Universitaires de France, 1987,

p. 35, the English translation provided for by B. Guiguet, "Citizenship and Nationality: Tracing the French Roots of the Distinction", in M. La Torre (ed.), *European Citizenship: An Institutional Challenge*, Springer, 1998, pp. 95, 98.

95 This *pouvoir constituant* is already mentioned in the Preamble: "(. . .) the German people, in exercise of their constituent power, have adopted this basic law. (. . .). Thus this Basic Law applies to the entire German People."

96 See e.g. R. Bartlsperger, "Verfassung und verfassunggebende Gewalt im Vereinten Deutschland", *DVBl.*, 1990, p. 1285; P. Häberle, "Verfassungspolitik für die Freiheit und Einheit Deutschlands – Ein wissenschaftlicher Diskussionsbeitrag im Vormärz 1990", *JZ*, 1990, Vol. 45, p. 358; B. Schlink, "Deutsch-deutsche Verfassungsentwicklungen im Jahre 1990", *Der Staat*, 1991, vol. 30, p. 163; J. Isensee, *Braucht Deutschland eine neue Verfassung? Überlegungen zur neuen Schlussbestimmung des Grundgesetzes, Art. 146*, Köln, 1992; H. Meyer, "Artikel 146 GG. Ein unerfüllter Verfassungsauftrag?", in H.H. v. Arnim (ed.), *Direkte Demokratie*, Duncker and Humblot, 2000, p. 67.

97 R. Scholz in Maunz and Dürig, op. cit., Art. 146 para 6.

98 Ibid., Art. 146 para 20.

99 Nevertheless, A. Roßnagel, "Die Änderungen des Grundgesetzes", *NJW*, 1989, p. 1325, might go too far when claiming that no constitution worldwide had been changed as often as the German Basic Law. Overview of all changes of the Basic Law by S. Menzenbach, A. Netterscheidt, M. Beckenbanze and L. Kuhn, "Änderungen des Grundgesetzes seit 1949. Inhalt, Datum, Abstimmungsergebnis und Textvergleich", Wissenschaftliche Dienste des Deutschen Bundestages, 2009, WD 3–380/09.

100 Busch, op. cit., p. 5.

101 Ibid.

102 Busch, op. cit., p. 9 with reference to K. v. Beyme, *Das politische System der Bundesrepublik Deutschland*, 1996, Piper, 8th edn, p. 45.

103 G. Robbers, "Die Änderungen des Grundgesetzes", *NJW*, 1989, p. 1325. English translation provided by Busch, op. cit., p. 10; K. Loewenstein, *Über Wesen, Technik und Grenzen der Verfassungsänderung*, Walter de Gruyter, 1961, used the metaphor of "filling constitutional gaps" (see p. 21).

104 Bryde, *Verfassungsentwicklung*, op. cit., p. 129.

105 Busch, op. cit., p. 11.

106 K. Hesse, *Der unitarische Bundesstaat*, Müller, 1962.

107 M. Herdegen, *Die Verfassungsänderungen im Einigungsvertrag*, Decker and Müller, 1991.

108 Pernice in Dreier, op. cit., Vol. II, Art. 23 para 1.

109 Ibid., Art. 59 para 5.

110 Busch, op. cit., p. 10; Bryde, *Verfassungsentwicklung*, op. cit., p. 121.

111 Häberle, "The Constitutional State and its Reform Requirements", op. cit., p. 80.

112 Ibid.

113 H. Kelsen, *Allgemeine Staatslehre*, Springer, 1925, p. 254.

114 Term shaped by P. Laband, *Die Wandlungen der deutschen Reichsverfassung*, 1895; Jellinek, op. cit., p. 6. For further reference see Dreier, op. cit., Vol. II, Art. 79 s 1 para 87.

115 M. Kenntner, "Grundgesetzwandel. Überlegungen zur Veränderung des Grundgesetzes und seines Bezugsrahmens", *DÖV*, 1997, p. 450.

116 Specifically for the context of basic rights ("Grundrechtswandel") Dreier, op. cit., Vol. II, Art. 79 s 1 para 38.

117 Ibid. Concerning a typology of constitutional changes see Bryde, *Verfassungsentwicklung*, op. cit., p. 283ff.

118 Term by K. Eichenberger, see G. Müller, *ZSR*, 1997, Vol. 116, I, p. 21ff. Further reference see in Dreier, op. cit., Vol. II, Art. 79 s 1 para 43.

119 G. Schmid, "Verfassunggebung in einer zusammenwachsenden Welt", in *Festschrift für Y. Hangartner*, Dike Verlag, 1998, p. 1043.

120 H. Kraus, *Die auswärtige Stellung der Bundesrepublik nach dem Bonner Grundgesetz*, Musterschmidt, 1950, p. 21. More than 50 years later, the Federal Constitutional

Court re-emphasized: "Das Grundgesetz hat die öffentliche Gewalt programmatisch auf die internationale Zusammenarbeit (Art. 24) und auf die europäische Integration (Art. 23 GG) festgelegt", *BverfGE*, Vol. 111, p. 318 – *Görgülü*.

121 Paradigmatically K. Vogel, *Die Verfassungsentscheidung des Grundgesetzes für eine internationale Zusammenarbeit*, Mohr, 1964. Later W. Rudolf, *Völkerrecht und deutsches Recht*, Mohr, 1967; R. Bernhardt, "Verfassungsrecht und internationale Lagen", *DÖV*, 1977, p. 45, in a cooperative perspective P. Häberle, "Der kooperative Verfassungsstaat", in Häberle, *Verfassung als öffentlicher Prozess*, 3rd edn, op. cit., p. 407. Furthermore H. Mosler, "Die Übertragung von Hoheitsrechten", *HStR*, 1992, Vol. VIII, 1st edn, para 175; U. di Fabio, *Das Recht offener Staaten*, Mohr, 1998; S. Hobe, *Der offene Verfassungsstaat zwischen Souveränität und Interdependenz*, Duncker and Humblot, 1998, and "Der kooperationsoffene Verfassungsstaat", *Der Staat*, 1998, Vol. 37, p. 521; K.-P. Sommermann, "Der entgrenzte Verfassungsstaat", in D. Merten (ed.), *Der Staat am Ende des 20. Jahrhunderts*, Deutsches Forschungsinstitut für öffentliche Verwaltung Speyer, 1998, p. 19ff.; with a special focus on the process of European integration, B. Beutler, "Offene Staatlichkeit und europäische Integration", in *FS E.-W. Böckenförde*, Dunker and Humbolt, 1995, p. 109; an instructive overview is provided by R. Wahl, "Der offene Staat und seine Rechtsgrundlagen", *JuS*, 2003, p. 1145.

122 One phrase of the federal Constitutional Court's Lisbon decision might foreshadow such an understanding (see Vol. 123, p. 344): "Mit der sogenannten Ewigkeitsgarantie reagierte das Grundgesetz einerseits auf historische Erfahrungen einer schleichenden oder abrupten Aushöhlung der freiheitlichen Substanz einer demokratischen Grundordnung. Es macht aber auch deutlich, dass die Verfassung der Deutschen in Übereinstimmung mit der internationalen Entwicklung gerade auch seit Bestehen der Vereinten Nationen einen universellen Grund besitzt, der durch positives Recht nicht verändert werden soll."

123 I. Pernice, "The Treaty of Lisbon: Multilevel Constitutionalism in Action", *Columbia Journal of European Law*, 2009, Vol. 15, p. 349; id., "Multilevel Constitutionalism and the Treaty of Amsterdam: European Constitution-Making Revisited?", *CMLR*, 1999, Vol. 36, p. 703.

124 N. Walker, "The Idea of Constitutional Pluralism", *Modern Law Review*, 2002, vol. 65, p. 317; M. Maduro, "Contrapunctual Law: Europe´s Constitutional Pluralism in Action", in N. Walker (ed.), *Sovereignty in Transition*, Hart, 2003, p. 501ff.

125 A. D´Atena, "The European Constitution's Prospects", in H.-J. Blanke and S. Mangiameli (eds), *The European Union after Lisbon. Constitutional Basis, Economic Order and External Action*, Springer, 2011, p. 13.

126 Pernice, "Multilevel Constitutionalism and the Treaty of Amsterdam", op. cit., p. 703; id., "The Global Dimension of Multilevel Constitutionalism: A Legal Response to the Challenges of Globalisation", in P.M. Dupuy, B. Fassbender, M.N. Shaw and K.P. Sommermann (eds), *Völkerrecht als Wertordnung. FS Ch. Tomuschat*, Engel, 2006, p. 973.

127 A.J. Arnaud, *Pour une pensée juridique européenne*, Presses Universitaires France, 1991.

128 J. Vanderlinden, "Le pluralisme juridique: essai de synthèse", in J. Gillissen (ed.), *Le Pluralisme Juridique*, Editions de l'université de Bruxelles, 1971, p. 19; K.v. Benda-Beckmann, "Transnational dimension of legal pluralsim", in W. Fikentscher (ed.), *Begegnung und Konflikt – eine kulturanthropologische Bestandsaufnahme*, Verlag der Bayerischen Akademie der Wissenschaften, 2001, p. 33; F. v. Benda-Beckmann, "Who's afraid of legal pluralism?", *Journal of Legal Pluralism*, 2002, Vol. 47, p. 37; A. Griffiths, "Legal Pluralism", in R. Banakar and M. Travers (eds), *An Introduction to Law and Social Theory*, Hart, 2002, p. 289.

129 As to the parallel public international law debate see A. Paulus, "Zur Zukunft der Völkerrechtswissenschaft in Deutschland: Zwischen Konstitutionalisierung und Fragmentierung des Völkerrechts", *ZaöRV*, 2007, Vol. 67, pp. 695–720.

130 G. Teubner, "Globale Zivilverfassungen: Alternativen zur staatszentrischen Verfassungstheorie", *ZaöRV*, 2003, Vol. 63, p. 1.

131 Pernice in Dreier, op. cit., Vol. II, Art. 26 para 13.
132 For the following Häberle, "The Constitutional State and its Reform Requirements", op. cit., p. 80.
133 This is the idea of implementation, see E.W. Vierdag, "Some Remarks about Special Features of Human Rights Treaties", in *Netherlands Yearbook of International Law*, T.M.C. Asser Press, 1994, p. 126ff. See also C. Walter, "Die Europäische Menschenrechtskonvention als Konstitutionalisierungsprozeß", *ZaöRV*, 1999, Vol. 59, p. 961ff.; id., "Nationale Durchsetzung der Grundrechte", in R. Grote and T. Marauhn (eds), *Handbuch des Grund- und Menschenrechtsschutzes*, 2005.
134 Häberle, "The Constitutional State and its Reform Requirements", op. cit., p. 82.
135 O. Sandrock, "Das Privatrecht am Ausgang des 20. Jahrhunderts: Deutschland - Europa - und die Welt", *JZ*, 1996, Vol. 51, p. 1ff.
136 Examples can be found in J. Hoffmann (ed.), *Begründung von Menschenrechten aus der Sicht unterschiedlicher Kulturen*, Iko-Verlag, 1991; S. Batzli, F. Kissling and R. Zihlmann (eds), *Menschenbilder, Menschenrechte, Islam und Okzident: Kulturen im Konflikt*, Unionsverlag, 1994. See also B. Fassbender, "The Better Peoples of the United Nations? Europe's Practice and the United Nations", *EJIL*, 2004, Vol. 15, p. 857ff.
137 C. Grabenwarter, *Europäische Menschenrechtskonvention*, 4th edn, Beck, 2009, p. 1.
138 H. Sauer, *Staatsrecht III*, Beck, 2011 p. 86.
139 R. Geiger, in R. Geiger, D.-E. Kahn and M. Kotzur (eds), *EUV/AEUV*, 5th edn, 2010, Art. 6 AEUV para 19.
140 Grabenwarter, op. cit., p. 36.
141 Geiger, op. cit., Art. 6 AEUV para 21.
142 Sauer, op. cit., p. 86.
143 *BverfGE*, Vol. 111, p. 307 – Görgülü.
144 Kotzur, in Geiger, Kahn and Kotzur (eds), op. cit., Anh. 1 GR-Charta Einf. para 3.
145 M. Nettesheim, in Th. Oppermann, C.D. Classen and M. Nettesheim, *Europarecht*, 5th edn, Beck, 2011, pp. 149ff.
146 Kotzur, in Geiger, Kahn and Kotzur (eds), op. cit., Art. 267 para 37.
147 P. Häberle, *Europäische Rechtskultur*, Nomos, 1994 and *Europäische Verfassungslehre*, op. cit.
148 M. Kotzur, in R. Schulze, M. Zuleeg and S. Kadelbach (eds), *Europarecht. Handbuch für die deutsche Rechtspraxis*, 2nd edn, Nomos, 2010, § 38, para 6.
149 P. Häberle, "Die offene Gesellschaft der Verfassungsinterpreten (1975/78)", in Häberle, *Verfassung als öffentlicher Prozess*, 3rd edn, op. cit., p. 155.
150 H. Sendler, "Richterrecht – rechtstheoretisch und rechtspraktisch", *NJW*, 1987, pp. 3240–2. Further reference T. Raiser, in N. Achterberg (ed.), *Rechtsprechungslehre*, Koln, 1986, p. 627ff.
151 Cf. M. Nettesheim, "Die Integrationsverantwortung: Vorgaben des BVerfG und gesetzgeberische Umsetzung", *NJW*, 2010, Vol. 63, pp. 177–83.
152 J.J. Weiler and M. Wind (eds), *European Constitutionalism Beyond the State*, Cambridge University Press, 2003; P. Häberle, "Neue Horizonte und Herausforderungen des Konstitutionalismus", *EuGRZ*, 2006, Vol. 33, pp. 533–40; Pernice, "The global dimension of multilevel constitutionalism", op. cit., pp. 973–1005.
153 H. Bauer, in Dreier, op. cit., Vol. II, Art. 20 (*Bundesstaat*) para 17.
154 See very early A. Verdross and B. Simma (eds), *Universelles Völkerrecht*, Duncker and 3rd edn, Humblot, 1984, paras 40ff.
155 Häberle, "The Constitutional State and its Reform Requirements", op. cit., p. 87.
156 Ibid. Furthermore P. Häberle, "Zeit und Verfassungskultur", in P. Häberle *Rechtsvergleichung im Kraftfeld des Verfassungsstaates*, Duncker and Humblot, 1992, p. 289.
157 G.S. Schaal and C. Ritzi, "Das Grundgesetz als umkämpfte Ordnung. Deutungsmuster in der massenmedialen Berichterstattung anlässlich der Jubiläumstage des Grundgesetzes", *Behemoth*, 2010, Vol. 3, p. 101ff.
158 With regard to the competition of different legal systems in general, A. Peters and T. Giegerich, "Wettbewerb der Rechtsordnungen", in *Veröffentlichungen der Vereinigung der*

Deutschen Staatsrechtslehrer, 2010, Vol. 69, pp. 7, 57; E. O'Hara and L.E. Ribstein, *The Law Market*, Oxford University Press, 2009.

159 J.L. Dunhoff and J.P. Trachtman (eds), *Ruling the World? Constitutionalism, International Law and Global Governance*, Cambridge University Press, 2009; A. Peters and K. Armingeon, "Introduction – Global Constitutionalism from an Interdisciplinary Perspective", *Indiana Journal of Global Legal Studies*, 2009, Vol. 16, p. 385; S. Kadelbach and T. Kleinlein, "Überstaatliches Verfassungsrecht", *AVR*, 2006, Vol. 44, p. 235.

160 P. Häberle, "Pluralismus der Rechtsquellen in Europa – nach Maastricht", *JöR*, 1999, Vol. 47, p. 79.

161 Häberle, *Verfassungslehre als Kulturwissenschaft*, op. cit., p. 459.

162 Hatchard, op. cit., p. 381; Dale, op. cit., p. 69 refers to "the creation of indigenous symbols of nationhood".

163 Hatchard, op. cit, p. 381.

164 P. Häberle, "Die offene Gesellschaft der Verfassungsinterpreten", in P. Häberle (ed.), *Die Verfassung des Pluralismus*, Königstein, 1980, p. 79.

9 Constitutional change in Greece

Xenophon Contiades and Ioannis Tassopoulos

History and evolution of the constitutional amendment procedure

Since the first Revolutionary Constitutions in the early nineteenth century, all Greek Constitutions have been written, generally recognized to be the supreme law, and difficult to amend. Nevertheless, the provisions regarding constitutional revision, though not ignored or rejected in principle, were never fully respected until the current Constitution of 1975 was enacted. This was primarily for two reasons: either the procedural and material limits were so demanding that they rendered necessary constitutional changes unfeasible unless such limits were breached, or constitutional changes resulted from serious political crises that were, in most cases, followed by changes in the form of government, alternating between crowned parliamentary government and the republic.

On the other hand, it is quite interesting and noteworthy that, although in violation of the amending procedures set out by the Constitution, Assemblies still clung to the title of "Revisional Assemblies," in an effort to emphasize continuity between the previous and the novel Constitution, thereby fostering their political legitimacy. It therefore emerges that the demanding amending formulas of Greek Constitutions did not serve constitutional stability (i.e. the exact aim it was supposed to serve). Yet the need to keep up the pretence of conducting a revision despite violations of the procedural and material limits expresses a desire to project respect for constitutionalism, since the absence of that respect would undermine the legitimacy and the authority of the new Constitution. Moreover, it is a common feature of all constitutions promulgated throughout modern Greek history that, even when enacted in breach of the pre-existing formalities and procedural limits, they were still democratically construed, in elected Assemblies following open, democratic dialogue.

The passage from absolute entrenchment to stringent amending procedures

After the recognition of Greece as a sovereign state in 1832, six Constitutions were enforced and applied—the Constitutions of 1844, 1864, 1911, 1927, 1952, and the current Constitution of 1975, amended in 1986, 2001, and 2008. The Constitution of 1844 was a contract between the monarch and the nation following an uprising initiated by the Greek army and supported by the people, who demanded a Constitution after the 10-year rule of King Otto as absolute monarch (1833–1843). The King had to accept the demand, thus elections were proclaimed for a constituent Assembly. The constitution-making procedure was concluded with the ratification and promulgation of the Constitution by the King.

The Constitution of 1844 was absolutely entrenched as it did not provide for its revision. Consequently, it could only be altered through a new Constitution granted by the monarch to the people (i.e. constituent power lay primarily with the monarch). In that sense, since the Constitution was designed to be absolutely entrenched, it was inevitably destined to be violated or even to collapse, as eventually happened.

The 1844 Constitution was never fully implemented in practice as King Otto systematically violated it. In 1862, the Greek people and the army revolted against Otto, who was dethroned; in March 1863, Prince George Wilhelm of Denmark was elected "King of the Hellenes" by the Second Constituent Assembly, which enacted a new Constitution in 1864. According to the entrenchment clause of that Constitution (Art. 107), a revision of its non-fundamental provisions was allowed after 10 years had elapsed from its enactment. The need for an amendment should be authorized and endorsed by Parliament in two consecutive parliamentary terms by a four-fifths majority of the total number of Members of Parliament (MPs), who also decided on the provisions that were to be revised. Following that decision, Parliament would automatically dissolve and a Revisional Assembly, consisting of twice as many members, would be convened to decide on the amendment.

The liberal Constitution of 1864 was influenced by the Constitutions of Belgium of 1831 and of Denmark of 1849, and proclaimed the principle of popular sovereignty. Therefore, a transition took place from constitutional monarchy to parliamentary democracy, and the competences of the monarch were restricted to those explicitly conferred by the Constitution. From 1864, all Greek Constitutions have enshrined parliamentarism, have provided the basis for the diffused system of constitutionality review, and, with the exception of the Constitution of 1927, have adopted monocameralism. Until its final resolution by the referendum of 1974, the most vexing, contested, and pervasive question regarding the constitutional debate had been the choice between a republic and crowned democracy, including the competences of the monarch, while in the post-1974 era it was replaced by the controversy over the extent of presidential powers.

In 1909, Greek army officers revolted, demanding the reorganization of the government and the army. This revolt resulted from a growing dissatisfaction with the traditional political parties of the time, clientelism, and state corruption. Nevertheless, the overthrow of the political system was not amongst its aims, but rather reforms including the dismissal of royal princes from the ranks of military authority. These events led to the revision of the Constitution of 1864, which took place in 1911, and was in reality the result of a constituent will, to the extent that the amending procedure set by the pre-existing Constitution had not actually been followed. Nevertheless, the use of the term "revision," regardless of the actual exercise of constituent power, was intentional, primarily reflecting the reluctance of the dominant political powers to allow the question of the form of government to be reopened, as it would inevitably arise in the case of a "Constituent Assembly," thereby causing severe political tension with the King.

The Constitution of 1864 was thus reformed and modernized; its liberal and democratic features, as well as the guarantees of the rule of law, were enhanced, thereby safeguarding judicial independence and public administration from clientelism. The revised Constitution of 1911 introduced a somewhat more flexible amending formula, yet remained quite complex and demanding. According to Art. 108, after the lapse of 10 years from its enactment, the Greek Parliament could resolve the amendment of the Constitution, specifying the provisions subject to change by a two-thirds majority of the total number of its MPs, in two ballots held at least one month apart. Following the resolution to amend the Constitution, Parliament would automatically dissolve and, following the elections, the new Parliament would decide the content of the amendable provisions in the course of its opening session by absolute majority of the total number of MPs.

The temporary simplification of the amendment process and the return to perplexity

The violent end of the Greek presence in Asia Minor in 1922, when Greece was defeated in a war against Turkey, led to a popular referendum held in 1924, officially dethroning the King. As a result, the republican form of government was adopted, with the Constitution of 1911 remaining in force with regard to the rest of its provisions. At the same time, a Constituent Assembly was convened and, although its workings were interrupted by a short-lived military dictatorship (1925–1926), it continued in 1927, leading finally to the promulgation of a new Constitution, which established a parliamentary republic with two legislative bodies (the *Vouli*, identified in Greek terminology with Parliament, and the Senate). Judicial review of the constitutionality of laws, which pre-existed as a constitutional custom, was explicitly adopted by the Constitution, a catalogue of social rights was introduced for the first time, while the Constitution also provided that the President of the Republic needed the Senate's consent to dissolve Parliament, a restriction stemming from the political experience of the National Schism. The amending process was simplified in the Constitution of 1927, which provided in Art. 125 that the non-fundamental provisions of the Constitution could be amended after the lapse of five years from its enactment. According to the new process, an amendment proposal required the approval of both legislative bodies by absolute majority of the total number of each body's members, followed by the convocation three months later of both Parliament and Senate in a Constitutional Assembly to decide on the amendment, by a three-fifths majority of the total number of its members. An optional constitutional referendum was also provided for: if the Constitutional Assembly so decided, it could submit its resolution to the people for approval.

From 1935 to 1949, Greece was in turmoil, closely following Europe's fate. In 1935, a series of military coups interrupted the normality of the parliamentary republic, forcing the Greek Parliament to issue a resolution temporarily re-establishing the Constitution of 1911, until the promulgation of a new Constitution and approval of a constitutional referendum over the form of government. Nevertheless, the workings of the newly elected Revisional Assembly were interrupted by the following events: after a rigged referendum in 1935, crowned democracy was re-established, while in 1936 the King actively supported the installation of a military dictatorship, which lasted until the occupation of Greece by the Nazis in 1941. After the country's liberation from German occupation in 1944, the conflict between the British-backed royal government on the one side, and left-oriented resistance organizations mainly controlled by the Communist Party on the other, deteriorated into a Civil War that lasted from 1946 to 1949, and with its repercussions lingering on for the next three decades. After defeat, the Communist Party was banned and anti-communist ideology influenced the function of the political system. In the meantime, the government had revived the Constitution of 1911 in an attempt to gain legitimacy, and elections were held for a Revisional Assembly. In 1946, a referendum over the form of government turned out in favor of crowned parliamentarism.[1]

Although the Assembly was called "revisional," in reality it was a constituent Assembly, since the amending process provided for in Art. 108 of the Constitution of 1911 had not been followed. The new Constitution enacted in 1952 was more conservative than the previous Constitution of 1911 in terms of allocation of powers as well as in terms of protecting fundamental rights. The legislative role of Parliament was downgraded in favor of the executive, while a departure from the liberal credo on constitutional rights was clear. The Constitution of 1952 set as material limits to its amendment "the provisions determining the form of government and the fundamental provisions." The meaning of the term "fundamental provisions," also appearing in all pre-existing Constitutions (of 1864, 1911 and 1927), was a constant source of dispute in constitutional theory. The amending process remained the same as that of the Constitution of 1911.

In the 1960s, once again the King's lack of respect for the "declared majority" (i.e. the conditioning of the Prime Minister's appointment on Parliament's confidence) led to a severe political crisis. Throughout that period, irregular centers of political power, under royal or military influence and overriding formal constitutional authority, operated energetically by obstructing the operation of the Constitution. This era of constitutional anomaly culminated in a seven-year military dictatorship (1967–1974). This dictatorship collapsed after the Turkish invasion and military occupation in Cyprus. Through a referendum conducted in 1974, the people expressed their choice regarding the form of government they preferred by overwhelmingly rejecting crowned democracy, and the so-called Third Republic was established. Thirty-five years after the end of the Civil War, the Communist Party was legalized. Although the Parliament elected in 1974 was called a "revisionary" one, in fact it exercised constituent power, promulgating the Constitution of 1975, which has been in force ever since. The enactment of the new Constitution concluded a period of repeated political and constitutional crises, which had began in 1915.[2] Although the Constitution of 1975 established a parliamentary republic, it vested enhanced powers in the President of the Republic in a configuration of presidential checks and balances dangerously bordering an Orleanist-type of regime, a choice strongly criticized by the opposition in the Constitutional Assembly. Thus, the President of the Republic, although elected indirectly by Parliament, was furnished with strong executive power enabling him to play a decisive role in the function of the political system. In the area of fundamental rights, the liberal character of the Constitution was restored with the adoption of an extensive catalogue of civil and social rights. Regarding the amendment process, the Constitution of 1975 maintained its traditional stringency (as with the previous Constitution of 1952), further expanding the material limits and adopting minor changes to the procedural ones.

The Constitution of 1975 was amended three times. The first constitutional revision, in 1986, was to limit the powers of the President of the Republic, concerning the dismissal of the Cabinet, even though it enjoyed the confidence of Parliament; the dissolution of Parliament; the proclamation of referendums against the will of the Cabinet; and the vetoing of a bill passed by Parliament in cases where the President disagreed with its content. Thus, the 1986 revision marks the passage from a potentially Orleanist system of checks and balances to a Westminster model of parliamentarism, diminishing the position of the President as a counter-balance against the power of the Prime Minister. In 2001, a second revision of the Constitution addressed a wide-ranging number of issues. The most important changes brought about related to: i) enhancing the protection of fundamental rights as new rights were enshrined, and rights already interpretatively derived by case law or legislation were formally constitutionalized; ii) the enshrinement of five independent authorities; iii) the provision for strict requirements for alterations in electoral law; iv) the addition of new incompatibilities for MPs; and v) the adoption of a more cumbersome procedure regarding prosecution of serving or former Cabinet members for criminal offences committed during discharge of their duties.

The third and final revision of the 1975 Constitution took place in 2008. Although an extensive revision was initiated, the major opposition party's refusal to participate in the amendment process led to the adoption of only four minor changes, the most important of which was the abolition of the incompatibility of any professional occupation of MPs, enshrined in 2001.

Convergences and divergences in the evolution of amendment restraints

An assessment of the evolution of amendment formulas in Greek history allows a series of interesting conclusions:

- With the exception of the Constitution of 1844, which was the first Constitution actually enforced in Greece, all subsequent Constitutions include provisions entrenching the Constitution's supremacy through material and procedural limits. The amendment model adopted by the Constitution of 1864 underwent several improvements, gradually becoming less complex, yet it remains the same in its basic structure, with the exception of the Constitution of 1927. Thus, the amendment process has two phases. In the first phase, Parliament decides on the need for amendment and determines its scope (i.e. the provisions to be amended); in the second phase, following general elections, the new Parliament is responsible for deciding on the content of the provisions.

- A comparison of the six Constitutions enforced in Greek constitutional history reveals a gradual relaxation of the stringency of the amendment process, while their fundamental provisions remain always absolutely protected and inviolable, beyond the reach of the constitutional legislator. Beginning with an absolutely entrenched Constitution granted by the monarch to the people in 1844, the passage to crowned democracy coincides with the appearance of the amending clause in the 1864 Constitution, which provides for a complex procedure involving three Parliaments and two general elections! This process is elaborated upon in the Constitutions of 1911, 1952, and 1975, while the short-lived Constitution of 1927 was the only one allowing the amendment to take place in the framework of just one parliamentary term.
- Excessive stringency amounted to a hardly applicable formality until 1986, when, for the first time, the provisions regulating constitutional revision were fully respected. Highly demanding formulas in the context of political turmoil had resulted in continuous violations. In that sense, although prominent constitutional scholars were of the opinion that the insistence of all Greek Constitutions on the previously discussed amending model had established a tradition, such a tradition could hardly exist because of the non-implementation of the relevant provisions. On the contrary, a continuous practice of non-abidance as regards the cumbersome amendment procedures points in the opposite direction—in other words that there may be, and might have always been, good reasons to re-examine the insistence on that particular model.
- Although the amendment process was not followed, the Constitutions of 1911, 1952, and 1975 were enacted by Assemblies self-proclaimed as "revisional." It is of particular interest that, although they violated the amendment procedure, the Constitutions of 1911 and 1952 did indeed, in principle, preserve the Constitution of 1864, retaining not only the form of government but also a significant part of its provisions. This shows that the choice of using the term "revisional" to draw legitimacy and to express constitutional continuity corresponds to true intentions to uphold this substantive continuity, mainly regarding the form of government. Characterizing an Assembly as "revisional" rather than "constituent" took the *form* of government off the agenda, ensuring that the permanent tension between republicans and royalists would not re-emerge in the context of the constitution-making process.
- All six of the aforementioned Constitutions resulted from major political conflicts. The conflict underlying the Constitution of 1844 was between an absolute monarchy and the claim for a Constitution and democracy, which

resulted in the imposition of constitutional restraints on the monarch. In 1864, this same conflict was re-fought, resulting in the defeat of the monarchy and the introduction of the principle of popular sovereignty. In 1911, the underlying tension was between the old populist, conservative political parties and the impetus towards modernization pursued by the rising new bourgeois classes; while in the Constitution of 1927, the victory of republicans over royalists was sweeping, and the form of government changed into a republic. By contrast, the Constitution of 1952 consolidated the defeat of republicans by the royalists, as well as the defeat of the Communists in the Civil War. Lastly, the Constitution of 1975 marked the prevalence of democracy and the rule of law, in particular of constitutional legality, not only over authoritarianism but also over the practice of constant constitutional violations during the period from 1935 to 1974.

- The examination of formal constitutional changes within their historical context suggests that, instead of safeguarding the Constitution, the constitutional arrogance expressed by extremely demanding amending formulas further intensified political crisis, leading not only to constitutional violations but also, in some cases, to the collapse of democracy.
- In all constitution-generating processes during the twentieth century, as well as in the amendments of the Constitution of 1975, the major political parties did not achieve consent. Thus, constitutional change in Greece was a product of confrontation rather than compromise, apart from the amendment of 2001, which was the only consensual revision. Moreover, when the Constitutions of 1911, 1952, and 1975 were voted on, the major opposition party abstained, which was also the case with the 1986 and 2008 amendments. Nevertheless, refusal to participate in the amendment process was never translated into overt questioning of the Constitution's legitimacy by those political parties who abstained from voting, nor did it undermine its effectiveness.

Informal methods of constitutional change

The demanding amendment procedure laid down by the Greek Constitution, especially the requirement that a new revision cannot be initiated within five years of the previous one, imposes a serious obstacle to constitutional updating. Thus, it appears *prima facie* that the difficulty of formal changes favors the informal ones. However, a number of particularities, both of the Greek legal system and of the legal culture, do not encourage informal change. Such features primarily concern the diffused system of judicial review in Greece, in combination with the existence of three supreme courts. Moreover, constitutional practice and customs are hardly recognized as sources of constitutional law. Persistent constitutional violations before the enactment of the current Constitution of 1975 explain the reluctance to entrust informal constitutional change in the hands of the political class and of the judiciary, relying only on formal constitutional procedure. The dominant opinion suggests that constitutional customs may only play a complementary role, where the Constitution and concomitant legislation leave room for such a development. In general, however, constitutional customs are not considered compatible with the existence of an entrenched, written Constitution, and they are not able to abolish or alter constitutional provisions. Nevertheless, in the past there have been examples of practices being attributed the status of constitutional custom by constitutional scholars and case law. After the enactment of the 1975 Constitution, all relevant issues are explicitly resolved by the text of constitutional provisions; thus, such constitutional customs have been set aside as it is accepted that there is no longer a need for their invocation.

With regard to judicial interpretation of the Constitution, the absence of a special constitutional court or sole supreme court (as opposed to three, in Greece) functioning as a supreme court with concentrated competence to decide on all constitutional issues, often results into a fragmented, unpredictable, uneven, and, to a certain extent, even incoherent case-law. In several cases where conservative approaches prevailed, Greece was taken to the European Court of Human Rights, which, on many occasions, played the role of a quasi-constitutional court, engaging in dialogue with the domestic lawmaker, in favor of a liberal reading of the Constitution. As a result, the actual source of informal change in Greece is the influence of the European Court of Human Rights and the European Court of Justice.

In any case, the ultimate responsibility for evaluating constitutional practices consolidated in the interim between constitutional revisions, as well as informal changes inscribed through constitutional interpretation into the corpus of domestic constitutional law or through the influence of the Strasbourg and Luxembourg courts, lies with the constitutional legislator when the task of constitutional revision is undertaken. Any informal change that has evolved is reconsidered in the process of a formal revision and may be explicitly included in the Constitution, or rejected, or left untouched to continue its course.

Formal constitutional amendment process

The Greek Constitution sets both material and strict procedural constraints on its revision in Art. 110. Indeed, Art. 110 para 1 differs from its predecessors in that it does not refer to the abstract notion of "fundamental provisions," which were immutable, and it sets material limits to the revision of the Constitution, excluding the provisions defining the form of government, as well as Art. 2 para 1 (respect for human dignity); Art. 4 paras 1, 4 and 7 (equality before the law, eligibility of Greek citizens for public service, and prohibition of titles of nobility or distinction); Art. 5 paras 1 (right to free development of personality) and 3 (personal liberty); Art. 13 para 1 (freedom of religious conscience); and Art. 26 (separation of powers). Nevertheless, entrenchment of the form of government poses difficult interpretive issues, given that Art. 110 para 1 of the Constitution leaves room for specifying which constitutional provisions and principles determine the basic features of the form of government that are being safeguarded. The dominant view regarding the non-amendable features of the form of government includes therein the system of parliamentary republic, the multi-party system, as well as the principle of the rule of law. As a result, the political system cannot change in order to become a crowned democracy, a presidential democracy, or a semi-presidential democracy. In contrast, the monocameral system may be replaced by a bicameral system, and the Westminster model may be modified through the intensification of the consensual features of the form of government. Furthermore, there is the explicit provision that Art. 26, which enshrines the separation of powers, is not subject to amendment and is considered to encompass judicial independence as well. On the other hand, it is also accepted that constitutional provisions concerning the economic system, such as socio-economic rights, fall beyond the scope of the material limits.[3]

The procedural limits set by Art. 110 paras 2–6 of the Constitution are strict. The organ vested with amending power is exclusively Parliament, without any interference by either the government or the President of the Republic. Constitutional revision takes place in two phases, between which general elections take place. It has traditionally been accepted that these elections ensure the indirect participation of the electorate in the amending procedure, choosing the majority that will proceed to the amendment of the Constitution during the second phase. It is important to stress that the timing of elections is not affected by the amendment process, contrary to pre-existing amendment procedures. Indeed, the fact that the decision to revise the Constitution does not lead automatically to the dissolution of Parliament reflects a degree of flexibility, facilitating the initiation of a formal constitutional amendment.

In the first phase of constitutional revision, at least 50 MPs submit a proposal entailing the amendable provisions, accompanied by a detailed report of the reasons that make their amendment necessary.[4] It is noteworthy that in the recent revisions of 2001 and 2008, the proposal for amendment submitted by the party having the majority of seats in Parliament was quickly followed by the submission of a proposal for amendment by the Opposition.[5] The Speaker announces the proposal for amendment to the House and distributes it to the MPs, then sets up the Constitutional Amendment Committee, which consists of 38 to 50 MPs, corresponding to the proportion of the political parties represented in Parliament. The Amendment Committee elects its Chair, Deputy Chair, and Secretary, and must elaborate on the amending proposal, submitting a relevant report within a deadline set by Parliament. Other MPs may also take part in the workings of the Committee, having the right to speak but not to vote. The Committee meets in public, unless it decides otherwise with the consent of the Speaker, and it may hear evidence from public functionaries, experts, social partners, etc. Following the discussion on the proposal and its elaboration, an open vote is held and a report submitted to Parliament, which nevertheless may carry on the amendment in case the Committee fails to submit its report within the time limit.[6] Next, the need for the amendment and its scope (regarding the amendable provisions) are discussed in the Plenum, and the first phase of constitutional revision is concluded with two votes by roll-call, held at least one month apart. Thus, the decision for a constitutional revision is ascertained by a resolution of Parliament, adopted by an absolute majority of the total number of MPs, or by a three-fifths majority, in both votes. This resolution specifically defines the provisions that are to be revised.

In the second phase, the next Parliament—traditionally called "Revisional"—proceeds with the amendment of the provisions, subject to revision. The Revisional Parliament is under obligation to finish its task within its first session. A Constitutional Amendment Committee is again established following the same procedure as described above. After the conclusion of the Committee's workings, the Plenum discusses and votes by roll-call, first the amendable provisions in principle, and second regarding each provision separately; and lastly, the revision as a whole is discussed, confirming conclusively the two former readings. The Revisional Parliament has the power to decide whether or not to amend the proposed provisions, and in practice it is not bound by the intended substantive direction of the amendments as envisioned by the previous Parliament. Thus, on numerous occasions, the Revisional Parliament ignored the previous Parliament's intended amending direction, going in completely the opposite direction.

According to Art. 110 paras 2 and 4 of the Constitution, in case a proposal for constitutional amendment has received the absolute majority of MPs' votes in the first Parliament, but not the three-fifths majority, the Revisional Parliament proceeds with the revision of the proposed provisions by a three-fifths majority of the total number of its members, and vice versa. This system of reversed majorities was first adopted in the Constitution of 1975, while the pre-existing procedures required an *enhanced* majority for the first Parliament's decision and an *absolute* majority of the total number of members for the Revisional Parliament. This alternative was considered to relax the stringency of the procedure, thereby allowing more options, while at the same time it was deemed to be more rational, since it equated both Parliaments taking part in a revision, without giving more weight to the decision of the first Parliament. However, the fact that the Revisional Parliament has the power to decide on the content of the amendable provisions, without being bound by any pre-existing direction, makes the achievement of consent imperative. This led to the formation of a practice that first appeared in the 2001 revision, and again in the 2008 process, according to which even if consent as to the amendment proposal and its direction was reached in the first Parliament, such consent was not expressed in a vote with the enhanced three-fifths majority of the total number of MPs, so that the Revisional Parliament would not have *carte blanche* to decide on the amendment merely with the absolute majority of the total number of MPs. Thus, it has been proved in practice that the Revisional Parliament outweighs the previous Parliament, since it has decisive authority on the content of the revision as well as the power to decide whether or not to continue the amending process.

Constitutional revision is concluded with the publication of the revised provisions in the government gazette within 10 days of their adoption by order of the Speaker of Parliament. According to Art. 110 para 6, revision of the Constitution is not permitted within five years of the completion of the previous revision. The rationale for this is to discourage hasty and continual constitutional changes. The dominant approach suggests that a new amending process cannot be initiated before five years have passed. Nevertheless, it has recently been argued that the five-year constraint dictates the time required before a new amendment is concluded. This latest approach has gained some support following the unsuccessful revision of 2008, which, despite its initial ambitious and wide-ranging proposals, resulted in the adoption of four amendments of minor importance, but in addition blocked the way for a future revision until 2013. In other words, the new, interpretative approach became attractive *after* it was shown in practice that a temporary lack of consent has the potential to block constitutional change for an extended period of time, even though developments in the domestic or international context require an amendment. Thus the interval may turn out in practice to be much longer than the constitutionally intended five-year period.

The role of the people

The answers to the questions of this section can be quite simple, if reduced to a dry legal analysis: in principle, the amendment procedure in Greece is framed according to the representative nature of modern democracy. As a consequence, the role of the people is guaranteed in the amendment process, but their participation is constrained and channeled within the limitations allowed by a strict application of the principle of representative government. The electorate intervenes indirectly, through general elections because, as already noted, the amendment to the Constitution is not completed by the same Parliament, but by a new one; as a result, the people are able to assess the position of the political parties on the questions of constitutional amendments and vote for or against them.

Some obvious features instantly strike the eye of the observer: a) the people do not themselves play any role in the initiative of a constitutional amendment; that initiative belongs exclusively to MPs; b) the electorate does not have a direct say on the final product of the revision, but only an indirect opportunity to express itself at an intermediate stage of the procedure, intervening, so to speak, between the two Parliaments who have the competence to amend the Constitution; c) at the level of state organs, however, the Parliament—being the representative organ of the people—has the exclusive competence to amend the Constitution.

Even the mere description of the aforementioned characteristics of the revision process reveals a great deal about the Greek constitutional tradition, including: an extraordinary emphasis on the representative system of government, and an unusual lack of elements of direct democracy, in particular the institution of referendums, which is practically absent from Greek constitutional tradition; the extremely powerful position of the political parties, which practically have exclusive control over the amendment process, being able to use it as a major pooling of political issues in framing their political agenda, and in showing their profound determination for modernization in their idealistic visions of ambitious constitutional revisions; the very insecure position of the electorate, which may end up with no say in the amendment process, according to the prevailing view (if the three-fifths majority is achieved in the first phase of the revision, and the Revisionary Parliament can decide with the absolute majority of 151 votes).

All these features add up to a very specific conception of majoritarian democracy, in what is basically a two-party political system: the party that wins two elections in a row, securing in either Parliament the required three-fifths majority necessary to amend the Constitution. The most alarming feature of the present system of amending the Constitution in Greece (i.e. the prospect of a simple majority of the second Parliament completely overturning a proposal previously voted by the supermajority of three-fifths) can only be explained through the assumption that the amendment to the Constitution will be the main issue of the electoral debate, and that voters will decide which party to choose on the basis of that party's constitutional policies, and additionally on the ground of their own constitutional views. Obviously, these assumptions may turn out to be erroneous on both grounds. The amendment to the Constitution may not be the major political issue of the day, and, even more likely, the citizens may not have clear views about these issues. If, however, they were asked in a referendum to directly assess the final product of a constitutional revision, it could be much easier to summarize in a nutshell the implications in principle and the practical consequences of their vote, helping them to make a relatively informed decision.

The aforementioned unusual lack of elements of direct democracy reflects the extremely limited role of civil society in Greece's process of constitutional amendment. In Greece, Abraham Lincoln's ideal of a "government of the people, by the people, for the people" is associated primarily with political participation through political parties, and with the Constitution's ascription of the majority's political will to the people, as a collective body, on the grounds of equal political rights for citizens who vote in free and fair general elections, and in practice elect the government directly, given that the first party usually receives the absolute majority of seats in Parliament.

The fact that the will of the majority is taken, by a legal and political fiction, to be the will of the people is well embedded in Greek political culture as an expression of a deeply shared democratic ideal. In principle, this fiction does not seem to be empty, fake, harmful, or dangerous. It is not empty, because, due to nationalism, it expresses the will of a present collective entity, an existing political entity (i.e. the Greek people and the Greek nation, which is highly conscious of its history)! It is not fake, because, as has been mentioned previously, it is formed and expressed by free elections and by democratic procedures, which are deeply rooted in Greek life. It is not harmful, because democracy is something good to have. And finally, it is not dangerous, because the will of the people is constitutionally sacred, given the principle of popular sovereignty; and the will of the majority, along Rousseauist lines of thought, tends to be right, or even if not right, it is at least legitimate!

Greece's constitutional tradition has been strongly egalitarian and democratic, based on freedom of political speech, universal suffrage, and general elections as the necessary and sole means to obtain and exercise legitimate political power.[7] But the impartiality of the political process (one man, one vote) is not coupled and combined in Greece with a matching and complementary social impartiality (i.e. of a strong and developed civil society of equal citizens). At the social level, the partiality of family ties, or of clientelism, or of partisan political affiliation and favoritism are quite powerful, and, from the private point of view, they can be quite effective. There are simple reasons that explain this. In an underdeveloped society, based on agriculture, the household was a strong economic unit. In addition, family life plays important social functions, with emotional and economic overtones (e.g. assimilating the new member into the family's social network, continuation of a small family business, offering assistance by having grandparents to look after the children, providing support in times of economic hardship, taking care of the older generations, etc.). Obviously, although these practices may have their advantages, their disadvantages exert an increasingly negative impact as society develops economically on the road of capitalism and becomes more impersonal and wealthier! Therefore, in Greece, a seemingly very effective political integration is undermined by an incomplete social integration, which is weak and ineffective from the point of view of social justice and impartiality.

Impartiality as a principle of social justice may accept in theory, and does accept in political practice, quite different interpretations regarding what Amartya Sen has called basal equality[8] (i.e. the selection of the fundamental aspect of equality, which becomes the principal focus of egalitarian concerns, such as liberties, rights, capacities, utilities, incomes, resources, etc.). Irrespective, however, of the political conflict over the dominant conception of equality and the specific mixture that may come to prevail in political life, shaping the model of social and economic relations in society, impartiality constitutes the irreplaceable foundation of public morality. Public morality is not simply the morality of those who hold public office, but, more broadly, the set of rules and principles that define the terms and determine the outcome of individual competition, failure, and success, thus regulating mobility on the social ladder. This is an issue of public morality because, ultimately, it depends on clear legal rules of justice that are consistent and strict, but not draconian to the extent of being unreasonable and therefore impractical and inapplicable, as is often the case in Greece.

Social impartiality is crucial for a complete social integration, and it constitutes the necessary background for a strong civil society that is able to play an important role in the amendment process. On the contrary, clientelism, partisan political affiliation, favoritism, and nepotism are sources of corruption, violating impartiality in its various aspects and inhibiting the development of civil society, which depends on respect for equal individual autonomy. In Greece, there is no embedded tradition of social contract theory, with all its moral and political overtones regarding social justice and an overlapping consensus.[9]

The role of experts

The Standing Orders of Parliament provide in Art. 119 for the discretion of the Constitutional Amendment Committees to summon and hear experts as part of the amending process, thus providing the legal basis for the active participation of experts in constitutional design. Nevertheless, this option has not been activated, and the role of experts in constitutional amendment remains underdeveloped in Greece. On the contrary, it could be argued that the political class has an underlying suspicion of the intervention of experts in constitutional amendment, which is viewed as primarily a political process rather than a legislative task requiring expert support. Thus, despite the fact that the majority of MPs have traditionally been jurists and lawyers, including constitutional law professors, the design and wording of constitutional provisions has often proved to be unfortunate and problematic. Taking into account the stringency of the amending procedures, such deficiencies caused by the limited role of experts acquire even greater importance.

The limited institutional role results in the unofficial, yet active, involvement of the academic community in the amending process, through conferences and publications. Furthermore, institutions such as the National Committee on Human Rights, the Bar Association, and the Magistrates' Association take initiatives and publicize reports on the amendment proposals. Informal consulting is also offered by the Plenum of the Supreme Courts, especially by the Supreme Administrative Court (the Council of State), expressing opinions on amendment proposals, particularly those related to the function of the judicial system, and on human rights issues.

Constitutional dialogue and informal opinions by consulting bodies, although never acquiring a formal, systematic involvement in the amendment process, achieved a considerable impact in all constitutional revisions of the Constitution of 1975. This influence has resulted from the publicity given to these opinions. The participation of experts is actually integrated into the political process of constitutional change, instead of providing technical support or even intervening under the guise of expertise.

How do international and european law and jurisprudence affect constitutional revision?

According to the juristic theory of the state, the "legal person" of the state has some necessary ontological features (e.g. a population, a territory), but, from the legal point of view, its most crucial and striking characteristic is sovereignty, analyzed externally as national independence, and internally as supreme and efficacious political power. State legalism on the basis of national sovereignty formalizes and institutionalizes national political power. From a structural perspective, unitary states are particularly adequate and propitious for the legal fiction of the nation's general will. Indeed, ideally, in a unitary, republican, nationally homogenous state, the collective body of the sovereign people, deliberating in Parliament through its representatives, would arrive at the formation of the *volonté générale*. In contrast, federal states break up and divide sovereignty into plural entities (e.g. states, *Länder*) whose federated constituencies have their own political say but, taken together, compose one nation, organized at the federal level. The federal constitution is the supreme law of the land, specifying the competences of the central government in a system normally guaranteed and regulated by a federal (constitutional) court.

Since its national integration, completed in the three decades between 1915 and the end of World War II, Greece has been a typical example of a unitary state:

republican, nationally homogenous, with the collective body of the sovereign people speaking with one voice, initially ethnocentric and then, following the collapse of Colonel Papadopoulos's dictatorship in 1974, republican and democratic. But the voice of nationalism in Europe also took the extreme form of aggressive totalitarian monologues, with the destructive consequences of World War II. To tame blind ethnocentrism and to prevent war, Europe moved away from the monological sovereignty[10] of national independence to the dialogical interdependence of European integration (intergovernmental, or according to community method), on the basis of political equality, solidarity, and responsibility. This change of paradigm was a necessary condition for the parallel consolidation of cohesive and democratic societies in European countries. In this respect, the European Convention on Human Rights (ECHR) has been the other pillar of European integration; Greece, as does every other member state of the European Union (EU), bears the burden to reconcile its constitutional order with that of the ECHR.

The profound impact of European law and the ECHR on the Greek legal order is beyond doubt. The relationship of Greek constitutional law to international and European law is regulated primarily by Art. 28 of the Greek Constitution, which provides the basis for Greece's participation in the EU. The judgment of 18 December 2008 C-213/2007 of the European Court of Justice (Grand Chamber) in the case *Michaniki AE v Ethniko Symvoulio Radiotileorasis* (National Radio and Television Council) is significant, after the decision of the Greek Council of State to refer questions to the European Court of Justice (ECJ) concerning the interpretation of Directive 93/37/EC on public works contracts, with a view to assessing the compatibility of the constitutional provision at issue (Art. 14 para 9) with European law. The Greek Constitution contains a provision that prohibits the award of public works contracts to undertakings whose shareholders, executives, or their spouses are also shareholders or executives of media undertakings. The ECJ concluded that, in principle, European law does not call into question the possibility for a member state to adopt measures to tackle the risk of favoritism in public procurement procedures towards tenderers who are also active in the media sector, but that a national provision such as Art. 14 para 9 of the Constitution is disproportionate and therefore unacceptable in the light of European law.[11] As a result of the ECJ's judgment, Art. 14 para 9 of the Constitution was rendered inapplicable, thus confirming in the most explicit way the principle of primacy of EU law.

It should be noted, however, that there are inherent constitutional limits to the primacy of EU law, set by the principles of democracy, popular sovereignty, and protection of fundamental rights, according to both Art. 110 and Art. 28 para 3 of the Constitution. As a consequence, Greece could not, constitutionally, agree to the introduction of a temporary waiving of the right to participate in the voting of the European Council as a political sanction for the violation of the economic provisions of the Stability Pact. The Greek Constitution cedes sovereignty, and therefore independence, for the sake of interdependence and integration, on the basis of reciprocity and solidarity. Integration, however, requires participation in decision-making.

A list with important provisions of the Constitution, whose language or interpretation has been affected by EU law or the European Convention on Human Rights (ECHR), reversing established views of Greek constitutional law and jurisprudence, follows below:

- Article 4 para 2, Art. 116 para 2: Adoption of positive measures for promoting equality between men and women does not constitute discrimination on grounds of sex. The state shall take measures for the elimination of inequalities actually existing, in particular to the detriment of women[12] (under the influence of EU law).
- Article 4 para 4: Only Greek citizens shall be eligible for public service, except as otherwise provided by special laws (EU law imposed an interpretation opening Greek public service to EU citizens).
- Article 4 para 6: Every Greek capable of bearing arms is obliged to contribute to the defense of the fatherland as provided by law. Interpretative clause: the provision of paragraph 6 does not preclude that the law provides for the mandatory performance of other services, within or outside the armed forces (alternative service), by those having a substantiated conscientious objection to performing armed service or, generally, military duties (ECHR imposing the provision for conscientious objection).
- Article 5A para 1: All persons have the right to information, as specified by law. Restrictions to this right may be imposed by law only insofar as they are absolutely necessary and justified for reasons of national security, of combating crime, or of private rights and interests of third parties (ECHR influence).
- Article 7 para 3: The general confiscation of property is prohibited. The death penalty shall not be imposed, except in the cases provided by law for felonies perpetrated in time of war and related thereto (ECHR influence).
- Article 9A: All persons have the right to be protected from the collection, processing and use, especially by electronic means, of their personal data, as specified by law. The protection of personal data is ensured by an independent authority, which is constituted and operates as specified by law (EU law).
- Article 12 para 1: Greeks shall have the right to form non-profit associations and unions, in compliance with the law, which, however, may never subject the exercise of this right to prior permission (ECHR, pressing for interpretations that offer protection to minorities).
- Article 13 para 2: Proselytism is prohibited (ECHR; the Greek cases inaugurated the Art. 9 jurisprudence of the Court in Strasbourg and reversed established Greek constitutional law).
- Article 14 para 9: The capacity of owner, partner, major shareholder, or managing director of an information media enterprise is incompatible with the capacity of owner, partner, major shareholder, or managing director of an enterprise that undertakes towards the public administration or towards a legal entity of the wider public sector to perform works or to supply goods or services (EU law rendered it inapplicable).

- Article 15 para 2: Radio and television shall be under the direct control of the state. The control and imposition of administrative sanctions belong to the exclusive competence of the National Radio and Television Council, which is an independent authority, as specified by law (ECHR influence and EU law).
- Article 16 para 5: Education at university level shall be provided exclusively by institutions that are fully self-governed public law legal persons (EU law is in direct conflict with it, leading to a problematic situation regarding the branches of European universities in Greece).
- Article 17 para 1: Property is under the protection of the state; rights deriving therefrom, however, may not be exercised contrary to the public interest. In order for works of a general importance for the country's economy to be carried out, it is possible that, by special decision of the court that is competent for the final or the provisional determination of the compensation, the execution of works even prior to the determination and payment of the compensation is allowed, provided that a reasonable part of the compensation is paid, and that full guarantee is provided in favor of the beneficiary of the compensation, as provided by law (ECHR complements the restrictive interpretation of the Constitution, and extends protection beyond real property to contractual rights and obligations of economic value).
- Article 19 para 2: Matters relating to the Constitution, the operation, and the functions of the independent authority ensuring the secrecy of paragraph 1 (secrecy of correspondence) shall be specified by law (EU law).
- Article 20: Fair trial and right to judicial protection (ECHR influence, e.g. in reversing the excessive procedural formalism of Greek courts).
- Article 25 para 1: Restrictions of any kind that, according to the Constitution, may be imposed upon these rights, should be provided either directly by the Constitution or by statute, should a reservation exist in the latter's favor, and should respect the principle of proportionality (ECHR influence and EU law).
- Article 28: Interpretative clause: Art. 28 constitutes the foundation for the country's participation in the European integration process (EU law).
- Article 51 para 3: The MPs shall be elected through direct, universal, and secret ballot by the citizens who have the right to vote, as specified by law. Article 102 para 2: Local government agencies shall enjoy administrative and financial independence. Their authorities shall be elected by universal and secret ballot, as specified by law (EU law introducing interpretations that allow EU citizens to vote in municipal elections).
- Article 57 para 1: The duties of MPs are also incompatible with the exercise of any profession. Para 3: MPs who accept any of the capacities or activities mentioned in this or in the preceding Article, and which are characterized as impediments to run for Parliament or as being incompatible with holding parliamentary office, shall forfeit that office *ipso jure* (ECHR, leading to its elimination by constitutional amendment in 2008).
- Article 62: During the parliamentary term, the MPs shall not be prosecuted, arrested, imprisoned, or otherwise confined without prior leave granted by

Parliament (ECHR, reversing the expansive and overprotective interpretation of the Greek legislature and courts).

- Article 70 para 8: The Standing Orders of Parliament shall specify the manner in which Parliament is informed by the government on issues being the object of regulation in the framework of the EU, and debates on these (EU law).
- Article 80 para 2: The minting or issuing of currency shall be regulated by law. Interpretative clause: Paragraph 2 does not impede the participation of Greece in the process of Economic and Monetary Union, in the wider framework of European integration, according to the provisions of Art. 28 (EU law).
- Article 103 para 2: Conversion by law of employees with private law employment relations in the wider public sector to permanent civil servants or conversion by law of their employment contracts into contracts of unlimited duration is prohibited (EU law).
- Article 103 para 9: Law shall specify matters relating to the establishment and activities of the Ombudsman, who functions as an independent authority (EU law led to the introduction and constitutionalization of Independent Authorities in Greece, including the Ombudsman).
- Article 106 para 4: The cost of purchase or the counterpart to the compulsory participation of the state or other public agencies must indispensably be determined by a court and must be in full, so as to correspond to the value of the purchased enterprise or the participation therein (EU economic constitution prevailed over Greek economic constitution).

The proposals discussed at the European level for a constitutional limit to public debt, and for constitutionally required balanced budgets, show how the penetration of European law into the national legal orders has not only increased, but has changed qualitatively. During the first era of European integration, the common constitutional traditions of the member states offered the catalyst for consolidating the European order, replacing the older paradigm of comparative law, which had been focusing mainly on the differences between the civil law countries themselves (France and Germany, primarily), and later, with the Anglo-American common law. The requirements of a European economic government, sustaining and supporting monetary union, and resolving co-ordination problems between the Euro-states, introduces a new era, where the European factor claims authority over the national constitutional orders, reshaping them more directly and more decisively in the course of deeper and further European integration. European constitutional law lives in the age of interdependence, when the isolation of full and intact sovereignty has been replaced by the advantages of combined but restricted sovereignty within the EU; and the European peoples are tasting the sweet and sour grapes of their common political itinerary.

Form of government, political conflict, and constitutional revision

The lag of social integration vis à vis political integration in Greece does not confirm the Tocquevillian hypothesis about a democratic civil society being the necessary social background of a stable democratic tradition. Greece does not have an embedded public morality of impartiality, but it does have a majoritarian political system, influenced by populism. An electoral system of the so-called "enhanced proportionality" favors the winner of the elections (i.e. the first party), which as a rule secures the absolute majority of parliamentary seats, leading to stable, one-party governments. In general, political parties are strong and extremely influential, generously financed by the state budget every year and during the elections,[13] but they lack internal democracy, and are quite centralized and focused on the personality of the leader, who is the party's candidate to become a powerful Prime Minister, at least in the case of the two main political parties contending for power.

In light of Greece's political system, it is not difficult to explain why referendums are taken to be antagonistic towards general elections and disruptive of the ruling party's political program rather than complementary and corrective; why the absence of popular initiatives and referendums for the ratification of constitutional amendments has been accepted as something natural; and why the amendment process is so dominated and controlled by the political parties.

Indeed, the representativeness of the National Assembly, which amends the Constitution, amounts to the representation achieved through the election of political parties. There is, however, one noteworthy qualification: as a matter of deontology, in parliamentary votes on questions of constitutional amendment, the party line does play an important, if not decisive political role, but there is no firm party discipline here; as a result, the deputies are allowed to play a more influential and active role than in regular legislative work in the amendment process. In particular, the group of deputies of the ruling party may even determine the outcome of the amendment process, especially through their inner discussions in preparing the party's line. So, in the most extensive amendment of the present Constitution, in 2001, the group of deputies of PASOK (socialists), the then ruling party, rejected the most controversial amendments on reforms of environmental protection, or judicial review of the constitutionality of the laws, proposed by the party's leadership.[14]

Democracy without the people is religion without God, which is something totally inconceivable, at least for a monotheistic system, or for a traditional conception of popular sovereignty. But who are "The People"? What is this supreme and sovereign collective being? The answer is clear: the nation. The Greek state is the nation-state of the Greeks. Next, what is the legally binding composition of the nation? Are there any constitutional limits or conditions on the issue of citizenship, in the name of national identity? Does popular sovereignty entail substantive constraints, regarding the configuration of the Greek nation? Traditionally, Greek citizenship has been particularly difficult to obtain, and the government enjoyed nearly unlimited discretion in declining applications for citizenship. This selectiveness was supposed to mean a lot to those who shared the privilege of Greek citizenship, but until recently it did not bother any others (who did not care), because it had not operated exclusively. As the term *diaspora* shows, Greeks have always been a nation of emigrants, while Greece was not the destination of immigrants. Since the 1990s, the fall of Communism, globalization, and Greece's participation in the EU have radically changed all this. Now, about 10 per cent of the population are immigrants. Does the unfettered discretion of the state to reject citizenship entail the equally broad discretion of the state to accept citizenship applications? A recent law provided a general and indiscriminate right of specific categories of immigrants to obtain Greek citizenship, as long as they fulfilled certain objective conditions. In this way, the law did not provide for an individual selection process of the candidates who applied for Greek citizenship, in a way that would show conclusively that they could (and should) become Greek citizens. On this ground, a decision of the Council of State in 2011 found the law unconstitutional:[15] national homogeneity took priority over social pluralism.

Another interesting and important implication regarding the (minimal) role of civil society in Greece's constitutional amendment process concerns the relationship between the Constitution's amendment and the exercise of constituent power. At the legal level, the two concepts are clearly distinguished. According to the traditional doctrine, the exercise of constituent power is legally unlimited and formally unconstrained, while the revision of the Constitution is a legal competence, a constituted power, subject to the procedural and substantive provisions of the existing Constitution. But the political dynamics of the power to amend the Constitution and the constituent power are quite different. In the nineteenth century, the first Professor of Constitutional Law at the University of Athens explained that the sovereign people does not fall asleep once the Constitution is enacted, but remains vigilant and alert to check and correct any violation of the constitutional order, retaining the exercise of sovereign power at any moment.[16] In the same vein, the last article of the Greek Constitution provides for the right to resistance against any attempt to dissolve the Constitutional order. Of course, the Constitution holds that sovereign power is to be exercised in the way specified by the Constitution itself. But the notion of active exercise of sovereign power by the people consolidates a tradition of political activism in Greece, which is significant for the unusual tolerance of a relatively high degree of political violence in clashes between demonstrators and the police.

However, there are obvious limits to the aforementioned approach. Political activism and voluntarism can easily turn into a type of Carl Schmitt's "decisionism."[17] But there is no reliable and credible way to speak in the name of the people other than free general elections. So, unless the political situation is that of a popular revolution against a dictatorship, the exercise of political violence in the name of the people, by any group or party whatsoever, is in principle illegitimate and clearly unlawful. This poses the question of democracy's normative constraints on constituent power and constitutional revision, derived from the inherent logical requirements and features of an impartial and inclusive democratic political process, without which the militant exercise of constituent power by some in the name of the people becomes not a case of heroism, but hubris and crime!

Popular sovereignty dominated by a polarized political system results in the positivistic view that the Constitution reflects the unstable equilibrium of the prevailing political forces of society.[18] Accordingly, the Constitution is ephemeral, exposed to changing historical circumstance and impervious political situations. In the light of the aforementioned discussions on the strength of electoral politics and on the weakness of social impartiality, this influential approach in Greece is, in some views,[19] clearly insufficient and unsatisfactory, both politically and legally. Of course, the political ideology of free elections and of an impartial political process may be supported by the larger part of society, contested by some, and opposed by a few; but the mere fact of such political division and disagreement does not render partisan and partial the Constitution's normative commitment to an impartial and inclusive democratic political process, whose perennial objective is to regulate and arbitrate the existing deep and divisive political disagreements in a fair, peaceful, and non-violent way.

Judicial review of constitutional amendments

All Greek Constitutions, as already noted, set material limits to constitutional amendments, additional to the procedural and temporal requirements. For this purpose, the older Constitutions of Greece provided that the fundamental provisions of the Constitution are not subject to revision. This was a notoriously vague and imprecise clause, and a constant source of interpretive friction and controversy. For the first time, the Constitution of 1975 replaced this clause as follows, in Art. 110 para 1: "The provisions of the Constitution shall be subject to revision with the exception of those which determine the form of government as a Parliamentary Republic and those of Art. 2 para 1 (human dignity), Art. 4 paras 1 (equality), 4, and 7 (prohibition of titles of nobility), Art. 5 paras 1 (free development of personality) and 3 (personal freedom), Art. 13 paras 1 (freedom of religious conscience) and 26 (separation of powers)." This is clearly an improvement over the previous situations, but there remain considerable uncertainties over the interpretation of the terms "determine the form of government." The Constitution provides that Greece is a republican, parliamentary democracy. The form of government does not have merely a formal meaning, indicating the principal state organs, which determine the identity of the regime (e.g. the electorate, the President of the Republic, the Parliament, the government, and the judiciary); it is also qualitative, capturing the liberal, democratic, and representative character of the regime. This combination of both the formal and the qualitative features offers a better understanding of the normative content of the clause in question. But, to give only one example, does the Constitution allow the amendment of the President's election process from indirect (through Parliament) to direct (by the people) democracy? Some argue that this would be inconsistent with the parliamentary nature of the regime; others argue that direct legitimacy does not transform the regime from a parliamentary into a presidential system, and comparative law supports them. If the President is devoid of competences, then no matter whether directly or indirectly elected, he or she cannot exercise power because he or she does not have any! It seems that an overall assessment of the final structural equilibriums of the regime, as affected by a constitutional amendment, is necessary before one draws the conclusion that the form of government has been amended unconstitutionally; there is no room for mechanical interpretations. This, of course, does not imply that there cannot be cases that are downright unconstitutional, such as a replacement of the Parliament by another organ, elected indirectly, or the abolition of the multi-party system.

A special question concerns the possibility of amending Art. 110 itself. It should be noted, in this respect, that the exclusion of Art. 110 from amendment is becoming more and more counterintuitive, as the impact of European law on the Greek legal order through Art. 28 of the Constitution dictates formal changes, or new interpretations, or renders inactive constitutional provisions, without the application of Art. 110, in what has been considered to be a parallel European amendment process.[20]

Over the question of whether the courts have the right, *per se*, to subject to judicial review the constitutionality of the amendments,[21] the prevailing view is in favor of this possibility; but there are also strong voices against this possibility, indicating that the Constitution guarantees judicial review of the constitutionality of the laws, and not of the Constitution itself, following its revision. The counter-argument is that Art. 110 is part of the Constitution, and actually the cornerstone of its rigid character, and therefore it would be unreasonable to be excluded from constitutional protection through judicial review. The discussion is naturally influenced by considerations regarding the necessity of checks and balances, or the threat of government by judiciary. Recent jurisprudence of the High Special Court (11/2003) has subjected to judicial review the content of constitutional amendments (regarding the incompatibility of deputy status with the exercise of any profession). Article 87 is also relevant because it expressly provides that judges are, on no occasion whatsoever, obliged to succumb to provisions posited in abolition of the Constitution. Finally, Art. 120 para 4 provides that: "Observance of the Constitution is entrusted to the patriotism of the Greeks who shall have the right and the duty to resist by all possible means against anyone who attempts the violent abolition of the Constitution." The abolition, or in literal translation, dissolution of the Constitution, differs from mere violation thereof, because it covers primarily cases of usurpation of the legislative authority by other than the constitutionally prescribed organs of the state. Dissolution, as opposed to mere violation, hints at the applicable standard of judicial review of constitutional amendments; it should not work as a substitute for the sovereign power of the people. Judicial scrutiny should show respect for the right of future generations to amend the Constitution, while guaranteeing the unhindered exercise of popular sovereignty.

Criticism of the amendment procedure

Ever since their introduction, the material and procedural limits provided in Art. 110 of the Constitution have been subject to criticism due to their overreaching stringency. In 1985, the amendment proposal, which led to the 1986 revision regarding the authorities vested on the President of the Republic, also included a new scheme amending the amendment process; the latter provided for the conclusion of the amendment process in one parliamentary term by a resolution taken by an enhanced majority of three-fifths of the total number of MPs. However, the vehement reaction of constitutional scholars and the opposition parties to that reform led to its withdrawal. Thus, an interesting controversy began regarding the possibility of amending the amending procedure itself. The dominant stance among constitutional scholars rejects as *contradictio in adjecto* the possibility of altering Art. 110 para 1 of the Constitution, which sets out the material limits to constitutional revision; accepting, however, that changes whose aim is to render the amending process more effective without endangering the Constitution's level of entrenchment may be realized by way of constitutional revision.

What seems to be a hands-off issue is the type and level of entrenchment, despite the fact that Greece's Constitution is one of the most difficult to change in Europe, and the excessive stringency of the procedures has caused trouble in the past, leading to violations of the amendment procedures in the era of political turbulence before 1975; while afterwards, it has inhibited the adoption of necessary alterations. This corresponds to a phobia against flexibility, in a problematic equation of stringent amending procedures with constitutional stability, explaining the fact that prior violations of the amending procedure were not viewed as an indication of the need to rationalize the process; on the contrary, they were viewed as a reason to safeguard the Constitution. Furthermore, polarization of the political system encourages distrust among political actors, setting a major obstacle for attempts towards greater flexibility.

Yet, the amending process has been under heavy fire from constitutional theory, especially in recent years, for three major reasons: first, setting a five-year interval for the initiation of a new amending process poses serious obstacles for the Constitution's ability to adjust to new developments at the national or international level. This may trigger informal amendments and even lead to violations of the Constitution, threatening legal certainty and undermining its very normativity. Second, the way in which the required majorities are structured does not facilitate consensual constitutional revision. In case a three-fifths majority in the first Parliament determines those provisions that are to be revised, the next Parliament may decide freely, and by an absolute majority of the total number of its MPs, on the content of the provisions under revision. This means that, if a political party has the absolute majority of seats in the Revisionary Parliament, it is in a position to determine at will the content of the Articles under revision; in this case, the final substantive outcome of the amendment is hardly the product of consent, thus undermining the legitimacy of the Constitution. Third, the participation of the electorate in the amendment process is not, in reality, served through the requirement of the intervening general elections, to the extent that voters in general elections do not vote based on the amendment proposals but rather following their political convictions, according to the general agenda of political parties, and their favorite candidate.[22]

Accordingly, the following suggestions for improving the amendment process have been made:

- Abolishment or reduction of the required minimum interval.
- The conclusion of the amending process in one Parliamentary session, with an enhanced two-thirds majority of MPs instead of the three-fifths provided for by the current arrangement.

- The conclusion of the amendment process in one Parliamentary session, plus the requirement of a referendum.
- The proposal and the decision on the amendment to be concluded by the first Parliament, requiring merely the confirmation of the second Parliament, following general elections.
- Enhancement of the role of experts in the amendment process and participation of civil society.

Contemporary debate on the need for a future constitutional revision

The recent severe economic crisis and the revelation of serious public debt, whose grave repercussions were largely unknown to the Greek public, have led to curtailments of sovereignty and infringements on fundamental rights, introduced by Greece's loan agreements with the European Union and the International Monetary Fund (the so-called "Memoranda"); and, inevitably, constitutional dialogue has been reoriented accordingly. As a consequence, a heated academic and political debate regarding the need for a new constitutional revision, as well as the need for amending the amendment procedure, is developing in the midst of the debt crisis and under its impact on the political system.

The basic suggestions for constitutional amendments fall into two major categories: proposals that are standard in all constitutional revisions, and those only recently framed either due to specific problems encountered in the application of the Constitution, or connected to the current political and economic crisis.

Thus, the following are repeatedly suggested proposals, several of which have managed to gain broad political consensus:

- Since the late 1990s, a debate regarding the need for establishing a Constitutional Court has been ongoing and the issue was twice brought before the constitutional legislature—during the constitutional revisions of 2001 and 2008—without however obtaining the required support. Arguments in favor of the establishment of a Constitutional Court stress the need for a more coherent and systematic constitutional review, while its opponents argue that the present model of judicial review of the constitutionality of laws has proved to be effective, and its change entails the danger of dismantling constitutional jurisprudence while creating a court more susceptible to politics.
- The increasing criticism of the concentrated power of the Prime Minister, and arguments in favor of further checks and balances, has led to proposals for enhancing the presidential competences as well as altering the presidential election process in order to detach it from the threat of general elections, if the necessary three-fifths majority of the total number of deputies is not achieved (Art. 32 of the Constitution). Among relevant proposals, direct election by the people has also been suggested.
- Appointments to the posts of President and Vice-President of the three Supreme Courts are decided by the Cabinet (Art. 90 para 5 of the Constitution),

through selection among the members of the respective courts. Criticisms regarding the above procedure have preoccupied the legal and political debate since the early 1980s, culminating during the 2001 revision. Selection by Cabinet has been considered a means through which the executive may exert influence on the judiciary. Such allegations also stemmed from the Cabinet's practice of bypassing seniority in appointing magistrates as Presidents of the Supreme Courts, suggesting possible influence of political criteria. Several ideas for changes to that system have thus been proposed, such as vesting the authority for the selection of Supreme Court Presidents in Parliament through heightened majority, or, as supported by the Council of State, conferring on the courts themselves the authority to select their Vice-Presidents and restricting the Cabinet's choice of the Presidents among the Vice-Presidents.

- According to Art. 16 of the Constitution, a university-level education is provided exclusively by institutions that are fully self-governed "legal persons" of public law, operating under state supervision. These provisions have triggered two major constitutional and political debates regarding their amendment: on the one hand, strong arguments have been made in favor of allowing the operation of private universities, at least regarding non-profit institutions; on the other hand, it has been argued that full self-government sets unwarranted impediments to university reform and modernization.

More recent proposals include:

- Special constitutional regulation of the criminal liability of members of Government is a feature of many modern democracies aiming to safeguard them from continuous criminal prosecutions hindering the performance of their duties. Nevertheless, Art. 86 of the Constitution sets up an overprotective safety net, which, in combination with its abuse in practice, leads to subverting any actual possibility of criminal conviction of members of Government. Therefore, this constitutional arrangement is subject to strong criticism and suggestions for it to be abolished in the next constitutional revision.
- The establishment of incompatibility between the office of MPs and Ministers is proposed in order to enhance separation of powers. But others suggest the exact opposite change—i.e. prohibiting the appointment of Ministers who are not MPs as a means of limiting the omnipotence of the Prime Minister.
- The introduction of new types of referendums has been proposed; for example, the adoption of referendums on bills passed by Parliament following a proposal voted for by at least one-third of the total number of MPs or the adoption of referendums initiated by the people.

The recent constitutional revision of 2008, conducted in times of blissful normality, turned out to be a wasted opportunity since consensus was not achieved and only a few minor changes were adopted. Only three years later, in the context of a multi-faceted crisis, the debate on constitutional amendment is at its peak;

nevertheless, it is highly questionable as to whether the current situation allows a sober reconsideration of the Constitution.

Conclusion

Greek constitutional and political history has been remarkably turbulent. Since 1822, the country's Constitutions have been written, entrenched, and codified. Nevertheless, the amending procedures were never respected before 1986, because of their extreme stringency and the persistent political polarization in an unstable institutional context from 1915 to 1975.

The current Constitution's amending formula lays down a slow and demanding process of revision, which becomes even more cumbersome when operating within the context of Westminster-style parliamentarism and a party system prone to political conflict. Therefore, since 1975, when the current Constitution was enacted, only three revisions have taken place. These revisions are dominated by the elites of the political parties, with the role of the people or of legal experts being of minor importance. Informal change is mostly effected through the impact of the jurisprudence of the European Court of Human Rights and the European Court of Justice, which exert influence on both legislature and judiciary.

Despite the difficulty of formal constitutional change, hindering the document's regular updating, lingering memories of the turbulent past in combination with a dominant tradition of legal positivism, maintain the perception of this very difficulty as an asset and as a means for protecting constitutional stability. This standard understanding seems to be constantly reconfirmed, whenever a proposal is made to alter the amending formula. Nevertheless, in light of the debt crisis, opinions in favor of making the amending formula more flexible have started to gain ground, at least with regard to the abolition of the mandatory five-year time lapse between two revisions. Major transformations of the political party system have been taking place since the end of 2011, leading to a coalition government and to an unprecedented fragmentation of the political forces. These developments may also affect the prevailing ideas regarding the engineering of constitutional change in Greece.

Notes

1 See more details in X. Contiades and A. Fotiadou, "Constitutional Law in Greece", in L.F.M. Besselink, P.P.T. Bovend'Eert, H. Broeksteeg, R. de Lange and W. Voermans (eds), *Constitutional Law of the EU Member States*, Kluwer Law International, 2012.

2 N. Alivizatos, *The Constitution and its Enemies in modern Greek History*, Athens: Polis, 2011 (in Greek).

3 See K. Chryssogonos, *Constitutional Law*, Athens-Thessaloniki: Sakkoulas, 2003 (in Greek); E. Venizelos, *Courses in Constitutional Law*, Athens-Komotini: Ant. N. Sakkoulas, 2008 (in Greek).

4 The amending procedure provided for in Art. 110 paras 2–6 of the Constitution is further specified in Art. 119 of the Standing Orders of Parliament.

5 This indicates that the constitutional amendment process in Greece is perceived as part of political party competition. See X. Contiades, *The Revision of the Constitution*, Athens-Komotini: Ant. N. Sakkoulas, 2000 (in Greek), p. 372ff.

6 P. Spyropoulos, *Introduction to Constitutional Law*, Ant. N. Sakkoulas, 2009 (in Greek), p. 91.
7 See G. Sotirelis, *Constitution and Elections in Greece 1864–1909*, Athens: Themelio, 1991 (in Greek).
8 See A. Sen, *Inequality Reexamined*, Oxford: Oxford U.P., 1995, p. 132.
9 See J. Rawls, *Justice as Fairness*, Belknap, Harvard MA, 2003, p. 32.
10 See N. Walker, "Late Sovereignty in the European Union", in N. Walker (ed.), *Sovereignty in Transition*, Oxford: Hart Publishing, 2003, p. 10. See, on the distinction between monologic and dialogic discourse, V. Brown, *Adam Smith's Discourse*, London: Routledge, 1994, p. 5.
11 See online. Available HTTP: <http://ec.europa.eu/dgs/legal_service/arrets/07c213_en.pdf>, for the summary.
12 Translated (all cited articles in the text) by Prof. Xenophon Paparrigopoulos and Stavroula Vassilouni, Directorate of Studies, Hellenic Parliament, 2008.
13 See Law 3032/2002.
14 See N. Alivizatos, "The Constitutional Revision of 2001", *To Syntagma*, 2001 (in Greek), vol. 5, p. 949.
15 See Greek Council of State, 350/2011, on Law 3838/2010.
16 See N. I. Saripolos, *Treatise of Constitutional Law*, Athens, 1851, p. 56.
17 See C. Schmitt, *Über die drei Arten des rechtswissenschaftlichen Denkens* (Greek Translation, H. Papaxaralambous), Athens: Papazisis, 2009, p. 151.
18 See A. Manessis, *Constitutional Law I*, Athens-Thessaloniki: Sakkoulas, 1980 (in Greek), p. 179.
19 See I.A. Tassopoulos, *The Ethicopolitical Foundation of the Constitution*, Athens – Komotini: Ant. N. Sakkoulas, 2001 (in Greek), p. 23.
20 See e.g. the discussion in J. Iliopoulos Strangas, *Greek Constitutional Law and European Integration*, Athens-Komotini: Ant. N. Sakkoulas, 1996 (in Greek), p. 37.
21 See e.g. the discussion in I.A. Tassopoulos, *Checks and Balances and the Revision of the Constitution*, Athens-Thessaloniki: Sakkoulas, 2007 (in Greek), p. 199.
22 See X. Contiades, *Deficient Democracy*, Athens: Sideris, 2009 (in Greek), p. 211ff.

10 Constitutional amendment in Ireland

Fiona de Londras and David Gwynn Morgan

Given the amount of popular and political attention currently being visited on the topic in Ireland, this is an opportune time for us to consider the normally arcane question of constitutional reform. This attention is largely driven by the country's recent fall from economic grace and the public reaction to it. The first part of this reaction was to remove from power (by a huge margin) the party that had formed the Government for 61 of the 79 years since it first came to office in 1932 (Fianna Fáil). In the general election leading to that party's removal, substantial attention was paid to constitutional reform, although the calls for constitutional change might fairly be described as more persistent than coherent at times.[1] The central elements of the clamour for constitutional change focus on more efficient control and accountability of public bodies, and the slimming down of the public sector and its emoluments. To some extent, these calls for change have emerged from non-constitutional experts, such as newspaper columns, and have tended to attach blame for Ireland's current economic straits to constitutional structures or the fundamentally misunderstand Constitution.[2] Notwithstanding that, the mood for constitutional change was seized on by political parties and fed into the establishment of some "popular" initiatives to debate and propose social change, including constitutional change. Preparations are currently under way for the establishment of a Constitutional Convention through which a range of individuals would draft a new constitution to be put before the people during 2016, the centenary of the Easter Rising against British Rule.

A notable absentee in this debate has been any call for change to the amending process itself. As we shall see, the major feature of formal constitutional change (which is partly a response to the ease with which the post-Independence Constitution [1922] could be amended) is a referendum of all qualified voters, and it is probable that, in these anti-politician times, this exactly suits the popular mood.

Part of the push for constitutional change is undoubtedly connected to the fact that Ireland's constitutions (the original Constitution in 1922 and its skeleton substantially retained in the present 1937 Constitution) were largely early Westminster (British) export models. In other words, in many respects, the form of government established in the Constitution is nearly a century old, and much of the updating that has occurred in the constitutional structuring of government has, in reality, been the product of two informal methods of constitutional change (judicial interpretation and organic law) and is not reflected in the constitutional text. As a result, there is a feeling that the text of the Constitution is somewhat outmoded, both in terms of governmental structure and statements of social values.

In outline terms, Ireland has a non-executive head of state, the President, who has certain functions as "Guardian of the Constitution," which she exercises at her own discretion. The executive power of the state is exercised by the "Government," which consists of the Prime Minister (Taoiseach) and 14 other members. The detailed administration of the executive function is carried out by the Departments of State, which are headed by members of the Government. The Government is responsible to, and may be removed by, the Dáil, which is the Lower House of the Parliament (Oireachtas) and is elected by universal suffrage. However, the Government is not responsible to the Seanad (the Senate, or Upper House). Finally, the judicial branch of Government is housed in a system of general (rather than specialized) courts. Although there is no formal constitutional court, as we shall see, the "superior courts" (i.e. the High Court and, on appeal, the Supreme Court) operate a strong system of judicial review of laws and administrative actions under the principle of constitutional supremacy.

History and evolution of constitutional amendment in Ireland

Between 1937 and 2011, 32 proposed amendments have been put to the people, of which 23 have been approved.[3] (There were also two "running-in" amendments achieved without referendum under Art. 51 of the Constitution, when it was possible to amend without a referendum.) In line with the way in which the rate of change has accelerated in the post-modern world, the pace of constitutional amendment has also increased exponentially. No successful amendments were put to the people until 1972 (although, as we shall see, three amendments were unsuccessfully proposed to the people). Then, during the 1972–1996 period (1996 being the year in which the Constitutional Review Group, explained below, commenced work), 18 proposals to amend the Constitution were put to the people. From 1996 to the end of 2011, there have been 11 more. So far as subject matter is concerned, they may be classified into the following six groups:

The European Union

Eight of the proposals relate to the European Economic Community (EEC) or the European Union (EU). First, in 1972, a constitutional amendment was held to enable the state to join the then EEC. In addition, a referendum is now held whenever substantial changes to the treaties are being undertaken at European level. Indeed, on two occasions the Irish people have been presented with "repeat referenda" on the same proposed treaty change (the Nice Treaty and the Lisbon Treaty).

Northern Ireland

Two amendments have (directly or indirectly) concerned Northern Ireland. This region, which remains a province of the United Kingdom, was partitioned from the southern two-thirds of the island, which became independent in 1921. Articles 2 and 3 of the 1937 Constitution had originally staked a territorial claim over the six counties that make up Northern Ireland. When, in 1998–1999, a compromise was reached on the status of Northern Ireland between Ireland and the United Kingdom, these Articles were substantially amended to read that "a united Ireland shall be brought about only by peaceful means through the consent of a majority of the people, democratically expressed in both jurisdictions . . ." In addition, the remodeled Art. 2 conferred an automatic right to citizenship on anyone born on the island, including those born in Northern Ireland. The 2004 citizenship referendum, considered in the next paragraph, partially rowed back on that change, by confining automatic citizenship to those born on the island of Ireland with "at least one parent who is an Irish citizen or entitled to be an Irish citizen."[4]

Human rights

Three amendments concerned the field of human rights. Two of these were enacted to allow for furtherance of international policy, namely prohibition of the death penalty (2001) and ratification of the Rome Statute of the International Criminal Court (2001). A further amendment reversed Supreme Court decisions,[5] which had stipulated that it would be unconstitutional to refuse an accused person bail, on the basis that it was suspected that the accused might commit an offence while on bail.

Voting

Seven referenda have concerned matters of electoral regulation and voting. The first three of these (all of which were unsuccessful) would have made a most fundamental change. Two (in 1959 and 1968, effectively the same proposal) would have replaced the current single transferrable vote system with a "first past the post" system for parliamentary elections, which would have had serious implications given the historical dominance of one political party in the state.[6] The third (again, 1968) would have permitted greater representation per resident in rural than in urban areas, and would also have had the effect of favoring the Government party. This would, in substance, have reversed the decision of the High Court in *O'Donovan v Attorney General*.[7] The remaining four referenda in this category were not controversial as between the parties or otherwise, and were passed by a large majority: lowering the voting age for parliamentary, presidential, and local authority elections (1972); permitting the extension of university representation in the Seanad (Upper House) to allow the graduates of new universities to vote[8] (1979); extending voting rights in parliamentary elections to certain non-citizens (in practice, the British who are resident in this state) (1984) and effectively reversing

Re. Art. 26 and the Electoral (Amendment) Bill 1983 [1984, IR 268]; and both recognizing the local government system and requiring local elections at least once every five years (1998).

Religious and moral matters

There have been eight referenda on what might broadly be called religious and/or moral–sexual matters, five of which were passed. The first of these, held in 1972, removed the provisions providing a "special position" to the Roman Catholic Church in Ireland and was relatively uncontroversial. The remaining seven all relate to abortion or divorce. In its original form, the Constitution banned the possibility of divorce. The first attempt to introduce divorce by referendum in 1986 was unsuccessful but a later proposed amendment in 1995 succeeded. In 1983, the Constitution was amended to protect the life of the unborn child, but following the finding in *Attorney General v X*[9] that some abortion was still permitted, further referenda followed. In 1992, two amendments to allow for freedom of travel for abortion and free availability of information relating to abortion succeeded, but two more proposals that attempted to restrict abortion to narrower parameters than those recognized by the Supreme Court in *X* were defeated in 1992 and 2002 respectively.

Institutions of Government

There have been only four amendments to modernize the institutions of Government. The first of these reversed careless *obiter dictum* from the Supreme Court in *M v An Bord Uchtála*,[10] which suggested that adoption orders issued by the Adoption Board might violate the separation of powers under Art. 34.1 (1979). The second stemmed from another Supreme Court ruling, to the effect that collective Government (aka cabinet) responsibility required confidentiality.[11] The Constitution was amended so that a public inquiry was no longer barred from inquiring whether a particular topic had been discussed at a Government meeting. Finally, in 2011, an amendment was passed allowing for judicial remuneration to be reduced in line with that of others paid from the public purse; and another, reversing a Supreme Court decision [*Maguire v Ardagh* (2002) 1 IR 385] that limited the capacity of parliamentary inquiries to make findings, was rejected.

Two general points emerge from this list of amendments. The first is that a substantial proportion of the amendments (on one count, eight out of 32[12]) were regarded as necessary in order to reverse statements of law resulting from unpopular judicial interpretations, or because of a judicial decision making it clear that a desired course of action would be possible only following a successful referendum to amend the Constitution. Second, a surprisingly small number of amendments related to institutional changes in regard to central government. We return to these features below.

Informal methods of constitutional change

In Ireland, there are two main mechanisms for informal methods of constitutional change: judicial interpretation and organic law.

Judicial "interpretation" of the Constitution

The ultimate arbiter of the meaning of the constitutional text in Ireland is the Supreme Court. Partly because of the inertia of the legislature in addressing and updating the socio-economic aspects of the legal system up to the 1990s, many developments that came about through either legislation, or even by way of constitutional amendment in other jurisdictions were in fact driven by constitutional litigation in Ireland. There are two contrasting aspects to this. First, we have already noted that judicial interpretations of the Constitution have sometimes been removed by means of a subsequent formal constitutional amendment uprooting them. But, in other cases, the Irish political branches have accepted significant judicial development of the Constitution. Without delving too deeply into general constitutional law, the following doctrines may be mentioned as significant elements of the *acquis constitutionnel*.[13]

First, substantial "unenumerated personal rights" have been deduced from Art. 40.3.1 of the Constitution.[14] These have given rise to about 20 aspects of protection of the person and personality, including rights to privacy,[15] to bodily integrity,[16] and to freedom from torture.[17] In large part, these rights were devised or discovered in litigation taken to challenge the constitutionality of older and outmoded legislation. Second, although the separation of powers is never expressly mentioned in the constitutional text, the three organs of government and their exclusive functions are outlined, and from these constitutional capsules the courts have woven a comprehensive separated powers doctrine that now functions as the spine of the Irish constitutional order.[18] Third, and as considered further below, it was a Supreme Court decision that resulted in Ireland needing a constitutional amendment before the state can ratify major developments to the foundation treaties of the EU.[19] Fourth, the prohibition of extra generous parliamentary representation for rural areas, prohibited by the High Court and subsequently rejected by the people in a referendum, has had immense consequences for the balance of political power in Ireland.[20]

This *acquis constitutionnel* comprises more than mere case law; together with the basic text, it is "the accumulated sense of legal tradition and case law, together with legal methodology and reasoning . . . which really counts"[21] when determining what the Constitution requires, permits, and prohibits. In that sense it is, of course, at the heart of governmental decision-making and the advice given by the Attorney General on the constitutional (im)permissibility of desired governmental action.

Organic law

Unless it intends to change something expressly governed by the Constitution, a Government will usually have to decide whether to bring about a desired change through organic law or through constitutional amendment. Generally speaking, Irish Governments have not been overly reticent in holding constitutional referenda where constitutionally entrenched systems or principles were candidates for reform.[22] However, there have been numerous occasions when substantial change to governance of the state was introduced by organic law because it did not interfere with existing constitutional provisions, even though constitutional amendment may have been more appropriate, given the nature of the changes in question. This has particularly been the case in relation to major changes in the government apparatus, including legislation: to control political parties; giving independent authority and responsibility to (civil servant) heads of government departments over (elected) Ministers;[23] vesting the selection of civil servants in a politically neutral body; creating an independent office of Director of Public Prosecutions; establishing an independent body to run the courts service; and proposed law on judicial standards and discipline.[24] These are changes that arguably belong within the constitutional text, as they go to the heart of constitutionalist values of transparency, accountability, and maintenance of institutional independence.

There are other situations in which changes introduced by organic law seem to grate against values outlined in the Constitution, creating a dissonance (and possibly even a fatal incompatibility) between the social values stated in legislation and those stated in the Constitution. The primary example is the maintenance of Art. 41.2.1, stating that ". . . by her life within the home, woman gives to the State a support without which the common good cannot be achieved" and Art. 41.2.2, providing that "[t]he State shall, therefore, endeavor to ensure that mothers shall not be obliged by economic necessity to engage in labor to the neglect of their duties in the home." These provisions are clearly out of sync with modern Ireland, but instead of removing this outmoded vision from the Constitution itself,[25] we have introduced a wave of legislation that tends to evince a more equal vision of society (including the Employment Equality Act 1998 and the Equality Act 2000), as well as a more socially appropriate framework of family law (including providing some protections for same-sex and unmarried couples in the Civil Partnership and Certain Rights and Obligations of Cohabitants Act 2010). Here, one might think that, although in most instances legislation has managed to provide *de facto* equality, constitutional (and therefore full *de jure*) equality remains unattainable without constitutional change. Moreover, one might even propose an argument, based on Art. 41.2, that such legislative innovations were unconstitutional. The legislature in such cases has failed to grasp the constitutional thistle of articulating a more equal vision of society in a constitutional referendum campaign, arguably leaving such political "hot potatoes" as gender equality and sexuality to the judiciary to resolve through any litigation that might arise.

Almost no attention has been paid in Ireland to the question of choosing between organic law and constitutional amendment. The 1996 Report of the Constitution Review Group serves as an exception.[26] Chapter 17 deals with possible "New Provisions" on the Ombudsman, local Government, the Irish Human Rights Commission, and the environment. The Ombudsman and system of local Government were well established, but not constitutionally entrenched.

The Committee concluded that "Constitutional guarantee for [the] independence [of the Ombudsman] would reinforce freedom from conflict of interest, from deference to the executive,"[27] and a majority recommended recognition of the system of local government in the Constitution. At the time of preparing the report, the Irish Human Rights Commission had not yet been established,[28] and the majority of the Group preferred that such a Commission should have legislative rather than constitutional status, at least until it had "bedded in" over a number of years. Finally, in Chapter 17, the majority of the Review Group recommended "inclusion in the Constitution of a duty on the State and public authorities as far as practicable to protect the environment," although "Legislation would remain the chief source of specific provisions aimed at safeguarding the environment." At the time of writing, the Ombudsman, local government, the Irish Human Rights Commission, and the environment remain established by organic law; although local government was recognized in a constitutional amendment in 1998.

The other official discussion of whether a change should be effected by constitutional or organic law centered on the question of the form in which to bring into Irish law the European Convention on Human Rights.[29] Two reasons against constitutional incorporation were given. First, it was felt that there might be unnecessary and unhelpful duplication of protections between the Convention text and the fundamental rights guarantees in the Constitution. Any such duplications, overlaps, or contradictions could be resolved through judicial ingenuity and clarification if the Convention had sub-constitutional status. But this would have been more problematic if the Convention was contained within the Constitution itself. Second, there was a legitimate concern that constitutional incorporation would make the domestic courts subservient to the European Court of Human Rights in a manner that would be problematic for the governance structure of the state itself, and for the workings of the Strasbourg Court. The Convention was eventually transposed by the European Convention on Human Rights Act 2003.

One might, of course, ask whether it matters if a change is introduced through constitutional or legislative means. First, does it matter to the Government? The answer seems clearly to be "yes." Referenda are costly in both time and money terms. They are also potentially costly in reputational terms. A Government that loses a referendum, or that wins by a lower than expected majority, will generally suffer some reputational damage. Additionally, there is always a risk that voters would use a referendum as an opportunity to "punish" a Government for reasons quite separate from the subject of the amendment. A further consideration is the consequences that flow from a provision being actually in the Constitution, since constitutional entrenchment will normally act as a limitation on a Government's power.

But these considerations see things mainly from the Government's viewpoint. From the perspective of what is good for a constitutional polity, there are reasons that, in the case of many of these changes, would favor making the change by way of amendment rather than organic law. First and most straightforwardly, if a change is made by way of organic law, there is the danger that it may be unconstitutional and ultimately be struck down. Second, one might argue that some issues are quite simply of such central constitutionalist importance, touching as they do on our capacity to properly limit state power by making it transparent, answerable, and accountable, that the institutions established to carry out these tasks ought to have their importance recognized (not to mention their existence safeguarded) by a headline in the Constitution. In addition, a constitution is not merely the basic law; it is also a statement of national beliefs, ideals, or aspirations. It is a symbol of the state by which the citizens say to themselves and to others "this is who we are." If changes are introduced through organic law and not through constitutional amendment, there is a danger of the Constitution becoming divorced from contemporary values and therefore undeserving of popular respect and support. The family law provisions already discussed are an appropriate exemplar here, encompassing as they do an antiquated constitutional vision of men as breadwinners and women as bread makers, which is vastly at odds with contemporary society. In *The State (Burke) v Lennon*, Gavan-Duffy J. famously stated: "[T]he Constitution, with its most impressive Preamble, is the Charter of the Irish People and I will not whittle it away."[30] Does the introduction of legislation focused on equalizing gender relations, coupled with concurrent maintenance of an unchanged text, not do precisely that?

A further matter that a Government might take into account is whether an international obligation to which it is committed requires constitutional change. This will, in truth, rarely be the case: indeed, many treaty provisions can be given domestic legislative effect by means of legislation, and, of course, the state will frequently ratify an international agreement and be bound to it internationally without ever giving it domestic effect at all. (Ireland's "dualist" [Art. 29.6] nature permits this.) That said, where what is involved is membership of an international institution that has some capacity to carry out a role that the Constitution has vested in a domestic organ, an amendment may be essential, or at least wise, as happened with Ireland's membership of the International Criminal Court.[31] There may be a different argument: that Ireland's membership of some international organizations is sufficiently central to our identity as a state that it ought to be ratified by constitutional amendment. For example, the Constitution declares Ireland's place among the peace-loving nations of the world,[32] the country has a long-standing position of neutrality ensured through the so-called "triple lock,"[33] and almost all military activity in which Irish Defense Forces are involved are peacekeeping. Does this not all suggest that membership of the United Nations properly belongs in the Constitution?

Formal constitutional change and judicial review of the process

The process of constitutional change in formal terms is fully prescribed by Art. 46 of the Constitution itself:

1. Any provision of this Constitution may be amended, whether by way of variation, addition, or repeal, in the manner provided by this Article.

2. Every proposal for an amendment of this Constitution shall be initiated in Dáil Éireann as a Bill, and shall upon having been passed or deemed to have been passed by both Houses of the Oireachtas, be submitted by Referendum to the decision of the people in accordance with the law for the time being in force relating to the Referendum.
3. Every such Bill shall be expressed to be "An Act to amend the Constitution."
4. A Bill containing a proposal or proposals for the amendment of this Constitution shall not contain any other proposal.
5. A Bill containing a proposal for the amendment of this Constitution shall be signed by the President forthwith upon his being satisfied that the provisions of this Article have been complied with in respect thereof and that such proposal has been duly approved by the people in accordance with the provisions of section 1 of Article 47 of this Constitution and shall be duly promulgated by the President as a law.

When assessed on a rigidity/flexibility scale, Art. 46 is decidedly rigid in terms of process, but entirely flexible in terms of content. No provisions of the Constitution are immune from amendment. Indeed, this has been confirmed in the High Court where Barrington J. held that "By Article 46.1 the people intended to give themselves full power to amend any provision of the Constitution and that this power includes a power to clarify or make more explicit anything already in the Constitution."[34] The same amending process is required irrespective of the scale of the amendment, or the particular provision being amended. There must first be an amending Bill, passed in both Houses. Because of the significance of an amendment, there are various safeguards in Art. 46. First, the amending legislation must deal solely with the act of amending the Constitution. Every Bill for amendment must start in the Dáil (the Lower House of Parliament). Next, the wording of the Bill has to be ratified in a referendum of the people, with the proposal being approved by simple majority of the valid vote. There is no required minimum turnout for a referendum. If the proposal is approved, the Bill is signed and promulgated by the President and the amendment becomes part of the Constitution.

The President has no discretion as to whether to sign an Act amending the Constitution once she is satisfied that Art. 46 has been complied with and the proposal has been approved.[35] It is now established that a constitutional amendment cannot itself be unconstitutional,[36] even if it interferes with what might be considered a precept of the natural law.[37] If the proposal is rejected, no amendment may be undertaken, although there is no legal impediment to proposing precisely the same amendment to the people once again almost immediately, and this has happened, twice in fact (Nice 1 referendum; Lisbon 2 referendum).

A practical difficulty arises from the fact that sometimes a good part of a voter's decision as to whether to support an amendment depends on material that is not in the amendment itself. One example lies in the organic law necessary to implement the amendment. Even if this has already been published before the referendum, a sceptical voter may say: "I must both see the small print and be sure that this will not be altered after the amendment has been safely banked." An attempt to meet this sort of concern was made in the proposed, but rejected, Twenty-fifth Amendment to the Constitution in 2002, concerning abortion. The Bill providing for the amendment contained, in a Schedule, the text of an associated Bill that was to have been put before both Houses of Parliament and, if passed, would have had constitutional status (and so could not have been changed by organic law), albeit not embodied in the text of the Constitution. Prior to the referendum taking place, the Bill was subject to an unsuccessful challenge in the High Court, in *Morris v Minister for the Environment*.[38] The main point in the case centered on the words already quoted in Art. 46. The High Court held that the words "variation [or] addition" could embrace free-standing constitutional norms of this nature, since the Constitution did not expressly require that an amendment must be contained in the body or text of the Constitution. Another practical difficulty arose from the fact that, after being passed, the Nineteenth Amendment of the Constitution of Ireland 1999, which was an element in the Northern Ireland peace process, was not to come into effect immediately; but was made conditional on reciprocal steps being taken by the UK Government, with reference to Northern Ireland, and these being confirmed by way of the Irish Government's declaration. The Supreme Court held that this was constitutional, on the basis that "[t]he People have a sovereign right to grant or withhold approval to an amendment . . . [t]here is no reason therefore why they should not . . . give their approval subject to a condition."[39]

Once the decision to try and achieve a certain end by means of constitutional amendment is taken, a process of drafting that proposed amendment will begin. Traditionally, the drafting process has been undertaken by the office of the Attorney General with very little general public consultation.[40] It is sensibly observed that "the devil is in the detail," and there have been many occasions when, even though the principle of an amendment appears to have been accepted, there has been substantial unease with the particular balance adopted in the amendment. In addition, there is the constant concern that the precise meaning of a proposed amendment might not be known until it is the subject of later litigation and judicial interpretation. Doubts of this character were well to the fore in the defeat of the 2011 proposed amendment regarding parliamentary inquiries, and in particular the meaning of the phrase "It shall be for the House or Houses concerned to determine [at a parliamentary inquiry], with due regard to the principles of fair procedures, the appropriate balance between the rights of persons and the public interest."[41] Considerable unease arose, with "no" campaigners arguing that this potentially excluded the possibility of judicial review of how one was treated by a parliamentary enquiry, and "yes" campaigners disagreeing, but, of course, the ultimate arbiters of meaning—the superior courts—were not able to intervene.

The influence of politics on constitutional amendment

While Irish politics is cast along party political lines, this does not tend to hold true for constitutional referenda. Generally speaking, opposition to proposed amendments has come from civil society rather than from political parties. Thus, initiation of the proposed referendum (in Parliament) has not generally been characterized by opposition, whereas the conduct of the referendum campaign has tended to be more divided. In the present section, we address the role of the political parties at three stages: the initiation of a proposal, the Oireachtas debate on the wording of the proposal, and the referendum itself.

Initiation

Constitutional amendments are initiated by Government through proposed legislation to amend the Constitution. Referenda have tended to be initiated because of the exigencies of EU membership, or to facilitate other international agreements. Others have been held to reverse unpopular, or seemingly unworkable, judicial interpretations. In addition, there have been two general reviews of the Constitution giving rise to recommendations for change. In both cases, Governments have ensured cross-party involvement. This is hardly surprising, since tension may exist, or be suspected, between a governmental interest in limiting firm restraints on its actions and the public interest in having adequate controls. In addition, Irish people and politicians esteem their Constitution as a symbol of their state and think of it as being above party politics. However, the reports and conclusions of both reviews held have not generally resulted in amendment or referenda.

The first of these two general reviews began in 1966. The three political parties in the legislature agreed that "an informal committee" of parliamentarians should be set up to review the Constitution, and this group reported in 1967.[42] The report identified 27 matters that ought to be dealt with. Where there was unanimity in the group, a change was proposed; where no unanimity could be achieved, the arguments for and against change were outlined. Although termed an "interim" report, a final report was never issued, probably because the Government decided to act on only one of the identified issues (the controversial change to the electoral system) and the proposed amendments were rejected by the people.

A further constitutional review was held in 1995–1996 by the Constitutional Review Group (CRG). This committee comprised non-political experts (although nominated by political parties) drawn from the fields of public administration, economics, education, political science, and sociology. However, the majority of the committee members were lawyers. The Group reported on 3 July 1996 and, on the same day, the All-Party Oireachtas (Parliamentary) Committee on the Constitution was established. That Committee has been re-established after every subsequent General Election, with a senior Government backbencher as Chairperson and the Deputy Chairperson coming from the principal opposition party. Although the recommendations of both general review groups are largely unimplemented, they have (over the past 15 years) worked their way through the CRG's proposals and have published reports, with recommendations, in respect of almost all aspects of the Constitution. Their reports remain the starting point for most discussions on constitutional change.

A further aspect in the initiation of constitutional referenda in Ireland is the particular position and concern with Northern Ireland. Long regarded as a lost province, various discussions about how the Constitution might be amended to make unification of the island more amenable to Northern Unions has sometimes taken place. For some time it was assumed that there were Catholic and confessional elements in the Irish Constitution (e.g. the ban on divorce; the special position of the Catholic Church) that made it unacceptable to the Northern Protestant community. Some reviews suggested that the Constitution might be amended to ameliorate these concerns,[43] but, with the possible exception of the divorce referendum of 1986, none of these reviews led to any concrete Bill to amend the Constitution.[44] And in the event, when peace came to Northern Ireland, it did so not in the form of Irish unity but of an internal settlement in which the only impact on the Irish Constitution was the removal of the irredentist claim on Northern Ireland.

Parliamentary debate

At the stage of parliamentary debate of a Bill to amend the Constitution (in which the wording to be put to the people is debated), the major opposition party in the state has usually supported the proposed change. Furthermore, party-political motivation has been surprisingly absent as the driving force for an amendment. It is notable, for instance, that the (Fianna Fáil) Government put forward the measure to reduce the voting age from 21 to 18 in 1972, even though it was generally felt that this would reverse Fianna Fáil dominance and usher in a youthful, socialist voting period in the 1970s. Proposing the change was seen as part of the "zeitgeist" in favor of youth, and the proposal had been recommended in the 1967 Report.

There are limited examples of party-political opposition to proposed amendments at debate stage. The first took place at the start of the history of constitutional amendments, when the Government party attempted to change the constitutional governance of the electoral system in three proposals (one in 1958, and two in 1969). In each case, the Government party would have been advantaged. Although the opposition parties lost the divisions in Parliament during debate on the bills to amend the Constitution, they successfully opposed the change (with media support) in the campaigns. Another case of the major opposition party opposing an amendment occurred in 1986. The Fine Gael–Labour Government proposed a referendum to remove the prohibition on divorce from the Constitution. Although the proposal was worded in very restrictive terms, Fianna Fáil—the major opposition party—opposed it, together with a number of conservative ad hoc anti-divorce groups and the Roman Catholic Church, and it was defeated by 63.5 per cent against to 36.5 per cent in favor. Interestingly, when divorce was introduced in Ireland—by means of the Fifteenth Amendment to the Constitution in 1995 (passed by a 0.5 per cent majority)—on this occasion, the opposition Fianna Fáil adopted a neutral stance, although the measure was cast in almost identical terms to that proposed in 1986.

Apart from these instances, the main parties have generally adopted a supportive approach to proposed constitutional change, although there has usually been some party-based opposition from "minor" political parties. This is particularly notable in relation to the amendments on the European Union, including the two "rerun" amendments relating to the Treaties of Nice and Lisbon. The first Nice Treaty, held in June 2001, saw every major political party (apart from the Green Party and Sinn Féin, who at the time were marginal parties with no history of significant electoral success) supporting the referendum.[45] A similar trend can be seen in relation to the first and second Lisbon Treaty Referenda. At the second referendum, the major political parties supported the campaign with (a little) more energy, and the information provision improved significantly.

The referendum

At the referendum stage, each political party has formally taken up the same stance as it did at the parliamentary stage, so that Government and main opposition parties are usually both pointing in the same direction. However, when it comes to encouraging their supporters to put in groundwork on the campaign, there have been impediments. First, as noted, the regular electors and even members of each party do not necessarily always agree with the party's stance on a referendum. Second, when it comes to expenditure, the party may well decide to preserve its treasure for an election, when the fortune of the party is more significantly engaged. The result of this reticence is that much of the action at the referendum campaign is often left to the Government party and the minor parties or ad hoc groups. On at least one recent occasion (the first Lisbon Treaty referendum) when the "yes" side lost, the principal opposition party blamed the Government party for failing to put sufficient effort into the campaign.

All of this raises the question of why it is that Irish opposition parties, normally zealous in adhering to the maxim (usually attributed to Lord Randolph Churchill) that "the duty of an Opposition is to oppose," should shrink back when it comes to a constitutional amendment. Three suggestions may be made. One is simply that the opposition parties respect the Constitution and know that the voters do so too and, therefore, it seems prudent not to "play politics" with it. Second, as has been said in a European-wide context, "most commonly, referendum issues are ones that cut across party lines,"[46] and this is certainly true of Ireland. Third, it is significant too that, in the Irish party-political system, there is little ideological difference between the major parties.[47] The result of these factors is that, while the representatives of a party in Parliament may support a bill for an amendment, opinion poll evidence (as well as the results of referenda themselves) shows that it by no means follows that a majority of that party's regular voters will support it at the ensuing referendum.

The role of the people

There are two stages at which the involvement of the people needs to be considered: the initiation of a proposal for amending the Constitution, and the conduct of the referendum itself.

Initiation

As mentioned, a constitutional amendment is usually initiated by the Government of the day. There is no mechanism by which the people can engage in a formal petitioning mechanism or initiate the referendum process themselves. Of course, a sufficient number of people could put political pressure on the Government or opposition parties to put the possibility of a constitutional referendum on the political agenda. The major example[48] of this is the 1982 abortion amendment. One of the roots of the amendment lay in US developments: a number of Irish intellectuals (supported by the Catholic Church, which still carried substantial political sway) noted that *Griswold v Connecticut*[49] (which established a right to use artificial contraceptives) had led to *Roe v Wade*[50] (right to abortion). They asked, rhetorically, whether there was not a danger that *McGee v Ireland*[51] (establishing the right to access artificial contraceptives as part of a right to marital privacy) would lead to an Irish equivalent of *Wade*, and proposed a constitutional amendment to prevent this from happening. This episode occurred at an auspicious time in the Irish political cycle (1981–82), when there were three General Elections during a period of 18 months. At this vulnerable time, the leaders of the two main political parties were fairly readily brought to commit their parties to supporting the necessary amendment in Parliament.[52] Although that constitutes an isolated example, as civil society develops in Ireland, there are various ways in which non-party politics can and do play a role in constitutional change, especially in the area of social progression and individual rights. The first is through the proposal for an amendment in the first place, and, increasingly, non-governmental organizations (whether concerned with constitutional and rights-based matters generally, or established to deal with particular issues) produce studies, reports, and proposals for constitutional change, including proposing the wording of possible amendments. As the rate of change accelerates and legal rights become increasingly central to public debate, the Constitution and, where appropriate, the possibility of its amendment moves center-stage.[53]

The referendum campaign

In general, people involved in referenda campaigns are organized as civil society organizations, frequently ad hoc but also often in existing bodies like religious groups. These groupings will naturally engage in the activities customary in a political campaign within a modern constitutional polity, such as writing opinion or explanatory articles and contributing to radio, television, and "live" debates. It is useful here to focus on a number of court challenges, mainly taken by civil society groupings or people closely associated with them, through which certain principles governing referenda campaigns have been laid down. In general, these principles reach across three areas: the expenditure of public money, the allocation of time to both sides by the public broadcaster, and the process of informing the electorate.

The first area—the expenditure of public money to support an amendment—came to prominence in the case of *McKenna v An Taoiseach (No. 2)*[54] on the divorce referendum. McKenna claimed that it was unconstitutional for the Dáil to have voted to spend £500,000 on promoting the "yes" arguments, but nothing on promoting the "no" arguments. Holding that the requirement of a referendum to change the Constitution could not have been intended to allow for the holding of an unfair referendum, and that the principle of equality laid down in Art. 40.1 of the Constitution included the notion of equal treatment of either side, the Supreme Court found that it was unconstitutional to spend public money on only one side of an argument. Thus, the principle that both sides should be equally funded—at least in terms of direct public spending on a referendum—was established.[55]

Second, the principle of equal expenditure almost inevitably raised questions about the allocation of air-time to both the "yes" and the "no" campaigns by the public broadcaster. Up until *Coughlan v Broadcasting Complaints Commission*,[56] the broadcaster had used the same formula to allocate time as was used in General Elections; that is, by reference to the strength of political party representation in the legislature. (Incidentally, this is an illustration of the point made elsewhere, regarding many people, politicians, or otherwise erroneously thinking of a referendum as a "General Election in drag".) Since all the parties in Parliament had supported the proposed amendment, the consequence was that the broadcaster allocated 42 minutes to the "yes" campaign but only 10 minutes to the "no" campaign. When this allocation was challenged, based on *McKenna (No. 2)*, the Supreme Court held that equal time is to be allocated to both sides in a referendum campaign.

The final, significant matter concerns how people are to be informed about proposed constitutional changes on which they will vote in a referendum. An attempt to establish that there is an obligation to provide sufficient explanatory material to the electorate was rejected in *Slattery v An Taoiseach*.[57] However, in the light of *McKenna (No. 2)*, it was clear that any public funds would have to be used to ensure that both sides of the argument came to light. The solution arrived at was to establish the Referendum Commission by the Referendum Act 1998.

The influence of European and international law

Inasmuch as international or European affairs influence constitutional change in Ireland, one's attention must immediately go to referenda relating to the EU. Joining the EEC (as it was then denominated) was approved by referendum in 1972. The case of *Crotty v An Taoiseach*[58] later established the principle that the ratification of membership by means of the original 1972 constitutional amendment did *not* bring with it an implied constitutional ratification of all treaty changes in the future. This important case constitutes informal amendment of the Constitution, as it makes ratification of major changes in the European treaties without a referendum potentially unconstitutional and politically fraught. In *Crotty*, the Supreme Court held that a referendum would be required before Ireland could ratify any new treaty by which the "essential scope or objectives" of the EU would be altered. This finding is limited on its own terms, but the exact parameters of what *Crotty* requires have never been tested. Instead, practically every change to the treaties (save for the establishment of the euro) has been put before the Irish electorate and, indeed, those changes have twice been rejected and then accepted on a "rerun," with some additional safeguards and promises from Brussels.

Whether or not *Crotty* has, in fact, required all of these referenda on European treaty changes is to some extent an open question as a matter of law. After all, there may be an argument that not every change is one that changes the "essential scope or objectives" of the EU. However, the default position seems to be to put all treaty changes to the people. There are three possible reasons for this. First, the dominant legal reading of *Crotty* sees it as having precluded "representative democracy," when it comes to the ratification of European treaties.[59] The second reason is a pragmatic one: that the Irish Government is now backed into a corner, in which they have to hold a referendum because of the possible implications at European level of ratifying a treaty without a referendum, and subsequently having that ratification found unconstitutional if the Supreme Court considers it to have altered the "essential scope or objectives" of the EU. As Barrett writes, "[t]he consequent invalidation of Irish ratification would have unthinkable consequences not alone for Ireland, but for the EU as a whole."[60] In this respect, whether or not a treaty change does make such a change to the EU itself is a question for determination as a matter of domestic law rather than as a matter of EU law; it is about whether, from the perspective of the scope of the constitutional authority given to the state when the people approved of Ireland joining in the first place, the change pertains to the essential scope or objectives of the EU. The third reason is that any party in Government that dared to ratify a treaty without a referendum might fear punishment by the electorate at the next available opportunity, especially given the expectation in the popular mind (after more than 20 years in which *Crotty* has gone unquestioned) that such treaty changes would be put to the people (although it bears noting that no general election has yet been significantly swayed by a constitutional matter).

Neither European nor international law has changed the process of constitutional amendment in Ireland, although they have inspired the content of proposed amendments at times. Apart from the EU, Ireland has also joined other international organizations and ratified international conventions without any constitutional change being required. This is possible because joining an international organization is a foreign affairs power, which is clearly within the executive function, and it is principally only when the membership of such an organization might undermine the sovereignty of the state in a functional sense that a constitutional amendment might be required. This would most commonly be the case if that international organization had the capacity to make law that has a direct effect in the domestic affairs of the state, or if the organization had within it a court (or some analogous arbitration mechanism) whose decisions would be binding in Ireland in terms of domestic law.

This, of course, reflects the dualist nature of the Irish legal system, laid down by the Constitution, Art. 29.3 and 29.6. As a general rule, the dualist nature of Ireland has been jealously guarded by the courts, in relation to matters that are particularly sensitive within the state; and in relation to attempts to import international decisions in a way that could undermine the domestic judicial function.[61] One might argue that membership of the United Nations is an example of an international or foreign affairs decision that required constitutional amendment, especially as Chapter VII Resolutions of the Security Council are fully binding on all member states, including Ireland, and, since 2001, have begun to take on a legislative nature inasmuch as they now often require the introduction of criminal offences or other legislative measures.[62] That said, the implementation of these Resolutions tends to be done by all EU member states together through EU law instruments,[63] and, as already mentioned, our EU membership has been authorized by constitutional amendment. Even if Ireland decided to implement the Resolution unilaterally, it would require an Act of the Oireachtas (although one in relation to which the Parliament would have relatively little flexibility), and, consequently, the exclusive law-making power reserved by the Constitution to the Oireachtas could be construed as being intact.

The role of experts in constitutional revision

Constitutional referenda attract enormous attention in Ireland and are, culturally at least, seen as an important part of popular sovereignty, even though voter turnout is increasingly low. Part of the attention that tends to be placed on proposed amendments comes from experts, particularly practicing and academic lawyers who are frequently invited to contribute to the media, by way of explanation or comment. With the growth in social media, it is now also common for online fora to either invite expert commentary or, indeed, to be established by experts for the purposes of reflecting on and debating particular constitutional matters. In the last four years, for example, three collaborative online exercises have been launched in which constitutional matters (among others) are discussed and expertise is disseminated in an easily digestible form: www.politicalreform.ie (run by political scientists); www.irisheconomy.com (run by economists and with a minimal focus on constitutional matters); and www.humanrights.ie (run by legal academics with a particular interest in the impact of constitutional structures on rights protection and enjoyment). In the context of the Twenty-Ninth and Thirtieth Amendments 2011 to the Constitution, a dedicated website was established by a private scholar to outline concerns with the proposals (www.irishreferendums.com). It is difficult to tell exactly what impact the input and involvement of experts has on voter turnout and behavior in referenda, but the various voter-sentiment analyses done after the unsuccessful Nice 1 and Lisbon 1 referenda show that a feeling of being uninformed was an important element in voters' decisions to either stay at home or to vote "no."[64]

In addition to the involvement of academic experts in referendum campaigns by their contributions to public debate, the Referendum Commission, established by the Referendum Act 1998, is increasingly becoming seen as an expertise-based contributor to such debates, although one that is decidedly neutral as to the result. The Chairperson of the Commission must be a judge or a former judge (with the other members being the Comptroller and Auditor General, the Ombudsman, and the Clerks of each of the two Houses of the Legislature).[65] It was previously the case that the Commission would produce a leaflet informing voters of the arguments both for and against proposed amendments, with more elaborate information usually being made available on the Commission's website. The Commission no longer has that role,[66] and, in 2011, a university-based group of constitutional scholars independently produced such guides online instead.[67] In the last two referenda campaigns (on Lisbon II and on the Twenty-ninth and Thirtieth proposed Amendments considered in the same campaign in 2011), the Chairperson appeared on the main morning news show in Ireland ("Morning Ireland") to answer questions on the referendum and its meaning. If this were to become a regular feature of constitutional referenda, it would presumably greatly increase the role that legal (and particularly judicial) expertise plays in the process of constitutional change, although presumably a judge who had acted as Chairman of the Commission and given his or her views in this way would recuse himself or herself, should any question as to the interpretation of the constitutional provision (if the amendment passed) arise in the future.

Criticisms of the constitutional amendment process in Ireland

The extent to which any system of constitutional change is subject to criticism is dependent, first of all, on what values and processes it is intended to establish as part of the constitutional culture in the state. In Ireland, one reason for a referendum is to entrench a culture of popular constitutional sovereignty. In this respect, history is important. Under the 1922 Constitution, the British monarch was head of state in Ireland (then a British Dominion), this provision having been insisted upon by the British Government. When the 1937 Constitution was established, one of the few changes from the 1922 Constitution was that the head of state should be a (non-executive) President, elected by universal suffrage. In significant contradistinction from the United Kingdom (where sovereignty resides in the "Queen in Parliament"), in Ireland sovereignty does not lie with the President. Rather, Art. 6 states that: "All powers of Government, legislative executive and judicial, derive, under God, from the people, whose right it is to designate the rulers of the State and, in final appeal, to decide all questions of national policy . . ." While this by no means signifies that there is direct democracy in Ireland, the popular nature of Irish sovereignty does manifest itself in the fact that the people, by a plebiscite, made the Constitution and have to be involved in the formal amending process. Thus, it is reasonable to say that one benchmark against which the "quality" of the Irish process might be judged is the extent to which it gives expression to popular sovereignty. It is true that the mechanism of constitutional change is not entirely participatory, because there is no formal initiative system through which proposals can be crystallized into referenda. However, the fact that the people are formally involved at the referendum stage naturally means that their voice is more likely to be heeded informally at the preliminary stage than would be the case with an organic law. Furthermore, public pressure can bring about a referendum (as it did with the abortion referendum) and the growth of non-party-political processes may yet develop into a more conventionalized participation pathway in terms of proposing referenda.

One might also judge an amendment process by its degree of rigidity/flexibility. The Irish process is rigid indeed: all formal changes must be effected by referendum. The question of whether a less stringent form of amendment should be available has arisen. But no authoritative person in Ireland has suggested the possibility of removing the requirement of a referendum from the general process of amendment. Moreover, even the suggestion of a non-referendum form of amendment for limited issues has been briskly rejected.[68] At one level, this is because the Irish enjoy their politics, and a referendum makes an adequate substitute where a General Election is not available. To put essentially the same point more seriously, a referendum is a central part of "the people's sovereignty" and confers legitimacy on any successful amendment. Any suggested change to this would be unpopular and, indeed, would most probably fail at the referendum that would be required to introduce it.

A fundamental question about "repeat referenda" arises here. Is popular sovereignty respected when a referendum on virtually the same amendment is effectively "rerun" shortly after it is rejected? In essence, this is most plainly observable when it comes to the Lisbon and Nice Treaty referenda, but it would be a mistake to suggest that the "reruns" were absolute facsimiles of the original referenda. In both cases, some additional assurances and clarifications had been provided at European level to respond to concerns expressed by voters, and voters generally considered themselves to be better informed about the Treaties and their implications for Ireland on the second referendum.[69]

Moving to a different and pragmatic basis for assessing a system of constitutional amendment, we can ask to what extent the Irish system has kept out undesirable amendments, while allowing in those that were desirable.[70] To take the first leg of the test: it seems reasonable to assume that amendments discriminating in favor of the party in Government should be kept out. The major exhibit here comprises the three amendments to the electoral system of 1959 and 1968, which, as already noted, were indisputably proposed for the advantage of the Government party. These proposals failed and are, in fact, the only clearly partisan amendments to have been attempted. Since these proposed amendments were rejected at the referendum stage, we may conclude that the amendment process worked satisfactorily on this occasion.

It is perhaps more difficult to assess the converse issue of whether the amending process prevented or discouraged desirable amendments. Two points arise here. The first is whether there have been desirable changes that were not made at all because the need for a constitutional amendment was thought to be too much of a barrier. In fact, there seem to have been relatively few "desirable" changes that were not made at all because of the need for constitutional amendment. The second issue is whether measures that might usefully or properly have been enacted though constitutional amendment were instead introduced by organic legislation, and whether this omission is connected in some way to the amendment process.

As to this, we have earlier reviewed the use of organic legislation to establish institutions, to regulate behavior (including in the civil service), and to introduce civil partnership and equality legislation. In most cases, so far as one can judge, these seem to have been popular and would have been passed at a referendum. However, because of the difficulties attendant on a referendum, they were introduced by way of organic law. The consequence has been to leave some of these measures in (at least academic) danger of being struck down and to leave the Constitution with an unfortunate and (misleadingly) out-of-date appearance.

Conclusion: contemporary debate on further constitutional revision

Although, as already noted, there seems to be no desire for the referendum to be abandoned as the means of constitutional amendment, preparations are currently underway for the establishment of a Constitutional Convention in Ireland through which a range of people, as yet undefined and unselected, would draft a new Constitution to be put before the people. Part of that process might well be to consider whether an additional, and limited, amendment process would be desirable in respect of minor changes, although this would have to be crafted in careful enough terms so as not to undermine the popular sovereignty that the referendum process brings with it.

In fact, judicial activity (or perhaps, even, activism) has had an appreciable impact on constitutional change in Ireland, and it seems worthwhile to dwell briefly on this by way of conclusion. In terms of the hierarchy of sources of amendment, if the judges stamp their interpretation on the Constitution, it must be respected by the Government unless it is reversed by the formal method. The Government can usually be confident of carrying the Houses of the Oireachtas with it, so that, in deciding whether it will go ahead and try to reverse a judicial interpretation, the calculation usually depends on two factors. The first of these is whether it wants to undergo the cost and delay that is inherent in a referendum process. The other factor is whether the Government expects that it can carry the popular vote. It is relevant that, on all bar two[71] of the occasions on which a judicial interpretation has, in effect, been referred to a referendum for reversal, that amendment has been passed.

In net terms, the superior court judges carry—and have not been afraid to exercise—a good deal of power to amend the Constitution, but that power is provisional, as, in line with the idea of popular sovereignty, the people have the last word. When a judgment that acts as an informal constitutional change is handed down, it is as if a draft melody, penciled on a piece of staff paper, has been composed. The Government then decides, usually in concert with other parties represented in the Parliament, whether or not to assemble the orchestra in readiness and, if so, to act the role of conductor by suggesting an alternative melody to the people. But it is the people, in the final event, who decide whether they prefer the judicial composition or that offered by the Government. This may or, more probably, may not have been what was intended when the Constitution was drafted. However, the result suggests that it is quite a successful method by which to manage the difficult task of constitutional amendment, provided that all the players understand—and take seriously—their part in the performance.

Notes

1 *Cf. King Lear* (2.4.305–9): "I will do such things/What they are, yet I know not: but they shall be/The terrors of the earth."
2 F. de Londras, "De Valera's Constitution Continues to Serve Us Well", *The Irish Times*, 12 May 2010.
3 For a full overview see Department of the Environment, Community and Local Government, *Referendum Results: 1937–2011* (2011). Online. Available HTTP: <http://www.environ.ie/en/LocalGovernment/Voting/Referenda>.
4 Article 9.2.1.
5 *The People (Attorney General) v. O'Callaghan* (1966) IR 501; *Ryan v Director of Public Prosecutions* (1989) IR 399.
6 With the exception of the last (2011) general election, there is one party (Fianna Fáil) which has fairly consistently commanded the support of mid-40s per cent of the popular vote (in contrast to the arrangement in Britain, where there happens to be two big parties who share, alternatively, the uncovenanted bonus in terms of parliamentary seats, which is the inevitable result of "first past the post"). The imposition of "first past the post" in Ireland would have created a dominant party vote.
7 (1961) IR 114.
8 In fact, even today, the necessary organic legislation to implement this change has not been enacted by the legislature, despite the huge increase in "new university" places.
9 (1992) 1 IR 1.
10 (1977) IR 287
11 *Attorney General v Hamilton (No. 1)* (1993) 2 IR 50.
12 The cases have been identified earlier. Specifically, there was one on human rights (bail); two on elections; one on abortion; and four on institutions of government. As regards the last category, there was no decided case in respect of the unconstitutionality of reducing judicial remuneration; but the Attorney General's advice was to the effect that such a change, without an Amendment, would have been constitutionally suspect. The two instances in which an Amendment to reverse judicial decisions failed are those on representation of rural voters and parliamentary inquiries.
13 G. Hogan, "The Constitution, Property Rights and Proportionality", *Irish Jurist*, 1997, vol. 32(1), p. 373.
14 Article 40.3.1 provides: "The State guarantees in its laws to respect, and, as far as practicable, by its laws to defend and vindicate the personal rights of the citizen." The development of this provision is analogous to the development of the concept of privacy in US constitutional jurisprudence.
15 *McGee v A.G. and Anor* (1974) IR 284.
16 Ibid.
17 *The State (C) v Frawley* (1976) IR 365.
18 D. Gwynn Morgan, *The Separation of Powers in the Irish Constitution*, Round Hall Sweet and Maxwell, 1997.
19 *Crotty v An Taoiseach* (1987) IR 713.
20 *O'Donovan v Attorney General* (1961) IR 114; *Re Art. 26 and the Electoral (Amendment) Bill, 1961* (1961) IR 169. It was held that, in any particular constituency, the variations from the national average regarding the inhabitants' representative ratio could not exceed +/– 5 per cent.
21 Hogan, op. cit., p. 373.

22 There are two examples where constitutional concerns have been expressly cited as the reason for not bringing about reform. One relates to the possible expansion of marriage to same-sex couples (currently the subject of constitutional litigation: *Zappone and Anor v Revenue Commissioners and Ors* [2006] IEHC 404). The other concerns the reform of the largely political system of judicial appointments, by introducing the Judicial Appointments Advisory Board on the justification that to go beyond an Advisory Board would violate Art. 35.1 of the Constitution. (This provision states that the judges must be appointed by the President, on the advice of the Government.)

23 Public Service Management Act 1997.

24 The example of judicial discipline is most germane. In 2000, a constitutional amendment was brought to the Oireachtas, which would have allowed for the introduction of a new, up-to-date system for disciplining judges, but when the Opposition withdrew its support, the Government withdrew the amending Bill and an agreement was reached that a judicial disciplinary system may be enacted by means of a simple organic law which, it is assumed, will be constitutional. As a further example, in 2010 the Government was in no way embarrassed to promise the establishment of an Electoral Commission by organic law (although this did not, in fact, come about).

25 Although Art. 41.2 has been earmarked for amendment, no proposal relating to it has ever been put before the people.

26 See generally online. Available HTTP: <http://www.constitution.ie/constitutional-reviews/crg.asp>.

27 *Report of the Constitution Review Group*, Dublin: The Stationery Office, 1996, p. 426.

28 Irish Human Rights Commission, Act 2000.

29 See generally F. de Londras and C. Kelly, *The European Convention on Human Rights Act: Operation, Impact and Analysis*, Dublin: Round Hall, 2010, Chapters 1 and 2.

30 (1940) 1 I.R. 136, 155.

31 Unlike joining the International Court of Justice (through membership of the UN), membership of the International Criminal Court required an amendment because it is a subsidiary court (acting where domestic courts are unable or unwilling to do so). When it does act, it has jurisdiction over matters that domestic courts also have jurisdiction over. As a result, it may well engage the administration of justice in a manner that invades on domestic courts to some degree. In contrast, the International Court of Justice is a court of consensual jurisdiction.

32 Article 29.1.

33 This requires approval by the Cabinet, the Parliament, and the UN before Ireland will engage in any military operations.

34 *Finn v Minister for the Environment* (1983) IR 154, 163. For discussion of this and other technical points, see G. Hogan and G. Whyte (eds), *J M Kelly: The Irish Constitution*, LexisNexis Butterworths, 2003, 4th edn, para. 8.1.01–30.

35 In the case of most other bills, the President has the discretion to send the Bill to the Supreme Court for what is known as an Art. 26 reference (a process of pre-emptive judicial review to check for constitutionality).

36 *Riordan v Ireland (No. 1)* (1999) 4 IR 321.

37 *Re Art. 26 and the Information (Termination of Pregnancy) Bill 1995* (1995) I IR 1.

38 (2002) 1 IR 326, 337

39 *Riordan v An Taoiseach (No. 2)* (1999) 4 IR 343, 354.

40 There are exceptions to this. In recent years, a long process in regard to a proposed amendment relating to the rights of children has been undertaken, which involved a special parliamentary committee that consulted widely and produced a proposed wording. No referendum has yet been held, however, and the final wording will emanate from the office of the Attorney General and will almost certainly not be the wording proposed by the committee.

41 Proposed Art. 10(4).

42 *Committee on the Constitution*, Interim Report, Dublin, 1967.

43 These included: the *Inter-Party Committee on the Implications of Irish Unity*, 1972; the *All-Party Committee on Irish Relations*, 1973; the *Constitution Review Body*, 1982 and the *New Ireland Forum*, 1983–84; only the latter of which, however, produced a report.

44 For more detail, see the *All-Party Oireachtas Committee on the Constitution*: First Progress Report (Pn. 3795, 1997), Appendix 1.

45 For a discussion of the political debate, including and beyond party politics, see J. O'Mahony, "'Not so Nice': The treaty of Nice, the International Criminal Court, the Abolition of the Death Penalty—the 2001 Referendum Experience", *Irish Political Studies*, 2001, vol. 16(1), pp. 204–6.

46 See also M. Gallagher writing on the Nice Treaty Referendum in *The Irish Independent*, 11 January 2001, p. 376.

47 The two largest parties (during almost the entire post-Independence period), Fianna Fail and Fine Gael, split from the original common trunk because of the Civil War of 1922–23, and throughout the post-Independence period there has been little difference, of a general ideological nature, between them. This is not to say there is no difference at all. In general, Fine Gael, which has spent substantially more time in Opposition than Fianna Fáil, has tended to act in a less opportunistic manner, which may help to explain why amendments were frequently supported by the Opposition.

48 For a distant example, note that the former provision of the Constitution, Art. 44.1.2, which established a "special position" for the Catholic Church was, in the circumstances of 1937, a considerable compromise, which was far from acceptable to a minority of Catholics. During the 1940s, a small Catholic organization, called *Maria Duce*, campaigned vigorously for a strengthening of this Article and, for a while, attracted support, some of its meetings being attended by crowds of thousands of people. In 1949, *Maria Duce* organized a petition urging an amendment to the Constitution. But without the backing of either a political party or the Hierarchy of Bishops, this campaign petered out. See B. Chubb, *The Constitution and Constitutional Change in Ireland*, Institute of Public Administration, 1978, pp. 61–2.

49 381 U.S. 479 (1965).

50 410 U.S. 113 (1973).

51 (1974) IR 284.

52 This is the merest outline of the histories involved. For fuller detail, see J. Schweppe, *The Unborn Child, Article 40.3.3 and Abortion in Ireland: Twenty-Five Years of Protection?*, Dublin: Liffey Press, 2008; J. Kingston, A. Whelan and I. Bacik, *Abortion and the Law*, Dublin: Round Hall Sweet and Maxwell, 1997.

53 See, for example, the centrality of constitutional discourse to the movement for marriage equality in Ireland, J. Pillinger and J. Walsh, *Making the Case for Marriage Equality*, Dublin: Marriage Equality, 2008.

54 (1996) 2 I.R. 10.

55 In traveling around the country to campaign for a "yes" (or, indeed, a "no") vote, members of the Government will frequently use public resources such as ministerial cars, drivers, and so on. The Court did not feel that this violated the Constitution. The case does not seem to place any restrictions on the amounts of private funds that can be spent on a referendum campaign. Nor, on the facts, was it asked to. This remains an important area, no doubt, for future litigation.

56 (2003) I.R. 1.

57 (1993) 1 I.R. 286.

58 (1987) I.R. 713.

59 G. Barrett, "Building a Swiss Chalet in an Irish Legal Landscape? Referendums on European Union Treaties in Ireland and the Impact of Supreme Court Jurisprudence", *European Constitutional Law Review*, 2009, vol. 5, p. 32.

60 G. Barrett, "Brief Reflections on the Holding of a Referendum in Ireland on the Treaty of Lisbon: A Response to Rossa Fanning". Online. Available HTTP: <http://ssrn.com/abstract=1125246>.

61 F. de Londras, "Dualism, Domestic Courts and the Rule of International Law", in M. Sellers and T. Tomaszewski (eds), *The Rule of Law in Comparative Perspective*, Wien: Springer, 2010, p. 217ff.

62 See e.g. A. Bianchi, "The Security Council's Anti-Terror Resolutions and Their Implementation by Member States", *Journal of International Criminal Justice*, 2006, vol. 4, p. 1044.

63 See e.g. C. Murphy, *EU Counter-Terrorism: Pre-emption and the Rule of Law*, Oxford: Hart Publishing, 2012.

64 See e.g. R. Sinnott, J. Elkink, K. O'Rouke and J. McBride, *Attitudes and Behaviour in the Referendum on the Treaty of Lisbon*, Dublin: Department of Foreign Affairs, 2009.

65 S.2, Referendum Act 1998.

66 S.1, Referendum Act 2001 inserting new s. 3(1), Referendum Act 1998.

67 UCD Constitutional Studies Group, *Guide to the 29th Amendment.* Online. Available HTTP: <http://www.ucd.ie/t4cms/Guide_to_the_29th_Amendment.pdf>; *Guide to the 30th Amendment.* Online. Available HTTP: <http://www.ucd.ie/t4cms/Guide_to_the_30th_amendment.pdf>.

68 Report of the Committee on the Constitution (December 1967), pp. 49–51. Report of the Constitution Review Group, 397405. The All-Party Oireachtas Committee on the Constitution, "Sixth Progress Report. The Referendum", 2001, pp. 43–4.

69 Sinnott, Elkink, O'Rouke and McBride, op. cit.; R. Sinnott and J. Elkink, *Attitudes and Behaviour in the Second Referendum on the Treaty of Lisbon*, Dublin: Department of Foreign Affairs, 2010.

70 At first sight, a logical person might object that the present test would necessitate some discussion as to what would constitute a desirable, or undesirable, amendment. In fact, there is no comprehensive discussion of this subject.

71 The two instances in which an Amendment to reverse judicial decisions failed are those on representation of rural voters and parliamentary inquiries: see Hogan, op. cit.

11 Constitutional revision in Italy

A marginal instrument for constitutional change

Tania Groppi

Introduction

A special procedure for constitutional revision was introduced for the first time in Italy in the 1948 Constitution, enacted by the Constituent Assembly after the fall of the Fascist regime and the end of the Second World War. The Constitution establishes a "constitutional democracy": that is, a form of government in which sovereignty belongs to the people, who are governed by a rigid constitution, entrenched within an aggravated amending procedure, requiring higher majorities than those requested for the enactment of ordinary legislation.

According to Art. 138:

> (1) Laws amending the Constitution and other constitutional laws shall be adopted by each Chamber after two successive debates at intervals of not less than three months, and shall be approved by an absolute majority of the members of each Chamber in the second voting. (2) Said laws are submitted to a popular referendum when, within three months of their publication, such request is made by one-fifth of the members of a Chamber, or five hundred thousand voters, or five Regional Councils. The law submitted to referendum shall not be promulgated if not approved by a majority of valid votes. (3) A referendum shall not be held if the law has been approved in the second voting by each of the Chambers by a majority of two-thirds of the members.[1]

In contrast, the next Article, Art. 139, establishes the only express limitation to constitutional revision: "The republican form of the state shall not be a matter for constitutional amendment."[2]

Both Articles are included in the part of the Constitution (Title VI of Part II) dedicated to the "Constitutional Guarantees," along with provisions on the structure and functions of the Constitutional Court.

Notwithstanding these provisions, one important feature of Italian constitutionalism lies in the fact that constitutional change has largely taken place by means of informal changes (i.e. outside of the rules provided for formal amendments) in a variety of forms: ordinary laws with constitutional effects (such as electoral laws or the Standing Orders of each Chamber); decisions of the Constitutional Court; constitutional conventions and practices; and European law. There are many reasons that concur in explaining this development, as we shall try to show in the following pages; these reasons are deeply connected with the specific features of Italy's constitutional culture and political system.

As for the constitutional culture, the most prominent Italian scholars endorsed since the very beginning a non-formalistic conception of the Constitution; according to these scholars, the meaning of the Constitution was supposed to reach beyond the mere written text, to become the product of the political, social, and economic groups that would uphold the written text at different historical moments and in different situations.[3] This has been the prevailing view throughout the life of the 1948 Italian Constitution,[4] together with a non-positivistic approach to constitutional interpretation,[5] which explains the important role played over the years by the creative interpretation of the Constitutional Court.

As for the political system, it should be noted that the 1948 Italian Constitution is the product of the political agreement reached between the various anti-fascist parties (the Italian Catholic party, *Democrazia Cristiana*, DC; the left-wing parties *Partito comunista* and *Partito socialista*; and some minor centrist parties): the amending formula contained in Art. 138 reflects this wide consensus by requiring a supermajority. However, since May 1947—that is, even before the entry into force of the Constitution—this agreement collapsed, due to the beginning of the Cold War at the international level. This event determined two sets of consequences. First of all, many provisions of the Constitution remained without legal implementation, as we will see below. Second, in the absence of a vast consensus, the prevailing opinion was that the constitutional revision procedure could be resorted to only for minor changes; thus, for major changes, other, informal avenues were eventually developed.

As a result of the aforementioned lack of legal implementation of several constitutional provisions, and of the limited recourse to the formal avenues for constitutional revision, the "living Constitution" in Italy today is very distant from the "written Constitution," a circumstance determined by the prevailing Italian constitutional culture.

In the paragraphs below, we shall touch upon the following issues: the history of the amending procedure, including the origin of the current amending formula in the debates of the Constituent Assembly; the formal constitutional amendment procedure and its interpretation; the material limits to constitutional revision; the practice of constitutional revision; the informal changes; and the debate on the possibility of amending the amending formula. Finally, we shall present some conclusions, addressing the current status and meaning of the Italian Constitution.

Historical precedents and origin of constitutional rigidity in Italy

A brief history of the constitutional revision under the previous Italian Constitution ("Statuto albertino")

Although defining itself in the Preamble as "the Monarchy's eternal and irrevocable fundamental law," the *Statuto albertino*—the previous Italian Constitution conceded by the King during the monarchic period (1861–1946)—did not expressly provide any rule for its amendment.[6] The prevailing interpretation considered it a "flexible constitution," since it did not require any special procedure—i.e. different from the ordinary legislative procedure—nor any parliamentary supermajority to be amended. In fact, in the absence of any entrenchment, many of its provisions had been derogated by acts of the King and the Parliament. The reasons behind this interpretation can be found in the central role played by the law (as an Act of the Parliament) in the nineteenth-century liberal state, together with a very deferential attitude adopted by the judiciary towards the political power, factors which prevented the development of a judicial review of legislation.[7]

The *Statuto*'s inability to resist changes enacted through ordinary laws became even more evident after the advent of fascism. The rapid succession of derogatory laws led to the emergence of a new authoritarian regime and the *Statuto albertino* soon found itself reduced to the status of "a piece of paper, devoid of authority."[8]

Constitutional revision in the debates of the Constituent Assembly

With only a few exceptions, the Constituent Assembly (elected in 1946 with the purpose of drafting and adopting the new democratic Constitution) did not directly address the issue of the opportunity to endorse constitutional rigidity. The need for constitutional supremacy was assumed, and also, consequently, the need to establish a special procedure for constitutional revision.[9] The preference for a rigid Constitution was, in large part, already achieved by the political parties in the period before the election of the Constituent Assembly, as testified by their respective electoral manifestos as well as by their statements within the pre-Constituent bodies and activities (such as the "Forti Commission").[10] The main reason lay in the idea that the flexibility of the *Statuto* had facilitated the rise of fascism,[11] even if it was clearly pointed out by an influential member of the Constituent Assembly that "if, during the period when fascism assaulted the Italian State, a rigid Constitution had been in force, fascism would have assaulted the Court of guarantee, rather than the legislative Chambers."[12]

A relevant part of the debate was devoted to the definition of the procedure to be followed in case of amendment, with the purpose of identifying an amending formula able to reconcile "the conflicting claims between the certainty and consistency of constitutional law and its adaptability to constantly changing needs," as Paolo Rossi, rapporteur on the constitutional revision, explained to the Constituent Assembly.[13]

Following an idea that had already emerged in the Forti Commission, the "Commission of the 75"[14] was initially oriented towards a formula inspired by the Belgian constitutional system, according to which approval of the draft amendment by absolute majority was necessarily followed by the dissolution of Parliament, and after the elections, the first act of the new Parliament should be to vote, without amendments and by simple majority, on the text of the draft amendment approved by the previous Parliament. From the very beginning, this proposal shared consideration with another, different proposal, requiring a double reading of the text of the draft amendment by each Chamber of the Parliament and a subsequent referendum.

In the course of the debate, a preference for a confirmative referendum rather than for new elections eventually emerged. It was pointed out that, following the Belgian formula, public concern would not have been focused on the revision, but rather on the election of the new Parliament.[15] Egidio Tosato was the only member who emphasized that, following the Belgian model, no guarantee for minorities would be provided, since it required approval by simple majority. In his speeches, it is possible to find a direct connection between the constitution-making process and the formula for constitutional revision.[16] When the debate over the quorum required for constitutional amendments began, he pointed out the need to postpone the final decision on the issue, in order to be able to foresee the actual majority that would support the approval of the new Constitution; if it had been a very large one, it might have been possible to think of an amending formula requiring a two-thirds supermajority.[17]

According to this view, Art. 130 of the draft Constitution incorporated the formula based on a double reading plus referendum, which eventually converged, with only a few changes, into the current Art. 138 of the Constitution.[18] The debate in the plenary session of the Assembly was limited, assuming a general consensus towards the mechanism developed by the Commission of the 75. The main speaker on the topic (Mr Martino) underscored the intention to make the Constitution changeable through a process that, at the same time, would allow only changes sufficiently considered and would deny political minorities a fully-fledged veto power. The double-reading requirement would have helped avoid changes based on demagogic or momentary impulses; in particular, the absolute majority requirement would have helped avoid minority coups and the referendum would have represented a guarantee for minorities.[19]

The provision, according to which the referendum cannot be required when the draft amendment is approved by the two legislative Chambers with a two-thirds majority in the second vote, is related to the consideration that a proportional electoral representation would have been established, and consequently the political system would have been fragmented. Thus, the Constituent Assembly assumed that the two-thirds majority in Parliament undoubtedly reflected the same, or even a larger, majority in the country. At any rate, in the course of the debate, someone raised the doubt that "in a country with a single-member electoral college system or where political trends are polarized around two political parties only, a two-thirds supermajority could possibly not necessarily reflect the country's real majority."[20] As we shall see later, this statement has been confirmed in Italy in more recent years, when the proportional electoral system, not included in the text of the Constitution, was modified.

The formal constitutional amendment procedure

The amending formula draws from the structure of the ordinary legislative procedure, introducing at the same time several additional requirements consisting of some necessary, and one optional, procedural "aggravations." The necessary additional requirements are as follows: a) the double reading (with a mandatory waiting period of three months between the readings) by each Chamber of the Parliament (for a total of four parliamentary approvals); and b) the mandatory requirement of approval by (at least) absolute majority, in the second vote.[21] The optional requirement is the possibility of a constitutional referendum to be held if, in the second vote by each Chamber, a two-thirds majority is not reached.

Procedural aggravations play a safeguarding role: they are designed to ensure that the Parliament, which is vested with the competence of constitutional revision, will resort to constitutional changes consciously, and only when there is a substantial political agreement. Minorities are not allowed to exercise a veto power, but they are granted the opportunity to request a referendum, an opportunity which also plays a safeguarding function.[22] Although early commentators noted that "the rules on the constitutional revision process [. . .] appear to be formulated in a clear and precise way and therefore no interpretive doubts can rise,"[23] experience has shown the emergence of several interpretive problems, on which we shall focus our attention analytically, devoting some consideration to ordinary legislation, parliamentary rules of procedure, and constitutional practice, in addition to the constitutional rules.

The phase of the initiative for the constitutional amending procedure is no different from that provided for the ordinary legislative procedure, as the Constitutional Court has repeatedly underscored.[24] In fact, Arts. 71, 99, and 121 of the Constitution also find application in the case of initiatives for constitutional laws. Thus, the Government, each Member of Parliament (MP), the National Economic and Labor Council (CNEL), and each Regional Council on regional issues are entitled to introduce constitutional law bills. The legitimacy of a regional initiative has been recognized by the Constitutional Court since decision 256/1989, and later confirmed, in a clearer and more strongly motivated manner, with decision 470/1992. More precisely, it is with the latter decision (and with the subsequent decision 496/2000) that, against a governmental denial of the regional initiative based on a reading of Art. 121 of the Constitution, the Court held that Regions can regulate the process (considered to be a regional internal affair) with a regional law for the formalization of the initiative. However, the Court continued, Regions are not allowed to submit proposals of constitutional revision for regional referendum, because the people—considered in its national entirety—can be called upon only as an ultimate source of decision within the revision process. Endorsing a different interpretation would lead to the conclusion that a regional electorate would be given the opportunity to express itself twice on the same question: firstly, in advance, during the consultative phase at the regional level; and secondly, subsequently as part of the national electorate, in the final optional part of the constitutional revision process.

The first "aggravation" constitutes, as previously mentioned, a double deliberation by each Chamber of the Parliament, within a waiting period of no less than three months. During the first deliberation, in both Chambers the ordinary legislative procedure is followed.[25] The vote is always public.[26] The first deliberation identifies a "complete legislative cycle," in which the two Chambers must approve the draft constitutional amendment in the same text. In case the second Chamber approves an amendment to the draft, the new text must be reapproved by the first House: it may therefore happen that the Chambers vote on the draft several times, until an agreement on the same text ("double conformity") is reached.[27]

According to Art. 138, the second vote is designed as a mere approval, requiring at least an absolute majority; that is, the supporting vote of the majority of the members of each Chamber. The second vote must take place after a waiting period of no less than three months from the first vote by the same Chamber. According to some commentators, this rule would imply the opportunity for each Chamber to start the procedure with the analysis in the Legislative Committee even before the period of three months has passed, as long as the vote takes place after three months from the first deliberation.[28] If, in the second deliberation, the draft constitutional amendment does not achieve an absolute majority in both Chambers, it is considered rejected.

The draft is approved if it is supported by at least the absolute majority of the members of each Chamber. In case the majority of two-thirds is reached, the approved constitutional amendment can then be promulgated and published, and enter into force according to Arts. 73 and 74 of the Constitution. Whenever a two-thirds supermajority is not reached in one (or both) of the two Chambers, but only the (necessary) absolute majority, a constitutional referendum can be requested within a three-month period after this decision. In this case, promulgation of the approved draft constitutional amendment will follow either with the expiration of the three-month term or, in the case of a referendum being requested, the positive vote expressed by the citizens in favor of the constitutional amendment.

The main issue regarding the promulgation phase includes the opportunity for the President of the Republic to use his or her veto power to send the draft constitutional law back to Parliament, pursuant to Art. 74 of the Constitution. In the absence of any constitutional practice, scholars hold differing views on this possibility. Most of the authors deny the possibility of the exercise of the presidential veto on constitutional amendments altogether, relying on several arguments, among which is the need for a double approval.[29] Conversely, others support the existence of a presidential veto power, linked to the presidential role of "guardian of the Constitution," even if in the case of constitutional amendments this power would need to be adapted to the peculiarities of the procedure under analysis.[30]

As mentioned, if on the second vote the draft constitutional amendment has been approved only by an absolute majority, the avenue to the optional referendum is open. The Constitution prescribes that the request for a referendum must be filed within three months "after the publication"; subjects allowed to file the request include one-fifth of the members of a Chamber, 500,000 voters, and five Regional Councils; the text subjected to referendum shall not be promulgated if it is not approved by a majority of valid votes. Further profiles of the referendum procedure are governed by Law 352/1970; up to that year, in the absence of rules regulating the practice of the constitutional referendum, all constitutional laws had to be approved by a necessary two-thirds majority, making the procedure even more rigid.[31] Once the optional referendum is requested and a majority of the voters approve the draft amendment, the President will then promulgate the constitutional law. Conversely, if the amendment is rejected by the voters, the outcome is published in the Official Journal and the constitutional law is not promulgated. Given the complexity of the procedure, several issues remain open, especially with regard to the general role played by the constitutional referendum within the framework described in Art. 138.

The Constitutional Court addressed this issue in the aforementioned decision on the possibility of regional governments submitting an initiative of revision at a regional referendum. As mentioned, this possibility was denied by the Court, which stated that "in our system, fundamental choices concerning the national community and inherent in the 'constitutional agreement' are reserved to political representation, on whose decisions people cannot intervene unless pursuant to the procedure indicated in Art. 138." In the Court's view,

> Art. 138 second paragraph of the Constitution not only provides a referendum on constitutional law only as an optional hypothesis, but (. . .), in preventing a popular intervention separated from the parliamentary procedure (. . .), circumscribes within strict time limits the exercise of the power of initiative (. . .) In the third paragraph, the same Art. 138 entirely precludes the possibility of popular intervention when it determines that "the referendum does not take place when the law has been approved in the second vote by a two-thirds majority of its members," thereby confirming that the power of constitutional revision belongs, first and foremost, to the Parliament. This situation does not mean that the debate over the most important rules for the life of the national community should be confined to political and institutional venues only. On the contrary, the diffusion (of the debate) in the public sphere is appropriate, with the parliamentary debate providing the cultural venue necessary to accommodate the revision process.
>
> However, there is no doubt that Art. 138 places the decision [on the constitutional amendments] primarily in the hands of the political and parliamentary representation. In fact, within the amending procedure, the people will act either only as a "check," with conservatory and safeguarding functions, or as a confirmatory force, with regard to an already perfected parliamentary will that, in the absence of a popular pronouncement, is nonetheless able to consolidate its legal effects.[32]

The different relationship between the Parliament and the popular intervention within the constitutional amendment process lies at the basis of the different qualification given to the constitutional referendum. Over time, the constitutional referendum has been variously defined as a referendum of "guarantee," allowing minorities to verify the correspondence between the will of the Parliament and that of the people; as an "opposing" referendum, which can be promoted to bring to a halt a constitutional amendment endorsed only by the Parliament's majority; and as a referendum of "control," with a preventive nature, against the possible malfunctioning of the constitutional legislation as a "confirmative" or "validating" referendum, which could be asked by the same majority that supported the reform, in order to strengthen its own legitimacy.[33]

Material limits to constitutional revision

The only explicit limit to constitutional revision is provided by Art. 139, according to which, "The republican form of the state shall not be a matter for constitutional amendment." This is the sole "eternity clause" included in the Italian Constitution. The Italian doctrine, however, has traditionally stressed the existence of implicit limits to constitutional amendments, referring to some principles that cannot be changed through the procedure described by Art. 138. These principles would represent the "core" of the Constitution and would qualify the form of the state. Thus, they fall within the purview of the "constituent power" (i.e. the constitution-making power), rather than within the competence of the "constituted" one (i.e. the constitution-amending power). According to this, absolutely dominant, point of view, a total revision of the Constitution is not allowed in the Italian legal system.[34] This common view is supported with different arguments by different scholars.

On the one hand, some scholars considered that the explicit limit to constitutional amendment provided by Art. 139 should be interpreted in a systematic way, together with Art. 1 of the Constitution: the concept of the "republican form of state" excluded from revision would refer not only to the selection of the head of state (a President of the Republic rather than a King) but also to the entire form of the state, namely democratic and social, as defined in Art. 1 (according to which "Italy is a democratic Republic founded on labor"). On the other hand, the existence of a "core" of unamendable principles was linked to the existence of a difference between the power to establish a new Constitution and the power to amend it. In this respect, the revision procedure could only be used to enact minor changes to the Constitution that did not affect the fundamental features of the system, while any legal avenue to change this fundamental document in its entirety would be excluded.

With decision 1146/1988, the Italian Constitutional Court explicitly dealt with the problem of the existence, within the Italian legal system, of supreme principles excluded from constitutional revision, qualifying such principles as implicit limits to constitutional amendments. In order to do so, the Court first had to recognize—against the text of Art. 134 of the Constitution, which lists the Acts subject to the Court's power of judicial review—its competence to review the constitutionality of constitutional laws, a typology of Acts not included in the list. The aforementioned decision stated that:

> The Italian Constitution contains some supreme principles that cannot be subverted or changed in their essential content neither by constitutional laws of revision nor by constitutional laws. These principles are explicitly provided by the Constitution as absolute limits to the power of constitutional revision,

> as the republican form of government (Art. 139 of the Constitution) as well as the principles which, although not expressly mentioned among those not subject to the constitutional revision process, belong to the essence of the supreme values upon which the Italian Constitution is founded.

These quite abstract statements are difficult to apply in the reality of cases; the Court has neither taken a position nor further elaborated on the constitutional foundation of the immutability of these supreme principles, nor has it provided an interpretative key for their precise identification, merely stating that those principles "belong to the essence of the supreme values upon which the Italian Constitution is founded."

An extensive debate is still current among scholars on the identification of these "supreme principles." This debate is strictly connected to the possibility of introducing a federal form of state, the direct election of the President of the Republic or the Prime Minister, and even the possibility of amending the provisions contained in some parts of the Constitution (such as the Part on "Fundamental Principles" or Part I). In this regard, it should be noted that the 1948 Constitution includes 12 articles under the heading of "Fundamental Principles," followed by Part I of the Constitution entitled "Rights and Duties of Citizens" (Art. 13–54). Part II of the Constitution addresses the "Organization of the Republic" (Art. 55–139), while some provisional and transitional dispositions (I-XVIII) can also be deemed relevant to the debate on the identification of the "supreme principles." Furthermore, scholars also debate whether it may be possible to amend the Second Part of the Constitution, if the amendments would impact indirectly on the First Part (as it would be the case for those changes in the organization of the Judiciary, regulated in the Second Part, which would indirectly impact on the right to defense, regulated in Art. 24 of the Constitution of the First Part). Finally, uncertainties also exist with regard to the possibility of amending even the amending formula entrenched in Art. 138: in this case, the majority of scholars support the view that the text of the Article (and the amending procedure outlined therein) can indeed be amended, but cautioning, however, that the principle of rigidity would be excluded from this possibility. In other words, according to them, the procedure regulated by Art. 138 could indeed be revised, with the only limit represented by a revision that would make the Constitution less rigid, as would be the case for a revision that would lower the majorities required by the original text of Art. 138.[35]

Since its pivotal decision in 1988, the Constitutional Court has not further specified the content of the category of the "supreme principles." The only other relevant decision is represented by a case in which the Court was asked to raise *ex officio* the issue of constitutionality regarding a constitutional provision, Art. 126, on the form of the regional government, claimed to be in contrast "with the supreme principle of parliamentarism." In the decision, the Court expressed the view that "the parliamentary form of government does not seem as such an unchangeable organizing principle of the constitutional system of government."[36]

The practice of formal constitutional changes

General considerations

Since 1 January 1948 (a period covering 16 legislatures), the procedure established by Art. 138 has been used to approve 34 constitutional laws,[37] only 14 of which are constitutional amendments.[38] The remaining 20 constitutional laws have been adopted mainly to regulate matters reserved by the Constitution for implementation by constitutional law, usually dealing with the autonomy of some Regions, although some constitutional laws may have an indirect impact on the text of constitutional provisions, as we will see later.

Constitutional laws that modify Articles of the Constitution usually contain an express indication of this function in their titles, which refer to the law as a "revision" or an "amendment." However, Constitutional Law 1/1999 explicitly modifies several provisions of Title V (Part II of the Constitution), without including any specific indication of its function of revision in the title, limiting the indication to "Provisions regarding the direct election of the regional president and regional statutory autonomy."

Limiting the analysis to the 14 constitutional laws self-qualified as "amending constitutional laws" (including 1/1999), it should be noted that—if the revision of Title V, Part II of the Constitution (completely rewritten through Constitutional Laws 1/1999 and 3/2001) is not taken into account—the number of revised provisions is limited to 14 out of 139 (to which the 18 articles of Title V amended or repealed should be added). Normally, with the exception only of the two constitutional laws previously cited, each amending law has effects on only a few (not more than three) homogeneous articles. This last remark, on homogeneity, also finds application with regard to the two constitutional laws wielding their effects on Title V of the Constitution; indeed, while modifying several provisions, they both present clearly identified thematic cores.

Most of the constitutional revisions enacted over the years affect provisions included in Part II of the Constitution or in the transitional and final provisions. Only three constitutional laws amend Articles contained in Part I of the Constitution: Constitutional Law 1/2000, on the right of Italian citizens residing abroad to vote, which added a paragraph to Art. 48; Constitutional Law 1/2003, which introduced in Art. 51 para 1 of the Constitution a new sentence on equal opportunities between women and men; and Constitutional Law 1/2007, which abolished the death penalty from the laws of war, amending Art. 27. As for the procedure, all constitutional laws with the sole exclusion of 3/2001, which was the result of a governmental bill, were introduced by MPs. Only in two cases was a constitutional referendum required (on this latter constitutional law and on a draft approved by Parliament in 2005 and eventually rejected by the people in the 2006 referendum). The following paragraphs will address the content of the laws of constitutional revision, the majorities reached and, more generally, the context of the revisions.

Different historical phases of constitutional revision in Italy

1948–1993: minor formal changes

Despite the difficulties implied in any establishing periods, it is possible to identify a first, long period in which Art. 138 of the Constitution, although rarely used, provided the framework for all formal revisions of the Constitution, and in which its formulation was never brought into question. This phase was characterized by the approval of eight constitutional laws of revision.

In the absence of a law regulating the constitutional referendum, the two-thirds majority for constitutional revision was deemed necessary until 1970, when the implementing law on the constitutional referendum was enacted. This interpretation found application to all four constitutional laws approved by the Chambers before that year. From that date onward, of the other four constitutional laws of revision enacted, two have been approved by absolute majority (1/1989 and 1/1992), and two have reached the broader consensus of two-thirds (1/1991 and 3/1993). In neither of these cases, however, was a constitutional referendum requested. The achievement of one or the other majority depended on totally random elements, mainly connected to the political moment that could either promote or discourage support from the opposing parties. Moreover, the eight constitutional laws of revision brought only minor adjustments to the text of the Constitution, with a limited political momentum, and mostly prompted by compelling reasons.[39] This situation is mainly true for the first four constitutional laws, enacted in the 1950s and 1960s. These were devoted to addressing some minor issues, such as: a) the establishment of a new Region, namely, Molise;[40] b) the reduction of the Senate's term from six to five years and the establishment of a fixed number of MPs;[41] c) the reduction of the term of the Constitutional Court judges from 12 to nine years and the establishment of new rules concerning the judges' immunity.[42]

Considerations regarding a "moderate" use of Art. 138 proposed by scholars—which found that the original constitutional system remained basically unchanged, at least from a formal point of view—appropriately describe this first historical period. Indeed, if changes were enacted, they were inconspicuous; they occurred due to the absence of implementation of many institutions established by the Constitution as well as through practices derogatory of the written constitutional provisions.[43] What happened afterwards was a long period without any constitutional reform. Paradoxically, it was at that point, in the 1970s, that an extensive debate on the need to reform the form of government began, and continued throughout the following decade, without, however, bringing any practical result.

At any rate, at the end of this period and since 1989, some constitutional laws have been enacted. Three of them were related, directly or indirectly, to the subject of parliamentary immunity. They were enacted at a moment when the Italian political system had started to change, also due to the investigation conducted on the widespread practices of corruption known as *mani pulite* ("clean hands"). This is the case of the constitutional amendments that allowed prosecution and trial of the members of the Government before ordinary courts,[44] introduced the requirement of a two-thirds majority in both Chambers to approve an amnesty law,[45] and allowed public prosecutors to proceed against MPs without any previous authorization.[46] The fourth revision approved in this period was devoted to detailing the power of the President of the Republic to dissolve the Chambers during the last six months in office.[47]

1993–1997: attempts at constitutional revision through procedures derogating Art. 138

The need for "a great constitutional reform" emerged during the 1980s and became stronger in the 1990s, coinciding with the collapse of the party system that had characterized the entire life of the so-called "First Republic." This system was based on coalition governments consistently led by the *Democrazia Cristiana* (DC) Party, which, since the 1960s, had also included the Socialist Party. The opposition was in the hands of the Communist Party, which, due to the particular international situation, was unlikely to be elected to the Government. Italian scholars defined this situation as a "*conventio ad excludendum*," referring to the practical impossibility of change in the Government due to the distrust of the Communist Party.[48] In this context, the proportional electoral system was considered an inviolable guarantee. The resulting fragmented political system thereby determined a consociationalist or power-sharing government, in which even the opposition party participated, although marginally, in the exercise of power. The electoral consensus was based on the increase of the public budget and debt. Governments were unstable and short-lived, and political crises frequent. This system was considered inefficient, and since the 1980s many proposals to change it had been presented, but an extensive revision became politically viable only after 1993. As a consequence of the fall of the communist regimes, in a few years all the political parties in existence since 1948 disappeared and a new political system began to develop. A new majoritarian electoral law was enacted in 1993 in Italy, and the political system began to function in a more bipolar manner.[49]

At any rate, the idea that the procedure outlined by Art. 138 could not, for several reasons, be used to promote a "major reform" prevailed in the political class.[50] It was indeed common opinion that, through this avenue, only limited and specific revisions could be achieved; Art. 138's procedure was considered responsible for the difficulties met in enacting a major reform, mainly due to the broad consensus required for change, which, if not reached, would have opened the way to a possible opposing referendum. Furthermore, in light of the far-reaching effects of the reform, it was generally felt that it would have been necessary to enhance popular participation in the process beyond the level provided by this provision.[51] During the 1990s, proposals aimed at derogating from the procedure outlined by Art. 138 multiplied and the idea of creating a new Constituent Assembly was proposed; these proposals are recognized in the message sent to the Chambers on 26 June 1991 by then President of the Republic, Francesco Cossiga, who advocated bypassing Art. 138 itself, stressing the need to initiate a reform process as soon as possible.[52]

Moving from these considerations, Constitutional Law 1/1993 and Constitutional Law 1/1997 were enacted, in order to derogate Art. 138, providing for the following: a) creation of a bicameral commission that would unify the referral phase of the two Chambers; b) drafting of an organic reform project of Part II; c) a limited time for the Commission's activities; d) confirmation of the need for double deliberation by each Chamber, even if with a highly simplified procedure (peremptory deadlines, prohibition of preliminary questions, open vote); e) the approval in second deliberation with an absolute majority; and f) a mandatory referendum on the entire project, regardless of the extent of the majority reached in Parliament's second vote.

These laws were highly criticized,[53] mainly due to the weakening of the Constitution's rigidity that they allegedly determined. In fact, an absolute majority approval would have been sufficient for the revision to be approved, although followed by the mandatory referendum. In the eyes of the critics, this procedure would have surrendered the constitutional revision to the hands of the political majority, and, therefore, to the hands of the Government—an even more problematic situation, if one considers the majoritarian electoral reform of 1993. In any case, due to the political context, these attempts at revision "in derogation" of Art. 138 eventually failed, notwithstanding the new electoral system. Indeed, for the "major reform" to be enacted, a large political consensus was still necessary, and that was not reached.

Since 1997: back to Art. 138

The failure of the attempts at revision "in derogation" of Art. 138 of the Constitution prompted a return to the ordinary procedure of Art. 138. Between 1997 and 2007, eight laws of constitutional revision were approved, five of them by absolute majority.[54]

New features emerged. First, even when the laws introduce specific changes, they enjoy great relevance and do not constitute mere improvement of the already existing text. Furthermore, Part I of the Constitution has been changed for the first time, with the amendment of Art. 27 of the Constitution, on the death penalty; as well as with the revision involving Art. 48 of the Constitution, dealing with the vote of those Italian citizens residing abroad; and Art. 51 of the Constitution, with the introduction of equal opportunities for men and women. In the case of these two latter provisions, their enactment is part of a specific constitutional policy, furthering an innovative concept of citizenship and equality. Similar considerations can be made with reference to Art. 111, concerning the right to a fair trial, whose amendment produced some effects on Art. 24 (on the right of defense), and to the law that brought an end to the efficacy of the XIII final and transitional provision providing restrictions affecting members of the House of Savoy. We mentioned it, although it could not properly be qualified as a "constitutional revision law" as determined the end, in a formal way, of an entire historical era.[55]

Second, new reasons for the amendments are related to the ever-evolving area of International and European law. The revision of Art. 111 of the Constitution appears as a consequence of the case law of the European Court of Human Rights, which frequently found Italy in violation of the Convention for the length of trials. The definitive abolition of the death penalty, even in case of war, which took place in 2007, appears to be the only case in which the reasons behind the reform find their justification in European law, in particular the Charter of Nice. In addition, in the most recent amendments, for the first time in Italian history the tendency has emerged to resort to constitutional revision to follow up on the Constitutional Court's decision, in order to modify the parameter used by the Court in constitutional review. While this well-known practice is resorted to in other jurisdictions, it has been considered a "risk" in the Italian legal system since the Constituent Assembly period.[56] This is the case of the amendment to Art. 51 of the Constitution, which was enacted after a decision in which the Court struck down an electoral law establishing quotas for women in the electoral lists, finding a violation of the principle of equality. The revision, providing the opportunity to enact specific measures "in order to promote equal opportunities for men and women" in access to public offices and elective positions, paved the way for the introduction of "affirmative action" in the electoral field as well.[57]

Third, the quality of the norms introduced changed compared with the previous phases. Article 111 of the Constitution (and some other provisions included in Constitutional Laws 1/1999 and 3/2001) also shows a tendency to verbosity and the constitutionalization of detailed rules, a practice clearly falling outside of the Italian tradition of a "Constitution of principles," a circumstance that can be traced back to some of the most recent developments and trends that, at the comparative level, have emerged with regard to the recent constitutions enacted in new democracies.

Fourth, for the first time, two extensive and articulated reforms were introduced changing the whole Title V of Part II (excluding Art. 133 of the Constitution). Constitutional Laws 1/1999 and 3/2001 appear to show that Art. 138 perfectly complements the implementation of major reforms when a political will in this sense is clear. It is worth underscoring that the second, extensive reform (3/2001), aimed at introducing federalism by changing the previous regional system, was enacted by mere absolute majority, and not by a two-thirds majority. According to some commentators, the approval of Constitutional Law 3/2001 represented a break with a constitutional convention requiring large political agreements for the enactment of a major revision, different from specific amendments.[58]

Finally, the constitutional referendum took place for the first time: the 2001 revision was confirmed by the electorate, receiving 64.4 per cent of positive votes, but that, at the same time, witnessed a very low participation (only 33.9 per cent of the whole electorate). A second referendum was held in 2006, on a draft constitutional revision previously approved by the majority in Parliament (and introduced by a governmental bill, the second example in Italian history), aimed at amending 50 Articles included in Part II of the Constitution, in the presence of a very hostile environment. The Opposition did not participate in the second deliberation and immediately rushed to request a constitutional referendum. For the first time in the history of the Republic, the referendum prompted the rejection by the electorate of the draft revision (with 61.4 per cent of negative votes), with a far higher turnout than the one reached in 2001 (53.6 per cent).

A few considerations on formal revisions

It should be noted at the outset that, in Italy, the subject of constitutional revision has been exclusively in the hands of the political parties and that the corresponding debate has occurred almost exclusively within the Parliament. Public opinion has played a role only in the two circumstances when a constitutional referendum was held,[59] and especially in the second case when the vote was perceived as a vote not only on the proposed constitutional revision, but also on the modernity of the whole Italian Constitution, a modernity and suitability confirmed by the citizens through the vote. In this process, scholars have undoubtedly played an important role, suggesting to the political parties the constitutional amendments to be enacted and providing constant support to their activity, especially in the case of the two bicameral commissions established in 1993 and 1997.

However, it should be pointed out that mixed bodies—composed of MPs and scholars—have never been created, nor committees formed, exclusively of experts. Even in the case of the two aforementioned commissions, which had been vested with the task of modifying the whole Second Part of the Constitution, they were composed only of MPs. The experts, therefore, have always performed an advisory function regarding the political parties and parliamentary groups; a situation that ended up raising some doubts on the expert's neutrality. Scholars are usually associated with either one or other political party. The Italian doctrine ended up losing an important part of its legitimacy due to this close connection with politics. What can be considered a paradox is that, while amending the text of the Constitution was proving extremely difficult, the "living Constitution" was intensely evolving through informal avenues.

Informal methods of constitutional change

Most constitutional changes in Italy have taken place without the enactment of constitutional amendment; that is, through informal changes that did not modify the text of the Constitution.[60] Some of them, however, developed "within" the legal framework of the written Constitution, due to the fact that the Constitution *does not regulate* all the "constitutional matter"; and, in any case, it contains general principles rather than detailed rules. The "open texture" of the Constitution[61] leaves room for other sources (such as electoral laws or Standing Orders of the Chambers) to step in and integrate the Constitution. The same could be said for constitutional conventions and mere common practices. This fact is especially the case for those constitutional norms dealing with the form of government, which allowed—through the amendment of the electoral laws—the development after 1993 of a majoritarian parliamentary form of government, which has eventually taken the place of the previous consociationalist or power-sharing form of government. These constitutional developments will not be addressed in this contribution, since, while belonging to the area of "constitutional changes," they do not influence the effectiveness of the written constitutional provisions.[62] Conversely, other constitutional changes developed "outside" of the text of the Constitution, in the sense that they affected the constitutional matter regulated by the written Constitution by *changing the meaning* of those written provisions.

The first, important way of informal change was determined by the lack of implementation of the written Constitution. After the entry into force on 1 January 1948 of the Constitution, many important laws were necessary to implement the Constitution, in order to establish both the new guarantor bodies and the various other instruments designed to limit the political majorities; and also, more generally, to favor the adaptation of the whole legal system to the new principles.

The elections on 18 April 1948 witnessed the electoral success of the DC Party, which, for several decades, ruled the country and showed little interest in the implementation of the Constitution. It took several years to establish the Constitutional Court (1956), the Superior Council of the Judiciary (1958), the ordinary Regions (1970), and the provision of an apparatus for the referendum (1970). In the absence of these bodies, the institutional system designed by the Constitution was not effective, due to its lacking several checks on the political majorities. This circumstance could be described as an attempt to modify the Constitution by making it an "empty shell." Furthermore, the very same political parties attempted to formally amend the Constitution, by means of an electoral law that would have awarded the coalition obtaining 50 per cent of the valid votes in a national election 64 per cent of the available parliamentary seats; that is, a majority of seats very close to the two-thirds supermajority needed to revise the Constitution.[63] This electoral law, termed "bribery law," was fiercely contested by the opposition parties. Since the 50 per cent threshold was not reached in the following national election, the law was then abrogated, prompting a return to the proportional system. From that moment onward, the majority abandoned the idea of rewriting the Constitution and initiated the long process of implementation.

The main avenue of informal change has been the jurisprudence of the Constitutional Court. Indeed, this played an important role not only in the implementation of the Constitution (striking down and expelling from the legal system all statutory laws enacted before 1948 that were inconsistent with the new Republican Constitution), but also in the adaptation of the Constitution to the demands of the changing Italian society. In many circumstances, the Constitutional Court, through constitutional interpretation, has gone far beyond the written text, an attitude that has generally been considered positively by scholars and political parties, but has also raised concerns about the risks of arbitrariness and juristocracy. In a few cases, the Court itself has shown a certain degree of self-restraint, explicitly stating itself to be bound by the black letter of the Constitution. This has been the case, for example, of the decision declaring the unconstitutionality of the system of reserved quota in the electoral lists (subsequently overcome, as mentioned, by a formal constitutional amendment),[64] and of the decision on same-sex marriage, in which the Court indicated that the text of the Constitution and the original intent of the Italian founding fathers precluded an evolving interpretation of marriage to accommodate same-sex couples.[65] A few examples of this activist jurisprudence include:

a) decisions recognizing that the rights guaranteed by the Constitution are not only those entrenched in the text, and that Art. 2 of the Constitution can be interpreted to promote the identification of new rights (right to housing, right to sexual identity, right to privacy, right to honor, right to marry);[66]
b) decisions recognizing that constitutional rights and duties (almost all but electoral rights) refer not only to citizens but also to foreign nationals (even if expressly referring only to Italian citizens in the text of the Constitutions);[67]
c) decisions identifying an undeniable core of fundamental rights (including social rights) connected to human dignity, in the absence of any express reference in the Constitution to the concepts of "undeniable core" and "human dignity";[68]
d) decisions recognizing that European law trumps inconsistent Italian legislation, including the Constitution, pursuant to the so-called "open clause" of Art. 11 of the Constitution referring to "limitations of sovereignty"; this clause has allowed ratification of the various European treaties, always conducted through ordinary legislation, without the need to modify the text of the Italian Constitution.[69] At the same time, the Court has identified in the "supreme principles of the constitutional system" a limit to the primacy of European law;[70]
e) decisions with which the Court has identified the material limits to constitutional revision and has indicated its power to review unconstitutional legislation;[71]
f) decisions with which the Court has "modified" the status enjoyed by international treaties in the Italian hierarchy of sources of law, modifying their status from primary legislation to intermediate sources of law (*norme interposte*); that is, norms that enjoy supremacy over legislative materials but remain subordinate to the Constitution, and whose violation determines automatically an indirect violation of the Constitution reviewable by the Court. This overruling was motivated by the Court with the change in the text of Art. 117 para 1 of the Constitution, determined by the constitutional revision prompted by Constitutional Law 3/2001, an interpretation not necessarily mandated by the new text of Art. 117 of the Constitution;[72]
g) decisions with which the Court introduced further limits to the abrogative referendum in addition to those expressly included in Art. 75 of the Constitution, giving rise to a practice of more stringent control on the admissibility of the requests of abrogative referendum, filed either by 500,000 voters or five Regions;[73]
h) the jurisprudence of the Court on the relationship between the state and the Regions, and particularly the decisions that identified the existence of an implicit constitutional principle of loyal cooperation[74] and introduced mechanisms (unknown to the written text of the Constitution) through which the state protects the principle of national unity. In this way, the allocation of

legislative competences contained in Art. 117 of the Constitution may be derogated by a national law;[75]

i) the decision recognizing the power of amnesty as a power belonging exclusively to the President of the Republic, even in cases when the Government opposes such grant (against the black letter of Art. 89 of the Constitution, requiring that every Presidential Act be countersigned by a member of the Government);[76]
j) the decision recognizing that the text of the Constitution may be integrated by "constitutional conventions", such as the one that provides the individual no-confidence vote against Ministers, notwithstanding that Art. 94 of the Constitution refers only to a no-confidence vote against the whole Cabinet;[77]
k) the decisions by which the Court added many new kinds of decisions of unconstitutionality (with different effects) to those provided by Art. 136 of the Constitution (according to which, "When the court declares a law or an act with the force of law unconstitutional, the norm ceases to have effect from the day following the publication of the decision").[78]

Other informal changes have been prompted by European law; its direct primacy over the Constitution, as recognized by the Constitutional Court, has produced important consequences, especially with regard to the so-called "economic constitution," promoting freedom of competition and, according to some scholars, determining the *desuetude* of some constitutional provisions (e.g. Art. 41 of the Constitution) aimed at imposing "socially oriented" limits to the freedom of enterprise. A good example is provided by the introduction of the right to vote in local elections for EU citizens, a right introduced through simple legislation (legislative decree 197/1996), in the presence of a constitutional provision (Art. 48 of the Constitution), explicitly granting the right to vote to Italian citizens only.

Finally, some constitutional laws that could not be qualified as revisions of the text of the Constitution have an indirect impact on it. Constitutional Law 1/1953, titled "Provisions on the Constitutional Court integrating the Constitution," in fact "integrates" the text of the Italian Constitution (in particular Art. 134, listing the Court's functions), without modifying it expressly. Constitutional Law 1/1958, titled "Expiration of the deadline established in the XI transitional and final provision of the Constitution," extends a five-year term provided for the establishment of new Regions. Constitutional Law 1/1967, addressing "Extradition for crimes of genocide," is designed as an interpretive law, establishing that constitutional provisions prohibiting the extradition for political crimes (Art. 10 last para and Art. 26 last para of the Constitution) shall not find application to the crime of genocide. Constitutional Law 1/2002 determines, as we said, the "Cease of the effects of paragraphs 1 and 2 of the XIII transitional and final provision of the Constitution."

Amending the amendment procedure

Article 138 itself has not been immune from proposals of revision. Constitutional Law 1/1993 did not consider Arts. 138 and 139 of the Constitution among the provisions susceptible to modification with the special procedure therein provided. Thus, it was not the same for Constitutional Law 1/1997, which referred, conversely, to the possibility of preparing a draft for the revision of the entire Part II, with express reference also to the "system of guarantees." In fact, during the first stage of the work of the Commission established on that basis, the issue of the amendment of Art. 138 was carefully considered. The "Parliament and normative sources of law" Committee, which dealt with the issue, submitted to the full Commission a text—approved on 9 June 1997 as a basic draft—proposing: a mandatory two-thirds supermajority quorum in the second vote of the Chambers; raising the number of signatures required for requesting a referendum and the introduction of a structural quorum in order for the referendum to be valid; involvement of the Regions in the amendment of the provisions of Title V of the Constitution, therefore introducing the concept of "variable rigidity"; introduction of a direct *a priori* recourse to the Constitutional Court with suspensive effects that could be lodged by one-fifth of the members of each Chamber to challenge draft constitutional laws.

However, the growing conflicts between the various political forces and the imminent expiry of the period within which the Commission was supposed to complete its activity eventually persuaded it to set aside the issue. Therefore, in the final proposal approved by the Commission (which was never approved by the Chambers), Art. 138 remained unchanged.[79] Moreover, even before 1997, consistent with critics on the effects of the introduction in 1993 of a majoritarian electoral system, which would have weakened the system of guarantees, proposals in the direction of a higher quorum had been submitted. For example, the draft Constitutional Law presented by a group of center-left deputies[80] advocated the need to always approve constitutional laws by a two-thirds majority.

Another element of concern addressed in this proposal was the constitutional referendum, which could be required only with specific provisions or groups of provisions addressing the same subject. It was determined that if "on the same provisions several requests for the referendum are presented, or if disputes on the aggregation of the provisions to be submitted to each referendum arise, the decision must be deferred to the Constitutional Court."

More recently, the issue of the reform of Art. 138 was once again raised. In 2003, in the presence of the risk to adopt a new "major constitutional reform" with the exclusive support of the government majority (as it finally happened in 2005), a group of center-left Senators submitted a proposal[81] incorporating the two main issues addressed in the previous draft. According to this new draft, the majority required in the second deliberation to approve the draft constitutional law would have been raised to mandatorily reach two-thirds of the members of each Chamber, while para 3 of Art. 138 of the Constitution would have been changed in order to allow referendums on homogeneous questions, vesting the Constitutional Court with the power to review their textual formulation.[82]

On the contrary, the Constitutional Law approved in a second deliberation on 16 November 2005 (but eventually rejected in the referendum of June 2006) decided to require a lower quorum. Its Art. 52 provided for the repeal of the last paragraph of Art. 138 of the Constitution, which excludes the possibility of the constitutional referendum in those cases when the two-thirds majority has been reached in the second deliberation. Thus, failing any incentive to the achievement of larger majorities, the guarantee of constitutional rigidity would have been left to the double parliamentary deliberation with absolute majority, and to the optional referendum. This project seemed to retain the idea that the Italian Constitution is difficult to modify due to Art. 138 and, therefore, that it would be necessary to simplify the amending procedure; an idea that, as we have tried to show in the previous pages, has no link to the practice of constitutional amendments in Italy.

However, conversely, it appears that the experience developed during the XIII (1996–2001) and XIV (2001–2006) legislatures has shown that the procedure pursuant to Art. 138 can indeed allow the realization of "major reforms," as long as a clear political will to do so actually exists. What Art. 138 of the Constitution has not been able to guarantee is the shared nature of the reforms and, with it, the maintenance of the consensual nature of the Constitution. The desire to restore this fundamental element, thereby preventing any random majority being tempted to make "their own" Constitution, justifies the proposals presented for increasing the quorum. In addition, whenever Art. 138 of the Constitution is considered adequate from a legal and factual standpoint to approve large revisions, the problem of constitutional referendum homogeneity will then arise: this is indeed another feature of Art. 138 of the Constitution that nowadays requires careful consideration.

Conclusions

The Italian experience shows a significant difference between the "written Constitution" and the "living Constitution." As previously noted, this difference is partly the product of the influence exerted by the Italian legal—or more specifically, constitutional—culture on the life of the Constitution, a culture which abandoned its original positivistic approach to embrace a concept and practice of constitutional evolution in which any idea of "maintenance" (that is, updating, adjustment to new demands, and realignment to dominant practices and interpretations) of the constitutional text is absent. Thus, in the factual experience, revisions finalized to the "maintenance" of the text are, with few exceptions, also absent.

In this chapter, however, we have tried to illustrate how the current status is also the result of an acceptance, by both scholars and politicians, of the idea that every constitutional revision aiming to go beyond the mere maintenance of the text requires a broad political consensus, larger than that required according to the text of Art. 138. In other words, Art. 138 of the Constitution does not outline an overtly complicated procedure for constitutional revision, but, over time, it has been interpreted as introducing (well beyond the textual requirements of Art. 138 of the Constitution itself!) a further degree of rigidity. This interpretation originates from a concept of the constitutional revision closely connected with the constituent process. Since the Italian Constitution is a negotiated document (i.e. a product of the agreement between the anti-fascist political parties), its changes must enjoy an analogous consensual character.[83] Whenever this broad consensus is missing, constitutional revision therefore becomes impossible.

In 2005, some new political parties—established in the 1990s, and unconnected to the traditional ideologies and political parties that participated in the Constituent Assembly—tried to impose a broad revision of the whole Second Part of the Constitution, with the mere support of the governmental majority. This attempted revision, as we have seen, was rejected by the people in the referendum held in 2006. This circumstance has reaffirmed the existence of a fully-fledged constitutional convention favoring consensual constitutional revisions.

The existence of such convention has recently been recognized in the current process of revision of Art. 81 of the Constitution, a revision aiming to include in Art. 81 of the Constitution a norm mandating budget equilibrium, pursuant to an express request by the European Union.[84] The constitutional revision was approved on 30 November 2011 by the Chamber of Deputies, in the first vote, with a large majority and no opposing votes,[85] and few days later by the Senate, with the same large majority.[86] The current state of necessity and urgency, which is due to external pressures—a consequence of the economic and financial crisis that invested the Eurozone in 2011—clearly favored the achievement of a broad consensus, which, in other circumstances, has proved considerably more difficult to reach.

Notes

1 An English version of the Constitution of the Italian Republic. Online. Available HTTP: <http://www.senato.it/documenti/repository/istituzione/costituzione_inglese.pdf> (accessed 5 December 2011).

2 Ibid.

3 The most influential book was C. Mortati, *La Costituzione in senso materiale*, Giuffrè, 1939. The author, Constantino Mortati, was later a member of the Constituent Assembly, and subsequently a judge of the Constitutional Court. He can be considered the most influential Italian scholar in Constitutional Law.

4 See recently, A. Barbera, "Ordinamento costituzionale e carte costituzionali", *Quaderni costituzionali*, 2010, no. 2, p. 311.

5 This approach is well summarized in G. Zagrebelsky, *Il diritto mite*, Einaudi, 1992, a book that deeply marked the last two decades of Italian Constitutional Law and has been translated into many languages (not in English).

6 The Albertine Statute ("*Statuto Albertino*") was the Constitution that King Carlo Alberto conceded to the Kingdom of Sardinia on 4 March 1848 (it is an example of nineteenth-century *octroyé* constitutions). In 1861, the *Statuto* became the Constitution of the now unified Kingdom of Italy and remained formally in force until 1 January 1948.

7 M. Bignami, *Costituzione flessibile, costituzione rigida e controllo di costituzionalità in Italia (1848–1956)*, Giuffrè, 1997, p. 11.

8 S. Trentin, "Dallo Statuto albertino al fascismo", in A.Pizzorusso (ed.), *Opere Scelte di Silvio Trentin*, Marsilio Editori, 1983, p. 146.

9 C. Pinelli, "Costituzione rigida e costituzione flessibile nel pensiero dei costituenti italiani", *Iustitia*, 1981, no. 4, p. 338, according to whom we are facing an almost *a priori* assumption of a rigid Constitution. A. Bozzi, a member of the Constituent Assembly (C.A.), in one of his first speeches in the plenary session during a general discussion on

the project on 4 March 1947, underscored that "a discussion whether the Constitution should be rigid or flexible was omitted. It was generally assumed that it should be rigid": *La Costituzione della Repubblica italiana nei lavori preparatori dell'Assemblea costituente*, Camera dei Deputati, 1970, vol. I, p. 148.

10 The "Forti Commission" was a study commission nominated by the Minister for the Constituent, Pietro Nenni, in order to analyze the problems related to the reorganization of the state. Ugo Forti was the Commission's President.

11 See the report by M.S. Giannini at the Forti Commission, in G. D'Alessio (ed.), *Alle origini della Costituzione della Repubblica italiana*, Il Mulino, 1979, p. 123, or G. Martino's speech, C.A., 11 November 1947, in *La Costituzione della Repubblica italiana*, op. cit., vol. V, p. 3785.

12 See P. Calamandrei, in C.A., Second Section, Second sub-committee, 14 January 1947, in *La Costituzione della Repubblica italiana*, op. cit., vol. VIII, p. 2025. See also M. Ruini, C.A., 12 March 1947, vol. I, p. 347: "even if there had been a rigid Constitution, the disaster would not have been avoided."

13 The intervention in the afternoon section is in this sense,14 November 1947, in *La Costituzione della Repubblica italiana*, op. cit., vol. V, p. 3893.

14 The "Commission of 75" was a special commission of 75 members, chosen among the members of the Constituent Assembly, with the task of drafting a proposal of a new Constitution. In its first period of activity, it worked through subcommittees. The Second Subcommittee was in charge of constitutional revision.

15 A. Piccioni, C.A., Second Subcommittee, 16 January 1947, in *La Costituzione della Repubblica italiana*, op. cit., vol. VIII, p. 1884.

16 In the sense that the provisions regulating the revision also assume "substantial value, reflecting and reproducing for the future the agreement between different political and social forces that gave rise to the constitutional text": A. Cerri, "Revisione costituzionale", *Enciclopedia giuridica*, Treccani, 1991, vol. XXVII, p. 3; R. Nania, "Intervento", in S. Panunzio (ed.), *I costituzionalisti e le riforme. Una discussione sul progetto della Commissione bicamerale per le riforme costituzionali*, Giuffrè, 1998, p. 486; T. Groppi, "Art. 138", in R. Bifulco, A. Celotto and M. Olivetti (eds), *Commentario della Costituzione*, UTET, 2006, vol. 3, p. 2701.

17 C.A., Second Subcommittee, I Section, 16 January 1947, in *La Costituzione della Repubblica italiana*, op. cit., vol. VIII, p. 1883.

18 See C.A., 3 December 1947, in *La Costituzione della Repubblica Italiana*, op. cit., vol. V, p. 4328.

19 Ibid., 14 November 1947, p. 3892.

20 Rossi, in *La Costituzione della Repubblica italiana*, op. cit., vol. V, p. 3894.

21 Conversely, in the first voting of each Chamber, approval can be by (at least) simple majority.

22 U. De Siervo, "Origini e significato della rigidità della nostra Costituzione", in E. Ripepe and R. Romboli (eds), *Cambiare Costituzione o modificare la Costituzione?*, Giappichelli, 1995, p. 5.

23 C. Mortati, *Concetto, limiti, procedimento della revisione costituzionale (1952)*, now *Note introduttive ad uno studio sui partiti politici nell'ordinamento italiano. Raccolta di scritti*, Giuffrè, 1972, p. 58.

24 Constitutional Court, decisions 256/1989, 470/1992 and 496/2000.

25 In this sense are Art. 97 para 1 of the Standing Orders (S.O.) of the Chamber of Deputies and Art. 121 para 1 of the S.O. of the Senate.

26 As inferred by Art. 49 S.O. of the Chamber of Deputies and Art. 113 S.O. of the Senate.

27 Italy's bicameral system is defined as "perfect": this means that both Chambers of the Parliament (*Camera dei Deputati e Senato*) must approve the text of every draft statute in order for this to become legislation.

28 S.M. Cicconetti, *La revisione della Costituzione*, Cedam, 1972, p. 136.

29 According to these scholars, the second vote, required by Art. 74 in order to overcome the presidential veto in the ordinary legislative process, would have already taken place. A. Pizzorusso, "Article 138", *Commentario della Costituzione Branca*, Zanichelli, 1981, p. 717.

30 P. Barile and U. De Siervo, "Revisione della Costituzione", *Noviss. dig. it.*, UTET, 1968, vol. XV, p. 7; V. Angiolini, "Revisione costituzionale", *Dig. Disc. pubbl.*, UTET, 1997, vol. XIII, p. 312.

31 See C. Fusaro, "Italy", in C. Fusaro and D. Oliver (eds), *How Constitutions Change, A Comparative Study*, Hart Publisher, 2011, p. 218.

32 Constitutional Court, decision 496/2000.

33 G. Ferri, *Il referendum nella revisione costituzionale*, Cedam, 2001, p. 153.

34 See E. Grosso, "Article 139", in Bifulco, Celotto and Olivetti (eds), op. cit., p. 2731ff.

35 A. Pace, *Potere costituente, rigidità costituzionale, autovincoli legislativi*, Cedam, 1997, p. 38.

36 Constitutional Court, decision 27/ 2004.

37 The count does not include D.P.R. 670/1972, the consolidated text of constitutional laws concerning the special statute for the Trentino-Alto Adige Region.

38 They are: Constitutional Law 2/1963 "Amendment of Articles 56, 57 and 60 of the Constitution"; Constitutional Law 3/1963 "Amendment of Articles 131 and 57 of the Constitution and Institution of the Molise Region"; Constitutional Law 2/1967 "Amendment of Article 135 of the Constitution and provisions on the Constitutional Court"; Constitutional Law 1/1989 "Amendment of Articles 96, 134 and 135 of the Constitution and of Constitutional Law of 11 March 1953, No. 1, and provisions on crimes provided by Article 96 of the Constitution"; Constitutional Law 1/1991 "Amendment of Article 88, par. 2 of the Constitution"; Constitutional Law 1/1992 "Revision of Article 79 of the Constitution on the granting of amnesty"; Constitutional Law 3/1993 "Amendment of Article 68 of the Constitution"; Constitutional Law 1/1999 "Provisions regarding the direct election of the President of the Region and the regional statutory autonomy"; Constitutional Law 2/1999 "Inclusion of fair trial principles in Article 111 of the Constitution"; Constitutional Law 1/2000 "Amendment of Article 48 of the Constitution regarding the institution of the 'Abroad' district for the exercise of the right to vote of Italian citizens resident abroad"; Constitutional Law 1/2001 "Amendment to Articles 56 and 57 of the Constitution on the number of Deputies and Senators representing Italian citizens abroad"; Constitutional Law 3/2001 "Amendment to Title V of Part II of the Constitution"; Constitutional Law 1/2003 "Amendment of Article 51 of the Constitution"; Constitutional Law 1/2007 "Amendment of Article 27 of the Constitution, concerning abolition of the death penalty".

39 S. Panizza and R. Romboli, *L'attuazione della costituzione*, Edizioni Plus, 2002, p. 8.

40 Constitutional Law 3/1963.

41 Constitutional Law 2/1963.

42 Constitutional Law 2/1967.

43 R. Tarchi, "Leggi costituzionali e di revisione costituzionale (1948–1993)", *Commentario della Costituzione Branca*, Zanichelli, 1995, p. 303.

44 Constitutional Law 1/1989.

45 Constitutional Law 1/1992.

46 Constitutional Law 3/1993.

47 Constitutional Law 1/1991.

48 L. Elia, "Governo (forme di)", *Enciclopedia del diritto*, Giuffrè, 1970, vol. XIX, pp. 634–75; G. Sartori, *Parties and Party Systems: A Framework for Analysis*, Cambridge, 1976.

49 A. Pizzorusso, "Disposizioni transitorie e finali I-XVIII. Leggi costituzionali e di revisione costituzionale (1948–1993)", *Commentario della Costituzione Branca*, Zanichelli, 1995, p. XLII.

50 S. Panunzio, "Le vie e le forme per l'innovazione costituzionale in Italia: procedura ordinaria di revisione, procedure speciali per le riforme costituzionali, percorsi alternativi", in A.A. Cervati *et al.*, *Studi sulla riforma costituzionale*, Giappichelli, 2001, p. 84 .

51 C. De Fiores, "La commissione bicamerale per le riforme istituzionali e l'art. 138 Cost.: i paradossi di una riforma", *Giurisprudenza costituzionale*, 1993, vol. 38, p. 1547.

52 See the message and the debate among constitutional scholars that followed in *Giur. cost.*, 1991, p. 3343. It has been described as "a textbook case-study on the violation of the Constitution": G.U. Rescigno, *Intervento*, ivi, p. 3317.

53 See F. Modugno, "Ricorso al potere costituente o alla revisione costituzionale?", *Giur. It.*, 1998, pp. 620, 624; Panunzio, op. cit., p. 163; G. Ferrara, "La revisione costituzionale come sfigurazione", *Politica del diritto*, 1998, vol. 1, pp. 93, 96.

54 Only Constitutional Laws 1 and 2/1999 and Constitutional Law 1/2007 reached the two-thirds majority.

55 The XIII final and transitional provision provided that "The members and descendants of the House of Savoy shall not be voters and may not hold public office or elected offices. Access and sojourn in the national territory shall be forbidden to the ex-kings of the House of Savoy, their spouses and their male descendants. The assets, existing on national territory, of the former kings of the House of Savoy, their spouses and their male descendants shall be transferred to the State. Transfers and the establishment of royal rights on said properties which took place after 2 June 1946 shall be null and void." Constitutional Law 1 of 23 October 2002 established that the first and second paragraphs of this provision ceased to be applicable as of the date of the entry into force of said Constitutional Law (10 November 2002).

56 In this sense see the intervention of Gaetano Martino: C.A., in *La Costituzione della Repubblica italiana*, op. cit., 11 November 1947, vol. V, p. 3780ff.

57 Reference is to Constitutional Court's Decision 422/1995.

58 On this convention see Fusaro, op. cit., p. 219.

59 On the contrary, Fusaro, ibid., emphasizes the role of public opinion also in the process that led to the enactment of the 1989–1993 amendments.

60 See S. Bartole, *Interpretazioni e trasformazioni della Costituzione repubblicana*, Il Mulino, 2004.

61 According to the words of R. Bin, "Che cos'è la Costituzione?", *Quaderni costituzionali*, 2007, no. 1, p. 11ff. In the tradition of Italian scholarship, this feature of the constitutional text is qualified as "elasticity".

62 On the contrary, see Fusaro, op. cit., p. 221.

63 See L. Lanzalaco, *Le politiche istituzionali*, Il Mulino, 2009.

64 Decision 422/1995.

65 Decision 138/2010.

66 See, among the many, decision 561/1987.

67 Since decision 120/1962.

68 For example, in decision 80/2010.

69 Since decision 14/1964.

70 Since decision 183/1973, and especially in decision 170/1984.

71 Especially in decision 1146/1988, quoted largely op. cit.

72 Especially in decisions 348 and 349/2007.

73 Since decision 16/1978.

74 Especially decisions19 and 242/1997.

75 Decision 303/2003.

76 Decision 200/2006.

77 Decision 7/1996.

78 See T. Groppi, "The Constitutional Court of Italy: Towards a Multilevel System of Constitutional Review?", *Journal of Comparative Law*, 2008, vol. 3, pp. 100–18.

79 See the 30 June 1997 text; in the 4 November 1997 text it was limited to substituting the words "Regional Councils" with "Regional Assemblies" for uniformity reasons with the remainder of the proposal; P. Passaglia, "Le proposte di modifica dell'art. 138 Cost.", in P. Costanzo et al. (eds), *La commissione bicamerale per le riforme costituzionali*, Cedam, 1998, p. 37.

80 See Chamber of Deputies, XII legislature, Constitutional Law Draft no. 2115, presented on 28 February 1995 on "Amendments of Articles 64, 83, 136 and 138 of the Constitution."

81 Senate of the Republic, XIV legislature, Constitutional Law Draft 1933/21 January 2003, on "Amendments of Articles 49, 51, 63, 64, 66, 71, 72, 74, 76,77, 82, 83, 88, 92, 94, 95, 134 and 138 of the Constitution and introduction Articles 58-*bis*, 81-*bis*, 82–*bis* and 98-*bis*, as well as of the XVII-*bis* transitional and final disposition of the same Constitution, on the form of government, constitutional guarantees, opposition statute and constitutional amendments."

82 Article 138 para 2 would provide that "if the constitutional law amends or repeals provisions included in more than one article of this Constitution, amending provision of rules included in each title or section are separately subjected to a referendum. The Constitutional Court may order that provisions included in the same title, section, or article are separately subjected to referendum provisions, if they concern non-homogeneous questions or institutions and if it is conducive to the clarity of the decision."

83 Ibid, para 2.2.

84 Articles 81, 100, 117, and 119 will be amended.

85 The amendment was approved by 464 out of the 630 members of the Chamber, with 11 abstentions and no opposing votes. The rest of the members of the Chamber were not present. It is the first voting; thus, from the legal point of view, the large majority reached was neither relevant nor necessary. The effectivity of the consensus will be checked on the second voting. However, there could be no doubt that the political consensus is generalized.

86 The amendment was approved by the Senate on 15 December 2011 by 255 out of 315 members, with 14 abstentions and no opposing votes.

12 Constitutional amendment in Luxembourg

Jörg Gerkrath

The Constitution of the Grand Duchy of Luxembourg is currently undergoing an extensive revision, which should result in a complete overhaul (in French: *refonte*) of the venerable text from 1868.[1] According to the intention of the parliamentary committee responsible, this procedure will give birth to a "new" Constitution, meaning that a revised and consolidated edition of the Constitution shall be published in the national official journal. The Constitution of 1868 is then to be repealed.

As Luxembourg's constitutional history shows, this would not be the first time that Luxembourg adopts a "new" Constitution following the formal revision procedure foreseen by the previous constitutional document. Local politicians and lawyers seem to take a pragmatic view, considering that the theoretical distinction between constitution making (by the will of an original *pouvoir constituant)* and constitutional revision (through a parliamentary procedure) amounts to a gradual difference rather than to one of nature.

History and evolution of the revision procedure

The genesis of the Constitution

Although the political existence of the Grand Duchy is a result of the Treaty of Vienna of 1815, Luxembourg's first "own" Constitution was not granted until 1841. Having analyzed Luxembourg's constitutional history, authors agree on dividing the process into two main phases.[2] There was indeed a first phase of instability from 1815 to 1868, during which the country was consecutively governed by five different constitutional documents, only the three most recent being genuinely Luxembourgish. The second phase starts with the Constitution of 1868, which, after numerous revisions, is still in place today.

Taking a closer look at the historic dates of one Constitution replacing another, it becomes obvious that, in addition to the first Constitution of 1841, the three subsequent documents of 1848, 1856, and 1868 are either the result of formal revision procedures (1848 and 1868) or at least are presented as such, while in fact major formal requirements had not been respected (1856). The Grand Duchy's existence as an independent and sovereign state was first stated in the Treaty of

London (19 April 1839). The Final Act of the Congress of Vienna declared Luxembourg a member of the German Confederation and conferred ownership and sovereignty on William I, King of the Netherlands and Grand Duke of Luxembourg.

1815–1840

In practice, and due to this personal union, from 24 August 1815 the Dutch *Grondwet* was applied to the Grand Duchy, which was administered by the King Grand Duke, as if it was part of the Netherlands like the (other) 17 Dutch provinces. From 1830 to 1839, during the Belgian Revolution, Luxembourg experienced a singular legal division. The fortress and the town of Luxembourg remained occupied by troops of the German Confederation, and thus governed by the Dutch Constitution, whereas the rest of the country became the Belgian province of Luxembourg and submitted to the new and liberal Belgian Constitution of 7 February 1831. This situation of "constitutional dualism" remained until the Treaty of London of 19 April 1839, under which Luxembourg regained its independence but lost two-thirds of its territory. It was uncertain whether this meant the re-entry into force of the Dutch *Grondwet* or the application of a transitional "quasi-Constitution" resulting from the royal grand-ducal order of takeover of possession of 11 June 1839.[3]

The first Luxembourgish Constitution of 1841

On 12 October 1841, William II granted the first national Luxembourg *Charter* called *Constitution of Estates* in harmony with the principles of the German Confederation. It resembled the Dutch Constitution of 1815 and gave the country administrative autonomy. The Grand Duke was declared sovereign, and all powers were vested in him. An Assembly of Estates with limited powers was established, whose members were indirectly elected for a period of six years. Article 52 of the Constitution conferred the power to revise it to both the King Grand Duke and the Estates "assembled in double number."

1848

Soon after the promulgation of the 1841 Charter, many Luxembourgers desired its revision. William II initially refused but had to give way under the pressure of the revolutions in France and Germany. Following the procedure laid down in Art. 52, and with the prior approval of the King Grand Duke, the Constituent Assembly adopted a new Constitution on 23 June 1848. Technically speaking, these proceedings may be considered as a general revision. The population received the 1848 Constitution—a faithful copy of the Belgian Constitution of 1831—enthusiastically, but not William III, who succeeded his father on 17 March 1849. From the very day of his coronation, the young sovereign proved to be a militant defender of the royal prerogatives against "parliamentary omnipotence."

The "coup d'état" of 1856

William III instructed the government to prepare a revision of the Constitution in view to restoring the monarchy. However, the Chamber refused to cooperate and was dissolved on 15 May 1854. The elections produced a majority hostile to the revisions the sovereign had proposed. After spending two years vainly attempting to win support for his position, the King Grand Duke staged a coup. On his own authority, he dissolved the Chamber and promulgated the revised text of the Constitution. The new Constitution restored the monarchy and abolished the parliamentary system. Although clearly adopted in breach of the formal requirements of revision of the 1848 Constitution, it was published by a royal ordinance from 27 November 1856, "carrying revision of the Constitution."

The Constitution of 1868

The 1856 Constitution remained in force for 12 years. Following the London Conference (1867), which had confirmed the independence and permanent neutrality of the Grand Duchy, the Grand Duke was forced to consent to a revision. The formal revision Act of 17 October 1868, "carrying revision of the Constitution of 27 November 1856," declares in Art. III that the revised text "constitutes for the future the text of the Constitution of the Grand Duchy." Again, the document dating from 1868 is in fact not a new Constitution but a revised version of the previous one. Constitutional history of Luxembourg during the nineteenth century reveals several revisions rather than a series of distinct Constitutions. Even the rupture of constitutional legality in 1856 should not be overrated: several core elements of the Constitution of 1856, for example the Council of State and the double constitutional vote, were conserved in 1868.

Evolution of provisions regarding constitutional revision

This evolution can be described in four steps. The 1868 Constitution contains its specific revision procedure in Art. 114. Initially, this procedure was a very rigid one: it implied dissolution of the Chamber, consent of the Grand Duke and the renewed Chamber, as well as a qualified majority of votes within the Chamber. This procedure was modified in 2003 and resulted in a new, more flexible procedure relying almost completely on the will of a qualified majority within the Chamber. In 2009, the Grand Duke lost his power to "sanction" Acts of Parliament, and therefore his power to "sanction" revision Acts. Recently, some are pleading in favor of a return to a more rigid procedure.

The initial revision procedure of Art. 114

Article 114 (Constitutional Revision)

(1) The legislature has the right to declare the need to revise any constitutional provision it specifies.

(2) Following such declaration, the Chamber automatically dissolves.
(3) A new Chamber convenes in accordance with Art. 74.
(4) This Chamber decides, by common consent with the Grand Duke, on the points to be revised.
(5) In such a case, the Chamber shall not proceed to the vote unless at least three-quarters of its members are present, and no revision may be adopted unless it is backed by at least two-thirds of the votes.

Each modification of the Constitution called for a three-step procedure. First, "the legislature," meaning the Chamber in accordance with the Grand Duke, had to declare that one (or several) specified articles of the Constitution needed to be changed. Such declarations were signed by the Grand Duke as part of the legislative process and published in the official journal. Second, the Chamber was dissolved and a new Chamber elected within three months. Third, the succeeding Chamber, often improperly called "*Constituante*,"[4] decided with a double qualified majority on the necessary modifications that still needed to be accepted by the Grand Duke. Finally, they were sanctioned, enacted, and published as revision Acts in the official journal. In theory, this procedure was very rigid and time-consuming. It was also criticized because of the need to identify in advance the Articles to be revised. It was considered to hinder the Chamber to realize a general revision, or to add new provisions.

The shift from constitutional monarchy to parliamentary democracy, due to a constitutional revision of 1919, did not alter the wording of Art. 114 but affected its spirit. As noted by the Council of State, "ever since sovereignty is residing in the nation, represented by the Chamber of Deputies, the role of the Grand Duke as the legislative body has in fact naturally disappeared to the benefit of the authority of Parliament." Similarly, the interventions of the Grand Duke in the revision process were considered from that date as mere formalities rather than expressions of a specific power. Without changing its terms, the revision of 1919 thus changed the understanding of Art. 114 and is the starting point of a genuine parliamentary revision procedure. In practice, the initial procedure, though conceived as very rigid, still allowed the revision of the Constitution 24 times between 1919 and 2003. The main hurdle, the need to dissolve the Chamber after a declaration of constitutional revision, was actually bypassed. The Chamber simply got used to adopting such declarations at the end of each legislative period.[5] Moreover, on some occasions these declarations mentioned many Articles at the same time. Thus, virtually any new elected Chamber was entitled to proceed to (some) constitutional revisions. Still, the old procedure made it impossible to revise the Constitution during a single legislative period. It also appeared to be an obstacle to a general revision and to reverse judicial review.

The revision of the revision procedure of 19 December 2003

First proposals to revise the revision procedure suggested distinguishing two separate procedures: one, simplified, for the needs of international and European integration; and another, more rigid, for internal use. The State Council, however, convinced the Chamber to maintain one single procedure. The question was raised as to whether Art. 114 allowed its own revision.[6] Bearing in mind that the revision power can neither ignore the substance of the Constitution nor repeal it, it should be estimated that an excessive easing of the procedure, which would align it with the legislative process, is not permitted. Such flexibility would deprive the Constitution of its superiority.

Since 19 December 2003, Art. 114 declares:

> Any revision of the Constitution must be adopted in identical terms by the Chamber of Deputies in two successive votes, separated by an interval of at least three months. No revision will be adopted, if it doesn't meet at least a two-thirds vote of the members of the Chamber; proxy votes not being admitted. The text adopted on first reading by the Chamber of Deputies is put to a referendum, which replaces the second vote of the House, if within two months following the first vote request is made either by over a quarter of the members of the Chamber or by twenty-five thousand registered voters on the electoral lists for elections. The revision is adopted, if it receives a majority of valid votes. The law shall regulate the details of the referendum.

The main motives for this reform were the need to adapt the Constitution more quickly to the requirements of international and European law; the wish to clarify the constitutional text in response to judicial review exercised by the Constitutional Court; and the desire to introduce a dose of direct democracy into the review process. The Chamber is now the unique holder of the revision power. The faculty to submit the text adopted on first reading to a referendum is to be regarded as a mere safeguard. As MP Ben Fayot noted: "The referendum appears as a barrier to easy revision and as a control of its Constitution by the people."[7] In the spirit of Art. 114, direct consultation of the people is an exception. It could either allow the expression of a popular veto against an unacceptable constitutional revision, or form an alternative to the second parliamentary vote to give greater solemnity to a major change agreed by consensus. In both cases, the people have no power to influence the content of the revision. Until 2011, this new procedure has been applied 10 times. Once, in 2009, an attempt was made by voters to request a referendum, but the required number of 25,000 signatures was not assembled.

The 2009 revision

The third change in the revision procedure results indirectly from the reform of Art. 34 by the revision Act of 12 March 2009. By ending the power of the Grand Duke to "sanction" Acts of Parliament, this revision also removed the last prerogative of the Grand Duke in the field of constitutional revision. Now constitutional revision Acts, like ordinary legislation, will simply be enacted "within three months of the vote in the Chamber."

Return to a more rigid procedure?

As shown above, Luxembourg moved away from a very rigorous procedure of constitutional revision to a very flexible one. In the current discussion about a general overhaul of the Constitution, some authors suggest a return to a more rigid procedure.[8] A possibility could be to introduce, as the Portuguese Constitution does, a certain period after each revision during which no further revisions are allowed. Another possibility would be to distinguish between general and simple revisions.

A history of constitutional revisions

Considering the dates of formal approval of each revision, 34 revisions took place between 1868 and 2009.[9] There appears to be a tendency towards an increasing frequency of constitutional revision: none from 1868 to 1899, five from 1900 to 1949, 16 from 1950 to 1999 and 13 from 2000 to 2009.

The 1919 revision

After the First World War, the Chamber decided to democratize the organs of state. Sovereignty was explicitly conferred on the Nation; the Grand Duke retained no powers other than those explicitly conferred on him by the Constitution or laws implementing it (Art. 32). Secret treaties were abolished. Article 52 of the Constitution conferred the right to a direct, single vote. Women, like men, were entitled to vote; restricted suffrage, based on property or income, was ruled out. The electoral system was based on proportional representation. Four articles were revised: Art. 32 (sovereignty of the nation and constitutional powers of the Grand Duke), Art. 37 (treaty-making power), Art. 52 (elections of MPs), and Art. 75 (allowances of members of the Chamber).

The 1948 revisions

Revision Acts from 28 April, 6 May, 15 May, and 21 May 1948: The right to work, the right to social security, and the freedom to form and join trade unions were included, as was the protection of the family. Most of these social and economic rights are declarations of principle. The other changes concerned the abolition of Luxembourg's neutrality, education (primary education was made compulsory and free of charge), the Grand Duke's assent to laws (the period for promulgation was reduced from six to three months), the Civil List, the language to be used in administrative and judicial matters, and the legal position of deputies (including a longer list of "incompatibilities").

The 1956 revisions

27 July and 25 October 1956: The term for which deputies are elected was reduced from six to five years. In Luxembourg, a founding member of the European

Community, the European Coal and Steel Community (ECSC) Treaty and the European Defense Community Treaty raised a number of constitutional issues. Consequently, Art. 49-bis was inserted in October 1956, providing that the exercise of powers reserved to the legislature, executive, and judiciary may temporarily be vested by treaty in institutions governed by international law.

The (26) revisions adopted since 1972

27 January 1972: The Chamber reduced the minimum voting age to 18 years and the minimum age for eligibility to 21 years (Art. 52). The residency requirement in relation to electoral rights was deleted.

13 June 1979: The revision of Art. 107 was intended to confirm municipal autonomy and the role of local government.

25 November 1983: The text of the oath, which the Grand Duke, the regent, deputies, and civil servants have to take when they accept office, was revised.

20 December 1988: The number of deputies was fixed at 60. Before that, the number depended on the size of the population.

31 March, 20 April, 13 June, 16 June, and 19 June 1989: The main change was that the Council of State was given constitutional status as an independent office. Until then, the Constitution referred to it as a "council advising the government." The other adjustments were intended to update the terminology of certain Articles.

23 December 1994: The Constitution was adapted in accordance with the Maastricht Treaty to enable non-Luxembourgers to exercise political rights.

12 July 1996: This major revision created a Constitutional Court (Art. 95-ter), and administrative courts to replace the Administrative Disputes Committee of the Council of State (Art. 95-bis).

12 January 1998: The Grand Duke's function as the head of state and the guarantor of the independence of the nation was included in the Constitution.

29 April and 2 June 1999: More than 20 years after the death penalty was abolished, an article was inserted in the Constitution providing that the death penalty cannot be introduced (Art. 18). The activities of the Court of Auditors were ruled in Art. 105.

8 August 2000: To enable approval of the statute of the International Criminal Court, Art. 118 was inserted.

18 February and 19 December 2003: The February revision reduced the necessary age to be eligible from 21 to 18 (Art. 52). The procedure to revise the Constitution (Art. 114) was changed in December 2003 in order to make it more flexible.

26 May and 19 November 2004: In May, minor modifications were made to Art. 24 (freedom of the press) and Art. 65 (modalities of voting in the Chamber). The November revision reorganized the regulatory power between the Grand Duke, the ministers, and certain public institutions entitled to do so. This became urgent because of a judgment of the Constitutional Court, which censured a practice contrary to the strict wording of the Constitution.

21 June 2005: A technical revision had to be added to Art. 37, Art. 51, and Art. 107 to take into account the 2003 revision of Art. 114 to which these provisions refer, in order to fix a qualified majority constraint for four types of specific laws.

1 June 2006: Reformulation of the rules regarding immunity of members of the Chamber and the conditions to waive immunity (Art. 68 and Art. 69).

13 July 2006: Art. 11 para 2 was revised in order to insert the principle of equality between men and women.

29 March 2007: Art. 11 and Art. 11-bis are revised in order to strengthen several human rights and to introduce new constitutional objectives like the protection of the environment.

24 October 2007: Following judgments of the Constitutional Court, Art. 16, on expropriation for public interest, is revised in the sense that financial compensation does not need to precede the expropriation.

31 March 2008: A new Art. 32–bis on the role of political parties is inserted.

23 October 2008: Conditions of naturalization of foreigners are simplified (Art. 9 and erasure of Art. 10).

12 March 2009: Revision of Art. 34: the Grand Duke loses the power to "sanction" Acts of Parliament. His involvement in legislation is therefore now limited to the promulgation of those Acts.

Summary

Compared to neighboring countries, this number of revisions does not appear to be exceptional. The Basic Law of the Federal Republic of Germany has in fact been revised more than 60 times since 1949, and the French Constitution 24 times since 1958. However, there is a growing consciousness in Luxembourg that the high frequency of recent revisions might alter the nature of the Constitution as the supreme law.

The quantitative impact of revisions on the text of the Constitution is not as great as one might expect. Altogether, 70 out of 121 Articles of the original text of the Constitution have never been revised, while 47 Articles have been revised once or several times. Article 11 (social and economic rights of the individual person and the family) and Art. 51 (Chamber of Deputies), for instance, have been modified five times each. Articles 10, 63, 73 and 121 have been abolished, whereas eight new Articles have been inserted. Despite the many constitutional revisions that have taken place since promulgation, the current Constitution still very much corresponds to the text of 1868.

From a qualitative perspective, the main revisions can be grouped into four categories: strengthening parliamentary democracy, adapting the Constitution to the needs of European integration, completing the catalogue of fundamental rights, and modernizing the Constitution according to the principle of "rule of law." All these four objectives are still not fully achieved, and the general revision procedure, which is currently in progress, aims to do that and to erase a number of old formulations and incoherencies that have resulted from the punctual modifications in the past.

Informal methods of constitutional change

Four modes of informal constitutional change may be identified in Luxembourg: institutional practice and constitutional custom; judicial interpretation; constitutional delegation to the Grand Duke regarding succession to the throne; and conclusion of international treaties transferring competences to international organizations.

Institutional practice and custom

Given the old age of the Luxembourgish Constitution, it is not surprising that constitutional change has also been undertaken through informal methods. The margin of interpretation of constitutional provisions tends to increase with their age. Therefore, political and parliamentary practice developed strongly outside of the explicit provisions of the Constitution, which was written for a monarchy. To mark the centenary of the Constitution of 1868, Alex Bonn published an article entitled "The forgotten Constitution." He developed the idea that in some respects, the text of the Luxembourgish Constitution was more or less ignored, giving three examples. In 1989, MP Georges Margue considered that "a superficial reading of the Constitution by a casual reader, who really would not know our society and our way of life and how we act in politics, could lead to misunderstandings." The gap between the written and the "living" Constitution is such that only a major overhaul could overcome it.

Many aspects of the relationship between the Grand Duke, the government, the Chamber, and the political parties are not determined by the constitutional text, but by political practice. Consequently, lawyers in Luxembourg concede an important place to customs *praeter legem*, established outside the written text to allow the necessary evolution of political life. However, the same authors generally admit that the authority of the Basic Law may suffer as a result of excessively gaping differences between the text and practice. The constitutional prohibition to suspend a provision of the Constitution figuring in Art. 113 prevents the validity of customary rules *contra legem*.

Judicial interpretation

Although ordinary courts do refer to constitutional provisions, this has not given rise to any consistent jurisprudence developing the wording of the Constitution by judicial interpretation. Committed to the principle of legality and the separation of powers doctrine, ordinary judges have refused to review the constitutionality of laws.

The introduction of the Constitutional Court could have been the starting point of a more dynamic interpretation of the Constitution, but such expectations were not met. Since its establishment in 1997 and until November 2011, the Constitutional Court has given 66 judgments. They do, of course, contain interpretations of the constitutional articles, which were applied by the Court. Nevertheless, the Court stuck from the very beginning to the method of a rather literal interpretation of the Constitution. According to its founding law, the Court perceived its function narrowly: controlling whether specific legal provisions are consistent with a constitutional provision or not. The only way to bring a case to the Constitutional Court is for an ordinary judge to ask a preliminary question about the consistency of a legal norm with an article of the Constitution, which this judge has to quote explicitly. Preliminary questions referring to the Constitution as a whole or to constitutional principles, without specifying the relevant constitutional provisions, were rejected.[10] The Luxembourgish Constitutional Court does not perceive its role in developing the meaning of the Constitution, but rather in a technical manner. Such judicial restraint is probably a consequence of the Court's composition by ordinary judges who, in addition, do act as constitutional judges.

Delegation given to the Grand Duke to modify the Pacte de Famille *from 1783*

Concerning the transmission of the Crown by inheritance, Art. 3 of the Constitution refers to the Nassau Family Pact of 30 June 1783 (*Nassauischer Erbverein*). This family agreement has become a kind of "extra Constitution." It has recently been changed by decision of the Grand Duke on 16 September 2010, introducing the principle of equality between men and women with regard to succession to the throne.[11] In written answer to a question asked by a member of the Chamber, the Prime Minister recently explicitly confirmed, that, at least in the opinion of the government, the Nassau Family Pact is to be considered as "having constitutional nature and value." Its content is "determined *proprio motu* by the Grand Duke," and modifications fall under the rules of the family pact itself.[12]

Constitutional change by conclusion of international treaties

Although the Constitution does not contain any clause regarding the value of international treaties within the national legal order, courts and scholars admit primacy of treaties over internal law including the Constitution.[13] According to its founding statute, the Council of State consequently monitors each draft bill on its compliance with all rules of "higher law." These are not only to be found in the Constitution, but also in international treaties and general principles of law. In addition, the statute of the Constitutional Court explicitly excludes treaty-approving laws from constitutional review. This is often explained with reference to the primacy of treaties. As a result, the conclusion of a treaty by the Grand Duchy may therefore induce constitutional change without revising the Constitution. This is, for instance, the case with human rights treaties adding rights to those guaranteed by the Constitution itself or modifying their scope.

Treaties conferring competences on international organizations, which the Constitution vested in domestic constitutional bodies, obey a special regime. Their parliamentary approval requires, due to Art. 37, the same qualified majority within the Chamber as the vote of a constitutional revision Act. Each conferral of competences to the European Union amounts in fact to an informal change of the Constitution. In a European legal order, which is founded on constitutional pluralism, any modification of the Union's Constitution necessarily affects the constitutional reality within the Member States.

Formal revision process

How is the revision process constrained?

Until 2003

According to the original procedure, the three major constraints were: the requirement to dissolve the Chamber after the adoption of a declaration to revise; the need to have the assent of the Grand Duke (even though this became a formality after 1919); and a positive vote from two-thirds out of a quorum of three-quarters of MPs being present. This, in practice, set the required majority to 30 out of at least 45 present members of the Chamber. Consequently, the main constraint was not this so-called "double-qualified majority," but the preceding phases of declaration, dissolution, and election.

Since December 2003

Luxembourg still has an entrenched Constitution, meaning that revisions require a special procedure, which is more complex than the legislative procedure. Any revision requires two consecutive votes of the Chamber by a majority of at least two-thirds of the members. Voting by proxy is not permitted. There must be an interval of at least three months between the two votes. If, within two months of the first vote, more than a quarter of the members of the Chamber (16) or 25,000 voters file a petition, the text adopted at first reading is put to a referendum. In this case there is no second reading in the Chamber, and the revision is passed if it receives a majority of valid votes.

As any revision of the Constitution takes the form of a law, the projects and proposals for constitutional reform follow the normal legislative procedure, unless specified otherwise. Since 2003 however, the procedure has become flexible to the point that, in comparison with the ordinary legislative procedure, there are only two significant differences left. The first difference results from the requirement in Art. 114 that the constitutional revision has to be adopted in the same terms "in two successive votes, separated by an interval of at least three months." It is true that Art. 59 of the Constitution provides more generally that "all laws are subject to a second vote" and that there will be "an interval of at least three months between the two votes." Section 114, however, departs from Art. 59 in that it does not allow waiving of the second constitutional vote. During the ordinary legislative procedure, the so-called "second constitutional vote" may be set aside, if the Council of State and the Chamber agree on this point. This has become the standard situation. The Council of State merely refuses to agree to the waiver, if it formulated a so-called "formal opposition" in its advisory opinion. This means that the Council identified a contradiction of the proposal with the Constitution or any other norm of "higher law."

The second difference results from the special rules of quorum and qualified majority for which the new Art. 114 ultimately adds to the requirements of the previous procedure. The former paragraph 5 required a quorum of three-quarters of the members (45 MPs) and a positive vote of two-thirds of the votes cast (30). The new para 2 of Art. 114 merely requires a majority of two-thirds of the members of the Chamber, without providing a quorum, but also without admitting proxy voting. Thus, the qualified majority required for the adoption of revision Acts was extended to two-thirds of all members of the House, 40 members in total. This is still a relatively high majority, maintaining the solemnity of constitutional revision and, thus, the rigidity of the Constitution. In practice, most of the revision Acts are adopted unanimously. There are four cases in which the special majority of Art. 114 para 2 is also required to pass specific laws. This is about ratification of treaties transferring sovereign competences (Art. 37 in combination with Art. 49-bis), declaration of war (Art. 37), determination of the number of MPs to be elected in each district (Art. 51), and nationality condition of mayors and their deputies (Art. 107). This situation, in which you have ordinary laws, constitutional revision laws, and a third category of law, adopted with the same majority conditions as the latter, somewhat blurs the distinction between the constitutional and legislative value of an Act.

Phases of the revising procedure

The procedure of constitutional revision follows the steps of the ordinary legislative procedure. Article 114 only provides for specific rules governing the adoption of a revision of the Constitution; that is to say, for those that deviate from the legislative procedure. The process involves five stages, namely: initiative, parliamentary procedure, advisory opinions, the referendum process, and enactment.

Initiative

The new procedure is primarily characterized by the abandonment of the prior declaration of revision. The current text of Art. 114 of the Constitution, however, is silent on the question of who may initiate a revision. Thus, as during the ordinary legislative procedure, the right of initiative belongs equally to the Chamber and the Government. The revision process will be triggered by filing a (parliamentary) proposal or, where appropriate, a (governmental) draft. Originally, the revision draft of Art. 114 provided that "it is the legislature alone that has the right of initiative for constitutional revision," excluding a "shared right of initiative between the Executive and the Chamber." It was the Council of State that suggested reflecting the balance achieved between the two powers. Thus, the executive branch gained the right to submit revision drafts! The parliamentary Committee on Constitutional Revision claims, however, a "precedence of the legislature to initiate revisions in the constitutional field." In order to support its point of view, it relies on the long institutional practice and indicates that the new provision "does not depart from this customary rule."

Other institutions, such as the Constitutional Court, can exercise some influence. The Court's jurisprudence is an important source of the parliamentary debate about possible revisions. This is notably the case when it comes to modifying the Constitution in order to "save" laws previously declared unconstitutional, or to take into account the possible interpretation of certain constitutional concepts by the Court. Luxembourg MP Alex Bodry stated accordingly that "the very conservative jurisprudence of our Constitutional Court, which is confined mainly to a literal interpretation of ancient texts, could push the Parliament to go further than the political context so requires."

Parliamentary procedure

Any proposal and any draft for a revision must follow the traditional stages of deposition, request, and deliverance of an opinion of the Council of State as well as of other advisory bodies. The Chamber's internal procedures are laid down in its rules of procedure in Arts. 55ff. Differences in the course of the procedure, depending on whether there is a proposal or a draft for a revision, apply in the same manner as for ordinary laws. Two types of legislative initiative are distinguishable. First, the *projet de loi*. This preliminary draft of a law is drawn up by the relevant ministry, approved by the cabinet, and then submitted to the Council of State for its opinion. Second, the *proposition de loi*. One or more MPs may bring in a bill, which is submitted to the Conference of Presidents of the Parliament, which in turn decides on its referral to a committee. The text of the proposal is submitted to the Council of State for its opinion and sent to the government for its position. Once the Council of State has given its opinion, the bill is sent to the relevant parliamentary committee for examination and to report to the Parliament.

The competent committee is the Parliamentary Commission on Institutions and Constitutional Revision. This committee has 12 members and is composed following the principle of proportionate representation of the political groups. The debate in the Plenary Session of Parliament is conducted in two stages: a general discussion and a discussion Article by Article. Any deputy may propose amendments. For adoption by the Chamber, the exact wording of each constitutional revision must pass two votes, separated by an interval of at least three months. This rule is meant to allow a reflection period and was instituted in order to provide a kind of surrogate for the lack of a second chamber. The law finally adopted enters into force after enactment by the Grand Duke, and publication in the *Mémorial*. Until the revision of Art. 34 in March 2009, it had also to be granted royal assent. The mandatory majority to pass a revision bill is a majority of two-thirds, proxy votes not being admitted. In practice, this means that 40 of the 60 Chamber members must vote in favor of the constitutional revision. The two political parties that together form the actual governmental coalition currently hold 39 seats in the Chamber.

Advisory opinions

The opinion of the Council of State, which is foreseen for any legislative Act, is compulsory, but its content does not oblige the Chamber. In practice, the opinions of the Council of State do have a strong impact and the legal arguments brought forward often strongly influence the content of constitutional revisions. If the Chamber wants to adopt amendments to the revision draft or proposal, they have to be submitted to the Council of State for a supplementary opinion. The Council of State is composed of 21 councilors. State councilors are formally appointed and dismissed by the Grand Duke on proposal by the government, Parliament, or the Council of State. In Luxembourg's unicameral system, the Council of State exerts the moderating influence of a second legislative assembly. It is required to express its opinion on all bills brought in before the Parliament prior to voting by the MPs. Its opinion must entail a thorough examination to ensure compliance of the draft texts with the Constitution, international conventions, and the rule of law. The role of the Council of State is one of persuasion rather than enforcement.

Furthermore, the opinion of the professional Chambers concerned must be sought on any bills falling into their sphere of competence. The composition of the professional Chambers is determined by elections within each socio-professional group represented. There are five professional Chambers in the Grand Duchy, three represent employers and two represent workers: the Chamber of Commerce; the Chamber of Employees; the Chamber of Civil Servants and Public Employees; the Chamber of Trades; and the Chamber of Agriculture. Finally, the Economic and Social Council can also introduce opinions with regard to revision Acts falling in its sphere of competence. This Council is an advisory body responsible for studying—either on its own initiative or at the request of the government—the economic, financial, and social problems affecting several economic sectors or the national economy as a whole.

Possibility of a referendum

Article 114 innovates by introducing the option for a referendum on the text of the revision bill as adopted on first reading by the Chamber. At least 16 MPs or 25,000 voters registered on the electoral lists for the parliamentary elections have to ask for it. Determining the conditions of implementation of this right for MPs did not cause any difficulties and has been enshrined in Arts. 191–197 of the internal rules of the Chamber. Regarding citizens, unorganized by definition, it was necessary to fix the rules according to which the required signatures are to be collected. The law of 4 February 2005 "on the referendum at national level" establishes not only the conditions for collecting signatures but also the rules for the conduct of the referendum itself. The start date for collecting signatures is decided by the Prime Minister on demand of "an initiative committee consisting of five voters at least, no later than the fourteenth day following the adoption of the text of the constitutional revision in the first reading by the Chamber." The maximum period of two months, reserved by the Constitution to collect signatures, is partly consumed by several preparatory operations, for each of which the law sets specific deadlines.

Given the large number of signatures that must be collected and the relatively short time within which this must be done, the success of a popular claim for a constitutional referendum seems quite unlikely. The future will show whether Parliament set excessively strict conditions. In January 2009, a claim for a referendum was launched for the first time by a citizens' committee: about 230,000 listed voters were asked to sign the petition calling for a referendum in their local village or city halls. As only around 500 signatures were collected, the referendum did not take place. With regard to the outcome of a hypothetical referendum, Art. 114 states that "the revision is adopted if it receives a majority of valid votes cast." This is clearly a decision-making referendum, not just an advisory one. The choice of the citizens will replace the vote of the Chamber as to whether to approve the text adopted on first reading or to reject it.

Enactment

To be legally perfect, the text of the revision law still needs to satisfy the requirements of Art. 34 of the Constitution, which says that "the Grand Duke enacts laws within three months of the vote in the Chamber." It should be recalled here that this constitutional rule has only applied since the revision of Art. 34 by the Constitutional Revision Act of 12 March 2009. Prior to this modification, constitutional revisions were subject to the signing of the Grand Duke, who proceeded simultaneously to the "sanction" (also called royal assent) and the enactment of any law. Following the events of 2008, when for the first time Grand Duke Henri refused to sanction a bill on euthanasia, the new wording now deprives the Grand Duke of any discretion, and enactment has become a pure formality. As enactment must be made under Art. 34 "within three months of the vote in the Chamber," this prescription could have been considered inadequate in the case of adoption of the revision through referendum. The Council of State indicated, however, that the wording that the possible referendum "substitutes to the second vote of the Chamber" was sufficient to allow the application in the state of Art. 34. The revision Act is finally inserted in the *Mémorial* "to be performed and observed by everyone." Publication is the logical complement of enactment. The latter, as proof of the existence of statutory law, only makes sense if it is made accessible to the public.

Do material limitations exist?

The Constitution of Luxembourg does not formulate any explicit material restriction to the Chamber's power of constitutional revision. There are, however, two provisions of the Constitution that ought to be mentioned. According to Art. 113, "no provision of the Constitution may be suspended." This provision can be considered, on the one hand, as a kind of corollary of the principle that the Constitution can only be revised following the procedure described by it in Art. 114 and Art. 115. On the other hand, it also tends to prohibit derogations to the constitutional functioning of the state and its organs during exceptional situations. Article 113 could also be construed as a prohibition of revising the revision procedure in such a way that it would be identical to the ordinary legislative procedure.

The idea of a "suspended Constitution" had also been mobilized in the context of the ratification of the Maastricht Treaty. It was criticized that ratification intervened without a prior revision (of Art. 9 of the Constitution) introducing the right to vote for EU citizens. Some lawyers argued that the Constitution should have been revised before the ratification of the Treaty. The Council of State considered that the Treaty did not directly organize the exercise of these rights but required the adoption of a directive. Finally, the Constitution was revised in December 1994. During the period between the entry into force of the Treaty and the final revision of the Constitution, the latter was somehow suspended.

Article 115 provided initially that "no change in the Constitution can be made during a regency." It was revised in 1998 in the sense that, from then on, only changes in "the constitutional prerogatives of the Grand Duke, his status and the order of succession" are prohibited. The restriction laid down in Art. 115 is simply a limitation *ratione tempori*, not *ratione materiae*. One can also wonder whether this provision has not lost its purpose since the revision of Art. 34 of the Constitution, in which the Grand Duke's power to sanction laws was removed. Now, the Grand Duke will never be able to oppose a revision of its powers, neither during regency nor in ordinary times.

Constitution drafting methods

Four different Constitutions have been established during the history of the Grand Duchy: two of them through the constituent power of the Grand Duke, the other two by following the pertinent revision procedures that necessitated the agreement of both the Grand Duke and the Chamber of Deputies.

The Constitution of Luxembourg does not know the distinction between partial and total revision, as do the Constitutions of Switzerland and Austria, by providing a specific procedure in case of a total revision. The 2003 revision of the revision procedure facilitated the way for a true reform of the Constitution as envisaged in the current revision proposal. It is no longer necessary to appoint, one by one, the provisions subject to revision beforehand. The wording of former Art. 114, which referred to the designation of a "constitutional provision" in the singular, did not prevent the Chamber from considering a general revision of the Constitution, in particular by designating in 1999 almost all the constitutional provisions. It relied on the opinion of Alex Bonn, published in 1978, who said that even under the ambit of former Art. 114, a total revision of the Constitution was possible. The Chamber of Deputies "could simply declare that it is necessary to conduct a revision of all articles of the Constitution by listing them from 1 to 121."[14] Yet, such a proceeding would have been contrary to the spirit of former Art. 114.

The general revision procedure in progress, as mentioned earlier, is meant to produce a renewed Constitution. One question that immediately arises is whether a complete revision of the Constitution may, in fact, give rise to a genuinely new Constitution. The term "reform" and the title of the proposed revision "revising and reordering the Constitution" suggest, *prima facie*, that the Constitution of 1868 would continue to apply as revised. The explanatory memorandum, however, states in the end that the committee on constitutional revision "will add during the review process a new article, providing for the repeal of the current Constitution and governing the issue of entry into force of the new Constitution." The subsequent working meetings of the Commission on Constitutional Revision reveal its intention to provide explicitly in the final text that the Constitution of 17 October 1868 "is repealed by the entry into force of the new Constitution." From a theoretical point of view, the exercise of the Constitution-revising power by the Chamber is not capable of giving birth to a new Constitution. At the price of a certain conceptual ambiguity, the constitutional history of Luxembourg seems to show, however, the contrary.

As the revision procedure of Art. 114 of the Constitution offers the alternative between a purely parliamentary procedure and a referendum, nothing would be more logical than to opt for direct consultation of the people when it comes to adopting this "new" Constitution.

The role of the people

Is the revision procedure assessed by the electorate?

According to former Art. 114, any constitutional revision required dissolution and subsequent election of a new Chamber. In theory, this should have meant that the electorate was called to intervene in order to elect MPs by taking into account their positions with regard to the coming revision. In practice, this was not the case. First, because declarations of revision were usually adopted at the end of a regular legislative period. In consequence, dissolution did not appear as an extraordinary event. Second, because the discussion about constitutional revisions almost never played a significant role during pre-election campaigns. Thus, the Chamber to be elected never appeared to the electorate as a true *Constituante*, but rather as an ordinary Chamber.

Since 2003, the new procedure creates the possibility of a referendum on constitutional revision. But, as mentioned earlier, this is merely an option submitted to rather strict conditions and therefore unlikely to happen in the course of limited revisions. The end of the current revision process will show whether the electorate will be consulted through a referendum in the course of a more general revision.

To what extent does civil society participate?

The degree of participation of civil society in the discussion about constitutional revision depends on its content. In 2008–2009, following the refusal of the Grand Duke to "sanction" a bill on euthanasia, public debate about a revision of the Constitution in order to withdraw this power from him was quite intense. Other revisions realized in the last couple of years have been passed without almost any public discussion. Amongst Luxembourgish newspapers, the weekly *Letzebuerger Land* and the monthly magazine *Forum für Politik, Gesellschaft undKultur* ("Forum for Politics, Society and Culture") regularly publish contributions on institutional and constitutional issues. In May 2009, the *Forum* dedicated a full issue (no. 286) to the planned general revision of the Constitution.

The professional Chambers as well as the Economic and Social Council, which play an advisory function in each constitutional revision procedure, do not deliver opinions on every revision, only on those that directly affect their competences. The same is true for the Bar Association and the courts and tribunals, which introduce opinions on constitutional revision from time to time. The *Institut Grand-Ducal*, with its section for "moral and political sciences," has already organized several roundtable discussions (1987, 1992, and 2010) on the subject of major constitutional revisions. In general, they are well attended by lawyers, judges, and MPs. Foreign experts are also invited to these discussions. Last but not least, the University of Luxembourg also provides a forum for public discussions on constitutional revision. In May 2010, an international conference was held in order to render a critical appreciation of the Constitutional Revision Proposal of April 2009.[15]

How does International and European Law affect constitutional revision?

Even though the Constitution does not explicitly stipulate the primacy of international over national law, it is widely recognized in jurisprudence and doctrine that duly approved international and European provisions precede national law on an infra-constitutional level. Priority over constitutional law is more controversial, although there seems to be a tendency in favor of it. In any case, the legislator has repeatedly affirmed its will to prevent discrepancies between international and internal law by adapting national law, including the revision of the Constitution if necessary. The eight examples enumerated hereafter in chronological order show how deeply European and international law has affected constitutional revision in Luxembourg.

Introduction of Art. 49-bis and revision of Art. 37 in 1956

Article 49-bis was introduced into the Constitution in 1956 in the context of the European integration process. The ECSC Treaty, as well as the European Defense Community Treaty, raised the pivotal question as to whether the Luxembourgish legislature, executive, and judiciary may transfer powers to international institutions. The government considered that the existing Constitution would cover the transfer of powers. The Council of State disagreed but decided not to oppose the approval of the Treaties as a "matter of expediency," although it urged the necessity of immediate revision of the Constitution. Thereupon, both Treaties were approved on 23 June 1952 and 24 April 1954 respectively, whilst the Constitution was revised in 1956 only, with the introduction of Art. 49-bis: "The exercise of the powers reserved by the Constitution to the legislature, executive, and judiciary may be temporarily vested by treaty in institutions governed by international law." According to the simultaneous modification of Art. 37, such treaties have to be approved by a law adopted under the same majority requirements as those that apply for constitutional revision (Art. 114 para 2). The regrettable wording of Art. 49-bis, allowing only temporary transfer of competences, is to be addressed in the course of the current revision procedure. A proposal made in 2009 to introduce a complete new chapter on the European Union was, in the end, not adopted.

Article 9 and Art. 107 paras 2 and 4: Right to active and passive voting in municipal and European elections granted to all EU citizens

In order not to risk the dissolution of the Chamber because of a revision of the Constitution pursuant to Art. 114, the Conseil d'État argued that Art. 8b para 1 Maastricht Treaty would not be in conflict with the Constitution, because it would not immediately grant rights that individuals could directly invoke before any tribune (see the second sentence of the Art.: "This right shall be exercised subject to detailed arrangements to be adopted before 31 December 1994 by the Council, acting unanimously . . .").

Articles 9 and 107 were only revised in 1994. Consequently, there have been two years of incompatibility between European and constitutional law entailing discussions about the compatibility of the Maastricht Treaty with the Constitution, and the procedure of revising the Constitution in virtue of Art. 114. Article 9 was completed with a new paragraph 3: "the law may confer the exercise of political rights to non-Luxembourgers." Article 9 para 3 confers henceforth to non-Luxembourgers the exercise of political rights (i.e. the "cardinal political right" of active and passive voting).

Article 95-bis: Judgment of the ECtHR in **Procola**

A judgment by the European Court of Human Rights (ECtHR) led to a change of attributions of the Council of State and a reform of administrative justice. Since its creation in 1856, the Council of State has in fact fulfilled a dual function: in its opinion, it has participated in the legislative and regulatory process, and, through the judgments of the Litigation Committee, it has dispensed administrative justice. However, critics of the system were increasingly vocal. It was by its *Procola* decision of 28 September 1995 that the ECtHR finally struck a blow to the existing system: a reform of administrative justice became inevitable. Through a constitutional reform of 12 July 1996, the jurisdiction of the Council of State was reduced to its advisory function. At the same time, a Tribunal of First Instance and an Administrative Court, having jurisdiction on appeals, were created.

Former Art. 11 para 2 (now Art. 10-bis para 2): Access to all posts in the public sector for EU citizens

The constitutional legislator decided to revise the Constitution in the aftermath of a decision of the European Court of Justice (ECJ) in 1996. The ECJ held that the general prohibition for non-Luxembourgers to work in the public service exceeded the limits of exception provided for in Art. 48 para 4 EC. In not complying with its obligation "to open the areas in question to nationals of other member states by restricting application of the nationality condition to only those posts which actually involve direct or indirect participation in the exercise of powers conferred by public law and duties designed to safeguard the general interest of the State or of other public authorities," Luxembourg failed its obligations under the Treaty.

In reaction to a revision draft introduced by the President of the Commission for Constitutional Revision, the Conseil d'État did not agree that a revision would be necessary, because the Constitution would not *formally* restrict the access of non-Luxembourgers to employment in public service and, hence, would not be in contradiction of Art. 48 para 4 of the (Maastricht) Treaty. So, no revision was adopted. However, in the context of the release of its recommendation relating to the project of law opening the public service to EU citizens, the Conseil d'État accepted the argument that this project would necessitate a previous revision of Art. 11 para 2 (now Art. 10-bis para 2). As a result, Art. 11 para 2 was then revised in April 1999.

Article 18: Abolition of the death penalty

With the ratification of Protocol No. 6 to the European Convention on Human Rights (ECHR), the reintroduction of the death penalty became impossible. In 1999, Art. 18 of the Constitution was revised and the former Art. 118 (about abolition of the death penalty in political matters) repealed. Thanks to the new Art. 18, the Constitution was already in accordance with ECHR Protocol No. 13, abolishing the death penalty in all circumstances.

Article 23 para 1: Primary education free of charge for every child

Pursuant to a revision of Art. 23 in June 1999, primary school education was guaranteed free of charge for every child living in Luxembourg. In its "amendment to the revision proposal no. 3903 of 23 April 1999," the parliamentary committee in charge of constitutional revisions notably proposed to limit the gratuitous access to primary education to "citizens." The Conseil d'État vigorously countered this approach, referring both to Art. 28 para 1, lit (a) of the Convention on the Rights of the Child, and to Art. 2 of the (First) Additional Protocol to the ECHR, because the limitation would violate international law. As a result, the limitation to "citizens" was not introduced into Art. 23 para 1: every person resident in the Grand Duchy enjoys henceforth the right of entry to primary education "free of charge."

Article 118: Approval of the Statute of the International Criminal Court (ICC)

The approval of the ICC Statute necessitated a previous revision of the Constitution as some of its provisions, namely Art. 4 (inviolability of the Grand Duke), Art. 68 and Art. 69 (immunity of the Deputies), as well as Art. 82 and Art. 116 (relating to the criminal liability of Ministers), were incompatible with Art. 27 of the ICC Statute, which stated that, with respect to criminal responsibility, there shall be no distinction made based on capacity. The Conseil d'État held that it would be too difficult to revise all Articles of the Constitution potentially affected by the ICC Statute. Therefore, it recommended introducing a new provision stating that the Constitution shall not be opposed to the ICC Statute. The Chamber finally shared this point of view.

Article 114: Constitutional revision procedure

In the context of the 1994 revision, there was an attempt to change the procedure of constitutional revision pleading in favor of a duality of procedures: where an article of the Constitution would be in conflict with international treaties' provision, an alleviated procedure should apply. However, the Conseil d'État argued in favor of a unique revision procedure. In 2003, Art. 114 was finally revised, following the argument of uniqueness of the procedure (i.e. renouncing the requirement of dissolution of the Chamber).

Form of government, political conflict, and constitutional revision

The Grand Duchy of Luxembourg, being a small monarchy with a parliamentary form of government, has developed a particular model of consensus democracy sometimes referred to as the "Luxembourgish model." This model of a *Konsensdemokratie* functions very well in a small country like Luxembourg, where the different interest groups are well organized through a system of professional Chambers. The political system is strongly characterized by stability, proximity to the citizens, and a common desire to take decisions based on consensus. This is particularly true for decisions on constitutional revision, which are usually supported by much stronger parliamentary majorities then necessary (40/60) and are very often taken unanimously. For instance:

- The revision of the revision procedure has been adopted in November 2003, for instance, by 59 votes in favor and one abstention.
- The revision of Art. 16 on expropriation was adopted in October 2007 by 50 votes in favor and five against.
- In March 2008, the introduction of a new Art. 32–bis on political parties was adopted by 47 votes in favor out of 47 MPs present.
- The revision of Art. 9 para 1 and Art. 10 was adopted in October 2008 by 55 votes in favor out of 55 MPs present.
- The revision of Art. 34 in March 2009 was adopted unanimously.

In Luxembourg's political system, executive power is exercised by the Grand Duke and the Council of Government. The latter includes the Prime Minister, who serves as head of the government. He is the leader of the political party or coalition of parties that has the majority of seats in the Chamber. Legislative power is vested in the Chamber, the members of which are elected directly for five-year terms. A second body, the Council of State, composed of 21 citizens appointed by the Grand Duke, advises the Chamber in the drafting of legislation. The Council's opinions have no binding effect, and the responsibilities of its members are in addition to their normal professional duties. The political culture favors consensus, and parties coexist within the context of broad agreement on key issues, including the value of European integration. Six political parties exist at the moment.

Since the end of World War II, the Christian Social People's Party (CSV) has been part of the governing coalition and is usually the dominant party. The CSV resembles Christian democratic parties in other western European countries and enjoys broad popular support. Its leader, Prime Minister Jean-Claude Juncker, in power since 1995, is the longest-serving head of government in the European Union. The Socialist Party (LSAP) is a center-left party similar to most social democratic parties in Europe. The LSAP defends state intervention in the economy and the sustainability of the welfare system. Part of the government from 1984 to 1999, it lost its junior coalition status to the Democratic Party, only to regain it in the 2004 elections. The center-right Democratic Party (DP) draws much of its support from civil servants, the professions, and the urban middle class. Like other West European liberal (i.e., libertarian) parties, it advocates both social legislation and minimum government involvement in the economy. In the opposition from 1984 to 1999, the DP overcame the LSAP to claim the role of junior partner in the government from 1999–2004. It is currently again in opposition. Other notable parties include the Green Party, which has received growing support since it was officially formed in 1983; and the ADR (Alternative Democratic Reform Party), which when elected in 2004 was known as the Action Committee for Democracy and Pension Rights. The Left (former Communist) Party has one seat in the 60-member Chamber of Deputies.

The Chamber includes 60 deputies elected from lists submitted by different political parties. Since 7 June 2009, following the legislative elections, the Chamber of Deputies has been composed of the following: 26 seats for the CSV (Social Christian Party), 13 seats for the LSAP (Luxembourg Socialist Worker Party), nine seats for the DP (Democratic Party), seven seats for *Déi Gréng* (the Green Party), four for *l'Alternativ Demokratesch Reformpartei* (ADR), and one for *Déi Lénk* (left-wing).

As constitutional revision requires at least 40 votes, it needs to be accepted by MPs coming from at least three different groups. The last constitutional reform, which took place in Luxembourg from December 2008 to March 2009, is an interesting illustration of how the political system influences revision of the Constitution. After the head of state, the Grand Duke of Luxembourg, had announced that he would refuse to approve a possible law on euthanasia that the democratically elected Parliament was about to adopt, the Government and Parliament decided *unanimously* to abolish the royal assent to laws that had existed in the Luxembourg Constitution since 1848.[16] In more detail, that meant that the second constitutional vote on the law on euthanasia was postponed until the modification of the Constitution took place. Then, the law on euthanasia was finally adopted by the Chamber and simply promulgated by the Grand Duke.

The role of experts

Experts can be consulted either by the parliamentary Committee on Constitutional Revision, or by the Council of State in order to prepare its advisory opinion. This possibility is explicitly foreseen by the internal rulings of the Chamber (Art. 26) and the Council of State (Art. 15). In practice, only the Constitutional Revision Committee of the Chamber has made use of this possibility. As a significant number of councilors within the Council of State hold a law degree, and some even a doctoral degree in law, the need for external expertise is probably considered less important by this institution. It must also be said that the written opinions of the Council of State frequently refer to legal writing, comparative law, or case law, especially of the ECJ and the ECtHR. The *a priori* control of constitutionality of laws and regulations is one of the Council's main tasks, acting as an advisory body within the legislative procedure. Quite naturally, the Council therefore considers itself as the guardian of the Constitution. Thus, in some respects, councilors holding a law degree can be considered as true experts in the field of Luxembourgish constitutional law themselves. The written opinions of the Council in any case constitute a precious source of information about constitutional law issues in Luxembourg.

Regarding modifications of the Constitution affecting the judicial power, the members of the Bar Association and the association of Luxembourgish judges have also taken the initiative to introduce their positions as experts of the judiciary by delivering advisory opinions to the Chamber. In general, both the Council of State and the Chamber are sensitive to the point of view expressed by foreign constitutional law experts. Roundtable discussions published by the *Institut Grand Ducal*, for instance, are quite often mentioned during parliamentary debates, as well as in committee and in plenary sessions. The Grand Duchy's Constitution was strongly influenced by the 1831 Constitution of Belgium and still contains a number of identical, or at least similar, provisions. Belgian constitutional law writings do, therefore, constitute a valuable source of expertise in Luxembourg.

The following three interventions of external experts have been officially mentioned by preparatory documents of the Chamber.

1994 report by Francis Delpérée

During the preparation of the constitutional revision of 12 July 1996, which introduced the Constitutional Court, the Committee on Constitutional Revision asked Professor Francis Delpérée, from Belgium, to prepare a report. This report, from September 1994, has become an official preparatory document of the Chamber and has influenced the final text of Art. 95-ter to quite a significant degree.

2000 report by Constance Grewe and Francis Delpérée

In 1999, there was an attempt to overhaul and restructure the Constitution. Professor Constance Grewe, from France, and, again, Professor Francis Delpérée (Belgium) were asked to present a draft structure for the new Constitution. They participated in a meeting of the Committee on Constitutional Revision, on 19 January 2000, and gave a written report in May 2000.

2009 Opinion of the Venice Commission

In a letter of 2 June 2009, the Chamber requested an opinion from the Venice Commission on its proposed constitutional review, geared to revising and reorganizing the Constitution (CDL[2009]131). The Venice Commission instructed a Working Group—comprising Mr Chagnollaud, Mr Colliard, Mr van Dijk, Mr Jowell, Mr Trocsanyi, and Mr Velaers—to prepare an opinion on this matter. The individual comments by the rapporteurs are reproduced in documents CDL(2009)129, 130, 158, 160, and 161.

On 14 October 2009, the Working Group held a meeting in Luxembourg with the Parliamentary Committee and the Conseil d'Etat. The Venice Commission adopted the written opinion at its eighty-first Plenary Session (Venice, 11–12 December 2009). In several meetings, the Committee for Constitutional Revision discussed this opinion in detail, and the position of the government from July 2011 also refers extensively to this document.

Judicial review of constitutional revisions

The constitutional revision of 12 July 1996 and a law of 27 July 1997 introduced judicial review of laws in the light of the Constitution. The Constitutional Court rules on the constitutionality of laws, excluding those that approve treaties. If a party questions the constitutionality of a law before a judicial or administrative jurisdiction, the matter must be referred to the Constitutional Court if the issue of constitutionality is deemed vital to the solution of a dispute. It should be noted that the public has no direct recourse to the Constitutional Court. The Court conducts concrete constitutional reviews *a posteriori*, and cases are referred to it for preliminary rulings.

As constitutional revision is finally effected by the adoption of a revision law (*loi de revision*), the question arises whether such a law could also be submitted to constitutional review. Only the laws ratifying international treaties were explicitly excluded from the Court's jurisdiction. Control of compliance with the Constitution of laws carrying constitutional revision does not seem excluded at first glance, especially if compliance with Art. 113, Art. 114, and Art. 115 of the Constitution is concerned. A revision Act adopted by a referendum, which replaces the second vote in the Chamber, would, however, constitute a special case. In this case, the revision actually emanates from the direct will of the people and cannot be equated with an expression of the legislature. However, if the possibility of such control can be considered in theory, a practical problem arises immediately. The Luxembourg model of control of the constitutionality of laws does not know a form of control *a priori*. Could an ordinary court ask for a preliminary ruling from the Constitutional Court about the constitutionality of a revision Act? This is more than doubtful. Indeed, from the moment of their publication in the *Mémorial*, revision laws somehow vanish from the legal order and what is left is merely the revised Constitution. Revision Acts, therefore, are not likely to be applied separately by ordinary judges and, consequently, cannot be deferred to the Constitutional Court as such. Although strictly speaking there is no judicial review of revision Acts, there is a sort of *ex ante* review carried out by the Council of State during the parliamentary procedure. While its advisory opinions are not binding on the Chamber, they are usually followed.

Criticisms

There are three main criticisms to be mentioned on the current constitutional revision procedure in Luxembourg, as follows.

Trivialization of constitutional revisions

Several authors, the Council of State, the Venice Commission, and even the Committee on Constitutional Revision itself have criticized the frequency of recent constitutional revisions. Aware of the dangers of too-frequent constitutional revisions, the Chamber decided on 11 December 2008 to abandon the practice of repeated selective constitutional revisions and to proceed to a global revision of the Constitution. Consequently, a list of 13 pending proposals and drafts of constitutional revisions has been deleted from the Chamber's roll of current affairs.

Severity of conditions for a constitutional referendum

According to Art. 114, a referendum may replace the second vote of the Chamber on a project or proposal of constitutional revision if more than one-quarter of MPs (16) or 25,000 registered voters ask for it. The requirement to find 16 members of the Chamber in favor of a referendum does not appear to be very difficult at first glance. After all, the minority of MPs who eventually voted against the revision could do this. In practice, however, most of the constitutional revisions have been voted for by more than 45 MPs, or even unanimously. Therefore, the request for a referendum would have to be made by deputies who supported the revision in the first vote, which is not very likely to happen for obvious reasons of lost time and political risk. The second possibility foreseen by Art. 114 is a popular request for a referendum. The number of signatures to be found is very high: 25,000 out of more or less 230,000 registered voters in fact represents almost 11 per cent. Such strong support for organizing a referendum cannot be reached without an active campaign by the main political parties.

Revisions of the Constitution as a reaction to judgments of the Constitutional Court

Since the establishment of the Constitutional Court in 1997, it has already happened twice that the Chamber revised the Constitution in order to take into account the Court's decisions declaring legal provisions inconsistent with the Constitution. According to the law of 1997 on the Constitutional Court, its judgments do not interfere with the legislative power, and the Court does not have the power to invalidate Acts of Parliament. It is up to the Chamber to decide on the matter. Surprisingly, on two occasions the Chamber decided to revise the Constitution rather than to modify the incriminated law. The current revision procedure should introduce a strict obligation for the Chamber to modify a law declared unconstitutional by the Court within a certain period; otherwise, this law should become void.

Contemporary debate

While several initiatives for a general revision have been undertaken since the 1970s, none has been successful. Between 1919 and 2009, no fewer than 34 revisions are listed, the last dated 12 March 2009. Occurring at different times and on various aspects, they have not always contributed to strengthening constitutional coherence. The Constitution still includes a majority of provisions dating back 160 years; it has been repeatedly modified and patched. Today, it is in many ways supplanted by international law and institutional practice, and it lacks transparency and consistency. Therefore, the Chamber Committee on Institutions and Constitutional Revision, chaired by Paul-Henri Meyers, has chosen the path of a true overhaul of the Constitution.

The proposal "revising and reordering of the Constitution" filed on 21 April 2009 constitutes an important step. A substantial reform is indeed indispensable, especially with regard to the chapters that have undergone few or no modifications since 1868. The drafters of the proposed revision put forward three reasons for their proposal: first, to modernize outdated terminology; second, to adapt the legal text to the political reality (i.e. to eliminate the "fictions"); and third, to incorporate into the written Constitution provisions relating to succession to the throne currently contained in a legal document of uncertain value, namely the 1783 Family Compact of the House of Nassau (*Nassauischer Erbfolgeverein*). At present, this revision, initiated in April 2009, is still under construction. The government has recently (21 July 2011) given its official statement, and the Council of State is supposed to give its advisory opinion before the end of 2011.

Notes

1 See "Proposition de révision portant modification et nouvel ordonnancement de la Constitution" of 21 April 2009, doc. parl. no. 6030.

2 Cf. P. Weber, *Les Constitutions du 19e siècle*, Livre jubilaire du Conseil d'Etat, 1957, pp. 303–62; L. Hommel, *Les étapes constitutionnelles du Grand-Duché de Luxembourg*, L'édition universelle, Bruxelles, 1935; G. Ravarani, "La Constitution luxembourgeoise au fil du temps", *Annales du droit luxembourgeois* nos. 17–18 (2007–2008), pp. 59–83; and J. Gerkrath, "Le mécanisme de la révision constitutionnelle au Grand-Duché de Luxembourg", *Journal des Tribunaux Luxembourg*, 2009, no. 6, pp. 174–80.

3 Cf. P. Eyschen, *Das Staatsrecht des Grossherzogtums Luxembourg*, 1890, p. 10; P. Majerus, *L'Etat luxembourgeois*, Imprimerie Editpress, 1990, p. 26, and Hommel, op. cit., p. 11.

4 In fact, the Chamber elected, after a dissolution according to Art. 114, had the same composition, attributions, and mandate as the previous Chamber, with the only difference that, in addition, it was entitled to decide on the revision of those Articles that the previous Chamber identified in its declaration.

5 Cf. A. Bonn, *Réflexions sur la révision de la Constitution*, Luxembourg, 1978, p. 7.

6 See N. Campagna, "Une révision de la Constitution sans la puissance souveraine?", *Forum*, no. 202, Septembre 2000, p. 5.

7 Cf. B. Fayot, *Les quatre référendums du Grand-Duché de Luxembourg*, Edition de la Petite Amérique, 2006, p. 14.

8 See P. Schmit, "Questions sur le nouvel agencement des pouvoirs voulu par les auteurs de la proposition de révision de la Constitution", in J. Gerkrath (Coord.), *La refonte de la Constitution luxembourgeoise en débat*, Bruxelles: Larcier, 2010, p. 158.

9 All revisions and also quoted laws can be found in the *Mémorial*, the Official Journal of the Grand Duchy, online. Available HTTP: <http://www.legilux.public.lu/leg/a/archives/index.html>.

10 See J. Gerkrath, "Compétence et recevabilité des questions préjudicielles", in J. Gerkrath (ed.), *La jurisprudence de la Cour constitutionnelle du Luxembourg 1997–2007*, Pasicrisie, 2008, p. 16.

11 Published in the German language, "Décret grand-ducal du 16 Septembre 2010 introduisant l'égalité entre hommes et femmes en matière de succession au trône". *Mémorial* B no. 55 du 23.06.2011.

12 Answer to parliamentary question no. 1538 from 21 June 2011 issued by MP Alex Bodry.

13 See P. Kinsch, "Le rôle du droit international dans l'ordre juridique luxembourgeois", 2010, *Pasicrisie*, nos. 1–2, pp. 383–99.

14 Bonn, op. cit., p. 9.

15 Gerkrath, op. cit., 2010.

16 Cf. L. Frieden, "Luxembourg: Parliament abolishes royal confirmation of laws", *International Journal of Constitutional Law*, 2009, vol. 7(3), pp. 539–43.

13 The constitutional revision process in the Netherlands

Sensible security valve or cause of constitutional paralysis?

Wim J. M. Voermans

> How an established society's fundamental institutional rules are revised ultimately determines the degree of liberty retained by its people.
>
> Charlotte Twight, 1992

Introduction

The Kingdom of the Netherlands has one of the oldest written constitutions in Europe.[1] It rode the crest of the first wave of post-revolutionary constitutions in Western Europe at the beginning of the nineteenth century. The Dutch Constitution dates back to 1814, with a first major revision in 1815 when what is now Belgium joined the Kingdom of the Netherlands following the Allied Congress of Vienna. The document is restorative in nature as well as post-revolutionary (Napoleonic), a typical example of the first wave of liberal constitutions in the West.[2] The Dutch Constitution of 1814 did not (and does not) have a preamble,[3] only a very limited list of fundamental rights, an institutional design based on the ideal division of powers (a checked and balanced legislative branch, a distinct executive, and an independent judiciary), an embryonic parliamentary system, and a firmly enshrined system of constitutional monarchy.[4] The restorative elements are to be found in the restored powers of self-government of municipalities and provinces, and the freedom of religion and conscience.

From the start in 1814, the Dutch Constitution has had a very rigid regime for constitutional revision. Article 142, through Art. 144 of the 1814 version, required a statute expressing that there was a need to amend (parts of) the Constitution and then a subsequent second reading, beginning with the convention of adjunct Members of Parliament (MPs) recruited from the Provinces (doubling the number of MPs—the "States General") to consider the proposal put forward by the statute. Only a two-thirds majority in this enlarged Parliament could then adopt and pass the amendment: a formidable double threshold indeed in a country famous for its many denominations, creeds, and factions.[5] There is no real explanatory note with the original Constitution so one can only speculate as to the reasons the founding fathers may have had to come up with a revision procedure like this one. It may have been to do with the experience of the volatile political situation at the end of the eighteenth century when, after the original Patriotic insurrection had been quashed,[6] the Batavian Republic was proclaimed in 1795 as the outcome of another popular revolution.[7] This revolution was brought about with the support of the French revolutionary army who invaded the Netherlands, at intervals, between 1793 and 1795. The end result of the French intervention was that, after a series of domestic coups, the Batavian Republic became a client state of France. After 1806, the Republic turned into a monarchy (Kingdom of Holland) under direct French rule, which in 1810 became part of the French Empire. Thorbecke, on the other hand, points out that Van Hogendorp, principal framer of the original Constitution of 1814, believed that a constitution that could not be revised was flawed. Actually, Van Hogendorp got the inspiration for the revision procedure, Thorbecke's notes, from an annex to the Batavian Constitution of 1798.[8]

This contribution will deal with the constitutional revision procedure in the Netherlands as such, but will also consider the wider perspective of the relative position of the Dutch revision procedure amidst other types of revision procedures, and will also discuss the effects of this kind of revision procedure and recent proposals to amend the revision procedure. To my mind, this wider perspective is needed if we want to be able to compare revision procedures in different jurisdictions.

Shapes and sizes of revision procedures: an overview to set the stage[9]

Constitutional revision: balancing flexibility and rigidity—theory and practice

One of the classical problems of constitutional law all over the world concerns constitutional revision. Modern constitutions are believed to express the political will of a people as regards the conditions and terms for political society. The received theory in our day and age is that a constitution is a consensual act by a sovereign nation or people empowered to do so[10] (a so-called *constituante*), resulting in one or more[11] written documents.[12] The rationale behind this theory is that of a temporary (mythical[13]) communion of individuals with different interests into one body with a common identity (nation or people) at a single moment, resulting in a balanced packaged deal. Most modern constitutions are based on this underlying notion of what I will call *constitutional singularity*. According to this theory, the revision of a constitution by a different body other than the *constituante* itself is problematic, and even then, revision is controversial because the *constituante* is not a mere body—it is an historic moment as well.[14] That may be the reason why they have annexed amendments to their Constitution in the United States rather than changing the original text itself. The revision of a constitution is not only problematic from the perspective of constitutional singularity, it may also compromise the balance and trade-offs in the package deal of the constitution itself. Modern contract theorists and political economists alike have pointed out that amendments or revisions to the original package deal of the constitution may render a post-constitutional state unstable, even reverting to anarchy, if rights in practice came to diverge substantially from people's "renegotiation expectations."[15]

Compared to the theories on constitution-making, there are virtually no theories on constitutional revision (apart from it being considered problematic).[16] What is the rationale or the justification for constitutional revision? According to one line of thought, it is not possible for a *constituante* to foresee everything, and therefore the work of this body is unfinished, or at least not perfected. Future legislators are therefore delegated by the *constituante* to finish the job and to perfect the constitution, within—of course—the confines of the mandate laid down by the *constituante.*[17] A second line is based on Fukuyama's theory of adaptation: political institutions need to adapt to changing circumstances in order to survive.[18] Constitutions as platforms and frames for political life need to adapt in order to keep the original will of the *constituante* intact.

Once we are clear on the *why* of constitutional revision, the question of *how* to revise presents itself. If a constitution is over-adaptive, it may risk compromising the original (package) deal and constitutional consensus (thus becoming futile as a constitution). On the other hand, too much rigidity may fossilize the constitution, or (as a result) trigger forms of bypass[19] or non-compliance. Balancing rigidity and flexibility (i.e. adaptation) is of course a question for political actors and not a theoretical consideration, although Cooter's "Minimax Constitution" strategy (originating from game theory),[20] in which a constitution and its revision procedure are set up in such a way that they minimize the harm when the worst political possibilities materialize, seems to explain the bulk of constitutional revision procedures in democracies.

Revision types

Most *written* constitutions in the world, to which I will limit my treatise, are equipped with revision procedures.[21] Classical constitutional doctrine makes a distinction between two types of constitutions based on the ease of a revision. *Rigid* constitutions are, according to this distinction, constitutions that are difficult to revise (e.g. because of a complex or difficult amendment procedure involving more than one reading, or qualified majorities or supermajorities), whereas *flexible* constitutions can be amended more easily.[22] This distinction, however, is confusing to a certain extent. First of all, because most of the many constitutions we regard as "flexible" in terms of their amendment procedure do set extra requirements on constitutional amendments compared with ordinary statutes, for example.[23] Even in countries where the fundamental constitutional rules are not enshrined in a single constitutional document, but in mere Acts of Parliament, for example, there is usually a certain degree of rigidity due to *de facto* respect for these parts of their Constitutions. For example, it is almost inconceivable that the Westminster Parliament would amend the Bill of Rights of 1688.

Moreover, the rigidity of a constitution involves more than the mere revision procedure. The rigidity of a constitution also reflects its fundamental nature.[24] This is in fact what distinguishes constitutions from ordinary statutes. Hans Kelsen already understood that a constitution that can be amended in the same way as any other statute results in a curious paradox. This constitution would be a constitution only in name, because any "unconstitutional" statute would, as a result of the operation of the maxim *lex posterior derogat priori*, lead to a change in the constitution, at least in terms of the sphere of validity of this statute.[25] Some jurisdictions, like India for instance, have expressed this by acknowledging that there are elements in their constitution that make up the "basic structure" of the document and, therefore, cannot be amended according to the normal (up to 1976 very flexible) revision procedure.[26]

A constitution may also impose different levels of amendability on different subject matter. The German Constitution, for instance, is famous for its *Ewigkeitsklausel* (eternity clause), which prohibits the amendment of the fundamental principles enshrined in Art. 1 and Art. 20 of the Constitution, and the division of powers between states and the federation.[27] Other countries have differing revision regimes for different subject matter/provisions in their constitutions.[28]

Constitutions can be rigid not only in terms of their amendment procedure but also in terms of their enforcement. Merryman and Pérez-Perdomo draw an illuminating distinction between formally rigid constitutions, which specify limitations on legislative power and define special requirements for constitutional amendments (but make no provision for enforcing these rules) on the one hand, and functionally rigid constitutions, in which an organ (court, council) can review—in one way or another—the constitutionality of legislative action on the other hand.[29] This functional rigidity also reflects the fundamental nature of a constitution.

More or less "rigid" revision procedures come in a wide variety of shapes and sizes. Procedural revision rigidity seems, however, to be the most common type.[30] Most of the time, qualified or supermajorities are required before an amendment to the constitution can be adopted, or there are procedural extras like a double parliamentary reading, new elections between the readings (e.g. the Netherlands), parliamentary enactment followed by a referendum (e.g. France), and adoption by Parliament and ratification by (a qualified majority of) territorial subunits (USA).

Heringa and Kiiver note that the formal rigidity of a constitution (the procedures) is not always a clear indicator of its substantive rigidity.[31] Changing customs and conventions in political practice may give, for instance, a different meaning to constitutional provisions. In the same way, judicial interpretation—notably that of constitutional courts—can play a crucial role in determining the substantial flexibility of a constitutional text.

The overview of revision types presented above is more or less classic textbook material. Recent literature seems to focus more on the actual ways constitutions are amended. A distinction between formal and informal revisions of constitutions then emerges. Formal revisions are, in this line of thinking, changes to a constitution brought about by amendments to the text of the entrenched written constitution, which have passed through a special procedure (that may include a qualified majority in Parliament or a referendum), or brought about by other written acts that can be regarded as of a fundamental nature.[32] Informal revisions, on the other hand, are changes made to the constitution (or impacts on it that yield the same result as change) that have not followed the path of the formal amendment procedure. Constitutional interpretation by courts, for instance, may (have the effect of) change the constitution, as may legislation or international treaties. On occasion, modern constitutional theory labels formal textual changes to a written constitution as "amendments" and informal changes as "revisions."[33] Donald Lutz has come across an interesting pattern while studying different amendment processes. He observes that in jurisdictions where it is "too difficult" (according to his Index of Difficulty) to formally amend the constitution, those jurisdictions will develop alternatives, including amendment by purported interpretation.[34]

The Dutch revision procedure

Chapter 8 of the Dutch Constitution deals with the revision procedure. In view of the procedural requirements it sets on revision, the Dutch Constitution qualifies as a rigid constitution. Any revision to the Constitution involves two parliamentary readings (with general elections in between), and a qualified two-thirds majority in both Houses of Parliament in the second reading.

There are different triggers for proposals for constitutional revision in the Netherlands. Proposals for relatively small amendments are commonly the result of incidents or the specific program of a political party. Major revision proposals are mostly preceded by studies and proposals by specially established government committees, although this is not mandatory. The role of experts is quite small. Proposals for revision are, almost always as a rule,[35] prepared by one or more ministerial departments.[36] The required skill and expertise is pooled within a special unit of the Ministry of the Interior. The Bureau of Constitutional Affairs and Legislation (*Constitutionele Zaken en Wetgeving*, or CZW for short) has a regular staff of a dozen expert civil servants who look into constitutional affairs. This central unit within government is consulted on constitutional issues that arise in the different ministerial departments; when it comes down to constitutional revision, this unit is responsible for drafting the proposals. Once a proposal is made by the Minister of the Interior, it needs to be discussed and agreed by the Council of Ministers: major legislation is a collegiate matter in the Dutch political system. After clearance by the Council of Ministers, the proposal is sent to the Council of State for consultation. The consultation must not be confused with judicial review of amendments as we know it in other constitutional systems (e.g. France or Italy). The Dutch Council of State gives a non-binding opinion; no more, no less. The Council of State's opinion is discussed in the Cabinet, and a subsequent report reacting to this opinion is added to the dossier (*nader rapport*). The proposal, the explanatory memorandum, the opinion of the Council of State, and the additional report with comments are then tabled before the Dutch House of Representatives (*Tweede Kamer*), the Dutch variant of a House of Commons in its bicameral Parliament (*Staten-Generaal*). The Houses at this stage deal with the bill proposing to amend the Constitution in a first reading. Since the bill after its first reading does not, in fact, amount to a constitutional revision (a subsequent second reading is necessary), we call this sort of first-reading bill a "consideration proposal" after the text of Art. 137 para 1 of the Dutch Constitution, which provides that a revision of the Constitution starts with the passage of a bill "stating that an amendment to the Constitution in the form proposed shall be considered." The consideration bill is debated as a regular bill in the first reading in the House of Representatives. Amendments can be made to it, and it is subject to regular voting procedures (i.e. a simple majority suffices for adoption). However, in most cases, constitutional revision in the Netherlands is an uphill battle.

Constitutional amendments tend to touch on principles, and the Dutch have a tradition going back more than 400 years of discussing (and most of the time disagreeing) on principles at length. This has resulted in a fragmented religious[37] and political landscape.[38] Political and ideological fragmentation combined with a rigid revision procedure has made it very difficult to amend the Constitution. It proved equally difficult to amend the revision procedure itself. A major revision to the Constitution in 1983, however, brought one innovation that tried to make constitutional amendment somewhat easier. Article 137 para 2 of the Constitution makes it possible to break up a bill proposing to amend the Constitution, which in turn makes it possible to save and readily pass uncontroversial parts of a proposal as a separate bill. Only the Government and the House of Representatives have this power to divide a first-reading consideration bill, not the Senate. After the House of Representatives has adopted the bill (the first reading stops upon rejection), it is tabled before the Dutch Senate, the other Chamber of Parliament. Under the Dutch Constitution, the Senate does not have the power to amend or break up the bill in its first reading. The senators have to deal with the bill as it stands, but they can try to persuade the Government to use its powers to alter or divide the proposals put forward in the bill. If the Government succumbs to this, an alteration or division has to travel the whole route again (Council of State and House of Representatives), before it can be dealt with again within the Senate. This method of "*novella*" to rally support in the Dutch Senate is controversial because, in the eyes of some, it is an extra-constitutional usurpation of the power to amend.[39] If the consideration bill is passed by the Senate, it becomes an Act of Parliament.[40]

When the Act becomes effective, by way of publication, Art. 137 para 3 of the Dutch Constitution provides that both Houses of Parliament have to be dissolved. The underlying idea is that of a plebiscite: the people need to be consulted on the proposed amendment. By ordering new elections, people can make up their mind as regards the proposed amendments and vote for the candidates who voice the position on the proposed amendment they prefer. This plebiscite theory has, however, been overhauled by the actual practice of the dissolutions for reason of constitutional amendment. The general practice throughout the last century or so has been to wait for the moment of the general election for the House of Representatives and only then to publish the Act putting forward the proposal to amend the Constitution. In this way, general elections and public consideration of the proposal to amend the Constitution can coincide. As we will see in the next paragraph, this method has resulted in the common practice that the general election totally overshadows the debate on pending proposals to amend the Constitution. The majority of voters are unaware of constitutional amendments during the general elections.[41]

After a series of changes in the way the Senate was elected and composed in the latter half of the twentieth century, the dissolution of both Houses of Parliament for the purpose of constitutional reform created problems. Because the members of the Senate are indirectly elected by representatives of the provinces, and (thereby) the terms of the House of Representatives and the Senate were no longer synchronous, even minor constitutional amendments could trigger mid-term provincial elections. This is indeed a very drastic consequence, and it is why the 1995 Act revised the dissolution procedure somewhat: only the House of Representatives has to be dissolved in the event of an Act proposing an amendment to the Constitution.[42]

After the election, the House of Representatives in its new composition convenes and considers the Act to amend the Constitution laid before it by the former session. The Houses of Parliament can no longer amend or divide this proposal during the second reading. The motion to amend the Constitution as put forward in the Act can only be carried if adopted in both Houses with a two-thirds majority of the votes cast. This way of conducting a second reading has proven to be a "killing field" for many proposed amendments, as one might imagine. The procedure gives 26 senators with a very indirect popular mandate the power to block any proposal.

If the proposal is adopted in second reading, it has, once again, to be ratified by the Government before it can come into force. Constitutional revisions, however, do not usually take immediate effect.[43] The amendments made to the Constitution may conflict with existing law, and, although Art. 140 of the Constitution enshrines a general transitory regime providing that existing legislation in conflict with an amendment to the Constitution remains in force until provisions are made in accordance with the Constitution (a form of deferred application), the Government generally tends not to let it come to this. Existing legislation is quite often tailored to the new constitutional amendments before the amendments themselves take effect. Constitutional amendments are promulgated by Royal Decree.

Processes and practices of constitutional revision in the Netherlands: past and present

Looking superficially at its history, one would not immediately conclude that the Dutch Constitution is very difficult to revise. Since its inception in 1814, there have been 23 revisions[44] to the Constitution. These revisions were not all equally important. Some are major in the volume of amendments (1848,[45] 1887,[46] 1983[47]) or major considering the political or constitutional impact of the amendments (1848[48], 1917[49] and, arguably,[50] the ones of 1956[51] and 1983[52]). The bulk of the amendments, however, represents minor changes and largely stem from the last 75 years.[53]

The nature of the revisions has changed over time as well, as Burkens notes. In the nineteenth and early twentieth centuries, debates on constitutional revisions were at the very heart of the political arena, and amendments to the Constitution acted as autonomous drivers for political change. After the major revision of 1917, which solved the stalemate debate over universal suffrage and equal treatment of public and private schools, there has been a tendency to leave the Constitution intact and only revise it after the political settlement of an issue. This is a transgression, in other words, from the Constitution as a driver of political change into a consolidating mechanism of political change after the fact.[54]

What has caused this deflation in the importance of constitutional revision in the Netherlands? There are two main explanatory perspectives here, expressing two different lines of thought. One group of commentators looks for the causes within the Constitution itself. They feel that the combination of the partial ban on constitutional review (Art. 120 of the Constitution); the nature of the constitutional provisions themselves;[55] the internationalization of human rights protection over the last 50 years, combined with the custom of submitting proposed amendments to the voters on the occasion of general elections (when the amendments get overcast by other political questions); and the rigid revision procedure have led to a steady decrease in the normativity of the Constitution, bordering on constitutional paralysis.[56] In 2006, the Dutch National Convention (a commission invited to reflect on constitutional and political modernization and reform) concluded that, if the Constitution is desired to be a "living instrument," the revision procedure and practice need to be reconsidered.[57]

Other commentators are less pessimistic and point out that the sober Dutch Constitution aligns well with the present political culture that the revision procedure is doing what it ought to do: protecting against whimsical change, protecting minority rights and the constitutional structure against chance majorities, and creating and maintaining political stability.[58] In this same vein, the most recent Dutch Government Commission on Constitutional Reform held that, at present, there is no real pressing need for constitutional revision to uphold the Constitution.[59]

Apparently, on the face of it, the Dutch seem content with their Constitution and the revision procedure. There is, however, somewhat more than meets the eye here, one could argue. First of all, the line of reasoning is a sort of conservative, self-fulfilling prophecy: the Dutch Constitution is not a living instrument, it is not critical for the political order, nor in any danger, so we are content with a procedure that effectively blocks change. Second, due to the complex revision procedure, a lot of constitutional settlements and regulation have taken place outside the Constitution itself. I have labeled this "covert constitution building."[60] This form of extra-constitutional settlement of issues is not unique to the Netherlands, but perhaps the volume is. In the Netherlands, some of the principal constitutional norms are largely unwritten (the rule of confidence governing the relationship between Parliament and Government, the principle of the rule of law, and the principles of legality, legal security, etc.). A lot of norms that curb present-day government action are not enshrined in the Constitution but in lower-ranking Acts of Parliament like the important General Administrative Law Act and the Act on the organization of the Judiciary. Acts of Parliament have been the instrument of choice for constitutional innovations and experiments, such as nationwide referenda,[61] over the past few decades. The long and winding road of constitutional revision has been deliberately evaded over the last 30 years. Only when an issue cannot be settled without compromising existing constitutional provisions or reserves[62] is the royal route of revision considered, but circumventing it seems to be preferred.[63]

Assessing the Dutch revision procedure and processes

In his book "Patterns of Democracy," Arend Lijphart discusses two important variables that have to do with the presence or absence of explicit restraints on the legislative power of parliamentary majorities:[64] first, the presence of a (rigid or flexible) constitution, and second, judicial review. The combination of the two variables characterizes the democratic system of a country. In the pure consensus model, a constitution is rigid (requiring supermajorities for amendments) and protected by judicial review. In the pure majoritarian model, a constitution is flexible and there is no system of judicial constitutional review. Analyzing 36 democracies between 1945 and 1996, Lijphart has found an empirical relationship between the two variables. The correlation co-efficient is 0.39—not exceptionally strong, in his view, but still statistically significant at the 1 percent level.[65]

Every Dutchman (including Lijphart, who is Dutch) would be suspicious of, or surprised by, a result that rates the country at the bottom of the league of majoritarian systems. Indeed, the Dutch constitutional system has—as discussed above—a ban on constitutional review of Acts of Parliament and Treaties (Art. 120 Constitution), and a rigid Constitution, but domestic observers would all stress the fact that the Dutch democratic system is an outstanding example of a true *consensus* democracy (which, by the way, is something a little different than a consensual system). Maybe this counter-intuitive outcome is (one of) the reason(s) why Lijphart concludes that the Netherlands present a *deviant* case as concerns this correlation.

The interplay between the variables combined with Dutch political culture is, however, to a high degree explanatory for the Dutch system. And the Netherlands do rate as a consensual system, if we take a closer look. We already saw that the Dutch Constitution is a rigid constitution. Any amendment needs to pass through two different Houses of Parliament, in two readings, with a plebiscite in between. Lijphart places the amendment procedure in the middle category of rigidity, among those requiring a two-thirds majority. Actually, the Netherlands could be placed in the highest category of rigidity that Lijphart adopts, among those requiring more than a two-thirds majority. The Dutch political system, for instance, has been highly fragmented for more than a century and was polarized until 30 years ago, which has resulted in a strong consensus culture. Political minorities do punch above their nominal electoral weight in everyday Dutch politics, due to this engrained culture of consensus and respect for minorities. There is even an official word for this consensus culture: *polderen*.[66] The flip-side of this culture is that a mere two-thirds majority in itself will not suffice for a constitutional amendment. This explains why the major revisions of the Dutch Constitution have been the result of significant trade-offs in package-deal amendments after decades of political discussion on the issue. It also explains why major constitutional innovations only succeed if there is a near total consensus. And it explains why most of the recent revisions concerned minor details of little importance: they were utterly non-controversial, and could therefore rely on (near) total consensus.

Consensus systems couple the rigidity of their constitution with judicial review, according to Lijphart's theory. The Dutch system, on the face of it, does not have judicial constitutional review. There is, however, more than meets the eye here. The ban on constitutional review enshrined in Art. 120 of the Constitution is only a partial one. Dutch courts are not allowed to review Acts of Parliaments and Treaties on their constitutionality, but they are free to review any other regulation. On the other hand, however, Dutch courts *are* allowed to review all domestic legislation—Acts of Parliament included—as to their compatibility with international Treaties and European Union (EU) law, and they do so very actively and frequently. The human rights catalogue of the European Convention on Human Rights (ECHR) and its protocols, which has direct effect and is directly applicable in the Netherlands, is invoked and applied frequently; actually, Dutch judges seem to favor the European catalogue over the constitutional domestic catalogue. It would be no exaggeration to say that—especially in view of the, normatively, relatively "weak" Dutch Constitution—the actual Dutch Constitution is comprised of the ECHR and EU Treaties as well. The Dutch Constitution presents a textbook example of a compound constitution. If we look through this lens, there is actually more judicial review, even constitutional review, in the Netherlands than meets the eye at first glance. And if we accept this, the Netherlands case would nowadays move towards a consensual-type system in Lijphart's characterization, rather than a more or less majoritarian system.

Revising the revision procedure: recent attempts

Is the Dutch revision procedure too rigid? Who is to say? The paradox, of course, is that the revision procedure itself is very difficult to change due to the rigidity of that very revision procedure. There have been initiatives to that end, though. In 1946, the Beel Cabinet proposed to elect a separate body for the second reading. It was believed that, with a dedicated Chamber for Constitutional Revision, the problem of general elections overshadowing the second reading of constitutional revision could be overcome. The House of Representatives, however, rejected the proposal during the second reading. In 1951, the Cabinet considered a reprisal of the idea of a dedicated Constitutional Revision Chamber, but the proposal was withdrawn at the first reading when it became clear that there was no majority to be found. In 1971, the influential Government Commission Cals/Donner, which came up with many of the proposals that found their way into the 1983 revision, floated the idea of a combined session of both Chambers of Parliament on the occasion of the second reading. The suggestion did not make it to an actual proposal.

A recent suggestion referred to above was put forward by the National Convention of 2006. During the first reading, the Convention proposed, the bill with the proposals for amendment to the Constitution should be debated in both the House of Representatives and the Senate, with the requirement of a two-thirds majority in both Houses. Upon adoption in both Houses, the Chambers would be dissolved and the proposed amendments then put up for a referendum, separate from the general election. If the proposal was adopted after the referendum, the Government would then ratify it, and thus it could come into effect. The suggestion was short-lived, however, and never made it to an actual proposal.

In conclusion, one might say that, in view of recent Dutch constitutional history, the chances for successful revision of the revision procedure seem very slim indeed.

Conclusion

The Dutch Constitution is equipped with a rigid revision procedure that has more or less withstood the test of time for over 150 years. The procedure involves two readings in the two Houses of the Dutch Parliament, with dissolution of the House of Representatives in between, in order to consult the electorate on the proposed changes. In the second reading, after the election, a proposal needs to collect a two-thirds majority in both Houses to be adopted.

Although the revision procedure seemed a formidable threshold at the outset, it has permitted 23 revisions in nearly 200 years, which amounts to more than one every decade. The nature of the revisions, however, has changed over time. Whereas in the nineteenth and early twentieth centuries, constitutional revisions were debated at the heart of the political arena and the revisions themselves were triggers of political change, the revisions of the last century followed and consolidated political change rather than spurring it on.

It is not easy to assess the effects of the Dutch revision procedure itself, since it is so intertwined with the political and constitutional culture. Causalities are difficult to define. Has the rigidity of the Dutch revision procedure caused a political culture that does not seem to overvalue the Constitution, or is it the other way around? If we try to assess the Dutch revision procedure in terms of effects, we can distinguish two different patterns. On the one hand, one might say that the revision procedure has been successful in protecting the basic constitutional structure against whimsical change of chance majorities. It has—in the eyes of many observers—created a level of political stability in a historically fragmented political landscape governed as a rule by essentially frail coalitions. Playing it down, especially on constitutional principle, seems to have paid off, with stability being the dividend. The revision procedure can also be perceived as successful due to its persistence: attempts or suggestions to revise the Dutch constitutional revision procedure seem to have a lot of trouble getting off the drawing board. Those that did have failed.

On the other hand, one might argue that the revision procedure suffocates the Dutch constitutional debate and paralyzes the Constitution as a living instrument. Evidence for this line of reasoning can be found in the lukewarm sympathy the Dutch have for their Constitution (if they know it at all), and their inclination to bypass the Constitution for constitutional change in the last decades. But then again, on a brighter note, one might argue that the Dutch political system in recent years has produced a revision procedure that already exists in other systems: a two-tiered revision procedure according to which changes to the constitutional core are governed by rigid revision procedures with supermajority requirements, and subsequent readings and run-of-the-mill adaptations that can be made by simple majorities in regular parliamentary Acts. But perhaps this perception is much too apologetic and conciliatory, because, from whatever angle we look at it, the Dutch *constituante* was never consulted on it.

Notes

1 The original Republic of the United Netherlands (1581–1795) did not have a written constitution in the modern sense of the word, although there were several constitutional documents and charters (e.g. The Union of Utrecht of 1579 and the Act of Abjuration of 1581). These documents typically had the character of medieval charters, edicts, or declarations and—by virtue of their character—they cannot be revised or amended.

2 The Norwegians boast that their Constitution is the oldest single-document national constitution in Europe, and the second oldest in the world, still in continuous force. But is it? The Norwegians adopted their present Constitution on 16 May 1814. The Dutch Constitution was adopted on 29 March 1814. It does not require "Dutch arithmetic" to see that this is more than a month before the Norwegian one. Admittedly, the Dutch Constitution had already been revised substantially in 1815 to implement the outcome of the Vienna Congress of that same year. But still, it was a revision of the existing Constitution of 1814, not a new one that came into force on 24 August 1815.

3 Recently (2009–2010), some scholars and politicians have lobbied for a preamble to introduce the Dutch Constitution as a means to boost and communicate Dutch identity, and the constitutional and political values underpinning Dutch Society. As of yet, these proposals have not been embraced by the majority of political parties.

4 C.A.J.M. Kortmann and P.P.T. Bovend'Eert, *Dutch Constitutional Law*, Kluwer Law International, 2000, pp. 17–18.

5 See R.B. Andeweg and G.A. Irwin, *Governance and Politics in the Netherlands*, Palgrave Macmillan, 2002, pp. 17–26.

6 With the aid of a foreign power – the Prussians. The Patriotic insurrection (or even "revolution") and its background have been depicted in an unparalleled way by S. Schama in his 1977 (first big) book, *Patriots and Liberators: Revolution in the Netherlands 1780–1813*, Harper Perennial, 1992.

7 On 19 January. The Batavian Republic replaced the Republic of the United Netherlands (originally the seven Provinces). Prince William IV of the House of Orange Nassau, Governor of the Republic of the United Netherlands, was deposed and had to flee.

8 Reglement Letter E. Bijlage bij de Staatsregeling van 1798, artikelen 27 e.v. See J.R. Thorbecke, *Aanteekening op de Grondwet (Comments to the Constitution)*, Part II, 2nd edn, Johannes Müller, 1843, pp. 305–7.

9 Some of elements of this paragraph have been taken from an article I wrote for the Indian Journal of Constitutional Law. W.J.M. Voermans, "Constitutional Reserves and Covert Constitutions", *Indian Journal of Constitutional Law*, 2009, vol. 3, p. 84ff.

10 By (pre-existing) law or in fact (by way of a declaration or political statement). In many preambles preceding constitutional texts, one may find declarations that try to justify why a nation or a people are entitled to define themselves as a political community and therefore empowered to constitution-making as well, especially when a legal title is missing. See P.B. Cliteur and W.J.M. Voermans, *Preambules (Preambles)*—a comparative study written at the request of the Dutch Ministry of the Interior and Kingdom Relations, Kluwer, 2009.

11 Sweden, for instance, has a constitution that consists of more than one single document.

12 This is the default method of sovereign constitution-making. There is also the method of post-sovereign making, in which the constituent power is not embodied in a single organ or instance with the plenitude of power, and all organs participating in constitutional politics are brought under legal rules. A. Arato, "Post Sovereign Constitution-making in Hungary: After Success, Partial Failure, and Now What?", *South African Journal on Human Rights*, 2010, vol. 26, pp. 19–44. I will not discuss this method separately in the rest of the contribution.

13 Perceived from a natural-law point of view, the constitutional moment is not merely a consensual moment, but also a moment of enlightenment and revelation, resulting in a common understanding of what natural law dictates.

14 According to some thinkers like Carl Schmitt, amendments cannot change the fundamental decision of the original revolutionary constituent power. Arato, op. cit., pp. 19–44, citing C. Schmitt's *Verfassungslehre* from 1928.

15 J.M. Buchanan, *The Limits of Liberty: Between Anarchy and Leviathan*, University of Chicago Press, 1975.

16 See C. Twight, "Constitutional Renegotiation; Impediments to consensual Revision", *Constitutional Political Economy*, 1992, vol. 3(1), pp. 89–112.

17 E.g. S. Levinson, "Introduction", in S. Levinson (ed.), *Responding to Imperfection—The Theory and Practice of Constitutional Amendment*, Princeton University Press, 2003.

18 F. Fukuyama, *The Origins of Political Order: From Prehuman Times to the French Revolution*, Profile Books, 2011, pp. 452–4.

19 For instance, in the form of what I have called "covert constitution building", Voermans, op. cit.

20 R.D. Cooter, *The Strategic Constitution*, Princeton University Press, 2000, pp. 11–12.

21 In 1978, only five of the then-existing 142 national constitutions lacked a provision for an amending process. H. van Maarseveen and G. van der Tang, *Written Constitutions: A Computerized Comparative Study*, Oceana Publications, 1978, p. 80. Although the data are more than 30 years old, it is highly unlikely that, in this day and age, more constitutions than back in 1978 will be without an amendment procedure, since the number of constitutions has grown since then, and most of the new constitutions tend to copy-cat best practices. See C. Saunders, "Towards a Global Constitutional Gene Pool", *National Taiwan University Law Review*, 2009, vol. 4(3), pp. 1–38.

22 K.C. Wheare, *Modern Constitutions*, 2nd edn (fifth impression of the 1966, 2nd edn), Oxford University Press, 1960, pp. 15–19.

23 Wheare points out that "flexible" is a relative concept. For example, the Constitutions of France, Austria, and Norway are sometimes regarded as flexible because, compared to the Constitutions of the United States, Denmark, and Australia, they can be amended more easily. However, in France, for example, a constitutional amendment is also subject to a much stricter procedure than that for ordinary legislative amendments (Art. 89 of the French Constitution). Wheare, op. cit., p. 16.

24 Sometimes the distinction between rigid and flexible constitutions is also defined in terms of the difference between entrenched and non-entrenched constitutions. Even though there is a difference in nuance, the essential characteristic of an entrenched constitution is the same as that of the rigid constitution (i.e. that it is more difficult to amend than a regular statute).

25 H. Kelsen, *General Theory of Law and State*, translated by A. Wedberg, 1945, reprint Harvard University Press, 1999, pp. 263–6.

26 In 1973, *Kesavananda Bharti v. State of Kerala* case (AIR 1973 SC 1461) the Indian Supreme Court ruled that certain principles within the framework of the Indian Constitution are inviolable and hence cannot be amended by Parliament, even if the Indian constitutional amendment procedure provided for simple majority amendment

by Parliament. The Supreme Court referred to this framework of inviolable principles as the "Basic Structure" of the Constitution.

27 Article 79 para 3 of the Basic Law of Germany (Constitution). Van der Tang calls this "supra-constitutionality", i.e. parts of the constitution that are not amenable to amendment, even not from changes by the *constituante*; G.F.M. van der Tang, *Grondwetsbegrip en grondwetsidee (Constitutional concept and idea)*, PhD thesis Erasmus University, Gouda Quint, 1998, pp. 344–5.

28 See for instance Art. 441 through Art. 444 of the Constitution of Ecuador, which entails different procedures for different sorts of revisions.

29 J.H. Merryman and R. Pérez-Perdomo, *The Civil Law Tradition*, 3rd edn, Stanford University Press, 2007, pp. 136–7.

30 At Leiden University we are currently analyzing and comparing all the constitutions of the world to see how different constitutions try to protect their "constitutional core", i.e. the essence of the constitutional order as it was, for instance, perceived by the *constituante*, the principal interpreter(s), or (constitutional) courts. We have restricted ourselves to merely looking at the text of the constitution itself, not the political or legal culture which are—evidently—equally important or even more important than the letter of the constitution itself.

31 A.W. Heringa and P. Kiiver, *Constitutions Compared*, Intersentia, 2009, pp. 6–7.

32 D. Oliver and C. Fusaro, *How Constitutions Change; A Comparative Study*, Hart Publishing, 2011, p. 4.

33 D.S. Lutz, "Toward a Theory of Constitutional Amendment", in Levinson (ed.), op. cit., p. 242.

34 Ibid., pp. 268–74.

35 Only very rarely is a proposal for an amendment to the Constitution tabled by a Member of Parliament. And it is even more rare that such a proposal survives the first reading. But very recently one proposal did actually survive. It was the proposal by the former member, Femke Halsema, to lift some parts of the ban on constitutional review of Acts of Parliament. See Private Members Bill 32334 (the number it has in the Dutch Parliamentary Papers). The initiative is now tabled for a second reading, but it is at this moment unlikely that it will gather a two-thirds majority in both Houses.

36 The Ministry of the Interior has a specialized section for constitutional affairs (CZW).

37 There are some 70 religions in the Netherlands, with more than 60 Christian denominations alone and more than 40 Protestant denominations to boot.

38 The House of Representatives in 2011 consists of 10 political groups, of which three support the coalition Cabinet of Prime Minister Rutte. To complicate matters, one party (the *Geert Wilders* Party for Freedom) is not fully committed to the coalition agreement but has only agreed to condone the Cabinet for its duration (on the basis of a separate agreement). Together, the three parties supporting the Cabinet hold a minute majority of 76 in the 150-member House of Representatives. This situation of tiny minorities supporting coalition Cabinets is not really unique in Dutch parliamentary history (although a minority Cabinet with a condoning partner is). It is an obstacle, though.

39 Heringa and Kiiver, op. cit., p. 4.

40 After the adoption by the Chamber, it still needs to be ratified by the Government (Art. 87 Dutch Constitution), but this is a mere formality.

41 E.A. Alkema, "Constitutional Law" (Chapter 16), in J.M.J. Chorus, P.H.M. Gerver, E.H. Hondius and A.K. Koekkoek (eds), *Introduction to Dutch Law*, 3rd edn, Kluwer Law International, 1999, p. 293.

42 *Official Journal* (Stb.), 1995, p. 403.

43 Kortmann and Bovend'Eert, op. cit., p. 30.

44 In 1815, 1840, 1848, 1884, 1887, 1917, 1922, 1938, 1946, 1948, 1953, 1956, 1963, 1972, 1983, 1987, 1995, 1999, 2000, 2002, 2005, 2006, and 2008.

45 238 amendments.
46 169 amendments.
47 Almost all of the 142 provisions.
48 The introduction of the parliamentary system, its attributes, the direct election of the House of Representatives, and the curtailment of the powers of the King as head of the executive.
49 The introduction of male suffrage (to be followed by universal suffrage in 1919 and the introduction of universal suffrage in the Constitution by 1922), the simultaneous introduction of a system of proportional representation to elect the House of Representatives, the States-Provincial, and the municipality councils. The religious parties traded the constitutional introduction of male suffrage—a long-standing demand of the socialists—for constitutional equality in state funding between public and denominational schools, ending the bitter Dutch School Wars, which had up until that moment antagonized Dutch political life for decades.
50 Kortmann and Bovend'Eert argue that only the 1848 and 1917 revisions were of "any real significance"; Kortmann and Bovend'Eert, op. cit., p. 30.
51 Accommodating the independence of Indonesia, introducing a new system of reception of international law (giving priority to some forms of international law over domestic law), enshrining a structure for semi-public collaborations that constitutes the basis of the consensus economy (the Dutch *Poldermodel*), the number of the House of Representatives members was increased to 150, and Senate members to 75.
52 As the result of a continuous modernization project starting in 1966, the Constitution was almost entirely rewritten (effective as of 1983). Many antiquated articles were abolished. Almost all of the provisions were redrafted (with the exceptions of Art. 23—the ever-controversial freedom of education—and other parts of Articles such as Art. 89) using new uniform legal terminology. The structure of the Constitution was also revised. There were also substantive amendments. Notably, the Bill of Rights was expanded with the prohibition of discrimination, the prohibition of the death penalty, the general freedom of expression, the freedom of demonstration, and the general right to privacy and social rights were added to the list too.
53 M.C.B. Burkens, "The Complete Revision of the Dutch Constitution", *Netherlands International Law Review*, 1982, vol. 29, p. 324. In his contribution Burkens discusses the revision of "1982". At the time of writing, in 1982, he could not know that the revision would only take effect as of 1983, so what he actually means is the 1983 revision.
54 Ibid., pp. 324–5.
55 Focused on institutions, and "shallow" according to some. Van der Tang, op. cit, pp. 91–7.
56 J.A. Peters, *Wie beschermt onze grondwet?* (*Who protects our Constitution?*), Inaugural lecture, University of Amsterdam, Vossiuspers UvA 2003, pp. 7–17.
57 Nationale Conventie, *Hart voor de publieke zaak (Commitment to the public cause)*, Dutch Ministery of the Interior—National Convention, 2006.
58 T. Barkhuysen, A.L. Dimitrova, M.L. van Emmerik, J.H. Gerards, H.M. Griffioen, M.M. Groothuis, T. de Jong, J.P. Loof, H.M. ten Napel, B. Steunenberg and W.J.M. Voermans, *De Nederlandse Grondwet geëvalueerd; anker – of verdwijnpunt? (The Dutch Constitution evaluated: anchor or vanishing point?)*, Kluwer, 2009. This report, based on literature and interviews in the public sector, shows that a majority of the respondents believes that the Constitution and its revision procedure perform quite well.
59 Staatscommisse Grondwet (Government Commission on the Constitution), *Rapport Staatscommissie Grondwet (Final Report of the Government Commission on the Constitution)*, Government Publisher, The Hague, 2010, p. 13.
60 Voermans, op. cit., 2009.
61 W.J.M. Voermans, "Voting for Europe: Lessons from Dutch Referendums", *Journal of the Japan-Netherlands Institute*, vol. X, 2010, pp. 220–43.
62 Voermans, op. cit, 2009.

63 Peters, op. cit.

64 A. Lijphart, *Patterns of Democracy; Government Forms and Performance in Thirty-Six Countries*, Yale University Press, 1999, p. 216ff.

65 Ibid., p. 229.

66 Meaning the inclination for prolonged negotiations until a compromise is reached that satisfies all parties. Derived from the word *Polder*.

14 The Portuguese Constitution of 1976

Half-life and decay

Jónatas E.M. Machado

> But as the Constitution of a State, when once it has been discovered to be no longer suitable, should be amended, either all at once, or by degrees as each defect becomes known . . .
>
> Niccolo Machiavelli

Written constitutions of the constitutional-state type tend to consist of a bill of rights and a bill of powers against a background of substantive principles of human dignity, freedom and equality, fundamental rights, democracy, the rule of law, and substantive and procedural justice. They also take into account the need to create protocols that articulate the local political community with larger projects of regional integration and cooperation within the international community as a whole. Speaking metaphorically, we may say that this is the typical "atomic nucleus" of the constitutional state. The Portuguese Republican Constitution (PRC) of 1976 lives up to these core requirements, although it has undergone a process of nuclear decay, generating different constitutional elements. After a short historical perspective, this chapter will address some aspects of these kinds of change and assess their impact on the nature of the PRC.

Portuguese history and constitutional change

Liberal revolution and constitutional monarchy (1820–1910)

Portugal felt the shockwaves of the French Revolution and the Napoleonic invasions. King John VI had to flee the country to Brazil in 1807 to escape the invading French army, and only returned to Portugal in 1821. It was in this turbulent context that the first Portuguese Constitution came about, following the "liberal revolution" of 1820.[1] This was the "Constitution of the United Kingdom of Portugal, Brazil and the Algarve," enacted in 1822.[2] It was based on the principle of the supremacy of Parliament over the King. Its coming into force was torpedoed by the independence of Brazil on 7 September 1822, as well as by the political struggle, violent confrontation and civil war that affected Portugal for several years. This situation was due to the polarization created by two sons of the deceased King John VI, Michael and Peter, who fought in both Brazil and Portugal to create a more authoritarian or liberal future for Portugal.[3]

In the process, the country saw a succession and alternation of constitutional texts, which included the above-mentioned Constitution of 1822, the Constitutional Charter issued by Peter in 1826, which was largely similar to the one he granted Brazil in 1824, and the Constitution of 1838, following the September revolution of 1836, which intended to bring about a compromise between monarchical and democratic forces. The main struggle was over the origin of constituent power as well as the monarchical or parliamentary supremacy within the Constitution. The 1838 Constitution, promulgated by Queen Mary II, left this struggle largely unresolved.[4] The political stalemate would only end with the revolution of 1842, led by the controversial conservative Costa Cabral, reintroducing the Constitutional Charter of 1826, which would remain in force with several amendments[5] until the republican revolution of 5 October 1910.

Liberal and authoritarian republican constitutionalism (1911–1974)

The republican Constitution of 1911 was premised on antimonarchical and anticlerical ideas, and inspired by the Portuguese Constitution of 1822 and the French Constitution of 1848, as well as by the later experience of the Third French Republic. Another source of inspiration was the Brazilian republican Constitution of 1891. The 1911 Constitution included a catalogue of civil and political rights, and affirmed the principles of national sovereignty, democracy, and separation of powers.[6] It also introduced the system of concrete judicial review. It was amended several times in 1916,[7] 1919,[8] and 1920.[9]

The republican regime did not assure political stability. The participation of Portugal in World War I, with the resulting political, economic, and social problems, was a permanent source of political instability, giving rise to the debate between republicanism and monarchism. *Laïcisme* was also a source of virulent cultural battles against the more conservative sectors. After years of political strife, a military coup established an authoritarian regime in 1926.

This event led to the 1933 Constitution, enacted by a referendum, albeit far from perfect.[10] It promoted the unity of the nation and the creation of a corporative State, known as the New State, which paid lip service to liberal principles.[11] Initially, the President was elected by universal suffrage, thus giving the office an important representative element. Little by little, with the restriction of political parties, unions and local autonomy, the apparent liberal dimensions gave way to an authoritarian form of government. The original constitutional text was subjected to several revisions.[12] In 1959, an amendment introduced the indirect election of the President, who assumed a more passive role. This move consolidated an authoritarian regime developed around Oliveira Salazar, the President of the Cabinet. The war in the African colonies, along with the repression in the metropolis, generated dissatisfaction within the army and the population at large, leading to the Carnation Revolution of 25 April 1974.

The Carnation Revolution and the 1976 revolution

The PRC of 1976 was the result of that revolution. The election of a constituent assembly was an important part of the revolutionary program of the Armed Forces Movement. The political parties, some of which had just been created, covered the different shades of the ideological spectrum: Christian Democrats (CDS), Social Democrats (PSD), Socialists (PS) and Communists (PCP). They were able to propose a platform of constitutional agreement that served as a basis for the PRC.[13] The original text was influenced by Marxist ideology and had a strong programmatic nature, although its structure and content reflected a political compromise.[14] This fact shaped the following debates.

The PRC consists of some fundamental principles[15] and four parts. Part I is a catalogue of fundamental rights and duties—including rights, freedoms and guarantees—with a negative character, and economic, social and cultural rights, with a positive nature.[16] Part II deals with economic constitutional elements, laying down the framework of a mixed economy and democratic planning of economic and social development, through the restructuring of property ownership and the pursuit of some agricultural, commercial and industrial policy objectives.[17] Part III devotes itself to the organization of political power, establishing a semi-presidential system, in which the President and the Members of Parliament (MPs) are directly elected by the people. The Government is politically responsible before the Parliament, while the task of the President is to supervise the regular functioning of the political institutions.[18] Part IV deals with the guarantee and revision of the Constitution, including different forms of judicial review and institutional, procedural, substantive and circumstantial limitations to the amendment processes,[19] followed by some final provisions.[20]

Historical development of the PRC

In the course of its existence, the PRC has formally undergone seven constitutional revisions.[21] They responded to both internal and external pressures. The first revision, through CA 1/82,[22] was the longest; it contains 249 Articles that altered a large number of provisions. Its main purpose was to correct the excessive Marxist and revolutionary underpinnings and to introduce a needed constitutional normalization. Although it extensively and profoundly altered the PRC, it was not seen as a new constitution. The second revision, made by Constitutional Act (CA) 1/89,[23] was a bit less extensive, including only 208 Articles, but they too were profound. It moved forward in the ideological neutralization of the PRC and opened new avenues of economic organization in addition to socialism. It went as far as changing some of the entrenchment clauses of the PRC. Both revisions dealt with values and principles that define the identity of the PRC.

The third revision was made through CA 1/92,[24] a small text with only seven Articles. It was an extraordinary revision, enacted less than five years after the previous revision. One of its triggers was the ratification of the Maastricht Treaty, creating the European Union and the need to allow for deeper European integration. It implicitly changed the traditional conception of state sovereignty, entrenched in Art. 288 para (a) of the Constitution, making it compatible with the "pooling" of public prerogatives at European level. The fourth constitutional amendment process culminated in an extensive revision, enacted by the CA 1/97,[25] a long text with 198 Articles. It came about through a secret agreement between the two major political parties (PSD and PS), sidelining the Parliamentary Commission for Constitutional Revision and the other political parties.[26] It adapted to the needs of European citizenship, introduced new mechanisms of popular participation, and altered the terms of the regional autonomy of Madeira and the Azores.

The fifth constitutional amendment came about through CA 1/01,[27] a short text with only seven Articles. It can be seen, in part, as a response to the Nice Treaty of February 2001, the events of 9/11 in the USA, and the creation of the International Criminal Court by the 1998 Rome Treaty. In 2004, the sixth constitutional revision, enacted in CA 1/04,[28] was composed of a medium-range amendment act with 45 Articles. It covered several topics, including the issue of European constitutionalism. The seventh and final revision came about a little later, via CA 1/05, with only three Articles, on the topic of a European referendum.[29] Since it is impossible to go through all the alterations, we will select some of the areas in which the most significant changes took place, affecting the atomic make-up of the PRC, its constitutional tissue and the traits of the political community. Space constraints force us to leave out subjects such as the administrative and regional organization of the Portuguese State and the political autonomy of the Azores and Madeira, although these topics have been subject to intense constitutional change over the years.

Demarxization

The original text of the PRC assumed an explicit commitment to building a socialist society according to the Marxist world-view.[30] Constitutional change brought about the gradual cooling of revolutionary fervor. CA 1/82 mitigated the Marxist doctrine of the collective appropriation and socialization of the means of production and wealth, as well as the programmatic nature of the PRC, while maintaining the goal of the transition to socialism. Instead, much heavier emphasis was placed on less ideologically charged goals, such as economic planning, welfare of the population, quality of life and participation.[31]

The second revision, through CA 1/89, moved forward in this process, in both a normative and semantic way. For instance, it abolished expressions such as "classless society," replacing it with the "building of a society based on freedom, justice and solidarity."[32] It abolished the constitutional goal of the transition to socialism, speaking now of the furthering of economic, social, cultural and participatory democracy,[33] and it freed private economic initiative from the constraints of collective progress.[34] Within this framework, it mitigated some of the promises made by social rights and introduced more flexibility in economic organization. This process of normative and semantic "desocialization" continued with CA 1/97, which introduced even more flexibility in economic organization and, among other things, the replacement of the "collective property of natural resources" by a reference to the "public property of natural resources."[35] The aspiration to the establishment of a socialist society remained, however, in the Preamble of the Constitution.

Demilitarization

The 1976 version of the PRC included a Council of the Revolution (CR), largely composed of representatives of the Armed Forces. Its mission was to protect the PRC and guarantee fidelity to the spirit of the 25 April Revolution.[36] The President of the Republic was the president *ex officio* of the CR. The first constitutional amendment, through CA 1/82,[37] dissolved the CR. The purpose was to return the political and legislative process to civil society, affirming the subordination of the military to democratically elected and accountable political institutions.[38] This move was described as a necessary step in constitutional normalization.[39]

Demilitarization demanded a reworking of the competences of the President of the Republic, which until then were closely linked to those of the CR, and a substantial revision of the statute of the Armed Forces, until then governed by it. Among other functions, the CR played a central role in the judicial review of legislative acts, with the assistance of a Constitutional Commission. Both were replaced by an independent Constitutional Court.[40] Later, through CA 1/97, the fourth revision eliminated the constitutional requirement of universal (male) conscription to military service. This change had more to do with cutting costs and adapting to new realities than with demilitarization *per se*.[41]

Improving the fundamental rights catalogue

CA 1/82 revised and clarified a significant number of fundamental rights provisions and, among other things, created a new chapter in the fundamental rights of workers.[42] CA 1/89 tried to improve and modernize the fundamental rights catalogue, enhancing its protective scope. For instance, in the face of emerging developments in computer technology, it created a right of habeas data.[43] It also created broader rights or public judicial action of the protection of health, environment and cultural goods.[44]

This modernization of the fundamental rights catalogue moved forward with CA 1/97, which, for instance, explicitly mentioned the goal of the promotion of gender equality, included the right to the free development of personality, reinforced the habeas data protection, inserted the right of genetic identity against genetic manipulation, and enhanced the rights of participation and information of workers and the due process rights of citizens before the public administration.[45]

In the aftermath of the terrorist attacks of 9/11, CA 1/01 reduced the protection content of certain fundamental rights such as the inviolability of domicile. At the same time, it broadened the inclusion to the members of the Community of Portuguese Speaking Countries, granting them substantial political rights.[46] The sixth revision, via CA 1/04, altered the PRC equal rights clause in a more contemporary way, inserting the prohibition of discrimination on the basis of sexual orientation.[47] It also inserted the constitutional goal of the conciliation of family and professional life.[48]

Enhancing democracy and adjusting the system of government

The Portuguese system of government is subject to the principles of democracy and the separation of powers. These principles can accommodate different institutional structures and allow for some constitutional adjustments. In the field of democracy, CA 1/82 reinforced the rights of the opposition parties.[49] The second constitutional revision, through CA 1/89, introduced the possibility of referendums. This change was instituted as a form of semi-direct democracy, since the calling of a referendum depends on proposals of Parliament and the Government, and it cannot deal with constitutional revisions or with fiscal, tax or financial questions.[50]

CA 1/97 addressed the problem of "political party governance," demanding more transparency and internal participation.[51] It also introduced the possibility of popular initiative in the referendum, although subject to the acceptance of the Parliament and the final decision of the President. It conditioned the binding character of the referendum on the participation of the majority of the registered voters.[52] Opposition political parties were given broader rights of information about public matters by CA 1/04.[53] The seventh constitutional revision, enacted by CA 1/2005, introduced the possibility of a referendum on the approval of any treaty regarding implementing and deepening European integration.[54]

Over the years, the system of government has demonstrated a remarkable stability, since it has only been subject to some minor changes. In the first revision, CA 1/82 limited the prerogative of the President to dismiss the Government to extreme cases of institutional disruption.[55] This modification reduced the power of the President to interfere in the political system, ascribing to the office a more neutral and balancing function. CA 1/92 reinforced the powers of the Parliament in the supervision of European integration.[56] CA 1/97 opened the door to a more significant change in the political and governmental systems, introducing the possibility of a German-inspired electoral system of personalized proportional representation, although it was never enacted by a legislative act.[57] CA 1/04 introduced super-majority requirements on more issues, forcing the agreement between the major political parties.[58]

Deepening the rule of law

The concept of rule of law (*Rechtstaat*) was introduced in the text of the Constitution by CA 1/82, after being viewed with suspicion by the revolutionary and military forces.[59] Among other things, it clarified the relationship between the different legislative and normative acts,[60] made some reforms in the judiciary,[61] and centralized the system of judicial review around the Constitutional Court.[62] CA 1/97 reinforced the fair trial and due process guarantees in areas such as legal counsel, reasonable time and special speedy proceedings for the protection of human rights in states of emergency. It also restructured the system of legislative acts, in order to better accommodate those requiring super-majorities.[63] Another important development was the guarantee of effective judicial protection, including preliminary injunctions against all forms of administrative conduct, positive and negative, including normative acts with an external effect.[64] Finally, it changed the duration of the term of the Constitutional Court justices, which is now nine years, non-renewable.[65]

Europeanization and internationalization

The PRC has also been pressed to adapt to European and international developments and global challenges. CA 1/82 opened the door for further integration into the international community and for future membership in the European Economic Community by allowing for the direct enforcement of legal rules of international organizations in Portugal.[66] Portugal signed the accession treaty to the European Economic Community in July 1985, which entered into force in January 1986. But it was through the third constitutional revision, in CA 1/92, that a major step was taken in order to adjust the PRC to the demands of the Maastricht Treaty of the European Union. It allowed for the necessary "pooling" of sovereign competences at the European level, within a framework of reciprocity and subsidiarity.[67] Changes were introduced to make it possible for European citizens resident in Portugal to vote in local elections and for the European Parliament. On the other hand, the Portuguese National Bank lost its exclusive prerogative to print money.[68]

The fourth revision, through CA 1/97, dealt with some of the issues currently being discussed in the light of European judicial cooperation and the possible creation of an International Criminal Court, such as international judicial cooperation and extradition, including that of Portuguese citizens.[69] This path was subject to further developments in the fifth constitutional amendment, through CA 1/01. This revision expressly included a reference to the European Space of Freedom, Justice and Security, and facilitated the direct application of the European norms on judicial cooperation. It also made possible the coexistence of the PRC with the supranational legal nature of the International Criminal Court.[70] CA 1/04 further promoted the space of freedom, justice and security, and the common external and defense policy, in light of the possible entrance into force of the projected European Constitutional Treaty, while at the same time assuring respect for fundamental rule-of-law principles.[71] This formal acknowledgment of the developments taking place in international law had a more profound impact than the length of the textual modifications would imply, since it encourages the interpreter of the PRC to regard it from a global perspective.[72]

Assessing formal revision and informal change

Amendment rules

The PRC encompasses formal, institutional and procedural rules regulating its amendment. Alongside these it includes a set of entrenchment clauses that identify some subjects whose norms cannot, in principle, be amended. It also provides for circumstantial limits to the exercise of the amendment power. These provisions open the door to the existence of unconstitutional constitutional norms.

Formal limitations

Article 287 para 2 of the Constitution establishes that amendments to the Constitution shall be combined in a single revision law,[73] called the Constitutional Act (CA). It follows a special sequence, different from that of the ordinary legislative acts. Each CA alters the text of the revised provisions of the Constitution. Article 287 paras 1–2 of the Constitution states that the amendments to the Constitution must be inserted in the proper place by means of replacements, eliminations and additions. A new consolidated version of the Constitution must be published along with the revision act. During the validation of the Constitution of 1933, revisions were made without the subsequent publication of a consolidated version.

Procedural limitations

a) *Initiative.* Article 285 para 1 of the Constitution prescribes that "[t]he competence to initiate revisions pertains to Members of the Assembly of the Republic." Thus, the Portuguese Parliament has the exclusive prerogative of amending the Constitution. Its individual members have a prerogative not extended to any other institution, organ, political party, parliamentary group, etc. This statement means that the President of the Republic cannot summon the Parliament to initiate a constitutional amendment process. In addition, the constitutional amendment process is not activated automatically. However, in many instances the amendment initiative belonged to the political parties, in isolation or through extra-parliamentary agreements, which weakens the Parliament and curtails the prerogatives of its members.[74]

   According to Art. 285 para 2 of the Constitution, "[o]nce a draft revision of the Constitution has been submitted, any others have to be submitted within a time limit of thirty days." This includes the possibility of amendments to the revision proposals as well as their removal. It allows a debate of all amendment proposals and their cross-examination by different social forces. Higher lawmaking will thus be reflected in the sphere of public discourse, where political parties, media outlets, political action groups, constitutional scholars, public intellectuals and regular citizens will engage in open dialogue about constitutional amendments.

b) *Exclusive parliamentary prerogative.* Article 284 para 1 of the Constitution establishes that "[t]he Assembly of the Republic may revise the Constitution five years after the date of publication of the last ordinary revision law." Portugal concentrates the amendment power in its Parliament, the primary representative institution.[75] There is no room for the institutional participation of the Government, nor of the autonomous regions of the Azores and Madeira. This procedure follows a pattern observed in the Portuguese Constitutions of 1822, 1826 and 1838. Constitutional amendment by a referendum is expressly rejected by Art. 115 para 4a of the Constitution. This move is probably a traumatic reaction to the Constitutional Referendum of 1933.

c) *Time period between revisions.* From a democratic perspective, Art. 284 para 1 of the Constitution's requirement of five years between each amendment to the PRC is understandable. A similar requirement had been introduced to the Constitutional Charter of 1826 (four years) in 1885 and was present in the Constitutions of 1911 and 1933.[76] This requirement makes more sense than trying to entrench a given political and economic arrangement. It distinguishes between constitutional politics and normal politics. It encourages reflection and deliberation before the enactment of a constitutional amendment, since the representatives know in advance that the next constitutional amendment will only take place five years after the previous one. From the CA 1/92 on, this five-year requirement applies only to ordinary revisions, not to extraordinary ones.[77] This solution encourages the derived constituent power to think twice before doing away with a fundamental constitutional provision. There is always the possibility of a fast-track procedure in case a constitutional amendment becomes a matter of urgent necessity to a broad consensus of members or Parliament. Article 284 para 2 of the Constitution determines that "by a majority of at least four-fifths of all the Members in full exercise of their office, the Assembly of the Republic may take extraordinary revision powers at any time." The rigidity of the PRC does not intend to freeze popular sovereignty at a point in time, but simply to protect it from passing political fancies.

d) *Super-majority.* Article 286 para 1 of the Constitution provides that "[a]mendments to the Constitution require passage by a majority of two-thirds of the Members of the Assembly of the Republic in full exercise of their office." The requirement of super-majority was absent in the previous 1911 and 1933 Portuguese Constitutions. Originally, in 1976, it required only a majority of two-thirds of the members of Parliament present, as long as it was larger than the absolute majority of the full membership. It was changed in 1982, in order to make it even more demanding.[78]

This requirement has an important effect on the political system, since it is impossible to enact a CA without the agreement of the two largest parties, PSD and PS. *De facto*, they have been sharing the *pouvoir constituant.* Their agreement is also needed to nominate most of the constitutional court justices, not to mention other crucial nominations (e.g. members of the media regulation agency) in which they also play a central role. This process encourages a cartel behavior of strategic cooperation, which allows these two parties to entrench themselves in the political and economic systems. It also renders the role of constitutional law experts practically irrelevant. The few who cooperate with the main parties often find themselves in the constitutionally unpalatable position of "useful idiots."[79] This fact does not totally obliterate the competitive nature of the amendment process. It simply encourages interest groups to try to influence them from within.

Because of the super-majority requirement for each amendment to the PRC—and contrary to what Art. 168 of the Constitution prescribes for ordinary legislative acts—the discussion and vote of each amendment takes place in a plenary session of the Parliament, with a vote for each specific amendment.[80] However, the previous discussion of the amendment proposals by a specialized commission is possible.[81] This procedure attempts a rationalization of the higher lawmaking debate.

Substantive entrenchment clauses

The identity and internal consistency of a constitution depends on the upholding of some core principles. They are its atomic nucleus. Constitutional legitimacy depends on its adherence to positively charged principles resistant to alteration, even by super-majorities. Therefore, it is not necessarily anti-democratic to affirm certain substantive limitations to the derived constituent power. Since they are nuclear elements of the PRC, changes to them may have important political and legal consequences, which can be compared with the radioactive effects of nuclear decay. Of course, this metaphor is just that. Constitutional change is an ideational process, not a physical one, and is powered by intellectual, political, social and economic factors, not by random physical or chemical processes.

Article 288 of the Constitution establishes a catalogue of substantive and institutional values, principles and rules that are entrenched and limit the amendment of the PRC.[82] Their purpose is to make certain amendments more difficult than others, if not impossible.[83] Since these entrenched values, principles and rules are constitutive of the identity of the PRC, their inclusion in Art. 288 of the Constitution is seen by some as merely declaratory, in the sense that each constitutional amendment would have to respect them anyway, or else we would be talking about a new Constitution and not a revised Constitution. Therefore, each revision must not create a new Constitution from scratch, but must respect the identity and integrity of the existing one. It must change the Constitution, without changing constitutions.[84] According to Art. 288 of the Constitution, each constitutional revision must respect central constitutional elements.

The entrenchment clauses cover the subjects of national independence and the unity of the State; the republican form of government; the separation between church and State; citizens' rights, freedoms and guarantees; the rights of workers, workers' committees and trade unions; the coexistence of the public, private and cooperative and social sectors of ownership of the means of production; the existence of economic plans, within the framework of a mixed economy; the appointment of the elected officeholders of the entities that exercise sovereignty, of the organs of the autonomous regions and of local government organs by universal, direct, secret and periodic suffrage; the proportional representation system; plural expression and political organization, including political parties, and the right of democratic opposition; the separation and interdependence of the entities that exercise sovereignty; the subjection of legal norms to review of their positive constitutionality and of their unconstitutionality by omission; the independence of courts; the autonomy of local authorities; and the political and administrative autonomy of the Azores and Madeira archipelagos.

The purpose of the entrenchment clauses of Art. 288 is to protect the substantive and institutional core of the PRC, the nuclear elements that define the Constitution, giving it "density and mass." They cover subjects related to the supremacy of the Constitution, the structure of the republican state, fundamental rights, economic organization, and the system of government. Whoever wants to change the PRC must preserve this nucleus of values, principles and rules in the new revised constitutional text. The possibility of a referendum or a super-majority to amend these entrenchment clauses is not allowed for. Theoretically, only a revolution, a legal *coup d'état*[85] or some type of constitutional moment[86] could do away with the entrenchment clauses and give birth to a new Constitution. However, some of the entrenched principles may even be said to be limitations on the primary constituent power.

It is possible that, apart from the express limitations derived from the entrenchment clause of Art. 288 of the Constitution, other implicit limitations can be deduced. For instance, the protection of territorial integrity can be derived from the unity of the state, and the principle of irresponsibility of judges can result from the principle of judicial independence and impartiality.[87] The fact that some values, principles and rules are constitutionally entrenched through Art. 288 of the Constitution does not proscribe some slight modifications to their specific concretization in the constitutional text, in order to adapt their content to new political, economic, social or environmental realities or security concerns—both local and global—as long as their core meaning is protected. Most of the entrenchment clauses purport to protect fundamental principles in an abstract way, regardless of their isotopic concretization in the PRC. The extent to which this is the case is a matter of interpretation of each specific entrenchment clause.

For instance, modifications of the fundamental rights provisions, entrenched in Art. 288 of the Constitution, must be allowed in principle. This fact is clear when these modifications broaden the range of application of fundamental rights and their protective power. However, the modifications may even include further restrictions of fundamental rights based on security concerns, as long as they do not eliminate the rights in themselves or substantially reduce their protection content. A fair and proper balancing of rights and interests against a background of new problems and concerns may result in further restriction of some rights to assure a satisfactory level of protection to other rights. The same reasoning applies *mutatis mutandis* to other principles. It should be possible to amend the structure of the system of government, or of the institutional structure and functioning of the judiciary, if the core of the principles of the separation of powers, judicial independence and judicial review remains intact.[88] In the same way, the fact that national independence is a constitutionally entrenched principle was never seen as a hindrance to deeper levels of economic, social and political integration in the European Union.[89]

Circumstantial limitations

Article 289 of the Constitution determines that "no act involving the revision of the Constitution may be undertaken during a state of siege or a state of emergency."

This provision is perfectly reasonable in the light of the "type" of the constitutional state and the republican character of the PRC. Its purpose is to preserve the integrity of the public and institutional spheres of democratic deliberation that should be in place in the realms of constitutional politics and higher lawmaking. It wants to guard the republican Constitution against self-proclaimed guardians who, in a decisionist mode, might want to take advantage of exceptional situations created by internal and external threats, to force the introduction of amendments not allowed by the PRC. The text and purpose of this provision seem to point to the total suspension of the constitutional amendment process, thus prohibiting any CA enactment-related activity in times of siege and emergency.[90]

Presidential veto and judicial review of Constitutional Acts

The PRC establishes a complex and prudent set of procedural rules, substantive entrenchment clauses and circumstantial limitations regulating the exercise of the constitutional amendment power. In other words, CAs that violate these amendment provisions are to be considered unconstitutional. They are real examples of "unconstitutional constitutional law." Oddly enough, the PRC does not expressly mention the possibility of a presidential veto of CAs, as it does in the case of ordinary legislative acts (Art. 136 of the Constitution). This oversight may still be understandable, considering the fact that the amendment power is an exclusive prerogative of the Portuguese Parliament. This being the case, it would not make sense to allow the President to veto a CA for political motives. The super-majority needed to enact a CA is additionally larger than that required for overriding a presidential veto (Art. 136 paras 2–3 of the Constitution).

However, Art. 286 para 3 of the Constitution expressly denies the President of the Republic the power to refuse to enact a CA. In other words, a presidential veto seems to be ruled out, regardless of political or constitutional grounds. Nor does the PRC expressly allow a presidential request for the preventive control of CAs by the Portuguese Constitutional Court (Art. 278 of the Constitution). In addition, it explicitly links the exercise of the presidential constitutional veto—ruled out by Art. 286 para 3 of the Constitution—to the initiation of proceedings of preventive judicial review of legislation, making it even more difficult to sustain the possibility of preventive judicial review of CAs on the basis of a presidential request thereof (Art. 279 para 1 of the Constitution).

If the textual and literal element of the Constitution was the only interpretative guide to be taken into account, one would have to conclude that both the President of the Republic and the Constitutional Court would be powerless bystanders in the face of a patently unconstitutional CA. The President would have to ratify the given CA without being able to call for an *ex ante* judicial review by the Constitutional Court and subsequently to exercise its constitutional veto power.[91] This would be a preposterous conclusion since the formal, procedural, institutional, substantive and circumstantial limits to the amendment power were put in place to protect the nucleus of the PRC and avoid the dangers of a constitutional meltdown. If the compliance with these limitations is not properly enforced by those most responsible for guarding the Constitution, then these limits to the amendment power would be downgraded to the dubious status of "soft law," if not "junk constitutional law." This absurd result calls for the invocation of teleological, rational and systematic elements of constitutional interpretation.

Some solutions have been proposed in order to mitigate this absurd result. According to one, CAs that violate the institutional and procedural amendment rules should be seen as not fulfilling the minimum qualifying requirements, and should therefore not be promulgated by the President.[92] According to another view, those same CAs should be treated as ordinary legislative acts and submitted to presidential political veto, judicial review and constitutional veto.[93] This interpretation would mean that a CA, which had been enacted by an incompetent organ or invalid procedure (e.g. Government, referendum) or by a competent organ without amendment powers (e.g. Parliament in violation of quorum, temporal and procedural limits), should be treated as inexistent—the most serious form of legal invalidity—although it would still need to be declared null and void by the Constitutional Court.[94] These two proposals are not that different from each other in practical terms.[95] However, it seems to be incoherent and systemically dysfunctional to allow for the veto and judicial review of CAs that violate procedural amendment rules and let those who violate substantive entrenchment clauses go unchallenged. A third possibility would be to proscribe an *ex ante* judicial review of CAs, in a strict reading of Art. 286 para 3 and Art. 279 para 1 of the Constitution, only to allow their successive or *ex post facto* judicial review by the Constitutional Court at the request of the President and other entities, in the case of abstract judicial review, or even by private entities and individuals in the case of concrete judicial review. This last possibility is also not clearly mentioned by the PRC, although one should recognize a right not to be subject to (un)constitutional provisions that have violated the procedural and substantive amendment rules. The problem with this view is that it would force everyone to wait until a patently unconstitutional CA is enacted and then react after the fact. From a rule-of-law perspective, this seems to be too little. It would make more sense to try to avoid that damaging result. A preventive law approach would be more reasonable, sparing the legal system the burden of putting up with patently "unconstitutional constitutional law" for a significant amount of time. This problem is further aggravated by the fact that both concrete and abstract forms of successive or *ex post facto* judicial review take much longer—sometimes several years—than *ex ante* judicial review, which at most takes 25 days (Art. 278 para 8 of the Constitution). *Ex post facto* review would also be too late.

Factors such as the supremacy of the Constitution as highest and hardest law, the need to assure its procedural and substantive legitimacy, the preservation of its substantive nucleus, the goal to avoid contradictory constitutional law, the need to guarantee the *effet utile* of the constitutional amendment rules, the presidential oath to uphold and enforce the Constitution, and the judicial review function of the Constitutional Court, all point to the acknowledgment of an implied constitutional power of the President to request the preventive judicial review of a CA by the Constitutional Court and to veto it on the ground of its unconstitutionality. Some scholars are open to this solution, at least when there are serious substantive doubts regarding the constitutionality of the CA.[96] This approach would require an interpretation of Art. 286 para 3 of the Constitution, which excludes the presidential refusal to promulgate CAs only when such refusals are based on strictly political reasons and not on minimum formal requirements or substantive constitutional questions. A preventive law approach seems to be entirely adequate in this area.

The nature of the amendment rules

The existence of constitutional limitations to the amendment of the PRC implies a distinction between the creation *ex novo* of a Constitution and the amendment or revision of an existing Constitution. That is, it presupposes the distinction between original constituent power and derived constituent power, and assumes that the amendment of the PRC is a secondary constitutional task that must comply with constitutional procedural and substantive limitations.

One question arises as to what extent that compliance should be absolute. In other words, it has been discussed whether it is possible to change or eliminate the amendment rules, both procedural and substantive, and then change the Constitution according to a new set of amendment rules or the lack thereof. Some hold that the constitutional amendment procedural and substantive rules cannot be changed or eliminated by the derived constituent power, since it makes no sense to establish rules that can be changed by those bound by them. According to this view, the derived and subordinated nature of the constitutional amendment power prevents it from changing the rules that bind the amendment process.[97] Others hold that constitutional amendment rules are constitutional norms like all the others. At best, they are self-imposed limitations to the constituent power that can be removed by it. It should therefore be possible to alter them in a first constitutional revision and then change the Constitution according to the new amendment rules in a second constitutional revision. This double-revision theory relies on the assumption that even the derived constituent power is still a sovereign power, with the responsibility of adapting the Constitution to a changing reality.[98]

In the second PRC revision by the CA 1/1989, not only did an amendment of the amendment rules take place, but it took place simultaneously with an amendment of the Constitution, all in the same amendment process, thus sidelining the double-revision theory. The context of this apparent constitutional infringement was that of the epic events of "Perestroika," "Glasnost," the fall of the Soviet Union and the collapse of Communism, which resulted in a constitutional moment that rendered many provisions of the PRC, including entrenchment clauses, totally irrelevant.[99] Some Portuguese constitutional scholars had already opposed the constitutional entrenchment of a specific economic organization that should be a legitimate part of a left-wing political party program but not of a constitutional text. In the aftermath of those epic events, it would not make sense to keep in the PRC those provisions that obviously had been declared dead and useless by the historical process. This means that, on some exceptional occasions, reality may speak louder than the theory and practice of constitutional law.

In spite of these developments, some think it may still make sense to distinguish between constitutional amendment rules that can be amended and those that cannot. However, this distinction is not without its shortcomings, since it has to appeal to fuzzy and contested concepts such as the "essence," "identity" or "internal logic" of the Constitution. We immediately see how vague and imprecise these concepts are, as they lead to controversial readings.

Amendment to procedural revision rules

According to Portuguese constitutional theory and practice, there can be amendments to the institutional and procedural amendment rules, as long as the fundamental principles of the PRC are respected. CA 1/92 enacted several amendments of this type without raising any serious objections from Portuguese constitutional scholars.[100]

Amendment to entrenchment clauses

Entrenchment clauses are the source of a strong nuclear force that maintains the integrity of the constitutional identity. Appealing to the above-mentioned criteria, some have held that substantive entrenchment clauses can be amended, as long as the nature, logic and identity of the PRC remain untouched. In some cases, the amendment of some substantive entrenchment clauses might even be necessary to remove contradictions between them. In Portugal, there were some inconsistencies between Marxist and socialist values on the one hand, and liberal pluralist ones on the other hand. This understanding would allow for some marginal modifications to the procedural amendment rules and to the entrenchment clauses, as long as the core constitutional principles they are deemed to protect are preserved. This view assumes that the entrenchment clauses are meant to preserve some fundamental principles in an abstract way, independently of their isotopic concretization in the PRC.[101] The problem is that the definition of concepts such as "marginal modification" or "core constitutional principle" is far from self-evident. There is room for significant disagreement. Furthermore, it may be that some entrenchment clauses intend to protect not only abstract fundamental principles, but also their exact concretization in the PRC.[102] To avoid becoming stuck in endless discussions on constitutional essentialism and metaphysics, it is probably safer to appeal to the "type" of the constitutional state in order to arbitrate between legitimate and illegitimate amendments to the entrenchment clauses. This "type" offers the possibility of a dynamic interpretation of the amendment clauses.

Limits to the amendment of entrenchment clauses

According to the above-mentioned criteria, calibrated by the "type" of the constitutional state, it may be said that some procedural and substantive constitutional amendment rules cannot be amended, at least not without limitations. This is because some constitutional amendment procedural rules are deemed to express the nature, essence, identity and internal logic of the Constitution. They simply declare the existence of inherent limitations to the amendment power that are constitutionally immanent. Therefore, such an amendment could lead to an inconsistent and self-contradictory Constitution, or to a Constitution that broke its connection with the "type" of the constitutional state. For instance, the amendment of a rule requiring a super-majority in Parliament to approve a CA so as to allow for constitutional revisions by simple majority would hardly be consistent with the higher law status of the Constitution, distinct from (and superior to) ordinary parliamentary or executive laws.

Creation of new revision rules and entrenchment clauses

In principle, the enactment of entrenchment clauses is a prerogative of the original constituent power (primary entrenchment clauses). The creation of new amendment rules and entrenchment clauses (secondary entrenchment clauses) by the amending power—i.e. derived constituent power—should be something exceptional. This question must also be discussed in light of the "type" of constitutional state. It may be possible to introduce secondary entrenchment clauses if these are seen as an adequate and necessary way to protect some fundamental constitutional principles that should remain sheltered from the erratic course of normal politics. In other words, the express insertion of secondary entrenchment clauses is constitutionally admissible if their only function is to declare the previous existence of implicit primary entrenchment clauses.[103] This means, for instance, that any change in the amendment rules that enlarges the nucleus of the Constitution with the purpose or effect of protecting the political or economic interests of a particular social group, political party or constellation of parties, should be considered unconstitutional. A conjunctural political majority should not be able to change the Constitution amendment rules, and then the Constitution, in order to perpetuate itself in power.

Relative distinction between original and derived constituent power

The above discussion allows one to draw conclusions regarding the relativity of the distinction between original and derived constituent power. In Portugal, not only has the amendment power changed the amendment power's substantive limits, it has also introduced new amendment limitations. At the end of the day, we cannot say that the different revisions were entirely faithful to the original principles of the 1976 PRC.

Current constitutional amendment debates

Since its inception in April 1976, the PRC has changed significantly, deactivating much of the revolutionary energy, building civil democratic institutions, and updating and upgrading the text in areas such as fundamental rights, democracy and the rule of law. The response to European and international changes and events has also been a very relevant factor in change. The question of the growing political autonomy of the Azores and Madeira islands, important as it is, was left out due to space constraints. However, this is not the whole picture when it comes to constitutional change. Constitutions do not live in isolation. They depend to a great extent on their environment. Changes in internal and external environments can significantly influence the atomic make-up of a constitution.

Deeper changes underneath

Underneath the formal and rules-compliant constitutional amendment processes, a deeper constitutional change seems to be going on. It will only cursorily be mentioned here. One aspect of it has to do with European integration. This process has slowly reshaped different areas of constitutional tissue and affected the nature of the organs themselves, as well as the traits of the political community. The Government is now institutionally integrated into the European Council, through the Prime Minister, and, at a ministerial level, in the EU Council and the Euro Group. The Bank of Portugal is now a part of the European System of Central Banks and of the Eurosystem.[104] In other words, the really important political, economic, and financial decisions and policies are made and defined by the European Union, it being the task of the Portuguese authorities to implement them.

The Portuguese Parliament is now part of a network of national Parliaments, in connection with the European Parliament, all united by a strong European magnetic field.[105] As such, the Portuguese Parliament is largely devoted to the secondary activity of transposition and execution of European directives, regulations and decisions, both legislative and non-legislative. National courts, whose constitutional function is to administer justice in the name of the people, have for a long time been co-opted by the European law as European courts. In a broad sense, they interpret national law in conformity with European law and enforce the Treaties and the legislative/non-legislative acts against contrary national law.[106] In doing so, national courts must comply with a system of cooperation with the Court of Justice of the European Union.[107] National competition authorities have been called to integrate the European Competition Network, centered on the Commission.[108] Consequently, the PRC regulates only some of the functions that the legislative, the executive and judiciary currently perform. On the other hand, the rules of the internal market, with its freed circulation of people, goods, services and capital, and its rules on competition and state aid, result in significant restrictions on state regulation, economic intervention and taxation, thereby restricting the ability to promote growth, protect the tax base, and reduce budget and current-account deficits. They have, little by little, deactivated the economic constitution of the PRC without ever formally revoking it. This situation was totally unintended by the 1976 PRC framers. The current sovereign debt crisis may be an opportunity to rethink the content and impact of the European Economic Constitution.[109]

Also unexpected are developments in the realm of human rights law, particularly at the European level. These developments are the subtle result of the subscription of the European Convention on Human Rights (ECHR) and of the Treaties of the European Union (EU). The application of the Charter of Fundamental Rights of the European Union brought into force by the Lisbon Treaty, along with the accession of the EU to the ECHR, will be very significant.[110] International human rights law and EU fundamental rights law tend to expand their range of application, extending their relevance and binding force to many areas traditionally covered by national Constitutions. The traditional hierarchies of norms have been disrupted and the Constitutional Court has lost its central role in favor of the ECHR and the Court of Justice of the European Union. This fact makes way for another source of informal constitutional change—judicial interpretation—through which important changes can be made to the way constitutional concepts are interpreted. This field is experiencing significant change with the rise of global constitutionalism and the proliferation of international organizations and international courts. The dynamics of treaty and customary law creation, along with the globalization of adjudication and the growing transjudicial dialogue, introduce new sources of normative variability from which international and national courts can select.

Judicial decisions can read unchanging constitutional concepts in the light of changing world views, presupposition, ideologies, and political and legal conceptions. Constitutional courts do it all the time.[111] For instance, in its recent decision on same-sex marriage,[112] the Portuguese Constitutional Court, when interpreting the concepts of family and marriage (Art. 36 of the Constitution), substituted the traditional natural law and Judeo-Christian conception of marriage, widely shared by many religious and secular world views, for a specific secular humanist conception based on different and hotly disputed assumptions about life, humanity, gender and privacy. In the long run, this interpretation can prove to be a profound constitutional change, raising all kinds of delicate constitutional questions about freedom of conscience, expression and religion, equality and privacy.[113]

These informal changes in the reading of the Constitution increasingly result more from the judicial decisions of the ECHR and the Court of Justice of the European Union. Some of the transformations thus operating are so fundamental that some refer to them as a *juridical coup d'état*.[114] They assume the existence of a new *Grundnorm*.

Debate on an eighth constitutional revision

For several months a debate has been going on about another forthcoming constitutional amendment. A proposal for an eighth constitutional revision, referring to a Constitution for the XXI Century, was introduced on 16 September 2010 by PSD, then the Opposition. Presenting itself as a response to the current economic crisis, the revision had the purpose of freeing the Constitution from its programmatic and ideological content. One topic of discussion was the removal of the word "socialism" from the Preamble of the Constitution, on the grounds that it might scare away foreign investors! It proposed to reform the social state and face the problem of public debt. An *ad hoc* Commission for Constitutional Revision was established to work on this matter and subsequent counter-proposals.[115] This initiative did not go forward since the largest parties, Social Democrats (PSD) and Socialists (PS), agreed to postpone it until 2013.[116] If it does go ahead at all, it will probably be conflated with a post-bailout constitutional debate.

Sovereign debt crisis and outsourcing of constituent power

The constitutional relevance of subjects such as financial justice and financial control has been neglected in Portugal and possibly in many other countries. It took a global sovereign debt crisis for many scholars to realize how dependent democratic self-government and internal and external sovereignty are on fiscal responsibility, government accountability and effective control of public expenses.

Against the background of a dire national and financial crisis, Portugal—as had happened with Greece and Ireland earlier—was forced to seek external financial help from the International Monetary Fund (IMF) and the European Union.[117] After some weeks of negotiations, on 3 May 2011 an agreement on a specific economic conditionality package in exchange for a 78 billion euro bailout was reached between the Portuguese Government and a "Troika," consisting of representatives from the IMF, the European Central Bank (ECB) and the Commission.[118]

The extent to which this agreement imposes a new constitutional revision has been disputed. Some say that the facilitation of the dismissal of workers is but one example in which a constitutional revision is due, whereas others hold that a revision is really not necessary since the Constitution can easily be subject *to death by a thousand qualifications*. One thing is certain: even without formal revision, the constitutional meaning of concepts and principles such as contract, tax, entitlement, settled expectations, ability to pay, redistributive justice, progressive taxation, government regularity, legal certainty, etc., have changed significantly in the face of urgent public-servant salary reductions and intensive, blind and retroactive taxation.[119]

More significant is the current debate, proposed by Nicolas Sarkozy and Angela Merkel, on the introduction of a constitutional debt limit, sidelining the electorate and constitutional scholars and experts.[120] The Portuguese President held that such a clause is a sign of distrust in the ability of politicians to cut the debt,[121] whereas others hold that it is necessary, since one cannot trust the politicians and must provide investors and lenders with extra-constitutional assurances. The debate about constitutional amendment is now an interactive issue involving at least the 17 member states of the Eurozone. The debt crisis has shaken constitutional structures and led to the outsourcing of derived constituent power.[122]

Critical assessment of constitutional change in Portugal

Constitutions are future-bound and purpose-driven social contracts. They enshrine the fundamental principles and rules that are to structure the political, economic and social life of a society. They establish a bill of rights and a bill of powers within a larger framework of collectively shared values and goals. As "social," they have to be adaptive in order to respond to the permanent challenges of society, some of which may be created by the Constitution itself, and to respond to the wishes and interests of future generations. As "contracts," they have to be rigid enough to guarantee their ability to constrain the political and legal processes. The idea that Constitutions are not unalterable stems from the infancy of modern constitutionalism.[123]

Pace, form, and causes of change

Constitutional change can be described as "development," "adaptation," or even "decline."[124] It results from a gradual accumulation of small informal changes, or from abrupt "constitutional moments" against a background of "punctuated equilibrium."[125] Portugal experienced a succession of sudden constitutional changes during the struggle between the monarchic and the democratic principles, the overthrow of monarchy (1910), the establishment of the New State (1926), and the Carnation Revolution, which led to the PRC of 1976. After that, constitutional change has been generally gradual, punctuated by yet another "constitutional moment" in 1989, mostly because of the collapse of Communism. During its life, the PRC has adapted to political, cultural, economic and social changes in its environment. Changes can be both formal and informal, resulting from the established amendment process as well as from judicial interpretation and application, at a national, European and international level. Portuguese constitutional change can only be understood as part of regional and international political and normative developments. They not only change the *content* of the Constitution, but also its *nature*. The PRC became a partial Constitution, a piece of a larger system of multi-layered constitutionalism.

Constitutional nuclear decay

There is significant room for the use of metaphors when dealing with topics such as constitutional offspring, entrenchment, cross-fertilization, transjudicialism, etc.[126] We will use the analogy of nuclear decay, bearing in mind that this is a physical process, whereas constitutional change—even when core principles are involved—is an intellectual, political and social phenomenon.[127] Both the possibility of constitutional change and its limits are ways to guard against a constitutional decay in a negative sense.[128] However, the expression "constitutional decay" does not necessarily have a negative meaning, since it refers to a change in the nature of a Constitution.

Chemical elements (e.g. hydrogen, carbon, uranium) come in a variety of forms, called isotopes (e.g. carbon may be ^{12}C, ^{13}C or ^{14}C). Most of them are stable, but some are unstable and decay. Some are less unstable (with longer "half-lives") and have a greater resistance to time and change. Others are more unstable and decay faster, as is the case with ^{14}C. They may decay to another isotopic form (e.g. uranium-238 to uranium-206) or to a different element altogether (e.g. carbon-14 to nitrogen-14), releasing heat and radiation in the process. In the process of decay, the initial isotope is called *parent* and the end product is called *daughter*.

Some constitutional principles may also exist in a variety of isotopes. This means, for instance, that there may be different substantive, procedural and institutional understandings of human dignity, liberty, equality, justice, due process, democracy, separation of powers, rule of law, judicial independence, entrenchment clauses, etc. Some of them are relatively stable, but others tend to decay into a different form. External pressures and the chemical environment may change the rates of decay of nuclear elements, up to a certain extent.[129] Something similar can be observed in the realm of constitutional change. Principles such as national sovereignty and democracy can acquire a radically new meaning in the context of the economic, political, legal and institutional developments in fields such as European integration, European human rights law or international criminal justice. In addition, they can rapidly decay when faced with pressures such as sovereign debt and external political dependence.

Using the atomic analogy, we can speak of a slow and sometimes hardly perceptible decay of some constitutional principles, including political and economic sovereignty, according to their varying half-lives. During the recent decades, the principles, rights and institutions of the PRC have slowly acquired a different isotopic form. The Treaty of Lisbon and the current debt crisis only accelerated the rates of constitutional decay. We could probably say that the PRC became a different element altogether, changing not only its *content*, but also its *nature*. The *parent* PRC started out as a sovereignty-based national Constitution, promoting the revolutionary ideals of the Portuguese people, whereas the *daughter* PRC is but a small part of a larger pool of constituent powers. This means that the PRC is now a partial, secondary and unstable Constitution, with a short half-life. Although constitutional decay is a non-physical phenomenon, with political and moral dimensions, it can be a subtle and continuous process or it can accelerate. The *parent* element of state constitutionalism seems to be giving way to a *daughter* element of European constitutionalism. The normative value and power of the PRC have substantially weakened.

Constitutional decay may release some political energy and radiation. Sometimes the heat is felt in the streets, with general strikes, angry demonstrations and even violent confrontation, as with the sovereign debt crisis. The degree of radiation and heat is variable, though. For instance, in Portugal, at least heretofore, low levels have been felt when the Portuguese state had to let go of its *golden shares* in several strategic corporations of the telecommunications and energy sectors because of the decisions of the Court of Justice of the European Union.[130]

Constitutional decay can have both negative and positive consequences. On the negative side, it may happen that the combined effect of constitutional revisions, legislative acts or judicial interpretative decisions—in domains such as campaign finance, political party governance, electoral systems and proportional representation, incompatibilities of MPs, administrative autonomy, financial control, media regulation and concentration, defamation of public figures, etc.—has a cumulative and degenerative impact on the quality of democracy. This was the Republican view of constitutional decay. It may also happen that the decay of national constitutionalism is not compensated by the establishment of strong institutions at European level, creating a situation in which the sovereignty of small states such as Portugal is lost, only to be retained by stronger member states and powerful economic interests. Its positive result should be the rise of a new European constitutionalism, with its form of democratic government and citizenship. The current decay chain signals the transformation of state-based constitutionalism into a regional and global multilevel constitutionalism. This seems to be the expected result, albeit intrinsically unstable. It will take a huge effort and quantity of political will to get there. This is where the analogy with nuclear decay ends. This new constitutional element can only be developed in a conscious, collective and forward-looking way.

Conclusion

After examining the rules of constitutional amendment of the PRC of 1976, and the constitutional revisions that have taken place since its inception, we noticed that a more subtle and profound structural change was occurring underneath. This slow and structural change led to the erosion of state-based constitutionalism and the transformation of national sovereignty. Constituent power has been, to a large extent, transferred to different regional and global levels. Constitutional debate and higher lawmaking are now a European and global issue. This situation forces us to look at the PRC in a completely different light, through European and global "lenses." In a sense, it is now a partial and unstable Constitution, with a relatively short half-life. Its main chapters have been inserted in a broader constitutional framework and, to some extent, outsourced. This process has changed not only the content of the PRC, but also its nature. However, there is a new kind of European and global constitutionalism, with its own political and legal challenges and dangers. Contrary to the process of nuclear decay, constitutional change can be a designed adaptation to new realities.

Notes

1 P. Bonavides, *História do Estado,* São Paulo, 2003, 5th edn, p. 66ff.
2 J.B. Gouveia, *Manual de Direito Constitucional,* Almedina, 2005, vol. I., p. 404ff.
3 D. Birmingham, *A Concise History of Portugal,* Cambridge, 2003, 2nd edn, p. 99ff.
4 Gouveia, op. cit., pp. 421ff., 436ff.
5 Constitutional Charter of 1826, amended by the Additional Acts (Actos Adicionais) of 1852, 1885, 1892, 1895–96 and 1907.
6 Gouveia, op. cit., p. 445ff.
7 Act (Lei) 635, 28–9–1916.
8 Act 854, 20–8–1919 and Act 891, 22–9–1919; G.J.J. Canotilho, *Direito Constitucional e Teoria da Constituição,* Coimbra: Coimbra Editora, 2007, 7th edn, p. 177ff.; Gouveia, op. cit., p. 461.
9 Act 1005, 7–8–1920; Gouveia, op. cit., p. 461.
10 Gouveia, op. cit., p. 466ff.
11 Ibid., p. 464ff.
12 A first set of amendments was introduced between 1935 and 1938, through different Acts (Leis) 1885, 2 March 1935; 1900, 21 May 1935; 1910, 23 May 1935; 1945, 21 December 1936; 1963, 18 December 1937; and 1966, 23 April 1938. In 1945 there

was a second revision through Act (Lei) 2009, 17 September 1945. A third revision was enacted by Act (Lei) 2048, 11 June 1951. A fourth revision was made by Lei 2100, 29 August 1959. The last revision was made by Lei 3/71, 16 August 1971. Gouveia, op. cit., p. 479ff.

13 Gouveia, op. cit., p. 488ff.
14 Ibid., p. 482 ff.; G.J.J. Canotilho and V. Moreira, *Constituição da República Portuguesa Anotada*, vol. 1., Coimbra: Coimbra Editora, 2007, p. 17ff.
15 Arts. 1 to 11 of the Constitution.
16 Arts. 12 to 79 of the Constitution.
17 Arts. 80 to 100 of the Constitution.
18 Arts. 101 to 276 of the Constitution.
19 Arts. 277 to 289 of the Constitution.
20 Arts. 290 to 296 of the Constitution.
21 Canotilho and Moreira, op. cit., p. 25ff.
22 Lei Constitucional (CA) 1/82, 30–12.
23 Lei Constitucional (CA) 1/89, 8–7.
24 Lei Constitucional (CA) 1/92, 25–11.
25 Lei Constitucional (CA) 1/97, 20–7.
26 Canotilho and Moreira, op. cit., p. 27ff.
27 Lei Constitucional (CA) 1/01, 12–12.
28 Lei Constitucional (CA) 1/04, 24–7.
29 Lei Constitucional (CA) 1/05, 12–8.
30 G.J.J. Canotilho, *"Brancosos" e Interconstitucionalidade*, Coimbra: Almedina, 2006, p. 155ff.
31 Art. 93 CA 1/82.
32 Art. 2 CA 1/89.
33 Art. 3 CA 1/89.
34 Art. 34 CA 1/89.
35 Art. 50 CA 1/97.
36 Art. 142ff. of the Constitution (1976).
37 Arts. 8 and 9 CA 1/82.
38 Art. 209 CA 1/82.
39 Canotilho and Moreira, op. cit., p. 25ff.
40 Arts. 160 and 161 CA 1/82; Canotilho and Moreira, op. cit., 2010, vol. 2, p. 28ff.
41 K.S. Ventura, "Os Direitos Fundamentais à Luz da Quarta Revisão Constitucional Portuguesa", *Boletim da Faculdade de Direito*, Coimbra, 1998, Vol. LXXIV, pp. 493–527.
42 Art. 19 CA 1/82.
43 Art. 20 CA 1/89.
44 Art. 27 CA 1/89.
45 Arts. 6, 28ff. and 182 CA 1/97.
46 Arts. 4 and 6 CA 1/01.
47 Art. 4 CA 1/04.
48 Art. 11 CA 1/04.
49 Art. 95 CA 1/82.
50 Art. 94 CA 1/89.
51 Art. 27 CA 1/97.
52 Art. 77 CA 1/97; M.B. Urbano, "O Impacto da Quarta Revisão Constitucional na Parte III do Texto da Constituição: A Organização do Poder Político", *Boletim da Faculdade de Direito*, op. cit., p. 431ff.
53 Art. 14 CA 1/04.
54 Art. 2 CA 1/2005.
55 Art. 151 CA 1/82.
56 Arts. 5 and 6 CA 1/92.
57 Art. 93 CA 1/97; Urbano, op. cit., p. 449ff.
58 Art. 24 CA 1/04.

59 Art. 2 CA 1/82.
60 Art. 93 CA 1/82.
61 Art. 161ff. CA 1/82
62 Art. 211ff. CA 1/82.
63 Arts. 8 and 74 CA 1/97.
64 Art. 183 CA 1/97.
65 Art. 145 CA 1/97.
66 Art. 7 CA 1/82.
67 Art. 2 CA 1/92.
68 Art. 4 CA 1/92.
69 Art. 16 CA 1/97.
70 Arts. 2 and 5 CA 1/01.
71 Arts. 2 and 3 CA 1/04.
72 R.D. Glensy, "Constitutional Interpretation Through a Global Lens", *Missouri Law Review*, 2010, vol. 75, p. 1171ff.
73 Gouveia, op. cit., p. 646ff.
74 J. Miranda, *Manual de Direito Constitucional*, Coimbra, 2003, Vol. II, 5th edn, p. 193ff.
75 Ibid., p. 171.
76 Ibid., p. 181ff.
77 Ibid., p. 182.
78 Ibid.
79 "Bacelar Gouveia critica processo de revisão constitucional", Agência Lusa, 2.9.2010. Online. Available HTTP: <*http://www1.ionline.pt/conteudo/76558-bacelar-gouveia-critica-processo-revisao-constitucional*> (accessed 21 November 2011).
80 Miranda, op. cit., p. 189.
81 Gouveia, op. cit., p. 647.
82 Miranda, op. cit., p. 199ff.
83 Gouveia, op. cit., p. 641ff.
84 Canotilho and Moreira, op. cit., p. 1011ff.
85 L. Corrias, "The Legal Theory of the Juridical Coup: Constituent Power Now", *German Law Journal*, 2011, vol. 12, p. 1553ff.
86 B. Ackerman, *We the People: Foundations,* Harvard University Press, 1991, vol. I and *We the People: Transformations*, Harvard University Press, 1998, vol. II, p. 3ff. and p. 312ff.
87 Canotilho and Moreira, op. cit., p. 1012.
88 Ibid., p. 1014ff.
89 Ibid., p. 1016.
90 Ibid., p. 1020; Gouveia, op. cit., p. 653.
91 Miranda, op. cit., p. 191ff.
92 Ibid., p. 194ff.
93 Canotilho and Moreira, op. cit., p. 1002ff.
94 Ibid., p. 1004ff.
95 Miranda, op. cit., p. 195.
96 Ibid., p. 197.
97 Canotilho and Moreira, op. cit., p. 1012ff.
98 Gouveia, op. cit., p. 643ff.; Miranda, op. cit., p. 221ff.
99 The CA 1/1989 changed the number of Art. 288 (which previously was 290), modified the wording of al. f) and g) and eliminated former al. j). In the original 1976 version of the PRC, al. f) entrenched, as a substantive limitation to the amendment power, the principle of the collective appropriation of the means of production, of the soil, of natural resources, along with the prohibition of monopolies and large rural estates, whereas al. g) entrenched the principle of democratic central planning for the economy. Former al. j) spoke of the participation of grass-roots popular committees in the local government. In the current version of the PRC, al. f) of Art. 288 of the

Constitution speaks of "the coexistence of the public, private and cooperative and social sectors of ownership of the means of production", and al. g) refers to the existence of economic plans, "within the framework of a mixed economy". These changes of the substantive amendment rules allowed CA 1/1989, among other things, to modify Art. 81 of the Constitution on topics such as nationalization and rural estate property, and to eliminate Title II of its Part II that dealt with the structure of the means of production. These and the other changes in the economic Constitution were largely the result of the collapse of Communism that was taking place at that time.

100 Miranda, op. cit., p. 185.

101 Ibid., p. 202ff.

102 Canotilho and Moreira, op. cit., p. 1014.

103 Ibid., p. 1012ff.

104 C. Nowak, *Europarecht nach Lissabon*, Baden-Baden: Nomos, 2011, p. 99ff.

105 Art. 12 TEU. A. Cygan, "The parliamentarisation of EU decision-making? The impact of the Treaty of Lisbon on national parliaments", *European Law Review*, 2011, vol. 36(4), p. 480ff.

106 Case 6/64, *Costa v ENEL*, 1964 E.C.R. 1251.

107 A. Pliakos and G. Anagnostaras, "Who is the Ultimate Arbiter? The Battle over Judicial Supremacy in EU Law", *European Law Review*, 2011, vol. 36(1), p. 109ff.

108 F. Cengiz, "Multi-level Governance in Competition Policy: The European Competition Network", *European Law Review*, 2010, vol. 35(5), p. 660ff.

109 C. Semmelmann, "The European Union's Economic Constitution under the Lisbon Treaty: soul-searching among lawyers shifts the focus to procedure", *European Law Review*, 2010, vol. 35(4), p. 516ff.

110 T. Lock, "EU Acccssion to thc ECHR: Implications for Judicial Rcvicw in Strasbourg", *European Law Review*, 2010, vol. 35(6), p. 777ff.

111 Two examples are landmark cases such as *Lüth*, 1 BvR 400/51, 15 January 1958; 7 BVerfGE 198, *Griswold v Connecticut*, 381 U.S. 479 (1965); A.S. Sweet, "The Juridical Coup d'État and the Problem of Authority", *German Law Journal*, 2007, vol. 8, p. 915ff.

112 Decision of the Portuguese Constitutional Court 192/2010.

113 A.L. Collins, "'I Will Not Pronounce You Husband and Husband': Justice and the Justice of the Peace", *Alabama Law Review*, 2010, vol. 61(4), p. 849ff.; J.L. Carleton, "Life, Liberty, and the Pursuit of Matrimony: The Constitutional Implications Of Arkansas's Amendment Concerning Marriage", *Arkansas Law Review*, 2011, vol. 64(2), p. 383ff.

114 Corrias, op. cit., p. 1554ff. and p. 1561ff.

115 Parliament Deliberation 2–PL/2010.

116 Público, 16 November 2011. Online. Available HTTP: <http://www.plmj.com/xms/files/noticias_imprensa/2011/Agosto/Tiago_Duarte_sobre_alteracoes_constitucionais.pdf> (accessed 2 September 2011).

117 *Washington Times*, 16 August 2011. Online. Available HTTP: <http://www.washingtontimes.com/news/2011/aug/16/merkel-sarkozy-meet-euro-economy-stalls/> (accessed 2 September 2011).

118 Portugal: Memorandum Of Understanding On Specific Economic Policy Conditionality, 3 May 2011.

119 Decisions of the Portuguese Constitutional Court 399/10, 27–10, and 396/2011, 21–9.

120 A constitutional debt limit has been proposed by J. Buchanan, *Constitutional Restrictions on the Power of Government. The Collective Works of James Buchanan, vol. 16: Choice, Contract and Constitutions*, Indianapolis: Liberty Fund, 2001, p. 42ff. and p. 309ff.

121 *Economics, NewsPaper*, "The President of Portugal, against the deficit limit in the Constitution", online. Available HTTP: <http://economicsnewspaper.com/policy/spain/the-president-of-portugal-against-the-deficit-limit-in-the-constitution-58749.html> (accessed 4 September 2011).

122 J.S. Baker, Jr. "Citing Foreign and International Law to Interpret the Constitution: What's The Point?", *Albany Law Review*, 2006, vol. 69(3), p. 683ff. The Sarkozy/Merkel political initiative of promoting a constitutional revision in at least 17 Eurozone member states would be the ultimate form of authority outsourcing.

123 Title VII 1 of the French Constitution of 1791.

124 S. Levinson, "Our Schizoid Approach to the United States Constitution: Competing Narratives of Constitutional Dynamism and Stasis", *Indiana Law Journal*, 2009, vol. 84, p. 1337ff.

125 D.W. Burnham, "Constitutional Moments and Punctuated Equilibria: A Political Scientist Confronts Bruce Ackerman's 'We the People'", *Yale Law Journal*, 1999, vol. 108, p. 2237ff.; M.C. Dorf, "Integrating Normative and Descriptive Constitutional Theory: The Case of Original Meaning", *Georgetown Law Journal*, 1997, vol. 85, p. 1765ff.; Levinson, op. cit., p. 1345, referring to a "punctuated equilibrium" view of the Constitution, in which certain dramatic changes are the result of basic transformations in the political order, often triggered by social, economic, or military crises".

126 A.-M. Slaughter, "Global Community of Courts", *Harvard International Law Journal*, 2003, vol. 44(1), p. 191ff.

127 The expression "constitutional decay" has been used in the context of Republican thought, linking it to political corruption and the weakening of social morality, M.J. Sandel, *Democracy's Discontent, America in Search of a Public Philosophy*, Cambridge, Mass., 1996, p. 169ff. Republicanism adhered to the "common belief that political corruption and constitutional decay festered most readily in societies where individuals had *lost their economic interdependence* and moral integrity"; J. Lauck, "After Deregulation: Constructing Agricultural Policy In The Age Of 'Freedom To Farm'", *Drake Journal of Agricultural Law*, 2000, vol. 5, p. 3ff. and p. 41.

128 J. McGinnis and M.B. Rappaport, "Originalism and the Good Constitution", *Georgetown Law Journal*, 2010, vol. 98(6), p. 1693ff.

129 G. Steinitz, O. Piatibratova and P. Kotlarsky, "Possible effect of solar tides on radon signals", *Journal of Environmental Radioactivity*, 2011, vol. 102(8), p. 749ff.; J. Mullins, "Solar Ghosts May Haunt Earth's Radioactive Atoms", *New Scientist*, 2009, vol. 2714, p. 42ff.; Roland M. Frye, Jr., "The Current 'Nuclear Renaissance' In The United States, Its Underlying Reasons, And Its Potential Pitfalls", *Energy Law Journal*, 2008, vol. 29(2), p. 279ff.

130 Case C-71/08, *Commission v Portugal*, 8–7–2010, Directive 2009/72/CE, EP and Council, de 13–7–2009; R. Lambert and C. Reekie, "European Union Electricity and Gas Markets. The Third Legislative Package", *International Energy Law Review* 2010, vol. 5, p. 135.

15 Constitutional change in Spain

Abraham Barrero Ortega and Irene Sobrino Guijarro

Introduction

The life of constitutional systems tends to oscillate between two poles. On the one hand, constitutions need to evolve by trying to adjust to social and political transformations, in order to avoid discrepancies with reality that could lead to eventual constitutional breaks while, on the other hand, constitutional stability benefits popular knowledge regarding the constitution as well as the development of a "constitutional feeling," given the indisputability of the symbolic and socially integrating force of a constitution. Therefore, constitutional reforms fulfill the need of adjustment of the constitution to a changing reality, but they do so through a difficult procedure, in the sense that the adjustment will necessarily depend on the achievement of broad political consensus. If such qualified consensus is not met, it is simply not worth it to compromise the integrity of the system.

Constitutional reform is a transcendental event, since it implies the modification of the decision of the constituent power (*originary*) regarding the political model. This fact explains why constitutions regulate the revision procedure that must be followed. Constitutional rigidity is the consequence of a constitution being accepted as a founding premise. Given that the constitution is the product of the constituent powers, only an analogous power, whose composition and functioning must be envisaged in the constitution, may proceed to such reform.[1] Nowadays, almost all constitutions have a rigid character. Therefore, rather than distinguishing between rigid and flexible constitutions, as James Bryce originally did, it would be more accurate to differentiate between constitutions with a higher or lower degree of rigidity.[2] In any case, constitutional revision procedures vary widely from a comparative law perspective. For instance, it is common for a revision procedure not to require the intervention of the sovereign power when the revision does not affect a transcendental matter or when it is restricted to technical questions. In those cases, the legislator acts as a constituent power (*derivative* or *constituted*) by virtue of its nature as a representative of the people.

Together with the constitutional revision, constitutional jurisprudence may also enable a certain constitutional evolution, yet through a slower path and of a more progressive character. Constitutional case law has acquired an undeniable salience and relevance in Europe, given the role developed by constitutional courts in most

European countries when acting as top interpreters of the constitution in the fashion adopted by the US Supreme Court from its early beginnings.

Such interpretation, by updating the content of the constitutional provisions, may effectively develop the role of adapting the constitution to society, which is, by definition, changeable. It is necessary to differentiate between the reform of the text of the constitution, and the *mutation* of the actual content of the constitutional norms, leaving its literal form intact, as a consequence of the dynamics of political reality. The need for the constitutional mutations is clearly appreciated in the case of long-standing constitutions, whose adaptation to reality cannot be automatic. However, since rigidity makes constitutional revision more difficult to achieve, the real changes are introduced as substantial interpretative mutations of certain constitutional provisions.[3] In certain legal systems with a concentrated system of constitutional review,[4] such as the Spanish model, the constitutional case law has an extraordinary relevance as the ultimate interpreter of the constitution.

This chapter does not aim to present the wide range of literature that deals with constitutional revision in the Spanish Constitution of 1978. Its scope is much more limited. We will try to advance some reflections on the topic, derived both from our readings and insights on such a tantalizing question, which embraces a large number of perspectives and possibilities. The references used, just a part of the existing total, will be the support to set out such questions and to provide attempted explanations. In order to do so, the discussion first needs to be framed within the history of the Spanish Constitution. Secondly, the way in which the current Spanish Constitution of 1978 regulates the constitutional revision will be analyzed from a procedural perspective. Thirdly, the influence of the political system in the articulation of the constitutional revision will be analyzed from a substantive approach as well as the decisive influence that European law has had on transformation of the Spanish Constitution. Finally, we will present some of the main proposals for reform suggested by Spanish scholars that heretofore, for different reasons, have not yet been introduced by the relevant legislative organs.

Needless to say, addressing the complex topic of constitutional revisions demands a wider reflection on the pondered decisions, hurdles and challenges encountered in the legal articulation of the democratic system within a diverse and pluralistic political community.[5]

Constitutional reform in Spanish constitutional history: rigid and flexible constitutions

Before the Constitution of 1978, Spanish constitutional history can be structured into several cycles that share a similar pattern: they would start with a liberal and ephemeral constitution (1812, 1869, 1873, and 1931), which would be followed by conservative and long-lasting constitutions that restored conceptions related to the constitutional monarchy (1837, 1845, and 1876), substituting the principle of constitutional monarchy for national sovereignty. The origin of each of these cycles lies in a crisis of legitimacy of the monarchy that has been identified as a triggering factor for the major changes in Spanish constitutional history.

Out of the diverse constitutional texts enacted over the two centuries, only the Constitutions of 1812 and 1869, the Project of 1873 and the Constitution of 1931 incorporated rigid mechanisms to undertake constitutional reform. However, the Constitutions that prevailed in the nineteenth century in Spain—the Constitutions of 1837, 1845, and 1876—were linked to the periods of Spanish constitutional monarchy, and, as a consequence, had a flexible character, as they did not envisage any requirements for constitutional reform that were differentiated from the ordinary legislative procedure. The Constitution in this period is understood as the result of the political pact between the monarchy and the civil society represented by the Parliament, and it is conceived as a mere political guarantee of the institutionalization of such a pact.[6] Constitutional flexibility implies the inexistence of any legal limits on the exercise of the constituted powers, so reform may therefore be carried out by the same procedures used to enact statutory law. The classical identification in monarchical constitutionalism of both the constituent power and the constituted powers as a consequence of the shared sovereignty was reproduced by the Constitutions of 1837, 1845, and 1876.

In sharp contrast to these Constitutions, the Spanish constitutional texts of 1812, 1869, and 1931 articulated diverse mechanisms in order to preserve the constitutional pact from the ordinary political decision-making of the constituent powers, as a direct projection of the principle of constitutional supremacy. However, the nature and ends of such rigidity of the constitutional revision were understood in different ways in each of the constitutional texts.

The constitutional text of 1812 is historically framed within the European constitutional revolutionary period. It departs from the acknowledgement of national sovereignty and the constituent power of the nation. The constitutional text aimed at symbolizing the break with absolutism and the start of a radical new manner of conceiving the state. Constitutional revision was therefore articulated as a means to protect the new state configuration through a highly complex procedure, whose result was very unlikely to be met in praxis. The Spanish Constitution of 1812, in the same manner as the initial Constitutions of the French Revolution—1791, 1793, and 1795—envisaged such mechanisms of reform as highly disconnected from the normal functioning of the institutions, with the result of making the reform almost impossible. The reform procedure was envisaged in Arts. 375–84 of the Constitution, and, among other requisites, these provisions established both the prohibition against revising the Constitution during the first eight years after its enactment, and the two-fold requirement that the amendment proposal be passed, firstly, by two-thirds of the legislative Chamber and, consequently, by the same majority in the following General Deputation.[7]

The founders of the Spanish Constitution of 1869 intended to devolve the rigid character to the Constitution, after the flexible models of the Constitutions of 1834, 1837 and 1845, which had converted the binding character of the constitutional text of 1812 into a mere pact between the political actors. As a consequence, in 1869 the Constitution was intended to reinforce the democratic focus, as well as to reframe the revision as a legal guarantee of constitutional supremacy. The Constitution of 1869 articulates the requirements of a rigid constitution according to the pattern of a limited monarchy. Within this framework, the Monarch together with the Chambers is entitled to propose the revision. However, the final decision remains with the Chambers (Arts. 110–112). Furthermore, all the acts of the Monarch, including his intervention in the revision procedure, must be countersigned by a Minister. Once the Chambers have adopted the Decree of revision, they will be dissolved and the proposed amendment may be adopted by a simple majority of the votes of the members of the constituent Chambers.[8]

The Spanish Constitution of 1931, in the Second Republic, constitutes the first experience of construction of a democratic and social state in Spanish constitutional history. Assuming the democratic paradigm and the corresponding mechanism needed to guarantee the constitutional pact against any majority in the Parliament, it establishes a new formulation for the protection of constitutional supremacy. On the one hand, it envisages a rigid mechanism of revision, and additionally it articulates a concentrated system of control of the constitutionality of the statutory acts through the "Guarantees Court" (*Tribunal de Garantías Constitucionales*). Regarding the revision mechanism, it establishes a reasonable "compromise" between an "excessive rigidity" and an "extreme facility" in order to proceed to a constitutional amendment.[9] The proposal for constitutional revision may be exercised either by the Government or by a quarter of the Members of Parliament (MPs). During the first four years after the Constitution was enacted, a two-thirds vote by the Congress was required, and after this period an absolute majority was required in order to adopt the constitutional amendment (Art. 125 of the Constitution of 1931). This was a very short constitutional experience, which was followed by the military uprising in 1936, the Civil War, and rejection of the constitutional system by Franco's dictatorship (1939–1975) until the democratic Constitution of 1978 was enacted.

Constitutional revision in the Spanish constitution of 1978: a procedural approach

The constitutional choice of not imposing material limits on constitutional revision

The Spanish Constitution of 1978 (CE) regulates in Title X (Arts. 166–169) two different procedures for constitutional revision. Similar to the Constitutions of 1812, 1869 and 1931, both procedures of constitutional revision have a rigid character; that is, they are different from and more complex than the legislative procedure. The procedure of revision in Art. 167 is the "ordinary" procedure of revision, while the one envisaged in Art. 168 is the "qualified" procedure, as it will channel the most relevant or complex revisions.

The existence of the two procedures of constitutional revision with a different degree of rigidity shows that the Spanish Constitution opted to make the constitutional revision more difficult for certain essential aspects of the democratic system rather than excluding certain provisions from the possibility of being revised. The latter option, known as the material intangibility clauses—according to which certain constitutional contents are excluded from constitutional revision—is actually an efficient means of preventing changes or political transformations. Regarding essential issues, the political action may eventually prevail over the constitutional provisions, making them void.[10] That is why the possibility of revision in the Spanish Constitution is also available for most relevant aspects of the constitutional system, as a useful means to channel possible transformation of the political regime and potentially avoid *de facto* actions. On the other hand, even from a formal perspective, the intangibility clauses are normally inefficient. As the transition to democracy proved in Spain (1975–1978), those provisions do not necessarily constitute an insurmountable obstacle to hinder the replacement of one political system by another founded on opposing principles (in the Spanish case, a dictatorship was replaced by a democratic system), while formally observing the procedures of constitutional revision (the legislation to revise Franco's Fundamental Laws).[11]

The inefficiency of establishing material limits of an absolute character explains why the Constitution has not yet established them. In any case, the essential aspects of the Spanish political system—the principles of the rule of law, the fundamental rights, the separation of powers, and the political decentralization—must be considered as implicit limits to constitutional revision, in the sense that the modification of these would imply the repudiation of the very concept of a Constitution in the context of an advanced democracy like the Spanish case.[12]

The only explicit limit established by the 1978 Spanish Constitution refers to the moment of constitutional revision—in this sense, it could be considered a *temporal* limit. The Constitution prohibits the amendment from being initiated in time of war or when any of the states outlined in Art. 116 are in operation (Art. 169). This limit aims to guarantee the development of a constitutional amendment debate in a situation of political normality, avoiding the potential interference of emotional reactions. This provision could be considered unnecessary, given the unlikelihood that the same Legislative Chambers that have declared any of the previous exceptional states decide, at the same time, to initiate a constitutional revision. However, the aim of the prohibition is to guarantee the normality of the political situation in which any of the reforms is undertaken.[13]

In any case, the limitation established in the Constitution is highly restricted, since it does not extend to any of the phases of the constitutional amendment, but only affects its initiation. The Constitution, therefore, only aimed to guarantee that there was a context of institutional normality at the moment of initiating the revision. However, the same arguments that apply to not considering the initiation of a constitutional revision adequate in a situation of instability could be equally valid in preventing its development or finalization, given that the aim is to achieve an absence of pressure on the individuals in charge of the reform.[14] This is the reason why the organic legislator excludes the possibility of celebrating any referendum, including those regarding the constitutional revision procedure, when the states of exception and siege are in operation, or 90 days after their finalization (Art. 4 para 1 of the Organic Law 2/1980 on the Regulation of the Different Modalities of Referendum). Some scholars have questioned the constitutionality of this legislative provision on referendums, on the grounds that the Constitution does not envisage such limits. Furthermore, it has been objected that the solution of the legislator could eventually be misused to obstruct the completion of a process of constitutional amendment through the declaration of some of the exceptional states.[15]

The proposal of constitutional revision

Regarding the right to propose a constitutional amendment, Art. 166 CE establishes that it shall be exercised under the terms contained in Art. 87 paras 1 and 2; that is, the procedure envisaged for any conventional legislative procedure. Thus, the right to initiate the constitutional reform belongs to the Government, to both the Chambers—Congress of Deputies and Senate—as well as, with important limitations, to the Assemblies of the Autonomous Communities. The right is altogether excluded in the case of lawmaking processes originated by popular legislative initiatives.

The parliamentary regulations implement the constitutional provisions regarding the right to exercise the constitutional reform initiative. In the case of the Government, it will submit the amendment bill proposal before the Congress of Deputies, to be processed as such subsequently by the two Chambers. Regarding the initiative of the Parliament, the Constitution attributes the right to the Chambers, hence not to the Deputies or Senators on an individual basis; therefore, it is each Chamber itself that exercises the right to initiate the constitutional amendment.

The Regulation of the Congress of Deputies envisages, as the only difference with the ordinary legislative procedure, that the proposals of the Chamber will have to be undersigned by two parliamentary groups, not just one, or by one-fifth of the Deputies (i.e. 70 of them), instead of 15 of them (Art. 126 para 1 and Art. 146 para 1). The Regulation of the Senate establishes that 50 Senators who do not belong to the same party may submit a proposal of reform, in contrast to the ordinary legislative procedure, which attributes the legislative initiative to a parliamentary group or to 25 Senators (Art. 108 para 1 and Art. 152).

The Assemblies of the Autonomous Communities may request that the Government adopt a bill or send a proposal of law to the Board of the House of Representatives, delegating a maximum of three members of their Assembly to that Chamber to defend it (Art. 87 para 2 CE). This possibility, like the ordinary legislative procedure, is a mere proposal that does not bind the Government to send the bill to the Chambers, or the Congress to consider the proposal of reform. Its position is, in effect, analogous to the role of the MPs when submitting a proposal of constitutional revision. Therefore, it could be deemed a limited initiative or a mere proposal of initiative.

The ordinary procedure of constitutional amendment

The ordinary procedure of constitutional amendment (Art. 167 CE) refers to all possible reforms with the exception of the contents specially protected (Art. 168

CE), and is articulated through various steps. In its basic modality, the bills on constitutional amendments (either as projects from the Government or as a proposal from the Congress or Senate) must be approved by a majority of three-fifths of the members of each Chamber (Art. 167 para 1 CE). Such a quota is computed with relation to the total (legal) number of its members, which in practice is reduced to the members with the full integral status of Senators or Deputies. Nevertheless, the Constitution also envisages the scenario of eventual disagreement of both Chambers on the text; in this case, if there is no agreement between the Chambers, an effort to reach it shall be made by setting up a Joint Commission of Deputies and Senators that shall submit a text to be voted on by the House of Representatives and the Senate, whose aim will be to agree on a text that will be submitted to the Chambers to be approved by a three-fifths majority of the members (Art. 167 para 1 CE).

In principle, if the bill did not reach the required majority in some of the Chambers—with or without the intervention of the Joint Commission—it should be understood that the reform initiative has failed. The same would be applicable if the Joint Commission could not agree on a text to be submitted to both Chambers. However, the Constitution envisages a second modality in the case that the bill submitted to the Chambers—again, with or without the intervention of the Joint Commission—is passed by both Chambers, but does reach a three-fifths majority of the Senate members. In that case, the Congress of Deputies may approve the amendment by a two-thirds vote (Art. 167 para 2 CE), provided that the text has obtained a favorable vote by an absolute majority of the Senate. That is, it is admitted that the reform is passed with a lower majority than three-fifths of the Senate, as long as the Congress of Deputies approves it with a two-thirds majority, since it may force the passage of the reform, even though counting only on an absolute majority in the Senate instead of the three-fifths majority. This possibility would be the last one in order to pass the initiated reform, with the consequence that if these majorities are not obtained, the reform will have failed.

The Constitution adds a third modality within the ordinary procedure: the intervention of the electorate. Thus, if so requested by one-tenth of the members of either Chamber (in principle, 35 Deputies and approximately 25 Senators), once the amendment has been passed by the Parliament it shall be submitted to a referendum for its ratification (Art. 167 para 3 CE). The request must be submitted within 15 days after its adoption by the Chambers. One of the main advantages of this option is the possibility that it provides for both the relatively modest parliamentary minorities and the driving political forces of the reform to resort to the electorate, if they consider that the popular ratification may be convenient. However, it exempts the reforms that count on a high degree of consensus among the political forces with parliamentary representation from the need to carry out a popular consultation.[16] The solution to the optional referendum does seem to be coherent with the idea of popular sovereignty, given that even in the ordinary procedure the electorate may participate, although it is possible to carry out the constitutional revision with the sole intervention of the political representatives in the case that none of the parliamentary forces consider it necessary to call a referendum.[17]

The only two reforms carried out so far in Spain have applied the channel of Art. 167 and have been founded on the Spanish commitments in the European process. In particular, the Articles that were the object of revision were 13 para 2 and 135 of the Spanish Constitution, and no referendum was held. Having been passed in Parliament, both were signed by the King and published the following day in the BOE (Official State Gazette).

The qualified procedure of constitutional revision

In contrast to the ordinary path, the qualified procedure of constitutional revision is highly rigid and complex. This procedure is applicable when a total revision of the Constitution is proposed, or a partial revision thereof, affecting the Preliminary Title Arts. 1–9, Chapter II, Section 1 of Title I Arts. 15–29, or Title II Arts. 56–65 (Art. 168 para 1 CE). While there are no particular difficulties in identifying what the specially protected partial areas are, it becomes very complex to identify the total revision. The criteria should probably be both quantitative and qualitative, considering that a total revision to an amendment implies a change in the essential elements of the constitutional text, on the grounds that it affects many constitutional provisions or even some of its main principles.[18]

The Preliminary Title states the principles and basic values of the constitutional legal order. Section 1, Chapter II of Title I regulates the fundamental rights and the public freedoms that have a reinforced constitutional protection, according to Art. 53 para 2 CE. Title II regulates the Crown. On the other hand, the expression "affect" used by Art. 168 implies that the qualified procedure will be required when the parts mentioned in the provision are amended even indirectly, although their text is not modified. Therefore, it is evident that the Constitution has identified the aspects that characterize the constitutional system in a most decisive way and has linked them to an amendment procedure as rigorous as if it implied a hypothetical total revision of the Constitution. The qualified procedure is due even though the reform of those parts is partial, or has a scarce relevance and does not imply any important modification of the constitutional system.[19]

The Constitution establishes that the decision to carry out a constitutional amendment according to Art. 168 must be approved by a two-thirds majority of the members of both Chambers (Art. 168 para 1 CE). Although the Constitution does not establish that the initiative of amendment must be constituted in a text, the Regulations of both Chambers establish that the project or proposals of reform will be subjected to a debate on the whole text. In the case that the principle of constitutional amendment is approved, both Chambers shall immediately be dissolved (Art. 168 para 1 CE). The elected Chambers must, firstly, ratify the decision by simple majority. Once ratified, they will proceed to examine the new constitutional text, which must be approved by a two-thirds majority of the members of both Chambers (Art. 168 para 2 CE).

Once the amendment has been passed by the Parliament, it shall be submitted to ratification by referendum (Art. 168 para 3 CE). As was mentioned above, the referendum will not take place under the states of exception, siege, or during the

90 days after the finalization thereof. It is therefore a notably complex procedure, which entails the intervention of two different Parliaments with two consultations to the electorate. The first Chambers must pass the proposal of constitutional revision by a large majority. However, these are not the members that must pass the reform, since that function is attributed to the subsequently elected Chambers. This procedure allows the electorate to express itself indirectly about the appropriateness of the revision itself, of its content, and about what the majority parliamentary forces will be in the constituent Chambers. Once the reform is passed, the electorate will have to ratify its content again, this time directly in a referendum.[20]

So far, after more than 30 years since the enactment of the Constitution, no constitutional revision has yet been proposed through Art. 168 that has gone beyond the doctrinal debate. Some authors have criticized the rigidity of Art. 168 and have suggested the need to reform it.

The participation of the people and the civil society in constitutional revision

Both the partial (Art. 167) and the total revision (Art. 168) of the Spanish Constitution incorporate the referendum within the amendment process. The direct intervention of the electorate has a different configuration in each process. Within the framework of the partial revision of the Constitution, the referendum is optional upon the request by one-tenth of the members of either House, within 15 days after the amendment has been passed by the Congress of Deputies and the Senate (Art. 167 para 3). However, in case of the total revision of the Constitution or the partial revision on specially protected areas, the referendum will have a compulsory character.

Although the Constitution does not refer to the question of the binding of the referendum in an explicit way, it is deemed that the decision expressed in the referendum will have a compulsory character for the legislature.[21] This characteristic of the amendment referendum, in addition to its logical differentiated nature given its constituent nature, would be the most salient differences in contrast to the consultative referendum on political decisions of special importance (Art. 92 of the Constitution). As already mentioned, the only two constitutional amendments undertaken in Spain, in 1992 and 2011, have been channeled through Art. 167, and did not apply the optional referendum within the revision procedure.

On the other hand, the lawmaking process begun by popular initiative is excluded in the Constitution as a mechanism to originate a constitutional amendment. The right to propose a constitutional amendment lies with the same bodies that can exercise the legislative initiative, explicitly excluding the popular initiative. The exclusion of the popular initiative to propose the constitutional revision was a question discussed at length in the constituent debates. The solution finally adopted by the constitutional text should be interpreted in light of the historic and political context that necessarily frames this concrete issue. Given the lack of a tradition of a consistent representative democracy in Spanish constitutional history, one of the main legal and political aims of the founders of the Constitution at this point was to effectively establish the roots of a representative democratic system. Hence, with this particular aim, the articulation of the right to initiate the constitutional amendment was subjected to the emphasis on representation.[22]

The impact of the political system on constitutional revision and the judicial review of constitutional amendments

The enactment of the Spanish Constitution of 1978 represents the fruits of the thorough and deliberate consensus amongst the constituent political actors to symbolize the break with the previous constitutional tradition and to initiate a differentiated stage in Spanish constitutional history, in which the supremacy of the Constitution as a binding and democratic framework for the political activity was beyond discussion. Specifically, the choice of a particularly rigid model of constitutional reform was a question that reached a general agreement in the constituent process.[23]

As has been analyzed previously, the Spanish Constitution articulates two different procedures in order to channel the constitutional amendment: the constitutional "reform" (Art. 167) and the constitutional "revision" (Art. 168). The basic pattern of the procedure envisaged for the constitutional "reform" falls in a coherent manner within the logic of the parliamentary type of political system in Spain. Certainly, the reform procedure configured in Art. 167 is basically parliamentary, given the fact that the legislative Chambers have a prevailing role over the electorate in the reform procedure. This process, however, should not be understood as a substantive primacy of the former over the latter in terms of the content of the decision, in case of an eventual contradiction between them. Rather, the prevailing role of the Chambers should be understood in strictly procedural terms; that is, the parliamentary organs intervene in the first place within the process of amendment and only if a certain percentage of its members disagree on the amendment bill will this opposition be subject to ratification by referendum. The rationale underlying this scheme is the futility of the referendum when it has previously reached unanimity over the reform in the Chambers.[24]

Within the framework of the reinforced constitutional revision (Art. 168) and, as an important exception to the *asymmetrical bicameralism* that rules the adoption of parliamentary decisions,[25] the role of the Senate is made equal to that of the Congress of Deputies in terms of required majority to approve both the proposed reform and the amendment bill (i.e. a two-thirds majority of the members of each House). Under the reinforced procedure, the total or partial amendments affecting specific questions will be made equivalent to a total revision of the Constitution.

Together with the constitutional regulation at the procedural level, the political parameter in the Spanish case has an extraordinary importance in order to shed light on the practical functioning and application of the revision instruments. In contrast with other constitutions in Europe, the Spanish Constitution has been subjected to strikingly few amendments. In this sense, it may be affirmed that there has been a "deficit" in the use of this instrument.

The decision on the monarchy and its constitutional configuration within the coordinates of the parliamentary system were not discussed at the time of the constituent debates but at a previous stage, through an agreement between the political parties that participated in the transition to the democratic system. In the case of the territorial distribution of power, the needed consensus to enact the democratic Constitution in 1978 was achieved to the detriment of the adoption of specific constitutional provisions on this question. The Constitution recognized autonomy as a right (Art. 2) and enabled diverse tracks for the territorial decentralization to be achieved (e.g. Arts. 143 and 151). Subsequent political pacts in 1981 and 1992 defined the type and content of territorial decentralization that would be channeled through the body of constitutional case law as a fundamental element in the construction of the current State of Autonomies. The flexible and dynamic system of the constitutional frame may have downgraded the need to proceed to the reform, but there are definitely questions on the constitutional text that need to be either updated or clarified in the light of the current state of evolution of the decentralized Spanish system.[26]

Notwithstanding the widespread political consensus on the need to revise certain constitutional aspects pertaining to these two questions, their amendment has never been initiated. It has been argued that the absence of a comprehensive constituent debate (a general transparent debate, unanimous consensus, and direct participation of the electorate) and, as a consequence, the lower levels of democratic legitimacy input applied on the constitutional configuration of these questions, would explain the almost non-existent resort to the amendment tools. This situation would only be the visible consequence of a deeper political–historical ambivalence that would refer to the unresolved question of the entitlement of the constituent power by the head of state and the territorial question present in Spanish history from the outset of the constitutionalist experience (beginning in the nineteenth century).[27]

Finally, although the constitutional review of the amendment process has not been envisaged in the constitutional text or in the Organic Law of the Constitutional Court, the literature has argued that the Constitutional Court should control the constitutionality of the process, as the amendment provisions are part of the constitutional text (Title X). Hence, should a constitutional amendment be challenged, the Constitutional Court would be legitimized to assess the constitutional validity of the revision. If the amendment had followed Art. 167, the scope of the control would extend both to the procedure and the substantive constitutional limitations (i.e. the "protected provisions" under the qualified procedure of Art. 168). However, if the constitutional revision had applied the procedure of Art. 168, the scope of control by the Court would be reduced to checking whether the rules of the constitutional procedure had been observed, since the Constitution does not envisage material limitations for the "qualified" procedure.[28]

The impact of European law on the Spanish Constitution of 1978: a substantive approach

European constitutional law

The Constitution of 1978 is framed within the context of classic constitutionalism, as a phenomenon framed within nation state boundaries. The 1978 Constitution "could be the alpha and the omega of our constitutionality," but "it has been a while since this is not the case."[29] Today, Spanish legal life is not bound exclusively by the national Constitution. Our Constitution is not the same as that of 1978. Both its content and its normative effectiveness have been profoundly altered. For obvious reasons, the incidence of international law on the Constitution of 1978 can easily be perceived in the case of European law.

All Constitutions intend to guarantee certain values: in the first place, the need to assume certain rules in the distribution and separation of the state functions; in the second place, the effective establishment of the dignity and freedom of the individuals. Without these values, the given text may be labeled a Constitution, although materially it will not be such. From such a material conception of the Constitution, it is not possible to identify the European constitutional law and the Lisbon Treaty as the arrival point of the process of political integration within the European Union. Certainly, the Lisbon Treaty, which manages to overcome to some extent the political gridlock of the Union as a consequence of the negative referendums of France and the Netherlands, constitutes the last step within the framework of the constituent process of the European Union initiated decades ago. What was "*de facto* [. . .] already a constitution [. . .], founded on certain dynamics rooted on the case law of the Court of Justice, yet admitted with different enthusiasm by the national Constitutional Courts," is turned now into a "*de jure* constitution, that is, a constitution in its own right."[30] The questions that were already present acquire constitutional translation: symbols, rights, political institutions, a supreme court of justice, provisions on the distribution of competences, and a special procedure for revision. In any case, it would be too simplistic to reduce European law or European constitutional law to the Lisbon Treaty, mainly because the European Convention on Human Rights has been forging a certain understanding of the values embedded in the idea of fundamental rights since 1950. The unstoppable internationalization of the fundamental rights after the Second World War led to the enactment by the Council of Europe of the Convention of Rome, whose influence in the growing interrelation of legal orders is undeniable.[31] The case law of the Spanish Constitutional Court confirms this statement.[32]

Any analysis on the influence that European law has had on the Constitution of 1978 should take into account an obvious fact: both of them are substantially coincidental. The Spanish Constitution of 1978 is founded on the same values and principles as those of European constitutional law. In spite of the substantive differences between the European legal order and the state-based legal orders, there is a nucleus of values and rules that share the same foundation and objective: the protection of the human being, without any distinction of nationality or personal circumstances, against arbitrary acts of power. The common aim is to effectively guarantee the rules of distribution and separation of state powers, and certain ethical values that have become fundamental rights. Both the European and Spanish legal cultures are founded on a universal paradigm. Peter Häberle refers to this process as the "European sedimentation,"[33] suggesting a certain degree of unity. And, in that sense, the Spanish Constitutional Court has stated that the European legal order "is constructed on the common values of the Constitutions of the integrated States of the Union and their constitutional traditions."[34]

In addition to this point, it is evident that the Spanish Constitution of 1978 manifested the firm will to join the European constitutional area. Also, the acceptance of democracy and fundamental rights was something assumed when the Constitution was enacted. These concepts were all legal realities that were non-existent in the previous political system and that were necessary to incorporate into the new constitutional order. The fact that Spain joined the Council of Europe, signed the European Convention on Human Rights, and ratified both Pacts of New York, clearly implied the wish to break with the past and found the basis for the transition towards a political order that was in compliance with the rule of law and individual rights.

The process of reception of Community law would start some years later. The Spanish Constitution had, however, already envisaged the instrument that would enable this integration: Art. 93. This provision is not only limited to the collaboration and cooperation with other states, but, very importantly, it also articulates the possibility to attribute to an international organization or institution the exercise of competences derived from the Constitution. In addition, the state powers ceased to be exercised by the national authorities and were then subjected to the decisions and law of a supranational organization. Although not explicitly mentioned by Art. 93, this provision was conceived and has been applied to facilitate the integration of Spain within the European Communities,[35] which was made effective from 1 January 1986.

Enlargement of the content

There is a very frequent phenomenon in the legal sphere that has been activated when interpreting the fundamental rights contained in Title I of the Spanish Constitution of 1978. This phenomenon refers to the attribution of new meanings and contents to a given text. The provision is stretched or dilated in order to adapt to the social reality. A basic instance of this logic is represented by Art. 10 para 2 of the Spanish Constitution, which refers to the tool of comparative law as an interpretative parameter for fundamental rights. In particular, this provision establishes that norms referring to basic rights and liberties that are recognized by the Constitution shall be interpreted in conformity with the Universal Declaration of Human Rights, but also, in close connection with the European Constitutional Law, in conformity with the Convention of Rome and the case law of the European Court of Human Rights (ECtHR). This has been a controversial provision since its enactment. It is complex, difficult, and open to a number of possibilities, amongst which there is the widening of its content. Some examples of this process will follow.

The Spanish Constitution does not explicitly envisage the prohibition of slavery contained in Art. 4 of the European Convention on Human Rights (ECHR). However, its inclusion was unnecessary given the function of Art. 10 para 1 and Art. 17. When Art. 18 was being drafted, it was not taken for granted that the protection of the inviolability of the home as well as privacy would be decisive arguments when protecting the individual from noise or acoustic pollution. Nowadays, that question is unchallenged on the basis of the case law of the European Court of Human Rights in Art. 8 ECHR, and, in general, through what has been called the "environmental content of the fundamental rights."[36] Finally, mirroring the Strasbourg Court, the Spanish Constitutional Court at an early stage also assumed the application of the jurisdictional guarantees of Art. 24 on administrative penalties.[37] It is important to underscore that the interpretation of Art. 10 para 2 in the light of sources of European law has implied the extension of some of the provisions of the Constitution of 1978.

Reduction of the content

On other occasions, the European Constitutional Law has, on the contrary, fostered the reduction or restriction of certain contents of the Spanish Constitution of 1978, mainly regarding Title I. In other words, it has led to an interpretation of the contents according to limits or restrictions generally admitted in the European sphere. It is undeniable that the Constitution does not support a regression of fundamental rights through international instruments. In this regard, the German or Italian experiences should be recalled in relation to the influence of European Community law on their internal law, and in particular, on their fundamental constitutional rights. These facts justify the importance of the interpretation of fundamental rights as general principles of law by the European Court of Justice. In contrast, the Constitution does protect the inverse logic that has just been analyzed: through the Treaties, it is possible to extend the level of protection of fundamental rights. Sometimes, however, such logic may project an ambiguous result, given that, while what may be interpreted by some as widening effects, may be perceived as a restriction on others. No right is absolute; limits and conventions will undoubtedly be needed when rights come into conflict with each other. Within the framework of the determination of internal and external limits to the exercise of the fundamental rights, Art. 10 para 2 and Art. 96 para 1 may be very useful. Although the general rule is the widening of the scope of protection, limitation is also possible. The provisions of international law establishing potential limits or restrictions on the exercise of certain rights should be excluded from the interpretation required by Art. 10 para 2, since the Spanish Constitution guarantees the given right or liberty to a higher degree.[38] These facts do not prevent the recognition of the influence of the Convention of Rome and ECHR case law regarding the limitations of the fundamental rights in the jurisprudence of the Spanish Constitutional Court. Let's see some illustrative examples of this question.

The freedoms of expression and information constitute consolidated and unquestionable values of democratic systems. However, regardless of their definite relevance, they are also subject to some limits and restrictions. Both the European system in general and the Spanish system in particular do impose limits on the exercise of both fundamental rights. Article 10 para 2 ECHR states that the exercise of these freedoms may be subject to such formalities, conditions, restrictions, or penalties. Article 20 para 4 of the Spanish Constitution specifies that these liberties find their limitation in the respect for the rights recognized and, especially, in the right to honor, privacy, personal identity, and protection of youth and childhood. More recently, Art. 52 para 1 of the Charter of Fundamental Rights has established a very similar content, according to which any limitation on the exercise of the rights and freedoms (therefore, also the freedom of expression and information) recognized by the Charter must be provided for by law and must respect the essence of those rights and freedoms. Hence, on the basis of Art. 10 para 2 CE, the Spanish Constitutional Court, following the jurisprudence of the Human Rights European Court on this point, has affirmed that "hate and despise [sic] towards a population or ethnic group are incompatible with the respect of dignity."[39] Any form of defense or justification of national, racial, or religious hatred is therefore banned.

In the same way, regarding the delimitation of the essential content of the freedoms of conscience (Art. 16 CE), the Constitutional Court has stated that the ideological and religious freedoms do not only include the right of the individual to freely choose an explanatory conception of existential realities. These freedoms also include conceptual room for the *agere licere*, by virtue of which the individual may act according to his or her free beliefs. Therefore, these rights include not only the freedom of beliefs through which the individual privately decides to follow a system of ideological or religious truths, but also the right to free social expression of their beliefs and freedom to behave in accordance with them. However, both the Constitutional Court and the European Court of Human Rights have dismissed the idea that the ideological and religious freedoms may lead to a general right of conscientious objection. Therefore, the ideological or religious freedoms would not include a potential right to fail to comply with the law whenever it is deemed to be against matters of conscience. This idea in itself would be contradictory to the basic postulates of the rule of law.[40]

In certain cases, the contrast with the Strasbourg doctrine has led the Constitutional Court to extreme caution when judging the legitimacy of the imposition of a limit to the exercise of a right. Privacy may be infringed upon through the resource to unauthorized entry to homes, or the use of wiretaps or similar devices. Public powers cannot freely implement actions of this kind: the intromission into private space is tolerated because there are superior reasons established by the law that impose conditions and that must be sufficiently precise.[41] Article 10 para 2 CE carries out an "especial [sic] function of guarantee"[42] of the constitutionally declared content of the rights and freedoms of Title I.

Mutation

On the other hand, it is important to underscore the deep transformation that European integration has brought about in the Constitution. Such transformation has not generally been reflected in the constitutional text of 1978 through a new intervention of the constituent power, but has taken place through new interpretations applied to the text. The accession of Spain to the European Communities on 1 January 1986 implied a constitutional mutation of this type. The constitutional text has not been formally amended, although it has undergone deep reforms. This process has been channeled through Art. 93. The transference to an international organization of the exercise of competences derived from the Constitution was adopted through the Organic Act 10/1995. Many constitutional provisions are nowadays interpreted in a different way, in order to allow the new political and legislative realities of European law to have effect in the unreformed and rigid domestic constitutional order. In this way, the difficult procedure that constitutional revision normally implies has been avoided.

The most transcendental result of all these processes is that a very important part of Spanish law derives not from the central state or regional legislative Chambers but from Brussels. Not only has the central state been altered, but the Autonomous Communities and Local Corporations have also experienced such effects. The territorial Spanish model has undergone a substantive change, since the central power and the Autonomous Communities have lost some of the legislative, decision-making power to European institutions.[43] While the Constitution has remained almost intact, the constitutional system has undergone a deep transformation. Moreover, this has been configured as an open process, as a process of mutation along a continuum, forged by successive organic laws before each amendment of the international treaties.

Reform

The influence of European Law on the Constitution of 1978 is made clearly evident through the constitutional reform brought about by European law. In front of an insurmountable contradiction between the Constitution of 1978 and European law, it is necessary either to reject that contradiction, or to proceed to a constitutional revision. It is important to emphasize the insurmountable character of such a contradiction, implying that it is not possible to overcome it through the integrative paths already analyzed. Article 95 para 1 CE guarantees the prevalence of the Constitution over any type of international law treaty: either the international treaty remains unsigned or the Constitution is reformed. And that is exactly what happened in 1992, on the occasion of the ratification of the Treaty of Maastricht, the Treaty of the European Union. This Treaty amended the Treaty establishing the European Community. It established that every citizen of the Union has the right to vote and to stand as a candidate in municipal elections in the member state where he or she resides. Hence, citizens will be able both to vote and to stand as candidates, in the same conditions as the nationals of that member state. The Spanish constitutional text had a specific provision in that regard: Art. 13 para 2 established some criteria for the exercise of the active suffrage by foreigners in the local elections, but it did not mention their right to stand as candidates; that is, passive suffrage.

Was it really necessary to revise the Constitution? Would it have also been feasible to make the Treaty of Maastricht compatible with the existent text? This question was extensively debated by legal scholars.[44] Some authors understood that the revision could perfectly be in accordance with the existent text at that time. However, the Constitutional Court, in response to the request of the Government (Art. 95 para 2 CE), declared that the Treaty of Maastricht was contrary to Art. 13 para 2 CE on the question of the attribution of passive suffrage rights in the local elections to the citizens of the European Union who were not Spaniards.[45] It was also clarified that the procedure required in order to achieve the adjustment of that provision to the Constitution was the one envisaged in Art. 167. Finally, on 27 August 1992, the reform was carried out.[46] It was a consensual, concrete, and simple reform that consisted of the addition of only two words to Art. 13 para 2 CE: "and passive."

To a great extent, the process of European integration motivated the constitutional reform of 2011. In this case, the reform was not necessarily required—i.e. there was not an insurmountable contradiction between a specific provision of European law and the Constitution of 1978—but it was deemed convenient to incorporate a settled principle of the European Union into the Constitution. The reform of Art. 135 CE aimed to guarantee the principle of budget stability, binding all the public administrations to this objective as well as reinforcing the commitment of Spain to the European Union, while, at the same time, guaranteeing the economic and social sustainability of the country. More than 30 years after the enactment of the Spanish Constitution, budget stability requires structural and conditioning evaluation of the ability of a state to maintain and develop its welfare state, as stated in Art. 1 para 1 of the Constitution, because as a current member of the Economic and Monetary Union, it must reinforce its competencies within the framework of a growing common governance. Such needs justified its constitutional incorporation, in order to limit and orient the activity of public powers. The current economic and financial situation emphasized the suitability of inserting the principle of budgetary stability into the Spanish Constitution, aiming to strengthen the trust in the Spanish economy in the short and medium term. The reform, also in this case, was implemented through Art. 167 and counted on the agreement of the two largest parliamentary groups, PSOE and PP.[47]

The debate on future reforms: proposals and obstacles

Spanish scholars have been intensively discussing the need for and opportunity of a constitutional reform over recent years. The proposals for reform and their importance are quite varied. It would go beyond the scope of this analysis to examine these proposals exhaustively. Therefore, we will only be focusing on both the proposals that have generated a greater doctrinal consensus and those that have evidenced a need to adapt the Constitution to the evolution of society or legislation.

Among the proposals that have gathered most support among scholars, we can highlight one that the Spanish Prime Minister, José Luis Rodríguez Zapatero, put forward at the beginning of the VIII Legislature, regarding the constitutional revision of four main areas. With this aim, a report was requested from the Council of State (submitted in February 2006).[48] The future political developments would not take that project into account; it was not even incorporated within the electoral program of the PSOE in the elections of March 2008. Since then, this question has not been dealt with in the political arena. However, given the great consensus aroused by the project, it may be interesting to recall the four points that needed to be revised according to the Government, some of which required revision through the qualified procedure of Art. 168. We are referring to the end of male priority in the succession to the Crown, the reform of the Senates, the inclusion of a provision on European integration, and the express mention of the denomination of the Autonomous Communities.

The end of male priority in the succession to the Crown

Article 57 para 1 CE establishes that the Crown of Spain is hereditary for the successors of HM Don Juan Carlos I of Borbon, legitimate heir of the historic dynasty. It also states that succession to the throne will follow the regular order of primogeniture and representation, the first line always having preference in the same grade, the male over the female. The priority of the male over his sisters, although he is the youngest, is a controversial point of the Constitution, and there is a high degree of consensus among Spanish social and political groups on the need to correct this question. This type of revision has already taken place in Sweden, Norway, and other European monarchies. The priority of the male is an unjustified discrimination contrary to contemporary logic and values, and it contravenes Art. 14 CE, which prohibits discrimination on the grounds of sex.

The complexity of the reform—it needs to follow the qualified requirement of Art. 168 CE—is well known since all referendums entail a risk of unpredictable consequences. It has thus far not taken place, in spite of the almost unanimous socio-political consensus on the question.[49] However, the circumstances of different historic events, such as the marriage of the Crown Prince and the question of his descendants, are exerting pressure to have this question resolved, since it may pose future controversies. Once it is decided to carry out the reform, it will be necessary to tackle the eventual questions, such as the retroactive application and acquired rights (or mere expectations of rights). Moreover, although the priority of Prince Felipe is beyond discussion, it would be appropriate to introduce a specific reference to this question in Title II.

The reform of the Senate

The Senate or second Chamber, as it is regulated in the Constitution (Art. 66ff.), is not a real second territorial Chamber in the federal sense, but rather a Chamber of *reflection* or *second reading* with little political weight. This type of Senate does not seem to be in accordance with the extraordinary process of political decentralization carried out in Spain. The circumstances have changed and the sub-national territorial entities exhort for a greater institutional and political presence. Within these parameters, legal scholarship insists on the need to proceed to the constitutional revision in order to tackle certain problems: the necessary cooperation between the central state and the Autonomous Communities, as well as the participation of these in the decision-making processes affecting their political autonomy.[50]

The next question would be the scope and limits of such reform. Should the new Senate be adjusted to the more or less diffuse functioning scheme of the Spanish Autonomous State? Or, on the contrary, should it be built upon a federal model that could actually challenge that scheme? There are some proposals consisting of turning the Senate into a governmental Chamber formed by representatives of each Autonomous Community, appointed by the respective presidents and subjected to their instructions. However, would this configuration be inconsistent with the constitutional idea of a Senate integrated within the legislative Chambers (Art. 66 para 1 CE), as well as with the prohibition of the imperative mandate or free condition of parliamentary representatives (Art. 67 para 2 CE)? It is necessary to reflect calmly on the *reduced* or *widened* scope of the reform. Very likely, comparative law is an optimal source in order to find elements to be included within our constitutional system (the German Bundesrat, Austrian Senate, Swiss Federal Council, etc). In any case, the reform of the Senate is not only a technical–legal problem, but also an unresolved political question.

In summary, it is essential to finalize the Spanish "territorial constitution" before proceeding to its reform; it is necessary to close the territorial decentralization process that began when the Constitution was enacted. This process of reflection will resolve the fundamental question of whether the model is heading towards a fully decentralized system structured in homogeneous sub-national entities, or whether the state is actually heading for a system in which these entities have certain differences, which would imply a totally different organic and allocation of power structure.[51]

The inclusion of a European integration provision

The ratification of primary European law by the Spanish state may conflict at the constitutional level, since the Spanish Constitution does not contain any reference to the European Union. It may be surprising that the Spanish public powers must apply European law lacking any specific provision on this question in the Constitution. This is a highly unsatisfactory situation that does require a unitary treatment of the European reality but may perhaps be resolved through an "integration provision" in our Constitution. In this sense, it would be necessary to "Europeanize" the Spanish Constitution.

It goes beyond the scope of this analysis to describe the possible formula that could articulate such need.[52] It is enough to point out that there are two questions that must be highlighted in order to proceed to such integration of European Union law within the Constitution. In the first place, it would be necessary to clarify whether it would be enough to include in Art. 93 or in other articles—outside the "hard nucleus" of the Constitution—some provision on the European integration, such as the one included in Art. 23 of the Bonn Grundgesetz or Art. 88 of the French Constitution, which would state the primacy of European law on certain transferred powers. In the second place, in the case that such a provision was not deemed sufficient, clarification would be needed as to whether a constitutional revision of Art. 9 para 1 should take place and therefore the application of the qualified procedure of Art. 168.

The explicit mention of the denomination of the Autonomous Communities

The Spanish Constitution recognizes the right to autonomy (Art. 2 CE), which has already been exercised. When the Constitution was enacted, it was evident that Catalonia, the Basque Country, and Galicia—and perhaps Andalusia—would have exercised their right to autonomy. The decentralized territorial model was extended to the whole country and, currently, the system is fully structured into Autonomous Communities. It would be advisable to explicitly include within the Constitution the names of the current Autonomous Communities.[53] This inclusion would be a channel to make explicit in the text of the Constitution what already exists on the constitutional order, which has been termed the "Territorial Constitution of the State" (Constitution and the Status of Autonomies). The reform, in this case, would aim at achieving a simple objective: the incorporation, in the most aseptic possible way, of a list of the Autonomous Communities that currently constitute the State of Autonomies. Thus, the introduction of any added information that could be misinterpreted as the establishment of diverse categories of Autonomous Communities would be avoided. The aim, therefore, would be to finalize the territorial design that was opened up in 1978, updating it to the present moment.

Regarding the potential location in the Constitution for such a list, it is considered that the Preliminary Title could present more hurdles than advantages, given the qualified procedure of reform required on that part. It might be sufficient if it could be included within the framework of Title VIII, specifically in Art. 137 of the Spanish Constitution. Regarding the order in which the Autonomous Communities should be named, there are two possible objective criteria: alphabetical and chronological. In our opinion, the latter could be useful to acknowledge the role that *historic nationalities* (Catalonia, Basque Country, Galicia, and Andalusia) have developed as a motor of decentralization.[54]

Other proposals for reform

There are other reform proposals that have not gathered the same level of general consensus as those that have just been analyzed. They constitute a set of heterogeneous proposals, of different legal–constitutional importance, and of minor relevance. To start with, the Constitution states the right of foreigners to vote in the local elections, in accordance with "reciprocity criteria"—just to the foreigners that have been born in countries where Spaniards are allowed to vote (Art. 13 para 2 CE). Keeping the criteria of reciprocity is debatable for two reasons. The first is the fact that many immigrants come from non-democratic countries. The second is that votes are normally more bound to calculations about the decisions that policymakers will make than to considerations regarding the place of birth. It seems evident, in any case, that it is a constitutional provision that had more significance when Spain was a country of greater emigration.[55]

Article 15 CE states the right to life and abolishes the death penalty "except in those cases which may be established by military penal law in times of war." The Organic Act 11/1995 excluded the death penalty from the Military Criminal Code. However, if the Constitution remained unreformed on this point, the death penalty could be potentially activated again in the Criminal Code, if there was a sufficient parliamentary majority. This point justifies why some scholars suggest this question to be definitively closed at the constitutional level. It is considered that the right to life in Art. 15 should not have any exceptions.[56]

The privileged relation of the state with the Catholic Church is a recurrent topic in the political and scientific debate. When Art. 16 CE mentions the relations of cooperation between the state and religious entities, there is a specific reference to the Catholic Church. However, it cannot entail a privileged legal status without justification for the Catholic Church; in this sense, it would be unconstitutional to attribute to the Catholic Church qualitative differences without an objective and reasonable justification. But it is also true that these differences do exist; the legislation that implements the constitutional text is more generous with the Catholic Church than with the rest of the denominations that form part of the cooperation agreements with the state (i.e. Jewish, Muslims, and Protestants). In order to tackle such a privileged position, the doctrine debates whether Art. 16 CE should be reformed, or whether it would be sufficient to proceed to a radical amendment of the agreements of cooperation with the Holy See of 1979.[57]

In 1978, the Internet did not exist, and the technological revolution that would take place later on could not even have been guessed at. Article 18 CE guarantees the secrecy of communications, particularly "postal, telegraphic and telephonic communications [. . .]"; it also mentions that "the law shall limit the use of information, to guarantee personal and family privacy [. . .]." Perhaps it would be advisable to adapt these provisions to the new challenges posed by the digital era. Scholars are divided on this point: some authors are in favor of its amendment, while others consider that those fundamental rights could be effectively protected by the legislator, without needing to proceed to a constitutional revision.[58]

Act 17/1999, of 18 May, on the Regulation of the Military Forces Staff, repealed compulsory military service. Therefore, it also seemed logical that it would cease to be regulated in Art. 30 para 2 CE, which envisages the right to conscientious objection. However, the doctrine is divided between those who believe that this mention should disappear from the constitutional text, and those, on the contrary, who believe that Art. 30 para 2 should not be amended.[59] In the same way that the legislator opted to abolish the compulsory character of military service, it should also have the possibility to restore it, if this happened to be the decision-makers' option. This question was initially configured as a legislative option and it should continue to be that way.

There are also some pro-autonomy proposals that aim at the constitutional revision of Arts. 148 and 149 CE in order to bring an end to the indeterminate and flexible character of the constitutional design on the distribution of powers that, according to the proponents, have generated a centripetal dynamic favorable to the state interest, on the grounds of constitutional case law. It is argued that the Constitutional Court, drawing upon the ambiguity of the terms used in Arts. 148 and 149 CE, have extensively interpreted the concepts of legislative framework and some horizontal powers of the central state, to the detriment of some specific powers of the Autonomous Communities. According to some authors, this dynamic has led to a "low-quality" political autonomy: the Autonomous Communities would be mainly implementing political decisions taken by the central state. In this sense, the constitutional revision would aim to improve the precision and clarification of those principles and competences, as well as to design some sort of exclusive categories of competences (i.e. with a single list of exclusive powers of the central state, on the understanding that the Autonomous Communities would count on exclusive powers over the rest of the subjects).[60]

Finally, acknowledging the infrequent character of constitutional revision in Spain, and the problems that this has generated in the adjustment of the Constitution to reality, different authors have suggested the revision of the qualified procedure of reform provided by Art. 168. Article 168 establishes an excessively rigid procedure that has been blocking the evolution of our constitutional system.[61] It is deemed necessary either to eliminate Art. 168 CE, or at least to add some flexibility to it. The reform of this Article, according to a literal interpretation of the constitutional text, could be accomplished through the ordinary procedure of Art. 167 CE.

Notes

1 F. Tomás y Valiente, *Constitución: escritos de introducción histórica (Constitution: writings on the historic introduction)*, Marcial Pons, 1996, pp. 40ff.

2 P. de Vega, *La reforma constitucional y la problemática del poder constituyente (The constitutional reform and problems regarding the constituent power)*, Tecnos, 1985.

3 Valiente, op. cit., p. 42.

4 P. Cruz Villalón, *La formación del sistema europeo de control de constitucionalidad (1918–1939) (The creation of the European system of constitutional review [1918–1939])*, Centro de Estudios Constitucionales, 1987.

5 F.R. Llorente, "La reforma de la Constitución" ("The constitutional revision"), *Claves de Razón Práctica*, 2008, no. 188, pp. 4–8.

6 J. Pérez Royo, *La reforma de la Constitución (The constitutional revision)*, Congreso de los Diputados, 1987, p. 74.

7 S.A. Roura, *La defensa de la Constitución en la historia constitucional española (The protection of the Constitution in the Spanish constitutional history)*, Centro de Estudios Constitucionales, 1998, p. 147; Pérez Royo, op. cit., pp. 74ff.

8 Roura, op. cit., pp. 173ff.

9 Pérez Royo, op.cit., p. 91.
10 A. Sant'Ana, "Un análisis sobre la intangibilidad de las cláusulas pétreas" ("An analysis on the intangibility of the stony provisions"), *Derechos y libertades*, 2010, no. 22, pp. 241–60.
11 A.J. Sánchez Navarro, *La transición política en las Cortes de Franco: hacia la Ley para la Reforma Política (1975–1976) (The political transitions in Franco's regime: towards the Political Transition Act [1975–1976])*, Instituto Juan March, 1990.
12 I. de Otto, *Defensa de la Constitución y partidos políticos (Protection of the Constitution and political parties)*, Centro de Estudios Políticos y Constitucionales, 1985, pp. 9–58.
13 R. Blanco, *Introducción a la Constitución de 1978 (Introduction to the Constitution of 1978)*, Alianza, 1998, p. 197.
14 Pérez Royo, op. cit., p. 154.
15 L. Ortega, "La inconstitucionalidad de la reforma de la Ley Orgánica de Referéndum" ("The unconstitutionality of the reform of the Organic Law on Referendum"), *Revista de Administración Pública*, 1982, no. 97, pp. 141–86.
16 Pérez Royo, op. cit., pp. 176–84.
17 Ibid.
18 Ibid., pp. 194–7.
19 Ibid., pp. 197–9.
20 Ibid., pp. 207–14.
21 M. Aragón, "Reforma constitucional" ("Constitutional Revision"), *Enciclopedia Jurídica Básica*, Civitas, 1995, vol. IV, p. 5653; Pérez Royo, op. cit., p. 180.
22 Pérez Royo, op. cit., pp. 142–9.
23 Ibid., p. 124.
24 Ibid., p. 184.
25 Together with the other two exceptions of Art. 150 para 3 and Art. 155 of the Spanish Constitution.
26 P. Cruz Villalón, "Constitución y Reforma" ("Constitution and revision"), *Claves de la Razón Práctica*, 2001, no. 115, pp. 4–7.
27 J. Pérez Royo, "Una asignatura pendiente: la reforma de la Constitución" ("A pending subject: the constitutional revision"), *Revista Española de Derecho Constitucional*, 2003, no. 69, pp. 119–233.
28 Aragón, op. cit., p. 5657.
29 P. Cruz Villalón, *La Constitución inédita (The unprecedented Constitution)*, Trotta, 2004, p. 13.
30 Ibid., p. 14.
31 L. Martín-Retortillo, *La interconexión de los ordenamientos jurídicos y el sistema de fuentes del Derecho (The interconnection between the legal orders and the system of sources of Law)*, Civitas, 2004.
32 J. García Roca (Coord.), *La Europa de los derechos: el Convenio Europeo de Derechos Humanos (The Europe of rights: the European Convention of Human Rights)*, Centro de Estudios Políticos y Constitucionales, 2005.
33 P. Häberle, *Libertad, igualdad, fraternidad. 1789 como historia, actualidad y futuro del Estado Constitucional (Liberty, equality, fraternity. 1789 as history, present and future of the Constitutional State)*, Trotta, 1998.
34 Declaration 1/2004.
35 Martín-Retortillo, op. cit., pp. 74–80.
36 SSTC 119/2001 and 16/2004.
37 STC 18/1981.
38 J.D. González Campos, "Las normas internacionales sobre derechos humanos y los derechos fundamentales y libertades reconocidos en la Constitución española (Art. 10.2)" ("The international provisions on human rights and freedoms on the Spanish Constitution [Art. 10.2]"), in P. Cruz Villalón, J.D. González Campos and

M. Rodríguez-Piñero, *Tres lecciones sobre la Constitución (Three lessons on the Constitution)*, Margablum, 1999, p. 46.

39 SSTC 214/1991 and 235/2007.

40 A. Barrero, *La libertad religiosa en España (The freedom of religion in Spain)*, Centro de Estudios Políticos y Constitucionales, 2006, pp. 410–18.

41 B. Rodríguez, *El secreto de las comunicaciones: tecnología e intimidad (The secrecy of communications: technology and privacy)*, McGraw-Hill, 1998, pp. 85ff.

42 González Campos, op. cit., pp. 52–4.

43 E. Aja and C. Viver, "Valoración de 25 años de autonomía" ("Assessment of 25 years of political autonomy"), *Revista Española de Derecho Constitucional*, 2003, no. 69, pp. 103–10; M. Holgado, "Cómo articular la participación de las Comunidades Autónomas en el proceso europeo de toma de decisiones" ("How to articulate the participation of the Autonomous Communities in the European decision-making processes"), *Revista Vasca de Administración Pública*, 2006, no. 74, pp. 299–313.

44 J.F. López Aguilar, "Maastricht y la problemática de la reforma constitucional" ("Maastricht and the problems on constitutional revision"), *Revista de Estudios Políticos*, 1992, no. 77, pp. 57ff.; E. Arnaldo, "El derecho de sufragio de los extranjeros en las elecciones locales" ("The right of suffrage of foreigners in the local elections"), *Revista Española de Derecho Constitucional*, 1992, no. 34, pp. 67ff.; F.R. Llorente, "La Constitución española y el Tratado de Maastricht" ("The Spanish Constitution and the Treaty of Maastricht"), *Revista Española de Derecho Constituciona*, 1992, no. 36, pp. 253ff.; M. Aragón, "La Constitución española y el TUE: la reforma de la Constitución" ("The Spanish Constitution and the TEU"), *Revista Española de Derecho Constituciona*, 1994, no. 42, pp. 9ff.

45 Declaration 1/1992.

46 Reform of Art. 13.2 of Spanish Constitution (BOE 08/28/1992).

47 Reform of Art. 135 of Spanish Constitution (BOE 09/27/2011).

48 Report of the Council of State (02/16/2006).

49 See the academic debates on the Crown, in F. Rubio Llorente and J. Álvarez Junco (eds), *El informe del Consejo de Estado sobre la reforma constitucional (Report of the Council of State on the constitutional revision)*, Centro de Estudios Políticos y Constitucionales, 2006, pp. 273ff.

50 See the academic debates on the Senate, in Llorente and Junco (eds), op. cit., pp. 709ff.

51 F.R. Llorente, "Sobre la conveniencia de terminar la Constitución antes de acometer su reforma" ("About the need to end the Constitution before embarking on its reform"), in F.R. Llorente, *La forma del poder (The shape of power)*, Centro de Estudios Constitucionales, 1993, pp. 165–73.

52 Llorente and Junco (eds), op. cit., pp. 457ff.

53 Ibid., pp. 565ff.

54 M. Medina, "La inclusión de las Comunidades Autónomas—y ciudades autónomas - en el texto constitucional (o sobre la conveniencia de preservar el principio dispositivo en la concreción de las Comunidades Autónomas)" ("The inclusion of the Autonomous Communities—and autonomous cities—within the constitutional text (or about the appropriateness of preserving the disposal principle when specifying the Autonomous Communities)"), in Llorente and Junco (eds), op. cit., pp. 609–10.

55 F. Vacas, "El principio de reciprocidad como condición del reconocimiento del derecho al sufragio de extranjeros en las elecciones municipales en España y sus implicaciones desde el Derecho Internacional" ("The principle of reciprocity as a condition to recognize the right of foreigners to vote in the local elections in Spain and its implications for international law"), *Revista de Derecho migratorio y extranjería*, 2009, no. 20, pp. 77–96.

56 M. Fuencisla, "Propuesta de reforma del artículo 15 de la Constitución" ("Suggestion for revision of Art. 15 CE"), in M. Carrillo and H. López (Coord.), *La Constitución Europea (The European Constitution)*, Tirant Lo Blanch, 2004, pp. 223–32.

57 Barrero, op. cit., pp. 410–18.

58 M.L. Fernández, "El impacto de las nuevas tecnologías e Internet en los derechos del artículo 18 de la Constitución" ("The impact of the new technologies and Internet on the rights of Article 18 of the Constitution"), *Anuario de la Facultad de Derecho de Extremadura*, 1999, no. 17, pp. 523–44.

59 G. Cámara, "Nota sobre el desarrollo de los derechos y libertades fundamentales a los veinticinco años de vigencia de la Constitución de 1978" ("Note on the development of the fundamental rights and freedoms 25 years after the enactment of the Constitution of 1978"), in M.L. Balaguer (Coord.), *XXV Aniversario de la Constitución Española: propuestas de reformas* (*XXV Anniversary of the Spanish Constitution: proposals for reform*), Diputación de Málaga, 2004, pp. 183–214.

60 Aja and Viver, op. cit., pp. 103–10.

61 P. García-Escudero, "El procedimiento agravado de reforma de la Constitución de 1978" ("The qualified procedure of constitutional revision in the Constitution of 1978"), *Revista de Derecho Político*, 2008, nos. 71–2, pp. 175–93.

16 Constitutional amendment in Sweden

Lars-Göran Malmberg

Introduction

Any discussion on amending the Swedish Constitution requires a brief introduction to the Constitution itself. It is not an easy task to understand or even detect what is referred to as the Constitution under the Swedish legal system. The biggest challenge is that of terminology in the Swedish legal context. There is no single document referred to as the Constitution, as normally seen in other European countries. Instead, four fundamental laws form the so-called Swedish Constitution. First and foremost of them is the Instrument of Government (IG);[1] second is the Act of Succession;[2] third is the Freedom of the Press Act;[3] and fourth is the Fundamental Law on Freedom of Expression.[4] These four fundamental laws were introduced in different periods and under varied circumstances. In the ensuing discussion, a brief background of these four laws is presented, as the main rules relating to the amendment procedures are laid down within the IG. Also notable in this context is the Riksdag Act, which is a piece of legislation between the fundamental laws and ordinary law. It is referred to as an in-between or quasi-fundamental law, because some of the rules pertaining thereto may be amended through a process similar to the fundamental laws, with the others following the amendment procedure of any ordinary law.

The development of the Swedish Constitution has been and is less dramatic than that observed in other European countries. The developmental process of this area of law is not very well researched and documented, although other areas relating to the Swedish fundamental laws have generated more interest amongst legal scholars and researchers. Therefore, it is difficult to find source materials to carry out a comprehensive study of the amendment procedures in Sweden. The most detailed discussions available on the subject are found in the study conducted by Professor Robert Malmgren in 1926 on the Swedish Fundamental Laws,[5] and that by the Swedish Riksdag published as 'The Swedish Constitution' with introductory chapters written by Judge Erik Holmberg and Professor Nils Stjernquist.[6] The latter is the only text available in English providing an in-depth analysis of the Swedish fundamental laws.[7]

Following the introduction, the first part of this chapter provides a brief historical overview of the development of constitutional legislation in Sweden starting from the fourteenth century onwards. The discussion on the developmental process also requires attention to be paid to the significant move that the 'Constitution' of 1809 provided, best described as a quiet revolution. The second part examines the amendment procedures found in the IG of 1809, which was subsequently replaced by the current IG. The third part describes the amendment procedures and also provides an in-depth understanding of these procedures, which foster democratic debate and participation by the civil society in the continuing development of the fundamental laws. The fourth part focuses on the constitutional amendment process and the role of the people. This part mainly examines the various possibilities to have a referendum on proposals on a fundamental law, which is held in abeyance over an election. The final part concludes the article with some closing remarks.

Constitutional history

Sweden has had a written constitution since the middle of the fourteenth century, when the first national legal code was drawn up by the reigning king at that time, King Magnus Ericsson. The code was called the *Landslag* or Magnus Ericsson's Law, after the King. The Royal Charter in this early legislation contained, among other provisions, rules regarding the election of the King, description of his duties, his powers to raise taxes, and the election and functions of the members of the Council of State. Later authors have described this as rules closely relating to the present IG. This law in a revised form was promulgated in 1442 as Kristofer's Law. Scholars tend to say that few alterations between the two laws are visible in the contemporary context. Over the ensuing years, additions to the Royal Charter were made during a period that could be described as the development of modern Sweden; such additions were succession pacts, which regulated the succession to the throne,[8] royal wills[9] and royal accessions charters.[10]

A notable change was made during the reign of Gustaf II Adolf. Even though his Accession Charter could be described as a capitulation on the part of the monarchy, his reign showed the opposite in the way that he took all the decisions that perhaps were to be taken care of by the Council of State. This situation changed when the King was killed in the Battle of Lützen in 1632, leaving as his heir his infant daughter Christina. To guide the regents, an administrative order was drawn up by the Chancellor, Axel Oxenstierna. This administrative order, named the Instrument of Government, was established in 1634. It did not, however, supersede the Royal Charter, and when Queen Christina took power, she did not adhere to the IG. When the second long regency was about to begin in 1660, however, a decision was taken to run the government in accordance with the IG from 1634. A protocol was added to the IG according to which the Parliament (the Estates) would convene every three years, which was a novelty. This is when the Parliament was established as an institution of the state and not as it had been previously (i.e. an institution that met the King at his bidding). But, at the time of his accession to the throne, Carl XI decided against the idea of making the IG a constitutionally binding instrument; instead, he had Parliament declare that the King was not bound by the IG and could alter it at will. This led to the establishment of the Carolingian era of absolutism, which ended with the death of Carl XII in 1718. After this period of autocratic rule, a period defined by a newly formed IG began. The new IG was enacted in 1719 and replaced in 1720 by another IG. In conjunction with the development of the new documents, a new Accession Charter was adopted in both 1719 and 1720. The power of the Parliament was strengthened through the IG of 1720 in the sense that the King had to obey the rule of the majority. Important parts in the IG were that the King possessed two votes and a casting vote in the Council of State. Nomination to the Council of the State was listed by a Committee of the Riksdag and, originally, the King could choose between three candidates, but this prerogative was later withdrawn from the King.

The Parliament was in the 'Age of Liberty', comprised of members from two different parties, Hats and Caps. Regulating the work in the Riksdag was set in the Riksdag Act. The first Act originated from 1617 when the work in the Riksdag was in the hands of the King. A second, in which the work in the Riksdag had to be more carefully regulated, was promulgated in 1723. The Act contained rules on procedure and forms for the business in the Riksdag. These rules formed the tradition upon which the Riksdag of today has its roots. In the same spirit, when the new Parliament was established, a completely new Freedom of the Press Act was promulgated in 1766, which established the principle of public access to official documents. At this time, there is also a clear distinction between basic laws (i.e. the fundamental laws) and other Acts of law. The clear distinction was that fundamental laws could only be changed after approval of two decisions by the Riksdag.[11] It should be stressed that, before 1867, all sessions were preceded by an election. From 1766 onwards, there are three different laws that form the fundamental laws of Sweden; the Instrument of Government, the Riksdag Act and the Freedom of the Press Act.

Sweden has not been excluded from political backlashes supported by over-ambitious legislators pushing democratic development too far. In the Swedish case, King Gustaf III conducted a first coup d'état in 1772, which led to a new IG establishing an instrument based on a division of power between the King and Riksdag. In 1789, a second coup d'état took place, and an Act of Union and Security was imposed, which in its terms led to the King becoming an autocratic ruler. This autocratic system ended in 1809, when Gustaf IV was deposed after an unfortunate involvement in the Napoleonic War and with the loss of Finland. A new IG was promulgated that same year. The new IG was based on the same division of power as was established by the IG from 1772. This could be divided into three different areas where this division of power was visible. The first area regarded the executive power, which was held by the King, and the Councillors of State maintained just an advisory role. The second area established a shared power regarding the legislative functions. The fundamental laws, civil laws, and criminal laws were shared between the Riksdag and the King, while economic and administrative legislation remained the exclusive prerogative of the King. The Riksdag was provided with the power over taxation and the budget, together with detailed power of supervision. In the Supreme Court, the King still retained his two votes but never really interfered in the Court's work. In 1810, Sweden saw a new dynasty established by Jean Baptiste Bernadotte, who ascended the throne in Sweden as Carl XIV Johan. Accession to the throne is regulated through the Act of Succession dated from 1810 and is still in force.

The fundamental laws of Sweden during the beginning of the nineteenth century were the IG (1809), the Riksdag Act (1810), the Act of Succession (1810) and the Freedom of the Press Act (1812). The IG from 1809 survived until 1974, when it was replaced by the IG prevailing today. The IG of 1809 was amended numerous times between 1809 and 1974, and the consequences of the amendments to the IG made it necessary to put an end to the second oldest constitution in the world. Today, the fundamental laws in Sweden are the IG (1974), the Act of Succession (1810), the Freedom of the Press Act (1949) and the Fundamental Law on Freedom of Expression (1991), and, as an in-between legislation (quasi-fundamental law), the Riksdag Act (1974).

Evolution of the constitutional amendment procedure

The discussion above makes clear that the amendment procedures were first introduced in the IG of 1809.The fundamental laws enacted between 1809 and 1812 were all a consequence of the coup d'état when King Gustaf IV was deposed from power. In the absence of a dominant monarch at the time of the establishment of the fundamental laws from this era, it was not difficult to firmly set the principles of a division of power in the IG. It is in this context that the amendment procedures should be investigated.

In most Swedish textbooks on public law, the discussions regarding the fundamental laws indicate that there should be a restricted use of the instruments to change these laws. Some constitutions are constructed in such way that the level of detail in the instruments withstands the change of time. In the Swedish IG, the level of detail is rather high, which means that there has to be a flexible system in the rules of revision of the text. It should be noted, however, that the revision of the IG as well as of the other three present fundamental laws are subject to the same procedures for revision or amendments.

In the IG from 1809, the provision on revision of the fundamental laws can be found in Art. 81. The substance of this Article reads as follows: this IG and other fundamental laws of the Realm could not be altered or repealed without the decision being taken by the King and two decisions by the Riksdag, and with a general election to the Riksdag between the two decisions. The safeguard provided was that two decisions were to be taken in the Riksdag and a general election to the Parliament held in-between the two decisions. This principle was already established in 1766, and the reason behind this was to enable a decisive referendum to be held on a matter of fundamental law. In Art. 85, the fundamental laws were named and enacted through a joint decision by the King and Parliament in accordance with the provisions described in the IG. From the text of Art. 81 of the IG of 1809, it was further stated that a revision of the fundamental laws could be initiated solely by either the King or the Riksdag. If the King would take the opportunity to initiate a proposal, this had to be announced to the Riksdag, which in turn had to be reported back to the King when the decision for approval was taken. On the other hand, if the initiative was taken by Parliament and this proposal was approved within the Riksdag, the decision had to be submitted to the King. To ensure that there were no delays in preparing the proposal, the King had to convene the Council of State[12] before the closing of the parliamentary meetings of the year. In ordinary matters of lawmaking, the King had an opportunity to reflect on the proposal to the next year's summoning of the Riksdag.

Robert Malmgren[13] writes that a decision to alter, amend, or abolish a whole law or an Act in the law has to be carried out through a decision made by the King and the Riksdag. Even if it is not clearly expressed in the IG, it is the fundamental understanding that the basic principle in the IG, that the country is ruled by the King and the Riksdag, should not be altered or abolished. Such a proposition should be rejected without any consideration in the Riksdag. This could be considered as a constitutional praxis. Furthermore, Art. 38 para 1 in the Riksdag Act stated that the Committee on Constitutions shall refrain from issuing proposals to amend the fundamental laws in any circumstances other than those in which it is absolutely necessary. Even though an amendment, adjustment or abolition of a fundamental law could not be performed without the consent of the King, it is not proper to describe this as a veto.

Regarding the meaning of the King, it should be noted that during the twentieth century there was a transfer of the rights vested in the King's power to the government in that the government was delegated the power in the name of the King. Decisions made by the government were named *Kungl. Majt.*, which is an acronym for the Swedish term for Royal Highness.

The most recent revision of the IG took place in 1974. It was a major change from the IG of 1809, leading to a modernized instrument with the move from division of powers to a more functionality oriented IG. Since its introduction in 1974, there have been revisions of the text more or less at the time of the general elections to the Riksdag. At the election to the Riksdag in 2010, a major revision of the whole IG of 1974 was carried out and the text was set in a more pedagogical manner. New chapters were introduced and some of the chapters were subdivided with special headings not seen previously. The text was also modernized.

Formal constitutional amendment process

The Swedish procedure for amending the IG or any other fundamental laws does not differ from amending any ordinary law in the Swedish legal system. Changing a law or a fundamental law starts with an initiative from either the Riksdag or the government. In the Riksdag, the members can initiate the process through submitting a proposal by means of a private members' motion. Private members' motions may be introduced once a year on any matter falling within the Riksdag's jurisdiction. This is called the general period for the introduction of private members' motions: it runs from the beginning of the Riksdag's session and lasts as long as a private members' motion may be introduced on account of the Budget Bill from the government. The other possibility for the members to table a motion arises from a Government Bill. A motion arising from a Government Bill has to be connected to the subject matter in the Bill. The other initiative that may start the revision of a particular legislation could be a report from one of the committees of the Riksdag. To handle matters connected with bills, written documentations, private members' motions and proposals from an agency under the Riksdag, a number of committees under the Riksdag are appointed for each electoral period among its members. There are three committees that could be described as standing committees, as they are mentioned in both the IG and the Riksdag Act.[14] At present, there are 15 committees in total under the Riksdag and they all hold different jurisdictions. Their right to present proposals is limited to their jurisdiction. If the Riksdag finds that a members' motion or a report from the committee has such importance that action by the government should be taken, the Riksdag can decide that the government has to start preparing a bill on the matter. The Committee on the Constitution, in their yearly report to the Riksdag, will then check whether the government has issued a directive to a committee to prepare the legislation or not. Since the government is responsible to the Riksdag,[15] the way to check how the government carries out matters presented to it is through the Committee on the Constitution. An initiative to start the process of drafting new legislation could also come from the government, either from within the government or from any of its administrative agencies. A possible way to initiate a change in the legislation could also come from a pressure group or a lobby group.

When the initiative has been approved and the process starts, a directive is issued by the Head of the Department in charge of the domain in which that legislation falls. The government is supported by a Government Chancery for the preparation of governmental business. This Chancery comprises ministries in different areas of activity.[16] Each ministry is led by a Minister who is generally referred to as the Head of Department in official documents and literature. In the case of a revision of the fundamental laws, the department in question is the Department of Justice. In the directive, the task of the assigned committee is formalized. The Head of Department provides instructions to the committee tasked with revising the legislation. In the instructions, the Head of Department issues a working timeline; normally a committee is allowed a two-year working period and should deliver their committee report within this time frame. In the instructions, the number of participants to the committee is decided. Furthermore, it is decided whether it should be a parliamentary committee or a committee within the department. Finally, the Head of Department issues detailed instructions regarding the legislation that is in focus for the revision.

The Working Committee established for the revision of the IG of 1974 was summoned in 2004. The directive was decided in a Cabinet meeting on 1 July 2004. In these instructions it was stated that the Committee should be a parliamentary one and should present its findings in a report by 31 December 2004. The Committee chairman will be the first to be empowered by the Head of Department, and then the members of the Committee will be nominated and empowered. The Committee will be calling experts to deal with special areas, making sure that people from academia are represented.

The Committee, as a parliamentary committee, will present a report in a series of Swedish Public Reports (originally referred to as *Sveriges Offentliga Utredningar* [SOU]). These reports are published on a yearly basis with numbering commencing each year. If it is a committee that works within the department, the report will be issued under a series called the Departmental Series (DS). When the report is presented to the Head of Department, the next step is to circulate it for consideration by the bodies tasked to review it. The bodies to which a proposed legislative measure is referred for consideration are both mandatory bodies and facultative bodies. Among the mandatory bodies we find the two supreme courts, namely the Supreme Court and the Administrative Supreme Court, the Parliament Ombudsman and a number of other courts. Among those that may be selected as consideration bodies are the law faculties of universities. In an important review such as the IG, the university will be selected but the task would be handed over to the Law Faculty by the Vice-Chancellor of the university. The main reason behind consideration by the bodies to the Working Committee's work is to find out if there would be any other considerations to the presented work. The author of this article was involved in presenting a consideration that stopped a proposal to the Riksdag from the government.

When all consideration has been collected by the government, preparation of a bill to the Riksdag is carried out. Before the proposed bill is presented, it will be scrutinized by the Law Council. The Law Council comprises judges from the two Supreme Courts. They evaluate the proposal, both from a constitutional perspective and also examining the critical views against the Working Committee report offered by the consideration bodies. The Law Council is as close to a Constitutional Court as the Swedish parliamentary system would tolerate, as it stands today. Even if the high judges from the Supreme Courts have their doubts about a special legislation, the Head of Department still has the last word in the proposal to the Riksdag. However, it is usually the case that the Head of Department will closely follow the advice of the Law Council on legal matters.

The next step is to put the Governmental Bill to the Riksdag. This bill is composed in the same way as an ordinary law proposal. According to the Riksdag Act,[17] the bill shall always be accompanied by the Cabinet minutes of the matter, by an account of earlier deliberation on the matter and by the opinion of the Law Council, if available. Bills relating to an amendment of fundamental law must be presented to the Riksdag, allowing sufficient time for the Committee of the Constitution to consider them, and also reasonably ahead of a general election to the Riksdag. The present wording in the IG, after the last revision in 2011,[18] may be summarized as follows: a fundamental law is enacted by means of two decisions with identical wording. Through the first decision, the proposal for the enactment of a fundamental law is adopted and held in abeyance. The second decision may not be taken until elections to the Riksdag have been held throughout the Realm. After the newly elected Riksdag has convened, a second decision shall be made. To make sure that there would be a proper debate around the proposal, both in the Riksdag and in Swedish society, there is a time bar between the two decisions, which requires that at least nine months shall elapse between the first submission of the matter to the Chamber of the Riksdag and the date of elections. If the timeline is not met, the Committee on the Constitution could grant an exception. Such a decision is to be taken no later than the committee stage and at least five-sixths of the members must vote in favour of the decision. It is further stated that the Riksdag may not adopt a decision held in abeyance over an election proposal for the enactment of a fundamental law, which is in conflict with another proposal concerning a fundamental law currently being held in abeyance. This could of course be corrected if, at the same time, the Riksdag rejects the proposal first adopted.[19]

When a Governmental Bill is presented to the Riksdag, it shall be referred to a committee for consideration. When the committee has deliberated over the bill, a report shall be notified to the Riksdag. After the notification to the Chamber, it shall be tabled twice at meetings of the Chamber before settlement. The Riksdag can determine, in response to a proposal from the committee or from the Speaker, that the matter shall be settled after having been tabled only once. It is important to note that a committee report shall not be notified to the Chamber before copies have been distributed to members of the Riksdag.[20]

Regarding the final settlement of a matter held in abeyance over an election under the rules laid down in chapter 8 of the IG, the matter has to be settled at the first parliamentary session of the electoral period, within which a final decision may be taken under the rules laid down in the IG, provided the matter has not already been rejected. This settlement may be deferred to another parliamentary session, but it has to be decided by the Riksdag. A decision of this nature may be repeated. The matter shall be settled finally before the next ordinary election to the Riksdag. If there should be an extraordinary election to the Riksdag, it may permit consideration of the matter to be deferred to the first parliamentary session of the next electoral period.

Pursuant to the rules under the IG and the Riksdag Act, the decision on a matter has to be made through two decisions with identical wording. It is also important to note that there has to be a proper time to discuss the content in the proposals. In the general election in 1991, a new party entered the Swedish Riksdag, and at the same time the Fundamental Law on the Freedom of Expression was held in abeyance, waiting for it to be settled under the first parliamentary session of the electoral period. The situation that emerged was that the new party, named 'New Democracy', requested time to review the proposal and to propose adjustment before the final decision. After being made aware of the actual wording in the IG regarding amendment procedures to fundamental laws, the parliamentary members of the 'New Democracy' party voted together with all other members to accept the Fundamental Law on the Freedom of Expression.

The system for amending the IG and other fundamental laws, as it was established through the introduction in the old IG from 1809, has been kept more or less in its original wording. Although the division of power between the King and the Riksdag was later modified to separating functions between the Riksdag and the government, the basic principle of a proposal for an amendment or an introduction of new legislation resulting in two decisions in the Riksdag with a general election to the Riksdag throughout the Realm has been kept intact. There has been little by way of academic discussion regarding this provision. There were no debates whatsoever during development of the IG of 1974, and the same goes for the latest review of the IG in 2010. A common conception of the provisions is provided by statements by the Head of Department and Committee on the Constitution that the provision for changing the Constitution is not meant to be an easy way to amend or change the fundamental laws over-eagerly.

Nevertheless, there have been constant revisions or amendments to the IG over the years. Looking at the number of changes to the IG, it is very rare to find no amendments awaiting a second decision after general elections. On the other hand, the elaborations necessary to finally achieve a version acceptable to all political parties for approval of the new IG in 1974 were, in certain cases, very difficult, and there were a lot of different articles and sections that needed further discussions and elaborations. Even after the latest major revision, there are still standpoints of different political parties to take into account for future revisions.

The role of the people

In the earlier parts of this article, a point was made regarding the different ways to provide for an initiative to amend or make changes to the fundamental laws. As already stated, it is the private members of the Riksdag, a Riksdag Committee, agencies under the Riksdag, and the government who have the right to present an initiative to the Riksdag. There are no such openings in Sweden for the ordinary citizen. One possibility is to try and get a private member of the Riksdag from the constituency to raise a motion during the general period for the introduction of private members' motions. The other possibility would be to act through some organization to promote a certain question. There are many organizations that have connections to the government and can thereby exert influence in different matters.

The only possibility for the common person to have influence in the process of amending a fundamental law is if the Riksdag decides to have a referendum on a proposal concerning fundamental law that is held in abeyance over an election. This would be held if a motion to this effect is supported by at least one-tenth of the members (i.e. 35 members), and if at least one-third of the members vote in favour of the motion (i.e. 117 members). This kind of referendum relating to a proposal on a fundamental law in abeyance *has never been held*. There are, in fact, few barring rules to make it difficult to carry out, but the initiative has never been used. The formal requirements, apart from the number of private members to vote in favour, is that the motion must be put forward within 15 days from the day the Riksdag adopted the proposal to be held in abeyance. The consequence of such a motion is that it should not be referred for preparation to a committee and that the referendum should be held simultaneously with general elections.

At the time of the referendum, the persons entitled to vote in general elections may declare whether they accept the proposal on fundamental law, which is being held in abeyance. To reject the proposal there are two criteria to fulfil: first, those taking part in the referendum and vote against the proposal are the majority; and second, this majority exceeds one-half of those who registered a valid vote in the election. If this is the case, then the proposal is rejected; in other cases, the proposal goes forward to the Riksdag for final consideration.[21]

The possibilities for the common person to affect the fundamental laws are, in other words, rather limited. The question is whether there is a need for more influence by the people outside the Riksdag. It is held that the present formulation of the IG contains enough elements to secure democratic stability through the discussions in the Riksdag, and the openness in the debates and access to public documents. It could be discussed whether the instrument for referendum should be used in the case of a fundamental law awaiting the final decision. The reason for not using the instrument cannot be based on the complicated manner or difficulties of handling it during the general election, since the procedures for elections are well established and the administrative authorities handling these issues are well prepared for such an event. A sense of insecurity prevails among the private members and the political parties in the Riksdag, prompting the argument that there will be difficulties in presenting the idea to the public to have a referendum on such an issue. It should be noted, though, that the number of referendums in local governmental matters is rising and the number of voters in these referendums is rather high. It may be that this will spill over to matters of more general questions, and that it would be possible to foresee referendums in matters relating to fundamental laws too.

Some critical and final remarks

In the introduction to this chapter, which relates to discussion on amendment to the Swedish fundamental laws, the author made a remark about the fact that the Swedish Constitution consists not of one but of four different laws. The amendment procedures, as they are described, follow a pattern more or less established in 1809, and very little changes have been made other than the change from a division-of-power philosophy to dividing different functions between the Riksdag and the government. Sweden has also been spared, since 1809, from the wars in Europe in such a way that there has not been a need to rethink the structures of the fundamental laws. In other European countries, as well as countries in the rest of the world, more discussions took place regarding the implication of legal cultures as a foundation for the reconstruction of the Constitution. This has been the fact for many of the emerging states after the fall of colonial powers in the middle of the twentieth century. The Swedish development of slowly establishing the state from the twelfth century to the present has been a process whereby the legal culture of Sweden has developed into the Constitution as it appears today.

A point worth making is that there have been very few academic discussions concerning the amendment procedures over the years. Even at the time when the revision of the IG of 1809 was carried out, during the 1970s, there were no traces of an in-depth debate on provisions for amending the fundamental laws. The setting in the IG for amending fundamental laws seems to be uncomplicated from a Swedish perspective. One of the few things that was stressed in the 1974 revision was the nine-month period between the two votes to make sure that the Riksdag is allowed enough time to debate the amendment.

While there has been a rather intense debate in Europe on different forms of majority voting for the change of treaties in international public law or within the EU, this has not been the case in Sweden. The main reason for this is that all parties are represented in the Working Committees that precede every amendment of the fundamental laws, and the rule on two decisions of identical wording makes it an effective block against a new party entering the Riksdag, after a general election, to vote against such a proposal.

The criticism that should be made concerns the relative ease with which the IG is amended. A fundamental law should be 'fundamental' in the sense that it is the backbone of the state and should be difficult (not impossible, but difficult) to amend or change. As the situation is with the present IG, there is an amendment to the text before every general election to the Riksdag. This indicates that too many Articles of a nature that dictates constant need of revision, as they seem to have a 'best-before/use-by date' built into them. Perhaps a solution might be that fundamental laws are contained in one document with a limited number of Articles, forming the backbone of the state, and the remaining set of Articles of lesser importance are placed in another document such as the Riksdag Act. Under the proposed arrangement, provisions of higher value may be amended following the same formalities as prescribed currently for amending a fundamental law, and provisions with a lower value may be amended as any ordinary law. This would perhaps give more formal stability to a text termed Constitution. Malmgren[22] noted in 1926 that legislation of a fundamental character should not be subject to constant revisions, and it is observed that the situation against which he reacted still persists.

Notes

1 In Swedish: Regeringsformen (1974: 152).
2 In Swedish: Successionsordningen (1809: 0926).
3 In Swedish: Tryckfrihetsförordningen (1949: 105).
4 In Swedish: Yttrandefrihetsgrundlagen (1991: 1469).
5 R. Malmgren, *Sveriges Grundlagar (The Fundamental Laws of Sweden)*, Stockholm, 1926.
6 The Swedish Constitution, published by the Sveriges Riksdag in 1996.
7 There is some other literature dealing partly with constitutional matters, but it is mostly to be considered as textbooks for foreign students to courses like "Introduction to Swedish Law". One such is M. Bogdan (ed.), *Swedish Legal System*, Norstedts Juridik, 2010.
8 First dated in 1544.
9 First dated in 1560.
10 First dated in 1594.
11 The terminology used in this text is the Swedish word for Parliament, i.e. Riksdag. This is the word used in both the Instrument of Government and in the Riksdag Act, which are the most commonly used legislative texts in this article.

12 Council of State in the 1809 IG is the same as the government today. In the old IG, the King ruled the country; this was changed to the government in the 1974 IG.
13 Malmgren, op. cit., p. 75.
14 These are the Committee on the Constitution, the Committee on Finance and the Committee on Taxation.
15 See IG Chap. 1, Art. 6.
16 See IG Chap. 7, Art. 1.
17 The Riksdag Act Chap 3, Art. 1.
18 See IG Chap. 8, Art. 14.
19 See IG Chap. 8, Art. 15.
20 See the Riksdag Act Chap. 5, Art. 1 and Supp Prov 5.1.1.
21 See IG Chap. 8, Art. 16.
22 Malmgren, op. cit., p. 74.

17 Constitutional revision

The case of Switzerland

Thomas Fleiner

Evolution of the constitutional revision procedure

Historical formation of the main features of constitutional change

Transformation of the confederation into federation

Switzerland calls itself a Confederation, but in 1848 it constitutionally became a federal country. Unlike Canada, it has developed its federal system from the bottom up, based on sovereign cantons that created the Swiss Confederation. Originally, Switzerland was a confederation of independent member states held together by the Treaty of 1813, which could only be amended by unanimous vote of its members. After a short civil war, the confederation was transformed into a federation, which maintained the title "Confederation of Switzerland" primarily for reasons of translation due to the four languages used there. However, unlike the United States or the European Union, the members of the Constitution Drafting Diet decided that the Constitution they were proposing to the people and the cantons could enter into force with the approval of a double majority: that of the voters and the cantons. Without formal legitimacy, they abolished the revision provisions of the Treaty of 1813, which could only be amended or revised with the unanimous consent of all cantons.

Thus, unlike the United States, which gave each state the opportunity to ratify and thus to incorporate the new Constitution, and required nine states to ratify in order to adopt the Constitution for those states, the Swiss citizens could only vote within their canton. Moreover, cantons that voted against the Constitution were nevertheless obliged to accept the vote of the majority of the cantons and the people. This procedure is now also the case for any revision of the Constitution. In contrast to the United States, where two-thirds of the state legislatures have to adopt any "amendment to" the Constitution, and to Canada, where each province has to adopt the most important constitutional provisions, the Swiss constitutional revision process is much more flexible. This procedure for installing the new Federation, which required the combined majority of the voting citizens and cantons, has basically remained unaltered since its foundation, although in the following two centuries it has been augmented with additional democratic rights for the citizens.

The system of constitutional revision in any federal country is of utmost importance for the understanding and functioning of its federal system. It indicates the position of the federal units and the federal legislature representing the federal power with regard to the constitution-making process. Furthermore, in addition to a Federal Constitution, many federal systems also enable the federal units to have their own constitutions, including special provisions for the revision of the constitution of each federal unit respectively. The harmonization of the revisions of the federal and cantonal constitutions thus addresses the most important procedural questions in regard to the revision of the constitutions of federal units and the supremacy of federal law.

Direct democracy as the main instrument for constitutional revisions

When Switzerland introduced its Federal Constitution in 1848, the drafters provided a legislative procedure for the revision of the Constitution, which, with the combined majority of both Swiss voters and cantons, was a compromise between the liberal centralists (opting for a simple majority) and the conservative federalists (opting for robust cantonal influence) regarding federal constitution-making. According to this compromise, any constitutional revision had to be proposed unanimously by the national Chamber (representing the majority) and the Council (representing the cantons). Therefore, any constitutional revision could only enter into force with the approval of the majority of Swiss voters and the majority of the cantons.

The Constitution of 1848 was inspired by the revolutionary spirit of the founding fathers, who were influenced by several cantonal constitutions that were adopted following the French Revolution of July 1830. The founders introduced important democratic rights for the people in the procedure of drafting the new Constitution. Thus, by popular initiative, 50,000 people could require the revision of the Constitution. In addition, if one Chamber of the legislature decided to revise the Constitution and the other Chamber rejected the proposal, the people had to make the final decision on this stalemate.[1]

Cantonal constitutions, which were established following the French Revolution, were primarily the result of a popular uprising against the entrenched political elites. While those insurgencies were initiated by liberal movements, the development of direct democracy was later undertaken by a more radical movement that demanded the installation of the citizens as the sovereign organ of the cantonal constitutions.

The Constitution of the Confederation followed the design already in force in most of the cantons. Consequently, the new Constitution could only enter into force after it had been approved through a constitutional referendum by the people and the cantons. Thus, the first Federal Constitution was approved by the majority of the people and the cantons. With regard to direct democracy, this Constitution only provided for two different possibilities in which the voters could intervene in constitutional matters. The most important was the fundamental right of the citizens to approve any constitutional decision. The second political right of the citizens was their right, through a general initiative, to require the two Chambers of Parliament to propose new constitutional amendments or to establish a totally revised new constitution.

Thus, since the establishment of the Federal Constitution in 1848, direct democracy has become the main instrument for any constitutional revision. All constitutional provisions and revisions have since been approved by the majority of the people and the majority of the cantons. The 1848 and 1874 Constitutions provided only the right of the people either to approve a constitutional decision by Parliament, or to require a concrete or general constitutional revision by a general initiative. The 1891 amendment, however, added the important democratic right to not only slow down reforms, but also to instigate reforms. This amendment guarantees the right to initiate concrete constitutional provisions to be included within the constitutional document after the initiative has been approved by the sovereign (that is, the majority of the voters and of the cantons). With this revision of such political and constitutional importance, the majority of the people and of the cantons became the real sovereign power and thus the most important organ in the constitution-making process.

Unlike many other states that have introduced direct democracy, in Switzerland no special quota of two-thirds of the voters, or even 50 per cent of the people with voting rights, have to vote. If the turnout of a vote is only 20 per cent and the majority does approve, the referendum is valid. If the majority of the voters (not of all the citizens with voting rights) approve the proposal and the majority of the voters in the cantons also approve, a constitutional vote is valid.

Actually, the Constitution provides for two instruments of direct democracy: the referendum and the initiative. With regard to the referendum, the Constitution distinguishes between optional and mandatory referenda. The optional referendum was introduced in the revision of 1874, with regard to the Parliament's legislative decisions. According to Art. 89 of the Constitution, 30,000 (but since the revision of 1977, 50,000) citizens could require that legislation approved by the two Chambers be submitted to the vote of the people. In such a case, the legislation could only enter into force when it was additionally approved by the majority of the people. In the case of a mandatory referendum, a decision can only enter into force if a popular initiative or a decision of the Parliament is approved by the majority of the people and of the cantons. This mandatory referendum is required for all constitutional revisions.

In order to have the right to vote or to sign a proposal for a popular initiative or an optional referendum, a Swiss citizen does not need to have any special kind of registration. Only his or her domicile in a Swiss municipality is needed in order to participate in elections and popular votes, or to sign for an initiative or a referendum. Swiss nationals living abroad must claim their right to be registered as a voter through the official representative of the municipality in which they had lived before moving abroad.

Flexible Constitution open for amendments

Although the revision procedure for the Constitution provided for a balanced representation of the cantons and the people with regard to the substance and content of constitutional provisions, the Constitution's founding fathers did not provide for any constraints. Thus, historically, Switzerland has principally opted for a flexible system of constitutional revision, open to any constitutional changes and restricted only by the procedure. Neither was there a provision guaranteeing perpetuity, nor did any provision prescribe a more cumbersome procedure for its revision as, for example, the Canadian Constitution does.

Article 112 of the original Constitution of 1848 provided a procedure for constitutional revision that was similar to the legislative procedure, with the important addition that any constitutional revision can only enter into force if it is approved by the majority of the voters and of the cantons. Originally, the Constitution did not distinguish between total and so-called partial revision. The original Constitution was totally open with regard to its revision. It had no provision guaranteeing perpetuity.

Stability of the system of government

After 1848, the Constitution was radically changed in 1874 and in 1999. In total, since 1848, the voters and the cantons have adopted almost 200 changes to the Constitution. However, even including the constitutional revisions of 1874 and 1999, principally the stability of the basic governmental system has never been redesigned. Neither democracy, nor federalism, nor the unique system of government has been overthrown. In contrast to the Basic Law in Germany, although the Swiss Constitution has been totally revised twice, there has never been a tendency to regard any of those Constitutions as merely provisionally valid. All of them have always been considered finalized settlements by the Swiss society.

Introduction of the popular initiative

Even when the Constitution was totally transformed in 1874, the original procedure for the constitutional revision was not changed. In 1891, the procedure was reconsidered, but only with regard to the introduction of the popular initiative to amend or introduce specific provisions into the Constitution. The constitutional amendment of 1891 was most important because it provided not only two different procedures for a total revision, but also a partial revision of the Constitution. In addition, it gave the citizens the opportunity to propose a concrete amendment to the Constitution, which ultimately had to be submitted to the people, and thus enlarged the voting rights of the citizens within the system of direct democracy quite radically. The introduction of the democratic right of the citizens to propose an amendment to the Constitution has been used for 392 different initiatives since 1891. It not only expanded direct democracy in Switzerland, but also provided for a transition of the actual function of the Constitution into a real political program to be followed by the Swiss legislature.

To sum up, one can observe the following main features with regard to constitutional revisions: the direct rights of the citizens with regard to constitutional revisions have been greatly expanded, with the right to propose not only a general revision of the Constitution, which was already established in 1848, but also to propose the exact wording of any new constitutional provisions that enter into force when accepted by the voting sovereign. This policy greatly strengthened the democratic rights of the citizens, and it even transformed the function of the Constitution, which in the twentieth century became not only an instrument to limit governmental powers but also to mandate that the legislature and the executive fulfill important tasks on behalf of the voting sovereign. With the introduction of the popular initiative to amend the Constitution, the Constitution provided for different procedures with regard to complete constitutional revision and partial revision for the first time.

Important moments in the development of the constitutional revision procedure

New constitutional body

Already in 1966, the sovereign included a new constitutional provision to foster a relationship with Swiss nationals living in foreign countries. Actually, the law of 1975 on political rights of Swiss denizens provides that Swiss nationals living in foreign countries can vote based on the municipality in which they either have citizenship or had been domiciled before living abroad. In the last vote on the expulsion of criminal foreigners, 2.4 per cent of the voters were living abroad.[2]

Only in 1971, after several failures on federal and cantonal levels, did the male sovereign finally accept the right of women to vote. With the introduction of women's suffrage in 1971, the sovereign body controlling the Constitution doubled.

After a negative vote in 1979, the sovereign decided in 1991 to lower the voting age of Swiss citizens to 18.[3] With this decision, the constituent body with the right to vote rose 2.8 per cent. Actually, on the cantonal level, several proposals have been made about giving voting rights to those foreigners who pay taxes and have a domicile in Switzerland. For the time being on the federal level, this political issue has not been raised.

Direct democracy in foreign affairs

In 1921, the sovereign changed the Constitution based on a popular initiative with a new provision introducing the democratic right of the citizens to require a referendum against the decision of the legislature to approve international treaties, which cannot be denounced.[4] This new provision marked the beginning of the new democratic rights of the people to also decide on international affairs, which has since been considerably enlarged, in particular with regard to international treaties with constitutional scope.

The new canton of Jura

In March 1978, Switzerland enlarged the constitutional body of the 25 cantons to 26, with the adoption of the newly founded canton, Jura.[5] Since then, the Senate—which is called the Council of States (cantons)—has two additional members representing the canton of Jura, and constitutional referenda also require the approval of at least 13.5 cantons.

Limiting the popular initiative

With the new Constitution, the democratic right to change this Constitution by popular initiative is limited to initiatives that do not violate mandatory provisions of international law. This new limitation of the popular initiative has since been the subject of many controversies, because three recently submitted initiatives appear to violate international law, in particular internationally protected human rights. The Parliament and the Federal Council, however, have considered that these initiatives did not violate mandatory international law, according to Art. 53 of the Vienna Convention on the Law of Treaties (*ius cogens*).

Procedure for parliamentary counterproposals

In the case of a popular initiative to change the Constitution, the legislature has three primary options. It can propose the voters' adoption of the new text or their rejection of it, or it can elaborate a so-called counterproposal that may take into account some of the initiative's ideas but may not be as extreme as the proposed text of the initiative. If the Parliament makes a counterproposal, the people can only vote either for the counterproposal or for the initiative. With the revision of 1987, the voters now have four possibilities: they can reject both proposals; they can adopt both proposals; they can adopt one proposal and reject the other one; or finally, they can decide, if initiative and counterproposal are adopted, which one should be introduced within the Constitution.[6]

Rejected proposals

Constitutional issues and controversies have not been limited to issues of concrete constitutional amendments. There have also been important issues debated with regard to the procedure of the revision of the Constitution that have not yet been approved by the sovereign. These important but unsettled debates can be summarized as follows:

a) *No constitutional review of federal legislation.* With the establishment of a Federal Constitution, the Swiss Constitution of 1848 provided for a non-permanent court that had jurisdiction predominantly in civil law cases only. It wasn't until 1874 that the new Constitution also installed a permanent Federal Court with constitutional jurisdiction over cantonal laws. Any constitutional review of federal legislation was excluded from the jurisdiction of the Federal Court. In 1939, the sovereign rejected a popular initiative aimed at installing constitutional jurisdiction of the Federal Court with regard to federal legislation as well.[7] Since then, several parliamentary initiatives have been launched to introduce a general constitutional review. In its proposal for a new Constitution, the Federal Council even suggested the introduction of the jurisdiction of the Federal Court to review the constitutionality of federal legislation in concrete cases also.[8] This proposal has not been accepted by Parliament. The issue has regularly been part of the constitutional debate but has not yet received the necessary approval by the majority in Parliament. Thus, the most important issue with regard to rejected proposals is still the issue of the constitutional review of legislation. For this reason, the legislature (the two Chambers of Parliament) is still the only body to decide on the constitutionality of federal legislation. The main argument against the constitutional review of federal legislation has always been direct democracy. Federal legislation, whether it is implicitly approved by the people or approved even after a facultative referendum, should not be reviewed by a limited body of judges who are merely elected by the Parliament.

b) *No emergency regulation.* The second important issue is the lack of a specific emergency regulation. The only regulation actually in force is the power of Parliament to decide that a statute can be enforced for a limited time without referendum. If such a law has no constitutional bases, it can only be declared urgent for one year. If it is to be valid for a longer, although also limited, period, it has to be submitted to a mandatory referendum.[9] Only if the majority of the voters and the majority of the cantons approve this statute in a referendum can the law remain valid for a limited time, but longer than one year. In addition, the unconstitutional bill has to be approved within one year by the majority of the Swiss voters and of the cantons. In all other cases, the legislature has to propose a new constitutional base in order to pass legislation regarding these matters. This is the only emergency regulation actually incorporated within the Swiss Constitution. Unlike most other countries, Switzerland has no emergency regulation provided in the Federal Constitution. However, during the First and Second World Wars,[10] the Swiss legislature transferred emergency powers to the executive without constitutional foundation.[11] During the First World War, this was done even without any specific discussion.[12] Although the Federal Constitution has no emergency regulation, at least some cantonal Constitutions have introduced special emergency regulations.[13]

c) *Unsatisfactory limitation of popular initiatives concerning constitutional amendments.* The actual Constitution, in Art. 193 para 4, states that popular initiatives concerning constitutional amendments should not violate mandatory provisions of international law. Recently, there have been three initiatives that were considered by a minority of the Parliament to violate mandatory international law. However, a majority in Parliament has argued that these initiatives may violate international law but not the limited term of peremptory norm of general international law.[14] Ultimately, all those initiatives have been adopted by an overwhelming majority of the voters and cantons.[15] Switzerland is still waiting to see what consequences this position will have, for example, on decisions of the European Court of Human Rights.

A short history of constitutional revisions

Looking into the constitutional revisions since 1891, one has to distinguish between total and partial revisions. The democratic right of the people to propose constitutional amendments by initiative has been used 392 times. Currently, 44 initiatives have been submitted and will have to be treated by Parliament. This democratic right has not only strengthened Swiss direct democracy, but has also changed the function of the Constitution. In many initiatives, the purpose was not only to enlarge the competences of the Federation, but also to mandate the legislature and the executive to fulfill certain tasks in a specific direction. From a total of 175 initiatives that have been voted on, only 18 have been adopted,[16] but one should not underestimate this popular right. Many initiatives that were ultimately rejected, have nevertheless had important political consequences and were at least partially implemented by legislation or by a constitutional amendment approved by the people as a counterproposal.

Total revisions of the Constitution

Revision of 1874

The first important total revision of the Constitution was approved by the majority of the voters and the cantons in 1874. This proposal was submitted to the sovereign after a first proposal had been rejected in 1872. The main issues of this revision were politically supported by the keywords "one army," "one legal system" and "one market." In addition, in order to gain the support of the French-speaking cantons against the Catholic conservatives, the revision introduced Articles prohibiting the order of the Jesuits and the foundation of new monasteries. With regard to the development of direct democratic rights of the citizens, the Constitution of 1874 introduced the right of the citizens to require that federal legislation be submitted to a popular vote. This has since been called the "facultative referendum."

Revision of 1999

The second total revision of the Constitution took place in 1999. This revision was proposed by the Federal Council and the Parliament as a mere revision of the editing and wording of the Constitution, without any major changes. However, with regard to federalism, this revision gave the Federation some new powers and responsibilities. In order to maintain federal and constitutional balance between shared rule and self-rule, the new Constitution added a new organ of the cantonal governments to participate in the decision-making process on the federal level.

Recent reform packages

The politicians favoring the new revision of the Constitution proposed some important additional partial revisions regarding improvement of the rule of law, improvement of direct democracy, and a new concept of federal distribution of powers between the cantons and the Federation, all of which amounted to a complete revision.

Rule of law and access to justice

By October 1999, the people and the cantons had approved an important revision with regard to the improvement of the rule of law on the cantonal and federal levels. With this revision, a new fundamental right providing access to justice was introduced. Cantonal constitutions were obliged to provide a court of final instance for any legal dispute. In addition, on the federal level, a new lower-instance court on issues of administrative law was introduced. However, some issues were rejected, such as the jurisdiction of the Federal Court with regard to the constitutionality of federal statutes (constitutional review). The new Art. 189 para 4 of the Constitution prohibits the Federal Court from reviewing the constitutionality of any decision made by the Federal Council and the Parliament, the only power of the legislature being to provide for exceptions. Other important revisions were the introduction of a Federal Criminal Court, a lower Federal Administrative Court, and the new competences of the Federation to issue civil and criminal legislation with regard to its substance and procedure.

Direct democracy

In 2003 a package strengthening direct democracy was adopted. It principally provided a new procedure of constitutional revision in case the Parliament wanted to submit a counterproposal to a popular initiative. In addition, it enlarged direct democracy in cases of international treaties to a certain degree. One new constitutional provision, concerning the democratic right not only to require change to the Constitution by popular initiative but also to amend or propose new legislation, was abolished in 2008 because it was considered too complicated within a federal system with two Chambers.

Fiscal equalization

The package on fiscal law concerning a prolongation of the competence of the Federation for direct and indirect taxes until 2020 was most important for the cohesion of the Federation. Both proposals, which contained almost 100 provisions of the Constitution to be amended, were adopted in 2004. This was almost a total revision of the Constitution. In particular, this constitutional reform provided a new concept of equalization of burdens and resources of the cantons, a disentanglement of federal and cantonal tasks and obligations, and institutionalized cooperation between cantons, and between cantons and the Federation. According to this new concept of equalization, the rich cantons were obliged to pay some of their income into a fund in order to mitigate the burden on cantons with few resources and higher expenditures.[17]

Education

An important package has been adopted on the issue of education, including professional and university education. This reform package was not initiated by the executive but by Parliament. With regard to education, since adopting this reform, the Swiss Constitution considers the entire country to be an education area, a policy which requires intense cooperation among cantons, the Federation, and even municipalities.[18] Cooperation between cantons and the Federation is now strengthened mainly in the field of university education, with a common council composed of the representatives of the canton governments and the Federation. In addition, the traditionally highly qualified professional education, which was formerly part of the economy, has been integrated within the traditional area of education.

Partial revisions of the Constitution

Popular initiative against the government

Since the constitutional amendment of 1891, which introduced the right of 50,000 voters to require a decision of the sovereign on a concrete text for the amendment to the Constitution, more than 220 constitutional initiatives have been submitted[19] and 26 initiatives are actually prepared for collection of signatures or to be assessed either by the Federal Council or by the Parliament.[20] This introduction of the right of the people to propose a concrete amendment text to be introduced in the constitutional document has been included by the Parliament, against the recommendation of the Federal Council.[21]

Limits of popular initiatives

The Constitution distinguishes between total and partial revision. The right to submit the wording of a concrete text to be introduced as an amendment into the constitutional document by popular initiative does not, however, permit the introduction of several constitutional amendments with one initiative. For this reason, up to now the Parliament has declared void any initiatives that violated the principle of cohesion of the subject matter, according to Art. 194 para 2 of the Constitution. Based on this principle, the Parliament has heretofore declared three initiatives invalid.[22] One initiative was declared invalid because it violated the *ius cogens* of international law.[23] Popular initiatives that violated international treaties, however, have been declared valid because international treaties could be cancelled.

The revised Art. 194 of the Constitution maintains that initiatives which are not coherent with regard to the subject matter and which violate *ius cogens* have to be declared invalid. Recently, several initiatives have been controversial, because a minority considered them a violation of *ius cogens* of international law. This controversy with regard to the constitutionality of initiatives has resulted in several proposals to introduce a constitutional court with jurisdiction on this issue or to limit the right of popular initiatives in general to international law.

Political agenda determined by popular initiatives

Regarding the relationship between the large number of initiatives (more than 220) on one side and the small number of only 17 initiatives that have finally been approved by the sovereign, one might draw the conclusion that the amendment of 1891 concerning the popular initiative has been a serious mistake, even a failure. However, one has to be aware of the fact that many initiatives that have been rejected had important political impacts. Either the Parliament has accepted some of the ideas of the initiative and has offered a counterproposal, or the substance of the initiative has been implemented by the legislature or by the administration. Looking into the political reality of Switzerland, one has to admit that a great part of the day-to-day political agenda is determined by discussions and controversies with regard to popular initiatives.

Low percentage of signatures required

The required number of signatures to submit an initiative was originally 50,000. Women's suffrage in 1971 doubled the constituency to 100,000. Today, almost 5.1 million citizens have the right to vote in Switzerland,[24] which means that actually only 2 per cent of the citizens with the right to vote are required to submit a popular initiative. In California, it is 8 per cent for a constitutional amendment. If Switzerland required the same percentage, it would have to raise the amount to almost 400,000 signatures.

Partial revisions since 2006

There are so many constitutional decisions amending, abolishing, or introducing new constitutional provisions each year that it would be impossible for an independent reader to keep up with all the information. Partial revisions, which included an entire reform package, have already been mentioned. We shall now deal with revisions that introduced only one reform issue into the Constitution. For this reason, we shall focus on the most recent revisions in the last few years, that is, since 2006. Thus, we shall distinguish among the following revisions: first, those based on popular initiatives that have been adopted against Parliament's recommendations; secondly, revisions that have been adopted following a procedure in which the sovereign had to decide between a popular initiative and a counterproposal made by Parliament; and thirdly, those that have been introduced based on a proposal by the Parliament and the Federal Council. To conclude, we shall consider popular initiatives that have been rejected by the sovereign.

Popular initiatives adopted by the sovereign against the recommendations of the Parliament

In recent years, there have been several popular initiatives adopted by the sovereign against Parliament's recommendation. Here, one must first mention the so-called popular initiative that introduced a provision in the Constitution to prohibit the construction of minarets. Several constitutional experts declared that this initiative is in conflict with a peremptory norm of general international law (*ius cogens*) according to Art. 53 of the Vienna Convention on the Law of Treaties of 1969, because it is discriminatory and violates the human right of freedom of religion. However, in its proposal to the Parliament to recommend that the people reject the initiative, the Federal Council put forward the initiative because it does not violate *ius cogens* of general international law.[25] Although the Federal Council and the Parliament clearly recommended that voters reject the initiative, it was adopted with 57.5 per cent voting "yes" and 42.5 per cent "no." The majority of the voters of 17 full cantons and five half cantons voted in favor of the initiative, and the voters of only three cantons and one half canton rejected the initiative. Most institutions predicting the outcome of the voting failed to forecast this result, which had not been foreseen by the political elite of the country.

According to Art. 53 of the Vienna Convention on the Law of Treaties, a peremptory norm of international law is "accepted and recognized by the international community of States as a whole as a norm from which no derogation is permitted and which can be modified only by a subsequent norm of general international law having the same character." Actually, international fundamental rights—such as the freedom of religion and, in particular, the obligation of states not to discriminate against any person based on religious beliefs—must be considered *ius cogens*. The Federal Council's argument that only those fundamental rights that are resistant to any emergency situation are considered as part of the *ius cogens* is not convincing, primarily for three reasons: first, there is no reference in the Convention with regard to the emergency situation; second, there is no emergency situation conceivable which could, for instance, justify the prohibition of the construction of a minaret; and third, freedom of religion and the principle of non-discrimination are part of the common and generally accepted international law, which could only be changed by a treaty having the same value as the international treaties guaranteeing human rights.

Popular initiative adopted by the sovereign against a concrete counterproposal

On 28 November 2010, the sovereign had to decide on two popular initiatives. One initiative supported by the Social Democrats proposed a new and, according to the initiators, more just system of taxation. This initiative was rejected by the majority of the people and the cantons with 58.5 per cent of the voters and 19.5 cantons. The second vote was on a popular initiative to expel criminal foreigners. This initiative is in conflict with the non-refoulement principle (i.e. the obligation of Switzerland not to expel asylum seekers to a country that uses inhuman treatment and torture), and it is also in conflict with the free-movement principle to which Switzerland has agreed in its bilateral treaties with the European Union. Instead of rejecting the initiative as a violation of the international *ius cogens*, the Parliament decided to offer the people a counterproposal that conformed with international law. However, the sovereign decided with a 52.3 per cent "yes" vote and 17.5 cantons in favor of the initiative and against the counterproposal. According to Art. 139b, the voters have to decide whether they accept the initiative, whether they accept the counterproposal, and, finally, if both proposals receive the majority, which proposal they would prefer. Since, in this vote, the counterproposal was rejected by the sovereign, the third question of preference became irrelevant.[26]

On 3 October 2010, the sovereign accepted the new Art. 118a, which requires the Federation to take not only conventional medicine but also alternative medicine into consideration with regard to mandatory health insurance. Based on an initiative, Parliament advanced a counterproposal. In order to have a better chance of gaining final approval from the sovereign, the committee in charge of the initiative can always renounce it, in which case, the sovereign can only decide on Parliament's counterproposal.[27] In this particular instance, the committee decided to withdraw on 15 October 2008.[28]

Rejected initiatives since 2006

Several initiatives have been rejected since 2006, such as the aforementioned initiative to provide a more just system of taxation to avoid abuses; the popular initiative against cruelty to animals and the introduction of access to justice for animals; the initiative against export of products to be used in warfare; the initiative to abolish the right of associations to sue in environmental issues; the initiative to introduce flexibility of retirement age; the initiative to provide a reasonable policy with regard to cannabis; the introduction of one united Swiss health insurance program; and the use of the profits of the National Bank for the Swiss social insurance for retired people. Such rejection by the sovereign cannot be interpreted as a general rejection of the issue. In many cases, Parliament takes ideas of a popular initiative into account without accepting a constitutional provision or formulating a counterproposal.

Revisions based on parliamentary proposals

The most important constitutional revisions have, however, still been proposed by the Parliament. An important revision focused on education and scientific research. Based on a parliamentary initiative, Parliament enhanced cooperation between the Federation, the cantons, and the municipalities with regard to all types of education. Since this reform, Switzerland must be considered one education area in which all different providers of education, such as cantons, municipalities, and the Federation, need to cooperate in order to have high-quality, internationally competitive, educational institutions.

In addition, the sovereign also adopted a proposal by the Parliament to revise the Constitution and to provide a better distribution of taxes imposed on air traffic. This proposal was also indirectly influenced by the popular initiative to limit military exercises by airplanes (noise) in touristic areas, which was rejected by the sovereign in 2005. Also, several adopted constitutional revisions in previous years have been implemented and introduced into the Constitution, such as financial reform, access to justice, centralization of procedure in civil and criminal law, and the decision on the limitation in law of sexual crimes and the lifelong imprisonment of pedophiles. Finally, some constitutional decisions have been taken with regard to foreign affairs, in particular the relationship to the European Union.

Informal methods of constitutional change

The entire Swiss Constitution is an open constitution that can easily be revised; there are no developed methods of informal constitutional change. Historically most important are the *de facto* emergency powers, which were decided unanimously by the two Chambers during the threats of World War I and World War II.

Moreover, one has to be aware of the fact that Switzerland has only a limited constitutional review conferred on the judiciary. Thus, it is basically Parliament that decides on the constitutionality of legislation. For that reason, the Federal Council, when it proposes new legislation, is obliged to comment on the compatibility of the proposed legislation with the superior law, the fundamental rights, and the European law. However, it remains within Parliament's power to interpret the Constitution and to decide whether legislative reform would also need a constitutional amendment. Thus, although there was no clear competence for a national library of the Confederation in 1992, Parliament issued a law on the national library, because such competence was not disputed and had been accepted since 1895.[29]

In a recent decision, the Supreme Court also reviewed a decision regarding the financial supervision of Switzerland and provided an extensive interpretation of the Federal Council's power to provide measures for internal and external security, even when there was no real threat of war but just a threat to the internal financial situation of Switzerland.[30]

The most important informal constitutional change by any standard is the procedure for electing the seven members of the Federal Council (executive). The governmental system of Switzerland is unique in the world. It has been influenced by the Executive Directory of the French Revolution, installed in France in 1795. Actually, there are seven members of the Federal Council, elected independently by the Federal Assembly (the joint Chambers of the Senate and the National Council). According to the Constitution (Art. 175), when electing the members of the Federal Council, the Federal Assembly has to ensure that all geographical and language regions are represented. In addition, according to a system developed since 1959, the Federal Assembly takes into account a fair representation of the different political parties. Thus, Switzerland has no coalition government but a government that acts as a council to decide by majority, thus representing not only different regions but also the strongest parties in the Federal Assembly.

Formal constitutional amendment process

How is the revision process constrained by the Constitution?

Amending the Swiss Constitution principally follows the ordinary process for general legislation and lawmaking. Thus, any constitutional amendment first needs to be adopted by both Chambers: the Swiss Senate and the National Chamber. In cases of disagreement, the issue has to be submitted to the people. If the majority of the people (not the majority of cantons) require a revision, a new Parliament (both Chambers) has to be elected.[31] The Federal Constitution, unlike some cantonal constitutions, does not provide for any special council to be elected for the purpose of proposing a new, revised Constitution. All amendment processes, including the two total revisions, have been elaborated within the ordinary legislative Parliament.

While legislation is always only submitted to an optional referendum, any proposal for an amendment of the Constitution has to be submitted to a mandatory referendum. The proposal is only valid if the majority of the voters and of the cantons approves it. Since 1848, this process has always been supplemented by additional political rights of the citizens. Already in 1848, 50,000 citizens could require, with a popular initiative from the Parliament, to elaborate constitutional amendments. Even though they required a concrete issue to be amended in the Constitution, the Parliament could submit the general question to revise the Constitution to the people.

The Parliament and even the Federal Council were not satisfied with this system. Thus, Parliament proposed a new system for revising the Constitution which made a clear distinction between a partial revision and a total revision. For a partial revision, Parliament introduced the popular initiative to require a concrete Article of the Constitution to be changed according to the wording of the initiative. This new system was adopted in 1891. Since this time, the people have the democratic right not only to propose a *total* revision of the Constitution, but also to propose a concrete amendment to be included in the constitutional document.

Phases of the amending procedure

With regard to the phases of the amending procedure, one has to distinguish between the procedure for the total revision and that of the partial revision. In both cases the revision can be instigated by the people based on an initiative to totally revise the Constitution, or based on a concrete initiative to change specific issues of the Constitution.

In cases of a popular initiative to change a concrete issue of the Constitution, a committee of at least seven and not more than 27 citizens can either submit a concrete text for a new constitutional Article, or formulate a general initiative to require a partial revision to be drafted finally by the Parliament.[32] In cases in which Parliament is not willing to fulfill the mandate of the initiative, the issue has to be submitted to the people. If the majority of the voters vote in favor of the initiative, Parliament is obliged to follow the will of the majority.[33]

With regard to the concrete popular initiative, the Federal Chancellery checks whether the proposed text with the signatures conforms with the legislation. The Chancellery can only formally inspect the text; it does not have jurisdiction with regard to the substance and the content of the proposed text. If needed, the Federal Chancellery will also look into the translation. Then the text will be published in the three official languages (German, French, and Italian) in the official publication of the Federal Council. When the text is published, the citizens proposing this text will have to collect the required signatures of at least 100,000 citizens within 18 months. After 18 months, the signatures have to be submitted to the Federal Chancellery. If the initiative has enough signatures, the Chancellery issues a decision that the initiative has been successful. Otherwise, the initiative has failed.

If the initiative has collected enough signatures, the Federal Council is obliged to submit a proposal concerning the initiative to the Parliament.[34] The Federal Council then has four different options:

a) It can propose that Parliament rejects the initiative because it violates mandatory international law, or because it does not respect the principle of coherence of subject matter.[35]
b) It can agree with the text and propose that Parliament makes a positive recommendation to the vote of the sovereign.
c) It can disagree and propose that Parliament issues a negative recommendation for the final vote of the sovereign.
d) It can offer Parliament a counterproposal that will have to be issued finally by Parliament and proposed as a counterproposal to the vote of the sovereign. In this case, the deadline for the Federal Council's proposal is extended from one year to 18 months.

   If Parliament issues a new proposal for a constitutional amendment, it follows the normal legislative procedure, the only difference being that the amendment can only become law if it is adopted by the sovereign.

Material limitations

As previously mentioned, there is one important material limitation that affects not only the content of the popular initiatives but also any total revision of the Constitution. Any revision must not violate mandatory provisions of international law.[36]

Constitution drafting methods

Methods have been established for drafting legislation. With regard to amending the Constitution, there are no established drafting methods. However, any proposal or initiative has to be written in German, French, and Italian. Article 57 of the Law of the Parliament requires that legislation must be drafted in plain, concise language. According to Art. 7 of the Federal Law on the national languages and the common understanding of the language communities,[37] the language must be coherent, understandable, clear, and user-friendly for the citizens.

With regard to popular initiatives, the initiative must respect the principle of consistency of the form according to Art. 194 para 3 of the Constitution. Other requirements are not provided in the Constitution.

Criticism of the amendment procedure

The only criticism about the amendment procedure refers to the limitation of the revision with regard to the *ius cogens*. There are many politicians, especially from left-wing parties, who favor stronger control of the actual limitation by a constitutional court and/or propose even stronger substantial limitations in particular for popular initiatives.

However, despite the fact that small cantons have the same weight in the constitutional vote as large cantons, such as Zurich, direct democracy is only seldom criticized. The vote of a voter in the canton of Appenzell Interior (the smallest canton, with two votes) is 37 times more important than that of a voter in the canton of Zurich, whose cantonal vote counts only one-half.

Besides, there is no vigorous debate with regard to the procedure for constitutional revision of the parliamentary initiative to introduce a constitutional jurisdiction of the Federal Court. In fact, a constitutional review would indirectly influence the revision process, as those formulating a constitutional norm would have to take into account the constitutional jurisprudence of the court. If Switzerland introduced a constitutional review, it would probably increase the competence of such an institution to review the formulation of popular initiatives as well.

The role of the people, the judiciary and experts

The role of the people

It is clear that, up to the present time, any constitutional revision has to be adopted in the end by the people. For this reason, any constitutional reform includes parties, churches, civil society, the economy, labor unions, and other non-governmental organizations (NGOs) within the constitution-making process. Article 147 of the Constitution formally provides a consultation procedure for any important governmental act, such as constitution-making, legislation, etc. Apart from the expressly mentioned cantons, parties, and interested groups, other communities, associations, or even private persons can be involved.

One has to mention in this context that, mainly with regard to the constitution-making process, direct democracy has had an enormous influence, not only on the everyday political debate, but also on the different institutions. The proportional electoral system as well as the unique system of government is directly or indirectly influenced by the system of direct democracy. Direct democracy is the key institution to understanding the Swiss political system.

Direct democracy has diminished the political power of the parties. As most important social conflicts are eventually solved by a direct democratic vote, most often aiming for constitutional revision, there is social and political stability in Switzerland. Indeed, the majority principle is not detrimental to minorities. In particular, the traditional minorities have a high likelihood of winning even important minority issues because of the small participation of voters in a vote directly concerning minority interests. The majority principle is only detrimental to minorities that are excluded from any participation, as women were before the introduction of women's suffrage, and foreigners currently are, since they have no right to vote.

The role of the people in the constitution-making process is of utmost importance. Direct democracy is, in effect, the key to any understanding of the Swiss procedures of partial or total revision of the Constitution. Even the Swiss political culture of political compromise, considered an asset rather than a weakness, is influenced by direct democracy. Since the voting sovereign is usually very conservative, it thus rejects even important reform projects, and the political elite is obliged to find compromises even with political adversaries in order to find enough support from the often very skeptical voters.

The role of experts in constitutional revision

The formulation of constitutional norms requires expertise with regard to the actual Constitution. In particular, the fact that Switzerland has no constitutional review of legislation makes it necessary for constitutional experts to be involved in the constitution-making process. However, those experts work behind the political scenes. For this reason, it is often unknown which experts are involved in formulating concrete constitutional norms. As far as a total revision of the Constitution is concerned, many constitutional experts have been involved in different committees. However, the final draft of the Constitution has been elaborated by the political representatives. Traditionally, the common people are rather reluctant to refer to any kind of academic expertise.

Judicial review of constitutional amendments

The constitutional jurisdiction of the Federal Court is limited. The Court has jurisdiction to review cantonal decisions concerning their compliance with the Federal Constitution. In addition, the Federal Tribunal can interpret federal legislation according to the Constitution. However, Art. 189 para 4 excludes the Federal Tribunal from challenging decisions made by Parliament or the Federal Council. However, one also has to admit that, indirectly, the review of the European Court of Human Rights (ECtHR) has a strong effect on the constitutional jurisdiction of the Federal Court. In particular, it influences the Federal Court to interpret federal legislation according to the jurisprudence of the ECtHR.

As there is no constitutional review of legislation, so there is no jurisdiction of the Court with regard to the constitutional limitations of the revision of the Constitution. There are actually moves to introduce some kind of control of popular initiatives and even to introduce a constitutional review of legislation, but, up to now, those moves have only a limited chance of finally being accepted.

How does international and European law and jurisprudence affect constitutional revision?

With regard to international law, the Swiss Constitution has introduced the important limitation that partial and total revisions of the Constitution have to respect mandatory provisions of international law. As previously mentioned, in practice this limitation has been interpreted very sparingly in order to respect the principle of direct democracy and sovereign independence, as much as possible. Thus, even initiatives violating human rights provisions of international law have not been annulled by the Parliament. Indeed, even European law and, in particular, the principle of free movement of persons agreed by Switzerland in the bilateral treaties with the European Union have not been considered as limiting constitutional revisions. The argument in those cases is invariably that if the majority of the sovereign have accepted such a revision that violates international treaties, then Switzerland always has the option of canceling the respective treaties.

Concluding remarks: does the political system influence constitutional revision?

Quite the reverse; it is the revision process and, in particular, the institutionalized popular initiative since 1891, which have had a strong influence on the political system. This tendency had already started, in fact, with several referenda at the end of the nineteenth and the beginning of the twentieth centuries. Since the Constitution of 1874 was in force, in only 45 years the people and the cantons rejected proposals made by Parliament more than 25 times. Thus, it became obvious that the majority in Parliament no longer reflected the majority of the people. For this reason, the electoral system had to be adapted so that Parliament somehow mirrored the effective fragmentation of the people in society. Majorities within Parliament should no longer be split with regard to the sovereign majorities.

This phenomenon required the adaption of the electoral system. Thus, in 1919 the Constitution was revised with a new concept of the electoral system, introducing proportional representation of the parties according to the majority of the people. Since then, the percentage of the parties within Parliament remained quite stable for a long time: one-third voted for left-wing parties and two-thirds for middle-class or right-wing parties. By 1890, a representative of the Catholic-Conservative party had joined the executive (Federal Council). Only in 1943 did a socialist become a member of the Federal Council, and only in 1959 was the Federal Council composed of two Socialists, two Liberals, two Christian Democrats, and one representing the party close to the farmers and middle class.

Since 2002, the Parliament has struggled to find a system of proportional representation for the large parties in the Federal Council, but it has not so far found a final consensus. In general, one can hold that the political system in Switzerland has retained an extraordinary stability. Since 1848, the executive government of Switzerland has never been replaced in its entirety. There have always been some members of the Federal Council remaining and others being replaced by newcomers, who were instructed by the remaining members of this body. No other countries in the world have had such stability throughout their history.

This extraordinary stability of the political forces in Switzerland is linked to the fact that people can always use their political rights to introduce new ideas and developments. Important political changes do not depend on the parties but rather on the instruments of direct democracy, and, in particular, on the openness of the process for revising the Constitution.

On the other hand, one also has to admit that there is still an important political deficit to be detected in this system of direct democracy. In principle, direct democracy lacks financial transparency, even today. Up to the present, committees that required referenda or proposed new constitutional articles based on the general right of popular initiative are not required to declare the financial support they received to prepare a popular initiative, or to collect the required signatures of the initiative, or to provide transparency with regard to the financing of efforts to win the support of the majority of the people and of the cantons in the final vote. Switzerland makes no obligation on political parties to render their finances transparent, nor does it require transparency for the financial support of campaigns to promote or reject proposals to change the Constitution.

Notes

1 Article 113 of the Constitution of 1848. Online. Available: <http://www.verfassungen.de/ch/verf48-i.htm> (accessed 22 July 2011).
2 See "Bundesgesetz über die politischen Rechte der Auslandschweizer" of 1975, Collection of Swiss laws SR 161.5 See also online. Available: <http://www.lexfind.ch/dta/19145/2/> (accessed 5 August 2011).
3 See the report of the National Council 30 January 1990. Online. Available: <http://www.amtsdruckschriften.bar.admin.ch/showDoc.do> (accessed 5 August 2011).
4 Online. Available: <http://www.admin.ch/ch/d/pore/va/19210130/index.html> (accessed 22 July 2011).
5 See also online. Available: <http://www.admin.ch/ch/d/pore/va/19780924/index.html> (accessed 22 July 2011).
6 See also online. Available: <http://www.admin.ch/ch/d/pore/va/19870405/index.html> (accessed 22 July 2011) and the new Art. 139b para 2 of the recent Constitution.
7 Online. Available: <http://www.admin.ch/ch/d/pore/va/19390122/det129.html> (accessed 25 July 2011).
8 Botschaft des Bundesrates für eine neue Bundesverfassung vom 20 November 1998. Online. Available: <http://www.amtsdruckschriften.bar.admin.ch/showDoc.do> (accessed 25 July 2011).
9 Article 159 para 3a and Art. 165 para 3 of the Constitution.

10 In both cases, both Chambers adopted the emergency competence of the Federal Council (executive in Switzerland) with unanimity, a fact that is regarded as providing legitimacy. See also discussion in Parliament, 30 August 1939. Online. Available: <http://www.amtsdruckschriften.bar.admin.ch/showDoc.do> (accessed 1 July 2011).

11 In an early case, the Federal Court refused to review the constitutionality of this decision, because it was decided by the legislature and thus could not be reviewed by the Court (BGE 41 I 551). The Court's main argument was that such indispensable measures for the public interest of the country were absolutely necessary and thus could only be reviewed by the legislature in cases where it was the only competent political body for such emergency issues.

12 R.P. Schmid, *Innere Sicherheit der Schweiz*, 2009, p. 194.

13 Ct. Glarus Art. 81, Ct. Jura Art. 60, Zug 84, Bern 91, Genf Art. 55.

14 It may be interesting that the English translation of "jus cogens" has been mandatory, although the relevant Art. 53 of the Vienna Convention on the law of treaties uses the term "peremptory".

15 See Art. 123a, Art. 72 para 3, Art. 121 paras 3 to 6 of the Constitution.

16 See information of the Federal Chancellery. Online. Available: <http://www.admin.ch/ch/d/pore/vi/vis_2_2_5_9.html> (accessed 19 July 2011).

17 See the information of the Federal Council on the voters 28 November 2004. Online. Available: <http://www.bk.admin.ch/themen/pore/va/20041128/index.html?lang=de> (accessed 18 July 2011).

18 Article 61a and following, see also information of the Federal Council of May 2006. Online. Available: <http://www.bk.admin.ch/themen/pore/va/20060521/index.html?lang=de> (accessed 18 July 2011).

19 Online. Available: <http://www.admin.ch/ch/d/pore/vi/vis_2_2_5_1.html> (accessed 26 July 2011).

20 Online. Available: <http://www.admin.ch/ch/d/pore/vi/vis_1_3_1_1.html> (accessed 29 July 2011).

21 Online. Available: <http://www.amtsdruckschriften.bar.admin.ch/showDoc.do> (accessed 26 July 2011).

22 Online. Available: <http://www.admin.ch/ch/d//pore/vi/vis_2_2_5_6.html> (accessed 26 July 2011).

23 Online. Available: <http://www.admin.ch/ch/d//pore/vi/vis223.html> (accessed 26 July 2011).

24 Online. Available: <http://www.bfs.admin.ch/bfs/portal/de/index/themen/17/03/blank/key/stimmbeteiligung.html> statistics of Switzerland (accessed 26 July 2011).

25 See message of the Federal Council of 27 August 2008. Online. Available: <http://www.admin.ch/ch/d/ff/2008/7603.pdf> (accessed 25 July 2011).

26 Online. Available: <http://www.admin.ch/ch/d/pore/va/20101128/index.html> (accessed 3 August 2010).

27 Article 73 Law on Political Rights, Bundesgesetz über politische Rechte, 17 December 1976. Online. Available: <http://www.lexfind.ch/?cid=1&eid=27> (accessed 3 August 2011).

28 Bundesblatt 2008, p. 8605, German edition. Online. Available: <http://www.admin.ch/ch/d/ff/2008/8605.pdf> (accessed 3 August 2011).

29 See proposal of the Federal Council of 19 February 1992, p. 33. Online. Available: <http://www.amtsdruckschriften.bar.admin.ch/showDoc.do> (accessed 8 August 2011).

30 Decision of the Federal Tribunal of 15 July 2011 NZZ. Online. Available: <http://www.nzz.ch/nachrichten/politik/schweiz/datenherausgabe_der_finma_war_rechtmaessig_1.11410970.html> (accessed 8 August 2011).

31 Article 193 of the Constitution.

32 Ibid.

33 Article 139 para 4 of the Constitution.
34 Article 97 of the Law of the Federal Assembly (Systematic collection of laws 171.10).
35 Article 194 of the Constitution.
36 Article 193 para 4 and Art. 194 para 3 of the Constitution.
37 Collection of Federal Laws 441.1.

18 Constitutional amendment in the United Kingdom

Robert Blackburn

In England the constitution can change constantly, or rather it does not exist at all.
Alexis de Tocqueville[1]

The pace of constitutional reform in the United Kingdom has accelerated in recent years. Yet, without a documentary constitution providing a special amendment procedure, legal changes to even the most basic aspects of the political and constitutional system can be made through the same process as an ordinary Act of Parliament. Conventions remain of special importance as an informal means of updating the constitution, but as a species of regulation they are in a state of decline, increasingly being superseded by ad hoc codes of practice. What has emerged is a constitution that is now overly flexible, and a number of improvements are now necessary in the process of reform.

The nature of UK constitutionalism

Considered from abroad, the most distinctive aspect of the UK constitution is the absence of it being contained within a written documentary source. Indeed, as a result, in the USA and other countries where great civic pride is expressed in the written document or basic law that regulates their system of government, with references regularly made to it in their politics and protection of civil liberties, the UK is widely regarded as having no constitution at all.

The UK's answer to this is to say that, in essence, a constitution is something more than a written document, and the term 'constitution' carries a variety of meanings.[2] One of these is certainly a document like the Constitution of the United States of America 1787, or the Constitution of the Fifth French Republic of 4 October 1958, copies of which one can buy from a bookseller. But another sense in which the term is used is simply that the constitution is the body of all those rules that govern the exercise and distribution of state power; or, as stated more elaborately by the House of Lords Constitutional Committee, 'the set of laws, rules and practices that create the basic institutions of the state, and its component and related parts, and stipulate the powers of those institutions and the relationship between the different institutions and between those institutions and the individual'. In this sense, the UK most certainly has a constitution, and one of great sophistication and antiquity. It has an uncodified and unwritten[3] constitution whose existence and scope must be established analytically.

It also helps to regard the UK system of government as having a 'traditional' constitution, one which has evolved and developed organically over the past 1,000 years, and whose history has been punctuated by major changes at various times, most notably in 1688 as mentioned below. There is no single theory that has shaped it, such as the separation of powers or government by the people, though fragments of these and other ideas have come to permeate the structure and processes of UK government. In the UK, political interests have generally driven and shaped constitutional change, and any constitutional doctrines[4] we possess tend to be in the nature of subsequent justification, making sense of what has already occurred.

Although the Magna Carta in 1215 remains the starting point for English constitutionalism, setting a medieval precedent for the concept of limited government and the rule of law generally across European and modern Commonwealth states,[5] the events of the Glorious Revolution of 1688 – when James II was forced into exile as Monarch and replaced on the throne by William and Mary – should be taken as fixing the foundations of the English constitution.[6] The Bill of Rights 1688 established Parliament's supremacy over the Crown and its prerogatives, and the Act of Settlement 1701 secured the independence of the judiciary, although one in which it was accepted that the common law performed a subordinate role with respect to parliamentary statute – a role in which statutory provisions were interpreted as to their meaning and application, but not reviewed as to their validity by reference to any higher law or body of legal principle.

Any understanding of the process of constitutional amendment in the UK must first appreciate certain special characteristics about the working of its legal system and structure of government. The first of these is the supremacy of an Act of Parliament as a source of law, involving its superiority over the common law and any judgments of the national courts. A second distinct, but associated, characteristic is that there is no body of fundamental or entrenched law that prevails over an Act of Parliament, and no court may override the provisions of a domestic statute by reference to it.[7] Indeed, there is no general legal or formal distinction between ordinary law and constitutional law at all.[8] The combination of these two features – parliamentary supremacy and the absence of any entrenched domestic law – also means that an Act of Parliament may not bind future legislative enactments. In any conflict between two parliamentary statutes, whatever their nature or level of importance, the provisions of the later one will always prevail.[9]

A third special characteristic that shapes the whole process of constitutional amendment in the UK lies in the institutional relationship between the executive and Parliament. The UK possesses a parliamentary executive, in the sense that government ministers (technically, ministers of the Crown) sit in the bicameral Parliament,[10] and collectively they dominate the proceedings of both Houses in a number of different ways. This domination in the House of Commons, by far the more powerful of the two parliamentary chambers than the House of Lords,[11] is largely the product of the simple plurality (First-Past-the-Post) voting system at general elections, which produces a wider deviation from proportionality than any other voting model, and usually results in an overall majority for one political party.[12] The initiation of public business and draft legislation, therefore, particularly on major issues including constitutional reform, lies with the executive, and Parliament is primarily a reactive body, approving measures after scrutiny, debate and discussion as presented it to it by ministers.[13]

Finally, the working of the UK constitution relies heavily on constitutional 'conventions', meaning political maxims and understandings regarded as binding upon those whom they describe or refer to, but which are not legally enforceable.[14] All countries rely upon such informal rules to some extent, in order to smooth the practice of politics, for no documentary constitution can hope to embrace absolutely every aspect of its politics and government. However, in the UK, conventions are of particular importance, firstly because of the sheer range of subject matter they address where no constitutional law exists. For example, there is no law that even provides for the office of the UK Head of Government, the Prime Minister, who is simply a creature of *de facto* political practice, and the convention that the Monarch will appoint a Prime Minister to preside over the executive government of the country. Secondly, conventions are of importance because they often make sense of obsolete or anachronistic laws that are still nominally in existence. For example, in common law the Queen has an untrammelled power to say 'Yes' or 'No' to any item of legislation passed up to her for Assent, but in practice no Royal Veto has been exercised since 1707 and the convention is that she will automatically give her Assent so long as all due parliamentary formalities have been complied with.[15] As is discussed below, conventions can play an important role with respect to informal methods of constitutional change.

The terminology of this subject needs a few words of explanation. In the past, and still today, the expression of an 'amendment' to the UK constitution, signifying some significant revision in its structure or operation, has hardly been used. This is mainly because it carries some connotation of a written constitution, arising from constitutions abroad, such as in the USA, having well-known 'amendments' attached to them. Constitutional 'reform' is the term most commonly adopted by UK politicians and writers to denote constitutional changes of some magnitude. Thus there are many books entitled this way,[16] and indeed some statutory measures effecting important revisions.[17] However, as Professor Jeffrey Jowell has pointed out, the term 'reform' connotes an intention of moving towards 'some higher plane or better world',[18] which may well be inappropriate in the view of others who disagree with its beneficial purpose or effects. Recently, for this reason, the term constitutional 'change' has often been used instead, as it is a more ubiquitous term, easily embracing gradual alterations in the theory and practice of the constitution (notably conventions) as well as measures implemented at a particular moment in time (notably Acts of Parliament or landmark judicial rulings). However, there is some merit in now speaking of reforms or changes to the UK constitution in terms of 'amendments', for it both firms up the idea that the UK does possess a constitution, and it clarifies the fact that major measures altering the political and constitutional status quo are indeed equivalent to revisions in foreign written constitutions elsewhere. The expression 'constitutional amendment' is therefore used regularly throughout this article, but this should not be taken to signify that it carries any technical meaning, any more so than the interchangeable terms of constitutional 'reform' or 'change'.

Major amendments and their political context

The changes that have occurred since the late seventeenth century have been evolutionary ones, reflecting new political realities. Ad hoc changes to the UK's traditional constitution have been made in an organic way, addressing some political problem as and when it has arisen. Many of these, which affected the working and machinery of government, were implemented by convention and a change in practice, such as the emergence of Cabinet government chaired by a Prime Minister in place of the Monarch,[19] and some landmark judgments were made in the courts, such as those affecting the liberties of the subject and the press.[20] However, most changes amending the relationship between the Crown, Parliament and the people were effected through Parliament, such as the three 'Reform Acts' of the nineteenth century – the Representation of the People Acts 1832, 1867 and 1884 – redrawing electoral constituencies and extending the franchise. This process was completed by the Representation of the People Act 1918, granting universal suffrage and votes for women for the first time.[21]

A selection of the most significant constitutional amendments over the past century is therefore a subjective exercise. In a recent study of constitutional legislation in the twentieth century, Professor Lord Norton, a former chairman of the House of Lords Constitution Committee, identified six major parliamentary enactments as being of special significance:[22] the Parliament Act 1911, the Representation of the People Act 1918, the European Communities Act 1972, the Human Rights Act 1998, the Scotland Act 1998 and the House of Lords Act 1999. Although there have been several other Acts of Parliament over the past century dealing with important aspects of the political and constitutional system,[23] these six statutes do indeed represent the most significant changes made to the UK constitution in recent times, on the grounds of their subject matter and the impact they have had on the working of the constitution as a whole.

The Parliament Act 1911

The Parliament Act 1911 was the product of a protracted political battle between the two Houses of Parliament: the elected House of Commons and the Conservative-dominated hereditary peers in the House of Lords. Possessing equal legislative authority as the Commons before the Act,[24] the Lords rejected the Liberal government's finance bill (the 'People's Budget') in 1909, which would have substantially increased taxation, including on landed estates. This came against a background of great controversy towards the end of the nineteenth century when the House of Lords had blocked an earlier Liberal government's plans for home rule for Ireland.[25] Two general elections were held in 1910, the latter expressly on the subject of curtailing the powers of the Second Chamber, and both elections were won by the Liberal government. The Parliament Bill, which substituted the legislative veto of the Lords with a two-year power of delay,[26] was finally agreed to by the Lords, after the Prime Minister obtained an agreement from King George V that, if they refused to pass the Bill, he would appoint sufficient new peers to flood the House with Liberal members and ensure a government majority in the Second Chamber to do so. Although it was passed in the same way as any ordinary Act of Parliament, this measure, more than any other constitutional amendment over the last century, was the subject of hugely lengthy parliamentary debates raising fundamental questions about checks and balances in the UK political system, and, as mentioned, a general election was specifically held on the subject, seeking a popular mandate behind restricting the powers of the Second Chamber.

The Representation of the People Act 1918

The Representation of the People Act in 1918 laid the foundations of the modern voting system in the UK, and dealt with a range of basic electoral issues including universal male voting, votes for women, the method of election (First-Past-the-Post, Alternative Vote or Single Transferable Vote) and the abolition of plural voting. As a major piece of legislation it was remarkable for having been prepared and passed whilst the country was in the middle of the most traumatic and devastating war ever faced. Yet this factor largely explained its success in terms of reaching agreement across the wide political division of opinion on its subject matter. The parliamentary passage of the Bill was marked by a spirit of concord amongst parliamentarians about the overriding need for civic reconstruction in the post-war era. The preparation of the Bill was preceded by conference in 1916–17, convened to agree its original terms, with a cross-party composition dominated by long-standing back-bench members of the House of Commons, under the chairmanship of the Speaker of the House.[27] This mechanism for reform was novel at that time, designed specifically as a device to secure political agreement on a number of sensitive issues. Subsequently, it provided a valuable precedent for the later Speaker's Conferences on electoral law that have been held.

The European Communities Act 1972

Of deep international significance for the UK constitution was the European Communities Act 1972, putting into legal effect Britain's membership of the European Communities (now Union). This was a subject where there were deep divisions within the two main parties, as well as across them. It was enacted under a Conservative administration, with the Labour opposition fiercely resisting the Bill, even though earlier it had agreed in principle to apply for EC membership itself. The House of Commons proved the battleground for the reform, narrowly won by the government, with the House of Lords comfortably supporting the measure. After the two general elections of 1974, with Labour returning to office, a referendum on continued membership of the EC was held in 1975 – the first ever held across the UK – in which parliamentary members and government ministers were allowed by their party leader to campaign freely as they wished, and which resulted in the UK remaining in the EC.[28] The constitutional consequences of the Act were to subject the domestic courts to the decisions of the European Court of Justice, a point that seems to have been unclear to parliamentarians at the time, and which created considerable controversy at Westminster following the *Factortame* case,[29] in which the Judicial Committee of the House of Lords accepted that the operation of a domestic statute, the Merchant Shipping Act 1988, was suspended by an inconsistent EC law.

The Scotland Act 1998 and the Human Rights Act 1998

The three other most significant measures of twentieth-century constitutional amendment were all enacted during the early years of the Labour government under Tony Blair's premiership, which began in 1997. Each of these was deeply controversial, but Labour had an overwhelming overall majority of 179 members in the House of Commons that guaranteed their passage. The background to the first of these, the Scotland Act 1998 – which devolved power to a Scottish executive and parliament for the governance of the region – was that an earlier Labour government in the 1970s had also attempted to introduce devolution. This had disastrously failed after insufficient support at a Scottish referendum held on the measure, and traumatically for the Labour Party had led to the collapse of the government itself.[30] This was therefore regarded as 'unfinished business' by Labour, and during 1997–98 it was fiercely campaigned for by ministers at a pre-legislative Scottish referendum held on the issue. Further strengthened by the positive outcome of that referendum, the Bill was pushed through Parliament on a three-line whip, controversially using a programmed timetable for the legislative process.[31] During the same legislative session of Parliament, there were other measures of devolution enacted for Wales and the government of London.[32]

There was a strong imperative behind the next major amendment to the constitution too – the Human Rights Act 1998, which incorporated the European Convention on Human Rights (ECHR) into domestic law. There were deep reservations within the Labour Party about this measure, because of the extension in power and influence it would give the judiciary. It substantially extended the scope of judicial review over the decisions and acts of public authorities, and the Bill's 'declaration of incompatibility' procedure would enable the courts to put pressure on the government over its legislative policy.[33] However, the policy of incorporation of the ECHR had been strongly advocated by John Smith, the much respected former Labour leader who died suddenly in 1994, and adopted by him as a centrepiece of his policy review on constitutional modernisation generally.[34] Implementation of this reform was therefore regarded within Labour as the 'moral legacy' of John Smith, whatever misgivings many within the Labour Party had about the measure. Passage of the Bill encountered few problems in Parliament, and the House of Lords – where the Bill was first introduced – was supportive of incorporation. No referendum was held on the issue, it having been included in Labour's election manifesto the previous year. The main source of criticism and pressure on the Bill came from groups outside Westminster, particularly the Church and media, leading to some revisions to the original form of the Bill.[35]

The House of Lords Act 1999

The next year, the House of Lords Bill 1998–99 sought to substantially amend the composition of the parliamentary Second Chamber. Removal of the hereditary peerage from the House of Lords had been the flagship policy in Labour's 1997 election manifesto section on constitutional reform, seeking to emphasise a distinction between 'modernising' Labour versus an 'out-of-time' Conservative government that defended the antiquated and anachronistic hereditary component remaining in the Second Chamber (most of whom took the Conservative whip). The Bill was comfortably passed by the House of Commons, but the real battle began in the Second Chamber where it encountered the opposition of almost all the hereditary peers and the Conservative opposition. However, if deference to the Salisbury–Addison convention of restraint on a matter of mandated government policy was widely accepted, there was a principled case that Parliament should not remove a large component of the House without first presenting its plans for an alternative method of selecting future members of the House. Less for this reason, and more because the government preferred a compromise on the Bill to losing it altogether that session, a scheme for 92 hereditary peers (out of a total of 750) to remain was agreed upon. No referendum was held on the issue, the government claiming a mandate on the subject from its overwhelming general election victory the previous year. One of the most unusual aspects of the reform lay in the negotiations and pressures within and across the parties outside Parliament. The compromise deal to keep 92 hereditary peers had originally been brokered by the Conservative leader in the House of Lords, Lord Robert Cranborne, directly with the Prime Minister at 10 Downing Street. However, this deal was repudiated by the Conservative Party's then national leader, William Hague, which led to Mr Hague sacking Lord Cranborne as party leader in the Lords. Nonetheless, the same agreement was put into effect later on during the Bill's passage, by way of a crossbench peer, Lord Weatherill, presenting it to Parliament as an amendment to the original form of the Bill.

It is important to make a final observation on the three constitutional changes that occurred in 1997–99, which is that the incoming government under Tony Blair in 1997 heralded a markedly different approach to constitutional change than had existed before. Earlier, individual constitutional amendments had generally emerged in reaction to some particular political problem or pressures. However, the Blair administration came into office with a wide-ranging programme of constitutional reform that it wanted to implement, including devolution to Scotland and Wales; an elected London mayor; incorporation of the European Convention on Human Rights; removal of the hereditary peers from the House of Lords; and a freedom of information statute.[36] In office, it then adopted an express policy of rolling constitutional change, with a new Department for Constitutional Affairs being created with a specific remit for modernising UK government and the constitution.[37] In other words, government attitudes towards constitutional change had become proactive, rather than reactive. Nonetheless, despite the breadth of the amendments undertaken, an ad hoc approach was taken by the government to each new measure, deliberately eschewing any coherent theory or overarching plan into which each constitutional amendment would fit with one other. As the then Lord Chancellor, Lord Irvine, the minister responsible for constitutional reform at that time, stated in the House of Lords, 'the correct road to reform was to devise a solution to each problem on its own terms'.[38]

The formal process for constitutional amendment

Because of the nature of the UK constitution, and the absence of formal distinction between ordinary and constitutional laws, as discussed above, the process and procedures by which the constitution is formally changed and amended is broadly similar to the passage of any other legislation.

A normal legislative process involves a Bill being presented in one of the two Houses of Parliament for a First Reading, which is purely formal; then a Second Reading debate follows at a later date, in which the general principles of the Bill are debated and voted on. Most Bills commence in the House of Commons, but some are chosen each annual session to start in the Lords for administrative convenience, making use of time in the Lords at the start of a session and avoiding overburdening it towards the end. After its Second Reading, a Bill then goes into a committee stage, in which its clauses are scrutinised one by one and amendments may be made. In the House of Commons, this stage is conducted by a Public Bill Committee comprising between 16 and 50 members,[39] chosen by reference to any special interest or expertise they may have in the subject of the Bill and the party composition of the House. In the House of Lords, the committee stage is usually taken in the whole house, but less important or non-controversial measures may be remitted to a Grand Committee to which all members may attend.[40] In the proceedings of each House, a Report Stage follows the committee, for consideration of its proposed amendments, if any. A final Third Reading then follows, sometimes taken immediately after the Report Stage, after which the Bill goes to the other House, if not already considered there. The Royal Assent then follows, which is a formality.

The Second Chamber, the House of Lords, has only limited legislative powers, being generally regarded by the political elite of the country as subordinate to the House of Commons. Under the Parliament Acts 1911 and 1949, the Lords may not veto a Bill of which it disapproves, and possesses only a power of delay of one year.[41] Therefore if the House of Lords rejects a Bill in two successive annual sessions, but the government is determined to enact the legislation, the Speaker of the House of Commons will certify that the provisions of the Parliament Acts have been satisfied, and the Bill is presented directly to the Monarch for Royal Assent. The Parliament Acts procedure to legislate without the consent of the House of Lords is only rarely used in practice, as the Lords generally acquiesce to the Commons' insistence on its measures or reversals of amendments in the House of Lords. There is a political custom, too, known as the Salisbury–Addison convention, under which the House of Lords will not vote down a government Bill whose main policy purpose was included in the governing party's manifesto at the previous general election.[42] Rarely, if the House of Lords has strong reservations about a Bill, particularly if it is initially presented to the Lords before the Commons, the Lords may refer the measure to a Select Committee, allowing greater time and more intensive scrutiny of its provisions and implications, followed by a formal report by the Committee for the benefit of the House. This happened over the controversial Constitutional Reform Bill 2003–04,[43] which in its original form sought to abolish the ancient office of Lord Chancellor without any proper prior consultation with the legal and judicial establishment.

Nonetheless, deadlock between the two Houses may occur, and governments have driven legislation onto the statute book in the face of objections by the House of Lords on a few occasions in our recent history. Such enactments include the Welsh Church Act 1914, the Government of Ireland Act 1914, the Parliament Act 1949, the War Crimes Act 1991, the European Parliamentary Elections Act 1999, the Sexual Offences (Amendment) Act 2000 and the Hunting Act 2004. It should be noted that each of these Bills was of a constitutional nature,[44] suggesting that the House of Lords is more assertive, even if ultimately ineffective, over subjects of a constitutional or civil liberties nature.

Some variations on normal legislative processes are applicable to Bills dealing with a major constitutional issue. One of these is that, in the House of Commons, it is customary for the Bill to go to a Committee of the Whole House, rather than a much smaller Public Bill Committee. This is so that a full ventilation of opinion on the Bill may be given. Examples in the current session of Parliament, 2010–12, include the European Union Bill, the Fixed-term Parliaments Bill, the Parliamentary Voting System and Constituencies Bill, and the Scotland Bill. The rigour of this custom has been diluted in recent times by a greater use of programme resolutions and time-allocation orders limiting the amount of time to be spent on parliamentary debate before the vote is put.[45] Another feature of such Bills is that, along with some particularly difficult or controversial measures, in recent practice they may be presented initially in the form of a draft Bill, allowing pre-legislative scrutiny by one or more Select Committees at Parliament. This is the case, for example, with the current draft House of Lords Reform Bill 2010–12, and earlier with respect to the draft Constitutional Renewal Bill 2007–08, which preceded the Constitutional Reform and Governance Bill 2008–09 enacted in 2010.[46]

There is one constitutional matter over which the House of Lords retains an absolute veto. This is any Bill to prolong the life of Parliament; in other words, to suspend general elections. This was expressly excluded from the provisions of the Parliament Act 1911.[47] No such veto has ever been exercised, but general elections were suspended during the First World War by the Parliament and Registration

Act 1916, the Parliament and Local Elections Act 1916, the Parliament and Local Elections Act 1917, and the Parliament and Local Elections (No. 2) Act 1917. The periods of suspension were, respectively, eight months, seven months, seven months and eight months. During the Second World War, general elections were suspended by Prolongation of Parliament Acts in each year from 1940 to 1944, each measure extending the life of Parliament by exactly one year. In the case of all these legislative measures, the House of Lords accepted the case for suspending general elections, being as they are a massive disruption to the population of the country, and the need for national unity between the parties that had formed a coalition government.

There are no requirements for special majority voting in either House over a legislative measure of any kind. Simple majorities are all that is required in the voting on the various stages in a Bill, however fundamental in nature. Indeed, there are only three special voting procedures required in UK parliamentary law at all. Two of these requirements are laid down in the Standing Orders of the House of Commons, being that 100 members must vote in favour of a Closure resolution, putting an end to a debate,[48] and 40 for a quorum in any division (vote).[49] Under section 2 of the Fixed-term Parliaments Act 2011, an early general election within each five-year interval between elections may be called if two-thirds of the membership of the House of Commons votes in favour of such a resolution.

Referendums are not a general requirement for constitutional amendment in UK law, but a few have been held on an ad hoc basis in recent times, mostly consultative in terms of endorsing government policy and proposals for legislation, but some as part of a legislative process. Most of these have concerned the regional government of the country, and the UK's relationship with Europe. The referendums in the 1970s involved consulting the electorate of Northern Ireland on whether it should remain part of the UK or join with the Republic of Ireland in 1973; on the UK's continuing membership of the European Communities in 1975; and on Scottish and Welsh devolution in 1979 as a procedural requirement before the Scotland Act and Wales Act that year could come into effect (which, in the event, lapsed because of insufficient support at the referendums). The Referendums (Scotland and Wales) Act 1997 later provided for further Scottish and Welsh referendums to endorse the new proposals for devolution under the Labour government headed by Tony Blair, which were forthcoming and led to the Scotland Act 1998 and the Government of Wales Act 1998. Later regional referendums were held on proposals for a London Mayor and Assembly in 1998, on the Northern Ireland Belfast Agreement in 1998, on a Regional Assembly in the North of England in 2003, and on further Welsh devolution in 2003. In 2010, a referendum was held on whether the present First-Past-the-Post method of electing members to the House of Commons should be replaced by the Alternative Vote, which returned a result in favour of the status quo. The European Union Act 2011 now requires an Act of Parliament and a referendum to be held before the UK government may agree to any treaty changes that represent an extension of the powers or competence of the EU or its institutions.

Constitutional amendment proposals may emanate from a number of different sources, most notably political parties whether in office or opposition, independent policy think-tanks (such as the centre-left Institute for Public Policy Research, and the centre-right Centre for Policy Studies), parliamentary select committees (particularly, at present, the House of Lords Constitution Committee, the Commons Political and Constitutional Reform Committee, and the Joint Parliamentary Committee on Human Rights), independent commissions (such as the Electoral Commission, and the Equality and Human Rights Commission), and the writings of university professors. Frequently, government legislative policy has its roots in sound but initially radical-sounding ideas that begin life on the margins of politics, particularly in the corridors of academe, which then slowly filter into the hearing and imagination of journalists, backbench MPs, party policy advisers, and eventually senior politicians and civil servants.

However, in the UK it is almost always the case that any constitutional change of major magnitude needs to be formulated and presented to Parliament by the government of the day. A Bill presented by an ordinary parliamentary member in the form of a Private Members' Bill in the House of Commons stands no chance of success unless the member secures time, which is done by winning one of the top six places in the annual ballot that takes place for prioritising such Bills in the limited time available,[50] and any such Bill is easily obstructed by the government through mobilising its majority in the House or declining to make the additional parliamentary time it will need available for it. In any event, it is a prevalent idea that on important matters a government minister should take responsibility, be able to harness the resources of the civil service in the preparation of the legislation, and be accountable to Parliament for shaping the Bill in its original form.[51] Private Members' Bills, even if unsuccessful, may have a role to play in building pressure behind a particular reform, and contributing to its eventual adoption, in revised form, by the government.[52]

Another customary idea is that difficult issues of parliamentary election law, particularly if they have a broad scope in terms of representation and are a matter of cross-party concern, are a suitable subject for referral to a Conference to be chaired by the Speaker of the House of Commons, with a view to recommendations being put forward for the government to consider acting upon. The first instance of such a Conference was in 1916–17, which was established to consider universal voting, the female franchise and the voting system. Most of its recommendations eventually found their way into the Representation of the People Act 1918, discussed above. A second such Conference was held in 1944 to examine the parliamentary constituency boundaries, reform of the franchise and conduct, costs and methods of election, which led to the Representation of the People Act 1944. Since then, there have been five further Speaker's Conferences, all dealing with matters of parliamentary representation and election law. The most recent was established in 2009 to examine female and ethnic minority representation, whether the voting age should be reduced to 16 years and on which day voting should take place.[53]

Changes affecting the monarchy may require special treatment. Where any Bill affects the royal prerogative,[54] it is customary for the government minister or parliamentary member to seek the permission of the Monarch first, before presenting the Bill to Parliament. The Monarch's consent will then be conveyed to each House when the Bill is presented for its Second Reading debate. For example, when introducing the Constitutional Reform and Governance Bill (affecting matters relating to the civil service, treaty-making and the peerage) on 24 March 2010, the responsible minister in the House of Lords said,[55] 'My Lords, I have it in command from Her Majesty the Queen to acquaint the House that Her Majesty, having been informed of the purport of the Constitutional Reform and Governance Bill, has consented to place her prerogative and interest, so far as they are affected by the Bill, at the disposal of Parliament for the purposes of the Bill'. This royal consent today is automatic, although it is always open to the Monarch to express her opinion privately to the Prime Minister of the day.[56]

Amendments to the law governing succession to the Crown are also subject to a special process, which is that those other countries where the Monarch serves as Head of State must be consulted and signify their agreement to the changes proposed by the UK government. These other 15 countries, known as the Commonwealth realms, are Canada, Australia, New Zealand, Jamaica, Antigua and Barbuda, Bahamas, Barbados, Grenada, Belize, St Kitts and Nevis, St Lucia, Solomon Islands, Tuvalu, St Vincent and the Grenadines and Papua New Guinea. A requirement for this multinational agreement stems from the Statute of Westminster 1931, which codified the principles agreed in the Imperial Conference declarations of 1926 and 1930 about the relationship between the UK and the self-governing dominions at that time. The Preamble to the Statute reads, 'Any alteration in the law touching the Succession to the Throne or the Royal Style and Titles shall hereafter require the assent as well of the Parliaments of all the Dominions as of the Parliament of the United Kingdom'. As this is not part of the text of the Act, this provision is not a legal rule as such, but a convention; one which in these circumstances is equivalent to an international treaty between all the self-governing nations retaining the Monarch as head of state. In effect, however, it is a legal requirement because unless the UK wishes to see the Crown divided – such that different laws govern the royal succession in the different Commonwealth realms, leading to different heads of state – it needs to secure the necessary changes in the constitutional law of each of the separate nations concerned. As each of the other 15 realms have their own written constitutions, with different processes for constitutional amendment, this could be a complex undertaking. However, such a process is currently underway following the public statement of the Heads of Government of the realms at its last Commonwealth meeting in October 2011, in which they agreed in principle to end the system of male-preference primogeniture and to remove the legal provision that anyone who marries a Roman Catholic shall be ineligible to succeed to the Crown.[57]

Informal methods of constitutional amendment

Whilst the great majority of important constitutional amendments take place by way of formal legislation through Parliament, as in the six cases considered above, other significant amendments do occur by what might be termed 'informal methods', notably judicial decision-making in matters of public law and changes in the constitutional conventions regulating the system of government. As a recent Council of Europe report has said, 'Formal amendment is not the only form of constitutional change, and in some systems not even the most important. Leaving aside revolutionary or unlawful acts, the two most important ways of legitimate constitutional change are through judicial interpretation and through the evolvement of unwritten political conventions supplementing or contradicting the written text. How this functions in a given constitutional system influences the formal amendment'.

In the UK this is certainly true, though in comparison with other countries it is less significant with respect to judicial decisions (in the absence of a constitutional court and constitutional text to interpret), and more so with respect to conventions (in the absence of a documentary constitution dictating the structure and working of government). The scope for judicial creativity in constitutional affairs is further limited by the UK's approach to legislative drafting, which is performed in great detail, generally attempting to provide for as many eventualities as may fall within the statute's scope as possible.[58] Nonetheless, important principles of constitutional law have been created by the judgments of the courts.[59] For instance, *Carltona Ltd v Commissioner of Works*[60] established the doctrine that statutory discretionary powers conferred upon a minister may lawfully be carried out by his departmental officials on his behalf, without express authorisation. Another famous example is *Council of Civil Service Union v Minister for the Civil Service*,[61] which not only authoritatively restated the grounds for judicial review of administrative action, but extended the scope of judicial review into the exercise of common law Crown prerogative powers, whereas previously this had been limited to statutory powers.[62] It is in the field of civil liberties that the judiciary has initiated most changes. *Entick v Carrington*[63] is an ancient landmark, establishing that a person's life, liberty and property can only be interfered with or forfeited if authorised by a power conferred by common law or statute, not under any general warrant signed by a minister. *Christie v Leachinsky*[64] laid down the doctrine that a person being arrested must be informed of the reason for his detention for it to be lawful, a principle codified into statute four decades later.[65] A line of cases developing from *Prince Albert v Strange* (1849) 1 Mac & G 25, including *Argyll v Argyll* [1967] Ch 302, established a doctrine of breach of confidence, enabling injunctions to be granted to suppress publication of private personal matters.[66]

Leading constitutional law judgments are often, in substance, pronouncements on the relationship between the executive and judiciary, and how the courts construe their role in interpreting ministers' powers or those of governmental bodies. Insofar as the courts are essentially the inventors of the common law, which includes its own subservience to Acts of Parliament under the doctrine of parliamentary sovereignty, they may qualify the terms of that relationship, albeit in a manner that is consistent with its doctrine of precedent (*stare decisis*).[67] In other words, the doctrine of parliamentary sovereignty as a dogma of the common law may be refined as time goes on.[68]

Only one parliamentary statute contains a code of constitutional principles, leaving it to the courts to develop and apply those principles in the cases that come before them. This is the Human Rights Act 1998, which incorporated the Articles of the European Convention on Human Rights into the domestic law of the legal systems of the UK. However, the creativity of the courts, in common with most other Council of Europe nation states, is limited by being strongly influenced by the judgments and reasoning of the European Court of Human Rights.[69] The judiciary's approach to its own law-making capacity is often itself a matter of statutory interpretation. Thus, section 2 of the Human Rights Act states that a court 'must take into account' the judgments of the Strasbourg Court, but this leaves open the question of the precise degree of influence and intensity upon the UK's national courts of that body of European jurisprudence. A leading judgment on the subject interpreted this section to mean, in the *dicta* of Lord Bingham, the senior Law Lord at the time, that any court should 'in the absence of some special circumstances, follow any clear and constant jurisprudence of the Strasbourg court'.[70]

An explanation of the special importance of conventions in the UK system of government has already been given. Because of their prominence in the working of the constitution, their nature, mode of coming into existence, establishment and means by which they are enforced (or not) have been the subject of extensive study by professors of constitutional law and political science.[71] The most authoritative analytical test for establishing the existence of a new convention is widely regarded as being that provided by Sir Ivor Jennings, who said there were three questions to ask: what are the precedents, did the actors in the precedents believe they were bound by a rule, and is there a reason for the rule? There are often difficulties in knowing precisely when a constitutional amendment by way of a convention has occurred, being either a change in the convention itself or the creation of a new one, because such rules often depend upon a series of precedents and evolve over a period of time, supported by changing political circumstances and ideas. Thus, one of the most basic conventions of political accountability in the UK is that all government ministers must have a seat in Parliament. With respect to the Prime Minister, the convention is more specific, that he or she must be a member of the House of Commons. The last Prime Minister to be appointed from the House of Lords was the Marquess of Salisbury in 1900–02. Over the next 50 years, there were occasions when a peer in the House of Lords was considered for appointment, such as Lord Curzon in 1923 and Lord Halifax in 1940, and in each case their peerage was undoubtedly a factor in another being appointed in preference to them.[72] That a convention had been firmed up on the matter was only conclusively proved in 1963, when Lord Home was appointed Prime Minister[73] but immediately renounced his peerage (as he was able to do, following passage of the Peerage Act 1963), and arrangements were made for his election as a member of the House of Commons.

However, conventions can be created by being declared, though they will require the support and acquiescence of all who are involved – they cannot be created by simple declaration of a minister unilaterally. A clear example of this happening was the Imperial Conference declarations of 1926 and 1930, followed by the principles set down in the preamble of the Statute of Westminster 1931, which stated that Commonwealth countries retaining the UK Monarch as head of state must agree to any changes in the law on royal succession and to the royal style or titles.[74] Another successful declaration of this kind was the Sewel convention in 1998, following Scottish devolution, which arose from the UK government and the Scottish executive publicly agreeing that the Westminster Parliament will not legislate on matters within the competence of the Scottish Parliament unless it has been previously agreed by the Scottish Parliament that it may do so.[75] An attempt in 2007–09 by the former Prime Minister Gordon Brown to declare a convention under which the House of Commons would need to signify its approval prior to any dissolution of Parliament floundered because the responsible minister, the Leader of the Commons, failed to secure cross-party agreement, or indeed interest, in the proposal.[76]

Another means of constitutional amendment by way of convention is the production by the government or one of its departments of an administrative circular containing a code of conduct. Many such codes have emerged in recent years, two important ones being the Ministerial Code dealing with the conduct of government ministers, and the Cabinet Manual describing the entire working of the UK government. Both these documents purport to be descriptive of the existing situation, and with each new edition will contain shifts in emphasis and practice. The code for ministers, originally called 'Questions of Procedure for Ministers', was first produced in 1945 but not made public until 1992, as a result of which it has acquired added status as a document of authority, descriptive and prescriptive. Its present version sets out 10 principles for ministers, covering such matters as the collective responsibility of ministers, requirements of accountability for their departments and executive agencies, and upholding the political impartiality of the civil service. The Cabinet Manual, prepared in draft by the Cabinet Office before the 2010 general election, and published in final form the following year, is also essentially an internal circular, but one which the media and public will *de facto* regard as an authority source of guidance on how government does and should operate. A significant amendment to previous constitutional practice declared in the draft Cabinet Manual in 2010 was that, following an inconclusive general election, an incumbent Prime Minister should perform a 'caretaker' role, with restrictions on what policies and decisions he or she could take, pending inter-party talks that the Cabinet Office would offer to the parties.[77] This subtly modified previous understandings about hung Parliament situations in which a Prime Minister had first opportunity to remain in office and attempt to form a coalition, with negotiations taking place at 10 Downing Street, but may resign straight away if he or she feels unable to continue in office, allowing the leader of the next largest party to be appointed Prime Minister with or without any pact with one or more of the smaller parties.[78] Earlier also, a prevalent theory maintained that the Monarch might have some personal role to play in government formation, as had been the case in 1931,[79] but the Cabinet Manual now rightly places emphasis on royal non-intervention.[80]

There are two further means of informal constitutional amendment that are of special significance in the UK. One is that several matters of considerable importance to the working of Parliament, which in foreign countries might well be included in their written constitution, are dealt with in the UK through simple resolutions of the House of Commons published as Standing Orders. Thus, the election of the Speaker of the House of Commons, the rules of debate, the existence and regulation of its Select Committees and the treatment of public petitions are all matters regulated and amended through such resolutions of the House.[81] A similar situation applies to the internal working of the House of Lords.[82] The other informal method to note is that amendments to the machinery of government and civil service may be made by the Prime Minister under the legal authority of the common law Crown prerogative. This means that departments of state, even the most important or longest in existence, may be modified by the Prime Minister without any formal parliamentary approval. In this way, the justice functions of the Lord Chancellor's Department and constitutional work of the Home Office were transferred to a newly created Department for Constitutional Affairs in 2003, which then had its responsibilities revised and was retitled the Ministry of Justice in 2007.[83]

Critique of current UK amendment practice

The whole process of constitutional amendment, together with the conduct of the Cabinet and centre of government in preparing its policy on constitutional affairs, is now a subject of major concern and discussion by parliamentary committees and university constitutional experts.[84] A number of serious criticisms of the way in which the UK government has carried out reforms to the constitution in recent years can indeed fairly be made. Even on matters of the utmost importance to the political system and its democracy, too many measures have been presented to Parliament without adequate prior consultation, and been rushed through both Houses on a three-line governing party whip, weakening the quality of genuine parliamentary debate and scrutiny of legislative proposals.

More broadly, an incoherence of guiding principles, a lack of clarity in governmental responsibilities and an inconsistency in the procedures chosen by the government for major constitutional amendment have been evident in the many changes made to the constitution in recent years. The vacuum of an established framework for constitutional amendment opens the way for an unscrupulous executive to make changes to the constitution for reasons of party self-interest and political advantage over its opponents. It breeds a culture of unethical conduct, in which other parties will seek to benefit and misuse their powers when in office, behaving in like manner. In the past, particularly up until 1997, an ad hoc and inconsistent approach to constitutional amendment was less of a problem as little attention was paid to constitutional reform generally. But, as has been mentioned, reform of the constitution has now become virtually a rolling exercise, with change – as in all contemporary bureaucracies, in the private or public sector – being regarded by those responsible as an inherent virtue in itself for managerial drive and success. The process of constitutional law reform has therefore become a matter of much greater importance, and there is now a pressing need to establish a proper system of procedures and safeguards to protect the fundamentals of the political system and life of its democracy.

A recent example as a case study is the Fixed-term Parliaments Bill, which reached the statute book on 15 September 2011. The purpose of this important constitutional amendment was to change the system for the timing of general elections – the main political event in the life of the UK, when the composition of both the executive and the dominant legislative chamber are chosen. The traditional system of election timing was that the Monarch dissolved Parliament upon the advice of the Prime Minister at some point within a five-year period, which in practice normally amounted to every four years (the average duration between elections over the past 100 years).[85] Under the government's proposals, elections would instead be held at five-yearly fixed intervals, subject to an earlier election in two specified circumstances of emergency.[86] In effect, this is prolonging the period between general elections, and weakening the political accountability of those who govern the country.

The government that presented the Bill is a coalition between the Conservative Party (having 306 seats in the House of Commons) and the Liberal Democrats (57 seats), giving it an overall majority in the House of 77 members. This amendment to the constitutional position on general elections had not been in the dominant Conservative Party's manifesto at the election only two months earlier in the year,[87] but it had been a Liberal Democrat policy for many years. Indeed, during the election campaign the Conservative leader, David Cameron, had made the contradictory promise for legislation to require a general election within six months of a new party leader taking over as Prime Minister, following the death or resignation of the previous incumbent within the lifetime of a Parliament (a reference to Gordon Brown taking over from Tony Blair as premier in 2007, although there had been several other occasions in British contemporary history of such a transfer of power taking place[88]). The political motivation behind the Bill, which everyone realised, was to cement the life of the government, both as a coalition between two parties who were not natural bed-fellows,[89] and in order to allow the Chancellor of the Exchequer as long as possible to preside over a recovery of the dire state of the national economy before having to face the electorate again.

Without any prior consultation, the Bill was published on Thursday 22 July 2010, only two working days before Parliament went into its summer recess on Tuesday 27 July. The government then set a date of Monday 13 September for the Bill's Second Reading debate, only five working days after Parliament had reconvened following the summer break. This allowed for negligible preparation by parliamentarians to consider and, if necessary, take evidence and expert advice on the proposal. Unsurprisingly, the specialist constitutional committees in both Houses of Parliament complained and were highly critical of the government's methods. Thus, the House of Commons Political and Constitutional Reform Committee, which had been established after the 2010 election specifically to scrutinise the coalition government's constitutional reform programme, and which had only a matter of days to prepare a report for the House, said:[90] 'The Fixed-term Parliaments Bill is ill-thought through, rushed and does not appear to provide a satisfactory solution, which ideally should be one around which there can be political consensus. It is unacceptable that a Bill of this legal and constitutional complexity has not been the subject of any prior consultation or pre-legislative scrutiny . . . It is acutely disappointing to us that we have needed to criticise the Government for the process it has chosen to adopt in the passage of its first two constitutional Bills,[91] the other being the Parliamentary Voting System and Constituencies Bill[92] . . . Bills of such legal and constitutional sensitivity should be published in draft for full pre-legislative scrutiny, rather than proceeded with in haste.'

The House of Lords, and its Constitution Committee, had more time to prepare for the Bill, which was received on 19 January 2011, with its Second Reading debate held on 1 March. The Report of the Committee was therefore more thorough than the Commons Committee had been able to conduct, but, in a similar manner to its sister body in the Commons, it concluded:[93] 'The speed with which the policy was introduced, with no significant consultation, no green paper and no detailed assessment of the pros and cons of a five-year term over a four-year term, suggests that short-term considerations were the drivers behind the Bill's introduction . . . We take the view that the origins and content of this Bill owe more to short-term considerations than to a mature assessment of enduring constitutional principles or sustained public demand.'

Both parliamentary committees complained that there should have been a thorough consultation process before the Bill was introduced, by way of a Green or White paper or a draft Bill, and both committees pointed out important issues in the Bill where there was little political and public support, particularly on the length of the interval proposed between general elections. The strong weight of evidence received by both committees suggested that the fixed interval between general elections should be four years, not five, reflecting existing normal practice.[94]

The accusation that the integrity of the government's process of policy formulation as manifested in the Bill was threadbare is supported by the peculiarity of its statements and erratic behaviour towards the reform in the months prior to its introduction to Parliament. As originally outlined in May 2010, the government said it would proceed by way of 'a binding motion' in the House of Commons, stating that the next general election would be held on the first Thursday of May 2015, and that this would be followed later on by legislation on fixed-term Parliaments after the present one.[95] This was then rescinded, upon the basis that, having thought further about the practicalities, this proposed binding motion could have caused difficulties for the Queen if a prime ministerial request for dissolution of Parliament were made subsequent to the resolution being made.[96] On the proviso for early elections within each fixed term, initially the government said that this would occur if 55 per cent of the House of Commons voted for this in a resolution.[97] Such a provision was also referred to in the Queen's Speech at the state opening of Parliament, setting out the government's legislative programme for the session. This prompted widespread confusion about how this vote on a parliamentary dissolution would synchronise with traditional 'No Confidence' motions in the House, and caused public controversy at the suggestion of the special majority required.[98] The government then changed its mind again, announcing a different scheme for early elections, which was set out in the Bill.[99]

The political imperative driving the Bill, being the mutual self-interest of the coalition partners in government, meant that the party managers in both Houses exerted maximum pressure on their parliamentary members to vote for the Bill, whatever their personal misgivings. Thus one Conservative member in the Lords amusingly stated later on:[100] 'The hallmark of our constitution is its flexibility . . . One of the things that we have done is to introduce fixed Parliaments. I do not know why we did it. I certainly did not agree with it, although I was seduced by the charms of our Chief Whip into voting for it. I am not in favour of fixed Parliaments at all. I can only think that the Chief Whip persuaded me to vote for it through the exercise of feminine wiles.'

The House of Lords disapproved of the measure, and inserted a 'sunset clause' in the Bill so that the fixed term was confined to the present Parliament only. A legislative 'ping-pong' process developed between it and the House of Commons until the Lords acquiesced, with the government agreeing to a provision for a review of the operation of the Act during 2020.[101] The interests of the coalition partners, then, were satisfied. For the Liberal Democrats, it guaranteed that the Conservative leadership would not renege on them at any time when their ratings in the opinion polls were riding high and advise the Queen to dissolve Parliament and call an election. For the Conservatives, it locked the Liberal Democrats into a five-year deal, giving long-term security to its position whilst implementing its unpopular economic programme of taxation rises and cuts in public spending. Compliance with good practice in the preparation and passage into law of a new, permanent constitutional structure for the timing of general elections in the future was very much a secondary consideration.

Many further case studies could be made of measures of constitutional law reform enacted through a poor process. Similar widespread criticisms about a flawed process being adopted by the government were made with regard to the Parliamentary Voting System and Constituencies Bill passed in the same session as the Fixed-term Parliaments Act.[102] Notorious earlier recent examples of major constitutional amendments presented with no or negligible pre-legislative consultation include the Constitutional Reform Bill in 2005 (seeking to abolish the ancient office of Lord Chancellor, remove the Law Lords from the Second Chamber and establish a Supreme Court, at the same time as establishing a Ministry of Justice under the authority of the Crown prerogative), and the Parliamentary Standards Bill in 2009 (establishing an external regulatory body over parliamentary members' financial affairs, at odds with the ancient tradition of parliamentary self-regulation).[103]

The way in which referendums have been utilised as part of a constitutional amendment process in the UK has lacked any consistency of purpose, and more often than not they have been used for crude political advantage by the party in office. Thus, some have been driven as a means to unite the governing party on an issue over which it is divided (such as Labour's referendum on Europe in 1975), and others as a means of neutralising political opposition to a measure the government is determined to put on the statute book (such as Labour's referendums on Scottish and Welsh devolution in 1997). On the voting system, the Labour government promised in its 1997 election manifesto an independent Commission to bring forward a recommended proportional alternative to the existing First-Past-the-Post (simple plurality) system that would be put to a referendum. The Commission duly reported in 1998,[104] favouring a mixed constituency and party-list system, but the Labour Cabinet then reneged on its promise and the referendum never took place.

However, in 2011 a referendum on the voting system took place under the present coalition government. This was driven by a political deal struck in the coalition agreement prior to taking office between the Conservatives and Liberal Democrats. In reality, the Conservative leadership oppose any change from First-Past-the-Post voting, and the Liberal Democrats support adoption of a proportional system, the Single Transferable Vote. Their political pact, however, grudgingly entered into by the Conservative leadership, was to hold a referendum offering the Alternative Vote, which neither party wished for as a long-term proposition. The electorate, therefore, was left in the position of not being offered an opportunity to express its voice on the full range of principal electoral systems[105] through which the country should be governed in future. Unsurprisingly, the country voted against change, even though there is evidence that public opinion does not support the status quo.[106]

Proposals for reform of the constitutional amendment process

There is now a real need for the UK to carry out a major reassessment of the direction in which it wishes its constitution to continue to develop, and the way in which future amendments to the political and constitutional system should be made. This is a wide-ranging subject that embraces issues of consultation in the preparation of public policy, establishing appropriate and consistent parliamentary procedures for scrutinising government proposals, and finding practical means of distinguishing measures of a constitutional nature that are to be treated differently from normal legislation. It also raises fundamental questions about the relationship between the two Houses of Parliament, and the future structure of the constitution itself.

It is not difficult to formulate schemes for improved norms of conduct, established as duties upon the government, in the preparation of new policies for constitutional change, and in the legislative and other processes through which they should be approved and come into effect. Thus, within the UK's existing constitutional framework, the following consultation procedures would command widespread parliamentary and popular support. There should always be a rigorous process of consultation, as with all significant public measures. The government's own Code of Practice on Consultation, which has existed since 2000, should actually be complied with, while at present it frequently is not.[107] Any measure identifiable as being constitutional in nature should be the subject of a formal Green (consultation) paper, followed by a White (statement and explanation of government intent) paper for public consumption and response. Greater care, and more genuine attempts, should be taken by ministers to ensure that relevant expertise and professional research to be found in the work of universities and elsewhere is taken note of, to supplement the preparatory work of the civil service. All constitutional amendment proposals should be the subject of collective discussion and agreement in Cabinet. A draft Bill on any constitutional proposals should always be presented to Parliament for pre-legislative scrutiny by each House and its committees. Only in genuinely exceptional circumstances, recognised and agreed by each House of Parliament, should these consultation procedures be departed from.

When a constitutional Bill is presented to Parliament for approval, it would be an improvement for the responsible minister to make an oral or written statement to the House in which it is first presented. This should, firstly, detail the consultation processes that the policy behind the Bill has gone through, together with a summary of the representations received and the government's response; secondly, it should indicate any unusual procedures through which the Bill will pass, such as a referendum, time allocation motions or departure from the House of Commons committee stage of the Bill being held by the whole House, giving their justification; and thirdly, it should give an assessment of the effect of the Bill upon existing constitutional arrangements.[108]

In present circumstances, the idea that governments might voluntarily apply a rigorous and consistent approach to their own proposed amendments to the constitution is regrettably an unrealistic proposition, for there is too often too much political self-interest in such measures for ministers to welcome hurdles and procedures that may obstruct or delay their implementation. Ministers are accountable to Parliament for all their actions and policies, but the political reality is that each House can only seek to persuade governments how to behave, they cannot dictate to it; and by virtue of the government's in-built majority in the legislature, coupled with the absence of any constitutional framework within which it and the legislature operates, the net result is that ministers may enact what measures they please and in whatever manner they please.

A more radical change in the conduct of parliamentary scrutiny of constitutional Bills would be to enhance the functions and powers of the House of Lords. Public discussion on reform of the Second Chamber has been a continuous exercise in British politics ever since the Parliament Act 1911, and since 1999 has been the subject of a Royal Commission inquiry and numerous government reports and parliamentary debates.[109] A draft Bill to introduce elections for membership of the Second Chamber is currently being considered by a joint parliamentary committee.[110] However, on the question of the role and powers of the Second Chamber, there is a curious consensus across the political elite that this should remain as it is at present, namely that it should continue to operate as a revising chamber, duplicating the work of the House of Commons (minus subjects of national finance), with minimal legislative power. In theory, at least, most accept that the House of Lords has a special role to play in scrutinising measures of a constitutional nature, and for this reason, for example, has a Select Committee on the Constitution. Yet the political parties' leaderships enthusiastically endorse no extension of the powers of the House of Lords over any kind of legislation, no doubt because they fear the obstruction this might cause them either in government or when in the future they return to office. However, there is a case for extending the powers of the Second Chamber over Bills of a major constitutional nature to one of a five-year delay, so that executive proposals giving rise to serious misgivings or controversy may be further reflected upon, and if necessary the opinion of the electorate expressed at a general election.[111] It would also enable the Second Chamber to more effectively supervise the constitutional amendment process and compliance by ministers with good practice in their preparation of constitutional Bills.

Crucial to any improvements in the amendment process will be to set down a means of determining what is a 'constitutional' Bill, to which prescribed consultation and parliamentary procedures apply. There is no shortage of authoritative definitions of what subject matter is constitutional in nature, or lists of what this includes.[112] It clearly comprises the general principles and institutions applicable to the executive (the Crown, ministers and civil service, together with their relationship and respective powers); the legislature (the composition and powers of each House of Parliament); the structure of central, regional and local government relations; the judiciary and courts (their composition, independence and powers); and the protection of citizens' fundamental rights and freedoms. However, it is no good arguing for 'a clear and consistent process . . . [to] apply to all significant constitutional change',[113] without providing a practical solution to how and whether any definition applies in any particular case. This will be particularly so where the government refuses to accept that a Bill is of sufficient constitutional importance to be covered by its terms, despite strong opinion to the contrary. Some mechanism for conclusive determination of the question is required, which means giving the responsibility to some suitable office-holder, similar to the way in which 'Money Bills' are certified by the Speaker of the House of Commons for the purposes of the Parliament Acts.[114] A suitable candidate for this task would be a permanent joint parliamentary committee, representing opinion across the political parties and in both Houses, chaired by the Speaker of the House of Lords.

Whatever common process or set of procedures might be agreed upon as desirable or necessary for future major constitutional change, it will almost certainly need to be set down in some single authoritative document. Such an initiative would be in tune with the ad hoc codification of several parts of our political and constitutional structure that has been underway for many years now. The Ministerial Code and Cabinet Manual, both internal government circulars but now relied upon as authoritative statements of constitutional practice, have been discussed above. An earlier Civil Service Code, existing as an internal government document, and the conventions on laying draft treaties before Parliament, have recently been developed and incorporated into statute by the Constitutional Reform and Governance Act 2010. There are codes of conduct for parliamentarians issued by each House of Parliament, reflecting customary ethics and standards.[115] In 2011 the system of general election timing was codified in the Fixed-term Parliaments Act, and the government appointed a Commission on a Bill of Rights to take forward its commitment to enacting a Bill of Rights to supersede the Human Rights Act 1988 and codify the indigenous rights and freedoms of UK citizens. There are many reasons driving this growing process of codification, but a search for clarity in our constitutional arrangements and regulation runs through them as a common thread.

Some would argue that the problem of poor process in political and constitutional reforms in recent years is symptomatic of a wider malaise, which is that the peculiarly flexible nature of the UK constitution, possibly a virtue in earlier times, is now no longer appropriate in the changed circumstances of today. In a time of modernisation and change, constitutional conventions as a species of political regulation are no longer as robust as they once were, and are in a state of decline.[116]

There needs to be a recalibration between flexibility and rigidity in the working of the UK constitution, which is the key question of balance that lies at the heart of any constitutional settlement. Although the UK is rightly proud of its historic reputation for good governance, it is likely that it has lessons to learn from comparative constitutional experience, especially as it has virtually no history of its own of obligatory or entrenched procedures governing constitutional change, apart from its interaction with the written constitutions in Commonwealth countries based on the Westminster system of government.[117]

This raises the wider question of whether the UK should now codify its constitution as a whole, a proposal that has steadily broadened its support across the political parties since a televised lecture calling for a written UK constitution by a former Conservative Lord Chancellor, Lord Hailsham, in 1976.[118] The Liberal Democrats have officially supported a written UK constitution for over two decades now, and the 2010 election manifesto of the Labour Party promised a commission on a written constitution if it were re-elected to office. Several suggested models for such a constitution have been produced in recent years.[119] Currently, the House of Commons Political and Constitutional Committee is engaged in an inquiry on 'Mapping the Path towards Codifying – or not Codifying – the UK Constitution'. The arguments for and against this proposal are diverse, and even the nature of the idea can be differently construed, either as a radical measure upsetting the status quo, or a conservative measure consolidating and protecting the UK's national traditions. A codified UK constitution would provide the occasion for expressing an overarching theory or updated set of principles underpinning the UK system of government, guiding its future development and settling the procedures by which constitutional amendments were to be made in the future.

Notes

1 A. de Tocqueville, *Democracy in America* (vol. 1, 1835, vol. 2, 1840), Fontana, 1994, p. 101.

2 For UK works on comparative constitutions, see K.C. Wheare, *Modern Constitutions*, Oxford University Press, 1966, 2nd edn; S.E. Finer, V. Bogdanor and B. Rudden (eds),

Comparing Constitutions, Oxford University Press, 1995; L. Wolf-Phillips, *Comparative Constitutions: Studies in Comparative Politics*, Macmillan, 1972. Apart from the two meanings or senses of the term discussed in the paragraph, a third may refer to the reality of a political system, particularly where this is at odds with the terms set out in a documentary constitution.

3 There has been some debate in the UK about the best shorthand terminology to refer to the nature of the constitution, many pointing out that to say it is 'unwritten' is, strictly speaking, misleading as many constitutional rules are to be found in written statutes or administrative codes, and a preferred approach today is to say it is 'uncodified'. See generally the House of Lords Constitution Committee, *Reviewing the Constitution: Terms of Reference and Method of Working*, 2001–02, HL 11.

4 Three such doctrines are those of 'parliamentary sovereignty' and 'the rule of law', on which see A.V. Dicey, *The Law of the Constitution*, Macmillan, 1885, 1985, 10th edn, and J. Jowell and D. Oliver (eds), *The Changing Constitution*, Oxford University Press, 2007, 6th edn, Chapters 1 and 2 and 'ministerial responsibility', on which see R. Blackburn and A. Kennon, *Griffith and Ryle on Parliament: Functions, Practice and Procedures,* Sweet and Maxwell, 2003, pp. 18–62.

5 See Sir I. Jennings, *Magna Carta*, Her Majesty's Stationery Office, 1965.

6 The government of Wales was united with England in 1536, and the kingdoms of England and Scotland were united into Great Britain in 1707. Ireland, whose governance was dominated by English rule since the middle ages, merged its legislature with Great Britain in 1798, and then in the twentieth century its greater southern part seceded into an independent Irish Free State (now the Republic of Ireland) in 1920, leaving Northern Ireland part of the United Kingdom. Today, Scotland, Wales and Northern Ireland have devolved systems of government in asymmetrical forms, operating under the overarching jurisdiction of the UK Parliament. The UK remains a unitary state, with no federal structure across its regions, having three separate legal systems (in England and Wales, Scotland, and Northern Ireland) subject to final appeal to the Supreme Court of the UK.

7 These two characteristics form part of the doctrine of 'parliamentary sovereignty'. Since the European Communities Act 1972, this principle has been qualified by UK membership of the European Union. See for example *R v Secretary of State for Transport, ex parte Factortame (No. 2)* (1991) 1 AC 603.

8 However, in some recent judgments, the courts have suggested that certain Acts of Parliament should analytically be regarded as constitutional statutes whose provisions carry a greater weight of authority to those of an ordinary statute. See *Thoburn v Sunderland City Council* (2003) QB 151.

9 Where the earlier statute has been analysed as being of a constitutional nature, express words to the contrary may be required in the later statute: *Thoburn v Sunderland City Council* (2003) QB 151.

10 Certain ministers, notably the Prime Minister and Chancellor of the Exchequer, today by convention must have a seat in the lower House, the House of Commons.

11 On the powers of the UK parliamentary Second Chamber (House of Lords).

12 Generally see R. Blackburn, *The Electoral System in Britain*, Macmillan, 1995, Chapters 1 and 8. This was not the case in 2010, however, when the general election resulted in no overall majority for a single party and the Conservative–Liberal Democrat Coalition government was formed, thereby giving the executive a working majority.

13 Generally see Blackburn and Kennon, op. cit., p. 5.

14 Generally see G. Marshall, *Constitutional Conventions*, Oxford University Press, 1984.

15 For discussion and a possible exception in cases where the Monarch's conscience is engaged, see R. Blackburn, 'The Royal Assent to Legislation and a Monarch's Fundamental Human Rights', *Public Law*, 2003, p. 205.

16 For example, R. Brazier, *Constitutional Reform*, Oxford University Press, 2008, 3rd edn, and D. Oliver, *Constitutional Reform in the United Kingdom*, Oxford University Press, 2003.

17 For example, Constitutional Reform Act 2005 and Constitutional Reform and Governance Act 2010.
18 Oral evidence to House of Lords Select Committee on the Constitution, *The Process of Constitutional Change*, 2010 12, HL 177, p. 8.
19 See J.P. Mackintosh, *The British Cabinet*, Stevens, 1977, 3rd edn.
20 For example *Wilkes v Wood* (1765) 19 State Trials 1153 and *Entick v Carrington* (1765) 19 State Trials 1029.
21 See R. Blackburn, 'Laying the Foundations of the Modern Voting System: the Representation of the People Act 1918', in P. Norton (ed.), *A Century of Constitutional Reform, Parliamentary History*, Wiley-Blackwell, 2011, p. 33.
22 Norton (ed.), op. cit.
23 Generally see V. Bogdanor (ed.), *The British Constitution in the Twentieth Century*, Oxford University Press, 2003.
24 Subject to conventions limiting the scope for Lords' intervention in matters of national finance: generally see R. Jenkins, *Mr Balfour's Poodle*, Collins, 1968.
25 See B. Harrison, *The Transformation of British Politics 1860–1995*, Ch. 3, Oxford University Press, 1995.
26 This was subsequently reduced to one year by the Parliament Act 1949.
27 James William Lowther.
28 For an account, see D. Butler and U. Kitzinger, *The 1975 Referendum*, Macmillan, 1976.
29 *Factortame v Secretary of State for Transport (No. 2)* (1991) AC 603 (EDJ and HL).
30 For a narrative, see D. Childs, *Britain since 1945: A Political History*, Routledge, 2006, Chapter 8, 6th edn.
31 See below for parliamentary procedures on constitutional legislation.
32 See Childs, op. cit., Ch. 12 and A. McDonald (ed.), *Reinventing Britain: Constitutional Change under New Labour*, Politico's, 2007, Ch. 7.
33 See R. Blackburn, *Towards a Constitutional Bill of Rights for the United Kingdom*, Pinter, 1999.
34 See R. Blackburn and R. Plant (eds), *Constitutional Reform: The Labour Government's Constitutional Reform Agenda*, Longman, 1999.
35 Generally see D. Feldman, 'Extending the Role of the Courts: The Human Rights Act 1998', in Norton (ed.), op. cit., pp. 65–84.
36 Blackburn and Plant (eds), op. cit.
37 See for example Department for Constitutional Affairs, *Justice, Rights and Democracy: DCA Strategy 2004–09* (DCA 2004).
38 *Lords Hansard*, 18 December 2002, col. 692.
39 *Standing Orders of the House of Commons, Public Business*, 2010 (New Parliament), No. 86, HC 539.
40 Divisions are not permitted in Grand Committees, and more important Bills including constitutional measures are almost always dealt with in a Committee of the Whole House. Generally see *Erskine May's Parliamentary Practice*, Butterworths, 2011, 24th edn, pp. 510–11 and pp. 612–23; Blackburn and Kennon, op. cit., pp. 723–24.
41 This one-year period is an approximation. The precise terms of the delay are that, 'If any Public Bill . . . is passed by the House of Commons [in two successive sessions] (whether of the same Parliament or not), and, having been sent up to the House of Lords at least one month before the end of the session is rejected by the House of Lords in each of those sessions, that Bill shall, on its rejection [for the second time] by the House of Lords, unless the House of Commons direct to the contrary, be presented to His Majesty and become an Act of Parliament on the Royal Assent being signified thereto, notwithstanding that the House of Lords have not consented to the Bill: Provided that this provision shall not take effect unless [one year has elapsed] between the date of the second reading in the first of those sessions of the Bill in the House of Commons and the date on which it passes the House of Commons [in the second of these sessions].'

42 For discussion, see Blackburn and Kennon, op. cit., pp. 708–11.
43 The Bill was enacted in the following session, 2005.
44 This includes the Hunting Bill as it was widely perceived as an attack on national traditions and civil liberty in the countryside.
45 See Blackburn and Kennon, op. cit., pp. 314–18.
46 Following a carry-over resolution pursuant to SO 80A, *Standing Orders of the House of Commons, Public Business*, 2010 (New Parliament), HC 539.
47 Section 2(1) Parliament Act 1911.
48 SO 37, *Standing Orders of the House of Commons, Public Business*, 2010 (New Parliament), HC 539.
49 In practice, this means 35 voting plus the Speaker and four tellers. SO 41(1), *Standing Orders of the House of Commons, Public Business*, 2010 (New Parliament), HC 539.
50 Thirteen Fridays each annual session are set aside for such legislative business: SO 14(4), *Standing Orders of the House of Commons, Public Business,* 2010 (New Parliament), HC539. Generally see Blackburn and Kennon, op. cit., pp. 539–55.
51 There are a few examples of successful Private Members' Bills on human rights and constitutional measures, such as the Abortion Act 1967 amending the law relating to the termination of pregnancies, and the National Audit Act 1983 extending the scope of public audit.
52 For example, several Private Members' Bills in the early 1990s on the human rights of the disabled resisted by the government were followed a few years later by the government-sponsored Disability Discrimination Act 1995.
53 See its Final Report, *Speaker's Conference on Parliamentary Representation*, 2010, HC 449.
54 The 'royal prerogative' comprises those powers, rights and privileges attaching to the Crown, recognised by the courts as having existed since time immemorial as a matter of common law.
55 Lord Bassam of Brighton, *Lords Hansard*, 24 March 2010, col. 959.
56 On the constitutional position of the monarchy generally, see R. Blackburn, *King and Country*, Politico's, 2006 and V. Bogdanor, *The Monarchy and the Constitution*, Oxford University Press, 1995.
57 For an analysis of this reform, see R. Blackburn, oral and written evidence to the House of Commons Political and Constitutional Reform Committee, *The Rules on Royal Succession*, 2010–12, HC 1615.
58 See generally M. Zander, *The Law Making Process*, Butterworths, 2004, 6th edn.
59 See the general works on constitutional law, such as A. Bradley and K. Ewing, *Constitutional and Administrative Law*, Longman, 2011, 15th edn and R. Blackburn, *Constitutional and Administrative Law*, *Halsbury's Laws of England*, Butterworths, 2012, vol. 20, 5th edn.
60 [1943] 2 All ER 560.
61 [1985] AC 374.
62 The power in question was that of regulating the position of civil servants, being in legal theory Crown servants, and whether or not they could belong to a trade union.
63 (1765) 19 Stat Tr 1029, which involved allegations of sedition.
64 [1947] AC 573.
65 Police and Criminal Evidence Act 1984, s. 28.
66 Respectively (1849) 1 Mac & G 25 and (1967) Ch 302. In the former case, this was in relation to personal etchings made by the Prince Consort of other members of the royal family; and in the latter case, of marital secrets between a wife and husband.
67 In 1966, the House of Lords qualified the rigour of the doctrine of precedent in its application to itself as the final court of appeal, so that while it would normally follow its own earlier judgments, it would henceforth in exceptional circumstances depart from them 'when it appears right to do so': *Practice Statement (Judicial Precedent)* [1966] 3 All ER 77.

68 See for example *Thoburn v Sunderland City Council* [2002] EWHC 195 (Admin) in which the court modified the common law doctrine of implied repeal where there are two conflicting statutes, so that where an earlier 'constitutional statute' was involved; a later statutory provision would only prevail if it contained express words to the contrary. Law LJ defined a 'constitutional statute' as one that conditions the legal relationship between citizen and State in some general, overarching manner, or enlarges or diminishes the scope of what we would not regard as fundamental rights. As examples, he cited the Magna Carta, the Bill of Rights 1689, the Act of Union, the Reform Acts that enlarged the franchise, the Human Rights Act 1998, the Scotland Act 1998, the Government of Wales Act 1998, as well as the European Communities Act 1972.

69 For a study of human rights law in the UK, see D. Feldman, *Civil Liberties and Human Rights in England and Wales*, Oxford University Press, 2002, 2nd edn and L. Lester, L. Pannick and J. Herberg, *Human Rights: Law and Practice*, LexisNexis, 2009, 3rd edn.

70 *R (Ullah) v Special Adjudicator* (2004) UKHL 26. For more recent judicial opinions on the precise level of influence of European Human Rights Court judgments, see the oral evidence session with Lord Judge (Lord Chief Justice) and Lord Phillips (President of the Supreme Court) before the Joint Parliamentary Committee on Human Rights, 15 November 2011.

71 See for example Marshall, op. cit. Two early influential jurists on the subject were Professor A.V. Dicey in *The Law of the Constitution*, op. cit. and Professor Sir I. Jennings in *The Law and the Constitution*, London, 1933.

72 Stanley Baldwin and Winston Churchill, respectively.

73 This was following the resignation through illness of his predecessor, Harold Macmillan.

74 The force of this convention is being followed today in plans to change the royal succession rules.

75 *Lords Hansard*, 21 July 1998, col. 791, when the minister Lord Sewel stated, 'we would expect a convention to be established that Westminster would not normally legislate with regard to devolved matters in Scotland without the consent of the Scottish parliament', and Cm 444, 1999, para 13.

76 Mr Brown's desire for such a convention was set out in the government Green Paper, *The Governance of Britain*, 2007, CM 7170, paras 35–6 and in his statements to the House of Commons, *Commons Hansard*, 3 July 2007, cols. 815–16. For commentary, see R. Blackburn, 'The Prerogative Power of Dissolution of Parliament: Law, Practice, and Reform', *Public Law*, 2009, pp. 766–89.

77 Cabinet Office, 2010, pp. 26–9.

78 See R. Blackburn, 'The 2010 General Election Outcome and Formation of the Conservative-Liberal Democrat Coalition Government', *Public Law*, 2011, pp. 30–55.

79 See R. Bassett, *1931: Political Crisis*, Macmillan, 1958.

80 For general discussion, see R. Blackburn, 'Monarchy and the Personal Prerogatives', *Public Law*, 2004, pp. 546–63.

81 For the current edition, see Standing Orders of the House of Commons (Public Business), 2010 (New Parliament), HC 539.

82 See Standing Orders of the House of Lords Relating to Public Business, 2010, HL 116.

83 For a critique of the 'near absolute power' of the Prime Minister in this respect, with reform proposals, see House of Commons Public Administration Committee, Machinery of Government Changes, 2006–07, HC 672.

84 See for example the reports of the Select Committee on the Constitution, *The Cabinet Office and the Centre of Government*, 2009–10, HL 30; *The Process of Constitutional Change*, 2010–12, HL 177, together with the written evidence from constitutional experts.

85 For a full study, see Blackburn, *The Electoral System*, op. cit., Ch. 2.

86 The provisions for an early election are where two-thirds of the membership of the House of Commons resolves that an election should take place, and where a 'No Confidence' resolution is passed in the government and 14 days elapse without any

alternative government being formed and receiving a 'Confidence' resolution in the Commons: section 2.

87 The election was held on 6 May 2010 and the Bill was given its formal First Reading in the House of Commons on 22 July 2010.

88 Previous precedents include John Major replacing Margaret Thatcher in 1990, James Callaghan replacing Harold Wilson in 1976, and Sir Alec Douglas-Home replacing Harold Macmillan in 1963.

89 For a detailed study of the election and formation of the Conservative–Liberal Democrat coalition, see Blackburn, 'The 2010 General Election Outcome', op. cit., pp. 30–55.

90 See House of Commons Political and Constitutional Reform Committee, *Fixed-term Parliaments Bill*, 2010–12, HC 436, for which the author presented oral and written evidence.

91 The Parliamentary Voting System and Constituencies Bill, reducing the number of MPs and rewriting the rules on constituency boundaries, was subsequently enacted the following year despite strong parliamentary opposition, especially in the House of Lords.

92 First Report from the Committee, Session 2010–11, Parliamentary Voting System and Constituencies Bill, HC 422.

93 House of Lords Select Committee on the Constitution, *Fixed-term Parliaments Bill*, 2010–12, HL 69, p. 9 and p. 43.

94 House of Commons Political and Constitutional Reform Committee, *Fixed-term Parliaments Bill*, 2010–12, HC 436, p. 9 and House of Lords Select Committee on the Constitution, *Fixed-term Parliaments Bill*, 2010–12, HL 69, p. 19. The majority view of the Constitution Committee added, 'the shift from a five-year maximum to a five-year norm would be inconsistent with the Government's stated aim of making the legislature more accountable, [and] inconsistent with existing constitutional practice'.

95 HM Government, *The Coalition: Our Programme for Government*, May 2010, p. 26. See also House of Lords Select Committee on the Constitution, *The Government's Constitutional Reform Programme*, 2010–12, HL 43, Q. 53.

96 Mark Harper, Minister for Political and Constitutional Reform, in evidence to the House of Lords Select Committee on the Constitution, *Fixed-term Parliaments Bill*, 2010–12, HL 69, Q. 116.

97 HM Government, *The Coalition: Our Programme for Government*, May 2010, p. 26.

98 There was a flurry of critical news reports and articles in the press. One was by David Davis MP, referring to the idea of fixed Parliaments as one of the greatest constitutional changes since 1911, yet the manner of its introduction being 'simply wrong', and the 55 per cent rule leaving the Commons with 'absolutely no authority'.

99 These early election events are to be two-thirds of the House of Commons' membership voting for an election, or a 'No Confidence' resolution followed by 14 days in which no new government could be formed and endorsed by the Commons.

100 Lord St John of Fawsley, *Lords Hansard*, 21 June 2011, col. 1208.

101 Section 7.

102 See House of Commons Political and Constitutional Reform Committee, 2010–12, HC 437 and House of Lords Select Committee on the Constitution, 2010–12, HL 58.

103 The view of the Lords Constitution Committee was, 'We are particularly concerned by the hasty manner in which policy-making has taken place, with negligible public consultation, and the subsequent "fast-tracking" through Parliament of a bill which will have major constitutional implications', 2008–09, HL 130, p. 3.

104 Report of the Independent Commission on the Voting System, Cm 4090, 1998.

105 These are, in addition to First-Past-the-Post and the Alternative Vote (a majoritarian, not proportional, system), the proportional Single Transferable Vote and the Additional (or Mixed) Member System (which incorporates proportionality through a party list system, alongside constituency-elected members).

106 In 2009, a YouGov poll for *The Sunday Times* showed 62 per cent of voters favoured a more proportional system of voting, and a BPIX poll for *The Mail on Sunday* found 60 per cent would prefer proportional representation to the current system.

107 The Code requires that: (1) Formal consultation should take place at a stage when there is scope to influence the policy outcome. (2) Consultations should normally last for at least 12 weeks, with consideration given to longer timescales where feasible and sensible. (3) Consultation documents should be clear about the consultation process, what is being proposed, the scope to influence and the expected costs and benefits of the proposals. (4) Consultation exercises should be designed to be accessible to, and clearly targeted at, those people the exercise is intended to reach. (5) Keeping the burden of consultation to a minimum is essential if consultations are to be effective and if consultees' buy-in to the process is to be obtained. (6) Consultation responses should be analysed carefully and clear feedback should be provided to participants following the consultation. (7) Officials running consultations should seek guidance on how to run an effective consultation exercise and share what they have learned from the experience (2008 edn).

108 The view of the House of Lords Select Committee on the Constitution is that a minister should issue a written ministerial statement giving his view on whether a Bill he or she is presenting to Parliament provides for significant constitutional change; and that if so, it should also state what the impact of the proposals will be upon the existing constitutional arrangements; whether and, if so, how the government engaged with the public in the initial development of the policy proposals and what was the outcome of that public engagement; in what way were the detailed policies contained in the Bill subjected to rigorous scrutiny in the Cabinet committee system; whether a Green Paper was published, what consultation took place on the proposals, including with the devolved regional institutions, and the extent to which the government agrees or disagrees with the responses given; whether a White Paper was published and whether pre-legislative scrutiny was undertaken and the extent to which the government agree or disagree with the outcome of that process; what the justification is for any referendum held, or to be held, on the proposals; and when and how the legislation, if passed, will be subject to a post-legislative scrutiny. See *The Process of Constitutional Change*, 2010–12, HL177, pp. 24–5.

109 Cabinet Office, *Reforming the House of Lords*, Cm 4183, 1999. Report of the Royal Commission on Reform of the House of Lords, *A House for the Future*, Cm. 4534, 2000; Lord Chancellor's Department, *The House of Lords: Completing the Reform*, 2001, Cm. 5291; Ministry of Justice, *The House of Lords: Reform*, Cm 7027, 2007; Ministry of Justice, *An Elected Second Chamber*, Cm 7438, 2008.

110 House of Lords Reform Draft Bill, Cm 8077, May 2011.

111 For further discussion on this proposal, see R. Blackburn, 'The House of Lords', Ch. 1, in Blackburn and Plant (eds), op. cit., p. 24ff. Bearing some similarity, the Labour Party's 1992 general election manifesto contained a proposal for 'an elected Second Chamber which will have the power to delay, for the lifetime of a Parliament, change to designated legislation reducing individual or constitutional rights', p. 117.

112 For discussion, see House of Lords Select Committee on the Constitution, *The Process of Constitutional Change*, 2010–12, HC177, pp. 8–11.

113 House of Lords Select Committee on the Constitution, op. cit., p. 11.

114 Parliament Act 1911, s.1(3).

115 House of Commons, *The Code of Conduct*, 2010, HC 735; House of Lords, *Code of Conduct for Members of the House of Lords*, 2011, 2nd edn.

116 See L. Wilson of Dinton, 'The Robustness of Conventions in a Time of Modernisation and Change', *Public Law*, 2004, pp. 407–20.

117 For literature on comparative constitutional engineering, see S. Levinson (ed.), *Responding to Imperfection. The Theory and Practice of Constitutional Amendment*, Princeton, 1995; R. Congleton and B. Swedenborg (eds), *Democratic Constitutional Design and Public*

Policy: Analysis and Design, Cambridge, 2006; D. Oliver and C. Fusaro (eds), *How Constitutions Change*, Hart, 2011; European Commission for Democracy through Law, *Report on Constitutional Amendment* (Council of Europe 269/2008).

118 *Elective Dictatorship* (BBC 1976). See also L. Hailsham, *The Dilemma of Democracy*, Collins, 1978.

119 Institute for Public Policy Research, *A Written Constitution for the United Kingdom*, Mansell, 1993; T. Benn, *Common Sense: A New Constitution for Britain*, Hutchinson, 1993; R. Gordon, *Repairing British Politics: A Blueprint for Constitutional Change*, Hart, 2010.

19 Constitutional revision in the United States of America

John R. Vile

Citizens of the United States take great pride in their Constitution, which dates back to 1787. Indeed, this pride borders on reverence that sometimes serves as an obstacle to further constitutional change.[1]

Whereas the first government that the colonies adopted required states to give unanimous consent to constitutional amendments, the new Constitution gave two-thirds majorities of both houses of Congress—or a Convention called by two-thirds of the states—the right to propose amendments, and three-fourths of the states the right to ratify them. Anticipating that the process would strike a middle ground between excessive flexibility and excessive rigidity, James Madison bragged in his essay Federalist No. 43 that the constitutional amending process "guards equally against that extreme facility, which would render the Constitution too mutable; and that extreme difficulty, which might perpetuate its discovered faults."[2]

History and evolution of the constitutional amendment procedure

Great Britain has an "unwritten constitution," but there were a variety of documents, including the Magna Carta of 1215, the English Bill of Rights of 1688, and a host of judicial rulings and other legal landmarks that both British and Americans cited in support of their rights. When Britain began to relax its policy of "salutary neglect" and assert a more active role in the colonies, the colonists affirmed their rights as Englishmen of "no taxation without representation."[3] Lacking actual representation within the English Parliament, colonists asserted that Parliament, which claimed virtually to represent all English citizens, had no power over them, and both the Parliament and the King resisted these claims. The Second Continental Congress adopted the Declaration of Independence in July 1776. It declared the right of the people to throw off governments that were not facilitating the rights to "life, liberty, and the pursuit of happiness," and replace them with governments that would.

As they asserted their independence, the former colonies began adopting written constitutions to secure their rights.[4] Over time, the standard procedure was to propose such amendments by special Conventions (rather than by ordinary legislatures) and ratify them by referendum.[5] Most such constitutions further provided for amending mechanisms, which provided possible national models. Four states relied on legislative action, three states on conventions, and two on Councils of Revision, which met periodically to review governmental practices.[6]

The nation's first government, the Articles of Confederation,[7] vested primary sovereignty within the individual states. Article II of the Articles thus provided that: "Each state retains its sovereignty, freedom, and independence, and every Power, Jurisdiction, and right, which is not by this confederation expressly delegated to the United States, in Congress assembled."[8] The national government had no power over interstate commerce and no power to levy taxes directly on the people, and key matters required the consent of nine or more state delegations within Congress, where each state had a single vote.

Once Congress proposed amendments, the legislatures of all 13 states had to ratify them before they became part of the Constitution. States agreed to the Articles in 1781. Although the inadequacy of national powers manifested itself relatively early, the state unanimity requirement prevented the adoption of any formal amendments over the next several years. Concern over the inadequacies of the Articles led to the Annapolis Convention, which examined commercial relations among the states, in September 1786. This Convention asked Congress to call the Constitutional Convention, which met in Philadelphia in the summer of 1787.[9] While recommending this meeting "for the sole and express purpose of revising the Articles of Confederation," Congress also tasked the Convention with rendering "the federal constitution adequate to the exigencies of Government and the preservation of the Union."[10]

In pursuing this latter goal, the 55 delegates who attended the Convention followed the initial lead of the Virginia Plan. It proposed devising a new system of government rather than simply repairing the existing Articles. The Convention thus moved from a role of *pouvoir constituant*, "the power that is created by and exercises power derived from the constitution," to that of *pouvoir constitué*, which is, "the power that creates [or in this case, proposes] the constitution."[11]

In place of a unicameral Congress, the Convention devised a system in which a bicameral Congress exercised expanded powers but was balanced by a single executive and by an independent court system. Delegates further substituted a more united federal system for the confederal system under the Articles. Two-thirds majorities of both Houses of Congress (or a convention called by two-thirds of the states) was required to propose amendments and three-fourths of the states to ratify them.

Delegates to the Convention specified in Art. VII of the document that the new government would go into effect among approving states only if nine or more approved in special conventions, thus bypassing the requirement for unanimity under the Articles of Confederation. The nation quickly divided into Federalist supporters of the document and Anti-Federalist opponents. Debates between proponents of these two groups resulted in numerous published arguments, the most famous of which are found in the Federalist Papers that Alexander Hamilton, James Madison, and John Jay wrote under the pen name of Publius.

Madison wrote most of the essays related to the amending process. In Federalist No. 38, he argued for the comparative advantage of the new constitution over the Articles of Confederation. In seeking to define the nature of the new government, in Federalist No. 39, he observed that the amending process was "in strictness, neither a national nor a federal Constitution, but a composition of both."[12] In Federalist No. 40, he argued that it was necessary for the delegates to exceed their instructions to revise the Articles at the Convention in order to make the government adequate to the exigencies of the Union. In Federalist No. 43, he argued for the propriety and moderation of the amending process. In Federalist No. 49, Madison critiqued a proposal by Thomas Jefferson that called for revising the constitution every generation, by arguing that such appeals would destabilize the government.[13] In Federalist No. 50, Madison also counseled against systems of periodic revision anticipated by the Pennsylvania Council of Censors.

Federalists were less successful in defending the new constitution against arguments that it should include a Bill of Rights. Federalists initially alternatively argued that such a Bill of Rights was either unnecessary or dangerous, in that an impartial list might leave omitted rights more vulnerable. In the final Federalist essay (No. 85), however, Hamilton observed that the amending process remained available should such changes be needed. Moreover, Jefferson insisted in correspondence to Madison that all people were entitled to having their rights enumerated. He further argued that a Bill of Rights could do no harm and would serve both to educate people about their rights and provide an instrument for upright judges to use to protect such rights.[14]

Evolution of the amending process

The states ratified the Constitution as a whole, the regime that the Constitution established remains intact, and formal methods of constitutional provision that Art. V of the Constitution articulated remain unamended. In 1913, the Seventeenth Amendment provided that the people, rather than state legislatures, would choose Senators, whose approval is needed to propose amendments. This made the process more responsive to popular wishes, but it otherwise remains unchanged. Especially during periods of American history in which no amendments were adopted, critics have expressed concern that the process is too difficult[15] and that it gives minorities too much power to adopt needed changes, but such criticisms are often muted in times of successful constitutional change.

A short history of revisions[16]

The Bill of Rights

James Madison introduced a Bill of Rights in the first Congress. Although Madison, who had not advocated such a bill at the Constitutional Convention, seems genuinely to have embraced some of Jefferson's arguments for such a bill, he also sought to take the initiative away from those who might either use such a

Bill of Rights to reduce federal powers or against those who sought a second Constitutional Convention that might undo the work of the first.[17]

In 1791, the states ratified 10 of 12 proposed amendments (the other two dealt with structural matters). The provisions of this national Bill of Rights focus on individual rights and are more prescriptive than precatory, approaching the language of Biblical commands. Congress accepted the arguments of Connecticut's Roger Sherman over Virginia's James Madison and added amendments to the end of the document rather than integrating them into the text. Although the arguments for following the former course were not altogether persuasive[18] and often require interpreters to examine several different sections of the Constitution to understand a single institution, the practice makes it much easier to trace the history of formal constitutional change in the USA than if changes been incorporated within the existing text.

The First Amendment unequivocally proclaims that "Congress shall pass no law establishing a religion or prohibiting the free exercise thereof." The Amendment further protected the rights of speech, press, peaceable assembly, and petition. The Second Amendment, recently interpreted by the US Supreme Court in *District of Columbia v Heller* (2008) as a personal right rather than a right tied to the militia,[19] proclaimed the right to bear arms, and the Third Amendment prohibited the quartering of troops in private households without their consent. The Fourth Amendment prohibited unreasonable searches and seizures, and established requirements for warrants. The Fifth Amendment provided protections for the accused including prohibitions against deprivation of "life, liberty, or property without due process of law" and a provision for "just compensation" for any governmental taking of property. The Sixth and Seventh Amendments outlined further protections for individuals at trial. The Eighth Amendment prohibited "excessive" fines or bail and "cruel and unusual punishment," the Ninth Amendment attempted to guard un-enumerated rights and reinforce the virtues of local government,[20] and the Tenth Amendment referenced the "reserved" powers of the states.[21]

The Eleventh and Twelfth Amendments

The Eleventh Amendment, ratified in 1795, reversed the Supreme Court decision in *Chisholm v Georgia* that had permitted states to be sued without their consent.[22] The Twelfth Amendment, ratified in 1804, corrected perceived defects in the Electoral College mechanism used to select Presidents. In addition to resulting, in 1796, in the election of a President (Adams) from one party and a Vice-president (Jefferson) from another, it also brought about an unexpected tie between the two Democratic–Republican candidates for President in the election of 1800.[23]

The Reconstruction Era Amendments

The amending process proved inadequate in quieting sectional conflicts raised by slavery. Only after the North defeated the slave states in 1865 were three amendments adopted to solve this problem. Congress used its power to decide which states were Republican (Representative) to require those that sought re-entry into the union to ratify these amendments as a condition of acceptance. Bruce Ackerman believes that this and other extraordinary "constitutional moments" are often characterized by departures from strictly legal forms.[24]

The Thirteenth Amendment, ratified in 1865, ended chattel slavery.[25] The Fourteenth Amendment, ratified in 1868, has five sections.[26] Section 1 overturns the notorious decision in *Dred Scott v Sandford* (1857),[27] which declared that blacks were not and could not become citizens, by extending formal citizenship recognition to all persons, including former slaves, born or naturalized within the United States. It also protected all US citizens against state invasions of their privileges and immunities, due process, and equal protection. Other provisions repealed the clauses that had counted individual slaves as three-fifths of a person; prevented former rebels from holding office; affirmed Union but not Confederate debts; and entrusted Congress with enforcement powers. The Fifteenth Amendment, ratified in 1870, further prevented states from denying voting rights on the basis of color.[28]

As concern over racial issues waned, many of the rights the Reconstruction Amendments had seemingly guaranteed received little more than lip service. Indeed, the Supreme Court more frequently utilized the amendments to protect corporations than it did the rights of African–Americans during this time period.[29] The Second American Revolution, or Second Reconstruction, would not arrive in full until the civil rights gains of the 1950s and 1960s. Meanwhile, however, the Reconstruction Amendments were extremely influential in expanding the scope of the Bill of Rights. *Barron v Baltimore* (1833) had asserted that the Bill intended only to limit the national government, thus exempting the states from its purview.[30] In a process signaled by the Supreme Court's application of freedom of speech to the states in *Gitlow v New York* (1925),[31] however, the Court began absorbing or incorporating the most important provisions of the Bill of Rights within the due process clause of the Fourteenth Amendment and applying them to the states. Today, almost all have been so incorporated.

Progressive Era Amendments

No amendments were adopted from 1870 to 1913, but the period from 1913 to 1920 saw the ratification of four amendments associated with the Progressive movement, which sought greater democratization. The Sixteenth Amendment (1913) overturned the Supreme Court decision in *Pollock v Farmers' Loan & Trust Co.* (1895)[32] and permitted imposition of a national income tax. The Seventeenth Amendment (1913) provided for direct election of US Senators.[33] The Eighteenth Amendment (1919) provided for national alcoholic prohibition but was repealed by the Twenty-first Amendment (1933).[34] The Nineteenth Amendment (1920) capped a movement for women's suffrage that had begun in the United States with the Seneca Falls Convention of 1848[35] by prohibiting denials of the right to vote on the basis of sex.[36]

The most recent Amendments

Most recent amendments have been less consequential. The Twentieth Amendment (1933) increased electoral accountability by speeding up the time that new members of congress and Presidents and Vice-presidents assumed their offices, thus reducing the power of so-called "lame ducks." The Twenty-second Amendment (1951) limited Presidents to two full terms. The Twenty-third Amendment (1961) provided for representation of the District of Columbia in the Electoral College. The Twenty-fourth Amendment (1964) limited the use of poll taxes. The Twenty-fifth Amendment (1967) provided for possible presidential disability,[37] and the Twenty-sixth Amendment modified a Supreme Court decision in *Oregon v Mitchell* (1970),[38] prohibiting discrimination in voting by the national government and the states against individuals who were 18 or more years old. Finally, the Twenty-seventh Amendment (proposed in 1789 as part of the original Bill of Rights but not ratified until 1992) prohibited the beginning of new congressional pay raises without an intervening election.[39]

Informal methods of constitutional change

The US Constitution is based on the natural rights principles that were articulated in the Declaration of Independence.[40] Similarly, one could not learn much about the operation of American political parties simply from reading the US Constitution. Some aspects of the Electoral College mechanism for selecting the President and Vice-president (for example, the fact that most states use a winner-take-all system rather than apportioning their votes proportionally) are better illumined by history and contemporary practice than by explicit constitutional provisions. William F. Harris II thus distinguishes between America's written large "C" Constitution and its larger unwritten small "c" constitution.[41]

Similarly, a review of constitutional amendments provides an admittedly partial key to understanding US constitutional change. The US Constitution is relatively short and was written at a time when such documents were largely devoted to establishing central governmental structures and outlining basic political rights rather than, as in many early twentieth-century constitutions, seeking to identify and guarantee a variety of social welfare entitlements. The USA's partial embrace of a social-welfare state that accompanied President Franklin D. Roosevelt's "New Deal" in the 1930s has thus left no visible imprint on the amending process.[42] The civil rights revolution of the 1950s and 1960s was triggered by Supreme Court decisions that interpreted existing post-Civil War amendments[43] and by the development of a civil rights movement rather than by new amendments. Americans ultimately rejected an amendment to extend equal legal rights to women, both because it believed that courts had already effectively utilized the equal protection clause of the Fourteenth Amendment to accomplish this purpose,[44] and because of fears that the judiciary might unduly extend such language. Similarly, recent decisions relative to the rights of homosexuals[45] are proceeding through legislative and judicial innovations utilizing existing constitutional language rather than through constitutional amendment.[46]

In recognizing the constitutionality of the national bank in *McCulloch v Maryland* (1819),[47] Chief Justice John Marshall paid deference to congressional decisions, which had twice established such banks after considerable debate. The Supreme Court's decision invalidating legislative vetoes in *Chadha*[48] shows that the age of a congressional practice will not always save it, but the Court usually defers both to legislative and executive practices that have developed within existing constitutional structures. Since 1937, the US Supreme Court has been particularly generous in sustaining congressional programs under its powers to tax and spend, and to regulate interstate and foreign commerce.[49]

The judiciary is the primary vehicle for ratifying or initiating informal change within the United States.[50] The judiciary asserted its power of judicial review of national legislation in *Marbury v Madison* (1803).[51] The judiciary affirmed the constitutionality of the national bank and of the states' inability to tax it in *McCulloch v Maryland* (1819).[52] The Court at first limited and later expanded the protections of the Reconstruction Amendments, and decided that they were an appropriate vehicle for extending the protections of the Bill of Rights against state action. The modern Court has similarly expanded protections of the equal protection clause not only to African–Americans but also to women and other minorities.

The comparative rigidity of the existing constitutional amending process increases pressure on the Supreme Court to render decisions to keep the constitution up to date. Some believe that the Court is too ready to "rewrite" the Constitution. Others suggest that institutional constraints—for example, the system for appointing and confirming judges and justices, impeachment and conviction mechanisms, and the possibility of reversing judicial decisions through the amending process—keep such decisions within respectable bounds.

Professor David Strauss has argued that extra-constitutional changes are so important, and amendments so rare, that the former are relatively inconsequential. He made four arguments:

> First . . . sometimes matters addressed by the Constitution change even though the text of the Constitution is unchanged. Second, and more dramatically, some constitutional changes occur even though amendments that would have brought about those very changes are explicitly rejected. Third, when amendments are adopted, they often do no more than ratify changes that have already taken place in society without the help of an amendment, rather than the other way around. Fourth, when amendments are adopted even though society has not changed, the amendments are systematically evaded. They end up having little effect until society catches up with the ambitions of the amendment.[53]

The author believes that Strauss underplays or ignores the process's "corrective function," its "checking function," its role in "domesticating revolution," its role in "legitimization," and its role in "publicity,"[54] but Strauss's critique is a reminder that amendments provide only a partial story of constitutional change in the United States.

The formal amendment process

Professor Donald S. Lutz found that the United States had "the second-most-difficult amending process,"[55] among 32 democratic countries on which he conducted statistical analyses. Foreign (mostly British) commentators writing in the late nineteenth century often commented negatively on this rigidity.[56] However, as much as Madison praised constitutional stability in Federalist No. 49,[57] the framers may not have intended for the amending process to be as difficult as it has become. Melissa Schwartzberg observes that "a supermajoritarian threshold for constitutional amendment provisions is *ex ante* indeterminate . . . these norms are only value before the process of constitutional making gives them shape."[58]

The amending process as outlined in the Constitution

The formal process for amending the US Constitution is found in Art. V of the US Constitution. It provides that:

> The Congress, whenever two-thirds of both Houses shall deem it necessary, shall propose Amendments to this Constitution, or, on the Application of the Legislatures of two thirds of the several States, shall call a Convention for proposing Amendments, which, in either Case, shall be valid to all Intents and Purposes, as Part of this Constitution, when ratified by the Legislatures of three fourths of the several States, or by Conventions in three fourths thereof, as the one or the other Mode of Ratification may be proposed by the Congress; provided that no Amendment which may be made prior to the Year One thousand eight hundred and eight shall in any Manner affect the first and fourth Clauses in the Ninth section of the first Article; and that no State, without its Consent, shall be deprived of its equal Suffrage in the Senate.

The two phases of the amending process

The most notable aspect of the language of Art. V is that it specifies two methods of proposing and two methods of ratifying amendments. The most notable aspect of the *practice* of amendments is how many are proposed and how few are ratified. During the course of US history, members of Congress have introduced more than 11,500 proposals to amend the document, although most of these proposals are redundant, and members of Congress have introduced some proposals—like those for an Equal Rights Amendment or for changes in the Electoral College—hundreds of times.[59] Of the 11,500+ proposals, however, Congress had only voted on 33 by the necessary two-thirds majorities, and the states have ratified 27 of these.[60] Congress, especially the Senate, is thus the primary obstacle to most proposals that its members have introduced. Most amendments are referred to congressional committees and never emerge from them.

The alternate provision whereby two-thirds of the states can petition Congress to call a constitutional convention to propose amendments has been remarkably quiescent, if not moribund. On occasion, threats to call such a convention have prompted Congress to take the initiative on its own, as in its decision to propose direct election of Senators,[61] but fears, perhaps largely unfounded,[62] about the possible scope of a convention[63] have prevented this mechanism from being used. Similarly, although some modern constitutional theorists have proposed that Congress would be obligated to accept amendments proposed and/or ratified by a popular vote,[64] no such amendments have been so introduced.

Article V allows Congress to specify whether amendments will be ratified either by state legislatures or by state conventions, and it has chosen the former route for all amendments other than the Twenty-first, which repealed national alcohol prohibition. The conventions that adopted the Twenty-first Amendment engaged in little actual deliberation and acted almost as plebiscitary bodies.

Entrenchment provisions

Article V contains two explicit entrenchment provisions. One, with a built-in expiration date, secured a compromise between the North and South over slave importation by limiting the taxes that Congress could impose on it for 20 years. The other perpetuated an even more important compromise by prohibiting any state from being deprived of its equal representation in the US Senate without its consent.

At the Constitutional Convention of 1787, authors of the Virginia Plan proposed representing states in both Houses of Congress according to population. Proponents of the New Jersey Plan favored perpetuating the scheme of representation under the Articles of Confederation by continuing equal state representation within a unicameral Congress. This debate was the most divisive at the Convention, and the Connecticut (or Great) Compromise was deemed to be so essential to the support of both sides of the controversy that the framers were determined that it not be displaced.[65]

While it provides for broad regional representation, the continuing equal state representation of states in the US Senate remains one of the most undemocratic aspects of the current Constitution,[66] and less-populated states have little incentive to give up their current representation. Adoption of a completely new Constitution might overcome the current system of representation. Reformers might also follow the letter, if not the spirit, of the provision by seeking first to remove the entrenchment clause—which does not itself appear to be entrenched—by amendment and *then* adopting yet another amendment to equalize Senate representation.

Most scholarly discussion on substantive limits on the amending clause has centered less on the two explicit entrenchment provisions of Art. V than on possible unstated implicit limits. The US Supreme Court has heard and rejected arguments, largely from conservatives,[67] challenging the validity of the Fifteenth, Eighteenth, and Nineteenth Amendments in *Myers v Anderson* (1915),[68] the *National Prohibition Cases* (1920),[69] *United States v Sprague* (1931),[70] and *Leser v Garnett* (1922).[71] More recently, Walter Murphy and John Rawls are among more liberal scholars who have hypothesized that some provisions relative to the protection of such rights as freedom of speech or press, or perhaps to equal protection, are so fundamental that to change them would effectively be to institute an entirely new constitution.[72] Eric Isaacson and Jeff Rosen have specifically argued that proposed amendments limiting flag-burning would be unconstitutional.[73] The author of this essay has argued that the dangers of granting the judicial branch the power to invalidate amendments are far greater than the rather remote possibilities that amendments might seek to void key civil rights and liberties.[74] Melissa Schwartzberg adds that "In disabling amendment, we may protect the reprehensible, instead of simply securing the precious."[75]

Constitutional drafting methods

Most constitutional change in America since 1787 has been piecemeal. The only national experience that the USA has in regard to constitutional drafting has been in the writing of the Articles of Confederation, which was done by the Second Continental Congress, and the drafting of the US Constitution and the Constitution of the Confederate States of America, which was done by conventions.[76] These experiences suggest that Congress could draft a new Constitution but that any completely new Constitution would more likely be proposed by a constitutional convention especially convened for that purpose. Consistent with the notion that such a document would be paramount to other legislation, it seems likely that such a document would be ratified by special state conventions or referenda. Notably, in commenting on the Virginia experience in his Notes on the State of Virginia, Thomas Jefferson denied that one "ordinary legislature" had the power to "establish an act above the power of the [another] ordinary legislature."[77] Depending on how such a Constitution proposed to change the existing system of federalism, such a Constitution might be subject to a popular plebiscite.

As indicated earlier, some states once provided for Councils of Revisions that would periodically review their constitutions and suggest changes. Although these have faded, some states have allowed constitutional commissions to propose new documents, subject to popular ratification.[78]

The role of the people

The Declaration of Independence proclaimed people's right to "alter or abolish" constitutions to secure popular rights. The US Constitution both rests on the sanction of "We the People" and also serves to constrain them. Part of this paradox is resolved through the constitutional amending process. Richard Albert observes that "the authority to amend the constitution is the best democratic answer to the enduring tension in constitutional statecraft between constitutionalism and democracy because the rules governing constitutional amendment unmistakably resolve this tension in favor of democracy—by giving citizens the key to unlock their constitutional handcuffs."[79]

James Madison suggested in Federalist No. 10 that the new republic utilizing a system of representation would be superior to ancient Greek democracies. Not only would representatives serve to "refine and enlarge the public views by passing them through the medium of a chosen body of citizens, whose wisdom may best discern the true interest of their country and whose patriotism and love of justice will be least likely to sacrifice it to temporary or partial considerations,"[80] but because such representatives would allow the government to embrace a larger territory, such a system would minimize the likelihood that any single faction or group of factions with interests adverse to common justice could dominate. The constitutional amending process further applies supermajoritarian requirements to such nationalist scope.

The Founders often equated conventions with the will of the people.[81] Significantly, the US Constitution was both written in a national convention and ratified by individual state conventions. Similarly, while some Founders favored popular election of the President and Vice-president, they ultimately settled for an indirect method of election. Although the Progressive Era brought about women's suffrage and direct election of Senators within individual states, it did not succeed in either replacing the Electoral College or in further democratizing the amending process, through initiative or referendum options or requirements.

The current system for proposing and ratifying amendments begins in Congress, the branch of the national government most accountable to the people, and ends in state legislatures or conventions, which are similarly accountable. Adoption of a new amendment is thus likely to require at least tacit approval by fairly large segments of the US population. Candidates for President or for Congress often run on platforms that call for changing provisions of the Constitution; for example, by imposing term limits, providing for the protection of prenatal life, allowing voluntary prayer in public schools, or in providing for equal rights for women.[82]

Amendments sometimes accompany successful political movements, like the triumph of Democratic–Republicans in the elections of 1800, the Republican victories during the Civil War, and Progressive gains in the early twentieth century. It is unlikely that two-thirds majorities of both Houses of Congress would propose, or three-fourths of the state legislatures would ratify, amendments that did not have substantial public support. By contrast, given the supermajorities required both to propose and ratify amendments, the fact that popular majorities, especially shifting majorities, favor a given amending proposal offers no certainty that it will be adopted.

In contrast to some states, the USA has no national mechanism by which the people can directly propose or ratify amendments. Acting as a circuit court justice, Chief Justice William Rehnquist upheld a Nevada Supreme Court decision permitting an advisory referendum on the state ballot in respect of the Equal Rights Amendment, but he stressed its advisory character.[83] Moreover, in *Cook v Gralike*, the US Supreme Court invalidated Missouri's attempt to instruct its representatives to press for an amendment supporting term limits and noting on ballots whether they had followed or disregarded such instructions.[84] However limited the role of referenda are in the current process, amendments are unlikely to be adopted without considerable deliberation and without fairly widespread geographic support. The difficulty of the system certainly privileges the perpetuation of existing structures.

The effect of international and European law on constitutional revision

The US model of constitutional government, derived both from and in reaction against preceding British and European models. James Madison spent considerable time examining the strengths and weaknesses of earlier democracies prior to advancing his own plans for reform at the US Constitutional Convention.[85] The US example has been copied throughout the world, and although many democratic nations prefer parliamentary systems, written constitutions are now normative.

Although it is not a part of the European Union, the United States has close ties with it and carries heavy responsibilities within the international arena. It has signed numerous treaties and is a member of the North Atlantic Treaty Organization (NATĐ). International developments influence the USA in a number of ways. Thus, American racial minorities returned from World War II determined that they would not, after helping fighting racism abroad, accede to it at home. Similarly, American professors teach, and students study, comparative and international law.

US Supreme Court justices have cited cases in foreign law in several recent relatively high-profile cases, including *Washington v Glucksberg* (dealing with physician-assisted suicide),[86] *Atkins v Virginia* (limiting execution of the mentally disabled),[87] *Grutter v Bollinger* (defining the parameters of affirmative action relative to college admissions),[88] *Lawrence v Texas* (invalidating state laws against consensual sodomy),[89] and *Roper v Simmons* (limiting the execution of juveniles).[90] These citations have stirred considerable controversy among justices, some of whom believe that they undermine their attempt to interpret the Constitution according to its original intent and among some legal commentators, who fear that over-reliance on foreign sources could undermine democratic accountability.[91]

The supremacy clause in Art. VI of the US Constitution is ambiguous. That clause specifies that "This Constitution, and the Laws of the United States which shall be made in Pursuance thereof; and all Treaties made, or which shall be made, under the Authority of the United States, shall be the supreme Law of the Land." In *Missouri v Holland* (1920),[92] the US Supreme Court suggested that the distinction between laws "made in Pursuance thereof" and Treaties made "under the Authority of the United States" might be consequential. Specifically, it ruled that the USA might by treaty limit state regulation of migratory birds in a manner that it could not do by congressional legislation, which was then thought to invade state sovereignty under the Tenth Amendment.

As the USA later engaged in a protracted Cold War, this case raised the specter that leaders might compromise civil liberties in an effort to appease communist or other foreign adversaries. One of the more popular amending proposals was the Bricker Amendment, which would have limited the capacity of such treaties.[93] Meanwhile, however, US Supreme Court decisions indicated that the domestic effects of treaties, like US laws, were subject to the US Constitution,[94] and this controversy has largely ended.

How does the US political system influence constitutional revision?

Despite periodic frustrations over the pace of both legal and constitutional change, and numerous proposals suggesting that the USA should adopt a new constitution, it has yet to do so.[95] Although the American Founders wanted a more energetic national government than the Articles of Confederation, they remained wary of concentrated power and its threats to liberty. They remembered that a putatively sovereign parliament had attempted to interfere with their natural and inalienable rights. As a consequence, the Constitution not only granted power, but also sought to limit it. Although the Bill of Rights and the Reconstruction Amendments imposed constitutional restraints on the national government, the constitutional structure itself imposes major obstacles to precipitous legal or constitutional changes,[96] and constitutional protections have limited benefit without a system of courts willing to enforce them.

The Founders divided powers among three branches of government with distinct but overlapping functions. According to Alexander Hamilton's arguments in Federalist No. 78, the US Congress exercises the power of the purse and the President exercises the power of the sword, but courts "have neither force nor will but merely judgment."[97] The Founders posed obstacles to the powers of the legislative branch, which they thought would be the strongest, by dividing the body into two houses and by giving members of the two bodies different terms. These two- and six-year terms, in turn, differ from the four-year terms that Presidents serve. Two political parties have dominated US politics throughout most of its history, although others are permitted, and the current Republican Party originated in the 1850s as an alternative to the Whigs. This system often results in periods of divided government in which the President is from one party and the majority of one or both Houses of Congress are from another. Although courts are less partisan, a majority of their members may have been appointed by members of one party while the other holds either the presidency or one or both Houses of Congress. Even apart from the supermajorities required by the amending process, the American system of divided powers thus often more effectively impedes than facilitates actions.

The amending process in Art. V is less tied to separation of powers in that it limits direct participation by national actors to supermajorities within both houses of Congress. *Hollingsworth v Virginia* (1798)[98] ruled that Presidents were not required to sign amendments in order for them to be valid. Although the Supreme Court ruled in *Dillon v Gloss* (1921) that state ratifications needed to reflect a contemporary consensus,[99] in *Coleman v Miller*, the Court declared that most issues relative to the ratification of amendments were "political questions" for Congress to resolve.[100]

By contrast, the federal division of power between the nation and the states is reflected in Art. V amending processes, which allow two-thirds of the states to request amendments and require three-fourths of the states to ratify them before they go into effect. After decades of centralization, recent years have witnessed increased attention to states' rights. Politicians often signal their opposition to decisions by national actors by proposing amendments to overturn them.

It is certainly possible, especially through the eyes of faith,[101] to interpret US history and, to a lesser degree, the history of constitutional amendments, as the progressive unfolding of the principles of democracy,[102] but this progress has not been, and is not destined to be, unidirectional in the future. Like the physical laws of inertia in which a body at rest stays at rest, the current system preferences existing provisions over proposed changes.

The role of experts in constitutional revision

The US Constitution identifies its constituents as "We the People." Drawing from Thomas Jefferson, pro-democracy advocate Christopher Phillips recently suggested that constitutional amendments might boil up from discussions of issues by ordinary citizens over coffee,[103] but the Document was written by an elite gathering, and the people can rarely act directly, and require institutions to act on their behalf in amending the Document.[104] Congress is relatively broad-based, and any member can introduce an amendment on the floor of either House. Congress does not sit, as some bodies once did over state politics, as a Council of Censors, and the Constitution neither authorizes nor prevents blue-ribbon commissions from suggesting amendments for congressional and state consideration. To date, all but one amendment that has been ratified has been approved by state legislatures, whose members are typically even less elite than those within Congress.

Although the Constitution does not outline a specific role for Presidents, they frequently support amendments. Puzzling over why a President supports amendments with little chance of adoption, H. Abbie Erler has hypothesized that his reasons might include "building or solidifying his electoral coalition, getting an issue on the agenda, pressuring Congress into less drastic action, or distancing himself from the opposition party or possible challengers."[105] Members of Congress might likewise use their sponsorship of amendments as ideological signals to their supporters.

The first 10 amendments were primarily the brain-child of James Madison of Virginia but reflected fairly widespread sentiments that had been expressed during ratification debates. Individuals like Ohio Congressman John Bingham and Indiana Senator Birch Bayh were particularly influential in the development of individual amendments (in Bingham's case, the Fourteenth Amendment and in Bayh's, the Twenty-fifth Amendment), but their success depended on widespread support. While the Twenty-seventh Amendment originated with James Madison, its ratification was largely the work of Gregory Watson, an otherwise fairly obscure aide to a Texas state representative. Madison argued that the Constitution should be interpreted primarily through a consideration of those who ratified, rather than those who proposed, the Constitution,[106] and once provisions are incorporated within the document, they largely lose their individual identity to become part of a larger, more collective whole.

American elites often cast a critical eye on constitutional proposals and interpretations, and judges ultimately decide what the words of the Constitution and its subsequent amendments mean. However, the people elect both the members of Congress and of state legislatures who propose and ratify amendments.

Judicial review of constitutional amendments

The USA has a vigorous system of judicial review, which has been exercised by all levels of national courts. The judicial assertion of the power to "say what the law is"[107] seems relatively secure. The Constitutional Convention of 1787 rejected a proposed Council of Revision giving the President and key members of the judiciary power to void legislation prior to its adoption,[108] but the same Convention gave the President the power a conditional veto of legislation and allowed the courts to examine "cases and controversies" that arose under the Constitution.

US courts have never invalidated an amendment, and it seems unlikely that they will embrace such a role in the near future. As they interpret both the original constitution and subsequent amendments, American courts have the responsibility of integrating such interpretations into a coherent whole. Courts cannot simply ask what framers or ratifiers might have thought in 1787, but must also consider those who came thereafter. While it is relatively obvious that the original Founders permitted slavery and those connected to the Thirteenth Amendment did not, courts have found it less obvious to decide whether the Fourteenth Amendment's guarantee of equal protection necessarily invalidates all forms of racial preferences or whether the guarantees of equal protection should be limited chiefly to distinctions based on race or color, or whether they should extend to gender equality and issues of sexual orientation.

Constitution amendments have overturned some judicial decisions. Thus, although it is difficult to locate the locus of sovereignty in a system that divides powers both vertically and horizontally, Lester Orfield has argued that, "In the last analysis, one is brought to the conclusion that sovereignty in the United States, if it can be said to exist at all, is located in the amending body."[109]

Criticisms of the amendment procedure

Criticisms of the amending process in the USA have waxed and waned. Decades of inaction often led to hand-wringing over the viability of amending mechanisms, followed by satisfaction that a new round of amendments proves that the process works. The most common criticisms are that the process is too difficult and insufficiently democratic.

Few individuals expect amendments to be adopted every time 51 per cent of the American population wants a change; most understand that the Constitution aims to encourage deliberation, seek amendments that reflect geographically dispersed support, and guard against temporary majorities. Given the prominent role that states play both in congressional representation and in ratification of the amending process, however, one can construct scenarios whereby individuals concentrated in one-third or more of the smallest states could oppose amendments that wide majorities in the two-thirds that were most populous favored. As a process that gives equal weight to the vote of two-thirds of senators, who are apportioned equally among the states regardless of their populations, the process is similarly subject to criticisms that it is insufficiently democratic.

During the Progressive Era, members of Congress introduced proposals to allow voters either to initiate or ratify amendments. More recently, Bruce Ackerman has proposed that second-term Presidents should be able to initiate amendments that three-fifths majorities of the voters could approve in the next two elections,[110] and Akhil Reed Amar has suggested that the principle of popular sovereignty already grants popular majorities the right to propose and ratify amendments.[111] Other proposals have called for reducing proposing or ratifying majorities. Rosalind Dixon suggests that courts should give weight to amendments that Congress proposes by the necessary majorities (what she calls "partial constitutional amendments"), even when the states do not ratify them.[112]

Other critiques of the amending process stem from unanswered questions. One such issue concerns the length of time that states have to ratify amendments. Although *Dillon v Gloss* suggested that such ratifications should reflect a "contemporary consensus," Art. V of the Constitution does not establish a limit on ratifications of amendments; *Coleman v Miller* identified this issue as a political question for the elected branches to resolve, and, with continuing state support and congressional consent, the Twenty-seventh Amendment was ratified more than 200 years after it was proposed. A number of proposed amendments have included seven-year time limits within their texts, where they are self-enforcing, but the proposed Equal Rights Amendment contained this limit only in the congressional authorizing resolution, which Congress subsequently extended. In *Idaho v Freeman*,[113] a US district court judge declared this extension to be unconstitutional, the requisite number of states failed to ratify the amendment, and the US Supreme Court has never resolved this issue.

It remains unclear whether states can rescind their ratifications of pending amendments. Some scholars argue that such rescissions of pending amendments should be just as valid as state decisions to ratify amendments they have previously rejected.[114] Others stress the value of finality[115] or fear that that this might encourage state legislators to treat ratifications less seriously than they should.[116]

Scholars continue to debate Art. V's unused mechanism to propose amendments through a convention. One debate concerns whether states have the right to limit the subject matter that such a convention considers, and, if not, whether state calls for such a limited convention should be counted with others. Charles Black has argued that the framers of Art. V did not contemplate such limited conventions and that "Applications asking for something other than what is meant by Article V are nullities, and 34 [two-thirds of the states] times zero is zero."[117] By contrast, William Van Alstyne has argued that the best way of honoring the framers' wishes is to construe such petitions generously,[118] and Russell Caplan has argued that "a national convention is in all likelihood constitutionally limited to proposing amendments described in the state applications that generated the call."[119]

Conventions called, and restricted, to limited purposes are less likely to become "runaway" bodies that might propose undesirable changes. Unless such a convention could persuade the nation to take extralegal actions, however, any recommendations would be subject to approval by three-fourths of the state legislatures, and other political safeguards diminish the likelihood of such a runaway body.[120]

If Congress called a convention at the request of two-thirds of the state legislatures, Congress would either have to decide, or allow the state legislatures to decide,[121] how representatives would be chosen, paid, and apportioned. Would it be proper for the legislators who called the convention to select the delegates, for the governor to select them, or should they be popularly elected; and, if so, on a district or state-wide, partisan or non-partisan basis?[122] Would the convention follow the precedent established in 1787 and give each state an equal vote, or would state delegates be apportioned according to population, or by a formula, similar or identical to that under the Electoral College, where states were represented according to their total numbers of representatives and senators?

Arguing that the quiescence of amending activity under the Art. V convention mechanism shows that the mechanism needs fixing, Michael B. Rappaport has proposed adding an additional amending procedure to the current mechanism. He favors allowing two-thirds of the state legislatures to propose identically worded amendments. He further favors an advisory convention of state delegates to work on such proposals, a requirement that such proposals would have to be ratified by states having three-quarters of the electoral votes, and a stipulation that this be done through popular ballots.[123] Timothy Lynch has proposed an amendment allowing simple majorities of both Houses of Congress to propose amendments or a simple majority of states to call a convention and only two-thirds of the states to ratify them.[124]

Contemporary debate on the need for future constitutional revision

Consistent with wishes that James Madison expressed in Federalist No. 49, most Americans continue to express considerable pride in the document. The last time Congress proposed an amendment by the necessary majorities (the Equal Rights Amendment) was in 1972, and the last time it ratified an amendment (the Twenty-seventh) was in 1992.

Proposals for more systemic reform

Throughout American history, a series of scholars and citizens have proposed changes that would require more than a single amendment or set of amendments. The most consistently cited proposal has been to establish a parliamentary system in place of the current system of separated powers. Such critics have often portrayed the parliamentary alternative as more accountable and responsive to public opinion, and less likely to result in governmental gridlock, which is often attributed to divided government.[125] Others have recommended elements of such a system, like the question hour in Great Britain, the establishment of a vote of no-confidence in the President, a shadow government, or presidential authority to appoint members of the national legislature to the cabinet. There have been hardly any proposals for a non-democratic or non-republican system of government.

Possible piecemeal reforms

Experience suggests that the most likely scenario for constitutional change is the adoption of relatively isolated amendments that correct, or tinker with, existing constitutional mechanisms. Reform of the Electoral College has been a perennial subject of proposed amendments. Amendments have often removed obstacles to the franchise or have democratized existing institutions. Similarly, there could be a renewed push for an Equal Rights Amendment,[126] for voting representation for the District of Columbia within Congress, for the expansion of victims' rights,[127] for more expeditious replacement of members in the case of a terrorist attack on the US Congress,[128] for repeal of the natural-born citizenship requirement for Presidents,[129] for an increase the size of the US House of Representatives,[130] for limiting pieces of congressional legislation to a single subject,[131] or the like.

America might also adopt a series of related amendments that signal a new political supermajority. Post-Civil War amendments and those of the Progressive Era have been introduced by Congress, but they might also be introduced by conventions. Journalist Richard Labunski is among those who have recently advocated such a path.[132]

Reforms favored by Liberals

Were liberals to achieve such a majority, they might choose to fashion voting into a positive right of citizenship. In line with a number of recent critiques of the Constitution,[133] they might further seek to democratize the Constitution. Such an effort might include: making the amending process easier;[134] providing for national initiatives, recalls, or referenda; providing for a more regularized system of primaries for nominating presidential candidates, perhaps giving less weight to small states with early caucuses and primaries; replacing the Electoral College with direct popular election; limiting the role of money in political campaigning;[135] requiring larger judicial majorities to invalidate legislation; eliminating the Senate filibuster and/or the requirement for 60 votes to invoke cloture;[136] or seeking (if they can overcome the entrenchment hurdle in Art. V[137]) to modify equal state representation in the US Senate.[138]

Alternatively, a new coalition of liberals might seek further security for social and economic rights or for the right to privacy, including abortion and gay rights, perhaps including national recognition of gay marriages. US Representative

Jesse Jackson, Jr. of Illinois, a Democrat, consistently proposes a series of amendments relative to the right to work and employment, high-quality healthcare, the right to a public education, equal rights for women, progressive income taxes, and voting rights.[139] Liberals might further seek to abolish the death penalty.

Most exercises of congressional power rest on a relatively few general clauses like those that give it authority over interstate and foreign commerce, war-related issues, or over taxing and spending or the enforcement clauses of the Fourteenth and Fifteenth Amendments, supplemented with the idea that it may exercise implied powers related to these. Individuals seeking to augment such powers and place them on firmer ground might seek to add more specific powers like power over manufacturing, agriculture, education, welfare, or the like.

Reforms favored by Conservatives

If conservatives garnered a supermajority, they could proceed in either a social/moral or fiscal direction. Were they to adopt the former, they might pursue amendments to: re-establish prayer and/or Bible reading in public schools; limit or prohibit abortion; define marriage as the union between one male and one female; outlaw desecration of the American flag; limit citizenship to individuals born on US soil with one or both citizen parents; or make English the official language.[140] Conservatives might even seek an amendment limiting judicial uses of precedents outside the USA or imposing term limits on members of Congress[141] and/or members of the judiciary, whom conservatives sometimes accuse of legislating from the bench.[142]

If, taking a page from the recent Tea Party Movement,[143] conservatives focused on fiscal matters,[144] they might seek to limit governmental taxation, expenditures, or debt; prohibit Congress from adopting fiscal legislation without supermajorities; support a presidential line-item veto;[145] or mandate a balanced-budget amendment.[146] There is a growing consensus that the current imbalance in the USA between taxes and expenditures and the resulting debt cannot be sustained over a long period of time, and such sentiment sparks constitutional reform, including reconsideration of current electoral incentives to tax and spend. Alternatively, amendments might seek to clarify which specific powers are reserved to the states. Professor Randy Barnett has recently proposed a "Bill of Federalism"[147] to restore federal powers. The most significant would grant two-thirds of the state legislatures the power to repeal federal laws.[148]

The lack of consensus

On 23–24 September 2011, a conference of representatives from both the right and the left met at Harvard University to discuss the possibly of calling an Art. V convention to propose reforms.[149] It achieved no consensus.[150] Formal constitutional change thus seems most likely to follow the traditional route. This process will remain difficult absent a reduction in the majorities required to propose and ratify amendments.

Notes

1 See M. Kammen, *A Machine That Would Go of Itself: The Constitution in American Culture*, Knopf, 1987. Christopher Phillips notes that "Americans venerate the Constitution, even if many of us don't actually seem to know what's in it".
2 A. Hamilton, J. Madison and J. Jay, *The Federalist Papers*, C. Rossiter (ed.), New American Library, 1961, p. 278.
3 J.R. Vile, *A Companion to the United States Constitution and Its Amendments*, 5th edn, Praeger, 2010, p. 2.
4 P.T. Conley and J.P. Kaminski (eds), *The Constitution and the States: The Role of the Original Thirteen in the Framing and Adoption of the Federal Constitution*, Madison House, 1988.
5 D.S. Lutz, "Toward a Theory of Constitutional Amendment", *American Political Science Review*, 1994, vol. 88, no. 2, p. 355.
6 J.R. Vile, *The Constitutional Amending Process in American Political Thought*, Praeger, 1992, p. 25. For specific information on the Council of Censors, see L.H. Meador, "The Council of Censors", *Pennsylvania Magazine of History and Biography*, 1898, vol. 22, pp. 265–300.
7 M. Jensen, *The Articles of Confederation*, University of Wisconsin Press, 1940.
8 W. Solberg (ed.), *The Federal Convention and the Formation of the Union*, Bobbs-Merrill, 1958, p. 42.
9 For accounts, see C. Rossiter, *1787: The Grand Convention*, W.W. Norton, 1987; R. Beeman, *Plain, Honest Men. The Making of the American Constitution*, Random House, 2009; C. Drinker-Bowen, *Miracle at Philadelphia: The Story of the Constitutional Convention May to September 1787*, Little Brown, 1966; J.R. Vile, *The Constitutional Convention of 1787: A Comprehensive Encyclopedia of America's Founding*, 2 vols, ABC-CLIO, 2005; D. Robertson, *The Constitution and America's Destiny*, Cambridge University Press, 2005; D.C. Hendrickson, *Peace Pact: The Lost World of the American Founding*, University Press of Kansas, 2003; M.M. Edling, *A Revolution in Favor of Government: Origins of the U.S. Constitution and the Making of the American State*, Oxford University Press, 2003.
10 Quoted from Proceedings in Congress of 21 February 1787, Solberg, op. cit., p. 64.
11 M. Payandeh, "Constitutional Aesthetics: Appending Amendments to the United States Constitution", *BYU Journal of Public Law*, 2011, vol. 25, p. 101.
12 *The Federalist Papers*, op. cit., p. 246.
13 Ibid., p. 314.
14 A.T. Mason, *Free Government in the Making: Readings in American Political Thought*, 3rd edn, Oxford University Press, 1965, pp. 318–28.
15 S.G. Fisher, *The Trial of the Constitution*, Da Capo Press, 1972 (reprint of J.B. Lippincott & Co. 1862), p. 21, critiqued the rigidity of the Constitution. For later critiques from the Progressive Era, see Vile, *The Constitutional Amending Process*, op. cit., pp. 137–56.
16 For histories, see R.B. Bernstein and J. Agel, *Amending America: If We Love the Constitution So Much, Why Do We Keep Trying to Change It?*, Random House, 1993; D.D. Kyvic, *Explicit and Authentic Acts: Amending the Constitution, 1776–1995*, University Press of Kansas, 1996; A.P. Grimes, *Democracy and the Amendments to the Constitution*, Lexington Books, 1978; K.E. Palmer, *Constitutional Amendments: 1789 to the Present*, Gale Group, 2000; T. Pendergast, S. Pendergast and J. Sousanis, *Constitutional Amendments: From Freedom of Speech to Flag Burning*, 3 vols, UXL (Gale Group), 2001; G. Anastaplo, *The Amendments to the Constitution: A Commentary*, The Johns Hopkins University Press, 1995; J.R. Vile, *Encyclopedia of Constitutional Amendments, Proposed Amendments, and Amending Issues. 1789–2010*, 3rd edn, ABC-CLIO, 2010.
17 P. Finkelman, "James Madison and the Bill of Rights: A Reluctant Paternity", in G. Casper, D.J. Hutchinson and D. Strauss (eds), *Supreme Court Review*, University of Chicago Press, 1990; R. Goldwin, *From Parchment to Power: How James Madison Used the Bill of Rights to Save the Constitution*, AEI Press, 1997; R. Labunski, *James Madison and the Struggle for the Bill of Rights*, Oxford University Press, 2006.

18 See Payandeh, op. cit., pp. 87–130.
19 554 U.S. 570 (2008). The Court interpreted this right as a personal right rather than simply as the right of states to recruit militia.
20 K.T. Lash, *The Lost History of the Ninth Amendment*, Oxford University Press, 2009.
21 J.R. Vile, "Truism, Tautology or Vital Principle? The Tenth Amendment Since United States v Darby", *Cumberland Law Review*, 1996–1997, vol. 27, pp. 446–532.
22 2 U.S. (2 Dall.) 419 (1793).
23 See T. Kuroda, *The Origins of the Twelfth Amendment: The Electoral College in the Early Republic, 1787–1804*, Greenwood Press, 1994.
24 B. Ackerman, *We the People: Transformations*, Harvard University Press, 1998.
25 E.M. Maltz, *Civil Rights, the Constitution, and Congress, 1863–1869*, University Press of Kansas, 1990; A. Tsesis, *The Thirteenth Amendment and American Freedom: A Legal History*, NYU Press, 2004; M. Vorenberg, *Final Freedom: The Civil War, the Abolition of Slavery, and the Thirteenth Amendment*, Cambridge University Press, 2001.
26 J.B. James, *The Framing of the Fourteenth Amendment*, University of Illinois Press, 1956; W.E. Nelson, *The Fourteenth Amendment: From Political Principle to Judicial Doctrine*, Harvard University Press, 1988; D.A.J. Richards, *Conscience and the Constitution: History, Theory and Law of the Reconstruction Amendments*, Princeton University Press, 1993.
27 60 U.S. 393 (1857).
28 W. Gillette, *The Right to Vote: Politics and the Passage of the Fifteenth Amendment*, Johns Hopkins Press, 1965.
29 See H. Gillman, *The Constitution Besieged: The Rise and Demise of Lochner Era Police Powers Jurisprudence*, Duke University Press, 1993.
30 32 U.S. 243 (1833).
31 268 U.S. 252 (1925).
32 158 U.S. 601 (1985).
33 See C.H. Hoebeke, *The Road to Mass Democracy: Original Intent and the Seventeenth Amendment*, Transaction, 1995; R.A. Rossum, *Federalism, the Supreme Court, and the Seventeenth Amendment: The Irony of Constitutional Democracy*, Lexington Books, 2001.
34 See D. Okrent, *Last Call: The Rise and Fall of Prohibition*, Scribner, 2010; DD. Kyvic (ed.), *Alcohol and Order: Perspectives on National Prohibition*, Greenwood Press, 1985; D.D. Kyvic, *Repealing National Prohibition*, University of Chicago Press, 1979; R.F. Hamm, *Shaping the 18th Amendment: Temperance Reform, Legal Culture, and the Polity, 1880–1920*, University of North Carolina Press, 1995.
35 V. Bernhard and E. Fox-Genovese (eds), *The Birth of American Feminism: The Seneca Falls Woman's Convention of 1848*, Brandywine Press, 1995.
36 See J.H. Baker (ed.), *Votes for Women: The Struggle for Suffrage Revisited*, Oxford University Press, 2002; M.S. Wheeler (ed.), *One Woman, One Vote: Rediscovering the Woman Suffrage Movement*, New Sage, 1995.
37 J.D. Feerick, *The Twenty-fifth Amendment: Its Complete History and Applications*, Fordham University Press, 1992.
38 400 U.S. 112 (1970).
39 R.B. Bernstein, "The Sleeper Wakes: The History and Legacy of the Twenty-seventh Amendment", *Fordham Law Review*, 1992, vol. 61, pp. 497–557.
40 Extra-constitutional norms are sometimes referred to as "usages". See H.W. Horwill, *The Usages of the American Constitution*, Kennikat Press, 1969 (reprint of 1925 edn). See also M. Foley, *The Silence of Constitutions: Gaps, "Abeyances" and Political Temperament in the Maintenance of Government*, Routledge, 1989.
41 W. Harris II, *The Interpretable Constitution*, Johns Hopkins University Press, 1993. For an alternate approach focusing on the manner in which institutions created by the text introduce change through "constitutional construction", see S.M. Griffin, "The United States of America", in D. Oliver and C. Fusaro (eds), *How Constitutions Change: A Comparative Study*, Hart Publishing, 2011, pp. 357–78, especially pp. 365–71.

42 Notably, although states failed to ratify an amendment that Congress had proposed to prohibit child labor, federal regulations have accomplished such a prohibition in the absence of the amendment. See S.B. Wood, *Constitutional Politics in the Progressive Era: Child Labor and the Law*, University of Chicago Press, 1968.

43 The most important was *Brown v Board of Education*, 347 U.S. 483 (1954). It overturned the decision establishing "separate but equal" accommodations for whites and blacks that the Court had approved in *Plessy v Ferguson*, 163 U.S. 537 (1896).

44 See M.F. Berry, *Why ERA Failed: Politics, Women's Rights and the Amending Process of the Constitution*, Indiana University Press, 1986; J.J. Mansbridge, *Why We Lost the ERA*, University of Chicago Press, 1986.

45 Thus *Lawrence v Texas*, 539 U.S. 558 (2003), invalidated state laws against consensual sodomy, reversing *Bowers v Hardwick*, 478 U.S. 186 (1986).

46 But see R.P. George, "The 28th Amendment: It Is Time to Protect Marriage, and Democracy, in America", *National Review*, 2001, vol. 53, pp. 32–4.

47 17 U.S. (4 Wheat.) 316 (1819).

48 *Immigration and Naturalization Service v Chadha*, 462 U.S. 919 (1983).

49 Both clauses are in Art. I, Section 8, of the US Constitution, which also includes the "necessary and proper clause", which allows for the exercise of various implied powers.

50 For a comparison of the advantages and disadvantages of various modes of change, see J.R. Vile, *Constitutional Change in the United States: A Comparative Study of the Role of Constitutional Amendments, Judicial Interpretations, and Legislative and Executive Actions*, Praeger, 1994.

51 5 U.S. (1 Cranch) 137 (1803).

52 17 U.S. (4 Wheat.) 316 (1819).

53 D.A. Strauss, "Commentary: The Irrelevance of Constitutional Amendments", *Harvard Law Review*, 2001, vol. 114, pp. 1457–59.

54 B.P. Denning and J.R. Vile, "The Relevance of Constitutional Amendments: A Response to David Strauss", *Tulane Law Review*, 2002, vol. 77, pp. 247–82.

55 Lutz, op. cit., p. 362.

56 See especially J. Bryce, *The American Commonwealth*, 3rd edn, New York: Macmillan, 1906, vol. I, p. 370.

57 *The Federalist Papers*, op. cit., pp. 314–15.

58 *Counting the Many: The Origins and Limits of Supermajority Rule*, under contract with Cambridge UP, Cambridge Studies in the Theory of Democracy, p. 14 of Chapter 5. Online. Available HTTP: <http://www.law.nyu.edu/ecm_div3/groups/public/@nyu_law_website_academic_colloquia_law_economics_and_politics/documents/documents/ecm_pro_067355.pdf> (accessed 6 May 2011). For factors affecting the rate of amendment, see R. Dixon, "Constitutional amendment rules: a comparative perspective", in T. Ginsburg and R. Dixon (eds), *Comparative Constitutional Law*, Edward Edgar Publishing Ltd., 2011, pp. 104–8.

59 Vile, "Number of Proposed Amendments", *Encyclopedia of Amendments*, op. cit., vol. II, pp. 343–5. For a complete compilation of the subjects of these amendments, see J.R. Vile (ed.), *Proposed Amendments to the U.S. Constitution, 1787–2001*, 4 vols, The Lawbook Exchange, 2011. The fourth Volume updates this list through 2010.

60 For the amendments that Congress proposed but that the states did not ratify, see M.J. Lynch, "The Other Amendments: Constitutional Amendments That Failed", *Law Library Journal*, 2001, vol. 93, pp. 303–10.

61 R.G. Natelson, who argues for a limited convention, in *Amending the Constitution by Convention: A Complete View of the Founder's Plan* (3 parts), Goldwater Institute Policy Report, 2010, notes in Part II, p. 21 that by 1912, 31 states (just one shy of those required) had called for a convention to propose direct election of Senators. Sara R. Ellis, Yusus Z. Malik, Heather Graves Parker, Benjamin C. Signer and Al'Reco L. Yancy argue that appeals for a convention to adopt a balanced-budget amendment led in part to the adoption of the Gramm-Rudman-Hollings Balanced Budget and

Emergency Deficit Control Act of 1985. See "Article V Constitutional Conventions: A Primer", *Tennessee Law Review*, 2011, vol. 78(3), pp. 667–8.

62 See P.J. Weber and B.A. Perry, *Unfounded Fears: Myths and Realities of a Constitutional Convention*, Praeger, 1989. Also see R.L. Caplan, *Constitutional Brinkmanship: Amending the Constitution by National Convention*, Oxford University Press, 1988.

63 W. Dellinger, in "The Recurring Question of the 'Limited' Constitutional Convention", *Yale Law Journal*, 1979, vol. 88, pp. 1623–40, has argued that conventions must be unlimited, whereas W. Van Alstyne, "Does Article V Restrict the States to Calling Unlimited Conventions Only? - A Letter to a Colleague", *Duke Law Journal*, 1978, vol. 1978, pp. 1295–306, argues that states may limit them. Natelson, op. cit., argues for Van Alstyne's view.

64 A.R. Amar, "Philadelphia Revisited: Amending the Constitution outside Article V", *University of Chicago Law Review* (Fall) 1988, vol. 55, pp. 1043–104; and "The Consent of the Governed: Constitutional Amendment outside Article V", *Columbia Law Review*, 1994, vol. 94, pp. 457–508.

65 See J.N. Rakove, "The Great Compromise: Ideas, Interests, and the Politics of Constitution Making", *William and Mary Quarterly*, 3rd ser., 1987, vol. 44, pp. 424–57.

66 A number of high-profile US scholars have in recent years argued that the current constitution in insufficiently democratic. See R. Dahl, *How Democratic is the American Constitution?*, Yale University Press, 2001; S. Levinson, *Our Undemocratic Constitution*, Oxford University Press, 2006; L. Sabato, *A More Perfect Constitution: 23 Proposals to Revitalize our Constitution and Make America a Fairer Country*, Walker and Company, 2007; D. Lazare, *The Frozen Republic: How the Constitution is Paralyzing Democracy*, Harcourt Brace and Company, 1996.

67 J.R. Vile, "Limitations on the Constitutional Amending Process", *Constitutional Commentary*, 1985, vol. 2, pp. 373–88.

68 238 U.S. 368 (1915). The case had challenged the validity of the Fifteenth Amendment.

69 253 U.S. 350 (1920).

70 282 U.S. 716 (1931).

71 258 U.S. 130 (1922).

72 See W.F. Murphy, "An Ordering of Constitutional Values' *Southern California Law Review*", 1980, vol. 53, pp. 703–60; C.A. Kelbley, "Are There Limits to Constitutional Change? Rawls on Comprehensive Doctrines, Unconstitutional Amendments, and the Basis of Equality", *Fordham Law Review*, 2004, vol. 72, pp. 1487–536.

73 See E.A. Isaacson, "The Flag Burning Issue: A Legal Analysis and Comment", *Loyola of Los Angeles Law Review*, 1990, vol. 23, pp. 535–600; J. Rosen, "Was the Flag-Burning Amendment Unconstitutional?", *Yale Law Review*, 1991, vol. 100, pp. 1073–92. The US Supreme Court had upheld the constitutionality of such desecration in *Texas v Johnson*, 491 U.S. 397 (1989) and *United States v Eichman*, 496 U.S. 310 (1990).

74 J.R. Vile, "The Case against Implicit Limits on the Constitutional Amending Process", in S. Levinson (ed.), *Responding to Imperfection: The Theory and Practice of Constitutional Amendment*, Princeton University Press, 1995, pp. 191–214.

75 M. Schwartzberg, *Democracy and Legal Change*, Cambridge University Press, 2007, p. 151.

76 W.C. Davis, *A Government of Our Own: The Making of the Confederacy*, The Free Press, 1994.

77 T. Jefferson, *Notes on the State of Virginia*, Harper & Row, 1964, p. 118. The italics are in the original.

78 See E.E. Cornwell, J.S. Goodman and W.R. Swanson, *State Constitutional Conventions: The Politics of the Revision Process in Seven States*, Praeger, 1975. See also, G.Đ. Tarr and R.F. Williams (eds), *State Constitutions for the Twenty-first Century: The Politics of State Constitutional Reform*, Vol. 1, State University of New York Press, 2006; F.P. Grad and R.F. Williams (eds), *State Constitutions for the Twenty-first Century: Drafting State Constitutions – Revisions, and Amendments*, Vol. 2, State University of New York Press, 2006.

79 R. Albert, "Constitutional Handcuffs", *Arizona State Law Journal* (Fall), 2010, vol. 42, pp. 663–5.

80 *The Federalist Papers*, op. cit., p. 82.

81 G.S. Wood, *The Creation of the American Republic, 1776–1787*, University of North Carolina Press, 1969, pp. 306–89; Payandeh, op. cit., p. 102, observes that representation "is never mimetic representation in which the representative entity is to be equated with the people, but is only symbolic representation, embracing the awareness that the representative body is not the same as the entity it is supposed to represent but only a representative in a symbolic way. The original Constitution, as well as the amendments to the Constitution, are therefore creations of representatives of the people, and both derive their ultimate legitimacy from the people as the bearer of popular sovereignty".

82 See, for example, E. Gillespie and B. Schellhas (eds), *Contract with America: The Bold Plan by Rep. Newt Gingrich, Rep. Dick Armey, and the House Republicans to Change the Nation*, Random House, 1994.

83 *Kimble v Swackhamer*, 439 U.S. 385 (1978).

84 531 U.S. 510 (2001).

85 See J. Madison, "Lessons of History: Of Ancient and Modern Confederacies", in M. Meyers (ed.), *The Mind of the Founder: Sources of the Political Thought of James Madison*, The Bobbs-Merrill Company, Inc., 1973, pp. 69–81.

86 521 U.S. 702, 734 (1997).

87 536 U.S. 304, 316 no. 21 (2002).

88 539 U.S. 306 (2003).

89 539 U.S. 558 (2003).

90 543 U.S. 551 (2005).

91 See A.L. Parrish, "Storm in a Teacup: The U.S. Supreme Court's Use of Foreign Law", *University of Illinois Law Review*, 2007, vol. 2007, pp. 637–80; G. Sitaraman, "The Use and Abuse of Foreign Law in Constitutional Interpretation", *Harvard Journal of Law and Public Policy*, 2009, vol. 32, pp. 653–93.

92 252 U.S. 416 (1920).

93 D. Tananbaum, *The Bricker Amendment Controversy: A Test of Eisenhower's Political Leadership*, Cornell University Press, 1988.

94 See *Rice v Sioux City Memorial Park*, 349 U.S. 70 (1955) and *Reid v Covert*, 354 U.S. 1 (1957).

95 J.R. Vile, *Rewriting the United States Constitution: An Examination of Proposals from Reconstruction to the Present*, Praeger, 1991; S.R. Boyd (ed.), *Alternative Constitutions for the United States: A Documentary History*, Greenwood Press, 1992, and Vile, *Encyclopedia of Constitutional Amendments*, op. cit.

96 See W. Connelly, *James Madison Rules America*, Rowman and Littlefield, 2010.

97 *The Federalist Papers*, op. cit., p. 465.

98 3 U.S. (3 Dal.) 379 (1798).

99 256 U.S. 368 (1921).

100 *Coleman v Miller*, 307 U.S. 433 (1939).

101 See J.M. Balkin, *Constitutional Redemption: Political Faith in an Unjust World*, Harvard University Press, 2011.

102 Grimes, op. cit.

103 C. Phillips, *Constitutional Café: Jefferson's brew for a True Revolution*, W.W. Norton & Company, 2011.

104 See R.S. Kay, "Constituent Authority", *American Journal of Comparative Law*, 2011, vol. 59(3), pp. 715–48.

105 H.A. Erler, "Article 5 and Executive Leadership: Predicting Calls for Amendments", Paper presented at the annual meeting of the MPSA Annual National Conference, Palmer House Hotel, Chicago, IL, 3 April 2008. Online. Available HTTP: <http://citation.allacademic.com/meta/p_mla_apa_research_citation/2/6/5/8/8/pages265888/p265888-1.php>, p. 7.

106 See J. Rakove, *Original Meanings: Politics and Ideas in the Making of the Constitution*, Alfred A. Knopf, pp. 17–18.
107 Quoted from *Marbury v Madison* (1803) 177.
108 C.F. Hobson, "The Negative on State Laws: James Madison, the Constitution and the Crisis of Republican Government", *William and Mary Quarterly*, 3rd ser., 1979, vol. 36(2), pp. 214–35.
109 L.B. Orfield, *The Amending of the Federal Constitution*, University of Michigan Press, 1942; M. Radin, "The Intermittent Sovereign", *Yale Law Journal*, 1930, vol. 39(4), pp. 514–31.
110 B. Ackerman, *We the People: Foundations*, Belknap, 1991, pp. 54–5.
111 Amar, op. cit. For a comparison to Jefferson, see J.I. Colon-Rios, "The Three Waves of the Constitutionalism–Democracy Debate in the U.S. (and an Invitation to Return to the First)", *Willamette Journal of International Law & Dispute Resolution*, 2010, vol. 18, pp. 1–37.
112 R. Dixon, "Partial Constitutional Amendments", *University of Pennsylvania Journal of Constitutional Law*, 2011, vol. 13, pp. 643–85.
113 529 F. Supp. 1107, 1981.
114 F.W. Grinnell, "Petitioning Congress for a Convention: Cannot a State Change Its Mind?", *American Bar Association Journal*, 1959, vol. 45, p. 1164.
115 Orfield, op. cit., p. 70.
116 S.S. Freedman and P.J. Naughton, *ERA: May a State Change Its Vote*, Wayne State University Press, 1978, p. 11.
117 C.L. Black, Jr., "Amendment by a National Constitutional Convention: A Letter to a Senator", *Oklahoma Law Review*, 1979, vol. 32, pp. 626–44.
118 Alstyne, op. cit.
119 Caplan, op. cit., p. 157.
120 Weber and Perry, op. cit., pp. 105–25. See also M. Stern, "Reopening the Constitutional Road to Reform: Toward a Safeguarded Article V Convention", *Tennessee Law Review*, 2011, vol. 78(3), pp. 765–88; M.M. Penrose advocates adoption of legislation on the subject in "Conventional Wisdom: Acknowledging Uncertainty in the Unknown", *Tennessee Law Review*, 2011, vol. 78(3), pp. 789–805.
121 Natelson, op. cit., Part I, pp. 22–3, suggests that these decisions should be made by the states themselves or by the convention itself, but decisions by the former might impact the range of decisions available to the latter.
122 Natelson, op. cit., Part III, p. 24, favors legislative selection.
123 M.B. Rappaport, "Reforming Article V", *Virginia Law Review*, 2010, vol. 96(7), p. 1514.
124 T. Lynch, "Amending Article V to Make the Constitutional Amending Process Itself Less Onerous", *Tennessee Law Review*, 2011, vol. 78(3), p. 830.
125 See, however, D.R. Mayhew, *Divided We Govern: Party Control, Lawmaking, and Investigations, 1946–1990*, Yale University Press, 1991. For a defense of the present system of separated powers, see J.W. Ceaser, "In Defense of Separation of Powers", in R.A. Goldwin and A. Kaufman (eds), *Separation of Powers – Does It Still Work?*, American Enterprise Institute, 1986, p. 168ff. For a study suggesting that parliamentary systems are more stable than presidential systems, see J.J. Linz and A. Valenzuela (eds), *The Failure of Presidential Democracy: Comparative Perspectives*, 1 of 2 volumes, The Johns Hopkins University Press, 1994.
126 See A. Bartow, "Proposed Amendment: An Equal Rights Amendment to Make Women Human", *Tennessee Law Review*, 2011, vol. 78(3), pp. 839–47.
127 V. Schwartz, "The Victims' Rights Amendment", *Harvard Journal on Legislation*, 2005, vol. 42, pp. 525–55.
128 *Continuity of Congress in the Wake of a Catastrophic Attack*, Hearings before the Subcommittee on the Constitution, Civil Rights, and Civil Liberties of the Committee on the

Judiciary, House of Representatives, One Hundred Eleventh Congress, First Session. 23 July 2009, Washington.

129 See S.P. Herlihy, "Amending the Natural Born Citizen Requirement: Globalization as the Impetus and the Obstacle", *Chicago-Kent Law Review*, 2006, vol. 81, pp. 275–300.

130 Brian Frederick favors a House of approximately 675 (rather than the current 435) members. See *Congressional Representation & Constituents: The Case for Increasing the U.S. House of Representatives*, Routledge, 2010, p. 36.

131 B.P. Denning and B.R. Smith, "Uneasy Riders: The Case for a Truth-in-Legislation Amendment", *Utah Law Review*, 1999, vol. 1999, pp. 957–1025.

132 R. Labunski, *The Second Constitutional Convention: How the American People Can Take Back Their Government*, Marley and Beck Press, 2000.

133 See the earlier references to Levinson, Sabato, Dahl, and Lazare. Also see S. Levinson, "Symposium: Is Our Constitutional Order Broken? Structural and Doctrinal Questions in Constitutional Law: Keynote Address: Has the Obama Presidency Vitiated the 'Dysfunctional Constitution' Thesis?", *Connecticut Law Review*, 2011, vol. 43, pp. 985–1002.

134 Levinson, *Our Undemocratic Constitution*, op. cit., pp. 159–66.

135 Since *Buckley v Valeo*, 424 U.S. 1 (1976), the US Supreme Court has considered most campaign expenditures to be a form of speech protected by the First Amendment.

136 J. Chafetz, "Symposium: Is Our Constitutional Order Broken? Structural and Doctrinal Questions in Constitutional Law: The Use of the Filibuster and Potential Senate Reform: The Unconstitutionality of the Filibuster", *Connecticut Law Review*, 2011, vol. 43(4), pp. 1003–40.

137 D.J. Levinson observes "a general paradox of constitutionalism", namely that "enduring constitutional rules and arrangements will tend to become both increasingly dysfunctional and increasingly difficult to change over time". See his "Parchment and Politics: The Positive Puzzle of Constitutional Commitment", *Harvard Law Review*, 2011, vol. 124, p. 714.

138 F. Zakaria has commended Iceland for considering a new Constitution (and using Internet resources to solicit popular ideas) and suggested that the US should consider changing both the Electoral College and the structure of the Senate. See "Is it Time to update the U.S. Constitution?". Online. Available HTTP: <http://globalpublicsquare.blogs.cnn.com/2011/06/20/is-it-time-to-update-the-u-s-constitution-2/> (accessed 20 June 2011).

139 J.L. Jackson, Jr. and F.E. Watkins, *A More Perfect Union: Advancing New American Rights*, Welcome Rain Publishers, 2001.

140 See R. Tatalovich, *Nativism Reborn? The Official English Language Movement and the American States*, University Press of Kentucky, 1995.

141 R.A. Epstein, "Proposed Amendment: Why We Need Term Limits for Congress: Four in the Senate, Ten in the House", *Tennessee Law Review*, 2011, vol. 78(3), pp. 849–57.

142 In *U.S. Term Limits, Inc. v Thornton*, 514 U.S. 779 (1995), the US Supreme Court ruled that the age, residency, and citizenship requirements within the Constitution were exclusive, that state attempts to impose congressional term limits were unconstitutional, and would require adoption of a constitutional amendment.

143 E. Price-Foley associates the movement chiefly with federalism. See her "Sovereignty, Rebalanced: The Tea Party & Constitutional Amendments", *Tennessee Law Review*, 2011, vol. 78(3), pp. 751–64.

144 In *Fed Up! Our Fight to Save America from Washington*, Little, Brown and Company, 2010, Texas Republican Governor Rick Perry advocates: limiting federal spending, a moratorium on earmarks, instituting biennial budgets, repealing the Sixteenth Amendment, imposing term limits on judges, allowing two-thirds majorities of Congress to override Supreme Court decisions, and adopting "clarifying" amendments limiting the scope of existing amendments, particularly the Fourteenth. See pp. 181–4. On p. 38, Perry questions the wisdom of the Seventeenth Amendment; on p. 102, Perry further

critiques the Supreme Court's decisions relative to prayers in public schools; on pp. 107–8, he opposes the Supreme Court decision on abortion, and on pp. 1, 8, and 10, he criticizes judicial decisions invaliding state sodomy laws and defining marriage to include same-sex couples.

145 See T.E. Cronin and J.J. Weill, "An Item Veto for the President?", *Congress & the Presidency*, 1985, vol. 12(2), pp. 127–51; *Clinton v City of New York*, 524 U.S. 417 (1998) invalidated a law that attempted to give the President such authority.

146 See M. Lee, *The Freedom Agenda: Why a Balanced Budget Amendment is Necessary to Restore Constitutional Government*, Regnery Publishing, 2011. For an analysis of the problems of addressing such an issue through amendment, see R. Ponnuru, "Credibility Deficit", *National Review*, 2011, vol. 63, pp. 16, 18.

147 R.E. Barnett, "A Bill of Federalism", *Forbes*, 20 May 2009. Online. Available HTTP: <http://www.forbes.com/2009/05/20/bill-of-federalism-constitution-states-supreme-court-opinions-contributors-randy-barnett.html>.

148 R.E. Barnett and W.J. Howell, "The Case for a 'Repeal Amendment'", *Wall Street Journal*, 16 September 2010. For a critique, see J.R. Vile, "The Case Against a 'Repeal Amendment'", *National Law Journal*, 3 January 2011. Online. Available HTTP: <http://www.law.com/jsp/nlj/PubArticleNLJ.jsp?id=12024766–6789&slreturn=1&hbxlogin=1>.

149 C. Shea, "Unconventional Meeting of Minds", *The Chronicle of Higher Education*, 23 September 2011, p. A1 and p. A4.

150 T.R. Eddlem, "Harvard Confab Fails to Convince Tea Party to Seek Constitutional Convention". Online. Available HTTP: <http://thenewamerican.com/usnews/constitution/9138-harvard-confab-fails-to-convince-tea-party-to-seek-constitutional-convention> (accessed 26 September 2011).

20 Models of constitutional change

Xenophon Contiades and Alkmene Fotiadou

> But I am constant as the northern star,
> Of whose true-fixed and resting quality
> There is no fellow in the firmament.
>
> William Shakespeare, *Julius Caesar* (3.1.58)

Constitutional change is a journey leading to complex, even labyrinthine relations and interactions between amending formulas, constitutional actors, and multiple centers of authority. Exploring the way in which constitutions change in 18 established liberal democracies, which represent what is traditionally conceptualized as the West, unravels the intricate correlations between players who pursue the final say in constitutional change, intended and unintended functions of amending mechanisms, and the interplay between formal and informal change. The comparative approach brings forth the way in which powers are articulated in modern constitutional states, fragmentation and concentration following a subtle rotation. On the basis of these correlations, distinct models of constitutional change are built. Classifying countries within models, in accordance with the way in which operative amending mechanisms connect, leads to a succinct portrayal of different modes of constitutional change engineering.

To follow Ariadne's thread, unfolding in the intricate paths of constitutional change, this chapter is structured in five parts: the first part explores the connection between *time and constitutions* in constitutional amendment narratives. In the second part, the *role of the players* who determine the route of constitutional development is analyzed, focus put separately on the judiciary, the political elites, and the people. Part three deals with *amending formulas*, which are assessed as to their capacity to capture the dynamics of constitutional change by setting up revision mechanisms that discipline change through constitutional rules. Attempting neither to overestimate nor to undervalue their impact on actual "levels of rigidity," light is shed on the relationship between amendment ratios and their consequences. In the fourth part, the interconnection between all actors, parameters, and factors involved in constitutional change is traced, revealing the variety of mechanisms employed and the existence of *five distinct models* of change: the *elastic* model, the *evolutionary* model, the *pragmatic* model, the *distrust* model, and the *direct democratic* model, within which countries are classified. In part five, the *concept of rigidity* is re-approached and alternative ways of comprehending it are explored, leading to overall conclusions regarding constitutional amendment engineering. Premised on the discussions being held at the moment in the countries under examination as to what constitutional reforms should take place, current tendencies are traced to pinning down divergences and convergences that can only be tested through their prevalence or disappearance over the passage of time.

Time, decisions, revisions

The relationship between time and constitutions is a reoccurring pattern in constitutional amendment narratives. Amending formulas regulate time, that is, channel change through time arrangements. Constitutional procedures designed to monitor revision will influence the evolution of constitutional change whether followed, bypassed, or violated. The observation of the function of amending mechanisms through the lens of constitutional history and the examination of the background of constitutional moments tracing the role played by constitutional actors is the starting point for comprehending the connection between constitutions and time. For formal change taking place through the amendment process, successful timing is a desideratum: to allow change when change is actually needed and to hinder it when wanton. Informal amendment has a more obscure connection to time. It may happen gradually, it may happen episodically, and perhaps it may occur through the combination of both tardiness and abruptness, forged slowly but coming to light and becoming apparent instantaneously. How long constitutional moments last is a contested issue: are these moments brief, rare moments that signal discontinuity,[1] or is there in such moments time for decisions and revisions that eventually surface as change?

Who has the strength to force constitutional moments to their crisis is perhaps even more important: moments of change are moments where the key players who have the power to change the constitution are revealed, and so is the actor who takes the lead and has the final word. Underlying the "how" and the "when" is the "who." The archetypal metaphor of constitutional moments,[2] widely embraced by constitutional scholars,[3] involves the people taking control over constitutional change. Yet, constitutional moments may be moments when the actor revealed to be in control is not necessarily the people. The questions that emerge thus are: how can density[4] of historical time be measured in constitutional moments—are they events or part of constitutional continuity? Do constitutional moments coincide with crisis, and how does the notion of crisis correlate with constitutional change?

Historical time with regard to constitutional change progresses at different speeds. Time moves fast with regard to *events*, slows down in constitutional *episodes*, and is slow in the realm of constitutional *culture*. Changing time density explains the difference between incremental updates and episodic shifts in constitutional continuance, which, when intermingled, produce constitutional change. Formal and informal amendment move in different times, and through their interrelation constitutions evolve. Formal amendment is also an attempt to freeze time, solidifying changes by placing them out of the reach of majorities and judges. Informal amendments are attempts to unfreeze time, introducing change through constructive interpretation reversing revisions. The dosage balance between formal and informal change is determined by a variety of factors: in the USA, a strong judiciary has undertaken the job of walking the unchanging constitutional text through time by way of informal amendment; UK legislative omnipotency stemming from parliamentary sovereignty allows total constitutional flexibility; German positivism favors explicit change over informality; the Swiss culture of referendums nourishes people-driven formal change; while in Spain it is the perplexed formula and a conflictual political culture that, in combination, block formal change, redirecting it through informal paths.

In conceptualizing the flow of constitutional time, notions of eternity sneak in through the entrenchment of eternity clauses, suggesting that *timelessness* is possible. Eternity clauses may be viewed from many aspects. They correspond to the image of a sanctified constitution, which resists the demystification that stems from disconnecting the amendment process from the memory of the constituent moment, the "quasi-religious communion of the amendment procedure with the founding moment of each political regime,"[5] and viewing it rather as a means of regular maintenance and updating. In a sense, eternity clauses are akin to constitutional moments as they are both visualizations of time that reproduce the *constitutional myth imagery*, in one case through eternality and in the other by transferring the memory of constituent moments to moments where the people are awakened to induce major constitutional changes.

Eternity clauses are something more than mere relics of the mystical constitution. They determine the balance between constitutionalism and democracy, shifting the weight towards constitutionalism. Creating an off-limits area, they narrow the scope of democratic deliberation. Material limits aspire to freeze time, yet often by including abstract core concepts of the constitution such as the form of government, the character of the polity, and fundamental rights, they inescapably abandon self-referential introvert inertia, craving dynamic understandings of concepts. At the same time, they open the door to judicial review with regard to the substance of constitutional amendments. Judicial competence to delineate the substantial limits of the amending power renders judges guardians of the "eternal" with authority to decide what is permanent, and further enhances their role, allowing them entrance into a space where the stakes of democracy versus constitutionalism are very high.

The extent to which judges may meddle with constitutional amendment is dependent on the type of the eternity clause, that is, its content and the function it is expected to perform. Eternity clauses, for example, may entail the polity or the spirit of the constitution, the core protection of fundamental rights, or they may aim to preserve forever or to transform constitutional reality towards a specific direction.[6] For example, Germany, Greece, France, and Portugal all have eternity clauses aspiring to entrench what matters most, ranging from the protection of the republican form of government or the inviolability of human dignity to the inclusion of more detailed directive principles and fundamental rights. Such choices stem from history and constitutional culture, yet a common thread that marks the reality of constitutional change in these countries is that it is political elite-driven, be it through conflict or through consensus. The absence of eternity clauses in Switzerland, Ireland, and Denmark, where the constitution vests in the people the final say on constitutional revision, suggests that this connection is not merely coincidental.

How a constitution responds to time is not determined by the intended "level of rigidity," nor can it be measured through amendment rates, but it depends on *multifaceted parameters* stemming from history, culture, and constitutional identity. Shared constitutional imageries may decide the way constitutional moments are played out. Whether the constitution is perceived as a mystical, sacred document inspiring constitutional fideism,[7] or a tool for coordinating political conflict that may be replaced by political actors if deemed or proved to be dysfunctional, is a focal differentiation. Predictions about the route constitutional change is going to follow provide as much certainty as historical predictions, and cannot be safely made on the basis of measurable factors such as the age and length of the constitution, or the hurdles set by the amending formula. Comparisons on constitutional amendment processes are only meaningful when attempting to grasp the zeitgeist and embracing the differentiations in constitutional ethos, which are not apparent by reading the amending formulas rather than engaging in futile juxtapositions of the seemingly similar arrangements found in constitutional texts.

The task becomes even more complex as, in times of constitutional transformation or reform, the interdependence between constitutional identity and extraconstitutional identities—political, religious, ethnic, etc.—accelerates.[8] Interacting constitutional and other identities thus develop a two-fold relationship to constitutional change as they speed up due to change but also determine change and have the force to expedite or slow it down. Constitutional change may only be explained through historical accounts entailing politics, economy, culture, identity, religion, and social customs. The non-measurable context of historical evolution and constitutional identity identification over time—entailing threats against national sovereignty, endangerments and violations of democratic institutions, constitutional patriotism and constitutional ethos—is where the answers with regard to constitutional change lie. All other parameters responsible for constitutional amendment (i.e. amending formulas, allocation of powers, judicial identity, party systems, etc.) are subject to the cunning of history while also being part of it. The cost of this comprehension is abandoning belief in the plausibility of predictions about constitutional change based on measurable variables.

Still, if narratives of constitutional change are bound to be historicist,[9] a question emerges regarding how big the distance is between this apprehension of the constitution and a more legalistic approach. In other words, it must be asked whether historical approaches mark a total shift in focus or whether they are reconcilable with legalistic understandings. Legalistic approaches do remain part of putting together the piles of the *constitutional change mosaic*, yet at a comparative level their value varies in relation to history. Conceding that the historical perspective is inescapable for understanding constitutional change in a liberal democracy like the US, which never underwent military coups and changes in the form of government, means that it is indispensable in any analysis with regard to constitutional orders with volatile political history. Accordingly, for the comprehension of the German entrenchment of human dignity through an eternity clause or of the particular weight afforded to the feasibility of explicit change, it is important to look into the traumatic experience of the fall of the Weimar Republic. It is thus at the comparative level that quantitative approaches are the most dangerous. If not measuring the immeasurable, in the selection of variables regarding both amendment rates and various parameters of rigidity lurks the danger of underestimating extraconstitutional parameters related to history, culture, and identity, which would potentially contradict the results of such studies.

Placing the constitution in the context of time and change evokes the relation of language with time. Words change, their meaning evolves, and as language transcends time so does the language of the constitution. The changing meaning of words and evolving notions about the very concepts enshrined in constitutions redefine their content, which may be studied either in a historicist manner meticulously placed in a specific constitutional background, or read also as a palimpsest of meanings, understandings, narratives, and uses transcending a constitution's era and historical context. Changing and contradicting definitions of what "peace, order and good government power" has been taken to mean in Canada displays the power of differing word definitions, which has the potential to alter the allocation of powers. More strikingly even, the text of the Danish Constitution would convey a totally misleading impression as to the function of the form of government to anyone who lacks knowledge of that country's constitutional practice, in accordance to which the word "King" is taken to mean the government: introversion results from distance between literal and actual meaning. Moments of change may thus be *moments of shifts in narrative* that may occur when the narrator changes. A concomitant problem is tracing who has control over time, that is, whether players can affect constitutional change by *accelerating or slowing down time with regard to change*, and to what extent this depends on the way time is regulated by the amending formula or determined by other parameters.

Identifying who has the final say in constitutional change is a tricky task. Amending formulas are often misleading with regard to the importance of the role played by actors, and there exist potential pitfalls in romanticizing the reality of who decides. Inherent in constitutional entrenchment is the issue of sovereignty. In modern constitutional states, no one appears to be the sovereign, at least not in the absolute, indivisible notion envisaged by classical theories of sovereignty. Sovereignty emerges fragmented, divided between many actors by the very constitution. Still, sovereignty has an intrinsic tendency towards concentration into the hands of one sole actor, apparent despite its institutional allocation. Fragmentation of sovereignty is not translated into multiple actors simultaneously taking multiple decisions on the same issue, but rather means that there is no sole actor who gets to decide on all issues.[10] By allocating authority to different actors in order to achieve checks and balances, the constitution does not stifle competition between them.

The possibility of change is the safety valve of modern constitutions, whether it occurs through constructive constitutional interpretation or through formal amending processes. Competition and conflicts between different actors take place within the boundaries set by constitutions. When such conflicts tend to exceed these boundaries, the constitution itself provides for the possibility of its change. Constitutional change is the supreme and most extreme conceivable moment of disturbance in the force of constitutional normality. To have the last word on the content of the text, which sets out the rules of the game through unsurpassable normative power, means to have the *authority to allocate authorities*. Even though constitutions lay down complex procedures for their revision, involving multiple actors (the parliament, the government, the judiciary, the electorate, experts, political parties, constituent states, etc.), the inherent tendency of power to concentrate still seems to prevail. Identifying who has the final say in constitutional change is an evasive goal, yet it is reachable and has crucial importance in understanding the balance each constitutional order endeavors to strike. Tracking down the equilibrium between key players in constitutional change sheds light on all aspects of state authority distribution, bringing forth new facets of power structure and the underlying conflicts.

Actors, roles, strategies

Juristocracy and constitutional change

When constitutional changes occur, the judge is always there. Judicial involvement in constitutional change appears in many forms: the judge may be the key player, informally changing the constitution, or he or she may trigger change by nudging the constitutional lawmaker to make reforms in response to creative constitutional interpretation, or he or she may legitimize directions of constitutional amendment by introducing shifts in judicial doctrine, lining up with the dominant political forces. The judge appears as the protagonist in three distinct yet closely interrelated areas of subtle tension: first is the strain between constitutionalism and democracy; second, the perpetual dialogue between lawmaker and judge; third, the competition between formal and informal constitutional change.

Although the role of the judge is usually invisible in amending formulas, informal change thrives within surroundings of slow-moving formal change. Yet, judge-made constitutional change should not be read solely as a side effect of the constitutional arrangements regarding formal change, as it is interwoven with *judicial identity*—the way in which a legal order perceives the role of judges and the way in which judges perceive themselves. Judicial appointment systems influence the role of the judge. It cannot be ignored that underlying US approaches of informal change are the way in which Supreme Court justices are appointed, which allows for describing them as instruments of political parties in the implementation of constitutional politics, but also facilitates considering them initiators of change, which corresponds to popular mobilization steering constitutional moments.[11] A striking distinction stems from the differences between common law and civil law traditions. Common law judges are at home with the idea of lawmaking, as it is the legal culture that bestows this role upon them—they are under no obligation to be, or pretend to be, the mouth of the law. Civil law judges had to cast themselves in the role, when strong constitutional and supreme courts started to engage in constitutional craftsmanship, demonstrating judicial activism.

Talk of juristocracy intensifies as the judiciary aims not only to have a say with regard to constitutional change, but seems also to claim the final word.[12] Having established a continuous dialogue with lawmakers[13] in which they demonstrate tendencies to impose on them specific lines of reasoning and exact ways to justify legislative choices under the threat of judicial review, judges upgrade the dialogue, transferring it to the constitutional level by opening up a conversation with constitutional legislators as well. International courts add extra flavor to juristocracy: the dialogue becomes internationalized through the jurisprudence of courts such as the European Court of Human Rights (ECtHR), which engage in direct communication with the constitutional legislators of the respondent states, pointing out necessary changes. As a rule, domestic courts eagerly enter this dialogical process. The transfiguration effected by the case law of the ECtHR on rights protection depends on the receptive reactions of each country: in Finland it turned the attitude of courts towards rights protection, leading to their legal enforceability, which amounted to a constitutional revolution; in Germany it triggered the Federal Constitutional Court to dictate that all courts must use the interpretative standards developed by the ECtHR, enriching interpretative possibilities; while in Austria it created a domino effect that caused such shifts in the Constitutional Court's interpretation of the Constitution that it eventually led to formal constitutional amendments. Manifest in such jurisprudence are the elements of a debate between judge and lawmaker, which is by far more distinct than the obscure erosion of constitutions through the national states' participation and integration in international institutions.

The competition between constitutional lawmaker and judge on shaping the constitution has the potential for perpetuity. The constitutional lawmaker's response to judge-made constitutional change may take two opposite directions: either to confirm and endorse informal change, or to reject it by constitutionalizing an opposing direction. Yet, formal amendments once adopted are not immunized from informal change; the judge may re-enter the game, producing new jurisprudence. Blocking change is also an option where judicial review of constitutional amendment is provided for.[14] Not blocking change is of equal importance: not getting in the way of change is an alternative way of judicial engagement in constitutional innovation.[15] Participants in discussions usually have one common characteristic: they all wish to have the final say. In dialogical patterns of constitutional change, it is important to trace who signals[16] the end of the dialogue, even if only a provisional end.

The appeal of informal amendment is that it allows refurbishing of the constitution without the possible side effects and collateral damages of formal change, and when its impact on the constitution or on politics is strong[17] it may even promise a way out of formal procedures. Yet, to assume that formal amendment is irrelevant on the basis that the constitution would look pretty much the same regardless of whether altered through formal or informal processes[18] seems to accept that all constitutional actors would change the constitution in the same direction, betraying a sort of subtle constitutional fatalism. However, the judicial way of approaching the constitution entails a legalistic interpretative discipline that, combined with the unique ethos of judicial self-restraint employed even by activist courts—if only as a pretence—differentiates judge-made change from change brought about by other actors. Litigation is a culture of its own,[19] and its particularities affect judicial decision-making.

What's more, the role played by the judiciary in constitutional updating inescapably activates the tension between constitutionalism and democracy, the permanently underlying question being whether judges are the ultimate, yet politically unaccountable, guardians of the constitution; and if so, whether this function is suitable for all parts of the constitution or whether some constitutional issues are best settled informally, while others are best served by formal amendment. Distinguishing between structural changes that affect the function of the form of government and the area of constitutional rights, as well as between changes involving value choices and technical improvements,[20] is a plausible approach. Judges seem to be best equipped to decide on rights and to provide constitutional maintenance, while decisions on the polity and distribution of constitutional powers that signal important shifts in values crave democratic legitimacy. Even if this allocation works, it can neither be binding nor left to the discretion of judges, and it does not necessarily provide a shield against juristocracy. The "democratic pedigree" of rules is what matters for those whose primary concern is democracy; no matter how just a rule might be, its origin and therefore its legitimacy are important.[21] Democratic legitimation acquires particular importance the more perplexed the matrix of formal and informal change is: Canada provides the ideal test case, since in a context encompassing multiple players (i.e. political actors, judges, subnational entities, legislators, etc.) operating at various levels of constitutional rule production, democratic legitimacy is of utmost importance. What this ultimately does is set the stakes for judicial work even higher. It is the difficult constitutional cases that demand Herculean skills from judges. Sorting out which cases best become informal change and what value choices are better off settled by other means and actors is indeed a Herculean labor.

The area more free from judicial trespassing seems to be that of constitutional review of constitutional revisions. When the judicial review system does not entail constitutional review, such interventions are out of the question. Where it would seem a reasonable possibility is where courts exercise rigorous constitutional review amounting to informal amendments, and material limits to constitutional revision exist. Yet, although strong supreme or constitutional courts have declared themselves competent to review the constitutionality of amendments (e.g. in the USA, Austria, Germany, and Italy), they seem reluctant to actually engage in such a review, which would lead to direct confrontations with constitutional legislators instead of the dialogical exchange emerging when they induce change through creative interpretation. Possibly this would jeopardize their legitimacy, a risk not worth taking, especially since at the level of constitutional design the interpretative task, when dealing with such abstract concepts as the republican form of government or the protection of human dignity, poses extremely difficult dilemmas.

Seen from a comparative perspective, the different balances struck in the interminable confrontations taking place between constitutional lawmaker and judge, between informal and formal change, and between constitutionalism and democracy shape different realities. This happens regardless of the existence of remarkable similarities in the wording and structure of constitutional texts, thus the wording of the constitution cannot be read outside the context of the unraveling confrontations; and if read, it does not say much about the way in which change actually occurs. It is a two-way street where an unending journey in two directions occurs—the particular features of each legal order orient the above confrontations, and the outcomes of the confrontations refashion legal orders. Comparative analysis turns into a "find the similarities" game, where within totally disparate icons of constitutional amendment from countries that belong to different models of change, similar amending formulas can be spotted. Tracking down similar formulas brings forth unmatched couples such as Germany and Portugal, or Greece and Finland. Suggestive of the impasses that block comprehension, met when constitutional amendment analysis uses the amending formula as the primary point of reference, such similarities question the notion of rigidity.

The political class: role-playing games in constitutional amendment

The rules of the political game are set out by constitutions, and those who play the game are bound to seek a decisive role in any rule resetting. The political class is diligent in pursuing a decisive role in constitutional change, a role dependent on the character of the political system and the function of the party system. Usually, according to amending formulas, parliaments are the designated key institutional actor in constitutional revision. Underlying formal authority conferred on parliament is the tension between different political actors. This tension between the exercise of political power and role allocation is far more acute and intricate in the context of constitutional revision than in the course of the normal lawmaking process. As the central locus of political conflict has moved away from parliaments and relocated in party-political competition, the role assumed by the political class in constitutional amendment is only conspicuous in the way in which the relationship between governing parliamentary majority and opposition is articulated.

Proposals for constitutional revision are actually formed, and frequently decisions regarding such proposals are taken by interacting major political parties that rotate in and out of power, or participate in coalition governments. Whether political parties accumulate and channel the constitutional beliefs of perspective voters[22] is highly dependent on the function and the malfunctions of the political system. Majority requirements dictated by the amending formula, along with the electoral system employed and the degree of polarization or consent in the party system, account for the engagement of the political class in role-playing games through the adoption of different constitutional narratives with regard to constitutional change.

Mapping out the roles assumed by the political class in initiating, negotiating, pushing forward, or blocking constitutional evolution, updating, and reforms inevitably starts off focusing on parliament. Basic ingredients of any constitutional stability recipe are the divergences and convergences between institutional and partisan actors. Competence to initiate the revision of the constitution is traditionally conferred on parliament. In some countries the parliament, beyond being the basic organ of the state vested with authority to revise the constitution, may enjoy—according to constitutional arrangements—exclusive competence to do so; constitutional lawmaking as opposed to normal lawmaking processes requires no participation from the head of state, the image being that of parliament acting alone. Nevertheless, this image is nothing but a *trompe l'oeil.* The parliament is far from being a sole player in this game, as the traditional separation of powers "government versus parliament scheme" seems to have been replaced by the conflict between governing parliamentary majority and opposition, not only in parliamentary but also in presidential regimes. The infrastructure of the relationship between governing parliamentary majority and opposition relies on the degree of party discipline, which is stricter in parliamentary and more relaxed in presidential systems,[23] the structure of the party system, and the Westminster or consensual type of government. UK-style parliamentary sovereignty seems to have also retreated, which means taking its persistence for granted might produce distorted images about how constitutional reform takes place.[24]

Party-system models[25] have great impact on constitutional change. Differences between dominant party, two-party, and limited or extended multiparty systems lead to different degrees of polarization and different modes of reaching consensus. Polarized two-party systems multiply the difficulty of formal change. This is, for example, the case in the USA, Spain, and Greece, where stringency of the amending formula is aggregated by the political rivalry between the two major parties. On the contrary, where a consensual culture of co-operation between political parties exists, reaching the necessary compromises and achieving consensus is far easier, which is the case, for example, in Luxembourg, Finland, and Sweden. These parameters are drastically influenced by electoral systems. Majoritarian electoral systems seem *prima facie* to facilitate the stronger political party to obtain the support of its opponents far more easily than proportional systems, where political fragmentation imposes consensus requirements involving a variety of diverse political parties. The abandonment of proportional electoral laws and the switch to a majoritarian electoral system after 1993 brought about significant changes in Italy in the operation of the political system that affected the way in which political parties tackled constitutional revision issues. Homogeneity and stability within political parties, as expressed by the degree of intra-party discipline, also exert important influence, since extreme diversity within political parties may impede the achievement of consensus during the amending process.

Different patterns of democracy[26] penetrate the amending formula, producing a variety of possible forms of co-operation between political parties. The political prerequisites for co-operation differ, depending on whether supermajorities or enhanced majorities are required. What also makes a remarkable difference is whether the process is concluded within one parliamentary term, or whether two consecutive parliamentary terms are necessary, the latter creating the context for political party competition and electoral tactics that influence constitutional amendment discourse. Thus, the correlation between procedural requirements and party-system particularities determines whether veto players exist,[27] who they are, and how they might put constraints on constitutional amendment. Veto strategies can often be a determinant factor in the pathway constitutional change takes in federal systems. The stakes in constitutional amendments multiply when subnational units enter the game, and the character of federalism, which differs across countries, plays a vital role. In the examples of Austria, Germany, Canada, Belgium, Switzerland, and the USA, federalism interacts differently with the rest of the factors that influence constitutional change.[28]

A distinctive feature of formal amendment is that decisions that matter are usually not taken by the governing majority, but require wider consensus. Thus, constitutional decision-making is set at the level of negotiations between parliamentary majority and opposition, the positions of which are determined by the corresponding political parties. Constitutional reform dialogue may be part of political party strategies, and formal change might be channeled or blocked through such tactics. Thus, the plausibility or implausibility of constitutional change is determined by political elites.[29] The burden of constitutional revision is borne (or sought to be borne) in most countries by mainstream political parties and not by anti-systemic populist parties or movements, commonly belonging to the extreme left and right, that either abstain at a regular basis from any dialogue regarding constitutional revision or support radical constitutional reform proposals.

The crisis of democratic representation paired with the inability of political parties to organize political representation affects constitutional change. An important side effect of that is the increasing importance of technocratic legitimation. Use of experts tends to expand into fields such as constitutional revision, traditionally characterized by the dominance of political discourse. Although in many countries political elites are still highly suspicious towards experts, expert involvement in the amending process seems to be steadily increasing. Perhaps the widest the participation of the people in constitutional revision is, the more suspicion towards experts exists. Thus, in Ireland and Switzerland, the people are rather distrustful of experts, whose involvement can therefore only occur behind the scenes, while in Germany or Finland openness towards expert participation exists. On the other hand, the stronger political elites feel, the less they seek to involve experts in the dialogue on constitutional reform. In that sense, it may be argued that underlying the use of experts is the concealed intention of political elites to reinforce the persuasiveness of their positions and add prestige to them, boosting their legitimacy through technocratic language. What remains unresolved is whether it is possible for experts to act independently of those who initially invited them into the amending game, becoming autonomous players able to adopt substantially different positions from their appointees. Mapping out expert involvement in the constitutional amendment process may thus reveal particular features characterizing political conflicts and the relationship between the people and elites, as well as the way in which the tension between democracy and constitutionalism is substantiated within a particular state.

Can the people have the final word?

Popular involvement in constitutional change can acquire many forms that are not all constitutionally prescribed. Several constitutions (e.g. in Switzerland, Denmark, and Ireland) provide that the decision concluding the process of constitutional revision is taken directly by the people by way of referendum. Other constitutions (e.g. in Italy, France, Spain, Austria, and Sweden) provide for the optional participation of the people, making referendums obligatory only under specific conditions, such as failure to achieve enhanced parliamentary majorities or at the request of the opposition. A stronger form of popular participation in constitutional referendums is the possibility of popular initiative (provided for by the amending formulas in Switzerland and Austria). In case the amending formula prescribes the involvement of two parliaments (e.g. in Belgium, Finland, Greece, and the Netherlands), the people participate indirectly in the amending procedure through their vote in the general elections held between the two phases of the process, which is presumed to express choices on the proposals of political parties regarding the pending constitutional amendment. An alternative way of popular involvement, irrespective of the amending formula arrangements, is effecting informal change. The people may be the driving force behind major shifts in constitutional evolution tantamount to informal amendments. In the US examples of constitutional moments, such as the New Deal Supreme Court jurisprudence, the people are perceived as the true initiators of change.

The place reserved for the people in the amending formula has much to say about the constitutional identity of each state and corresponds to different conceptions of the constitution, rooted in political culture and collective experiences. Constitutional arrangements regarding popular participation in the amending process correspond to choices about which constitutional actor is best equipped to decide on constitutional change, related to notions and ideas about the function of democracy. Highly dependent on how their intended purposes are realized in practice, such arrangements risk producing adverse results since, when the designed procedure fails to ensure that decisions are indeed taken by the people, decisions are inevitably taken elsewhere. To begin with, the vote of the people in the intervening elections held in the midst of the amending process is ideally conscious of constitutional change, yet as a rule the choices of the electorate are mostly influenced by the agenda of political parties on other public policy issues and also by the popularity of candidates. Besides, the outcome of general elections is not binding on the parliament vested with the task to conclude the amendment process, while the will of the people on the specific constitutional issues at stake is not clearly discernible. What remains is merely the use of constitutional reform discourse by political parties as part of their political strategy. In constitutional referendums, decision-making consciousness is certain, yet the catch is that the actual fulfillment of their purpose relies on the way in which they are staged. An important question is who can initiate constitutional referendums. For example, popular sovereignty with regard to constitutional issues works differently in Switzerland, where popular initiative exists, and in Ireland where politicians pick and choose which issues on which to hold referendums, usually avoiding issues of governance.

A question lingering ever since the mid-war period is whether popular participation in the amending process through referendums is nothing but the expression of imaginary sovereignty, since constitutional questions are posed by the political elites in a dilemmatic form addressing issues of a highly technical nature, while the information provided to the people is not always either adequate and objective, nor does it give a fair account of the conflicting choices.[30] If that is indeed the case, popular participation would perform a mere placebo function with regard to the legitimation of the constitution. What's more, if the electorate's participation is low or the majority obtained marginal, an additional issue emerges as to whether and to what extent the legitimacy of the constitution and the consensus on its content are indeed enhanced. Taking this argumentation one step further, constitutional referendums could be regarded as a Trojan Horse for constitutionalism, since the assumed popular will could overturn guarantees placed beyond the majoritarian premise. The Swiss ban on minarets through referendum provides an excellent example of minority rights left to the discretion of the majority.[31] This argument is reinforced by taking into consideration the danger of demagogy used by politically active minorities to lure the majority.[32] Such agonies might account for the fact that in many legal orders, which share common features with regard to legal culture and political system, use of referendums differs greatly as it ranges from constituting an inherent part of the amending process to being entirely left out of the amending formula, while it is also possible that the use of referendums may not exist at all.

Serious argumentation against suspicion towards constitutional referendums exists, not giving up on the possibility of the people collectively mobilizing to express their will on matters of high importance. It might be a mistake to group objections against legislative referendums together with criticism on constitutional referendums, because the stakes are different and because in constitutional issues it is arguable that questions can be much more straightforward and less technical. Substantial deliberation might therefore stand a much better chance of taking place in the context of constitutional referendums.[33]

To assess the degree of actual popular decision-making, the stage in which the people get involved in constitutional revision and the details of the procedure are of vital importance. As a rule, the phase of elaboration, discussion, and vote on the reform proposal in parliament precedes popular participation. In some countries, various preventive control mechanisms for the elaboration of revision proposals that are to be put before the people exist. On the other hand, technological development has facilitated the spread of new methods of popular deliberation and exchange of information, allowing the conduct of public debate with the participation of civil society and limiting the danger of populism. Thus, variables depending on the character of each polity, and its specific assets and malfunctions, determine how successful constitutional referendums are in establishing popular deliberation and participation on constitutional issues. What is very dubious is whether, even if the role of the people is enhanced, it might be read as the final say on the amendment process.

The people are traditionally considered to have spoken during the exercise of the *pouvoir constituant*. Amending formulas may be perceived as replications of the constitutional moment where the *pouvoir constituant* was exercised, being attempted simulations of that primordial, constitution-making function. Constituent assemblies, elected directly by the people to draft constitutions during the first era of constitutionalism, created an archetypal icon. This original constitution-making process is embellished with great symbolic force, the reproduction of which during every constitutional revision would be unfeasible. Yet, desire to somehow preserve the spirit of that moment is often apparent in constitutional arrangements that risk sacrificing practicality for symbolism. Practicality is, however, crucial if the people are to have a role. Conceptualizing the people either as a totally fragmented entity or as a romanticized sovereign does not contribute towards delineating this role.

Growing concern about juristocracy underlies the tendency of re-examining possibilities to enhance the role of the people. Strengthening popular participation in constitutional revision has won many supporters, who see in it a remedy for both the crisis of representative democracy and juristocracy. The people are depicted as a rival against the discredited political class and those detached from society cartel parties. Under this rationale the discussion on participatory democracy, which has been ongoing since the 1960s with increasing appeal, can be transferred almost unaltered at the level of constitutional revision, yet with a twist: in the heart of constitutionalism lie safeguards against temporary majorities, both parliamentary and electoral. The exact opposite issue is posed by popular participation if regarded as a counterweight against the expansion of judicial power. What is at stake here is whether a constitutional democracy can react against the power of the judge to informally change the constitution, which transforms the constitutional state into juristocracy.[34] In that sense, the people could indeed have the final say in constitutional change, an elusive finality anyway, lasting until the judge or the lawmaker would again endeavor to bring about informal change. The question raised here is how best to assess the will of the people on constitutional issues. Judges can be viewed as go-betweens connecting the people and the constitution: underlying the judicial stance at constitutional moments were shifts in popular constitutional ethos. But the very need for judges to act this way stems from the institutional incapacity of the people to directly impact constitutional change. Perhaps it is not merely a coincidence that the stronger arguments in favor of enhancing popular involvement are articulated in countries where the judiciary plays a crucial role in guaranteeing constitutionalism, that is, primarily in common law jurisdictions.

Formulas, intentions, consequences

Ratio and irrationalities of amending clauses

Amending formulas set up mechanisms that endeavor to tame constitutional actors and encapsulate the relationship between the constitution and the passage of time. To do so, they have limited resources that may be—and indeed are—used in indefinite combinations. Procedural and material limits interwoven in different blends provide a wide variety of attempts to reconcile stability and change, signifying different understandings of constitutionalism, while in reality suggesting underlying patterns of distrust between constitutional actors. There is an element of romantic quest in the faith that an ideal balance may be stuck between safeguarding the stability of the constitution against the political will of temporary majorities, while allowing constitutional change. This quest, juxtaposed to the crudity of reality, may perhaps account for the astonishing variety of amending formulas, which is also influenced by the degree of distrust between political and constitutional players at the time when the provisions regulating constitutional revision are framed.

No preferred archetypal amending formula exists and the variety in design seems to suggest that the ideal formula is but an evading goal, and perhaps, in designing formulas, constitutional legislators tend to focus inwardly, putting more weight on their polity's idiosyncratic features. What formulas are up against is the volatility of power equilibrium between the players whose role in constitutional change they attempt to delimit. This equilibrium may determine the operation of the amending formula in practice. A probability also exists that formulas may at any time default due to bad design, leading to failure to fulfill their intended purposes. Such default of amending clauses may have more perplexed consequences than bad design in other constitutional provisions, because they are potentially self-defeating due to their entrenchment and the impediments they might set to their own correction.

Possible elements of the equation set up to control constitutional change are time and players articulated in different combinations, which provide the following criteria for building a typology of amending formulas: whether the formula is an attempted simulation of the constituent moment endeavoring to imitate the exercise of *pouvoir constituent*;[35] whether it includes eternity clauses; if and to what extent it provides for popular participation in the amending process; whether constitutional revision is concluded within one parliamentary term or involves two parliaments and intervening general elections; whether it provides for supermajorities or enhanced majorities; whether, besides the parliament, the head of state or the cabinet also has a role in constitutional revision; whether, in addition to organs of the central state, organs of constituent or peripheral states participate; and whether it provides for a mandatory lapse of time between the conclusion of an amending process and the initiation of a new one. Infinite combinations of such arrangements may be found within constitutions.

Evaluating formulas presupposes tracing their ratio and the intended level of constitutional stability. Scrutinizing amending formulas in search of their purpose and in light of the *de constitutione ferenda* dialogue on their change provides the ideal context for the tension between constitutionalism and democracy to make a grand appearance. Leaning toward constitutionalism craves for the guarantees offered by a demanding amending formula, while pursuing higher levels of democracy within the constitutional state favors strengthening popular participation and increasing the flexibility of the amending process.

The fundamental goal that amending formulas openly aim to serve is ensuring the supremacy, stability, and continuity of the constitution, while at the same time allowing its adaptability to the demands of historical evolution. Regular maintenance and keeping up with major social changes are very important. Constitutional continuity is pursued through the adoption of material limits such as the non-amendability of fundamental constitutional principles, the form of government, or specific rights and principles—as is the case in Germany, Portugal, France, Italy, Greece, and the USA—or by imposing an explicit obligation to the constitutional legislator to respect constitutional consistency, as in Switzerland. Constitutional consistency's best companion is consensus, the achievement of which is part of the amending formula's ratio. Qualified majority rules are techniques designed to block temporary majorities from changing the constitution at will, but they also have autonomous value as they are the conditions for the wider possible acceptance of the document, which lays down the ground rules of the political game. Alternatively, low majorities may suffice but popular approval is required, as happens in Denmark and Ireland, which creates a different type of hurdle. Invariably, the balance between constitutionalism and democracy is difficult to strike, and amending formulas often betray their ratio.

The amending formula may not be the only determining factor with regard to the level of difficulty with formal constitutional change, yet it certainly does greatly affect it, and in that sense it affects the way in which the constitution generally works as well as the relationship between political actors. Constitutional theory and political science usually draw conclusions regarding the rigidity of constitutions on the basis of the amending formula, through an analysis of the complexity of the procedure, the number of different stages provided for, the number of state organs involved, and the type of majorities required, etc. At first glance, such approaches seem to be based on solid ground. A complex multifaceted amending process appears to render the constitution stable and enduring. Taking a step back from that first reading, however, seems to reveal that the importance of the amending formula is compromised, being dependent on the operation of a number of external, interrelated factors. In practice, the ratio that the formula is designed to serve is bypassed or eroded due to imperfections in the amending mechanisms, while several formulas produce severe unintended consequences with regard to the function of the constitution and the political system.

Ultimately, the normative content and operation of amending formulas turn out to be highly versatile, unpredictable, and interacting with parameters that the constitutional legislator had failed to afford their due consideration. Recent changes in the political party landscape of Austria, which have increased the difficulty of constitutional amendment,[36] provide a vivid example: since the two major parties lost their two-thirds parliamentary majority due to the rise of a third party, the long-standing mode of reaching compromises is disturbed. In Italy, as the party system has gone through transformations, the practice of the amending formula has also changed, allowing the possibility of major reforms when the political will to induce them exists. What is not realized through this practice is the intention of the formula to foster the consensual character of reforms. Such unpredictable turns in the use of amending formulas do not mean that formal amendment is less important than informal constitutional change, but rather that amending formulas are best understood if read within their wider context, while informal change can only be understood by also exploring causal relationships between formal and informal amendments.

Unintended consequences of amending formulas

The reason why no such thing as the ideal amending formula exists, or can ever exist, is that the way formal change works in practice depends on a country's legal culture, party system, judicial review system, constitutional ethos, etc. Once agreed that no ideal amending formula exists, what follows is acceptance of the amendability of amending formulas, which may adapt to transformations of states and constitutions as long as they are revisable themselves. Evaluating formulas in accordance with the actual realization of their intended consequences is one way to start. Nonetheless, assessing their unintended consequences is equally important. Formulas may have entirely the opposite consequences to the ones they were designed to produce, yet the amending processes might still work well or suit the needs of political actors.

Here is an example: the often cited Jefferson–Madison disagreement on constitutional amendability demonstrates how far back the tension between constitutionalism and democracy dates, expressed by the difficulty of making the choice between a difficult-to-revise constitution (which finally prevailed, as put forward by Madison) and the Jeffersonian concept that each generation should rewrite its constitution. In addition, it shows that the route constitutional change follows is determined by the formal amendment mechanism, but not necessarily in the direction it sets. The endurance over time of the US Constitution and the stability of the US constitutional order are widely attributed to the hurdles established by the formal amending process. Yet, perhaps in reality it is Jefferson's ideal that silently prevailed, each generation indeed having its own constitution due to the very stringency of the amending formula. Difficulty in formally changing the constitution opened the way to informal amendment through emblematic judicial interpretation, casting the judge in the key role within constitutional evolution, as the judiciary imprinted important changes in the constitution through new readings in each historical era: changes so daring that perhaps they would never be introduced by way of formal amendment. Other constitutional actors also played key roles; the President, political parties, and social movements had their say in reshaping the Constitution, yet to do so they had to interact with the judiciary.

What the constitutional history of several among those countries approached in this volume seems to reveal is that, in the past, over-stringent amending formulas have brought about the exact opposite result from the one intended (i.e. they led to violations and even abolition of the constitution), while in modern constitutional states, the usual result of adopting complex and time-consuming formal amendment processes is that the constitution ends up being constantly subjected to informal alterations either by the legislature or by the judiciary. Where the perplexity of the amending formula is complemented by limited possibility of informal constitutional change, as happens for instance when the system of constitutional review does not leave much room for creative judicial interpretation of the constitution, the adverse result may even go as far as the development of a body of para-constitutional rules operating beyond the constitution or in parallel with it. Finnish "exceptive enactments," Dutch "Acts of Parliament," and Belgian "special laws" are examples of such legislation. Demanding amending processes may prove not to be in the service of constitutional coherency and continuity, but contain the potentiality of the exact opposite. At times of acute political crisis, mandatory time delay may induce the same paradox, triggering instabilities in the constitutional order.

Faulty constitutional engineering in the amending formula may also lead to failure to serve the ratio of consensus, which is perceived as a basic device for safeguarding constitutional stability. Enhanced parliamentary majorities might not be the product of agreement between political parties, but may on the contrary result from the use of a majoritarian electoral system. Conversely, in countries where the electoral system is not constitutionally enshrined, its modification towards a more majoritarian direction could render the majorities required by the formula unfeasible. Another unintended consequence may be seen when the amending formula's operation causes changes in the way in which political antagonism takes place, either by favoring co-operation or by intensifying conflict. For example, the prerequisite of intervening elections between deciding and concluding a constitutional revision, prescribed by numerous amending formulas, often magnifies conflict in polarized political systems, leading to the constitutionalization of politics and vice versa.

Holding constitutional referendums in countries where the culture of referendums is not deeply imbedded may lead to explosions of populism induced by the discourse on constitutional reform, reducing the degree of consensus and the legitimation of the constitution, or even end up blocking proposals for constitutional change that have high consensus among political elites. Bad design with regard to constitutional referendums risks turning popular participation and enhancement of the role of the people into something completely different. On the other hand, in several countries, political tricks are employed to bypass the perplexity of the amending formula. Examples of this kind of "cheating" are apparent in the Netherlands, where the vote on constitutional revision is held right before the end of the parliamentary term so that Parliament is not prematurely dissolved; and in Luxembourg, where the hurdles of the amending process—up until its relaxation in 2003—were evaded by a vote opening the way to constitutional revision, which always took place before the dissolution of Parliament.

Amending clauses may have the best of intentions, but prove to be impossible—or even dangerous—to implement when the rest of the parameters influencing constitutional amendment have not been paid due attention, or when the formula itself has a genetic defect with regard to the way it engineers constitutional change. Political actors may always contrive ways to bypass the amending formula, while unintended consequences may prove to be more important than the very changes introduced by constitutional reforms. It is thus possible that the use of the amending formula may produce *perverse incentives*. The recent trend seems to be towards the simplification of amending formulas, since the constitutional state no longer fears its enemies, and it is becoming increasingly apparent that perplexed formulas in a rapidly changing world entail significant perils for the constitution. Such trends are particularly strong in countries where it has become obvious that faulty constitutional engineering of the amending formula leads to its direct or indirect bypass, or to the erosion of its meaning and ratio.

To fully comprehend the engineering of constitutional change, it is important to take into account that amending formulas do not delimit the role of the judge in formal and informal change. By not addressing the role played by the judiciary, amending formulas seem to have an inherent defect. In most constitutions, the originally designed formulas were repeatedly reproduced almost unchanged, despite the fact that the modern constitutional state, and the role played by state organs and political actors, have undergone multiple transformations since the end of the nineteenth century. It is thus inevitable that they often fail in successfully regulating constitutional change.

Amending formulas nonetheless provide a map for exploring the way in which the multiple actors who exercise power interact. Glimpses of sovereignty sparkle in the course of that exploration. Underlying the amending formula is an *allocation of sovereignty*, as he who decides on constitutional change seems to perform a task that belongs to the sovereign. Pinning down who actually changes the constitution, whether this is done by the book or informally, can be read as a sign of sovereignty—the more perplexing the game is and the more numerous the players, the better the chance of understanding how fragmentation of sovereignty works, by placing focus on the processes of constitutional change.

Mechanisms, correlations, models

Mechanisms of constitutional change

Constitutional change is accomplished through the operation of mechanisms consisting of actors, amending formulas, and other constitutional arrangements that interact in various combinations and work together to channel change. The actors involved and the means employed to effect change connect to form a mechanism. Mechanisms may be simple or elaborate, and may operate simultaneously, alternatively, or complementarily. The set of operative mechanisms within a legal order amounts to an overall amending model, corresponding to distinct profiles of constitutional change. Comparative analysis reveals the following mechanisms, which often co-exist within different models operating in combination, in parallel, or antagonistically:

- Political elite-driven change by following the steps of the amending formula. Success of this mechanism relies to a great extent upon the *formula's design and rationality*. Impediments set out by amending clauses in the form of material or procedural limits guide the steps of constitutional change. Possible gaps between the ratio of the formula and the results it brings about are often the basic problem in the operation of this mechanism. A simple, clean-cut formula facilitating formal constitutional change, as long as it is explicit and consensual, allows the two leading political parties in Germany to routinely update the Basic Law. The rationality of the amending formula, which fits well within the political system, upholds constitutional normativity aligned with the German positivist tradition. Eternity clauses in the German example do not set impediments to constant maintenance, since they capture the essence of the constitutional culture and counterbalance a lack of perplexed procedural impediments. Conversely, the situation in Greece comprises political elite-driven revisions in an environment of political polarization, guided by a stringent amending formula, where political contingencies govern the operation of the formula producing unintended consequences. A system of reversed majorities (i.e. a three-fifths majority in the first Parliament leading to a decision by absolute majority in the second Parliament and vice versa) means that in case a three-fifths majority of seats is achieved in the first Parliament, an absolute majority suffices in the second Parliament, which decides on the content of the Articles under revision. Thus, the intended broad consensus is not achieved, since a political party that obtains the absolute majority of seats is then in a position to determine at will the crucial issues.
- Political elite-driven consensual or conflictual bypass of the formula. Impediments to change may be set aside by cunning implementation of the formula when political agreement on relaxing its stringency exists. *Relaxation without violation* relies on practices adopted by consenting political elites that enjoy the luxury of an absence of distrust. The Luxembourgish practice (until the 2003 revision of the amendment procedure) of bypassing the amending formula's hurdles, by ensuring that an option of revision always exists, suggests that when there is consensus there is a way. Another vivid example of bypassing the formula is the way in which the mandatory dissolution of both Houses of Parliament upon the publication of the Act to revise the Constitution is handled in the Netherlands. Although the intended purpose is to involve the people in the amending process in a quasi-plebiscite manner, it became normal practice not to publish the Act until the moment of a general election. Thus, the side effects of parliamentary dissolution for the political class are escaped, albeit sacrificing the intended emphasis on revision issues that are doomed to be overshadowed by the political agendas of the general election. The ingenuity of the political class appears at its best when political considerations require stretching amending formulas to their limits.

- People-driven constitutional revision by means of popular initiative and constitutional referendum provided for by the amending formula. Direct democratic mechanisms that aim to infuse more popular participation into the amending processes may provide an alternative to political elite-driven or judge-made changes; nevertheless, it is only within the context of a fully-fledged direct democracy that they reveal their full potential as well as the dangers they entail. A textbook and emblematic example of direct democracy, Switzerland demonstrates that the people can have the lead role in constitutional change, yet this seems to be dependent on the overall ethos of direct democratic decision-making, while it cannot but entail an extra risk where fundamental rights of the few are at stake.
- Political elite-driven change of flexible constitutions, by way of passing new legislation. Parliamentary sovereignty is the key feature of this mechanism, as shifts in its understanding signal shifts in the way in which the constitution changes. Tracing which legislation is tantamount to constitutional norm is correlated with a deeper conception of what the constitution is, in the absence of the criterion of entrenchment. The UK is the point of reference with regard to constitutional flexibility, as any Act of Parliament can change the constitution. A government having the majority of seats in the House of Commons can alter the constitution at will. The difference between constitutional legislation and ordinary legislation is not a matter of form and process but one of substance. In addition, no standard practice has been as yet established as a convention, or even the proper means to introduce constitutional change, and no differentiation exists between major and minor changes. Different degrees of parliamentary scrutiny and popular involvement through referendums may be employed. Parliamentary supremacy provides a mechanism through which the political party having parliamentary majority may change the constitution but cannot entrench such choices against future change.
- Change through *political practice*: the way in which political actors operate the constitution reshapes it. Such practices may acquire the form of constitutional conventions, although not necessarily. In Denmark, rarity of formal constitutional change in combination with the reluctance of the judiciary to enter the role of substitute constitutional legislator renders political practice extremely important in terms of constitutional change. Thus, the practice of political actors is a source for renovation of the constitutional rules, while it may also create constitutional conventions, allowing an aged Danish Constitution to retain its functionality. In Austria, where formal and informal change add up to an overall scheme of efficiency-oriented incremental constitutional updating, the practice of state organs transforms the Austrian Constitution. For example, the federal President's refusal to sign legislation due to substantial unconstitutionality being accepted by the other state organs created a precedent, which impacts the Constitution.
- Quasi-constitutional rule production outside the constitution induced by the legislator, usually requiring enhanced parliamentary majorities. The basic

feature of this mechanism is the presence of veto players empowered to block change. On the basis of explicit constitutional provisions or by ignoring the amending procedures, constitutional change takes place *beyond the constitution*. In Belgium, the allocation of powers between state organs is effected through special laws, requiring a two-thirds majority vote in both Houses of Parliament. In Finland, constitutional change was commonly effected through the possibility of adopting legislation contrary to the Constitution, under the requirement of following the process of constitutional revision while having the status of ordinary legislation. Exceptive enactments viewed as a mechanism of "digging holes" in the texture of the Constitution are a distinct feature of the Finnish paradigm.

- Informal change brought about by the legislator by way of normal lawmaking processes. Legislation may reshape the constitution through interpretation and is a mechanism often used when formal change is difficult. An excellent example is provided by Ireland, where political-elite reluctance to follow the path of formal amendment, which involves popular participation through referendums, is conspicuous in the use of organic laws as a mechanism of constitutional change. In particular, alterations in the way basic institutions of the state operate and relate to each other are usually effected through organic laws and the risk of involving the people is thus avoided. The Netherlands provides another example of such a mechanism, since change mostly occurs through Acts of Parliament and not in accordance with the demanding amending formula.
- Judge-made informal change through constitutional review. The system of judicial review in combination with judicial identity determines the features of this mode of change, which is either supplementary to formal change or may even become its substitute. This mechanism is equally important for achieving constitutional updating and for radical interventions to the constitution. Being the primary mechanism for constitutional evolution in the USA, it unfolds its full potential, blurring the distinction between constitutional change and constitutional interpretation. Constitutional dialogue is inevitably focused on constitutional adjudication, and interpretative methods acquire heightened importance; so do methods of judicial appointment. A clear characteristic of this mechanism is that it disciplines change through the distinct modes of judicial rationality and justification, and filters it through the judicial idiolect. Landmark constitutional cases are also stories, have a background of underlying battles fought, and thus understanding constitutional change goes through a process of narrative comprehension. In Italy, where a system of centralized constitutional review exists, a strong Constitutional Court constitutes a European version of judicial interpretation, providing the primary mechanism of constitutional evolution. Constitutional law revolves around jurisprudence, and the Italian Constitution is perceived as an open-textured, living document. Constitutional updating through case law is done mainly by recognition of implied rights, extension of rights-holders, and identification of constitutional conventions.

- Subnational entity-driven change in federations by way of inducing informal constitutional change through altering regional constitutions or legislation.[37] Stringency of the amending formula, the complexity of which is enhanced in federal states by the multiplicity of strong players, leads to informal change originating at the subnational level. In Spain, where the Constitution is characterized by difficulty and rarity of formal change, implicit change is induced by the Autonomous Communities, which, by enhancing their competences and reforming their statutes, transform the constitutional order while the text of the federal Constitution remains intact.[38] In Austria, practices of the Federation states actuate informal changes to the Constitution. In the Canadian example of province-induced informal change, such transformations are assimilated in the overall conception of the Constitution as an organic process. The multinational character of Canadian federalism dictates interminable adjustments, intergovernmental negotiations, and agreements that all exert influence on the Constitution.
- Informal change induced by the international or European legislator. Pinning down the actor is the trickiest part in exploring that mechanism, which is open to the obscurity and democratic deficit issues that go hand in hand with international and European lawmaking processes. European Union (EU) membership exerts continuous influence on all member states, which, depending on the particularities of their constitutional culture, react differently towards this source of transformative power. The examples of Germany and Portugal illustrate different aspects of the same phenomenon. Openness of the German Constitution towards international and EU law is paradigmatic of informal absorption of global developments in the notions of human rights protection and the rule of law. European integration is a primary source of informal change in the case of Portugal, which has been experiencing a transformative redefinition of constitutional meanings rendered more profound due to the recent economic crisis. The impact of EU membership has been a major source of constitutional transformation in Finland. Triggering compatibility judicial review, it eroded the traditional parliamentary supremacy principle, which dictated absence of judicial review, changing the fundamental rights-protection landscape and leading eventually to the constitutional adoption of judicial review in 2000.
- Informal change as a result of international or European court jurisprudence. This is judge-made change, yet the way in which it is channeled may involve various actors in secondary roles. The rulings of the European Court of Justice have a profound impact on all member states, while the jurisprudence of the European Court of Human Rights (ECtHR) has changed the geological landscape of rights, and its influence exceeds even the boundaries of its jurisdiction. Having the distinct characteristics of judge-made law, furnished with the additional trait that it addresses a multiple audience of potential dialogue partners, international courts impact constitutions through various channels, primarily by dictating changes to the lawmakers or by influencing domestic courts' jurisprudence. The particular example of ECtHR case law

influencing constitutional change has many facets due to its interaction with different systems of constitutional review, depending also on the existence and character of constitutional catalogues of rights. The incorporation of the European Convention on Human Rights into domestic law in the UK, where rights-based constitutional review did not exist, placed a new weapon in the hands of a strong and experienced judiciary that made full use of the ECtHR case law. From the opposite standpoint, the Spanish Constitutional Court's approach to rights protection makes full use, in its jurisprudence, of the ECtHR interpretative elaboration of human rights with regard to their doctrinal analysis, their protective scope, but also their limitations, breathing new meanings into the provisions of the unchanging Constitution. The Federal Constitutional Court of Germany complements its interpretative toolkit with the ECtHR judge-made interpretational standards, dictating also that all German courts should make use of them. Operating as primary, substitute, or complementary means of informal change, international case law acquires different shapes, chameleonically adapting to each legal order's needs.

Mechanisms of constitutional change are subject to a series of parameters that determine their modus operandi, the way they relate to each other, and their "market dominance." This happens because these parameters shape the role and status of the actors involved, and account for the specific features of the means used by the actors to induce changes. Tradition and polity, state structure, ethnic, linguistic and religious composition, party system and patterns of democracy, polarization and consent, constitutional ethos, and a judicial review system along with the requirements of the amending formula—all determine how mechanisms of change are assembled and operate, as well as which mechanism shall be switched on, and when. Amending formulas function as catalysts for change, whether that occurs through the formula or outside it, since informal amendment is often a side-product of a stringent formula. The basic ingredients an amending formula may contain—that is, the organs involved in amending processes, referendums and intervening elections, eternity clauses, time constraints, and the possibility of judicial review—may also function independently as parameters that guide both the internal working of mechanisms and their external coordination with each other.

Models

Constitutional change models emerge from the observation of mechanisms of change under the prism of the parameters that influence them. Criteria that allow creating a taxonomy through their combined use are the exact equilibrium between formal and informal change, pinning down the winner in the competition over the final say on constitutional change premised on the distinction between triggering change and actualizing it, and the true degree of difficulty of change construed by eternity clauses, time limits, and other constitutional hurdles viewed along with the empowerment of actors. These criteria take shape under the continuous influence of political culture, the prevalent constitutional ethos, and political antagonism.

It might be that the use of elaborate criteria serves only as confirmation of an intuitive classification of constitutional change within models: a model exists when reflection on constitutional amendment may be expressed laconically by a word that captures its essence. If such an abstraction is possible, a model appears. Verification testing is feasible, since these single words are bound to epitomize the ongoing and perhaps permanent constitutional dialogue taking place within each polity. Distinct models of constitutional change under that rationale, which stand out as characteristic of a pattern of change, can be built around the words *elastic, evolutionary, pragmatic, distrust*, and *direct democratic*, describing different paths of change.

Models are *descriptive*, not normative. Analysis therefore focuses on the particular features of each model, the articulation of mechanisms and actors, and the way the whole consort works, as well as its malfunctions. It is possible that some countries have discernible features of more than one model, albeit with the basic weight placed on one. Alternatively, hybrid combinations involving features of two and even perhaps more models might also exist. This happens because the taxonomy is not based on the hurdles set by the amending formula (since formulas might be identical and yet countries belong to different models), nor on quantitative data analysis, but on *correlations* between amending processes, political system, constitutional ethos, and legal culture.

The elastic model

The elastic model encompasses mechanisms operating under an unentrenched constitution, which may be altered through the normal lawmaking process, having no procedural limits and no eternity clauses. The way an uncodified constitution lacking an amending formula undergoes formal and informal change may serve as a test for preconceived notions of rigidity, amendment rates, formal/informal change correlations, constitutional continuity, and self-restraint. Parliamentary supremacy is the key feature of the elastic model, thus its transformations influence constitutional change mechanisms. The legislator is omnipotent, as no obstacles to revision exist other than self-restraint flowing from legal culture, tradition, and political accountability. In addition, judicial self-restraint emanating from respect for parliamentary sovereignty is a fetter to judicial activism. The judge is no rival for the legislator with regard to constitutional reforms. Yet, common law judges accustomed to lawmaking are involved in constitutional change without claiming the lead. Actors responsible for formal change are thus the dominant political elites, and the judiciary, which plays a supplementary role bringing about informal change. Mechanisms of normal lawmaking are therefore used as mechanisms of constitutional change, differentiated only by requirements stemming from the nature of the subject they are tackling. The key subject is of major importance, since lack of an amending formula means that tracing constitutional change is subject-dependent, and not always an easy task.

The UK paradigm stands as an example of flexibility. Ordinary Acts of Parliament as well as Conventions may amend the constitution, so to take the initiative and change the constitution can be easy to do, but difficult in the sense that lack of entrenchment carries the cost of taking full responsibility for any reform. Pinning down what counts as constitutional change is not always straightforward, since the constitution itself is difficult to define. This is perhaps best illustrated by the fact that even in the Select Committee report on constitutional reform,[39] one of the plausible answers referred to is the "I know it when I see it" definition—both elusive and tangible at the same time. The very recommendations of the report elucidate elasticity by stating, as their aim, cultural change with regard to constitutional legislation. Constitutional decision-making as culture and an indisputably living constitution appear as a self-evident reality, whilst in other legal orders they are but working hypotheses in need of support.

In the UK, constitutional change is more about the "who" than about the "how." Parliamentary sovereignty enables political elites to change the constitution at will.[40] Shifts in parliamentary sovereignty dictate reconsidering the manner in which the constitution can change. Flexibility lies in the centre of UK constitutional debates. More so, since on the one hand constitutional reform has become much more important in recent years, while on the other hand a traditional self-restraint ethos seems to give way, revealing the dangers of flexibility in the hands of unscrupulous political elites.[41] Discussion about abandoning flexibility[42] is related with attempts to misuse it. Elasticity in order to thrive must be supported by self-restraint that is deeply imbedded through tradition, an attitude that must be demonstrated by all constitutional actors. The focal role of Parliament determines the role of the judiciary. Common law ability to make the law enjoyed by a strong judiciary does provide a secondary mechanism of constitutional amendment. Although common law had moved in the direction of fundamental rights protection in line with international rule of law trends even before the Human Rights Act, and which led the judges into a dialogue with the ECtHR, judicial review never took the form of a competition over constitutional change. Informal amendment in the context of an uncodified, unentrenched constitution[43] is of particular interest, as it cannot be considered as the side effect of a stringent formula, nor as a product of the traditional scheme of constitutional review. It is therefore linked to different types of impediments to change that are remedied by judicial intervention, or can only be understood in relation to its subject matter—a possible reminder that certain types of constitutional change best become judicial reasoning[44] because of the subject that must be dealt with. The role of experts is also a crucial parameter in this model. Need for legitimization in the context of fluidity opens up a job for experts, whose opinion seems to gradually acquire important influence.[45]

The evolutionary model

The evolutionary model entails the dynamic evolution of a formal change-resistant constitution through informal change. Underpinning this model is the combination of a strict amending formula with the status of a very strong judiciary. Judge-made change is the basic feature of the evolutionary model, brought about by the judge who has both the will and the legitimacy to alter the constitution. Textual changes are rare and may result from a dialogue between constitutional lawmaker and judge, as a reaction to judge-initiated changes that push the lawmaker to act in order to either adopt or overturn them. Dynamic interpretation lies in the heart of that model, where constitutional change is meticulously construed through legal reasoning as befits judicial justification. Judge-made change may not be attributed exclusively to the judge; political elites or the people might be the driving force behind judicial constitutional evolution.[46] Nonetheless, constitutional change is filtered through judicially accomplished decision-making, rendering the judge the key player in this model. Constitutional review operates as a mechanism of constitutional change. Informality of change covers alterations that range from being perceived as constitutional revolutions to incremental maintenance. Constitutional moments mark major changes occurring outside the formal amendment process, which plays a role in this model mainly by causing outsourcing of constitutional amendment to the judiciary.[47]Through constant elaboration by the judiciary, the constitution remains ever awake, and is attributed the characteristics of a living organism with the ability to adapt to changing times and demands.

Political polarization extending to issues of constitutional politics underlies the evolutionary model. Disputed constitutional issues decided by the judiciary are often issues that cause major political disagreement, so judicial resolution towards one or the other direction covers areas where political consent is unfeasible. Judicial filtering provides a special configuration for constitutional changes, marked by the distinct style of judicial reasoning. Eternity clauses do not occupy a special position in this model, which, however, presents a unique interplay with notions of the eternal, since stringency of the amending formula signifies intention of remarkable time endurance of the constitution. Demands for consensus conditions similar to those of the original constitutive moment may furnish formal constitutional change with extra symbolic weight. Theories of judicial interpretation acquire specific significance in this context, where the boundaries between interpretation and amendment are obscure, and the way the task is described and perceived by actors is equally important with what it is in reality.

The US and Canada both fit into the evolutionary model of constitutional change, where judge-made change molds the constitution into what it is. In the USA, where the "judiciary is the primary vehicle for ratifying or initiating informal change,"[48] textualist, originalist, and interpretivist approaches[49] measuring degrees and ways of departure from or adherence to the constitutional text and meaning are the product of the model where the judge can remodel the US Constitution. Underlying these theories that deal with ways in which the Constitution must be approached, and the vast scholarship and controversies built around them that exert influence in a much wider context than US constitutional law, is a subtle discomfort in dealing with the actual role played by the judge in constitutional change. Grand theories[50] are created exactly because what they are attempting to explain and account for is not merely judicial interpretation but informal amendment. At the very least, judges have taken on the job of filtering the actions by lawmakers or Presidents that impact the Constitution, and by legitimizing them they informally amend the Constitution.[51] Recent scholarship suggests the possibility of even reconciling originalism with living constitutionalism. Judges are attributed their true role, no longer seen as mirrors or reflections of popular opinion or presidential policies but as "independent actors."[52] Profound respect for the idea of the constitution is characteristic of the American culture, as neither the age of the Constitution nor informality of change have had a negative impact on its symbolic grasp or its normativity. The price to pay for the extra-textuality of constitutional change is that the actual text of the Constitution has become quite distant from the reality of operation of government and rights protection.[53] The US Constitution can only be understood in combination with the vast bulk of adjudication that infuses life into its provisions and the theoretical approaches that elaborate on case law.

The living tree imagery of the constitution and the dialogical model of exchanges between judge and lawmaker stem from the Canadian perception of judge-made constitutional change. To begin with, the amending formula is complex, providing for a variety of procedures, and has in itself been open to judicial interpretation. The co-existence of a general amending procedure, a unanimity procedure, a some-but-not-all-provinces procedure, and a federal Parliament alone procedure, while each provincial legislature has competence to amend alone the constitution of the province, creates many pathways for formal amendment. Textual rigidity of the Canadian Constitution did not translate into a sanctification of the document, the legal culture being more open to the unwritten and fluid. It did, however, facilitate the courts in becoming "the preferred site for effecting important changes in the constitutional order."[54] The addition of a Bill of Rights in the Canadian Constitution in 1982 had a profound impact on the texture of constitutional change, giving the people a much stronger stake in constitutional politics and the courts much more room for creative jurisprudence. Informal constitutional amendment brought about through judicial interpretation[55] fits well in a conceptualization of the Constitution as an organic process,[56] where not everything needs to be written and constitutional law is built through the dialogical communication between lawmaker and judge.[57] Coming to terms with an evolutionary view of constitutional arrangements is inherent in the identity of a federation where one province, the French-speaking Quebec, never ceased to envisage the possibility of secession and took no part in the patriation of the Constitution. The judicial approach to the issue according to which, in case there is a clear democratic vote in Quebec in favor of secession answering a clear question, Canada is under obligation to enter into negotiations with Quebec, demonstrates how the inevitability of change is rationalized and how important dialogical processes are at all levels.

The question here is whether it is possible for living constitutionalism to also emerge from a non-common law environment. Italy provides an example of a living constitution thriving without the need for a common law judge. The Italian

Constitution is perceived as a living organism due to random use of formal avenues of constitutional revision[58] and the dynamic interpretation of the Constitution by the Constitutional Court. Due to its stringent amending formula, which is placed within conflictual political surroundings that foster distrust, Italy displays numerous features of the distrust model. The imaginary simulation of the *pouvoir constituant* pursued by the amending formula, which requires wide consensus, in a context of political conflict would lead to manipulation of the formula or to constitutional inertia if it weren't for the constitutional culture of Italy, which is open to informal change. The formula itself is demanding, requiring a double reading (with a mandatory three-month gap between readings) by both the Upper and the Lower House, and approval by absolute majority. In case the second vote does not achieve a two-thirds majority in each House, a constitutional referendum is held if claimed by one-fifth of the members of either House, 500,000 voters, or at least five regional councils. Only one eternity clause exists, complementing procedural stringency by entrenching the republican form of the state. The demanding amending formula, within an evolving political context making a transition from fragmentation to bipolarism, stood in the way of formal change, while attempts at revision "in derogation" of the formula did not succeed.[59] A paradox exists, since on one hand the stringent formula was traditionally interpreted as even more demanding than its text suggested, dictating a very high degree of consensus and, as a consequence, ruling out routine constitutional maintenance, while on the other hand the Constitution itself has always been perceived as open-textured, allowing expansion and growth without formal amendment. A strong Constitutional Court played the key role in this direction, while a dialogue between constitutional legislator and judge has begun to emerge. It is through Italian living constitutionalism that the Constitution of Italy retains its status and glamor. Political conflict and distrust are thus not allowed to stifle constitutional evolution, still Italy is a hybrid combination having strong features of the political distrust model; and the possibility that these features prevail always remains open.

The pragmatic model

The pragmatic model allows constitutional change to take place smoothly, with efficiency of formal change being the most striking feature of the way the system works. The basis of pragmatism is either the amending formula, or a consensual political culture, or both. Constitutional arrangements may *per se* point in the direction of easily achieved constitutional maintenance, or practicality may be fostered by compromise expressed through the co-operation between political parties, which provides a consensual background for the operation of constitutional change mechanisms. Slow, gradual change and updating are characteristic of the pragmatic model. When the amending formula allows constitutional revisions to become daily routine in political life, efficiency and adaptability of the constitution are promoted, sheltered even against the possibility of deeper political cleavages lurking beneath the surface of agreement on constitutional updates. Such differences may, however, block dramatic changes to the constitution. Maintenance in the pragmatic model is thus distinct from structural constitutional changes. When agreement on constitutional issues is encouraged by the amending formula, this leaves a clearly discernible imprint on the political system, and it is quite possible that the dictated co-operation may also exert a wider influence.

Many variations of the way consent or compromise work to bring forth change exist. The amending formula may be demanding, designed to secure constitutional stability; nevertheless, constant change is feasible due to a consensual constitutional ethos. It is possible that the formula is bypassed, stretched to its limits, and eroded to serve the needs of constitutional maintenance. Political elites may tamper with the amending formula to produce the practical results that best serve constitutional adaptability. In this line of changes the amending formula is not violated but twisted to fit the requirements of the co-operating political class, while constant change is allowed without normally amounting to major shifts or reforms. Amending formulas may thus lead to unintended, yet widely accepted consequences. The symbolic status of the constitution within the legal culture varies, mainly dependent upon features of the political system that lie outside the constitution. In other words, constant constitutional change may in theory work in two directions: it might enhance respect for the constitution, through ensuring that whenever alterations are needed the mechanisms for making them are available, or it may have a negative impact on the glamor or even the normativity of the constitution.

A strong judiciary is a feature of this model; nevertheless, there is no need for constitutional review to operate as a substitute for formal amendment. Either the formula itself permits constant change or political compromises allow meeting the requirements set by the formula, so change is not sidetracked and channeled through judicial interpretation—change can be effected by way of revision, although in some cases differently from the way revision was originally designed to function. Judicial interpretation plays a complementary role and is not the primary vehicle of change. The role played by the people is secondary as well, since it is the consenting political elites that pull the strings of constitutional change and have the final say on it. Use of experts fits well in the pragmatic model, consensus signaling lack of distrust towards experts and practicality dictating reliance on expertise for better results.

A moderately stringent formula—which requires wide consensus but nevertheless allows remarkably constant change exactly because such consensus is feasible, due to the way in which the party system operates—underlies the German version of pragmatism with regard to constitutional amendment. Deeply rooted in historical experience, and in concordance with its positivist tradition and the traumatic Weimar constitutional past, German procedural hurdles are accompanied by eternity clauses protecting human dignity and fundamental rights. The amending formula's rationale is simple. Firstly, it obeys the demand for any change to the Constitution to be explicit, a prerequisite in line with positivist rule-of-law dictates but also with a commitment to block any possibility of a silent turnover, which is the result of fears stemming from historical experience. Secondly, by providing for approval by both the Upper and the Lower House, it requires a cross-party consensus[60] for constitutional change. No extra procedural hurdles are provided for, so if the consensus requirements are met, expediency is easily achieved. In the current political reality, this usually translates to an agreement between the two dominant political parties. Formal amendments to the Constitution are routine practice, ensuring constitutional updating and maintenance. It is noteworthy that the Federal Constitutional Court is a strong court, deeply engaged in constitutional review, and plays a very important role as the primary dialogue partner of the constitutional legislator. Yet, its task appears to be that of guarantor and protector of the Constitution, especially in the area of fundamental rights. Accordingly, it does not compete for the role of constitutional change initiator. The difference is subtle, since the Court does claim the role of the ultimate interpreter of the Constitution, possessing competence to exercise abstract constitutional review and providing in-depth, comprehensive constitutional interpretation, which may be perceived as quiet constitutional change. Where conflicts between the federal government and the governments of the subnational units exist, the Constitutional Court also enters another role, that of arbiter,[61] which results in a dialogical mode of change. Comparable in strength and influence to the US Supreme Court, the Federal Constitutional Court[62] clearly differs with regard to the judicial selection system, the whole process being far less political than in the USA. Justices, being elected by the two Houses by a two-thirds majority, are in practice selected through a compromise between the two major political parties. Compromise thus also underlies the composition of the Constitutional Court. What decides the locus of constitutional change, however, is the amending formula, which in combination with the consensual attitude towards constitutional amendment provides a mechanism for constant change, as opposed to the US amending formula, which blocks formal change.

The World War II experience has forged the co-operation between Austrian political parties, which is a prerequisite for ensuring constant constitutional change. The Constitution evolved through this consensual pragmatism, with the two major parties identifying issues of great importance and entrenching them in the Constitution after reaching compromise.[63] The amending formula allows routine formal amendment, as it only requires a majority of two-thirds in the Lower House with half of its members present. Furthermore, the Constitution allows the enactment of formal constitutional legislation outside the Constitution in the form of individual constitutional Acts. Subject exclusively to total revision are the core principles of the Constitution. The striking adaptability of the Austrian Constitution is underpinned by the correlation between the amending formula and the political system.[64] Yet, beneath its adaptability lies major difficulty in achieving radical change, as such intervention requires higher levels of political consensus and trust, not a mere ethos of expediency-oriented compromise. The process provided for total revisions that aim to alter the fundamental principles of the Constitution is more stringent, including a referendum requirement. The inability to adopt a bill of fundamental rights due to unfeasibility of agreement on an issue that demands more than mere pragmatism is the result of such deeper ideological divides. Where Austria seems to deviate from the clichéd scheme of reverse analogy between flexibility and informal change—i.e. not adhering to the stereotype that rigidity fosters informal change while flexibility obliterates the need for it—is in the paradox that constant formal change is complemented by informal change brought about by both legislator and judge. The Constitutional Court, especially in the area of fundamental rights, produces dynamic jurisprudence, equipped with power to exercise both abstract and concrete constitutional review. Where political compromise fails to push constitutional change forward, other actors intervene to fill the gap.

Pragmatism in the examples of Germany and Austria is substantiated by a continuum of incremental maintenance supported by amending formulas that fit well into the political party system, securing consensus on constitutional revision. The status of the constitution is thus upheld, further supported by constitutional review. An excellent example of an amending process designed to render formal change difficult, but relaxed in practice with the synergy of consenting political elites, is the case of Luxembourg. Practical necessity spells out what needs to be done, and finding the most efficient way to do it encapsulates the way constitutional changes take place. The Constitution thus draws legitimacy exactly because it works and because it never fails to serve the purposes it has to fulfill. The amending formula operating up to 2003 was originally designed to foster constitutional stability; however, the Constitution was constantly revised through consensual bypasses of the formula. The requirement to dissolve the Chamber following a declaration of constitutional revision was deactivated through the simple practice of always adopting such declarations at the end of each legislative period, sometimes even with regard to numerous articles, thus allowing every new Chamber to revise the Constitution.[65] Even following the increased flexibility of the amending process in 2003, political elites still bypass hurdles to amendment consensually whenever deemed necessary, displaying how the "rigidity level" of a constitution cannot be traced by a simple reading of the text, as it is dependent on the way the actors involved choose to operate it. The stance of the courts is interrelated with the lack of need for inducing constitutional change. Ordinary judges never got involved in the business of creative constitutional interpretation, as they do not engage in constitutional review, while the Constitutional Court does not perceive itself as a driver of constitutional change, adopting a highly technical role in line with practicality as the optimal function.

Elite-driven continuous change of a Constitution comprising four basic fundamental laws plus one quasi-fundamental piece of legislation is the form in which pragmatic maintenance appears in Sweden. Political stability creates the environment for a high rate of changes, since in practice amendments to the text of the Instrument of Government are proposed before every general election. The amending formula provides for two decisions of identical wording taken by Parliament with a one-half majority, the second decision after intervening general elections. A mandatory nine-month gap between the first submission of the matter to the Parliament and the date of the election is provided for, to foster debate between political parties. The possibility of a referendum also exists, but it has never been activated so far, the hurdle being a speed requirement (i.e. the motion for referendum must be put forward within 15 days from the date the relevant proposal is adopted). Key players are thus political parties that have established a pattern of interminable change through thorough debate on the amendment proposals, which eventually reach a level of consent that makes it improbable for a political party entering Parliament following the intervening elections to vote against the proposed change. A diffused system of constitutional review exists; courts do not, however, exercise vigorous constitutional review. Nonetheless, the Law Council, comprised of judges from the two supreme courts, scrutinizes bill proposals and its opinion is held in great respect; expert opinions are also respected and exert an influence on amendment proposals.[66] The overall picture of a political party-driven pragmatic approach to constitutional change seems to be closely related to lack of traumatic turmoil in Sweden's political and constitutional history, which permits constant maintenance without much contemplation about altering the basic structures of the fundamental laws that form the Constitution.

Emblematic as a paradigm of constant constitutional change, France adheres to the ideal of every generation having its own constitution. An ever-changing constitution transforming constantly to serve the needs of the people seems to fulfill the Jeffersonian aspiration through a pragmatic approach to change. Pragmatism does not flow from the amending formula itself, but from the way it is applied in practice. Approval by both Houses of Parliament, followed by approval by a special joint session of both Houses by a three-fifths majority or a referendum, are the requirements set out by the formula, while for the republican form of government it is the sole eternity clause. Although the formula is demanding, the Constitution of 1958 has been modified 24 times, while this succession of formal changes is a sign of enhanced constitutional stability since, before the 1958 Constitution marking the Fifth Republic, constitutions were normally replaced rather than revised. What is unique about the French version of pragmatism and efficiency is that consensus evolves around the notion of sovereignty in relation to the distinction between *pouvoir constituant* and *pouvoir constitué*. The Constitution has significant symbolic power, but it must also serve the needs of the sovereign people. Notwithstanding the theoretical point of reference being popular sovereignty, amendment is driven by the political elite and usually constitutes a weapon in the hands of the executive power.[67] Prevalence of efficiency has to maintain a low profile due to the overarching grip of the popular sovereignty, or general will, concept. Incessant formal change in the French example does not obliterate informal change, since the French Constitutional Court plays a vital role in constitutional evolution. Yet, as opposed to their common law counterparts, judges appear laconic in their utterances, conveying the impression that what is expressed through unanimity is the will of the state and not merely the opinions of judges.[68] The balance of power between major political actors in the context of semi-presidentialism underlies the case in France, where a distinct conflictual edge is present, and antagonism is ever ready to surface and render the pragmatic approach fragile.

A stringent amending formula involving two parliamentary votes with intervening elections and enhanced majority in the second vote, without the possibility of any material change of the proposed bill, and a fragmented political system should not *prima facie* allow the possibility of pragmatism in constitutional change. The Finnish example, presenting features that could block the efficiency of formal amendment, demonstrates the extent to which it is the exact correlation of mechanisms and political culture that determine the profile of constitutional change. Finnish consensus stems from homogeneity expressed by the absence of ethnic, cultural, political, or religious controversies, and allows constitutional reforms to take place smoothly. Respect for the Constitution never faded in Finland, where political parties from both the left and the right wing traditionally reach agreements on constitutional amendment. The proportional electoral system allows a multitude of political parties to enter Parliament, which results in stable coalition governments. A legal positivist tradition, in combination with the high esteem in which the Constitution is held, facilitates consensus.[69] Expert involvement in the amending process is remarkable, which is also characteristic of the pragmatic model. The mechanism of exceptive enactments (i.e. the adoption of legislation in substance contrary to the Constitution without its amendment, but requiring approval in accordance with the procedure prescribed for constitutional enactments) has provided a parallel path for channeling change outside the demanding amending formula.[70] Thus, constitutional updating was possible without betraying the legal positivist culture, and changes could be eventually affirmed by constitutional revision. For many years, bypassing the formula allowed adaptability, primarily serving international integration while leaving the Constitution intact, only to give way in the area of fundamental rights protection in the late 1990s as consensus pointed in the direction of safeguarding rights. The only recent (in the 2000 revision) adoption of constitutional review by the courts has but a complementary role, and constitutional evolution does not emerge from the courtrooms.[71] Still, both in the areas of allocation of powers and of human rights protection, the strong impact of EU membership provides a parallel mechanism of constitutional evolution, gradually gaining more ground and fitting into the consensual context. Finnish history of constitutional change places it in the pragmatic model, yet this classification relies greatly on the balances of the political system, which might be in a process of polarization following the augmentation of the right-wing populist party at the last general election.

The distrust model

Demanding and complex amending formulas, political elite-driven change, and difficulty in reaching compromises on constitutional issues are the basic ingredients of the distrust model. Their mixture within a political environment characterized by conflict, distrust, veto player strategies, and in many cases polarization, leads to a model of change that has essential differences from the efficiency-oriented, pragmatic model. The constitution is entrenched by stringent amending formulas containing eternity clauses and setting up perplexed procedures. Often aiming at an imaginary simulation of the legitimacy existing at the constituent moment, formulas demand a fictitious consensus, which is out of place within the polarized political system. Disharmony between the ratio of consensus and political reality causes dysfunctionality. Formal constitutional change is rendered difficult by the amending mechanisms and/or by strong political antagonism and the existence of a conflictual constitutional ethos. Constitutional reform narratives are often used by political elites as part of their political agenda, and exploited to gain political support in the context of political party competition.

Popular participation in the form of intervening elections or even referendums is usual, yet the separation of constitutional issues from the wider political choices is not always ensured. Rarity of formal amendment boosts informal changes introduced by the legislator, who often bypasses the constitution, reshaping it through legislation. Distance between the constitution and legislation may create issues of constitutional normativity. Nonetheless, the symbolic status of the constitution is usually high and plays a central role in political discourse. The possibility of judge-made informal change providing an alternative path depends on the position held by the judiciary and the way judges themselves define their task. As a rule, regardless of the strength of the judiciary, which varies, the leading role in constitutional change is left to competing political elites. Distrust of experts results from political polarization, as constitutional change is regarded highly political in nature and not suited for technocratic decision-making or even support. The conflictual context somehow renders neutrality an almost inconceivable quality and, in that sense, experts cannot but be treated as part of the political tensions. Distrust as a basic element of this model might also create a pattern of *ex post* confirmation of legislatively induced changes that are eventually adopted by the text of the constitution.

An utterly stringent amending formula comprising three successive stages, involving four organs (the two Houses of Parliament, the federal government, and the people), and most importantly entailing the automatic dissolution of Parliament upon the publication of declarations for revision, renders the Constitution of Belgium extremely difficult to modify, accompanied also by material limitations. Originally enacted in 1831 and designed to secure democratic participation, it has never been amended despite its multifaceted and obvious dysfunctionality, as it is entrusted to preserve the "fragile cohesion"[72] of a country where two linguistic communities (the Dutch speaking and the French speaking) are deeply divergent on a great number of issues, and where opinion polls indicate that among Flemish parties 46 per cent of voters would opt for the independence of Flanders. The environment of political distrust affects political life, since even the installation of a new government proves to be an adventure due to lack of will to reach a compromise. Thus, the amending formula can neither change nor can it be consensually applied in a way that would facilitate constitutional change. In such a polarized context, intervening elections cannot but serve other purposes than actual popular participation in the amending process, while mandatory parliamentary dissolution is either a threat for those who do not want to lose their parliamentary seat, and perhaps fear a shift in the political equilibrium, or a tool used to trigger elections for political purposes. In other words, intervening elections are anything but an infusion of democracy in the amending process. The classic notion of an amending formula aspiring to balance the need for stability with the necessity of change does not apply in that case, dysfunctionality and obstacles to constitutional change becoming the guardians of delicate balances. The price to pay is that part of the fundamental rules governing the country's institutional structure and the organization of the state lie outside the Constitution, while all important reforms take place elsewhere, beyond the Constitution. Substantial functions and changes of the Constitution are conducted through special laws that are of primary importance to the function of the state. Notwithstanding being legislative enactments, special laws require a two-thirds majority in both Houses of Parliament. In a context of distrust, the extra hurdles set by the amending formula make structural changes difficult to achieve.

Along with Belgium, Greece is characterized by difficulties with formal constitutional change. Although stringency of the amending formula had led historically to a series of replacements of the Constitution or revisions that were in violation of the formal process, and to constant bypassing of the Constitution, this was hardly regarded as signaling the need for rationalizing and relaxing the formula due to the context of political polarization; on the contrary, it was deemed to dictate safeguarding the Constitution through maintaining a demanding amending process. The current amending formula lays down a series of stringent procedural hurdles, containing numerous material limits. Competence to revise the Constitution is vested in Parliament, which decides on the need for revision by a three-fifths majority of the total number of its members, and following intervening elections the next Parliament decides on the proposed amendments by an absolute majority of the total number of its members, while reverse majorities are also possible. Although an obligatory dissolution of Parliament is not provided for, a serious time limit is set as initiating a revision of the Constitution is not permitted within five years of completion of the previous revision. The structure of the majorities provided does not in itself fetter consensual revision. The fact that Parliament is not dissolved automatically does not create the problems obvious in the example of Belgium; nevertheless, it further distances the issues of revision from the people who barely consider them when casting their vote at the general election.[73] Distrust underlies the tendency to regard stringency of the formula as an asset despite the lack of practicality and efficiency of the amending process. Constitutional maintenance is rendered even more difficult because, in Greece, despite the existence of a well-established system of diffused constitutional review, the judge never substantially entered the role of informally amending the Constitution. The price to pay is that when amendments to the Constitution are proved to be necessary, it might take a long time for them to be made.

Enhanced majorities and eternity clauses are the basic ingredients of the Portuguese profile of constitutional amendment. The amending power is vested exclusively in Parliament, requiring a two-thirds majority of all members. A mandatory five-year gap between constitutional amendments amplifies procedural difficulty, while the only way out is through a fast-track process, which requires very broad consensus (i.e. a majority of four-fifths of all members of Parliament). The whole amendment game is played by the major political parties, which initiate amendment and are the key players throughout the process, while the wide consensus requirements that aim to promote democratic legitimacy and popular participation actually enhance the power of the two major parties, placing amendment in the context of negotiations and agreements between them. Political distrust facilitating and, at the same time, stemming from this "cartel behavior"[74] allows constitutional change to slip away from formal processes and even from informal change through the jurisprudence of the Constitutional Court, leaving the door open for international and European law to slowly erode the Constitution, as state-based constitutionalism is being replaced by its European and international versions. This is a major shift in a constitutional culture where the Constitution not only occupies a central position, but historically follows the transformations of the will of the people, expressing their political and cultural aspirations.

Difficulty with formal change is a basic feature of the Spanish Constitution. A complex and demanding amending formula provides such hurdles for total revision that it has never been used since the enactment of the Constitution in 1978, while the partial revision process has only been used twice. Being a product of the consensual optimism that followed the restoration of democracy, the amending formula dictates the existence of agreement between political parties. However, in an environment of intense political polarization, it is not possible to reach such agreements. In this context, referendums included in both processes (i.e. mandatory referendum in case of a total revision or partial revision of certain issues, and optional referendum in the process for partial revision) have never been used. The text of the Spanish Constitution remains static, while the political system evolves and change is inevitably sidetracked.[75] What's more, when it does occur formally, it is burdened with extra significance precisely because of its rarity. For example, the recent inclusion of a deficit cap in the Constitution to ensure budget stability was bound to stand out more than it would in a system where constitutional amendment is more routine. Compromise allowing constitutional reform was rendered possible under the pressure of the financial crisis, putting even more emphasis on the stringency of the amending process. Distrust combined with enhanced consensus prerequisites for constitutional change incites the political elites to channel change through legislative paths, while the Constitutional Court is also a leading driver of informal change, reflecting international developments in the area of fundamental rights and mirroring the jurisprudence of the ECtHR. Despite the great importance of the Constitutional Court's jurisprudence, it has not transformed the constitutional text into a living document to an extent akin to US judicial interpretation. Neither informal change induced by the legislator, the Autonomous Communities, and the Constitutional Court, and taking place under the strong influence of EU law, nor rarity of formal amendment have imbedded the idea in the Spanish constitutional culture that the place where constitutional change normally happens is beyond the Constitution.

In the Netherlands, the amending formula dictates two parliamentary readings with intervening general elections and a qualified two-thirds majority in both Houses of Parliament in the second reading. Changes in the second reading are not possible, thus in light of the enhanced majority requirement this reading is usually the "killing field"[76] for many proposed amendments. The combination of a stringent formula with a strong underlying notion that constitutional revisions are about principles, and an environment of political and religious fragmentation that goes back centuries, lead to constitutional inertia. As a result, constitutional change has been channeled in practice through Acts of Parliament over the last 30 years. Yet, there is a price to pay for the normality of bypassing the Constitution, which seems to have lost its grasp on the people.[77] Judge-made change and political, elite-driven change differ in quality: judicial change can bring about constitutional development whilst the Constitution not only remains intact, but maintains its decorum, acquiring even stronger symbolic value. This happens because in the exercise of rigorous constitutional review, judges strongly affirm in their *dicta* that it is the Constitution they are applying. Conversely, as happens in the Netherlands, constitutional change taking place openly outside the Constitution and led by the political elites (without being filtered by the judicial idiolect) may inflict wounds on the status of the Constitution. Lack of constitutional review of Acts of Parliament and treaties does not translate into weak courts, as courts may review all domestic legislation, including Acts of Parliament, as to their compatibility with international treaties and EU law. Thus, judicial review dealing with constitutional issues, including the area of human rights protection, does occur—without, however, exerting influence on the Constitution. The Dutch paradigm is a unique case of distrust, which is centered on constitutional amendment where deeper fragmentation flowing from diversity blocks change, while the exact same diversity otherwise fosters a strong consensual political culture. It might be argued that this consensus, flowing from diversity, works at the level of ordinary politics, but is somehow transformed into distrust at the constitutional level. This suggests that distrust in the area of constitutional revision *is not necessarily the product of polarized and conflictual politics*, but may exist within a consensual model of democracy.

The direct-democratic model

In the direct-democratic model, the people have the final say on constitutional change, as well as also being able to initiate change. Constitutional referendums are mandatory, not just optional. Eternity clauses setting substantive obstacles to revision do not exist. The political party system is characterized by fragmentation and diversity, while it is the people who are the designated drivers of change. Popular decision-making lies at the heart of this model, which is built around the concept of substantiating popular sovereignty with regard to constitutional change. In that context, distrust of experts is in line with the direct-democratic ethos. It appears that in a culture where the people get to take the decisions on constitutional reforms, experts can only play a supportive and highly technical role. The design and qualities of referendums are of great importance, while the role of political elites and courts is influenced by the fact that the ultimate amending power lies with the people. A test area for different facets of constitutionalism and civic participation emerges, as the side effects of the people retaining the final word on constitutional revision are revealed.

The impact of direct-democratic features on constitutional change is fully displayed in the Swiss case, where referendums are deeply imbedded in the legal and political culture. It is the people of Switzerland who are in the position to continuously rearrange their Constitution, while the only substantial limits they have to respect are mandatory international rules. The operation of a directorial system of government facilitates this unique system of popular involvement in constitutional change. The federal Constitution of Switzerland may be totally or partially revised at any time. An amending formula that allows constant revision without demanding enhanced majorities operates within the context of a consensus-based democracy. Approval by the people and the cantons is necessary for both total and partial revisions.[78] Popular initiative not only allows the people to play a key role, but seems to have a distinct impact on the political agenda as well. By initiating constitutional change, the people get the opportunity to set the political agenda highlighting the issues at stake, even if they fail to impact the Constitution. Reform proposals may thus shape the political debate as opposed to political competition-premised models, where elites use constitutional change discourse as a pretext, and where constitutional change dialogue is swept away by ordinary politics. Whilst in the direct-democratic model it is people-driven constitutional discourse that sets the political agenda, in the distrust model—even in elections where the electorate is asked to decide on constitutional reforms—other political choices take over in the context of polarization, leaving choices regarding the constitution completely out of the picture.

Diversity reconciled with consensual decision-making (as it is the people who play the key role instead of political parties) and a Constitution open to change and modification suggest that it is feasible for the people of Switzerland to retain the role of key actor in constitutional change. In combination with the absence of constitutional review of federal legislation, this majority dominance inevitably poses the issue of fundamental rights and liberties protection. The role of recognizing and protecting fundamental rights and liberties was undertaken by the Federal Supreme Court, which built a body of jurisprudence under the influence of the European Convention on Human Rights—guarantees that were subsequently codified in the Constitution by way of total revision. Albeit that its constitutional importance was not heralded or feared as informal constitutional revision, the absence of judicial review of constitutionality was not allowing the judge to be treated as a player in constitutional change. What's more, the fact that popular initiatives can be successful despite the opposite recommendation of Parliament on one hand may be read as a materialization of people-driven constitutional change, yet also displays the flip side of majority decision-making on constitutional issues, which is the possibility of endangering fundamental rights, especially those enjoyed by minorities. The recent introduction by popular initiative of a provision in the Constitution that prohibits the construction of minarets seems an archetypal example of what happens to minority rights if left in the hands of majorities. Although in violation of the core values of the Constitution, since there is an obvious violation of international law obligations to respect religious freedom, the ban of minarets approved by referendum serves as a reminder of the tension between democracy and liberty. Absence of constitutional review enhances this tension, while it also leads to a paradox: direct democratic reflexes rule out open reliance on experts; in reality, however, their role in drafting constitutional provisions is essential, due to the lack of subsequent expert interpretation. Consequently, the silent, non-conspicuous work of experts is rendered indispensable.

Textual inertia resulting from the mode of entrusting to the people the final word on constitutional amendment is the direct-democratic model's mirror image. The Danish Constitution dates back to 1849 and has only been amended four times since then, acquiring its current form in 1953. In conformity with the direct-democratic rationale, no material limits exist so the people may change all the content of the Constitution. The amending formula requires a majority in two consecutive Parliaments, with intervening general elections. In addition, a popular vote is prescribed requiring approval by at least 40 per cent of the voting population. The apparent difficulty of getting such an approval and mobilizing such a great percentage of the people, and the concomitant political dangers of a failed referendum, lead to constitutional inertia. The aged Constitution retains its symbolic value, yet its very language is inaccessible to citizens: by remaining unchanged in a changing political environment, this causes a gap between its content and the operation of the political system it organizes. So how does constitutional change occur? No constitutional court exists in Denmark and, despite having the power to perform concrete constitutional review in a diffused system of judicial review, Danish courts are reluctant to engage in finding legislation unconstitutional, adhering in that respect to the Scandinavian tradition. Thus, it is in the hands of the political actors who operate the Constitution to change it through its application. Such distance between the written document and its application is a puzzling and unexpected consequence of constitutional arrangements, aspiring to render the people drivers of constitutional change, while in actuality the people become obstructors to change, since only proposals certain to succeed are put before them.[79] The existence of a consensual culture among the political elite allows the smooth operation of the system on the basis of constitutional language conversion, which ensures adaptability to the requirements of progress. In that sense, Denmark bridges the distance between constitutional text and constitutional practice, achievable only through agreement.

In Ireland, an amending formula vests the final say in the people, resulting in sidetracking a considerable amount of constitutional change through other routes. A hybrid combination of strong direct-democratic and evolutionary elements, the Irish example demonstrates how the hurdle of mandatory constitutional referendum, in a context of political polarization, instead of achieving the intended purpose of popular participation actually blocks constitutional maintenance through the formal process. Amendments to the Constitution must be passed by both Houses and subsequently approved by referendum. No eternity clauses exist, so the Constitution is amendable in its totality. Political polarization on constitutional issues in the context of Irish politics is not located within the political class—as political elites do manage to find ways to compromise—but lies instead in the realm of civil society. Opposition to constitutional referendums is not channeled mainly through political parties but rather through civil society organizations. A strong civil society, which has the potential to block change against the will of the political class, is a determinant factor in the route that constitutional change follows in the case of Ireland. Although the people may not formally initiate change, they can exert pressure to induce a referendum. The direct-democratic ratio of constitutional amendment is clear, but still political elites and judges claim a major part in determining the route of constitutional amendment by way of informal change. The Irish Constitution of 1937 has been amended 23 times, a large number of those instances being in response to judge-made changes. Few amendments address the organization of powers, thus the way the organs of the state operate has become quite distant from the relevant constitutional arrangements.[80] Political elites in power are reluctant to risk unfavorable referendum outcomes, and prefer to channel change through legislation. Informal change, which thus acquires primary importance, takes place by means of organic laws and constitutional litigation in the Supreme Court. As a result, constitutional change proceeds through a dialogue conducted mostly between lawmaker and judge, yet leaving the final say to the people who are the designated drivers of change. Since popular participation is not subdued to such an unreachable goal as the Danish requirement for 40 per cent of the voting population, the pending proposals for a major reform in the context of the financial crisis shall show whether the people can retain their role and engage in updating their Constitution. The correlation of mechanisms in the Irish example rests on a fragile equilibrium: the Supreme Court claims the role courts have in the evolutionary model, political elites channel change through legislation when afraid to bear the cost of unsuccessful referendums, and the people are present and claim to be expressed through civil society organizations, not willing to give up their direct involvement in constitutional amendment. Popular sovereignty emerges thus as the primary feature in Ireland, maintained through the continuous competition and interaction between the people, the judiciary, and the legislature.

Correlations

The categorization of countries within models, built on the correlation between mechanisms of change and the elements of the constitutional and political culture that influence their operation, relies on changeable interfaces. Transformations of the party system or the system of judicial review, changes in electoral laws, etc. may signal correlation shifts potentially leading to the abandonment of a model and the adoption of a new one, or a move towards hybrid combinations. Some countries present stability in the relationship between the features comprising a model, while others are more susceptible to volatility. The correlation stability factor is in itself a tool for understanding the constitutional amendment profile of a legal order. Profiling modes of change through breaking down and analyzing the variety of components that interact entails the comprehension of facts that are sometimes susceptible to multiple understandings. The same facts could be read differently, resulting in divergences with regard to the way in which each country's particularities are perceived.

By monitoring modes of constitutional change through the use of models, it is possible to trace the difference between conscious, deliberate choices to change the existing model through the obvious route of altering the amending formula, which seems to be a rarity, and unintentional transformations caused by changes in the equilibrium of the parameters that add up to a model. Constitutions, being open-ended projects, involve multiple actors and multiple possible directions. The five models of constitutional change, by encompassing a multiplicity of parameters, allow a profiling of countries that stresses rather than obliterates their idiosyncratic features, as they are based on holistic approaches of constitutional narratives.

Models of constitutional change may provide a prism for the analysis of much broader issues. For example, it is discernible that countries classified under the pragmatic model have prosperous and stable economies, while the economies of countries that belong in the distrust model are weaker.[81] An obvious differentiation exists: the pragmatic model, in which political elites manage to reach agreements and effect constitutional change smoothly, is linked to strong economies, while unstable economies usually relate to the distrust model, where obstacles to constitutional change are set by distrust reflexes. Such links suggest that the way in which constitutions change mirrors the overall balance of the constitutional organism and the polity, which in turn interrelates with the economy.

Undoubtedly, European integration has affected all member states, but constitutional change mechanisms employed in these states have retained their close connection to the idiosyncratic elements of each constitutional order. The existence of fundamentally different models of constitutional amendment within the old EU member states corresponds also to differentiations in political systems and constitutional ethos. Use of models additionally allows mapping out of the differentiations that affect the way in which the notion of the constitution is perceived.

Rigidities, predictions, illusions

Rigidity has long been the term employed in legal scholarship to signify how a constitution is revised. Distinctions between rigid and flexible constitutions, and between formal and informal change, emerge as polar opposites used to encapsulate the possibilities of constitutional change. The rigidity/flexibility scheme translates to levels of rigidity, often approached through the use of quantitative analysis based on different methods of measurement. The formal/informal dipole, also described as reform/evolution or explicit/implicit, indicates the distinctions between changes to the text of the constitution and changes in its meaning through interpretation and practice. Age in combination with brevity or verbosity are some of the variables used in comparative constitutional law and political science literature as indices to explain, and even to forecast, change.

Rigidity, however, is an overused concept, which provides but a small prism through which to look at the constitution, and may even distort the true image. Under the umbrella of "super-rigidity" are the constitutions of countries such as the USA, the Netherlands, Greece, and Denmark, which are all very different with regard to history, legal culture, political system, and the way in which their constitutions change. US "rigidity" is not comparable to Greek "rigidity"; and yet it is typical of constitutional law textbooks to begin by stating that the constitution is "written and rigid." A plurality of meanings underlies the generality of rigidity. It may be used to declare stringency of the amending formula and the existence of eternity clauses, but it is also possible that it may indicate slow-moving processes or procedural dysfunctionalities, or it might simply describe the rarity or difficulty of change stemming from a combination of parameters. Often, rigidity implies the feasibility of measuring non-measurable and non-comparable factors. Use of the terms "rigidity" and "rigid," especially when unaccompanied by an appropriate epithet to characterize them more specifically, is an easy way out of the hardship of providing precise analysis of complex realities.

Thus, "new conceptual glasses"[82] are needed to view the complexity of constitutional change. In terms of expressing what the constitution is, rigidity proves to be no more than an empty shell, signifying everything and nothing at the same time. That is because there is no singular, self-sufficient form of rigidity; instead, a plurality of *rigidities* exists. Rigidity may be re-conceptualized through breaking it down into its component parts and analyzing them separately.

Rigidities are different shapes in which hindrances to constitutional change appear. Rigidities cutting down the possibility of changing the constitution are varied: they may be formula-driven, as in the example of Spain, where the stringent amending formula renders formal amendment exceedingly difficult. *Procedural rigidity*, in combination with the dynamics of informal change, created the basis for the US Constitution to become one of the oldest constitutions in the world. Rigidity, however, does not explain what the US Constitution is in reality; that is, a highly esteemed, working document that has evolved through jurisprudence.

In the case of Denmark, *people-driven rigidity* blocks formal amendments. The requirement that constitutional revisions must be approved through popular vote by at least 40 per cent of the voting population means that only alterations that have the appeal to massively mobilize the people to vote for them stand a chance of being proposed. Making it this difficult to change is not the amending formula's intention, which is instead to enhance popular participation, but nevertheless it results in people-driven rigidity. *Culture and practice-driven rigidity* appears in the UK, demonstrating that political self-restraint may fetter change even in the absence of an entrenched written document. For an uncodified constitution to operate through its total elasticity, it requires those who change it to respect the idea that it is a constitution they are handling.

In Greece, for example, there is a *political system-driven rigidity* by way of political conflict and polarization. Political party polarization and conflictual constitutional ethos affect constitutional revisions since discussion on change is framed in terms of distrust and competition. This may even block changes that are considered necessary by both major political parties, but about which they cannot afford to demonstrate agreement, constitutional politics usually succumbing to ordinary politics. In the Netherlands, *judicial review system-driven rigidity* is caused by absence of constitutional review. When the model of judicial review and/or the tradition of the courts does not encompass rigorous constitutional review, the constitution automatically loses one route of development, therefore acquiring a form of rigidity. Reversely, *judicial activism-driven rigidity* may appear where the task of changing the constitution is undertaken by the judge, obliterating the need for textual modification. *Diversity-driven rigidity* appears in cases where ethnic and linguistic diversity, when profound enough—as in the case of Belgium, may generate a distinct form of rigidity. The constitution is left intact so that underlying cleavages shall not be stirred. This rigidity stems from giving priority to preserving constitutional serenity over being updated and issues of practicality.

Multiple rigidities may co-exist since they are not self-referential but operate within models of constitutional change. Where rigidity fails to explain how constitutions change, rigidities in the context of the evolutionary model, the pragmatic model, the elastic model, the distrust model, or the direct-democratic model will succeed. The mythology of rigidity is simply a convenient delusion. As a characterization in terms of change, rigidity conveys that some sort of procedural hardship is prescribed, whereas it offers nothing tangible beyond that. It is but an illusion of defining the identity of constitutional change, but instead it only evades, and sometimes obscures, its comprehension. Abandoning the use of the dyads rigid/flexible and formal/informal as the basic comprehension tool, to turn toward studying *multiple rigidities* in the context of the five models of constitutional change, refocuses the analysis to when, how, by whom, why, and in which direction a constitution is amended.

Rigidities can be either *institutional* or *factual*. Institutional rigidities are institutionally embedded ways of increasing the difficulty level of constitutional change. The amending formula is the most obvious among such rigidities, while the system of government and the judicial review system, with regard primarily to constitutional review, also fall into this category. Factual rigidities are sources of impediments to constitutional change situated in the practices, attitudes, and behavior patterns of different actors, which emerge through the application of institutional requirements, or address areas that fall outside the scope of institutional regulation, or stem directly from the political, legal, or social culture and constitutional ethos. A crucial dimension of factual rigidities is the existence or absence of political credibility. Political credibility translates into trust in political acts aiming to give effect to constitutional goals, and this trust is built when the stated purpose of such acts is the institutionally intended one.[83]

The distinction between the two categories of rigidities cutting through the formal/informal landscape allows understanding of the matrix of variables that determine constitutional change. Institutional and factual rigidities are *communicating vessels*, and the exchange between them is unavoidable. Consequently, changes at the institutional level influence factual rigidities and vice versa. The rapport between rigidities is crucial for the dynamics of constitutional change: if the relationship between them goes bad, the unintended consequences produced may be detrimental. The ultimate evaluation criterion is the compatibility between institutional arrangements and political or legal culture—in case of mismatch, multiple dysfunctionalities may emerge.

The interaction between institutional and factual rigidities may be exploited to address detected dysfunctionalities by intentionally inducing change. At the institutional level, modifications are effected formally and intentionally, and can be used with the additional purpose of transforming political culture-induced rigidities. For example, it is often the case that in polarized political systems, amending formulas prescribe that intervening elections must be held before Parliament decides on an amendment proposal. This inevitably fosters the constitutionalization of politics, as the constitution becomes an arena of political confrontation. What is not substantiated through this practice is the expression of popular will on constitutional issues. Not only are constitutional issues inevitably sidetracked by other political issues when voting in general elections, but they are most often twisted by the confrontational spirit. The conflictual political culture is therefore nurtured by the amending formula: modification of the formula may impact the way in which political conflicts are articulated.

The reciprocal relationship between institutional and factual rigidities, and the assessment of their incompatibilities with regard to the model of constitutional change, allow the evaluation of the amending formula and reflection on the desirability of its modification, which may be pursued either directly or indirectly by changing the parameters that determine its function. Engineering constitutional change entails understanding how *mechanisms* of change work and how *rigidities* interact. *Models* of constitutional change facilitate this task by providing guidance as to the parameters that require consideration. A complex machine can operate effectively as long as all its parts are functioning; and even replacing the smallest part affects the overall performance. *De constitutione ferenda* approaches should place extra significance on the fact that any alteration in the manner in which a constitution changes impacts the whole constitution. This is true for the way in which state organs are set up, and it is also true for the ambit of their powers: they do not depend solely on the provisions that regulate them, since awareness of by whom, how, and when they can be changed defines them as well.

Along with the "third wave" of global democratization, starting from Southern Europe in the mid-1970s, the democratic transitions in Latin America in the 1980s, and Eastern Europe in the 1990s, came global acceptance of the constitution as the indisputably appropriate tool for the realization of democratic governance. The constitution is no longer a luxury but an everyday commodity, not threatened by enemies of democracy but evaluated in accordance with its ability to provide service to democracy and the rule of law. Consequently, a constitutional and political culture has prevailed in which the constitution is not perceived as a totem but as an indispensable instrument. Protecting the constitution and safeguarding its unity and continuity no longer rely mainly on stringent amending procedures and other institutional rigidities, but are increasingly founded on factual rigidities (i.e. on political behavior demonstrated and practices employed in the application of the constitution). Factual rigidities acquire greater importance for constitutional stability, while strict, complex, and slow-moving procedures of formal constitutional change are becoming a remnant of the constitution's childhood years. The enhancement of factual rigidities thus allows the relaxation of institutional rigidities.

Discussion on the possibility of changing the amending formula is ongoing in many countries, including the USA, the Netherlands, Belgium, Denmark, Greece, etc. Such discussions often remain at the theoretical level, since fear of the unknown usually prevails. For example, the successful modification of the amending process in Luxembourg was, in reality, the constitutionalization of a long-employed consensual practice that had worked smoothly, so there was no fear of unexpected consequences. Nevertheless, although it is impossible to make safe predictions on constitutional change *per se* due to the complexity of interacting factors, it is feasible to perform impact assessment with regard to suggestions to alter the mode of change, based on the analysis of these multiple factors. The possible consequences of altering the amending formula can be identified, while changes to other institutional rigidities that influence constitutional change, such as the system of judicial review or the electoral system, can also be assessed as to their potential side effects with regard to constitutional change. The whole consort of rigidities is re-arranged through every modification, and it is crucial to be able to predict the outcome.

To do so, the purpose of modifications must be clear. The purpose is important precisely because no instruction manual exists. For example, adding stringency to the formula does not in itself say much about the direction any change will take. It is possible that if a concentrated system of constitutional review exists, the judge will take on the job. Nevertheless, this is not inevitable. The Austrian Constitutional Court has used its power to push through its case law on political parties in the direction of achieving consensus on constitutional issues. Relaxing the formula, on the other hand, does not guarantee in itself that amendments will be carried out efficiently. Even where the power to reform the constitution lies entirely in the hands of the political class, as in the case of a totally unentrenched constitution, this does not guarantee that constitutional reforms address the requirements set by changes in the political context. Although politicians do have, in theory, the ability to accommodate constitutional rules to the demands of political and social reality, it does not necessarily follow that things work this way. Factual rigidities emerge even in the context of absolute constitutional elasticity, as political elites might choose to avoid changes that would create obstacles to their policy-making, regardless of their necessity. Continuous discussions in the UK about drawing some limits to amending modes, substituting factual with some kind of institutional rigidities, seem to suggest this.

Impact assessment thus relies on awareness of the character, ethos, and culture of all involved actors, and on having an overall picture of the correlations of mechanisms within the specific model of constitutional change in which a country belongs. Such awareness also facilitates the use of comparative data, which may be evaluated under the prism of models. All attempts to analyze a country's mechanisms for constitutional amendment seem to lead to a study of its fundamental constitutional and political features. What is protected against change is often the most valued, but also the element most susceptible to change. Comparative analysis is a there-and-back-again journey, and models provide the map for visiting the correct places to collect experience that may be of use back home.

The necessity or desirability of changing or preserving the amending process as it stands relies, therefore, on evaluations and impact assessment based on matching the amending formula with its working environment. The tension between democracy and constitutionalism lurks behind such considerations, as choices between endurance, durability, adaptability, fluidity, and even replaceability of the constitution are put on the table. In case there is a one-size-fits-all ideal, measuring constitutional endurance[84] could be the optimal way to constitutional self-analysis. A constitution undergoes a subconscious evaluation when viewed within lists of constitutions compiled on the basis of their endurance, accompanied by data on dates and numbers of revisions, while crises of all sorts are presented as the major threats against constitutional endurance, which account for breaks in continuity. A strong craving for longevity is thus created. Endurance is conceptualized as a virtue and a strength, something beyond mere continuance in time. This, however, downplays the importance of constant reconsideration and questioning of values inherent in democracies.[85] Endurance in itself might suggest totally diverse things in different constitutional cultures. While it is therefore indispensable to understand constitutional history, it could prove misleading if being considered the ultimate sign of constitutional health is set as the primary goal of the amending formula.

A trend seems to be emerging toward reflection on the functions of amending formulas, which as a rule are those constitutional provisions less friendly to reconsideration and most resistant to change. This tendency ensues from transformations of the constitution, which no longer needs to proclaim its supremacy and normativity through the extreme difficulty of formal change. Virtually commonplace, the notion that constitutions are the fundamental laws of all modern democracies, providing the framework of government and regulating all aspects of organized social co-existence, gradually became, in the post-World War II period, incontestable. As the prevalence of the constitution has been firmly established, what is expected of it is not a demonstration of authority but one of efficiency: proof of capability to meet the challenges of rapidly changing circumstances.

Conclusion

Constitutional efficiency is valued as much as symbolism of authority; it is of great importance that constitutions work well. Contemporary challenges to the power of the constitution do not originate from parliaments and legislators, but rather from international integration and the concomitant erosion of national sovereignty, democratic deficits, crises of the welfare state, persistent malfunctions in political representation, and the spectrum of new technologies. What is at stake is the scope for application of the constitution, and that has more to do with effectiveness and adaptability than the demonstration of symbolic power associated with the connotation of rigidity. As the authoritative power of the constitution has become self-evident, it is supported by efficiency and endangered by lack of it.

Constitutions are faced with the risk of becoming obsolete when they cannot keep up with the pace of developments at the international and domestic political, economic, and social environment. Rigidity in its traditional sense gives way before the *mosaic of multiple interacting rigidities* that correspond to the complexity of constitutional change. Stamina of the constitution requires energy and aptness of response, which are *model-specific*. Functionality can only be assessed in light of the particular features of a model that determine the level and mode of a constitution's adaptability. Mechanisms of change set in motion by multiple actors and the parallel operation of rigidities in the opposite direction are not static themselves, but they can nevertheless be captured through the lens of different models of constitutional change.

Differing concepts of the constitution and polity emerge from each model. Focusing on change brings out distinct conceptualizations of the constitution. Ability to change and adapt to the environment is a feature of living systems. The constitution is a living organism and, as such, it may malfunction and require repair. Detection and contemplation of malfunctions could take the magic out of the constitution. Discovering the divergences in its apprehension could deconstruct its myth. Analysis of constitutional change engineering through models, instead of envisioning constitutive and amending power in motion, demystifies processes. And yet the grasp of the concept of the constitution remains firm. Demystification does not translate to enfeeblement of the notion of the constitution; on the contrary, it reinforces its appeal, which is no longer premised on its sanctity but on its accessibility and efficacy.

Notes

1 "Brief and rare" moments marked by discontinuity and transformation are the way in which constitutional moments are perceived by N. Walker, "After the Constitutional Moment", in I. Pernice and M. Maduro (eds), *A Constitution for the European Union: First Comments on the 2003 Draft of the European Convention*, Baden Baden: Nomos Verlagsgesellschaft, 2004, p. 23ff.

2 To explore the fundamental conception of constitutional moments, see B. Ackerman, *We the People: Foundations*, Harvard University Press, 1991, vol. 1; Id., *We the People: Transformations*, Harvard University Press, 2000, vol. 2; Id., "2006 Oliver Wendell Holmes Lectures: The Living Constitution", *Harvard Law Review*, 2007, vol. 120, p. 1737ff.

3 On approaches revealing the grasp of Ackermanian moments on constitutional scholarship, see S. Choudhry, "Ackerman's Higher Lawmaking in Comparative Constitutional Perspective: Constitutional Moments as Constitutional Failures?", *International Journal of Constitutional Law*, 2008, vol. 6(2), pp. 193–230; S. Levinson, "Transitions", *Yale Law Journal*, 1999, vol. 108, p. 2215ff.; A. Sajó, "Constitution Without The Constitutional Moment: A View From The New Member States", *International Journal of Constitutional Law*, 2005, vol. 3, p. 243ff.; M. Tushnet, "Misleading Metaphors in Comparative Constitutionalism: Moments and Enthusiasm", *International Journal of Constitutional Law*, 2005, vol. 3, p. 262ff.

4 On time density and the way time moves, see F. Braudel, *Grammaire des Civilizations*, Paris: Champ Flammarion, 1993.

5 D. Baranger, "The language of eternity. Constitutional review of the amending power in France (or the absence thereof)". Online. Available HTTP: <http://www.juspoliticum.com/The-language-of-eternity,319.html>.

6 See R. Albert, "Constitutional Handcuffs", *Arizona State Law Journal*, 2010, vol. 42, pp. 664–715, who distinguishes between preservative, transformational, and reconciliatory entrenchment. Eternity clauses potentially can lock again the constitutional handcuffs that citizens can unlock by the key of amendatory power.

7 J. Balkin, *Constitutional Redemption: Political Faith in an Unjust World*, Harvard University Press, 2011.
8 This acceleration is pinned down in M. Rosenfeld, "The Problem of Identity in Constitution Making and Constitutional Reform", Cardozo Legal Studies Research Paper No. 143, analyzing the way in which the relation of constitutional identity to extra-constitutional identities varies depending on the historical situation.
9 On the importance of historical methodology to understand constitutional evolution, see S. Griffin, "Constitutional Law Outside the Courts". Online. Available HTTP: <http://www.aals.org/profdev/constitutional/griffin.html>.
10 See P. Kondylis, "Epilegomena", in C. Schmitt, *Political Theology* (Greek trans.), Athens: Leviathan, 1994, p. 128ff.
11 L.D. Kramer, *The People Themselves: Popular Constitutionalism and Judicial Review*, Oxford University Press, 2005; L.A. Powe, Jr., "Are 'the People' Missing in Action (and Should Anyone Care)?", *Texas Law Review*, 2005, vol. 83(3), p. 855ff.
12 On juristocracy, see R. Hirschl, *Towards Juristocracy: The Origins and Consequences of the New Constitutionalism*, Harvard University Press 2007; C.N. Tate and T. Vallinder (eds), *The Global Expansion of Judicial Power*, NYU Press, 1995.
13 On the model of dialogue, see P.W. Hogg and A. Bushell, "The Charter dialogue between Courts and Legislatures", *Osgoode Hall Law Journal*, 1997, vol. 35, pp. 75, 79.
14 See G.J. Jacobsohn, "An Unconstitutional Constitution? A Comparative Perspective", *International Journal of Constitutional Law*, 2006, vol. 4(3), p. 460ff.
15 Judicial constitutional updating by getting out of the way after the New Deal is analyzed in A. Vermeule, "Constitutional Amendments and the Constitutional Common Law", University of Chicago, Public Law Working Paper No. 73, 2004.
16 See M. Tushnet, "Popular Constitutionalism as Political Law", *Chicago-Kent Law Review*, 2006, vol. 81, pp. 991–1006, who insists on the importance of "who signals the conversation is over."
17 K.M. Sullivan, "What's Wrong with Constitutional Amendments", in L.M. Seidman and V.E Sloan (eds), *Great and Extraordinary Occasions: Developing Guidelines for Constitutional Change*, New York City: The Century Foundation Press, 1999, p. 39.
18 See D. Strauss, "Commentary: The Irrelevance of Constitutional Amendments", *Harvard Law Review*, 2001, vol. 114, p. 1457ff.; B.P. Denning and J.R. Vile, "The Relevance of Constitutional Amendments: A Response to David Strauss", *Tulane Law Review*, 2002, vol. 77, p. 247ff.
19 R. Dworkin, *Freedom's Law: The moral reading of the American Constitution*, Harvard University Press, 1997, p. 171.
20 Vermeule, op. cit.
21 A. Hutchinson, in this volume, referring to Canada.
22 J. Balkin and S. Levinson, "Understanding the Constitutional Revolution", *Virginia Law Review*, 2001, vol. 87(6), pp. 1045–104, 1077.
23 G. Sartori, *Comparative Constitutional Engineering*, NYU Press, 1997, p. 203.
24 As put by N.W. Barber, "that Parliamentary sovereignty continues to occupy our attention is hazardous; it risks distorting the answers we give to questions of constitutional reform . . .", see N.W. Barber, "The afterlife of Parliamentary sovereignty", *International Journal of Constitutional Law*, 2011, vol. 9, pp. 144–54. On the current state of parliamentary sovereignty, see also J. Goldsworthy, *Parliamentary Sovereignty: contemporary debates*, Cambridge University Press, 2010.
25 See political party typologies in G. Sartori, *Parties and Party systems: a framework for analysis*, ECPR Press, 2005.
26 A. Lijphart, *Patterns of Democracy: Government Forms and Performance in Thirty-Six Countries*, Yale University Press, 1999.
27 G. Tsembelis, "Decision Making in Political Systems: Veto Players in Presidentialism, Parliamentarism, Multicameralism, and Multipartyism", *British Journal of Political Science*, 1995, vol. 25, pp. 289–326; B. Rasch and R. Congleton, "Amendment

Procedures and Constitutional Stability", in R.D. Congleton and B. Swedenborg (eds), *Democratic Constitutional Design and Public Policy. Analysis and Evidence*, Cambridge, Massachusetts: MIT Press, 2006, pp. 319–42; B. Rasch, "Foundations of Constitutional Stability: Veto Points, Qualified Majorities, and Agenda-Setting Rules in Amendment Procedures", ECPR Joint Sessions of Workshops, Rennes, France, 11–16 April 2008.

28 On the particularity of constitutional change in federal systems and differentiations between the above-mentioned federal states, see A. Benz, "Joint-decision traps and beyond: Varieties of constitutional change in multilevel systems". Online. Available HTTP: <http://www.sv.uio.no/arena/english/research/news-and-events/events/tuesday-seminars/2011/benz-08-03.html>.

29 See J. Balkin, "How Social Movements change (or fail to change) the Constitution: The Case of the New Departure", *Suffolk University Law Review*, 2005, vol. 39, pp. 27, 52, where he points out how political parties help produce what is constitutionally plausible or implausible.

30 P. Krause, "Verfassungsrechtliche Möglichkeiten unmittelbarer Demokratie", in J. Isensee and P. Kirchhoff (eds), *Handbuch des Staatsrechts*, 2005, Müller, Bd. III, pp. 61–8; O. Jung, *Grundgesetz und Volksentscheid*, Westdeutscher, 1994, p. 51ff.

31 T. Fleiner, in this volume, referring to Switzerland.

32 U. Berlit, "Soll das Volk abstimmen? Zur Debatte über direktdemokratische Elemente im Grundgesetz", *Kritische Vierteljahresschrift*, 1993, vol. 76, p. 335.

33 S. Tierney, "Constitutional Referendums: A theoretical inquiry", *MLR*, 2009, vol. 72(3), pp. 360–83.

34 A.C. Hutchinson and J. Colon-Rios, "Democracy and Constitutional Change", *Osgoode CPLE Research Paper Series*, 2010, Vol. 06, No. 11, Research paper No. 48.

35 For example, by vesting the competence to revise the constitution to an ad hoc organ of the state. This option exists in the USA, where the legislatures of two-thirds of the federal states may call a Convention for proposing amendments; however, it has never been used in practice. Nevertheless, it does still occupy the imagination of constitutional scholars. In France, the President may submit an amendment proposal to the Bureau of Congress (i.e. both Houses of Parliament convened in Congress).

36 See M. Stelzer, in this volume, referring to Austria.

37 See an overall account of different patterns of constitutional change in federal states in N. Behnke and A. Benz, "The Politics of Constitutional Change between Reform and Evolution", *Publius: The Journal of Federalism*, 2009, vol. 39, pp. 213–40.

38 For a comprehensive analysis on the role of Autonomous Communities in constitutional change in Spain, see C. Colino, "Constitutional Change Without Constitutional Reform: Spanish Federalism and the Revision of Catalonia's Statute of Autonomy", *Publius: The Journal of Federalism*, 2009, vol. 39, pp. 262–88.

39 Online. Available HTTP: <http://www.publications.parliament.uk/pa/ld201012/ldselect/ldconst/177/17702.htm>.

40 See the expression of serious doubts regarding the possibility of a rational people agreeing today with the Diceyan concept of absolute, unbridled legislative power given to parliamentarians, subject only to an assessment of their overall performance every five years or so, in D. Feldman, "Comparative Reflections on sovereignty and constitutionalism" (W.G. Hart Legal Workshop, Sovereignty in Question, June 2011), online. Available HTTP: <http://www.law.cam.ac.uk/people/academic/dj-feldman/723>.

41 R. Blackburn, in this volume, referring to the UK.

42 See the evidence given by Prof. R. Blackburn at the House of Lords Select Committee on the Constitution, stressing how process has developed into a constant problem, Constitution Committee, 5th Report (2010–2011): The Government's Constitutional Reform Programme (HL Paper 43), Q 9.

43 R. Blackburn, in this volume, referring to the UK.

44 Vermeule, op. cit.

45 See the expert evidence given to the House of Lords Constitution Committee, online. Available HTTP: <http://www.publications.parliament.uk/pa/ld201012/ldselect/ldconst/177/17702.htm>.
46 See Ackerman, *We the People: Transformations*, op. cit.; S.M. Griffin, *American Constitutionalism: From Theory to Politics*, Princeton University Press, 1998; Balkin and Levinson, op. cit., p. 1045.
47 See M. Tushnet, *Taking the Constitution away from the Courts*, Princeton University Press, 2000.
48 J.R. Vile, in this volume, referring to the USA.
49 For a critical account of the vast literature on the topic, see S.M. Griffin, "Rebooting Originalism", *University of Illinois Law Review*, 2008, vol. 4(4), p. 1185ff.; G. Huscroft and B.W. Miller (eds), *The Challenge of Originalism. Theories of Constitutional Interpretation*, Cambridge University Press, 2011.
50 On the grand style of such theories, see J. Harvie Wilkinson, *Cosmic Constitutional Theory. Why Americans Are Losing Their Inalienable Right to Self-Governance*, Oxford University Press, 2012.
51 See the thoughts expressed by S. Levinson in discussing H.K. Gerken, "The Hydraulics of Constitutional Reform: A Sceptical Response to our Undemocratic Constitution", 2007. Online. Available HTTP: <http://digitalcommons.law.yale.edu./fss_papers/351>.
52 See J. Balkin, *Living Originalism*, The Belknap Press of Harvard University Press, 2011, p. 287, where he analyzes why the Supreme Court is a player and not a mirror.
53 See S.M. Griffin, "Constitutionalism in the United States: From Theory to Politics", in S. Levinson (ed.), *Responding to Imperfection*, Princeton University Press, 1995, p. 56. Recently, a Supreme Court justice dramatically encapsulated the essence of the evolutionary model in an interview with regard to how a new constitution should be drafted, stressing the non-exportability of the US Constitution in the year 2012 due to its age. The reason behind this is that the US Constitution has evolved since its enactment but this evolution is not incorporated in its text. The mere text, stripped of its judicial elaboration and the concomitant practice and theory, does not provide the transplantable elements of American constitutionalism. On the decline of the transplantability of the US Constitution, see also D.S. Law and M. Versteeg, "The Declining Influence of the United States Constitution", *New York University Law Review*, 2012, vol. 87(3), online. Available at SSRN: <http://ssrn.com/abstract=1923556>.
54 A. Hutchinson, in this volume, referring to Canada.
55 As stated by I. Greene in "Constitutional Amendment in Canada and the United States", in S.L. Newman (ed.), *Constitutional Politics in Canada and the United States*, State University of New York Press, 2004, p. 249ff., following the reform of 1982 it is "commonplace for academics to conclude" that, "like the United States, Canada has succumbed to judicial supremacy, in part because the domestic amending formula has made the Canadian Constitution as difficult to amend as the US Constitution."
56 A. Hutchinson, in this volume, referring to Canada.
57 It is not by coincidence that the dialogical model is greatly discussed in Canada. See Hogg and Bushell, op. cit., pp. 75 and 79. See also, on the model of dialogue, C. Manfredi and J. Kelly, "Six Degrees of Dialogue: A Response to Hogg and Bushell", *Osgoode Hall Law Journal*, 1999, vol. 37, p. 513ff.
58 T. Groppi, in this volume, referring to Italy.
59 Ibid.
60 M. Kotzur, in this volume, referring to Germany.
61 On the role of the Federal Constitutional Court as an arbiter, see Behnke and Benz, op. cit., p. 225.
62 On the competences and function of the Federal Constitutional Court and its role in constitutional change, see W. Heun, *The Constitution of Germany, A Contextual Analysis*, Hart Publishing, 2011, pp. 159–89.

63 See M. Stelzer, *The Constitution of Austria: A Contextual Analysis*, Hart Publishing, 2011, pp. 13ff., 40ff.
64 M. Stelzer, in this volume, referring to Austria.
65 J. Gerkrath, in this volume, referring to Luxembourg.
66 L.G. Malmberg, in this volume, referring to Sweden.
67 W. Mastor, in this volume, referring to France; S. Boyron, "France", in D. Oliver and C. Fusaro (eds), *How Constitutions Change: A Comparative Study*, Hart Publishing, 2011, pp. 115–42.
68 For the role of the French Constitutional Court and for the way judges draft their opinions without showing they express "the opinion of a lawyer, be he a constitutional judge," see Baranger, op. cit.
69 See T. Ojanen, in this volume, referring to Finland.
70 This practice started to wane after the 2000 revision.
71 See M. Suksi, "Finland", in Oliver and Fusaro, op. cit., pp. 87–114.
72 C. Behrend, in this volume, referring to Belgium.
73 X. Contiades and I. Tassopoulos, in this volume, referring to Greece.
74 J. Machado, in this volume, referring to Portugal.
75 A. Barrero Ortega and I. Sobrino Guijarro, in this volume, referring to Spain.
76 W. Voermans, in this volume, referring to the Netherlands.
77 Voermans, op. cit., talks about "lukewarm sympathy," as the Constitution "suffocates no longer having the ability to function as a living instrument."
78 See T. Fleiner, in this volume, referring to Switzerland.
79 H. Krunke, in this volume, referring to Denmark.
80 F. de Londras and D.G. Morgan, in this volume, referring to Ireland.
81 The Netherlands are an obvious exception to this remark, since they belong to the distrust model yet have a prosperous economy. An explanation could be that the aged Constitution has a minimal role in the polity, having been substituted by international and European law, in the framework of a strong consensus democracy.
82 L. Wittgenstein, *Remarks on the Philosophy of Psychology*, Oxford: Blackwell, 1980, Vol. II, 525.
83 On the concept of political credibility as a constitutional principle, see D.T. Tsatsos, *Von der Würde des Staates zur Glaubwürdigkeit der Politik*, Berlin: Nomos, 1987.
84 See the comprehensive comparative study on constitutional endurance in Z. Elkins, T. Ginsburg and J. Melton, *The Endurance of National Constitutions*, Cambridge University Press, 2009.
85 See Hutchinson and Colon-Rios, op. cit.

Appendix

Table 1 provides a summary of the basic features of each model of constitutional change analyzed in the comparative chapter. Table 2 presents a taxonomy of countries based on the five distinct models of constitutional change.

Table 1 Models of constitutional change: main features

Elastic	*Evolutionary*	*Pragmatic*	*Distrust*	*Direct democratic*
• Unentrenched constitution • Subject matter-dependent definition of the constitution • Parliamentary supremacy • Any law can change the constitution • Political, elite-driven change • Influential judiciary • Self-restraint of all actors	• Informal change as main mechanism • Demanding amending formula • Drivers of change: strong judiciary • Rarity of textual changes • Constitutional lawmaker/judge dialogue • Judicial filtering of political elite-driven or people-driven changes • Influential theories of interpretation	• Efficiency of formal change comes through compromise • Pragmatism stemming from amending process and/or consensual political culture • Political, elite-driven change • Feasibility of constant constitutional updating • Reluctance towards major reforms • Use of experts • Strong judiciary (supplementary role)	• Stringent amending formula • Difficulty with formal change • Political, elite-driven change • Unwillingness to compromise on constitutional issues • Political exploitation of constitutional reform narratives • Veto player strategies • Distrust of experts • Conflictual constitutional ethos	• The people have the final say • Mandatory constitutional referendums • No eternity clauses • Distrust of experts • Fragmentation of political party system • Civil society involvement

Table 2 Models: taxonomy of countries

Elastic	*Evolutionary*	*Pragmatic*	*Distrust*	*Direct democratic*
UK	Canada Italy USA	Austria Finland France Germany Luxembourg Sweden	Belgium Greece The Netherlands Portugal Spain	Denmark Ireland Switzerland

Index

Printed in the USA/Agawam, MA
April 25, 2014
588455.112